SCULPTURE OF Angkor AND ANCIENT Cambodia

Millennium of Glory

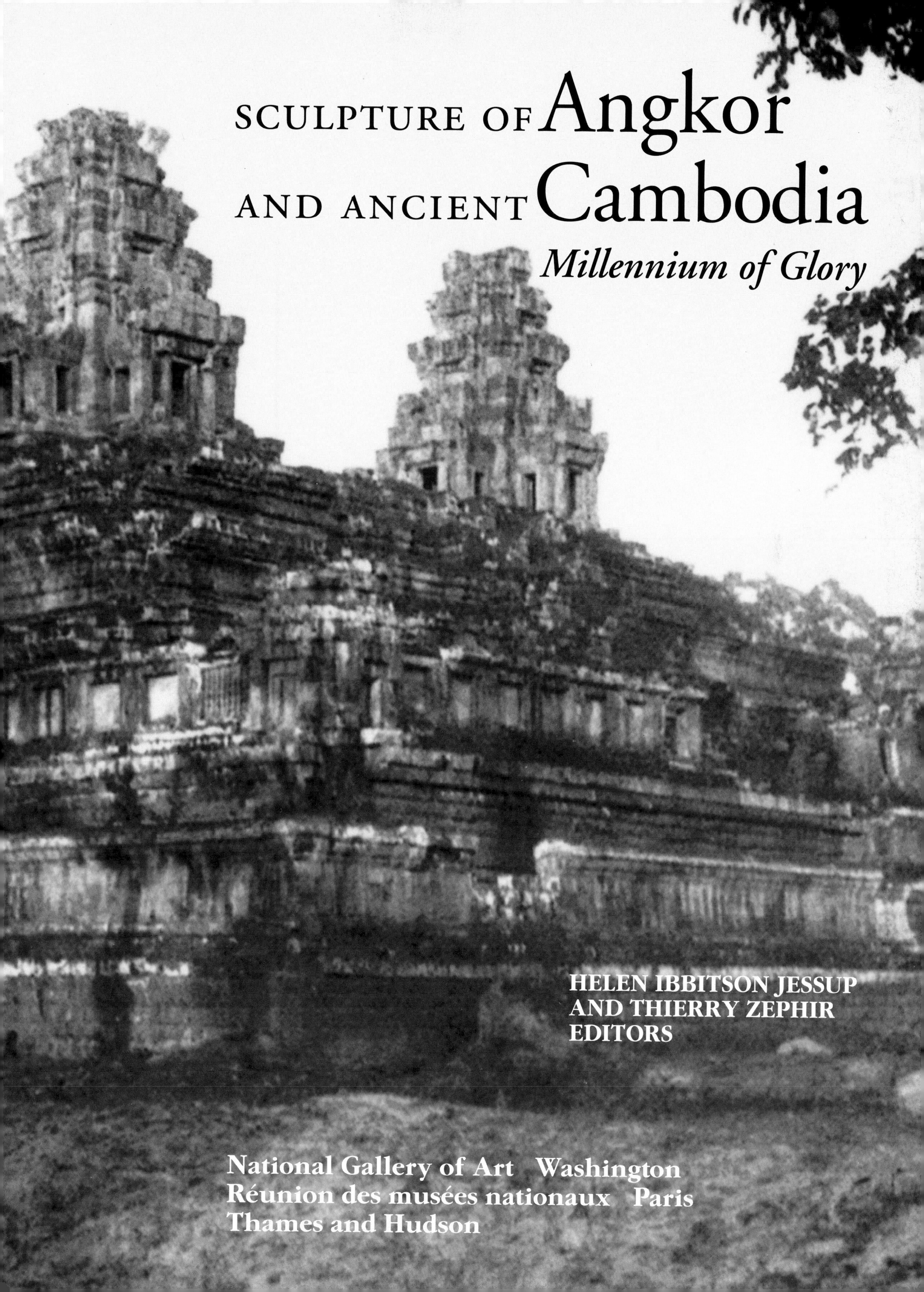

SCULPTURE OF Angkor AND ANCIENT Cambodia

Millennium of Glory

HELEN IBBITSON JESSUP
AND THIERRY ZEPHIR
EDITORS

National Gallery of Art Washington
Réunion des musées nationaux Paris
Thames and Hudson

The exhibition is made possible by The Henry Luce Foundation, The Marjorie Kovler Fund, and The Rockefeller Foundation.

Galeries nationales du Grand Palais, Paris
January 31 – May 26, 1997

National Gallery of Art, Washington
June 29 – September 28, 1997

Tokyo Metropolitan Art Museum
October 28 – December 21, 1997

Osaka Municipal Museum of Art
January 15 – March 22, 1998

The exhibition is supported by an indemnity from the Federal Council on the Arts and the Humanities.

The exhibition is organized by the National Gallery of Art, Washington, the Royal Government of Cambodia, and the Réunion des musées nationaux/Musée national des Arts asiatiques-Guimet, Paris.

List of Contributors
Ang Chouléan A. C.
Kamaleswar Bhattacharya
Jean Boisselier
Jacques Dumarçay
Maud Girard-Geslan
Jean-François Jarrige
Helen Ibbitson Jessup H. J.
Albert Le Bonheur
Wibke Lobo W. L.
Pich Keo
Saveros Pou
John Sanday
Son Soubert S. S.
Ashley Thompson
Thierry Zéphir T. Z.

Editor-in-chief, Frances P. Smyth
Senior editor, Mary Yakush
Editors, Susan Higman and Julie Warnement
Production manager, Chris Vogel
Translations by Willard Wood, John Stowell, and Amy Ryan, with Helen Ibbitson Jessup and Thierry Zéphir
Photographs by John Gollings with assistance from Isamu Sawa and Fabrice Lépissier, except as otherwise noted
Typeset in Eurogaramond by World Composition Services, Inc., Sterling, Virginia
Designed by Bruno Pfäffli
Printed in France by Kapp Lahure Jombart, Évreux

First published in the United States of America in 1997 in hardcover by Thames and Hudson Inc., 500 Fifth Avenue, New York, New York 10110

First published in Great Britain in 1997 by Thames and Hudson Ltd, London

Library of Congress Catalog Card Number 96-61815

British Library Cataloguing-in-Publication Data
A catalogue record for this book is available from the British Library

ISBN 0-500-23738-7

cover: Cat. 89
back cover: Cat. 92
pages ii–iii: Ta Keo, Angkor, late 10th-early 11th century
page vi: National Museum of Cambodia, Phnom Penh, 1917–1918
page x: Bayon, Angkor Thom, late 12th-early 13th century
pages xii–xiii: Baphuon Temple, Angkor, 3d quarter of the 11th century
page 1: Angkor Vat, Siem Reap, 1st half of the 12th century
page 33: Phnom Bakheng, early 10th century. The top of the pyramid, viewed from the central shrine
page 79: Banteay Srei, Siem Reap, 967–968
page 129: Sūryavarman II on his throne, Angkor Vat, west section, south gallery
page 141: Cat. 18
page 187: Cat. 47
page 235: Cat. 60
page 279: Tower Faces at Bayon, Angkor Thom, late 12th – early 13th century
page 333: Cat. 117

Contents

I wish to express my profound gratitude to France, to its President of the Republic and to its Government, and to the United States and its President and Government, and to the distinguished officials and staffs of the Réunion de musées nationaux and the Musée national des Arts asiatiques-Guimet, and the National Gallery of Art, for the singular honor that they bestow upon the Royal Kingdom of Cambodia and its people in organizing an exhibition of Khmer art, beginning February 1, 1997, in the prestigious setting of the Grand Palais in Paris, and continuing in June at the National Gallery of Art in Washington. The exhibition is destined, I am convinced, to be a great success and will make better known and appreciated the thousands of years of history and civilization of my country, Cambodia.

N. Sihanouk

His Majesty Norodom Sihanouk
King of Cambodia

THE PRESIDENT OF THE REPUBLIC

Few names possess for the French as strong an evocative power as that of Angkor. A fabled province, a legendary site, and without a doubt one of the most beautiful archaeological complexes in the world.

On the occasion of the great *expositions universelles* hosted by our capital, hundreds of thousands of visitors were able to admire the majesty of the temples of Angkor thanks to remarkable reconstructions. Since the beginning of this century, a close collaboration between the École française d'Extrême Orient and Cambodian experts has made possible the restoration and preservation of this unique patrimony.

This exhibition presents a particularly fascinating aspect of this patrimony with a selection of masterpieces of Khmer sculpture. It is indeed the first time that the major works of the two most prestigious collections of Khmer art, that of the National Museum of Cambodia, Phnom Penh, and that of the Musée national des Arts asiatiques-Guimet, have been brought together. This exhibition is, therefore, a truly historic event for it offers to the public the most complete survey of the marvels of Khmer sculpture from the sixth to the seventeenth centuries.

I would like to thank His Majesty Norodom Sihanouk, King of Cambodia, for generously agreeing to lend to France works that belong to the national treasures of the kingdom and which are remarkable expressions of human genius. I hope that this exhibition will give our compatriots the opportunity to discover for themselves the "magic of Angkor," celebrated by the first explorers of the temples.

Jacques Chirac

THE WHITE HOUSE

WASHINGTON

MARCH 19, 1997

The people of the United States of America are most grateful for the generous loan by the Royal Kingdom of Cambodia of these beautiful treasures representing a millennium of its civilization.

The sculptural tradition of Cambodia is imbued with grace and spirituality, transcending time and place and embodying universal human values. The unprecedented collaboration among the Kingdom of Cambodia, the Republic of France, and the United States of America gives even greater importance and significance to this superb collection.

I encourage visitors to view the exhibition in a spirit of friendship, cooperation, and admiration, remembering the good faith and trust that the people of Cambodia have shown by sharing with us their splendid national treasures.

Bill Clinton

Foreword

From time to time, extraordinary historical moments converge. *Sculpture of Angkor and Ancient Cambodia: Millennium of Glory* is such a moment, bringing together one of the world's most remarkable sculptural expressions as the result of propitious circumstances.

The emergence of Cambodia into the open fellowship of nations, after two decades of political turbulence, has made it possible for the National Museum of Cambodia to lend its treasures. The temporary closure for renovation of the Musée national des Arts asiatiques-Guimet has permitted the loan of major works from its collection. For the first time ever, therefore, it will be possible to exhibit together works from the two greatest collections of Khmer art in the world.

We are delighted that the longstanding friendship between the Republic of France and the United States of America has been enhanced by this fruitful collaboration with the Royal Government of Cambodia. For the people of France the exhibition is an affirmation of an old friendship; for the people of the United States it permits new insight into one of the most distinguished ancient civilizations of Asia.

We thank the museum staffs in Paris, Washington, and Phnom Penh. The Réunion des musées nationaux/Musée national des Arts asiatiques-Guimet is grateful to Lyonnaise des Eaux and GTM-Entrepose for support of the exhibition in Paris. The National Gallery of Art, Washington, is most grateful to The Henry Luce Foundation, The Marjorie Kovler Fund, and The Rockefeller Foundation for their dedication to this project and significant grants in support of the exhibition in Washington.

We owe a profound debt of gratitude to His Majesty King Norodom Sihanouk and Her Majesty Preah Reach Akka Mohesei Norodom Monineath Sihanouk, and the government and the people of Cambodia, who have entrusted us with a valuable part of their priceless national heritage.

Françoise Cachin
Director, Musées de France
President, Réunion des musées nationaux

Earl A. Powell III
Director
National Gallery of Art

Lenders to the Exhibition

The Asia Society, New York
Asian Art Museum of San Francisco
Musée national des Arts asiatiques-Guimet, Paris
Staatliche Museen zu Berlin, Museum für Indische Kunst
National Museum of Cambodia, Phnom Penh
Philadelphia Museum of Art

Acknowledgments

Throughout the four years of this exhibition's evolution, we have enjoyed the sustained enthusiasm of many colleagues and the constant inspiration of the extraordinary sculpture of Cambodia. We thank the Royal Government of Cambodia for its unprecedented generosity in lending its sublime sculptural heritage, and the Musée national des Arts asiatiques-Guimet for sharing its own precious collection.

The exhibition would not have been possible without the unflagging support of many friends and colleagues in the diplomatic community. The exhibition received the official sanction and guidance in Cambodia of Minister Vann Molyvann, his chief of cabinet, Soeung Kong, and Minister Nouth Narang, as well as that of H. H. Prince Sisowath Sirirath, Ambassador to the United Nations, and H. E. Var Huoth, Ambassador to the United States. We are grateful for the efforts made by Pich Keo, director of the National Museum of Cambodia when the exhibition was in the planning stages, and his staff, including Kak Chanthat, Lim Yi, Long Thol, Meas Khim, Phy Sakhoeun, Sum Sovannarith, Thlang Sakhoeun, and Sam So Phy, as well as Khun Samen, present director. In Siem Reap, the governor was helpful, as were Oung Vorn of the Depot for the Conservation of Angkor, and Ouk Sun Heng and Thep Vattho of Apsara. We were aided in Phnom Penh by Eng Sun Kerya, Ashley Thompson, and Siv Samnang. We are grateful to Ambassador Gildas Le Lidec, Alain Freynet, and Michel Igout of the Embassy of France in Phnom Penh. At the United States Embassy in Phnom Penh, we received help from Ambassador Kenneth Quinn and his predecessor Ambassador Charles Twining, Damaris A. Kirchhofer and her predecessors Franklin Huffman and David Miller, and Helen Hudson, as well as from their colleagues at the State Department in Washington. Also in Washington, we thank Sovan Thun, Phavann Chhuan, and Natalie Chhuan. During the UNTAC period we received great help in Cambodia from Tim Carney, now Ambassador, Vicki Butler, and Janos Jelen.

It has been a privilege to collaborate on this catalogue with many of the great scholars of Khmer art. For the texts that they contributed, we are grateful to Kamaleswar Bhattacharya, Jacques Dumarçay, Maud Girard-Geslan, Jean-François Jarrige, Wibke Lobo, Pich Keo, Saveros Pou, John Sanday, Son Soubert, and Ashley Thompson, along with Jean Boisselier and Albert Le Bonheur whose essays are published here posthumously. The catalogue will, we hope, provide readers with insight into the remarkable civilization of the ancient land of Cambodia. The occasional divergence of opinion about dates and themes reflects the current state of Khmer studies. Thus we have included some apparent contradictions, normal in any field where certainty is the long-gestated child of scientific evidence and patient scholarship.

Space limitations preclude an exhaustive list of the museum colleagues in Washington and Paris who helped us so freely and often. At the National Gallery of Art, Earl A. Powell III, director, has from its inception given his support and commitment to this exhibition, as have Alan Shestack, deputy director, Roger D. Mandle, former deputy director, and Carol Kelley in the director's office. Many others at the National Gallery of Art worked tirelessly toward the realization of the exhibition: D. Dodge Thompson and Ann Bigley Robertson in the exhibitions office, aided by Jennifer Fletcher Cipriano, Michelle Tuplin, Jonathan Walz, and Stephanie Fick; our inspired designer Mark Leithauser, and Gordon Anson, Jay Brown, Linda Heinrich, Gina O'Connell, and Jane Rodgers, as well as the late Gaillard F. Ravenel, all of the department of installation and design; Ross Merrill, Mervin Richard, and Shelley Sturman in the conservation department; Sally Freitag, Lauren Mellon Cluverius, Michelle Fondas, and Daniel Shay in the registrar's office; Susan Arensberg and Isabelle Dervaux, with Elyse Kunz and Rolly Strauss, in the department of exhibition programs; Neal Turtell, Theodore Dalziell, Lamia Doumato, Thomas McGill, and the circulation staff, in the library; Philip C. Jessup, Elizabeth A. Croog, Marilyn T. Shaw, and Montrue Conner of the office of the secretary-general counsel; and Ruth Anderson Coggeshall, her predecessor Laura Smith Fisher, Melissa McCracken, Cathryn D. Scoville, and Melanie J. Wolfe in the development office, as well as Deborah Ziska and Nancy Starr in the information office, and Genevra Higginson of the department of special events, all under the leadership of Joseph Krakora head of external affairs.

Many individuals brought expertise and considerable energy to the English edition of the catalogue, most notably Frances Smyth, Mary Yakush, Chris Vogel, Susan Higman, and Julie Warnement, as well as Janet Blyberg, Mariah Seagle, Maria Tousimis, and Jennifer Wahlberg of the editors office of the National Gallery of Art; Vidya Daheja, and Stephen Allee, Woodman Taylor of the Arthur M. Sackler Gallery, Smithsonian Institution; and Michelle Peters and Pilar Wyman. Willard Wood translated the texts written in French into English, aided by Amy Ryan, and John Stowell translated the German texts into English. Eleanor Mannika read and commented upon the manuscript. The catalogue was produced in collaboration with the département de l'éditon de l'image of the Réunion des musées nationaux, Paris, where hearty thanks are owed to Anne de Margerie, Marie-Claude Bianchini, and Nicolas Përrier, as well as Gaëlle Masse, Sandrine Cousson, Marie Lionnard, Jacqueline Menanteau, and Carolyn de Lambertye. The book has been enhanced by photographs by John Gollings, assisted by Isamu Sawa, Fabrice Lépissier, and Thomas Renaut. Bruno Pfäffli designed the catalogue, and to him and his staff we are profoundly grateful.

At the Réunion des musées nationaux, Paris, the exhibition unfolded under the brilliant guidance of Irène Bizot, ably supported by Ute Collinet and Bénédicte Boissonas, with Agnès Takahashi and Jean Naudin. The support of Jean-François Jarrige, director of the Musée national des Arts asiatiques-Guimet has been, needless to say, the *sine qua non* of all our efforts. At the research laboratories of the Musées de France we thank Jean-Pierre Mohen, Thierry Borel, David Bourgarit, and Benoît Mille. We are much indebted to Pierre Batiste, Jérôme Ghesquière, Dominique Fayolle, Thierry Ollivier, Anne Micard, Madeleine Bonnat, and Émilienne Jacob. We wish to acknowledge as well the cooperation of Roland Mourer of the Museum of Lyon, Gwénaël Rimaud, Van Duong Thanh, Tran Ky Phuong, Wolfgang Felten, and Jaroslav Poncar.

For their inspiring efforts in conserving the sculpture from Phnom Penh, we thank France Dijoud and Roland Coignard with his family team members Benoît, Olivier, and Sandrine, as well as Claude Forrières, Bertrand Porte, Emmanuel Desroches, and Raphaëlle de Cointet. The conservation of the works will be an enduring legacy of the exhibition. Special thanks are due to Kenro Izu for graciously allowing us to use his photographs in the Washington exhibition, and to David Chandler for his unstinting enthusiasm and support. Personal thanks are offered to Sichan and Martha Siv, Hervé de la Bâtie, Amy Poster, and Francesca Cook, as well as Giuliocesare Barzacchi, and Philip Jessup.

Unfortunately, we cannot mention all who helped us in fellow institutions throughout the world. We would like to praise the collegial support of all those who lent to our exhibition: The Asia Society, New York, Asian Art Museum of San Francisco, Musée national des Arts asiatiques-Guimet, Paris, Staatliche Museen zu Berlin, Museum für Indische Kunst, National Museum of Cambodia, Phnom Penh, and the Philadelphia Museum of Art. Thanks, too, to colleagues at the Museum of Fine Arts, Boston, the Art Institute of Chicago, the Cleveland Museum of Art, the Los Angeles County Museum of Art, the Metropolitan Museum of Art, the Nelson Atkins Museum, the Arthur M. Sackler Gallery, Smithsonian Institution, the St. Louis Art Museum, and the Walters Art Gallery. The guidance of Michael Brand and others at the Australian National Gallery was most important. In addition we would like to express our gratitude to the Rautenstrauch-Joest-Museum für Völkerkunde, Cologne, the Linden-Museum, Stuttgart, the Rietberg Museum, Zurich, the Historical Museums of Hanoi and Ho Chi Minh City, the Cham Museum, Danang, the National Museum, Bangkok, the British Museum and the Victoria and Albert Museum in London, and the Centro Cultural Arte Contemporaneo, Mexico City. We thank Bruno Dagens, Jacques Dumarçay, Christine Hawixbrock, Nadine Dalsheimer, Bruno Bruguier, and Olivier de Bernon, as well as other members of the École française d'Extrême-Orient who were helpful in both France and Cambodia. We are grateful to UNESCO, especially to its former director in Phnom Penh, Richard Engelhardt, and the team of the World Monuments Fund in Cambodia, especially John Sanday and John Stubbs.

Ang Chouléan, Helen Ibbitson Jessup, and Thierry Zéphir

Introduction

Jean-François Jarrige

Since World War II, an important exhibition of Khmer art has not been seen in Paris, nor in the United States or Japan. It will doubtless be remembered that the prestigious site of Angkor, thanks to monumental replicas of its "pagoda," was one of the great curiosities and attractions of the universal and colonial expositions occurring from the end of the nineteenth century until the independence of Cambodia. From the beginning of the 1960s, with the growth of air travel, the site of Angkor was accessible to an increasing number of tourists who were all dazzled by the spell of the temples in their splendid natural setting. The tragic civil war cast a mantle of silence over the region of the temples, broken by bursts of machine gun fire and detonating mines. When a measure of political stability returned, work could be resumed at Angkor, notably by an Indian team, and in 1992 *The Age of Angkor*, an exhibition comprising thirty-five pieces from the National Museum of Cambodia, was organized in Canberra, Australia.

Since reentering power in 1993, the royal government of Cambodia has attached great importance to restoring all of Angkor's monuments, which are once again drawing numerous visitors. Even as I write, grandiose projects for marketing the site of Angkor are under discussion, sparking lively debate between potential investors, on the one hand, and foreign and Cambodian experts, on the other, who fear that "the magic of Angkor" may not survive the proposed development, which could prove disastrous in the long term. For its part, the École française d'Extrême-Orient has resumed the task of restoring some of the monuments of Angkor. Teams of various nationalities, including Japanese, British, American, and Italian, among others, are currently participating in a range of restoration projects, in close collaboration with the Cambodian authorities and actively partnered by UNESCO. But much work remains to be done if these monuments, neglected during the period of tumult, are to be restored and maintained and the looting stopped over an archaeological area of some 150 square miles (400 km^2). Given the size of the task, it is appropriate to draw as much international attention as possible to this extraordinary cultural heritage. The idea came to our colleagues at the National Gallery of Art in Washington and to ourselves of proposing to Cambodia a great exhibition of Khmer sculpture that could provoke a virtual rediscovery of the extraordinary art of Cambodia, which had been somewhat forgotten during long years of political unrest. The project immediately received the support of the Cambodian authorities, in particular Vann Molyvann, minister of state responsible for cultural patrimony, and Nouth Narang, minister of culture. During an audience most kindly granted to us, His Majesty King Norodom Sihanouk assured us of his benevolent interest in the project. The administrateur général of the Réunion des musées nationaux, Irène Bizot, personally undertook the often complex negotiations both in Phnom Penh and in Paris, and directly oversaw all the stages of this ambitious project. Yet the realization of this exhibition owes a great deal to the French ambassador in Phnom Penh, Gildas Le Lidec, to the cultural division of that embassy, and especially to Alain Freynet, counselor, head of the cultural division, and to Michel Igout, cultural attaché. We thank them for the vast time and energy needed to shepherd the project through its many steps, and for managing at every turn to surmount the numerous difficulties that inevitably attend so large an effort. The ambassador of the United States was kind enough also to support our efforts, as was Helen Ibbitson Jessup, guest curator for the exhibition at the National Gallery of Art. We are also pleased that, thanks to the participation of NHK and the Asahi Shimbun, this exhibition will travel to Japan, a nation that is currently very active in the conservation of the Cambodian cultural heritage.

It must be acknowledged that, after the initial enthusiasm for this project, voices were raised to signal anxiety about the departure of so many prestigious works from the national heritage. But the authorities in Cambodia, very concerned about the quality of this exhibition and about the role it could play internationally, acceded to our requests for loans with exceptional generosity. Naturally we had no intention of exposing the objects to the slightest risk. Several delegations of experts studied the condition of the works, obliging us to renounce transporting several important works. Under the sponsorship of the Ministry of Foreign Affairs and the Ministry of Culture, Christian Dupavillon, coordinator of French aid to the Cambodian cultural heritage, established a restoration workshop directed by Bertrand Porte at the National Museum of Cambodia, to provide training for a team of Cambodian conservators. Roland Coignard, along with his sons Olivier and Benoît, and with the help of France Dijoud, chief conservator of the national patrimony and director of restoration for the museums of France, has overseen all restoration efforts and addressed the problems of transporting the artworks. Claude Forrières, at the Arc'antique laboratory in Nantes, has been responsible for restoring the bronzes, receiving help with radiography from the Laboratoire des musées de France and with nuclear imaging from the Centre d'energie atomique at Sarclay.

The Goals of the Exhibition

The aim of this exhibition has been to reunite the masterworks of two museums, the National Museum of Cambodia and the Musée Guimet in Paris, whose collections are for historical reasons complementary. Successive generations of eminent scholars, in Paris as in Phnom Penh and at the Depot for the Conservation of Angkor, have ensured that these two museums should provide the best possible view of Khmer art. In addition, the closure of the Musée Guimet for renovations encouraged us to eschew leaving its Khmer collections in storage and to allow certain of its most important works to travel after the exhibition at the Grand Palais.

While we wished to associate this exhibition with the potent symbol of Angkor, its true title is *Ten Centuries of Khmer Art,* since many of the major works belong to a time before the founding of Angkor at the end of the ninth century. There was no question of trying to evoke the site of Angkor in this exhibition, as was done at universal and colonial expositions in an era when travel was difficult, by means of casts and monumental reconstructions, if only because we lacked the space to do so. Instead, the exhibition will provide the opportunity to see or to review films and other documents relating to the Khmer temples and the history of the Depot for the Conservation of Angkor, whose giant labors have brought so many monuments through a long period of civil war without their suffering irreparable damage.

We have therefore sought to present as complete as possible a panorama of Khmer sculpture, drawing primarily on the two museums with direct historical links to the discovery and appreciation of the Cambodian cultural heritage, and giving preeminence to works from Phnom Penh. Khmer sculpture without doubt has been studied more closely by generations of French specialists than any other field of Asian art. The chronology of Khmer monuments was largely reconstructed by Philippe Stern, chief curator of the Musée Guimet from 1954 to 1965. By painstakingly studying the sculpture and decorative elements, using a method of analyzing the evolution of forms devised by Henri Foçillon, Stern was able to determine the order of succession of monuments that usually lacked epigraphic evidence permitting accurate dating. This is only to suggest what detailed scrutiny and annotation the sculpture in this exhibition received, following often lengthy discussions among the most eminent scholars in the field. Among these we might cite Pierre Dupont, who in 1935 wrote the catalogue for the Musée Guimet's Indochinese collections. Later one of the foremost members of the EFEO (École française d'Extrême-Orient), Dupont would publish in 1955, the year of his death at age forty-seven, his seminal reference work, *La statuaire préangkorienne*.

The exhibition attempts to pay homage to these generations of renowned scholars and researchers, using their work to present the clearest possible synthesis of Khmer sculpture for the benefit of all those who do not have the leisure or the possibility to consult specialized literature such as articles from *BEFEO (Bulletin de l'École française d'Extrême-Orient)* or the journal *Arts Asiatiques*. Thierry Zéphir and others have provided detailed bibliographies at the end of each catalogue entry, for those interested in discovering more on the subject. It was naturally unthinkable to present Khmer statuary out of context, particularly as we have the means of displaying some very fine architectural elements and some important inscriptions. A number of specialists have been enthusiastic about writing catalogue essays evoking the architectural, religious, and linguistic background of the works on display. For the historical segment, an area still dominated by the work of George Cœdès, we have turned to a text written some years ago by Albert Le Bonheur. A former student of Philippe Stern, Le Bonheur was in charge of the Musée Guimet's Southeast Asian collections for almost thirty years, before illness claimed him at the start of 1996. It is certain that if his health had allowed it, Albert Le Bonheur would have provided a fresh contribution to this exhibition, which, on the French side, has fallen to the supervision of Thierry Zéphir, his assistant for many years at the École du Louvre and the Musée Guimet, and who is thus indirectly the heir to the teaching of Philippe Stern. We would also like to mention the pleasure we have experienced in working in close collaboration with our colleague Helen Ibbitson Jessup, who has, on behalf of the National Gallery of Art in Washington, provided curatorial direction, with the valuable help of Ang Chouléan, member of the EFEO, and Pich Keo, of the directorate of Khmer patrimony, who, during the time the exhibition was in preparation, was the director of the National Museum of Cambodia.

Historical Overview

This exhibition also provides the opportunity, as we have said, to remember that the formation of the collections of the Musée Guimet and the National Museum of Cambodia was directly linked to the history of research into Khmer civilization, first at Angkor, then in many other areas of present-day Cambodia, Thailand, and Vietnam. In the light of considerable talk today about the looting of the Khmer artistic patrimony and the problems of the restitution of art objects, and of the frequent mention of the unfortunate Malraux affair, sometimes blown up in popular imagination beyond its true proportions, it might be useful to recall the motivations of the pioneers, scholars, and curators who were responsible for the establishment of these two museums.

The European discovery of Angkor, which brought the first works of Khmer art to France, has been ably told by Bruno Dagens in his well-documented and well-illustrated *Angkor: Heart of an Asian Empire* (New York, 1995). The early thirteenth century, following the reign of Jayavarman VII and his immediate successors, marks an end to the great royal foundations and the spread of a branch of Buddhism known as the Lesser Vehicle. Yet the Chinese traveler Zhou Daguan describes Angkor in 1296 as a flourishing city, despite its constant wars with the neighboring countries. Although the city was largely abandoned afterward, the great Hindu temples were transformed into Buddhist sanctuaries of the Lesser Vehicle, and Angkor remained a center of pilgrimage until the eighteenth century. Missionaries who visited the site in the sixteenth century attributed the ruins of Angkor to the cultural influence of Alexander the Great or the Romans, and a missionary from the seventeenth century described it as the equivalent in Asia of Saint Peter's in Rome.

In about 1850, accounts began to trickle in from European travelers who had visited Angkor. They were either surprised by the bizarre aspect of the monstrous sculpture, or enthusiastic about the romance of the ruins among the extraordinary tropical vegetation. The naturalist Henri Mouhot, who visited the kingdoms of Siam, Cambodia, and Laos between 1858 and 1861, left wonderfully lyrical descriptions of his visit to Angkor and particularly of the temple of Angkor Vat. "At the sight of this temple, one feels one's spirit crushed, one's imagination surpassed. One looks, one admires, and, seized with respect, one is silent. For where are the words to praise a work of art that may not have its equal anywhere on the globe?. . . What genius this Michelangelo of the East had, that he was capable of conceiving such a work" (*Le Tour du Monde* 2 [1863], 299).

But the discovery of Khmer art truly begins with a mission organized in 1866–1868 by Doudart de Lagrée, in collaboration with Louis Delaporte and Francis Garnier, to study the navigability of the Mekong River. Delaporte, a naval officer known for his draftsmanship, was dazzled by his first visit to Angkor, which, at the time, was under the sovereignty of the king of Siam. Delaporte's descriptions, accompanied by drawings, were published as Mouhot's had been earlier in successive installments of *Le Tour du Monde;* they provoked enormous public interest. Abandoning comparisons to Greek and Egyptian art, Delaporte stressed the originality of Angkor's monuments, which offered "another form of beauty." Following his first visit, he conceived a project that was to have considerable consequences, and which he summed up in a single sentence: "I could not contemplate these monuments of a long-ignored art without experiencing the liveliest desire to make them known in Europe and enrich our museums with a collection of Khmer antiquities, that they might assume their rightful place beside the antiquities of Egypt and Assyria" (*Voyage au Cambodge—L'architecture khmère* [Paris, 1880], 12). At this point, Delaporte entered upon a veritable campaign to "bring Angkor into the museums" and have Khmer sculpture and architecture recognized as major constituents of world art (Zéphir, "Le Cambodge de Louis Delaporte," in *Ages et visages de l'Asie*, Musée des Beaux-Arts de Dijon, 1996). In 1873, he headed a new expedition to make plaster impressions and bring back the first set of original works from Angkor and such provincial sites as Beng Mealea and Koh Ker. In Paris, Delaporte learned that the Louvre had no interest in his Khmer collections, and the packing cases stayed on the sidewalk for almost a month. They were finally deposited at Compiègne, where the castle's guardroom became the first museum of Khmer art. After the triumph of the universal exposition of 1878, and the restoration of the Giants' Causeway at Angkor's Preah Khan, a temple built by Jayavarman VII in 1191, Delaporte set out on a final mission to Cambodia in 1881, from which he brought back a number of casts and seventy original works. In 1882, the Khmer collections were transferred from Compiègne to the Palais du Trocadéro in Paris, where they were installed on two floors of the Passy wing, which became the Indochinese Museum. On his retirement, Delaporte served as volunteer curator of the Khmer collection at the Trocadéro from 1889 to 1924—a year before his death at the age of 83. When no longer able to undertake expeditions to Asia, he encouraged others to do so, among them the architect Lucien Fournereau, who returned from his 1887–1888 expedition with casts and original pieces, but also some remarkable watercolors of the Khmer monuments, preserved today in the École des beaux-arts in Paris. By the time Stern succeeded Delaporte in 1925, the Indochinese Museum at the Trocadéro possessed a rich collection of casts and original pieces, supplemented by an abundant collection of photographic documents, which would prove particularly valuable to the new curator in gathering the information he needed to establish a chronology of the principal monuments of Cambodia.

Across town, the museum on the Place d'Iéna founded by Emile Guimet in 1889 boasted "several Brahmanic casts and sculptures" of Khmer art, which it displayed in a first-floor gallery on the courtyard (1897 catalogue). Etienne Aymonier, with the financial support of the Académie des inscriptions et belles-lettres, would mount three successive expeditions from 1882 to 1885, in the course of which he assembled a large collection of Khmer sculpture, including such masterpieces of pre-Angkor art as the famous Harihara from the Asram Maha Rosei, which went first to the Ethnography Museum before being transferred to the Musée Guimet in 1890. As the collection grew, Joseph Hackin, the curator from 1923 to 1941, created the first Khmer gallery in the Iéna wing, where a number of original works and photographs of Angkor Vat were installed.

In Indochina, the time had long since passed when an expedition could venture into the jungle, then ruled by the king of Siam, and wrest elements of a lost civilization from its dark recesses. The EFEO was founded in Hanoi in 1898, under the direction of Louis Finot and Alfred Foucher. In 1907, the Indochinese archaeological mission was established in Saigon, from where it was able to extend its activities to the site of Angkor. In the same year, King

Sisowath I, with the support of France, reclaimed the full extent of his territory from Siam. Under the leadership of the first "curator" of Angkor, Jean Commaille, who was assassinated by brigands in 1916, the temple of Angkor Vat was cleared of brush and rubble, with the Angkor Thom complex soon to follow. This work continued for the first half of the century, and the names of an extraordinary sequence of personalities are associated with it—curators of Angkor such as Henri Marchal and Maurice Glaize, and directors of the EFEO such as George Cœdès. The chief aim was to develop the Khmer artistic patrimony to its full extent in situ, while not neglecting to complete the Paris collections, increasingly used for teaching purposes.

The inauguration of the Albert Sarraut Museum in Phnom Penh was held on 13 April 1920. With the clearing then under way at Angkor, a large number of statues and inscriptions had been uncovered, and these were brought for safekeeping to the Depot for the Conservation of Angkor. The most important pieces, either from an artistic or a historical point of view, were then transported to Phnom Penh and displayed alongside the major finds from all over the country in the museum built by George Groslier, the director of Cambodian arts. Thus were formed the exceptional collections of what is today the National Museum of Cambodia, which still occupies the same traditional-style building. The directorship of the EFEO and the curators of Angkor made it clear that it was impossible to remove any portion of the monuments, whose restoration had now become the active concern. The famous Malraux affair illustrates this. In 1923, André Malraux obtained official authorization to carry out archaeological investigations in Cambodia. When he reached Hanoi, the interim director of the EFEO, Léonard Aurousseau, warned him that any discoveries he might make in the forests of Cambodia would have to remain in place, following a directive passed to protect the cultural patrimony. Malraux's expedition traveled through the tropical forest toward Banteay Srei, a small temple discovered in 1914 and described scientifically by Henri Parmentier in 1919. (As it happens, Parmentier met Malraux and his wife Clara on their way through Siem Reap and was impressed by the young writer's culture.) With a handsaw, then using a chisel and crowbar, they dislodged "seven stones," which were subsequently transported to Phnom Penh via the Tonle Sap. On 24 December, Malraux was arrested with his friend Chevasson. Without passing judgment on this affair or on Malraux's motives, we would like to suggest that this incident has often been wildly exaggerated, to the point where Malraux is imagined to have cut the heads off innumerable Khmer statues, some of which would be now in the Musée Guimet. In fact, the famous seven stones were confiscated. And as a direct and happy consequence of this ill-fated expedition, it was decided to restore Banteay Srei, whose ruined state and isolation in the impenetrable depths of the forest had warranted, in Malraux's eyes, the removal of a small number of carved stone blocks.

The restoration of Banteay Srei was undertaken by Parmentier and Goloubew in 1924, and in 1931 a technique of restoration new to Cambodia, anastylosis, was tried by Marchal in the Angkor region. During a visit to Java, Marchal had seen Dutch architects dismantle ancient monuments, having first carefully numbered each stone. They then rebuilt the monument around a reinforced internal structure, thus managing to replace any stones that might have fallen or been dislodged by creeping vegetation. Only when a stone was actually missing was it replaced by new materials. The trend today is to point out the flaws in this technique, but when we observe how well

Angkor's monuments have withstood twenty years of neglect, we must give all due credit to men such as Marchal and Bernard-Philippe Groslier who practiced this method of restoration on a grand scale. And we must applaud Jacques Dumarçay and his team for continuing their reconstruction of the Baphuon, after a hiatus of twenty-five years. When renovations started at Banteay Srei, however, it became apparent that some pavilions were beyond reconstruction. Two pediments that could not be returned to their original place were brought to the Depot for the Conservation of Angkor. The one considered, perhaps for subjective reasons, the more beautiful was sent to the museum in Phnom Penh and the other to the Musée Guimet. In the present exhibition, they are reunited.

In France, meanwhile, 1927 proved an important year for the Musée Guimet. Its curator, the archaeologist Hackin, and Stern decided to transfer fifty-three original works from the Indochinese Museum to the Musée Guimet. In 1931, the remainder of the collection also went to the Guimet. In 1936, Stern undertook an important mission for the Musée Guimet, traveling to Indochina to collect documentation for the courses offered at the École du Louvre and for his own study of the stylistic evolution of architectural decoration, which would establish a relative chronology of Khmer monuments. A further goal of the expedition was, "in cooperation with the governing bodies (École française d'Extrême-Orient), to identify from among the works with doubles that could be sent to France those that might usefully complete the collections of the (Guimet) museum." In the report of the national museums for that year, 1936, René Grousset succinctly summed up the spirit in which works were sent to France: "It was decided that no unique piece should leave Indochina, in order that the integrity of the artistic patrimony be preserved." He also observed that a decision had been taken several years earlier that, from each series, only

> a limited selection of typical examples would be sent to the Musée Guimet, in order to complete the existing collections and to form a sort of anthology of Khmer and Cham art.... Several consignments reached the museum in 1936 and were presented to the council of national museums on November 24. The council agreed, partly by way of thanks and partly because of the important findings stemming from the excavations and constructions of the École française d'Extrême-Orient to vote a subsidy to support these excavations and constructions in Indochina.

The accessions to the Musée Guimet's holdings in Khmer art were very much in keeping with the spirit of the times. In the Near East, for instance, and in such countries as Iran and Afghanistan, the French government made sizable contributions toward French archaeological research, in exchange for which it regularly received a share of the antiquities, although the unique works always went to the country of origin. This helps to explain authorization given by governors of Indochina after a colonial exposition, such as that of 1923, to allow certain works to remain in France to complete the teaching collections at the Musée Guimet. Grousset also stressed in his report the importance of the Musée Guimet's collections for tourism, a potential economic asset for Cambodia.

In 1938, the inner courtyard of the Musée Guimet was covered and the greater part of the first floor was devoted to Khmer art and the art of ancient

Champa (the Indianized south of Vietnam). In essential respects, the Musée Guimet's collection had by then been formed, and Stern, who succeeded Grousset in 1954, turned his attention to expanding the photographic archives and to the publications and teaching programs. The Conservation of Angkor, under the leadership of Groslier, experienced a period of flourishing activity and an increased level of funding, while Jean Boisselier, and later Madeleine Giteau, followed up the work initially undertaken by George Groslier, Bernard-Philippe's father. The work of the archaeologists, curators, and architects who labored at Angkor and throughout the country would not have been possible without the collaboration of generations of Cambodian experts, foremen, and workers. The climate of respect and confidence in which they worked was such that Marchal, for instance, remained in his adoptive country until his death at Siem Reap in 1970.

This exhibition does not include many masterpieces now in other museums and private collections, although several will be shown at the National Gallery of Art in Washington. But the joint presentation of a substantial set of major works from Phnom Penh and a series of major works from the former Musée indochinois and the Musée Guimet provides a comprehensive panorama of ancient Cambodian art. It will also sidestep the potential for debate and controversy that could be provoked by works that have appeared suddenly on the art market outside a scientific context, some of which, by their handling or in certain details of their iconography, raise questions that have no place in this exhibition.

Certain topics in Khmer art remain problematic, and each is richly deserving of its own thematic exhibition. For instance, it is not known how forms that originated in India were transmitted to other countries. The very rare wooden Buddhas at the Historical Museum in Ho Chi Minh City (Saigon), dating in all likelihood from the fifth or sixth century, that had been preserved in the marshes of Vietnam's Plain of Reeds, provide a glimpse of an entire area of documentation that has now been practically obliterated. The resumption of archaeological investigations in the full complement of countries that came under the influence of ancient India may allow certain questions to be reexamined, such as whether some sculpture is truly ancient, in which case the dates of the works might be related to the dates of their Indian models, or whether, as other specialists have held, they exhibit archaistic features and are of relatively more recent date.

Our hope, which we believe justifies our requesting such generous loans from the National Museum of Cambodia, is to make available to a very wide public the most beautiful possible insight into one of the major art traditions in the history of humankind. It is worth pointing out that it is rare for stone sculpture in the Indianized world to be free of walls and steles and to be fully three-dimensional. The exhibition makes it possible to follow how Khmer sculpture gradually became liberated, first from supporting frames, then from braces, to become true sculpture in the round. Yet our view of Khmer statuary remains incomplete. The presence in the exhibition of a bronze statue of the upper portion of Viṣṇu's body (cat. 68), originally resting on the serpent Ananta, which would have been some twenty feet (6 m) long in its complete state, really gives us an idea of how the most prestigious sculpture of Angkor might have looked, a statuary which today, save for this fragment in Baphuon style from the West Mebon temple, has totally disappeared.

These many centuries of statuary, from the pre-Angkor works that Groslier dubbed "Greco-Gupta" to the enigmatically smiling Buddhas and

Bodhisattvas of the Bayon style, allow us to retrace the history of Khmer sculptural art through its long succession of strongly marked styles. The jutting hips, sensual forms, sweet smiles, and meditative faces of certain works contrast markedly with the hieratic, frontal poses of others, almost mineral in nature, with their hardened faces and sharp eyebrow arches. Khmer sculpture eludes simple definitions.

The fact that Khmer sculpture was in the service of religion, and most often a royal or aristocratic one, should not be overlooked. The divinities presided over the dark labyrinths of chambers and galleries, organized to this day according to the great cosmic diagrams mirrored by the temples' architecture. The civil war, the looting, the conversion of certain temples into Buddhist sanctuaries of the Lesser Vehicle, and the crumbling of the monuments have dispersed the statuary, and for obvious security reasons the Conservation of Angkor has not attempted to return statues to their proper places, with rare exceptions. But if we were to judge these statues solely according to our aesthetic criteria, we would fail to understand their power and quality as representations of the divine. When an icon in the hieratic style of Bakheng or Koh Ker appears somewhat cold to our Western eyes, we should not forget the importance in the Indian world of such phenomena as *āsana,* an ascetic technique for transcending the human condition to become invulnerable to the external world. The infinite possible positions of the human body are reduced to one archetypal and iconographic position, which certain sculpture in the exhibition illustrates superbly. Alterations in style can also result from the fluctuation of ideas and of attitudes toward worship, and textbook discussions in terms of decline and renewal largely miss the point. The Bayon figures with their columnar legs may, according to our criteria, represent a decline in the art of modeling and signal the final exhaustion of Khmer art, overburdened by the countless foundations Jayavarman VII had commissioned. Yet was it ineptness that caused representations of the human body to conform to a more abstract architecture at a time when the tower shrines of Angkor were being transformed into gigantic faces? All the spirituality, all the mystique of the period, was rather concentrated in those heads, which stand among the finest ever created by man and offer us, in a style far different from that of earlier periods, a further splendid illustration of *āsana.*

The National Museum of Cambodia

Pich Keo

The distinctive building that houses the present National Museum of Cambodia opened in 1918 as part of the École des Arts Cambodgiens (School of Cambodian Arts). Its original purpose was to store and exhibit Cambodia's national treasures—stone, bronze, and wooden sculpture. In the early days, only the front rooms were used for display purposes. The side and rear halls were used as general workshops and for student accommodations. On the basis of a royal decree signed by King Sisowath on 12 April 1919, however, it was renamed the Musée du Cambodge (Museum of Cambodia). The official inauguration ceremony took place on 13 April 1920, the first day of the Khmer New Year, under the auspices of King Sisowath and the French representative to Cambodia, Mr. Baudoin. On 10 April 1920, King Sisowath issued a decree changing its name once more, to the Musée Albert Sarraut, in honor of the French governor-general of Indochina.

A forerunner, the Musée Khmer (Khmer Museum), had existed since 1905. It displayed only Khmer archaeology, however, while the main Indochinese museum was located in the Vietnamese city of Hanoi. The Musée Khmer was organized and run by the French when Cambodia was a protectorate of France. In 1909 the French had brought together more Khmer sculpture in a house within the compound of the former Sisowath High School, which they named the Musée de Phnom Penh. The house was filled with 150 works of Angkor-period sculpture, which the French had excavated. All of this sculpture was given to the new Musée Albert Sarraut after the inauguration ceremony in 1920.

Before 1951, all museum operations and architectural restoration work in Cambodia were conducted under the control of the French governor-general of Indochina. Subsequently, the French transferred the direction of archaeology to the Cambodian authorities, while technical conservation support was provided by the French Department of Museums. After the Musée Albert Sarraut was transferred from French to Cambodian authorities, it was renamed the National Museum of Cambodia. French control of the museum ended in October 1966, when a Cambodian, Chea Thay Seng, was appointed director.

The National Museum is located to the north of the Royal Palace and faces the Tonle Sap River across the former royal cremation site. Designed in a rich adaptation of traditional Khmer architecture by the French archaeologist George Groslier, with help from the staff of the École des Arts Cambodgiens, the rectangular structure (66 x 54 meters) is built around a beautiful interior courtyard featuring four ornamental ponds filled with flowering lotus plants. The whole building sits on a plinth 2.5 meters above ground level, and the roof, including the center spire, reaches a height of 38 meters. All of the architectural ornamentation is the work of Cambodian artists, with the wooden doors and window shutters made by the teachers and students of the École des Arts. The museum's two imposing front doors, which weigh more than a ton and measure 5.1 by 2.4 meters, took eight teachers and students forty-five days to complete. The design on the doors is copied from the tenth-century temple of Banteay Srei.

In 1920 the collection included more than one thousand objects: bronze and stone sculpture, traditional costumes, jewelry, weapons, palanquins, coins, and ceramics. The museum housed an information office, a workshop that made reproductions of famous Khmer sculpture in the collection, and a museum shop. The library contained three hundred books on Cambodia, its temples, and archaeology, and its reading room was open daily.

In 1969 the museum was renovated. The central part of the front eastern wing was demolished and rebuilt in concrete in the same style. This alteration made it possible to divide the eastern wing into three levels: a newly created basement for storage, the ground floor for gallery space, and the upper floor for offices, files, and the library and reading room.

The collection of the museum has increased dramatically since 1920. By 1975 it numbered in the thousands and ranged from prehistoric and ethnographic works to the arts of the later post-Angkor period. Many objects were given to the museum by the king, tribal people, temples, the Depot for the Conservation of Angkor, and generous individuals, while other works were purchased. The display is now divided into two parts, archaeological and ethnographic. The archaeological section is further subdivided into three parts: bronze, stone, and ceramic. The ethnographic section includes wooden ornaments from temples, old musical instruments, and weaving looms.

By 1970 several Cambodian provinces had established their own museums. Battambang, for example, had two. During the civil war, between 1970 and 1975, much bronze and stone sculpture was brought to the National Museum for safekeeping and conservation treatments. In 1975, the conservation workshop was destroyed, and three Khmer conservators who had studied in France were killed. Between 1975 and 1979 the National Museum was abandoned and the staff forced to leave Phnom Penh, and Ly Vouong, the museum's director, was killed, tragically. Many objects were also damaged or stolen. The museum's electrical wiring system had become unreliable and dangerous.

The liberation of Phnom Penh on 7 January 1979 revealed that the entire museum compound was filled with dust and vegetation, and the collections were in disarray. The roof and ceiling were on the verge of collapse, while wild trees grew amid the empty ponds in the interior courtyard. The whole building was also filled with bat dung and its repulsive odor. The condition of the national collection was a disgrace that caused the Cambodian people much anguish. Thanks to the work of six staff members who had survived the civil war and others who were related to former staff, the buildings and compound were cleaned, and the sculpture put back in order. The National Museum officially reopened to the public on 13 April 1979, on the day of the Cambodian New Year, under the auspices of Heng Samrin, president of the Cambodian People's Council.

Recently, the Australian government has entirely rebuilt the museum's roof and replaced the electrical system. This is an encouraging development and a much-appreciated first step on the long road to the museum's rehabilitation. Much remains to be done, however. The southern, western, and northern parts of the building are old and rotten, and urgently need repair. The library of approximately one thousand books has also deteriorated and is infested by insects. In fact, everything needs restoration, but how are we to manage this? The museum staff lacks the expertise and resources to repair and conserve the sculpture, or to catalogue the collection.

All of the problems mentioned above can only be rectified with international help. For this reason I would like to use the opportunity of this exhibition to make an urgent plea for assistance, so that the National Museum can resume a leading role in the preservation of Cambodia's national culture, the precious heritage from our ancestors.

Adapted from *The Age of Angkor: Treasures from the National Museum of Cambodia*, Canberra, 1992, by kind permission of the National Gallery of Australia.

Chronology

	Non-Cambodian	Cambodian
1st century AD	Indian culture spreads throughout Southeast Asia Decoration of the portals of the great *stūpa* at Sāñcī 78: śaka era begins 79: Destruction of Pompeii	
2d century	Furthest extension of Roman Empire Amarāvatī *stūpa* Buddhist reliefs, classical phase 1st half: Villa Hadrian mid: Bacchus temple at Baalbek late: Linyi kingdom (the future Champa) appears in Chinese records	PRE-ANGKOR PERIOD from early in the Christian era until the end of the 8th century
3d century	Funan appears in Chinese records Pyu dynasty in Burma 212: Construction of Caracalla baths begins in Rome 220: End of Eastern Han dynasty in China c. 225: Sassanid dynasty in the Middle East 2d half: Inscription of Vo Canh in Khan Hoa province, Vietnam	Oc Eo established as center of maritime power of Funan
4th century	Classical phase of Mayan Empire begins in Central America 320: Gupta period begins in India 330: Founding of Constantinople	
5th century	c. 400: Brahmanistic inscriptions of Mūlavarman in Kutei, Kalimantan early: Barbarian invasion of northern China closes land route and stimulates maritime route to the advantage of Funan and the kingdoms of the Indonesian archipelago c. 450: Inscriptions mention hydraulic works by Pūrṇavarman in West Java 451: Defeat of Attila the Hun Image of Teaching Buddha at Sārnāth late: Hun domination of India begins (through 6th century)	484: King of Funan sends the Buddhist monk Nagasena to China
6th century	532: Construction of Hagia Sophia begins in Constantinople	Chinese records mention Zhenla dominance over Funan

	c. 550: Cālukya dynasty in India (until 750) end: Elephanta cave in India	514–539: Rudravarman (?) c. 550: Bhavavarman I late: Construction of Bhavapura as capital of Bhavavarman
7th century	Height of Pallava dynasty in India (600–850) Rise of Śrīvijayan Empire in southeastern Sumatra 607: Construction of Horyuji temple begins at Nara, Japan 618: Tang dynasty in China Height of Ellora cave art in India Earliest buildings at Mi Son, Champa 671–695: Buddhist pilgrim I Tsing visits Southeast Asia late: Earliest known inscriptions in Malay recorded in Sumatra	1st half: Reign of Īśānavarman at Sambor Prei Kuk Construction of temples at Angkor Borei and Sambor Prei Kuk Phnom Da style Sambor Prei Kuk style c. 616–635: Īśānavarman I 635–656: Bhavavarman II 2d half: Prei Kmeng style late: Prasat Andet style
8th century	Moors arrive in Spain Pālā dynasty in India Buddhist Śailendra dynasty in Central Java 732: Inscription mentions construction of a *liṅga* by Sañjaya in Central Java 794: Kyoto becomes capital of Japan	early: Construction of Prasat Ak Yum, the first temple-mountain c. 790: Return of the future Jayavarman II, founder of the Angkor dynasty, from "Javā" Kompong Preah style
9th century	800: Coronation of Charlemagne in Europe c. 800: Construction of Borobudur in Central Java Normans invade Europe 845: Proscription of Buddhism by the Taoists in China 856: Inscription in Central Java celebrates victory of a Śivaite monarch mid: Brahmanic temple group built at Prambanan, Central Java	ANGKOR PERIOD 802–1431 802–after 830: Jayavarman II 802: Installation of *devarāja* on Phnom Kulen (Mahendraparvata) by the Brahman Śivakaivalya 1st three-quarters: Kulen style after 830–at least 860: Jayavarman III 877–889: Indravarman II; establishment of Hariharālaya as the capital Preah Ko style 879: Preah Ko temple 881: Bakong temple-mountain 889–early 10th c.: Yaśovarman I 893: Lolei temple, built as an island in the *baray* Indratatāka
10th century	c. 900: Decline of Mayan Empire and abandonment of its great ceremonial centers Shift of royal power in Java to East Java Cola Empire in India Danes invade England 960: Song dynasty in China Temple construction begins at Pagan, Burma	early: Yaśovarman I establishes his capital, Yaśodharapura, on Phnom Bakheng Construction of the Bakheng temple-mountain 1st quarter: Bakheng style Phnom Krom and Phnom Bok, contemporary with Phnom Bakheng 912–922: References to Harṣavarman I 921: Prasat Kravan 925: Reference to Īśānavarman II 921/928–942: Jayavarman IV; reigned at Koh Ker (Chok Gargyar) 942–944: Harṣavarman II; reigned at Koh Ker

		944–968: Rājendravarman II; return of capital to Angkor 3d quarter: Pre Rup style 952: East Mebon temple 961: Pre Rup temple-mountain Beginning of Royal Palace in Angkor 967: Consecration of Banteay Srei by the Brahman Yajñavarāha last quarter: Banteay Srei style 968–1000/1001: Jayavarman V
11th century	c. 1000: Khaṇḍāriya Mahādeva temple at Khajurāho, India Lost-wax bronze casting in Ife, Nigeria 1019–1049: Reign of Airlangga in East Java 1025: Cola raid on Śrīvijaya 1066: Norman Conquest of England	early: Ta Keo temple-mountain (see also 1002–1010) 1002: Udayādityavarman I 1002–1010: Jayavīravarman I (Ta Keo; completion of monument ?) 1002/1010–1049: Sūryavarman I Construction of Preah Vihear temple Modifications to Phimeanakas, royal temple in grounds of Royal Palace (?) 1050–1066: Udayādityavarman II Construction of western *baray* Baphuon temple-mountain 1010–c. 1080: Baphuon style 1052: Inscription of Sdok Kak Thom, from temple of that name in Prachinburi province in present-day Thailand, records the installation of the first *devarāja* on Phnom Kulen in 802 1066–1080: Harṣavarman III 1080–1107: Jayavarman VI
12th century	High Gothic period in European architecture early: Decline of Toltec Empire, rise of the Aztec 1st quarter: *Song of Roland* in France 1170: Murder of Thomas à Becket in Canterbury 1193: Sultanate of Delhi in India 1194: Construction begins on Chartres Cathedral	1107–1113: Dharaṇīndravarman 1113–at least 1145: Sūryavarman II 1st half: Construction of temple-mountain of Angkor Vat Construction of Beng Mealea, about 60 miles east of Angkor Banteay Samre 1st three-quarters: Angkor Vat style after 1150–1165: Yaśovarman II 1165–1177: Tribhuvanādityavarman (killed during battle against Chams) 1177: Cham capture of Angkor 1181–1218 (?): Jayavarman VII Mahāyāna Buddhism established as state religion Construction of Banteay Kdei 1186: Ta Prohm temple, dedicated to mother of Jayavarman VII 1191: Preah Khan temple, dedicated to father of Jayavarman VII Construction of Jayatatāka, *baray* of Preah Khan, with Neak Pean in its center last quarter: Construction of Angkor Thom late: Construction of Bayon temple-mountain

		Srah Srang, royal bathing pool last quarter of 12th–1st quarter of 13th: Bayon style Construction of Banteay Chmar temple in northwestern Cambodia
13th century	c. 1200: Rise of first Incan emperor, Manco Capac 1215: Genghis Khan conquers northern China 1244: Fall of Jerusalem Islam arrives in northern Sumatra 1292: Marco Polo visits northern Sumatra late: Sukhothai kingdom in Thailand 1299: Ottoman Empire in Turkey	1219–1242: Indravarman II 1243–1295: Jayavarman VIII; Brahmanism restored as state religion 1296–1297: Chinese traveler Zhou Daguan visits Angkor Construction of some temples in the Preah Pithu group
14th century	End of power of Śrīvijaya in Sumatra Emergence of Majapahit Empire in East Java Vijayanagara Empire in India 1305: Construction of Alhambra palace begins in Spain 1321: Death of Dante in Italy 1325: Founding of Tenochtitlán, capital of Aztec Empire 1347: Black Death throughout Europe 1350: Ayuthayā kingdom in Thailand 1365: *Nāgarakṛtāgama* in East Java 1367: Hundred Years War begins in Europe 1368: Ming dynasty in China 1398: Timor invades India	Thai raids on Angkor Growing importance of Theravāda Buddhism in Cambodia
15th century	Height of Inca power in South America 1400: Death of Chaucer 1416: Chinese pilgrim Ma Han visits Java 1421–1434: Duomo of Florence by Brunelleschi 1453: Fall of Constantinople 1492: Columbus arrives in the New World late: Benin Empire in Nigeria	1431: Abandonment of Angkor; location of capital in Srei Santhor region to the south Buddha of Tep Pranam (possibly later)
16th century	First Roman Catholic conversions in Southeast Asia 1511: Melaka captured by the Portuguese 1520: Süleyman the Magnificent comes to power in Turkey	1516–1566: Ang Chan I 3d quarter: Temporary reoccupation of Angkor by Ang Chan I and his successor
17th century	Major European colonial expansion in Southeast Asia 1602: Establishment of the Vereenigde Oost-Indische Compagnie in the Netherlands 1603: Death of Elizabeth I of England 1616: Dirk Hartog's ship arrives off the coast of western Australia 1638: Louis XIV ascends throne in France 1684: Phra Narai of Thailand and Louis XIV exchange ambassadors	

Note to the Reader

For Sanskrit, the usual Latin transcription with diacritical marks, fixed at the 10th Congress of Orientalists in Geneva (1894), has been adopted.

In general, all letters are pronounced, including diphthongs (*ai, au*).

A horizontal mark above a vowel (*ā, ī, ū*) indicates a long vowel.

The *ā* is pronounced as the *a* in *hard.*

The *ī* is pronounced as the *ee* in *see,* but lightly.

The *ū* is pronounced as the *oo* in *tool.*

The *ḷ* (vocalized *l*) is pronouced with the tip of the tongue on the hard palate.

The *ṛ* (vocalized *r*) is pronounced with back palatal contact similar to the *r* in French.

A dot above *ṅ* denotes nasalization of the preceding vowel.

A dot below a consonant (with the exception of vocalized *ḷ* and *ṛ* and of *ṣ*) does not strongly affect normal English pronunciation.

The *c* and *ch* are pronounced *tch,* lightly aspirated, as in *choose.*

The *j* and *jh* are pronounced *dj,* lightly aspirated, as in *judge.*

The *g* is always hard, as in *guard.*

The *h* is pronounced, as in *hope.*

The *ñ* is pronounced *ny,* as in *piraña.*

The *s* is pronounced as in *hiss.*

The *ś* is pronounced as in *shout.*

The *ṣ* is pronounced as in *ash.*

For Khmer, a simplified transcription has been adopted, omitting accents. In some instances, this transliteration is followed by the scientific transliteration in parentheses: for example, *phnom* (*bhnaṃ*); *prasat* (*prāsād*). Readers may be surprised to find the use of *v* where formerly *w* was used in English transcriptions (as distinct from French transcriptions, where *v* has always been used). This is particularly noticeable in *Vat,* also widely spelled *Wat.* This transliteration represents more accurately the sound in the Khmer language: a slight contact of the upper teeth with the lower lip, resembling the half-formed *v* of words like *vary, volley* rather than the more fully articulated *v* in *view.*

In general, all letters are pronounced, including diphthongs, according to the guidelines for Sanskrit above.

The *ph* is pronounced *p,* never *f* (for example, *phnom, Baphuon*).

The familiar forms have been retained for topographic and geographic names (for example, *Banteay,* not *Pandāy; Angkor,* not *Aṅgar; vat,* not *vatt*).

In texts in English one frequently finds the terms Vaiṣṇava or Vaiṣṇavite, and Śaiva or Śaivite, whereas we have used Viṣṇuite and Śivaite. Our use of the latter terms conforms with the usage of our French colleagues, and at the same time with the terminology adopted by Bhattacharya to define the distinction between the sects within Viṣṇuism and Śaivism of which Vaiṣṇava and Śaiva are but two among many.

For Chinese, in accordance with similar recent international standards, Pinyin has been adopted. In some texts the former transcription of EFEO has been added in parentheses: for example, *Zhou Daguan* (*Chou Ta-Kuan*).

For the occasional Vietnamese and Indonesian words in the book, the current standard international form has been adopted.

The order of the given dimensions of objects is height followed by width followed by depth. Dimensions are given in centimeters. One inch is equal to 2.54 centimeters.

History

The Khmer territory in pre- and protohistory. Summary map
■ Sites of the pre- and protohistoric periods
▲ Sites from the beginning of the historic period
● Modern cities
Dangrek Mountains (Chaine des Dangrek)
Cardamom Hills (Monts des Cardamomes)
Elephant Hills (Monts de L'Elephant)
Plain of Reeds (Plaines des Joncs)
Oc Eo (Oc-Éo)
Ho Chi Minh City/Saigon (Hochiminhville)
Gulf of Thailand/Gulf of Siam (Golfe de Thaïlande)

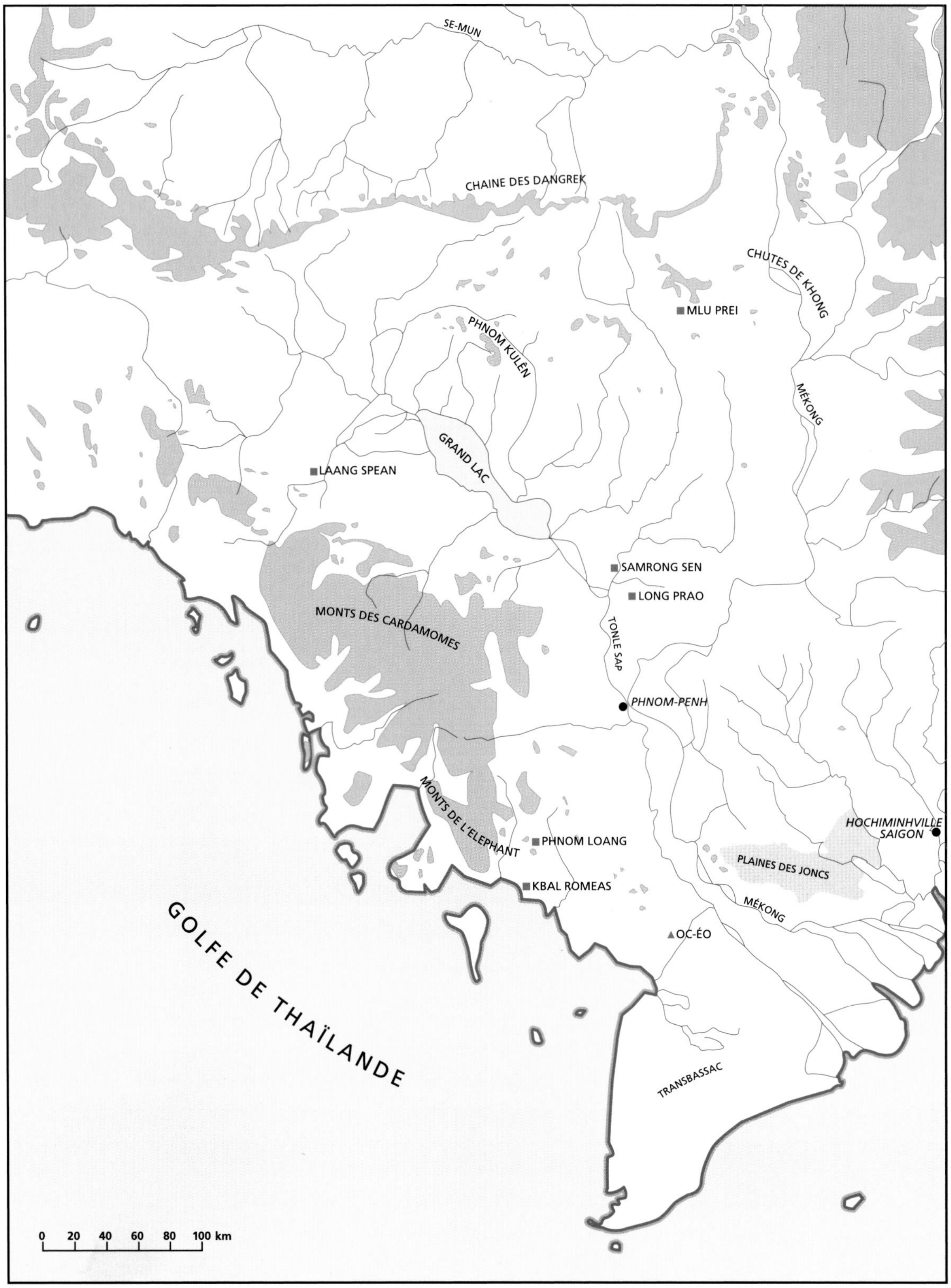

Cambodia from Its Beginnings

Maud Girard-Geslan

I. Land and People

Centered in the south of the Indochinese peninsula, at the crossroads of the mainland and islands of Southeast Asia, Cambodia lies between longitude 102.5° and 107.5° and between the 10th and 15th parallels. It is bounded on the north by Laos, on the east by Vietnam, and on the west by Thailand; to the south, it opens onto the Gulf of Siam. The country occupies at present only a portion of the territory it held at the time of the Khmer empire's maximum expansion, when it also included what today are southern Laos, northeastern Thailand, and the southern part of Vietnam.

The heart of the country, then and now, is a vast lowland region, the great central plains of Cambodia (77,500 square miles or 125,000 km²), surrounded on all sides by hills and mountains. To the southwest, the Cardamom Range, rising to 5,810 feet (1,700 m), and the Elephant Range, rising to 3,280 feet (1,000 m), separate this immense low-lying area from the Gulf of Siam. On the west, the Pailin Heights link the southern mountain ranges to the Dangrek Mountains in the north, which form a long escarpment marking the country's northern border with Thailand. To the east are the high plateaus of Indochina, the southern extremity of the Annam Range, separating Cambodia from Vietnam and effectively marking the boundary between the Indianized and Sinicized worlds. Lower down, the Mekong delta extends its marshy plain toward the southeast. Around the delta's western branch, the Bassac, would develop the first Indianized kingdom in Indochina, a kingdom that would become the ancestor of Angkor period Cambodia.

The climate is tropical, alternating between a dry and a rainy season. From November to April, the dry season, with its monsoon winds from the northeast, is extremely hot and debilitating. During the rainy season, from May to October, plants, animals, and men revive under the beneficial effects of the southwest monsoons. Differences from region to region are considerable. The Phnom Penh area, where the sun shines 240 days a year, receives an annual rainfall of approximately 56 inches (1,400 mm). The sea side of the Cambodian mountain ranges and the northeastern plateaus, however, are lashed by the full force of the monsoons; rainfall there is much more abundant, reaching 152 inches (3,800 mm). Arriving as sporadic storms at the start of the season, the rains become torrential in September and October, causing widespread flooding.

Cambodia's most distinctive physical characteristic and the one most responsible for its development is its complex hydrography. By first putting its waters to admirable use, then managing and exploiting them, Cambodia's inhabitants were able to compensate for the naturally poor soils that are common to most of the Indochinese peninsula.[1] Crossing Cambodia from north to south is the Mekong River, the third longest in Asia after the Yangtze and the Ganges. It is 2,600 miles (4,200 km) in length, rising in Tibet at

1. See Groslier 1979, 161-202.

16,000 feet (4,875 m) and traversing the western reaches of the Chinese province of Yunnan as the Lancang River.[2] The Mekong's middle course irrigates Laos, alternately passing through narrow whitewater defiles and broadening out in the plains. Near the Cambodian border, the Mekong flows over the Khong Falls, then runs south through Khong to Kratie, where it turns toward the west, and, as a mighty, silt-laden river, irrigates Kampong Cham and Phnom Penh. From there it flows southeastward to the sea, crossing the vast Plain of Reeds and ramifying into a thousand channels once over the Vietnamese border, where it is known as the Sông Cuu Long, or Nine Dragon River.

Between the last rapids at Sambor and the sea, the river crosses a distance of 300 miles (500 km) with only a very slight drop in elevation. Beginning in June, melting Tibetan snows combine with the onslaught of rain from the southeast monsoons, enormously increasing the quantity of water to be flushed out through the lower course of the Mekong. The river is unable to handle the volume, despite the myriad rivulets fanning out across the lower peninsula. The colossal surge of water spills into one of the Mekong's tributaries, the Tonle Sap, and reverses its course. This river then floods the lake also called Tonle Sap (Great Lake), which grows from 1,800 to 6,200 square miles (3,000 to 10,000 km^2) just a few months into the rainy season. At the height of the floods in October, the Tonle Sap holds 80 billion cubic meters of water. At Phnom Penh the river crests at 26 feet (8 m) above low water level. Starting in mid-October, the floods recede and the Tonle Sap resumes flowing in its natural direction. The reservoir releases water laden with silt, which is deposited on the lowlands bordering the river, and leaves fish in the ponds and puddles lying between the low ridges partitioning the fields. The flooding greatly assists both agriculture and fishing. Fishermen and rice growers can prosper, setting aside food surpluses against the shortfalls of the dry season.

Cambodia's first inhabitants seem to have been Australoid peoples, who were pushed out or infiltrated by "Indonesian"[3] groups from the north during the Neolithic era. Cambodia then found itself within the sphere of activity of the Mon tribes, also from the north, who settled an area from the mouth of the Irrawaddy River to the Mekong delta and pushed back the earlier inhabitants into the forested areas and mountains. The Khmer arrived next and subsequently intermingled with the Mon to create the brilliant civilization whose art is the focus of this exhibition.

Today certain groups of mountain peoples living in the Dangrek Mountains, the Cardamom Range, or the Elephant Range (the Samre, Pear, and Kuy) and certain groups living in eastern Cambodia near Mondolkiri and Ratanakiri represent the last descendants of the Australoid, "Indonesian," and some proto-Mon tribes. Most speak languages belonging to the Mon-Khmer family. However the majority of the population (almost 80 percent) is Khmer, descendants of the Angkor civilization who practice wet-rice farming in the great plain.

II. Prehistory and Protohistory

The overall picture of the prehistory and protohistory of mainland Southeast Asia is becoming clearer.[4] Since the 1960s major discoveries have

2. This was not without significance for the cultural exchanges that occurred, particularly during the earliest periods of civilization.
3. This term is problematic. These "Indonesian" peoples were related to the present inhabitants of maritime southeast Asia but cannot be specifically identified as Indonesians as we currently understand the term.
4. See especially the works of Janice Stargardt on Burma; those of Chester Gorman, Donn Bayard, Pisit Charoengwongsa, Joyce White, and Charles Higham on Thailand; and those of Hà Van Tân, Diep Dinh Hoa, Pham Minh Huyên, and Nguyên Van Buu on Vietnam.

been made in the countries adjoining Cambodia—southern China, Burma, Thailand, and Vietnam. With the unsettled conditions in Cambodia resulting from the Vietnam War and its aftermath, however, fewer excavations have been carried out there than one would like. The most recent work relating to Cambodian prehistory is still that of E. Saurin, J.-P. Carbonnel, and the Mourers, from the 1960s and 1970s, which continued the research begun in the colonial period.[5] Excavations in the Mekong delta and lower Dong-nai basin[6] by Vietnamese archaeologists resumed in 1975. They have produced evidence, however still marked by frustrating lacunae, consistent with the notion that a koine, or set of cultural attributes, belonging to Southeast Asia is independent and distinct from the koine of China or of the Indianized world. Its particular nature may serve to explain the lateness with which the countries of this region came to statehood and entered the historical period.

The Paleolithic Period

Few habitation sites dating to Paleolithic times and used by hunter-gatherers are known in Cambodia. In the eastern part of the country, the terraces overlooking the Mekong were occupied by peoples who practiced a primitive technology.[7] On the highest terraces, where occupation dates back 600,000 years, pebbles worked on one face only have been found, while on the lower terraces, where habitation is more recent, worked stones and flakes have been found with a few rare bifaces among them.

Elsewhere nothing is clear. In western Cambodia, the most ancient stratum of the Laang Spean cave, twenty-five miles (40 km) west of Battambang, dates from 8500 (±900) B.P., which could indicate that it was inhabited during the Upper Paleolithic. The dating of the southern Phnom Loang (Kampot) site to the Paleolithic by Carbonnel is disputed by Mourer.[8]

Everywhere on the Indochinese peninsula, throughout its long history, archaic techniques persisted even after more advanced ones were introduced, coexisting on the same site or on neighboring sites. This tends to blur an already incomplete picture of Southeast Asian prehistory.

The Hoabinhian Period[9]

Though it is difficult to determine the boundaries between the different phases, it is possible to find Hoabinhian remains in Cambodia. In the vast area extending from southern China to the Malay Peninsula, hunter-gatherers were starting to practice a primitive form of cultivation. The Laang Spean cave, which was excavated on two separate occasions and in several locations by Mourer, gave rise to a number of scientific datings that indicate occupation from 8500 (±900) B.P. to 1200 (±70) B.P. The lithic technology (fig. 1), in which polishing is unknown, is characterized by tools made from single-faced pebbles (sumatraliths) or from flakes produced on site. Pottery starts to appear in Level II, which dates from the fifth millennium B.C., in a purely Hoabinhian lithic context. Varied in form and reddish in color, the pottery becomes abundant between the third and the first half of the first millennium B.C.

5. Roland Mourer has published a remarkable article entitled "Contribution à l'étude de la préhistoire du Cambodge" (see MOURER 1994), which David Chandler was kind enough to pass on to me, along with Michael Vickery's article on Zhenla (see VICKERY 1994).

6. The study of this region, which was taken from Cambodia during the nineteenth century, appears to be of great importance for understanding the history of the Khmer civilization and the civilization of Southeast Asia in general. Hà Van Tân, Vo Si Khai, Luong Ninh, Dô Dinh Thuât, Lê Xuân Diêm, Nguyên Van Long, Nguyên Duy Ty, Dao Ba Hac, and Pham Duc Manh, to mention only a few, have worked on this region and the question of Funan. We are unfortunately unaware of any synthesis in a western language on the archaeology of Oc Eo and Funan that takes into account the recent and highly promising work performed by the Vietnamese. Only a portion of the documents published in Vietnam, access to which remains very difficult, have been read by us. The presentations on this subject made at the December 1992 colloquium in Hanoi are as yet unavailable to us, as is the collection of essays gathered and published by Hà Van Tân under the title *Van hoa Oc-eo và cac nên van hoa cô o dông bang sông Cuu Long*, Long Xuyên, 1984.

7. See E. SAURIN, "Le Paléolithique du Cambodge oriental," *AP* 12 (1966), 27–41.

8. See MOURER 1994, 165.

9. The Hoabinhian, which takes its name from the eponymous site of Hoa-binh in northern Vietnam discovered by M. Colani in 1927, is characterized by stone tools made of pebbles worked on one face only (sumatraliths).

Fig. 1
Short ax made of hornfels, from a layer dated 6240 ± 70 BP (4290 ± 70 BC). Laang Spean. Hoabinhian period. Height 9.3 cm, width 8.2 cm. C. and R. Mourer excavations. Inv. 80000751. Collection of the Lyon Museum

Fig. 2
Bowl with a circular base. Pottery decorated with spirals on a stippled background. Samrong Sen. Late Neolithic period. Height 15 cm, diameter 28.5 cm. Collected by L. Jammes 1887–1888. Inv. 80000751. Collection of the Lyon Museum

The Neolithic Period and the Bronze Age

In the third millennium B.C., numerous settlements along rivers and in hilly areas throughout continental Southeast Asia show that dry or naturally flooded rice cultivation was practiced side by side with hunting and gathering. In Cambodia, several Neolithic kitchen middens (shell mounds, so-called *kjökkenmöddinger*) are known in the Tonle Sap region. The midden site at Samrong Sen, known since the nineteenth century, has been excavated several times in this century by H. Mansuy. There, as at Long Prao, many objects were acquired off-site from villagers.[10] Though damaged because its shells have been extracted for lime since time immemorial, the kitchen midden at Samrong Sen has yielded a rich variety of chipped and polished stone objects, including axes, adzes (sometimes with a tang for attaching a handle), chisels, and personal ornaments. Among the latter is a bracelet with a T-shaped cross section of a type also found in Vietnam, Thailand,[11] and southern China. Bone implements are also present.

The pottery, built up by hand, comprises containers with rounded or footed bottoms (fig. 2). In the oldest strata of the midden, the pottery has little or no decoration, but in the higher levels the decoration becomes more com-

10. See MANSUY 1902 and 1923.
11. At Ban Chiang, this bracelet appears in bronze and in stone, with both versions worn concurrently by the same corpse. See WHITE 1982, 79 and 84, fig. 59.

plex; always geometrical, it sometimes consists of smooth, broken, or wavy bands on a dotted background.

Bronze objects are also present. Many, however, were obtained off-site from local villagers, and dating them on any basis other than style is impossible. Axes with sockets, chisels, knives, arrowheads, fish hooks, rings, and bells give the picture of a village society endowed with a certain level of prosperity and complexity.

Unlike the coastline of Vietnam, rich in this kind of shell mound, the coast of the Gulf of Siam apparently features only a single kitchen midden at Kbal Romeas, dating from 5370 (±140) B.P.[12] Near Mlu Prei, south of the border with Thailand and Laos, three open-air sites excavated in 1938 by P. Lévy[13] have yielded fine stone tools of chert, quartz, and sandstone, generally polished but sometimes chipped, comprising adzes, axes, and chisels, some of which have tangs. One also finds sickles made of shale, bone, and bronze, including a fairly large number and variety of bronze objects with high copper content. The tools, which all have sockets, consist of axes, chisels, and sickles, either whole or fragmentary. The presence of crucibles and two-part molds made of sandstone[14] indicates that these bronze objects were made locally. The refined decoration of certain bracelets has an aesthetic quality comparable to that of Dông-son or Ban Chiang. A few iron objects that are impossible to date also appear there.

The ceramic ware consists of round-bottomed or footed containers, decorated by impression or incision, as well as spindle whorls, anvils, beaters, and *bolas*.

Samrong Sen and Mlu Prei, like many other Neolithic sites in Southeast Asia related to them by their technology, were inhabited in the Bronze Age, without any apparent interruption in their development. The origin of metallurgy still remains to be discovered. It is not impossible that it was invented locally (either with or without an external stimulus from China or India) even if, given the paucity of data on Cambodia, the question of where the ores came from has not even been broached. Copper and tin are abundant in the neighboring countries, particularly in Yunnan, where metalworking flourished even before the Chinese conquest (109 B.C.),[15] and both are present in Cambodia, copper in the northeast and tin in the south. However, no early mines have been discovered to date.[16] It is possible that when small village societies wanted to produce bronze objects locally for their own use, they extracted ore from available alluvial deposits by simply washing them. Or, metal may have been bought in ingots or in the form of scraps at villages near collection sites or along trade routes. This is conceivable even in those areas rich in ore, as trading for metal may well have been more economical than extracting and refining it.

Whether or not based on the practice of melting down existing metal, metalworking had already attained a high level in the prehistoric period, implying familiarity with different metals and techniques. But no site has yet been discovered in Cambodia that is equivalent either in the abundance or quality of its production to those in Yunnan or to the Dôngsonian sites in Vietnam. The predilection for spiral motifs (see bracelet illustration, Boisselier, *Manuel*, 1966, 27, fig. 2 c-f), as found on a knife blade and on small bells and bronze bracelets from Samrong Sen and Mlu Prei, is common to all continental Southeast Asia in the Bronze Age and the early Iron Age.[17] Clearly the different cultural centers from Yunnan to the Malay world were exchanging goods and ideas both along river routes such as the Mekong and across sea routes.

12. See CARBONNEL, "Recent Data on the Cambodian Neolithic: The Problem of Cultural Continuity in Southern Indochina," in SMITH and WATSON 1979, 223.
13. LÉVY 1943.
14. One of the molds is for a sickle that bears a resemblance to the sickles of Phung Nguyên in northern Vietnam. The molds are of stone, as are most of those found in Vietnam in the Red River and Sông Ma basins as well as at several southern sites: Hàng Gon I, Dâu Giây, Cù Lao Rùa, and Dôc Chùa (3845±130 B.P.), see *KCH* 1977, 4:44–48. At Nhommaiat in Laos and at Non Nok Tha in Thailand (WHITE 1982, 48–49), and in southern China in the Wucheng culture of Jiangxi, stone molds have also been recorded. In northern China, molds are generally ceramic.
15. Metallurgy was common not only in the region of Dian Lake but also in the Erhai Lake region, which is in the watershed of the Lancang River before it becomes the Mekong. Yunnan has yielded a great number of bronze objects of remarkable quality and diversity, much superior to what has been found farther to the south. Interestingly, a small bronze bracelet aesthetically very close to Indochinese bronzes decorated with a series of spirals looking like concentric circles was excavated from tomb 209 at Aofengshan in Jianchuan, to the north of Dali, an area of Yunnan Province that belongs to the Lancang (upper Mekong) River system. The tomb could date back to a period close to 2420 ± 80 B.P. See *Wenwu* 1986, 7:9, fig. 31. For the province as a whole, see *Ancient Bronzes from the Yunnan Provincial Museum* (Tokyo, 1981, Japanese-language text). For the Dian region, see M. PIRAZZOLI-t'STEVENS, *La Civilisation du royaume de Dian à l'époque Han*, EFEO (Paris, 1974); and H. BRINKER, *Dian Ein versunkenes Königreich in China* [exh. cat., Museum Rietberg] (Zurich, 1986). China's possible stimulation of Thailand, Cambodia, and the former Cochin China may have occurred from western Yunnan and radiated through the river valleys. See TRINH SINH 1979, 49–68.
16. See BRONSON 1992, 78–81.
17. Spirals are found from the Yunnan cultures (fifth to second century B.C.), the Dôngsonian civilization of north and central Vietnam (fifth century B.C. to second century A.D.), the prosperous villages of northeastern Thailand, and even the sites in the Dong-nai basin. See the group of *ge* halberds (an originally Chinese form that has spread to the outskirts of China) from Lông Giao, Xuân Lôc (Dong-nai) in PHAM DUC MANH 1985, 37–38. These weapons date from 2495±50 B.P. Characteristically Southeast Asian in their ornament, they are in shape close to the Chinese *ge* halberds of the Warring States period (fifth to third century B.C.). This period may have constituted a golden age for the village societies and chiefdoms in the entire region.

In the general imprecision attending the protohistory of Southeast Asia, one group of very fine bronze objects stands out as a landmark between the Bronze Age and the start of the historical period. Apparently ritual in purpose, and as yet undated[18] because none was discovered in a scientific archaeological context, they also mark the cusp between metalworking to produce tools and personal ornaments and that to cast statues.[19] On the one hand, the objects consist of receptacles in the shape of flattened skin vessels, biconvex or lentil-shaped in section, with incurving neck and rounded bottom; some still have three rings, for hanging from a cord or chain.[20] Another group comprises bells, quite ample in size and lacking clappers. Two examples exist in Cambodia: the Kandal urn (fig. 3), twenty-two inches (56 cm) in height, and the Samrong bell (fig. 4), twenty-two and one half inches (57 cm) in height, both now at the National Museum in Phnom Penh.[21]

All these objects are decorated with refined, basically geometric motifs, in which broad bands of spirals (sometimes looping vertically, sometimes horizontally) play an important part in conjunction with animal figures, which may

18. GROSLIER 1961, 32, assigns the Kandal urn to the fourth century B.C. and several years later, in 1966, to the fourth to second centuries B.C.
19. See MALLERET, *Objets du bronze*, 1956. At the time, three were inventoried, whereas six or seven are known today.
20. For example the urn in the collection of Georges Ortiz, see GIRARD-GESLAN, "La Protohistoire," in *L'Art de l'Asie du Sud-Est* (Paris, 1994), fig. 16.
21. They have been found in Burma, Thailand, Malaysia, Indonesia, and Cambodia. There are two known bells in Vietnam (Môt-son and Viêt-khê, the latter closer in resemblance to the classic Dông-son bells). I. Glover reports that an urn very similar to the Kandal urn was found in Thailand near Chaiyapun, in the Petchabun Hills, inside a small cave surrounded by pottery, see GLOVER 1992, 221.

Fig. 3
Kandal urn. Bronze. National Museum of Cambodia, Phnom Penh

Fig. 4
Samrong bell. Bronze. National Museum of Cambodia, Phnom Penh

Fig. 5
Ring with the figure of a bull. Gold. Oc Eo. Historical Museum of Ho Chi Minh City (Saigon)

have functioned as emblems. A certain affinity with Dôngsonian civilization seems to be recognizable—despite the differences in the objects, so apparent in the drums and situlae (ritual bronze buckets)—in the use of related motifs, though these are treated in a distinctive way and with a totally original organization of decorative space. A wide, symmetrical ax blade ending in two upturned points, similar to axes common in Indonesia[22] and related to certain Dôngsonian axes, is represented on the Kerinci urn (Sumatra). A boat with an upturned prow appears on the urn in the Ortiz collection and on the Kandal urn. The motif is reminiscent, in a simpler form, of the boats often represented on the shoulder of Heger type 1 drums, on Dao-thinh jars, and on situlae from Viêt-khê[23] and the tomb of the king of Nanyue in Canton.[24]

Given the high quality of their casting and ornament, the urns and bells presumably belonged to religious and political leaders and may well have fulfilled a function similar to that of the drums and situlae in Dian and Dông-son. Perhaps they held water or grain for ritual use during an agricultural or funerary ceremony.[25] Whatever the circumstances, their flattened shape makes them unsuitable for burial urns other than in secondary interment except in case of cremation. The decoration is not entirely unlike certain Dayak baskets from Sarawak and Kalimantan.

The urns and bells, as ritual objects or symbols of high social rank, may well have functioned within a chiefdom system in which the political structure was considerably more complex than a simple village society. This was a world that was clearly ready to integrate the knowledge of metalworkers conversant with statue-making, as well as to absorb the Indian cultural message and to progress toward state formation.

III. The Early Historical Period

The precise moment when Cambodia came into being as a historical entity cannot be stated with precision, any more than with other countries in the region. The Kingdom of Funan is traditionally considered the first Indianized state in the region and the ancestor of the Khmer Empire that produced Angkor. According to a legend preserved in Chinese annals, its founding resulted from the union of an Indian Brahman and a local princess of divine extraction. But the location of Funan, its size, even its name remain to this day questions of great uncertainty, as are the site of its capital, its political organization, the ethnic composition of its population, the length of time it existed, its relations with its neighbors, and the connections between its coastal and interior regions.[26]

22. See R.P. SOEJONO, "The Distribution of Types of Bronze Axes in Indonesia," *Bulletin of the Archaeological Institute of the Republic of Indonesia* 9 (Jakarta, 1972), fig. 2, type IB, VA.
23. See L. BEZACIER, *Le Viêt-Nam* (Paris, 1972), 198, fig. 114a (drum from Ngoc-lu), 155, fig. 76 (Viêt-khê, c. third century B.C.).
24. See Archaeological Institute and Museum of the Province of Guangdong, *Xihan Nanyue Wang Mu* (Peking, 1991), 54, fig. 37 (second century B.C.). Although bronze drums from various sites are preserved in the National Museum of Phnom Penh, it is clear that Cambodia does not fall within the Dôngsonian cultural sphere; however, like southern Vietnam and maritime Southeast Asia, Cambodia was involved in trading with Dông-son.
25. MALLERET, *Objets du bronze*, 1956, 317, notes that an urn of the same shape but made of pottery was discovered in central Java, at Gunung Wukir, in the ruins of a building excavated "in connection with a new reading of an inscription dated A.D. 732." As it happens, Gunung Wukir is the site of a temple dedicated to Śiva in the form of a *liṅga* (an image of kingly power) by King Sañjaya. Whatever the date of the object or its relation with the bronze pieces, the context in which it was found is a religious one. Only further archaeological research will enlighten us as to the date and function of these mysterious objects.
26. One of the difficulties in using Chinese sources for information about Southeast Asia is that the Chinese language, both phonetically and in its written characters, is unsuited to the transcription of polysyllabic Sanskrit names. Only when archaeological exploration uncovers actual inscriptions for epigraphers can a Chinese name be made to coincide with a particular geographical or political entity. The Chinese name "Funan" is apparently a transcription of the local term *bnaṃ*, which would become *phnom* (*bhnaṃ*) (mountain) in Khmer, and the ruler perhaps bore the title "King of the Mountain." See PELLIOT 1903, 251, and PELLIOT 1925, 252. G. CŒDÈS in his *The Indianized States of Southeast Asia* relies on this pioneering work. JACQUES 1979 observes that a critical reading that takes into account all available Sanskrit and Khmer inscriptions is needed for all Chinese documents.

Chinese historians mention a kingdom called Funan, which had vassals and was visited by Kang Tai and Zhu Ying, envoys of the Wu emperor (222–252). From this it is possible to situate Funan in the general area of the lower Mekong basin, from the coast of Vietnam to the Angkor Borei region in southeast Cambodia and perhaps as far as the deltas of the Chao Phraya and the Irrawaddy,[27] but its exact boundaries are unknown.[28]

It is thanks to the excavations conducted by L. Malleret in the Mekong delta that Funan has taken on a more tangible existence.[29] At the coastal site of Oc Eo lies an immense city, rectangular in plan, 1.9 by 1 miles (3 x 1.5 km) in size, and connected to its port city, Ta Keo, by a large central canal that penetrates its earthen ramparts. The site has yielded religious remains, building foundations primarily made of brick, vestiges of ports, and objects of diverse geographical origin. Beads made of glass, crystal, and various kinds of stone such as are found in a trail along the coasts of South and Southeast Asia, Indian-style gold (fig. 5) and tin ornaments, intaglios, stones carved with *Brāhmī* characters, Roman coins (of Antonius the Pious, dated 152; and representing Marcus Aurelius), and fragments of Han mirrors combine to form a picture of a large and rich port settlement that drew on a well-managed rice-growing hinterland[30] from whose hills came the spices and precious raw materials that were sought in both the East and the West.

The inhabitants of Funan—prosperous traders, lovers of luxury, living in houses set on pilings, builders of warehouses—erected temples of brick and stone to honor their gods, who came from India. Hindus who worshiped Śiva and, to a lesser extent, Viṣṇu, the Funanese were also touched by Buddhism. They undoubtedly created an original art that was the ancestor of the art of Angkor, but is still difficult to characterize. The Funanese were perhaps at the head of a loose confederation of settlements of the same sort as Oc Eo, which though somewhat cosmopolitan were also well integrated with their hinterlands. These entrepôt ports along the coast of the Gulf of Siam and the Malay Peninsula, peopled according to their location by proto-Indochinese, Mons, or Austronesians, were in all likelihood governed by princely families that were partially Indian in origin and related to one another. Dominance was perhaps temporary in nature and a function of changing circumstances.[31]

Situated at the crossroads of all the great sea trading routes between the Mediterranean and the China Sea,[32] and between continental and archipelagic Southeast Asia, Oc Eo unquestionably traded with Rome, India, and China starting in the second century; indeed, trading had very likely occurred for a number of centuries before the beginning of the Christian era.[33] At some as yet undetermined point, the port silted up.[34]

Malleret's excavations confirm the information gathered by Chinese envoys to Funan. Its inhabitants, they said, were builders of large seagoing vessels and experienced navigators who traded with India and the West according to the rhythm of the monsoons, and who built temples for the worship of their gods.

Although five separate embassies from Funan were sent to China in the third century prior to the year 287, the impact of the great civilization to the north, which is very apparent on neighboring Vietnam, was virtually nil on the southern Indochinese peninsula. The cultural influence of India, for all that no statues dating from before the sixth century (at the earliest) have been found in Funan, appears to have been continually renewed. In 478, a trade mission returning from southern China was raided by the Chams of

27. Luong Ninh, in his latest summary article (LUONG NINH 1993, 29), calls attention to the fact that coins from Oc Eo are found as far afield as these two deltas. On the subject of objects typical of Oc Eo culture found on the site of Tha Muang at U-Thong, see also H. LOOFS-WISSOVA, "Problems of Continuity in Central Thailand," in *Early Southeast Asia* (Oxford, 1979), 342–351.

28. Different Chinese texts give the distances between Funan and other contemporary countries, as well as itineraries and the lengths of sea journeys, all of it well summarized in COLLESS 1978, 25–26, 27.

29. See MALLERET 1959–1963. The excavations did not provide absolute proof identifying Funan with Oc Eo, in the form of a name in a dated inscription, but they did provide a corpus of data that was in agreement with the information contained in the Chinese chronicles.

30. A *nāga*-king, the father of the first queen, drank all the water covering the kingdom, thereby making it fit for development. The extraordinary network of canals that extended over the delta was intended for agriculture as well as trade; it provided water to the cities and linked them together. See GROSLIER 1961.

31. WOLTERS 1979, 429. An outline of this kind announces what is known of the maritime power of Śrīvijaya in the Southeast Asian archipelago.

32. Chinese archaeologists have discovered in Canton the site of a boat yard that was in operation during the Qin and Han dynasties (third to first centuries B.C.). Seagoing vessels were built there, which is proof that maritime trade operated in both directions, see *Wenwu* 1977, 4:1–22. Several Han tombs in Canton, including the tomb of the king of Nanyue, provide indications that exchanges took place with the Persian world and most likely with the Indonesian archipelago, see *Wenwu* 1977, 4:346–347, and *Les Ors de l'archipel Indonésien* [exh. cat., Réunion des musées nationaux—Musée Guimet] (Paris, 1995), 25–26, note 14.

33. See GROSLIER, "Archéologie des échanges commerciaux," in *Archéologie, Grand Atlas Universalis* (Paris, 1985), 254–255.

34. A comparable phenomenon occurred at a later date on the west coast of the Malay Peninsula. It ended with the disappearance of the center of a very lively South Sea entrepôt civilization in South Kedah (fifth to fourteenth centuries). See M. JACQ-HERGOUAL'CH, "Un exemple de civilisation des ports-entrepôts des mers du Sud," *Arts Asiatiques* 67 (1992), 47.

Linyi. In 484, by royal order, the Indian monk who had survived the preceding mission left again for the Chinese court. In the sixth century nine embassies were sent to the northern countries. The title of General of the Pacified South was conferred by the Liang Emperor on the king of Funan, Jayavarman. The last trade missions are reported during the Tang dynasty, from 618 to 626 and from 627 to 649.

From Chinese annalists, again, we know that the decline and end of the kingdom of Funan occurred during the sixth century with the emergence in the north of a related vassal principality named Zhenla, which was equally Indianized. Nothing in Khmer epigraphy permits us to confirm that a military conquest of one state by another took place, or that one disappeared and was replaced by the other.[35] The consensus today seems to be that Funan and Zhenla were neighboring political entities, flexible and complex in nature, existing contemporaneously at least for a time, and that one succeeded the other in having hegemony over a certain number of small principalities, all of them Indianized. Funan's economy, which was essentially based on trading and oriented toward the sea, declined, possibly because of a change in maritime trade routes between China and India when a Malayan or Sundanese route was adopted, or possibly because the port and canals of the delta silted up. This may have led to the decline of its political fortunes to the advantage of Zhenla (whose indigenous name is still not known), a profoundly agrarian state oriented toward the interior.[36]

35. See VICKERY 1994, 197–212.

36. Pamela Gutman of Sydney, Australia, has kindly made available to me a copy of an unpaginated booklet published in December 1987 by the Department of Culture and Information of the Province of Long-an (*So van hoa và thông tin tinh Long An*), in which Vo Si Khai gives an account of the excavations for that year. He reports that the region of Duc-hoa alone yielded more than fifty sites belonging to the Oc Eo culture, which were found to be rich in pottery fragments, religious images, and architectural remains in brick and stone. In particular he mentions and cites a Sanskrit inscription engraved on a thin gold plaque measuring 8.26 by 1.57 inches (21x4 cm) that could be of great importance if the meaning he assigns to it is correct. The plaque had been placed at a depth of more than 5.5 feet (1.7 m) at the center of a temple that has been uncovered at Go Xai, in the Duc-hoa District on the Plain of Reeds, along with a number of other objects, twenty-six of them gold. The inscription, according to the Vietnamese translator, would have been signed by the copyist, and states that King Bhavavarman I proclaimed an edict ordering the retreat of an army of a hundred thousand men, and that before the order was executed the people buried their wealth, precious metals, jewels, and objects of lesser value such as bronzes. Elephant emblems, ancient bracelets, textiles, and elephant tusks would have been offered to the gods and to Indra. The retreat toward a very distant place then began. On this occasion, the king reminded his subjects to submit voluntarily to a newly established faith. The text went on to praise Brahmā, who led a conquered people to follow the established religion. Of great importance for Cambodian history, the inscription—the translation of which might be erroneous and is strongly challenged—might pertain to or may concern the attack by the army of Citrasena, king of Zhenla, on Vyadhapura, the capital of Funan, and his invasion of that country. This event is well-known from the Chinese annals of the Sui and Tang dynasties. Curiously enough, Luong Ninh (1993) does not mention this information, which if confirmed would not only reinforce the accuracy of the Chinese sources but also provide key archaeological evidence on the "prenatal" history of Cambodia.

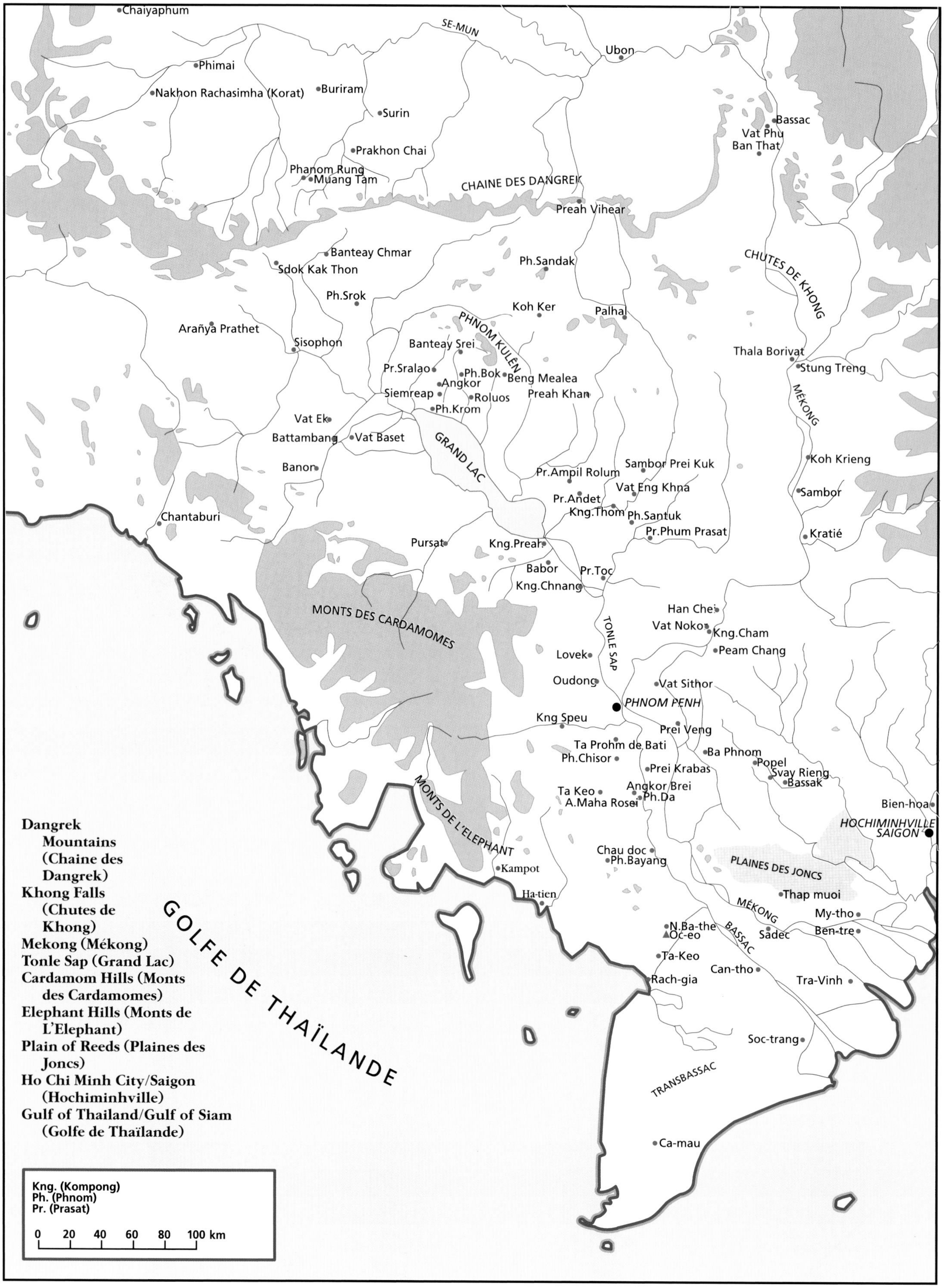
Chaiyaphum
SE-MUN
Ubon
Phimai
Nakhon Rachasimha (Korat)
Buriram
Surin
Bassac
Vat Phu
Ban That
Prakhon Chai
Phanom Rung
Muang Tam
CHAINE DES DANGREK
Preah Vihear
Banteay Chmar
Sdok Kak Thon
Ph.Sandak
CHUTES DE KHONG
Ph.Srok
Koh Ker
Palhal
Arañya Prathet
Sisophon
PHNOM KULÊN
Banteay Srei
Thala Borivat
Stung Treng
Pr.Sralao
Ph.Bok
Beng Mealea
Angkor
Siemreap
Roluos
Preah Khan
Ph.Krom
MÉKONG
Vat Ek
Battambang
Vat Baset
GRAND LAC
Koh Krieng
Banon
Pr.Ampil Rolum
Sambor Prei Kuk
Vat Eng Khna
Sambor
Pr.Andet
Chantaburi
Kng.Thom
Ph.Santuk
Pr.Phum Prasat
Kratié
Pursat
Kng.Preah
Babor
Pr.Toc
Kng.Chnang
Han Chei
MONTS DES CARDAMOMES
Vat Nokor
Kng.Cham
TONLE SAP
Lovek
Peam Chang
Oudong
Vat Sithor
PHNOM PENH
Kng Speu
Prei Veng
Ta Prohm de Bati
Ba Phnom
Ph.Chisor
Popel
Prei Krabas
Svay Rieng
Bassak
Ta Keo
Angkor Brei
Ph.Da
A.Maha Rosei
Bien-hoa
Dangrek Mountains (Chaine des Dangrek)
Khong Falls (Chutes de Khong)
Mekong (Mékong)
Tonle Sap (Grand Lac)
Cardamom Hills (Monts des Cardamomes)
Elephant Hills (Monts de L'Elephant)
Plain of Reeds (Plaines des Joncs)
Ho Chi Minh City/Saigon (Hochiminhville)
Gulf of Thailand/Gulf of Siam (Golfe de Thaïlande)
MONTS DE L'ELEPHANT
HOCHIMINHVILLE SAIGON
Chau doc
Ph.Bayang
PLAINES DES JONCS
Kampot
Ha-tien
Thap muoi
MÉKONG
My-tho
GOLFE DE THAÏLANDE
N.Ba-the
Oc-eo
BASSAC
Sadec
Ben-tre
Ta-Keo
Can-tho
Rach-gia
Tra-Vinh
Soc-trang
TRANSBASSAC
Ca-mau
Kng. (Kompong)
Ph. (Phnom)
Pr. (Prasat)
0 20 40 60 80 100 km

Ancient Cambodia: A Historical Glimpse

Albert Le Bonheur

Like many other countries in Southeast Asia, Cambodia was heavily influenced by India. Through trade relations, which probably originated in prehistory, some of the hallmarks of Indian civilization—its religions (Hinduism, primarily of the Śivaite but also of the Viṣṇuite sects, and Buddhism); Sanskrit, the language of religious texts and the higher forms of Indian literature; and even certain social structures—made their way to Cambodia. There, they were adapted, transformed, and expanded when necessary to fit the ambitions of the local elite.

Khmer art, which, in the forms that have survived, is primarily religious in nature, borrowed its logic, its forms, and its procedures from India. Very rapidly, however, Khmer art distinguished itself from its models. As early as the seventh century, the date of the oldest extant monuments of importance, Cambodia was producing works that were true to its own creative spirit, in many cases displaying qualities unknown in India.

The history of Cambodia can be divided, for convenience, into three major periods: the pre-Angkor period, from the beginning of the Christian era to the end of the eighth century; the Angkor period, from the ninth to the thirteenth century, in which royal power become progressively more centralized while the capital, with one exception, remained in the Angkor area; and a post-Angkor period, dating from the city's abandonment in the face of Thai aggression (c. 1431) to the present.

The Pre-Angkor Period

From the first or second century until the mid-seventh century, the Chinese records refer to a kingdom of "Funan." The name appears in embassy reports preserved in the dynastic archives, as well as in accounts by Buddhist pilgrims, but its local name is still not known. The kingdom, at any rate, seems to have held dominion over the southern portion of present-day Cambodia and the Mekong Delta, and doubtless over part of the lower Menam Basin (in today's Thailand) and the Malay Peninsula. Funan's wealth came from commerce, as excavations led by Louis Malleret in various sites around the Mekong Delta demonstrate. At Oc Eo, in particular, where a network of canals and a port for maritime trade were found, objects have been recovered that originated in Rome and the Mediterranean world, as well as in Iran, India, and China.

The Indianization of Funan seems to have occurred slowly. Only the names of its later kings, as transcribed by the Chinese, bear any relation to the Sanskrit royal names that survive from ancient stone inscriptions—for instance, Chö-ye-pa-mo (in the EFEO transcription), the Chinese equivalent of Jayavarman.[1] One of Funan's capitals, possibly its last, is generally held to have been at Angkor Borei, near the *phnom (bhnaṃ,* mountain)

Opposite, simplified map of the Khmer territory

1. Khmer royal names are Sanskrit compounds that end in the word *varman*, meaning "shield." Jayavarman is therefore the king "protected by *jaya* (victory)," and Iśānavarman the king "protected by Iśāna (a name for Śiva)," etc.

Da, where Viṣṇuite temples related to the city are found. Beginning in the middle of the sixth century (according to Chinese sources), Funan experienced a decline and was succeeded by a former vassal, Zhenla, a name the Chinese would apply to Cambodia until the thirteenth century. The cradle of Zhenla seems to have been in the area of Vat Phu (southern Laos) and along the Se Mun. To this period, in the seventh century, the earliest stone inscriptions that are partially written in Khmer, rather than wholly in Sanskrit, are datable.

In the first half of the seventh century, the great monarch Īśānavarman reigned at Sambor Prei Kuk (fig. 1). His influence extended over the states neighboring Cambodia to the west (the Chantaburi area) as well as to the east (the Indianized kingdom of Champa). Yet during the pre-Angkor period—and to some extent also the Angkor—the allegiance to a sovereign state must, in many cases, have been in name only, as many principalities wanted to retain or recover their independence. This state of affairs may be reflected in pre-Angkor art of the seventh century, and in the eighth century, the tendency seems to have become even more pronounced. Inscriptions carved in stone, of which a greater number were conserved, indicate that several parallel royal lines existed in Cambodia simultaneously. Further, certain Indonesian kingdoms to the south (Malay Peninsula and Sumatra), whose powers were then expanding, seem to have inherited the former commercial empire of Funan and to have exercised power over the south of the country.

Fig. 1
Sambor Prei Kuk. Octagonal shrine 7, south group (S7). Brick. First half of the seventh century

The Angkor Period

The founder of the Angkor royal line, Jayavarman II, appeared toward 790. Having come from a region under the dominion of "Javā," he united a number of different principalities under his rule and was consecrated as the "universal monarch" in 802 on *phnom* Kulen, a hill somewhat to the northeast of the future site of Angkor, in a place referred to as Mahendraparvata, "the mountain of the great Indra." In Indian theology Indra was the king of the gods in heaven, just as Jayavarman II, who had now freed his domain of the overlordship of "Javā" and become emperor, was king of kings on earth. The ceremony took place under the direction of Brahmans of the Śivaite sect, and henceforth king and his kingdom would be under the protection of an eminent form of Śiva living on the mountain. In religious art, this concept was expressed in the *liṅga,* an "immaterial" form of Śiva, housed in a temple at the summit of a mountain and, eventually, in a terraced pyramid representing the mountain.[2] Most of the subsequent Angkor kings would trace their ancestry to Jayavarman II, whose posthumous name of Parameśvara indicates that he was personally consecrated as a Śivaite so that after his death he was considered to have been reintegrated with the bosom of Śiva in his "supreme" form (Parameśvara, "supreme lord," is an epithet of Śiva).

While the religious basis of the Angkor monarchy is attributable to Jayavarman II, it was under his second successor, Indravarman (877–889), that the great religious foundations typical of the centralized Angkor state began to appear. This coincided with an intensive use of the land for irrigated rice paddies that necessitated vast agricultural water projects. At his capital (Hariharālaya, with the Roluos group temples, 9 miles, or 15 km,

2. Originally a phallic emblem, the Śiva *liṅga* had become an abstract representation of the divinity by the Angkor period. A column with square base, octagonal central section, and round upper segment, corresponding, respectively, to Brahmā, Viṣṇu, and Rudra, it represented a diverse form of the supreme deity, in this case Śiva.

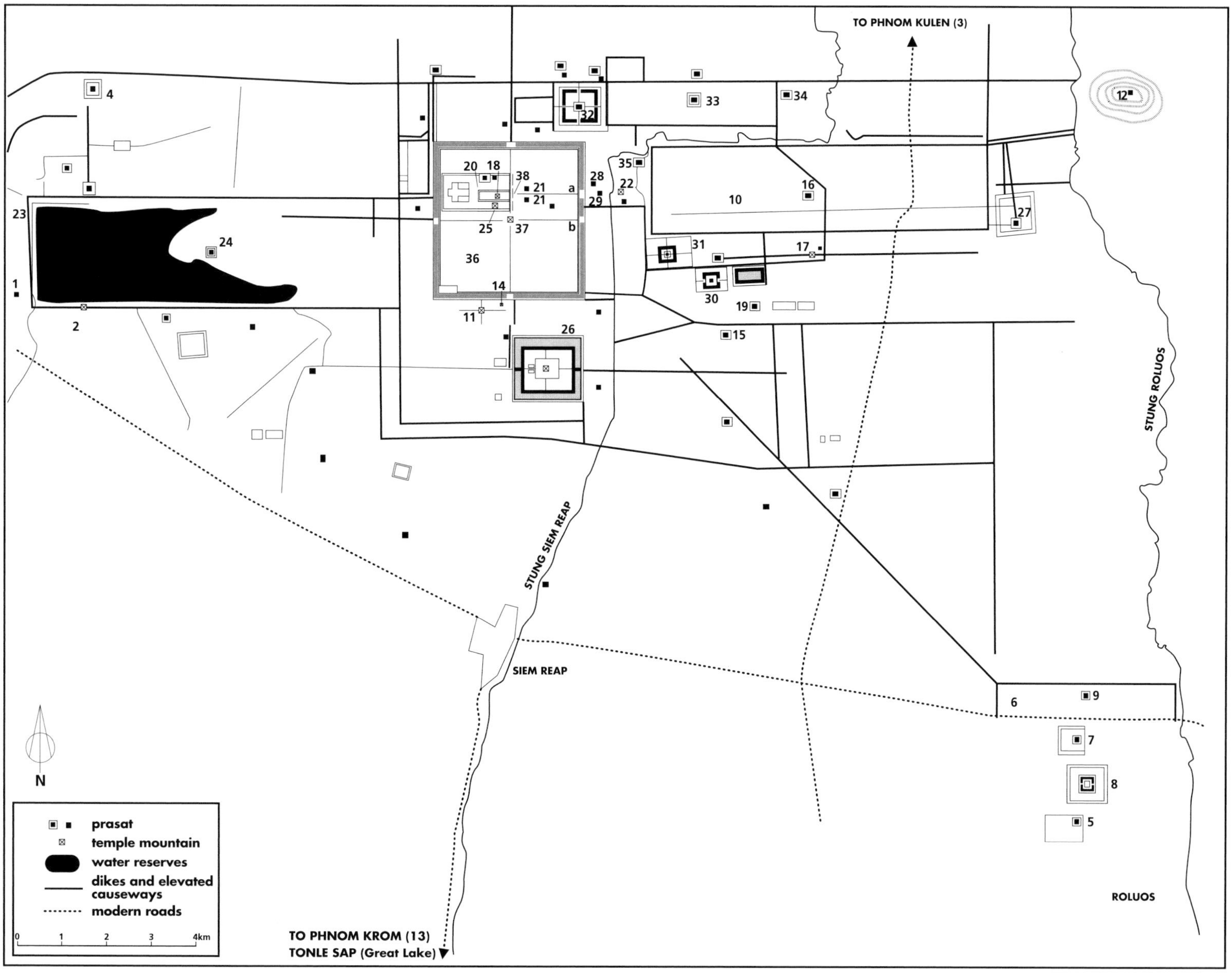

Site of Angkor (monuments are numbered in chronological order)

1 Prasat Prei Kmeng, 2d half of the 7th century
2 Prasat Ak Yum, 8th century
3 Phnom Kulen (many monuments)
4 Prasat Kok Po (for the most part)
5 Prasat Prei Monti (in Hariharālaya/Roluos)
6 Indratatāka (in Hariharālaya)
7 Preah Ko, 879 (in Hariharālaya)
8 Bakong, 881 (in Hariharālaya)
9 Lolei, 893 (in Hariharālaya)
10 Eastern *baray* (Yaśodharatatāka), founded by Yaśovarman
11 Phnom Bakheng, c. 900, founded by Yaśovarman
12 Phnom Bok, contemporary with Phnom Bakheng
13 Phnom Krom, contemporary with Phnom Bakheng
14 Baksei Chamkrong
15 Prasat Kravan, 921
From 928 to 944, Angkor ceased to be the capital; it was replaced by Koh Ker
16 East Mebon, 953
17 Pre Rup, 961
18 Phimeanakas (the pyramid)
19 Prasat Bat Chum
20 Royal Palace
21 North and South Khleang
22 Ta Keo
23 Western *baray*
24 West Mebon
25 Baphuon
26 Angkor Vat
27 Banteay Samre
28 Thommanon
29 Chau Say Tevoda
30 Banteay Kdei
31 Ta Prohm, 1186
32 Preah Khan, 1191
33 Neak Pean
34 Ta Som
35 Ta Nei
36 Angkor Thom, the enclosure
a) Victory Gate
b) Gate of the Dead
37 Bayon
38 Royal Terraces

Fig. 2
Phnom Bakheng. Early tenth century. Aerial view from the southeast

Fig. 3
Phnom Bakheng. The top of the pyramid, viewed from the central sanctuary. In the foreground, northeast tower of the quincunx

Opposite, Fig. 4
Garuḍa from Koh Ker (Prasat Thom). Sandstone. Height 213 cm. National Museum of Cambodia, Phnom Penh (image reversed)

southeast of the future site of Angkor), Indravarman ordered the construction of dikes for a huge rectangular reservoir, measuring 2.5 miles (3800 m) east to west and .5 miles (800 m) north to south. In addition to its agricultural use, the reservoir fed the moats of two temples—such public works were effective only because they were also primarily religious foundations. The six stuccoed brick towers of the Preah Ko monument were consecrated in 879, containing three images of Śiva and three images of the Goddess, in homage to three of Indravarman's predecessors (Parameśvara among them) and their wives, considered protectors of the kingdom. In 881 a *liṅga,* a form of the god Śiva, associated by its name, Indreśvara, to the reigning king, was consecrated at the summit of a temple-mountain, the five-tiered pyramid of Bakong. Indravarman seems to have had a peaceful reign, and his authority extended from the Se Mun in the north to the Chau Doc region in the south. Indravarman's son and successor, Yaśovarman (889–at least 910), in the course of completing and expanding his father's program of religious construction, built the first city of Angkor. Its ancient name, Yaśodharapura, "the city where glory resides," is related to his own. After constructing the four brick and stucco towers of the "ancestors' temple" at Lolei (893) on an island in the center of the reservoir of Hariharālaya, Yaśovarman moved northwest. There he ordered the construction of dikes to make a rectangular reservoir four times larger than that of his father (4 miles, or 7 km, east to west, and 1.5 miles, or almost 2 km, north to south), the eastern *baray* of Angkor. The center of his new capital was some distance to the southwest, marked by a natural hill, Phnom Bakheng. On its summit he built a temple-mountain, a pyramid with five terraces and 109 sanctuary towers, an explicit representation of Mount Meru, which, in Indian cosmology, is the center of the universe and the abode of Indra and the gods (figs. 2, 3). On the summit of Phnom Bakheng was a shrine to the *liṅga* Yaśodhareśvara. According to the inscriptions, Yaśovarman's authority was recognized from Vat Phu in the north to Hatien in the south. The two sons who followed him lived and reigned only briefly. One was responsible for building the small temple-mountain of Baksei Chamkrong, with its single tower shrine capping a terraced pyramid, situated to the northeast near Phnom Bakheng. A representation of Kailāsa, Śiva's mountain, it contained images of Śiva and the goddess erected for the spiritual benefit of King Yaśovarman and his queen. In 928, Jayavarman IV, the maternal uncle of the two previous kings and a great feudal landholder, ascended the Cambodian throne. He chose, however, to retain his own city as his capital: Koh Ker, 53 miles (85 km) northeast of Angkor (fig. 4). He had retired there in 921 and within a few years built many colossal sanctuaries dedicated to the form of Śiva known as the "master of the three worlds." The old capital, meanwhile, was abandoned for some twenty years. It is thought that the *prang* Jayavarman IV added to the great architectural ensemble of Prasat Thom at Koh Ker at the time of his consecration was a five-tiered pyramid thirty-five meters high intended to hold the royal *liṅga*.

After the death of Jayavarman IV's son and successor, Rājendravarman (944–968), another nephew of Yaśovarman, returned the capital to Angkor. On the east side of the site he constructed two temple-mountains. The first, the East Mebon (953), rises from an artificial island in the center of the eastern *baray* and is consecrated to the *liṅga* Rājendreśvara and to the spiritual welfare of his parents. The second, the temple of Pre Rup (961), is south of the eastern *baray*, and is dedicated to the *liṅga* Rājendrabhadreśvara, whose name simultaneously evokes Bhadreśvara, the deity of Vat Phu, a Khmer holy site since pre-Angkor times, and the king himself. When Rājendravarman died, in 968, he had been at war with Champa, and his death may not have been a natural one. The dignitaries gained more and more importance, particularly the Brahmans, who acted as spiritual masters, chaplains, and counselors to the king. In the reign of Rājendravarman's son and successor, Jayavarman V (968–1001), who ascended the throne at a young age, the king's guru, Yajñavarāha, held enormous power, as the shrine he founded a dozen miles (20 km) north of Angkor is the famous temple of Banteay Srei, to which the best artists and artisans in Cambodia had been assigned.

Fig. 5
East *gopura* of the royal palace at Angkor Thom. Sūryavarman I had the famous "oath of allegiance" engraved on this monument, which was probably built under Jayavarman V. In this inscription, more than two hundred officials swore the loyalty oath to the sovereign

The eleventh century opened with a civil war. Of the two kings vying for power, the first, Jayavīravarman, was ultimately bested but left the unfinished temple mountain of Ta Keo at Angkor, while the second, Sūryavarman I (1002–1050), founded a new dynasty and left great temples both in the north (Preah Vihear) and in the south (Phnom Chisor), though not in Angkor itself (fig. 5). The first Khmer expansion into the Menam Basin occurred in his reign, and either he or a successor (Udayādityavarman II, 1050–1066) constructed the vast reservoir of the western *baray* at Angkor (5 miles, or 8 km, east to west, and more than a mile, or 2 km, north to south). His successor ordered the temple mountain of the Baphuon, a "mountain of gold similar to Mount Meru, at the center of the capital, for a gold Śiva-*liṅga*." Meanwhile, various revolts troubled the country. In the reign of Harṣavarman III (1066–1080), Cambodia fought against Champa and was defeated. Then, at the behest of the Chinese, Cambodia became Champa's ally against the Dai Viet[3] but was again unsuccessful. In 1080, Jayavarman VI established a new royal line, and was responsible for building the very fine temple of Phimai. The events of the period that followed are confused, but in 1113 the king Sūryavarman II (1113–1145; fig. 7) is said to have seized power from two kings. He would lead the Khmer armies far afield, against Champa, against Dai Viet, and into the Menam Basin. As a follower of Viṣṇu, Sūryavarman II's greatest construction was to be the celebrated temple-mountain of Angkor Vat (fig. 6). During his reign many important sanctuaries were erected, notably

3. The first Vietnamese Empire after emancipation from Chinese sovereignty.

Fig. 6
Angkor Vat. First half of the twelfth century. View of the pyramid from the west-northwest

Fig. 7
Angkor Vat. Gallery of the third enclosure, known as the gallery of bas-relief. South gallery, west side Paramaviṣṇuloka (Sūryavarman II). Detail of the "historical procession"

Fig. 8
Angkor Thom, west facade of the west entrance. Early thirteenth century

Fig. 9
Bayon. Naval scenes on the exterior gallery, east gallery, south face. Early thirteenth century

Fig. 10
***Chedi* from Preah Khan at Pursat. Approximately seventeenth century. This *chedi* is one of the oldest reliquary monuments of the Thai architecture of Ayuthayā**

Beng Mealea, built on the same plan as Angkor Vat but without the pyramid. At Angkor, he built Banteay Samre and several temples of the Preah Pithu group. It is not known precisely when the last great sovereign of Angkor Cambodia, Jayavarman VII (r. 1181–1218), was born. During his youth he fought in Champa, and the king at Angkor was, in the meantime, ousted by a usurper. Champa took advantage of this to invade Cambodia, Angkor being occupied in 1177 by the Cham king, who put the usurper to death. It was at this time that Jayavarman VII appeared. After four years of fighting, he drove the Chams from Cambodia and was consecrated king (1181). In turn, he would occupy Champa, and during his reign the territory and influence of the Khmer Empire were more extensive than ever before. Yet all of Jayavarman's warring and politicking would have been invalid without the religious protection of the empire, and this was secured by founding new sanctuaries. Jayavarman VII made Mahāyāna Buddhism the state religion, and a great number of monuments were built during his reign according to a very distinct iconography and highly admired new style (the famous "smile of Angkor"). Among these are most of the monuments on the present site of Angkor (figs. 8, 9): the walled city of Angkor Thom (7 miles or 12 km in periphery), at the center of which is the Bayon, celebrated for its towers with faces; the temples of Banteay Kdei, Ta Prohm (1186) and Preah Khan (1191), along with the dependent constructions of the last; and other great temples in the provinces (part of Preah Khan of Kompong Svay and Banteay Chmar).

The Post-Angkor Period

The thirteenth century marks a turning point in the history of Southeast Asia. While the Mongols of Kublai Khan were invading China and its southern neighbors, the Thai in the Menam Basin had liberated themselves from the Khmer and from then on threatened to overrun a weakened Cambodia. The Angkor dynasties ended, and the kings that succeeded them were of humbler origin. Hinduism and Mahāyāna Buddhism, with their aristocratic cults, lost ground in the face of Theravāda Buddhism. Originally from Sri Lanka, it also had the sponsorship of the Thai monarchs and gained popularity at every level of the population. Thai aggression became more frequent, however, and Angkor, captured several times by the Thai king of Ayuthayā, was finally abandoned in 1431 for more southern and less exposed capitals. In the face of attacks by the Vietnamese as well, and, from the end of the sixteenth century, the first encroachments of the West, Cambodia would thereafter come increasingly under the cultural influence of Thailand. Its Buddhist religious art—monasteries of light or mixed construction, statues, paintings, manuscripts, etc.—would bear the strong imprint of Thailand, though certain Khmer elements would remain constant (fig. 10).

Changing Perspectives: Cambodia after Angkor

Ashley Thompson

Sources

The middle period of Cambodian civilization—some five hundred years between the fall of Angkor and the establishment of the French Protectorate—has been almost completely obscured over the course of history. One has the impression, at least in the West, of two Cambodias: that of the ancient past, which once intrigued Europe and, above all, France; and Cambodia since 1975, when political turmoil led to a modern tragedy that still horrifies the world. European scholars have spent more than a century researching ancient Cambodia, while others in the English-speaking world focus on the modern period. Although exchange between these fields is increasing, it has been difficult to overcome the limitations of their approaches, which continue to define research in Khmer studies today.[1]

The work of an independent Khmer scholar demonstrates that it is possible and, above all, valuable, to recover that which has been forgotten. In her extensive work on the development of Khmer language and literature, Saveros Pou has proved the reality of a coherent and singular civilization spanning the pre-Angkor period to modern times. Her careful research on the middle period has been essential to this enterprise, bringing to light the specificity of the epoch and the mechanisms and forms of transition. Disparate translations and studies have also been made of Khmer chronicles, which recorded events of this period retrospectively and often with much imagination.[2] Bernard-Philippe Groslier used Portuguese and Spanish sources to arrive at a more comprehensive understanding of sixteenth-century Cambodia,[3] and post-Angkor art has been formally investigated by one art historian, Madeleine Giteau.[4]

Drawing on these various sources, this essay aims to contextualize middle Khmer art. Yet the primary source for such an endeavor must be the cultural landscape itself: only through study of the physical, social, and "spiritual" environment in which it developed can this art be understood. The social and cultural forms proper to modern Cambodia—a Theravāda Buddhist nation growing out of a long Brahmanic history built upon indigenous tradition—saw their first manifestations in the middle period. Middle Khmer art thus offers invaluable insight, as a material and spiritual reflection of its time, into the complex transition between Cambodia's past and Cambodia's present.

The Khmer people continue to reflect on images of the past. For unlike the kingdom of Champa, a former neighbor to the east, Cambodia never disappeared, either as a nation or as a civilization. The sociocultural context of Khmer art runs continuously from ancient to modern times, and as art cannot be fully understood out of context, neither can the Cambodian context be understood in the absence of its artistic heritage. In particular, as an example of how the persistence of cultural tradition can be forged from the

1. This is, of course, a generalization; exceptions to the rule have existed and have produced some of the most insightful research on Cambodia. In any case, these stereotyped views are increasingly enhanced and will undoubtedly be altered, notably by rising Asian perspectives. Japanese scholars are presently developing singular and complementary approaches to Khmer studies. Most importantly, Khmer national scholarship, until now largely nourished abroad, promises to grow on Khmer soil over the coming decades.
2. Written mostly in the nineteenth century, that is, centuries after the events they recount, these chronicles are themselves attempts to recuperate lost history. See the work of F. Garnier, J. Moura, A. Leclère, M. Vickery, Khin Sok, and Mak Phoeun. A short article by Cœdès (1918, 1–28) explains the historical background of these documents.
3. Groslier 1958.
4. Much of this research is brought together in Giteau 1975.

very loss it attenuates or modulates, of how radical rupture in this tradition reconfirms its necessity and can set the mechanisms of its perpetuation in motion, middle Khmer perspectives may prove useful in probing the workings of Khmer culture in general.

The Post-Angkor Landscape

Historically, the end of the Angkor Empire is marked by the loss of the capital city to Siamese invaders in the fifteenth century. Khmer civilization, however, did not disappear with the fall of Angkor. By that time, dramatic transformation in the Khmer cultural complex was already well under way. Political realities and concomitant religious developments had served from as early as the thirteenth century to progressively temper Angkor aspirations to eternal power and glory. A physical and spiritual retreat characterizes this period, during which a dynamic civilization began a transformation into the founding memory of a people.

From a twentieth-century viewpoint, it is the relative absence of new cultural undertakings after Jayavarman VII that is most striking. There are virtually no new constructions, the production of statuary drops sharply, and stone inscriptions become rare. Accompanying a rise in Siamese power proportional to the Khmer decline, Theravāda Buddhism seems to announce an end: the end of sophisticated engineering projects; the end of delicately carved architectural elements; the end of artistic and linguistic perfection. The wild iconographic intermingling of the vegetable, animal, and human that announces the divine above each sanctuary threshold is gone. Images of fantastic creatures and powerful gods no longer populate the landscape. Sanskrit verse is no longer composed. To many, this material loss would seem to reflect a spiritual or intellectual decline. Loss in formal diversity would reflect a loss in intellectual liberty. Abstract conceptions—Śiva's *liṅga,* the human and animal avatars of Viṣṇu, dancing gods with multiple heads and arms—as well as the sensuality and majesty of the divine virtually disappear from the Khmer cultural landscape.

However, a closer look at this negative image reveals obscured detail. Having rapidly diminished over the thirteenth and fourteenth centuries, cultural production had apparently come to a standstill by the fifteenth century, when the court retreated south. Yet the engineering, architectural, artistic, and literary works that together had translated Brahmanic fervor into the Khmer space over centuries remained in the land and in the hands and minds of its inhabitants. As the seat of power shifted between Angkor and sites on the southern river plains, a movement to reappropriate ancient space for the new Theravāda sect, which had begun long before the fall of the capital, continued. The ephemeral nature of the early Siamese occupation was to allow Cambodia ample time to develop a unique practice and expression of Theravāda Buddhism, nourished by a rich and ever-present past.

The sixteenth century saw in many ways the culmination of this movement. A reaffirmation of political unity and military prowess was accompanied by a marked renewal of cultural expression. Not surprisingly, this revival of Angkor modes, where religious art underlined political unity, came to fruition in the Angkor region itself. The Angkor heritage was reanimated, physically and conceptually, by the Theravāda movement. Undoubtedly enhancing the sacred value of new artistic production, the

Angkor tradition also gave aesthetic inspiration to Buddhist expression. The finest artistic production of this period demonstrates a harmonious synthesis between Angkor virtuosity and Buddhist serenity. Not until the seventeenth and eighteenth centuries, with the decline of political and military power, would Siamese, and also Lao, influences begin to obscure the Angkor aesthetic heritage.

Signs of Change

The relative paucity of artifacts from the post-Angkor period is a result not only of reduced production but also changes in media. After the reign of Jayavarman VII in the thirteenth century, wood largely replaced stone as a construction material in architecture and sculpture. The few extant stone structures thought to date from this early transitional period are notably modest in scale. Dubbed "Buddhist terraces" by modern researchers, most are, in fact, the foundations of Buddhist sanctuaries or *vihāra,* wooden pavilions that supported a tiled roof and housed sacred images.[5] Like much statuary, architectural elements that had at one time been carved in stone, such as lintels or pediments, were rendered in wood, which is an impermanent material.[6]

A few statuettes of gold, silver, bronze, or other alloys demonstrate the continued practice of lost-wax casting and embossing techniques. The extent of middle-period statuary production is difficult to gauge, however. As with wooden images, these statuettes would have been easily transported during war. Many were surely melted down for their monetary value. Certain traditional practices continue to contribute to the destruction of religious imagery. Considered to possess therapeutic powers, fragments of old wooden statues are still used in healing potions. The sacred value of

5. See MARCHAL 1918.
6. The use of stone by ancient Khmer architects involved certain construction techniques appropriate only for working with wood. This fact, which in some cases has accelerated the degradation of monuments, has bewildered and even angered generations of scholars. Given the enormously sophisticated nature of Angkor composition and design, it seems unlikely that this "deficiency" was derived from technical or, as is often implied, intellectual incapacity but rather from intentional imitation. Why? Part of the response would undoubtedly arise from better understandings of wooden architecture in the Angkor period itself.

Fig. 1
Monument 486 at Angkor Thom, viewed from the southwest. Tenth century, altered later by Buddhists

modern metal Buddhas is also enhanced by the incorporation of material from the past. Thus, precious metal objects are melted down and mixed with other materials to be recast as a new image.

Reduced resources in the thirteenth century may have been seconded by Theravāda's fundamental belief in impermanence, and the idea that the art object itself was inseparable from its spiritual expression. From this perspective, however, the relative absence of artifacts signifies a very real spiritual presence. The negative image often projected of middle Khmer artistic production can be seen as a distorted view of what was, in many ways, a positive cultural reappropriation of the ancestral tradition.

Buddhist temples were often built on ancient religious grounds, integrating existing sanctuaries into the new religious complex. In contrast to the Brahmanic central sanctuary, which housed sacred images and was accessible only to the elite, the *vihāra* was a larger, more open construction designed in accordance with the populist tenets of Theravāda Buddhism. Typically, the early *vihāra* were built directly east of the ancient sanctuaries. At Monument 486, for example, in the southwestern quadrant of Angkor Thom, an existing tenth-century Brahmanic sanctuary was repaired and modified: two lateral sanctuaries were added and a *vihāra* was raised at the eastern entrance. There are few examples in Cambodia of this typically Brahmanic design—three sanctuaries aligned on a north-south axis—conceived for the Theravāda movement.[7] The sacred Buddhist space was marked by border stones implanted around this hybrid configuration (fig. 1).[8]

Architectural modification of the structure was accompanied by changes in iconography, with sculpture serving as a principal agent of religious change. The central sanctuary of Monument 486 boasts delicately carved Brahmanic scenes of the tenth century and Theravādin reliefs of a later date, but the iconography of the two lateral sanctuaries is strictly Theravādin. Similar bas-reliefs, perhaps as early as the thirteenth century, adorn a number of other Angkor temples. Preah Palilay and Ta Tuot (Preah Pithu X), in the northwestern and northeastern quadrants of Angkor Thom, also demonstrate architectural and iconographic appropriation of ancient ground. While in technique and treatment of form these reliefs clearly descend from Angkor models, especially the Bayon style, Siamese influence begins to appear in such details as costume design.[9] The practice of Buddhism remains active at these two temples, which still carry names distinctly associated with Theravādin mythology: Palilay is indirectly derived from the Pāli Pārileyya, a legendary Buddhist forest; Pithu is the Khmer pronunciation of Vidhūra, the Bodhisattva hero of a well-known *jāṭaka* tale. Such Buddhist appellations of Angkor temples are notably rare.

Transformation was, however, gradual, and there is no evidence of iconoclastic or otherwise belligerent religious confrontation. A lintel from a sanctuary at Preah Pithu (cat. 112), also dating from the thirteenth century, depicts a lively Brahmanic scene. Just as other forms of Buddhism had coexisted in ancient Brahmanic Cambodia, so did Brahmanism and Theravāda Buddhism mingle on neighboring grounds as the middle period began.

Remaining statuary exhibits this same religious tolerance and stylistic exchange. What little stone carving exists dates primarily from this early transitional period. The sandstone Buddha found at the Mahāyāna complex of Preah Khan at Angkor (cat. 113) represents a remarkably elegant synthesis of Angkor artistic authority, expressed in the corpulent and stately forms, and the aesthetic serenity of Theravāda Buddhism. Generally said to be of the

7. Another form of this tradition can be seen at Vat Sithor in Srei Santhor, where the monarchy first resettled after the fall of Angkor in the fifteenth century. The alignment of three modern sanctuaries on a north-south axis suggests that the Theravāda sect here modeled itself upon preexisting architectural design. A tenth-century Buddhist inscription found at Vat Sithor indicates, moreover, that this site may long have been favored by a Buddhist sect associated with the court, and that conversion was subsequently made from the Mahāyāna to the Theravāda faith. The ancient Buddhist tradition may, in fact, have motivated the choice of this site for the new seat of the Buddhist monarchy. For more on this inscription and Cambodia's ancient Buddhist tradition, see E. Sénart, cited in Aymonier 1901, 261–271.
8. See Marchal 1918, 1925.
9. The exact dating of Preah Palilay is particularly problematic. See Marchal 1922 and Dupont 1935.

"Commaille type,"[10] several post-Bayon Buddhas, represented both standing and seated in meditation, bear features like those of the Preah Khan image: dimpled chin, well-defined lips and sharp nose, heavy eyelids, smoothly arched eyebrows, hair and conical *uṣṇīsa* covered in small raised curls. Though indisputably Khmer in stature and expression, this type is thought to show the influence of the Dvāravatī school. In this example, Dvāravatī style is marked by a tendency to depict the Buddha in *abhayamudrā* (a gesture indicating the absence of fear) with the monastic robe covering both shoulders, and employing a technique whereby the lower arms were carved separately, sometimes in wood, and attached to the stone body.[11] The relatively poor quality of sandstone available in this period must also have contributed to the adoption of this particular technique. Representing a more stylized version of the "Commaille type," the Buddha head from Preah Palilay again demonstrates Angkor aesthetic refinement to convey a sense of profound inner peace. This Buddha's gentle expression, his eyes nearly closed to the world, infuses Theravāda's remarkable humility with the tradition of Jayavarman VII.

As early as the thirteenth century there is a great reduction in thematic variety—it is primarily the Buddha (or abstract representations thereof) and his disciples who merit iconographic representation—but the production of Brahmanic sculpture was never entirely abandoned. And just as Angkor aesthetics and technical skill continued to influence Theravādin representation, Cambodia's western neighbors also influenced, in terms of style, Brahmanic production of the period. For example, the elaborate costume of the bronze Viṣṇu from the northern Khleang of Angkor Thom evinces a departure from Angkor aesthetics within the very perpetuation of Angkor tradition (cat. 115). A collection of post-Angkor sandstone divinities was conserved until recent wars in Buddhist temples in the southern region of Srei Santhor. It is in this region, which would seem to have been long favored by a royal Buddhist sect, that the monarchy resettled immediately after the fifteenth-century fall of Angkor.[12] Not surprisingly, these pieces are considered the earliest post-Angkor vestiges to have been found outside the Angkor region. Giteau, who studied this statuary in the 1960s and 1970s, distinguished a style characterized by Angkor boldness of form and facial expression, with a Siamese influence primarily in the carved motifs of the decorative elements (e.g., necklaces and tiaras; figs. 2, 3).

Evolution in statuary decor can be followed over the course of the middle period, and provides a reference for relative dating. Decorative motifs carved on a statue, or into its black, red, and gold lacquer coatings, often bearing glass or shell inlays, became increasingly elaborate over time, and show Angkor and Siamese influences.

Buddhism itself, which had accompanied the development of the Khmer civilization from its inception, took on unique expression as the Theravāda faith flowed into Cambodia's deep cultural molds. Cambodia's ancient divinities—and, most important, ancient concepts of the divine—did not disappear with Theravāda's arrival. In orthodox terms, Theravādins—and all Buddhists—reject the attribution of "divinity" to the Buddha. Yet in Cambodian practice the Buddha becomes the god of gods.[13] Viṣṇu, primarily in the form of Rāma or Nārāyaṇa, and Indra developed great importance. While the twelfth-century Viṣṇuite temple of Banteay Samre bore numerous Buddhist bas-reliefs, the neighboring modern Buddhist temple of Pradak bears a Viṣṇuite scene atop its entrance gate. Powerful reminders of the

10. So named after a Buddha discovered by Jean Commaille, the first conservator of Angkor. See Boisselier, *La Statuaire khmère*, 1955, pl. 100.
11. For a first discussion of these influences, also apparent in certain bas-reliefs of Preah Palilay, see Dupont 1935, 63. Though reconsidering chronological development, other scholars have drawn on Dupont's studies to further analyses of the historical evolution of Khmer art. See, in particular, the work of Boisselier and Giteau.
12. See note 7.
13. This has, of course, long been true for the practice of Theravāda elsewhere. Interesting reflections on the growth of Theravāda out of Indian tradition and into Southeast Asia, and particularly in Cambodia, are raised in numerous studies by F. Bizot. On the Khmer Buddhist statuary tradition, see Bizot 1994, 101–139.

Fig. 2
Adorned Buddha. Vat Sithor, north sanctuary. Worshiped today as Srei Sar Chor (a deified heroine of mythology). Cast in cement from an ancient image that was recently destroyed

Fig. 3
Viṣṇu. Vat Sithor, north sanctuary. Recently restored

Brahmanic tradition, Śiva, Umā, and Gaṇeśa still play a central role in modern religious practice, often even figuring in the Buddhist context. While a tenth-century inscription recounting the foundation of a Buddhist monastery at Angkor begins with an invocation to Śiva,[14] modern healing rituals performed, for example, under the patronage of Gaṇeśa, inevitably begin with an invocation to the Buddha. This transformation, through which Brahmanism was preserved in subordination to Buddhism, with ancient divinities safeguarding the religious power and intensifying the sanctity of Khmer Buddhist practices, undoubtedly came about during the middle period.

A fourteenth-century inscription, found in the Angkor region, illustrates the complexities of this transformation.[15] This inscription, composed of two texts, one in Pāli and the other in Khmer, recounts the foundation of a Buddhist temple under the auspices of King Śrīndravarman following his abdication from the throne. The Pāli text—the earliest inscription found in Cambodia in this language, which remains the vehicle of the Theravāda faith—formally records the names, dates, and events. The Khmer text provides the same information, but in greater detail. Names that figure in Pāli in the former appear in Sanskrit within the Khmer text. For example, the Pāli text calls the king Sirindavamma, and the Sanskrit gives the divine epithet *deva,* Śrīndravarmadeva. The Khmer text, moreover, names the statue of the Buddha image placed in the newly erected temple: Śrīndramahādeva. In conformity with Angkor tradition, and in pointed contradiction to Theravāda tenets, the king and the Buddha are intimately associated, the latter bearing the royal name. In fact, the Pāli text records only the erection of the statue, not its name. While the foundation of this temple clearly served to convert the surrounding region from Brahmanism to Theravāda Buddhism—one village serving the temple is even said to have been formerly "under the authority of the sanctuary of the honorable *Suvarṇaliṅga* (gold *liṅga*)," a version of the Śivaite phallus—ancient tradition was not abandoned, but rather continued to inform religious practices.

In artistic terms, the theme of the adorned Buddha, associating the Buddha with royalty, had been well known in Cambodia from as early as the twelfth century. Middle Khmer art was to develop new forms in perpetuation of this

14. K. 290. See CŒDÈS, "La stèle," 1908. The importance of this inscription in understanding the context of Buddhism in Cambodia is multiple. Recording the foundation of a Buddhist monastery under the reign of Yaśovarman, this inscription was conserved in the modern Buddhist temple of Tep Pranam in Angkor Thom, a site which is known to have harbored a Theravāda sect since at least the sixteenth century, and which adjoins the temple of Preah Palilay, a Theravādin site since at least the thirteenth. While there is no confirmation that the Tep Pranam stele was originally erected at Tep Pranam, or that the tenth-century monastery in question was founded on these very grounds, the idea is enticing. This scenario would tend to suggest that the post-Angkor Theravāda tradition may literally have grown from Angkor Buddhist roots.

15. K. 754. For translation and commentary, see CŒDÈS 1936.

singular tradition. The concept of divinity may be rejected by orthodox Theravāda philosophy, yet in Cambodia the Buddha and, to some extent, the king himself, continue to be associated with the divine.

Affirmation of Tradition

A symbolic and, at times, spectacular reappropriation of ancient sacred space by the Buddhist sect was to be made over the course of the sixteenth century. Renewed artistic and epigraphic production, primarily though not exclusively in the Angkor region, testifies to the firm establishment of Theravāda Buddhism in a specifically Khmer tradition. During this period, literary composition in the Khmer language began to take form. The abandonment of Sanskrit composition in the fourteenth century, in conjunction with the introduction of the more populist Theravāda religion, provided the conditions necessary for literary development in the Khmer vernacular. Cambodia's most remarkable literary works in Khmer verse date from the sixteenth to the eighteenth centuries. Of particular note are the Khmer Buddhistic version of the Indian Viṣṇuite *Rāmāyaṇa,* known to have existed in Sanskrit in ancient Cambodia, and an original epic poem recounting the mythical construction of Angkor Vat.[16] Here again, changes in cultural production from the ancient to the middle period, which are most often presented as irreversible loss, can be seen, instead, to reflect positive appropriation of ancient tradition.

Continuous artistic development is evident at those monuments that had been consecrated to the Theravāda faith as early as the thirteenth century. At Preah Palilay, Ta Tuot, and Monument 486, later bas-reliefs can be identified by a decline in technical skill and stylistic refinement, while both form and decor reflect an increased but not yet overwhelming influence from Siam.

The colossal sandstone Buddha head discovered on one of the Buddhist terraces of Angkor Thom, now in the Musée Guimet (fig. 4), suggests the scope of an art that continues to inspire artistic production in Cambodia. A number of colossal Buddha statues, some of which incorporate only fragments of their middle-period predecessors, are worshiped on the Buddhist terraces of Angkor Thom today. Measuring as much as six meters in height, these enormous statues were either carved out of monoliths or numerous sandstone blocks stacked together. Some of these images may have been coated with a sort of stucco to smooth over the joints or irregularities of the stone.

One example of the way in which Buddhism was consciously founded on the past is seen in the colossal Buddha of Tep Pranam, a Buddhist temple adjoining Preah Palilay in Angkor Thom. An anastylosis was performed in the 1950s on this Tep Pranam statue, thought to date from the fifteenth or sixteenth century. The base of the image was filled with primarily Buddhist sculpture fragments dating from as early as the twelfth century. The remarkable head, the features of which resemble those of Jayavarman VII, was, in fact, discovered here, buried and so preserved by the Theravāda foundation of Tep Pranam (fig. 5). Like the sacred deposits buried within Angkor religious foundations, as well as those of the present day, this collection of statues clearly served to accumulate sacred energy in the colossal Buddha image.[17]

16. For a complete translation and explication of the middle Khmer *Rāmāyaṇa* text, see POU, *Rāmakerti,* 1977; and *Etudes,* 1977. Pou also edited two versions of the text in Khmer (1979, 1982). AYMONIER (1878) published a Khmer version of the epic poem mentioned above, along with a summary translation entitled "Edification d'Angkor Vat."

17. See the July 1950 report of the Conservation of Angkor. Collections of the fragments discovered are pictured in BOISSELIER, *La Statuaire khmère,* 1955, pl. 114. Boisselier suggests that this sacred deposit was made during a restoration of the Tep Pranam Buddha by local inhabitants around the turn of the century (290–291).

Other giant images of the Buddha were literally carved out of ancient temples. Archaeological research carried out in the 1960s revealed at the Baphuon's western base the presence of a monastery, probably dating from the fifteenth and sixteenth centuries, and indicated that it was at about this time that the western facade of this temple was transformed into an enormous reclining Buddha.[18] Just outside the walls of Angkor Thom, the Bakheng temple underwent similarly dramatic transformation. Ancient temple blocks were relaid to form a seated Buddha atop the pyramid's summit. Measuring thirty meters in width, the Buddha engulfed virtually all that was left of the original temple's five sanctuaries. The remains of this statue were dismantled by French restoration teams in the 1920s; gazing now at the ruins of the Bakheng, one can only imagine the presence this Buddha must have imposed on the surrounding plain.

Sacred deposits found under the Bakheng Buddha during the restoration process are also of note. In a sandstone receptacle at the bottom of a shaft under the central sanctuary were a number of Buddha statuettes measuring up to nine centimeters in height and made of silver or gold leaf molded around a resin-based substance. Other gold and silver statuettes were found in the masonry of the colossal image.[19] Though perhaps relatively common in the post-Angkor period, this type of image has rarely survived to the present day. Such ritual burial of sacred objects has proved to be one of the most successful methods of preservation.

Sixteenth-century inscriptions further testify to the importance of the Bakheng site, and to artistic production, in the evolving cultural complex. One pilgrim, recording such pious deeds as statue repair and donations to Phnom Bakheng and Oudong, prays for the perpetual peace of Kampuchea under the guidance of the ruling monarch and in continuation of the royal line.[20]

18. J. Dumarçay, personal communication.
19. DUMARÇAY, *Phnom Bakheng*, 1971, 14–16.
20. K. 465. For full translation and commentary, see POU 1989, 20–25.

Fig. 5
Sculpture found under the pedestal of the Buddha at Tep Pranam during restoration work in the 1950s

Fig. 4
Head of the Buddha. Buddhist terrace I at Angkor Thom. Sandstone. Height 100 cm. Musée national des Arts asiatiques-Guimet, Paris

Less spectacular but equally significant examples of sculpture as a primary agent of religious change and political affirmation can be seen throughout the region. Middle-period Buddha images continue to animate Angkor from Phnom Kulen in the north to Phnom Krom in the south in such seemingly minor sites as Baksei Chamkrong or Ta Prohm Kel.

The temple of Angkor Vat, however, harbored the most extensive Buddhist sect. Religious pilgrims from Cambodia, as well as other Southeast Asian nations and Japan, are known to have visited the temple. Some forty inscriptions on the walls and pillars record the pious acts and donations made by pilgrims between the sixteenth and eighteenth centuries. Although the epoch was predominantly Buddhist in nature, the Viṣṇuite bas-reliefs carved on the walls of the temple's northeastern first-level gallery have proved to be one of the monumental achievements of the period. All but this section of the continuous gallery had been carved with Viṣṇuite scenes at the temple's founding in the twelfth century. The historical importance of this act far exceeds its aesthetic value; for while indisputably less refined in technical terms, the sixteenth-century bas-reliefs demonstrate a remarkable continuation of ancestral tradition. One of the few post-Angkor artistic works to be dated, these bas-reliefs have served as a basis of comparison in understanding the artistic evolution of this period.

Opposite, Fig. 6 Angkor Vat. Preah Pean in the 1920s. The chaotic aspect is deceptive. In fact, everything is arranged to allow the worshiper full participation: prostrate behind the statues in the foreground, he is physically integrated into the scene

In homage to the actions of her royal son in "restoring [Angkor Vat] to its ancient glory," one queen mother records her own pious acts there. She shaves her hair and burns it in ceremonial offering. The ashes are used to make a sort of lacquer, which she then uses to adorn statues of the Buddha.[21] As in ancient times, the fabrication and constant care of religious imagery was a principal act of devotion in the middle period, as it still is today. Through such ritual practices, statues come to incorporate the spirit of the devotee (fig. 6).

In these middle-period inscriptions, the term "a Thousand Buddhas" first appears. This designates a gallery on Angkor Vat's second level where statues were, and indeed still are, sheltered and worshiped. Late nineteenth- and early twentieth-century visitors reported that this gallery, as well as other passageways and sanctuaries, were full of Buddhist images. While some post-Angkor sandstone statues, primarily Buddhas standing in *abhaya-mudrā,* remain in situ, most of the wooden images found in the temple were transferred to the reserve collection of the Angkor Conservation for safekeeping or the National Museum for display over the course of this past century. Research on middle Khmer art has largely been based on this singular collection. In her study of post-Angkor iconography, Giteau identifies a Siem Reap school in this collection. She demonstrates that while the Siem Reap school is generally characterized by an increasing rigidity and stylization in form and costume, which betrays considerable Siamese influence, artists in the ancient capital nonetheless developed a distinctive style recognizable in small detail. Even into the seventeenth and eighteenth centuries, with the Khmer court's retreat into the interior of the country as the domination of Cambodia intensified—by the Siamese to the west and the rising Vietnamese to the east—Siem Reap remained a center of original artistic production.

The Angkor elegance of several wooden Buddhist images from Angkor Vat has long attracted the attention of art historians, casual observers, and Khmer pilgrims alike. Indeed, these images demonstrate a technical mastery and refinement worthy of any Angkor artist. In fact, the ornamental motifs, majestic stature, full features, and supple curves of two "royal" Buddhas, which

21. IMA 2. For full translation and commentary, see LEWITZ 1970. The Khmer text is reproduced in MAHĀ BIDUR KRASSEM 1984, 2–4.

closely resemble eleventh- and twelfth-century design, have led more than one specialist to date them to the Angkor period.[22] If the statues were not actually carved in the twelfth century, their forms and decor were nonetheless directly inspired by Angkor models, and were to inspire a series of wooden images in the sixteenth and seventeenth centuries.

The decidedly Theravāda nature of the devotee in prayer (cat. 117) leaves no doubt as to this image's post-Angkor production. Often considered the jewel of middle Khmer art, the statue harmonizes with extraordinary delicacy an ancient tradition of religious devotion, expressed through unmannered aesthetic assurance, with the profound humility of Theravāda. A cavity carved into the figure's stomach may once have held sacred deposits: gold, silver, or

22. See Boisselier, "Note," 1950.

bronze; personal belongings; small Buddha figures; relics; or perhaps palm-leaf texts. Placed before the "thousand Buddhas" of Angkor Vat, this image was undoubtedly the representation of a particular devout donor, his devotion enhanced through this singular offering of eternal prayer. At Angkor Vat, in the Phnom Penh museum, and now on view in this exhibition, this pilgrim from the past carries forth a living memory even as he turns back to pray to an ancient cultural heritage.

Religion, Epigraphy, and Iconography

The Religions of Ancient Cambodia

Kamaleswar Bhattacharya

When we talk about the religions of ancient Cambodia, we are mainly talking about Hinduism and Buddhism, the two great religions of India. These religions arrived in Cambodia as part of their general expansion into Southeast Asia, to Indochina (Burma, Thailand, Cambodia, southern Vietnam, Laos), the Malay Peninsula, and the islands of Indonesia.

We know very little about the early stages of this religious expansion, which subsequently led to a great cultural expansion. We know equally little about the cultures and beliefs that were in place prior to the Indianization of what we sometimes now call Greater India.

Our knowledge of ancient Cambodia's religions derives from epigraphy (in both Sanskrit and Khmer), iconography, Chinese dynastic histories, and accounts of Chinese travelers. Yet we cannot fully understand the information these documents contain without comparing them whenever possible with the relevant Indian documents. Herein lies the difficulty in studying the subject for anyone unwilling to settle for a few vague generalities, as scholars did before the publication of *Les religions brahmaniques dans l'ancien Cambodge, d'après l'épigraphie et l'iconographie* in 1961, a book written under difficult circumstances that still stands as a reference work in the field. Aside from a few additions to its documentation and interpretations by the author himself, or others, the study of Cambodia's religions has remained at practically the stage where the author left it thirty-five years ago. Since then, however, many documents have been discovered and many Indian texts have become available that could shed light on matters in Cambodia. Furthermore, the book discussed only the Brahmanic or Hindu religions, leaving the systematic study of Buddhism still to be addressed. The author, who had promised himself to do it, has renounced the project. For all that was said,[1] he was never admitted to the circle of "Khmerologists," and has never even visited Cambodia—surely there is irony in his now being called to write these pages! He then very soon turned to other research, more exigent, that placed him far from Khmer studies. In the meantime, no Khmerologist has stepped forward to do the necessary work on Buddhism, although Khmer studies have never suffered interruption because of the political turmoil in Khmer lands. And the field is currently bustling with Khmerologists. The reader should know, then, from the outset, that this summary, an imperfect one, is not everything that might reasonably have been hoped for today.

The Indian expansion into Southeast Asia began around the first century of the Christian era. While no documents attest to this specifically, a variety of indications bear it out. The period was exceptional in the history of India, marked by great transformations and the expansion of India's commerce and culture to the north and east.

The source documents on ancient Cambodian religion date from several centuries later. Among them, Sanskrit epigraphy holds an essential place. It is

1. Groslier 1976, 28; Filliozat 1979, 41.

the only literature, strictly speaking, that survives from ancient Cambodia, a literature written over nearly a thousand years (from the fifth to the fourteenth centuries) by Indians and by Khmer writing in Sanskrit, the cultural language of both India and Cambodia. In addition to the historical facts they relate, Sanskrit inscriptions are our only source for the religious conceptions and the culture of their authors and, along with, doubtless, part of the population of ancient Cambodia. (The name derives from the Sanskrit *Kambudeśa,* "Country of Kambu," or *Kambujadeśa,* "Country of the descendants of Kambu," which in abridged form becomes Kambuja or Kampuchea.) It is therefore appropriate, before turning to the religions, to describe very briefly the history of Sanskrit epigraphy.

The oldest Cambodian inscriptions, which date from the fifth and sixth centuries, are all written in Sanskrit, using scripts that originated in south India. Khmer, the local language, began to be used in the seventh century. The poetic and philosophical texts, however, were still written in Sanskrit. Scripts and inscriptions in Khmer will be discussed later in this volume. Quite often, the poetic and philosophical component of an inscription is in Sanskrit, and the part devoted to material and technical questions is in Khmer. The same division, between Sanskrit and Dravidian, can be found in dual-language inscriptions from southern India. But the very existence of Khmer inscriptions proves that the Indian religions they concern were not practiced in Cambodia solely by an educated elite, although what proportion of the population subscribed to these religions is unknown.

The first to publish and translate Sanskrit inscriptions from Cambodia was the great Dutch Sanskritist Hendrik Kern, between 1879 and 1882, on the basis of rubbings sent to him by a French explorer.[2] Systematic work on the inscriptions truly began with the French Sanskritists Auguste Barth and Abel Bergaigne, whose brilliant work *Inscriptions sanscrites de Campa et du Cambodge* was published in 1885 and 1893. Their lead was followed by Louis Finot and George Cœdès, who published and translated Khmer inscriptions as well. In 1966, three years before his death, Cœdès published the last installment of a work that had first started to appear in 1937, his *Inscriptions du Cambodge.* Its eight volumes manage with a very few exceptions to avoid duplicating inscriptions in previous or parallel publications. This work marks the end of the great period of Cambodian epigraphy, although there has been a great effort to develop scholarly programs in the field.

To be sure, not everyone can be a George Cœdès who in 1906, at the age of 20, had already published a long Sanskrit inscription from Cambodia, and who over the next sixty years, would publish and translate hundreds of Sanskrit and Khmer texts that were often difficult and wide-ranging. At the same time, he devoted a great deal of other fundamental research to Southeast Asia, which resulted in two brilliant historical summaries, among other works. The current level of activity, in contrast, seems derisory when one considers that only four or five moderate-sized Sanskrit inscriptions have been published and translated in the last thirty years, one of them in Thailand by a Thai scholar.[3] One might believe that what remained to be done had been accomplished. However, several Sanskrit inscriptions discovered since the completion of Cœdès' *Inscriptions du Cambodge* still await publication, and more are constantly being discovered, apparently. Above all, the works of the old masters—Barth, Bergaigne, Finot, and Cœdès—admirable as they are on the whole, often need correction. This is a gigantic task that

2. See *Annales de l'Extrême-Orient,* 1879–1882.
3. Prapandvidya 1990, 11–14.

requires, beyond an excellent command of the Sanskrit language, a vast knowledge of Sanskrit culture. Only one part of this has been accomplished, and it was essentially outside the context of the institutions that were charged with the task. Thus, the epigraphist must not only be able to decipher texts and gather historical information from them (assuming that one still knows when to look for it and when to refrain from doing so): the epigrapher must also be capable of understanding the literary, philosophical, and technical themes that abound within them.[4]

The inscriptions, despite their richness and extent (one of them is some 298 stanzas long), cannot compensate for the absence of a true literature. Any description of the religions of ancient Cambodia is thus condemned to remain fragmentary, in contrast to the religions of Indonesia, for example, where a genuine body of literature survives. The deficiency is all the more striking in that certain important inscriptions have come down to us in a partially destroyed state.

The question that has always troubled scholars is which of the two religions of India, Hinduism or Buddhism, first spread to Southeast Asia. In the context of India, one more readily associates Buddhism with a missionary zeal; it is a more universal religion and less tied to the intimate structure of Indian society. Various indications do seem to bear out that Buddhism was indeed propagated in Southeast Asia first. The door was opened by seagoing traders, who may or may not have been Buddhist themselves.[5] The Brahmans, however, were not long in joining this movement. From the earliest epigraphic evidence, dating to the fourth or fifth century, one already finds Hinduism established in one form or another in the different Indianized states of Indochina and Indonesia.[6] A Chinese text relates that in the third century more than one thousand Brahmans lived in a certain kingdom on the Malay Peninsula in fealty to Funan (an ancestor to Cambodia).[7] And still in the ninth century a Brahman who arrived in Cambodia from India declared that he had made his way there "in order to purify the land of Kambu, worthy of great praise."[8]

Unfortunately, the beginnings elude us, and one would like to know the circumstances under which the Indian religions first took root in Southeast Asia. Remarkable as these events were, India, curiously, has lost all memory of them, and by the time the first documents appear in Southeast Asia (and not in Cambodia alone), the Indian religions are already solidly established there.

According to the Sanskrit epigraphy, iconography, and Chinese dynastic histories, Hinduism and Buddhism existed side by side in Cambodia during the fifth and sixth centuries. The main religion seems to have been Śivaism, one of the two major branches of Hinduism, but the other branch, Viṣṇuism, also had adherents in the royal family.

According to Chinese dynastic histories, the kingdom of Funan was a great center of Buddhism, frequented by missionaries from India. It was from Funan that the famous scholar Paramārtha, a native of Ujjayinī in central India, left for China in 546 with 240 bundles of Buddhist texts.[9] But there were also monks native to Funan living in China; they worked on translating sacred texts from Sanskrit into Chinese in various localities there, at least one of which bore the telling name "Office of Funan."[10]

Paramārtha was an adept of the idealist-meditative school (Vijñānavāda/Yogācāra; page 45), the branch of Buddhism usually called Mahāyāna, or the

4. See, among others, Bhattacharya 1961; Bhattacharya 1984, 475–484; Bhattacharya 1994, 225–228.
5. Lévi 1929, 19-39. Reprinted in Lévi 1937, 133–144.
6. Bhattacharya 1961, 20. See also Barth 1882, 251, reprinted in Barth 1914, 352; and Renan 1884, reprinted in Renan 1992, 418–419.
7. Wheatley 1961, 17.
8. See note 43.
9. Pachow 1958 14–15; Cœdès 1964, 118.
10. Pelliot 1903, 284–285; Bhattacharya 1961, 14.

"Greater Vehicle," with its extensive and complex pantheon of gods. Yet epigraphy and archaeological remains, as well as Chinese dynastic histories, suggest that the Buddhism in Funan was of the more sober form called Hinayāna, or "Lesser Vehicle." People honored the Three Jewels, namely, the Buddha (c. 560–480 B.C.), the Law (*dharma*), and the monastic community (*saṃgha*), and offered homage to images of the Buddha and "holy relics."[11]

While Buddhism can point to its founder, the origins of Hinduism are lost in the abyss of time. A descendant of the old Vedic religion, and perhaps even going back beyond the Vedic period, Hinduism was impregnated, as it spread across the Indian continent, by many autochthonus, non-Aryan elements. We shall see that this process went on in other countries.

The most remarkable element of classical Hinduism is the conception of the trinity (in Sanskrit, *trimūrti*, "form of three"), composed of the gods Brahmā, Viṣṇu, and Śiva, respectively responsible for the cosmic tasks of creation, preservation, and dissolution. These three are considered emanations of the Supreme God, who is sometimes imagined as Viṣṇu, sometimes as Śiva, and sometimes, though rarely, as Brahmā. In a given case, one of the three gods becomes the most important member of the trinity, its central god, the one considered the most complete emanation of the Supreme God, while the other two are relegated to a lesser rank. Thus, two great religions are organized within the heart of Hinduism—Śivaism and Viṣṇuism—each with its own theology, mythology, and rituals. A "Brahmanism" must also have existed, but it had small success in India and left no trace at all in Cambodia.[12]

Despite its undeniable popular polytheism, Hinduism at the superior level is therefore a monotheistic religion. Often it is even monistic, in the sense that it recognizes no duality between God and the world, the world being the manifestation of God, who is at the same time its material and efficient cause. This God is sometimes identified with the Impersonal Principle, the Absolute Being (*brahman*) of the most ancient Indian thought, contained in the *Upaniṣads*. The religious speculations appearing in the Sanskrit epigraphy of Cambodia clearly demonstrate that such Hinduism also prevailed in that country.[13]

Viṣṇuism had followers among the royal family during the Funan period. From Vedic times, Viṣṇu had been intimately associated with royalty in India, and, according to a happy theory of Cœdès', the installation of a *viṣṇupada*, or footprint of Viṣṇu, installed in the Plain of Reeds in Cochinchina by Guṇavarman, a prince of Funan, marked the reclamation "of a region, by drainage and partial filling, which is still today very marshy and flooded for a part of every year."[14] The inscription says that the prince was named governor over a region "rescued from the mud."[15] Just as in Java, continues Cœdès, "the footprints of Pūrṇavarman, rather than Viṣṇu, perhaps marked the formal act of possession of the country after a military conquest."

A late inscription from Phnom Da,[16] near Angkor Borei, links a series of Viṣṇuite images to a certain king Rodravarman, possibly a middle-Indian form of "Rudravarman," as the last king of Funan was called.[17] Some of the images mentioned in the inscription may correspond, at least in part, to the oldest of the figures discovered at Phnom Da, among them a Viṣṇu with eight arms symbolizing the eight directions of space, or Viṣṇu in his cosmic aspect. This statue is very likely the one referred to in the inscription by the

11. BHATTACHARYA 1961, 12–14.
12. BHATTACHARYA 1961, 125.
13. BHATTACHARYA 1961, 57–70; and BHATTACHARYA 1970, 98–101.
14. CŒDÈS 1964, 117.
15. CŒDÈS 1931, 6, VII; BHATTACHARYA 1991, 65, no. 249.
16. *IC* 2: 155–156.
17. BHATTACHARYA 1991, 9.

significant name Hari Kambujendra, meaning "Hari (Viṣṇu), Lord of the Kambujas (Cambodians)," or "of Kambuja (Cambodia)," identifying the king with Viṣṇu, in accordance with a well-known Indian tradition.[18]

Adopting a religion implies adopting its ideology. Thus, the inscription by Queen Kulaprabhāvatī[19] that invokes Viṣṇu lying on the serpent Ananta (or Śeṣa)—a motif that would become very popular in ancient Cambodia (cat. 68)—informs us that the queen, "much beloved of King Jayavarman" (of Funan), realized the vanity of the world and, probably, retired to a hermitage that she had built for herself following historical events that are known to us.[20]

The Guṇavarman inscription refers to Viṣṇu as *Cakratīrthasvāmin,* "Lord of Cakratīrtha," after a well-known Viṣṇuite holy place in India.[21] Numerous inscriptions from the pre-Angkor period, when Indo-Khmer civilization was developing, designate Śiva sanctuaries with names borrowed from the holy places of the Indian tradition.[22] These indications, along with facts gleaned from a Sanskrit inscription being issued by a probably foreign king, lead us to think that the first Hindus in Cambodia hastened to create a new Hindu world by founding holy places bearing Indian names on the Indian model.[23] Similar phenomena are found in other parts of Southeast Asia (see, for instance, the legend that Mount Meru, the axis of the world and abode of the gods, was transferred to the island of Java).[24]

The epigraphy does not relate the full story, however. No surviving inscription from the Funan period refers to Śivaism. Yet according to Chinese dynastic histories, it was the predominant religion, in fact the state religion, of Funan. The same sources inform us, furthermore, that a synthesis of Śivaism and the indigenous cults had been achieved.

One of the chronicles states: "It is the custom of the country (Funan) to worship the god Maheśvara (Śiva). The god ceaselessly descends onto Mount Modan."[25] Another, which provides information prior to 589, says of Zhenla: "Near the capital is a mountain called Ling-kia-po-p'o [Lingjiabopo], on whose summit, under the perpetual guard of one thousand soldiers, sits a temple dedicated to a spirit named P'o-to-li [Poduoli], to whom human sacrifices are made. Each year the king enters the temple and himself performs a human sacrifice at night."[26]

The mountain this last Chinese text calls Lingjiabopo is none other than the Liṅgaparvata of epigraphy. This is the mountain dominating the site of Vat Phu, in what is now southern Laos. Poduoli, for his part, has been construed as Bhadreśvara. It was under this name that Śiva was worshiped at Vat Phu—Liṅgaparvata, according to epigraphy. This was, in a sense, the national god of the Kambujas throughout Cambodian history. The text suggests that the religion celebrated on Liṅgaparvata was an indigenous cult adopted by Śivaism. The "spirit called Poduoli" was certainly a mountain spirit, but identified with Śiva. And it was possible, even natural, to make this identification, because Śiva himself was a "mountain spirit." He was *Giriśa,* "He who lies down on the mountain," and *Girīśa,* "Lord of the mountain," and *Giritra,* "Protector of the mountain." His wife was *Pārvatī,* "Daughter of the Mountain," *Haimavatī,* "Daughter of the Himalaya," and *Śikharavāsinī,* "She who lives on the summits." The mountain is, in effect, "the place where the mysterious potency of the earth and hence of all natural life, is concentrated," as was once said of Mesopotamia.[27] And the mountains played an important role in the chthonic religion practiced in Funan, where the kings were called *Śailarāja* or *Parvatabhūpāla* (Khmer, *Kuruṅ Vnaṃ?*), "Monarchs of the Mountain." The Chinese name for the kingdom has a similar derivation: Funan (*b'iu-nâm,* old

18. Bhattacharya 1964, 72–78.
19. Cœdès 1937, 117–121.
20. Cœdès 1964, 117.
21. Bhattacharya 1961, 122.
22. Bhattacharya 1961, 169.
23. Majumdar 1959–1960, 22–26. Jacques 1962, 249–256. Wolters 1979, 438–440. Salomon 1990, 160–176.
24. Gonda 1975.
25. Bhattacharya 1961, 12–13; Wheatley 1974, 101–102; Wolters 1979, 442, note 15.
26. Bhattacharya 1961, 20–24.
27. Frankfort 1954, 54.

Fig. 1
Vat Phu, viewed from the hill

Khmer *bnam* [*vnam*], the present *phnom,* "mountain"). Funan's sacred mountain was the one the Chinese called Modan, the mountain on which the god Maheśvara "ceaselessly descended," and it is almost certain that Śiva was identified with the spirit of the mountain in Funan.

This affinity between Śivaism and the beliefs that were widespread in Southeast Asia was at least a major reason Śivaism succeeded so well in that part of the world. Another was the religion's liberal outlook toward classes and castes, which contributed to the success of Śivaism even in India itself by making it easier for the population at large to enter into Brahmanic society.

Human sacrifice was characteristic of the chthonic cult found throughout "monsoon Asia."[28] Until the end of the nineteenth century, there persisted the memory of an annual human sacrifice performed on Ba Phnom, a hill several miles southeast of Phnom Penh that was known in the tenth century as *Vraḥ Vnaṃ,* or Sacred Mountain. The capital of Funan is now thought to lie somewhere in the vicinity of this "Śivaistic place of worship with its traces of pre-Indian ritual."[29] This mountain is also doubtless the one the Chinese call Modan, the one on which the god Maheśvara "descends ceaselessly." Later epigraphy seems, in effect, to confirm that Śiva was worshiped there under the name of Giriśa, "He who reclines on the mountain."

The role of human sacrifice in the worship of the earth has been well described by Paul Mus: "The earth god is the deification of the energies of the soil." This god is impersonal, amorphous, but he can be made tangible, and communication can be established between this abstract god and the community around him. The sacrificial victim is his incarnation. "The victim is not served to the god, who is no cannibal. The victim simply provides the divinity with the vehicle of a person for the duration of the ceremony. The intangible thus finds bodily form and becomes exorable. The community can then communicate with the divine through the intermediary of its leader, who is also its priest."[30] This description accords with what the Chinese text

28. Mus 1934, 367–410.
29. Dupont 1955, 17. See also Chandler 1974, 207–222.
30. Mus 1934, 8–11.

says: "Each year, the king enters the temple and himself performs a human sacrifice at night."

In India, human sacrifice was often practiced in honor of the terrible forms of the Great Goddess and it is significant that certain texts state categorically that the sacrifice must be performed by the king and only the king, and that Brahmans have no right to do it.

The situation here is thus the same within India and outside it: A non-Aryan cult has been assimilated by Hinduism but rejected by the orthodoxy. It is difficult to say how long this situation lasted in Cambodia. The orthodoxy undoubtedly worked to bring it to an end and thereby assert its supremacy, though without violence, and using the king himself, who was also the high priest of the official cult described in the Chinese document. The most efficient solution was to make the king an incarnation of Śiva and establish the cult of the *devarāja*, or "god-king," as the official religion. Its priest would naturally be a member of the orthodoxy (page 42).

As well as Viṣṇuite images (page 38), the soil of Cambodia, particularly in the area of the lower Mekong Valley where the kingdom of Funan was centered, has yielded numerous *liṅga* that may date from the Funan period.[31] It was in this form that Śiva was primarily worshiped. A phallic emblem, "descended from the uncarved stones of earth cults," the *liṅga* symbolized the fertilizing energy of the god.[32] In later speculation, however, the *liṅga* represents the sky, and the *yoni* (female organ), the basin into which it is inserted, the earth;[33] further, the *liṅga* represents the cosmic light of Śiva.[34] The anatomically naturalistic appearance of the early images would be replaced by a stylized form.

Śivaism and Viṣṇuism, therefore, both existed in Funan. And the Harihara, or mixed image of Śiva and Viṣṇu, found at Phnom Da suggests—if we accept the oldest Phnom Da works as belonging to the time of Rudravarman—that the Hinduism of Funan in its last years was a syncretic religion that blended Śivaism and Viṣṇuism (page 51).

The seventh century saw a new influx of ideas. The ancient Śivaite school of the Pāśupata (who worshiped Śiva under the name of *Pāśupati*, "Lord [*pati*] of the beasts [*paśu*] = souls"), which was then flourishing in India and had spread as far as Central Asia, appeared in Cambodia for the first time.[35] Pāśupata spiritual leaders found favor with the kings of Cambodia. They were well-versed in grammar, as they tell us in surviving Sanskrit inscriptions, and in the various philosophical systems current in India, including Buddhism.[36] The grammatical work of Pāṇiṇi, the greatest grammarian of antiquity, was highly prized in Cambodia, particularly among Śivaites. An Indian tradition held that it was Śiva himself who had revealed the secrets of grammar to Pāṇiṇi.[37] Indian documents also attest to the ecumenical spirit of the times, as when Śivaites are cited as studying Buddhist philosophy.[38]

The Pāśupata reappear in Cambodia, though for the last time, toward the end of the ninth century in the reign of Yaśovarman I. They lived side by side with the Śivaite school known simply as "Śaiva" (Śaivite) which seems to have appeared in Cambodia shortly after its creation in India. Yet while one of Yaśovarman's inscriptions mentions the Pāśupata doctrine beside the Śaiva doctrine, there are no specific elements of Pāśupata thought in the Śivaite doctrine as it is revealed in the Sanskrit epigraphy of Cambodia. Nor do we learn anything from this epigraphy about the particular rites of the Pāśupata, while the Śivaite iconography of Cambodia contains no trace of their passage.

Fig. 2
Angkor-period *liṅga*. Sandstone. Height 46.5 cm. Late ninth century. Musée national des Arts asiatiques-Guimet, Paris

31. O'Connor 1972, 24.
32. Mus 1934, 23–24.
33. Bhattacharya 1961, 71. *Kāraṇḍavyūha* 265.
34. Bhattacharya 1961, 71.
35. Bhattacharya 1961, 44. Wolters 1979, 431.
36. Bhattacharya, "La Secte," 1955, 479–480. (At 480, 4, read "acquired a sure knowledge of the true meaning of grammar, of Vaiśeṣika and of Nyāya" instead of "gave a sure meaning to grammar..."[Cœdès].)
37. Bhattacharya 1961, 48.
38. Bhattacharya 1955, 488, note 3.

Śivaite theology, on the other hand, was classically expressed in Cambodia for the first time in a magnificent invocation to Śiva found on an inscription of 624. Personal god of grace, endowed with supernatural qualities, Śiva is identified at the highest level of spiritual experience with the absolute Brahman; this is an idea that had appeared in India at the very dawn of Śivaite thought.[39]

On the Viṣṇuite side, the important school of the Bhāgavata ("devotees of the Blessed") already appears in the inscription of the Funan prince Guṇavarman (page 37). Also known as Pāñcarātra or Sātvata, the school had elevated Kṛṣṇa Vāsudeva, originally a tribal "hero," to the rank of Supreme God by identifying him with the Vedic Viṣṇu. It was not long since the school had been formed in India. But rudiments of its doctrine, taken from Indian texts, were first expressed in Cambodia in an inscription from the reign of Jayavarman I.[40] This inscription also mentions the dogma common to all the religions of India, namely, that a man may progressively purify himself in the course of his various existences so as to free himself from successive rebirths, either good or bad, resulting from action (*karman*).[41]

As to Buddhism, finally, the situation seems to have been the following, as far as we can now tell.[42] The Amarāvatī-Nāgārjunakoṇḍa region in southern India and the island of Sri Lanka (Siṃhala, Ceylon), with which it had close ties during the first centuries of the Christian era, played a preponderant role in spreading Buddhism throughout Southeast Asia. The contribution made by northern India should not be ignored, however. In the seventh century, both the style of the Buddha statues and the epigraphy give proof of new influences arriving in Cambodia, on the one hand, from Sri Lanka and, on the other, from the kingdom of Dvāravatī (in what is now central Thailand). Thus the statue of the Buddha from Tuol Preah That (cat. 4) reflects the Dvāravatī style. On its back is an inscription that reproduces—as do countless monuments and images of the Buddha in India, Central Asia, and China—the famous stanza in which one of the Buddha's immediate disciples so well summed up the "Four Noble Truths" (Suffering, the Origin of Suffering, the Cessation of Suffering, and the Path that leads to the Cessation of Suffering), a stanza so succinct that it was elevated to the level of becoming Buddhist credo. But this inscription is written in Pāli, the canonical language of the Theravāda school (belonging to the Lesser Vehicle), that was established in Dvāravatī.[43] The Greater Vehicle appears first in the epigraphy and iconography of Cambodia during the seventh to eighth centuries. It would soon displace the Lesser Vehicle until Theravāda Buddhism was reintroduced to Cambodia after the Thai invasions at the end of the thirteenth century (pages 49–50). In the last quarter of the eighth century, Mahāyāna Buddhism also spread to the Malay Peninsula and Java. This expansion was perhaps not unrelated to the rise, in the east of India, of the Pāla dynasty (which we know for certain to have had close relations with Indonesia) and the activities associated with the great University of Nālandā, located to the east of Patna in the valley of the Ganges.

The great political event of 802, the founding of the Angkor dynasty by Jayavarman II and the establishment of the cult of the *devarāja,* was doubtless, as suggested previously, also a great religious event. The relation of it comes to us from an inscription written exactly 250 years later, but there seems no reason to doubt its authenticity. The famous Sdok Kak Thom inscription, dated 1052,[44] relates that the magic rites intended to liberate Cambodia from

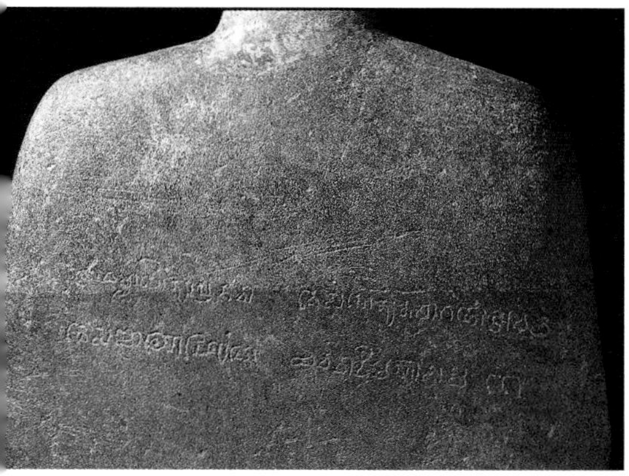

Fig. 3
ye dhammā hetuprabhavā[1] tesaṃ hetuṃ tathāgato avaca/tesañ ca yo nirodho evaṃvādī mahāsamano
"Of all things derived from a cause (*hetuprabhavā*), the Tathāgata (Buddha) has told the cause; and he has also foretold their end, great monk that he is" (new translation by K. Bhattacharya)
1. A Sanskritism also found elsewhere. See *Epigraphia Indica* 28 (1900), 220-226

39. BHATTACHARYA 1961, 57–58.
40. BHATTACHARYA 1961, 97–98. See also BHATTACHARYA, "Sur une stance," 1965, 407–409.
41. *IC* 2: 194 and 195, VIII.
42. BHATTACHARYA 1961, 16–19, 27.
43. BHATTACHARYA 1961, 17. See also *IC* 7: 108. An inscription from the Prachinburi region of Thailand, not far from the Cambodian frontier, cites three stanzas from a non-canonical Pāli text composed in Sri Lanka. It is said to be in Old Khmer and to be dated 761. We do not have the materials, however, to verify this information. See ROHANADEERA 1987, 59–73. At any rate, there are known instances of inscriptions in Old Khmer written outside the borders of ancient Cambodia (see CŒDÈS 1958, 125–142).
44. CŒDÈS and DUPONT 1943–1946, 57–134. See also CHAKRAVARTI 1980.

its vassalage to Java and unify the country under the rule of a universal king were performed in accordance with four Sanskrit texts. The names of these texts are known in India; it is even likely that a recently discovered and published text represents one of them, perhaps the most important one.[45] The basic elements of this text correspond, in part, to those mentioned in the Sdok Kak Thom inscription, although the word *devarāja* itself does not appear in it.

Much has been said on the score of the *devarāja,* and no other subject in Khmer studies has so consistently fascinated scholars. As it will be discussed elsewhere in this volume, only a few points will be emphasized here. First of all what does *devarāja* mean? In attempting a definition, the great scholars of the past, in their wisdom, considered both the Sanskrit word and its Khmer equivalent as it appears in the Sdok Kak Thom inscription, *kamrateṅ jagat ta rāja,* and came to the conclusion that the word meant "god-king." Two other interpretations have been proposed in recent years: "king of the gods"[46] and "god of the king."[47] But the first, a normal meaning in Sanskrit, agrees poorly with the Khmer; and the second, a possible meaning in Khmer, is an absolute impossibility in Sanskrit. This suggests that we retain the interpretation "god-king." In Java, it is worth noting, there is a similar expression used in the same way: *devaprabhu.*[48]

If the word *devarāja* and its Khmer equivalent appears only in the Sdok Kak Thom inscription, the king in ancient Cambodia was considered an incarnated portion of Śiva as early as the seventh century (Jayavarman I).[49] In India, the king was sometimes considered a partial incarnation of Śiva, and sometimes a partial incarnation of Viṣṇu.[50] And the Viṣṇuite version of this idea must have existed in Cambodia during the Funan period, if the twelfth-century inscription that links Hari Kambujendra with King Rudravarman can be trusted.

In 802, what had been only an idea became an institution. The magic rites performed on this occasion were intended, as we have seen, both to free the country and to unify it, but might not one think, without too great temerity, that by establishing a state cult whose officiating priest was a member of the orthodoxy, that orthodoxy was attempting to bring an end to the cult practiced on Liṅgaparvata and in so doing strengthen its own authority?

Underlying this idea of the "god-king" was perhaps the classical Indian idea that the earthly king is a reflection of the heavenly king Indra, the king of the gods (which is the usual meaning of *devarāja),* just as this world is a reflection of the world beyond, both participating in the Eternal Order that holds both macrocosm and microcosm and creates an intimate bond between man and the Divine. Is it by chance that the founding rites were performed on Mount Mahendra (present-day Phnom Kulen)? There is a well-known mountain of this name in India that is associated in texts from north and south India sometimes with Śiva and sometimes with Indra.[51]

But a host of problems arises in connection with the *devarāja,* and it is ill-advised to ally one's self (as too often happens) with one or another of the hypotheses proposed. It should be noted that the post of officiating priest to the god-king was exclusively reserved for male or female members of the maternal line of Śivakaivalya, a priest instructed by the cult's founder, the Brahman Hiraṇyadāma.[52]

One must avoid overinterpreting the evidence: There is no text of Cambodian epigraphy into which one may read, forcing it somewhat, that the

45. GOUDRIAN 1985.
46. FILLIOZAT 1966, 95–106. Reprinted in LAGHUPRABANDHAH 1974, 454–465.
47. POU 1993, 168.
48. NAGARAKRTAGAMA 43, 1. See PIGEAUD 1960, 1: 32; 3: 49.
49. *IC* 1: 8 AND 10, III. BHATTACHARYA 1964, 78.
50. BHATTACHARYA 1964.
51. BHATTACHARYA 1991, 54–55 no. 178. Also, FILLIOZAT 1966, 102–1974, 461 (FILLIOZAT, followed by WHEATLEY 1974, 105, has not always reproduced the information correctly.)
52. CHAKRAVARTI 1980, 20–21, XXXI.

king's "subtle essence" (*moi subtil*) resided in the *liṅga*, Śiva's emblem.[53]

Despite the installation of a Śivaite "god-king," Viṣṇuism continued to prosper. The religion found favor with Jayavarman II, and his son and successor, Jayavarman III, was Viṣṇuite.[54] It was under the latter's reign that the Brahman mentioned earlier came to Cambodia (page 36). This Viṣṇuite Brahman left an inscription that has survived in mutilated form, but where one reads, nevertheless, that he had come "to purify the country of the Kambus, who were worthy of high praise, though in the celebrated country of his birth he had become a very knowledgeable expert on the Vedas."[55] But the theory claiming that, in the following reign, the spiritual master of the king, Indravarman I, voyaged to India to study with the Vedānta philosopher Śaṅkara, who was reputed to be the greatest philosopher in India, seems to rest on a misinterpretation.[56] No text that we are as yet aware of mentions such voyages.

In the time of Yaśovarman, the founder of Angkor (889–c. 900), the inscriptions reflect the predominance of Śivaism. They further reveal a syncretism, not only between Śivaism and Viṣṇuism, as before, but between Śivaism and Buddhism,[57] a phenomenon that would recur during the following centuries. The edicts promulgated by Yaśovarman to regulate the organization and governance of his temples and hermitages (*āśrama*) give us precious insights into the religious, social, and cultural life of the time. One remarkable text quotes a passage from Manu, the legislator of Hinduism, exalting knowledge above all other "acquired virtues."[58] In the three great hermitages built near the capital and devoted respectively to Śivaites (Śaiva and Pāśupata), to Viṣṇuites (Vaiṣṇava, Bhāgavata, Pāñcarātra, Sātvatas), and to Buddhist, "the common people without exception—children, the old, the infirm, the poor, the neglected" were to be "cared for with food, medicine and other needful things."[59] The worship of the brown cow, *kapilā*,[60] is also mentioned, as are funerary offerings performed according to Indian rites—even for "those who fell in a devote cause on the field of battle, devotees who have expired, those who died without the right to normal funerary offerings (for lack of relatives), the deprived, the neglected, infants and the old."[61] The Indian tradition in effect allowed the king, as the "relative of all," to order such offerings.

Curiously, these edicts have not, for all their uniqueness, received the attention they deserve from historians. It is true that Bergaigne's translation, despite its harsh revision by Barth (page 35), is not always accurate. One stanza, which prescribes nonviolence (*ahiṃsā*) and forbids meat-eating in or near hermitages, has continued to be misunderstood for more than a century now (page 36). Cœdès, following Bergaigne as corrected by Barth (1893), still translated it as follows in 1932: "No person shall be made to die here, not by deed, by thoughts nor by words; nor will any person be revealed to his pursuer, either within or without the hermitage."[62] But the stanza means: No person shall kill any being here, either by actions, by thoughts or by words; nor will one offer meat (*āmiṣa*) on any account to any person, either within or without the hermitage.

During the troubled period following Yaśovarman's death, Viṣṇuism enjoyed something of a revival among the country's dignitaries. A number of them, for instance, founded the Viṣṇuite temple of Prasat Kravan in 921.[63]

The reigns of Rājendravarman (944–968) and of Jayavarman V (968–1001) produced a great period in religion as well as in literature and

53. Bhattacharya 1966, 2: 7–9. See also Filliozat 1981, 65–66.
54. Bhattacharya 1961, 28.
55. *IC* 4: 41 and 42, XIV.
56. Nagaswamy 1967, XVI.4, 342–343. See also Bhattacharya 1971, 99, note 1.
57. Bhattacharya 1961, 30.
58. *ISCC* LVI, C1, 8-9. See also Cœdès, "Études," 1932, 98.
59. *ISCC* LVI, C1, 10; Cœdès 1932, 99. (Translation slightly altered here.)
60. *ISCC* LVI, C1, 11; Cœdès 1932, 99.
61. *ISCC* LVI, C1, 13; Cœdès 1932, 99. (Translation altered here.)
62. *ISCC* LVI, D, 9, 431 and note 2; Cœdès 1932, 103.
63. Bhattacharya 1961, 30.

Fig. 4
Prasat Kravan. Relief carving in the central tower sanctuary. Eight-armed Viṣṇu

philosophy. Śivaism predominated as before, but the monistic tendency that had been present in Śivaite theology since the seventh century seems to have received new strength. An inscription from Banteay Srei, dated 969, is entirely devoted to defending the monism of the Vedānta against the dualism of the logical school of Nyāya and certain *Āgama* (Śivaite texts).[64]

This monism, inspired by the Śaṅkara school (page 43), subsequently had a general influence on thought. King Rājendravarman, echoing his illustrious predecessor Yaśovarman, exhorted his successors to protect his religious foundations as though they were their own.[65] Why should they do this? It is the notion of the "unity of the self" that provides the theoretical foundation of those exhortations to the author of the Pre Rup inscription, the longest Sanskrit inscription ever composed in Cambodia (page 36). In poetic terms of which the following translation gives only a pale reflection, it says:

"In multiple bodies, there is only one Self (*ātman*) that acts and feels. O you who are wise, may you come more and more to consider all meritorious works as your own.

64. Bhattacharya 1961, 60–63, 161–162. (Bhattacharya 1970, 81–83.)
65. Bhattacharya 1991, 56–58 no. 189.

"The idea that each individual reaps the rewards of his own acts arises from distinguishing between agents. Yet this distinction is only imagined—owing to the distinction between contingent appositions (*upādhi*). It is therefore a secondary distinction, and one that should be dissipated by an awareness of the Ultimate Truth, as darkness is dissipated by the sun's brightness."[66]

The author of this inscription is also familiar with the doctrine, among others, of the idealist-meditative school of Buddhism, or at least with its central tenet, namely, that our representation of the external world is merely a thought, unconnected to any object. But he rejects the notion, citing this "thought without object" in the context of Yaśovarman's entreaties, which had proved ineffectual ("devoid of any object"), since his capital and his foundations had been abandoned.[67]

On the whole, however, the relations between the religions were good, and this sometimes led to syncretism. Buddhism, which had been more or less neglected by succeeding kings after Yaśovarman's death, made great progress during the reigns of Rājendravarman and Jayavarman V. It was given new life by the learned master Kīrtipaṇḍita, a follower of the idealist school, in fact, who not only restored a large number of broken images and erected new ones but "drew from abroad a host of philosophic books." Its influence penetrated to the royal family itself.[68]

Viṣṇuism is represented as before by the Bhāgavata school (Pāñcarātra, Sātvata), and several inscriptions from this period expound its doctrines. In particular, one finds the concept of the *vyūha,* or "emanations," but described in terms that betray a certain lack of understanding. The divine emanations are assigned the three qualities of nature, whereas the qualities they possess are in fact "supernatural."[69] Another example of this kind of misunderstanding appears in one of the inscriptions at Bat Chum from the reign of Rājendravarman. The author of the inscription finds a contradiction between the doctrine of the negation of the individual self, *nairātmya,* and the idea of the Supreme Self, *paramātman,* the absolute, impersonal, or suprapersonal self. Yet the author says himself, following his reading of fundamental Buddhist texts, that the Buddha taught this very doctrine of *nairātmya* as a "means of attaining the Supreme Self."[70]

Such mistakes, owing to imperfect assimilation of often highly complex Indian doctrines, are in fact rare in Cambodia's Sanskrit inscriptions and are unlikely to have impaired faith or devotion of worshipers. Thus we read in another stanza from this same Bat Chum inscription—a stanza misunderstood by Cœdès in 1908 and again in 1952[71]—that the famous architect in the king's service, Kavīndrārimathana, offered up the temples he had built to the Divinity as substitutes for the lotus of his own heart.

Aside from two classical Buddhist texts, the inscription of Kīrtipaṇḍita at Vat Sithor (or Srei Santhor)[72] mentions texts that are as yet unidentified. These would seem to be "Tantric" texts. At any rate, according to the tendency of the time, the pure doctrines of the negation of self (*nairātmya*) and of "nothing-but-thought" (*cittamātra*) that the master Kīrtipaṇḍita propounded were well adapted to Tantric ritual, mixed with Hinduism. Among other notable aspects of the Vat Sithor inscription are the references to "formulas" (*mantra*), "gestures" (*mudrā*), the lightning bolt (*vajra*), and the bell (*ghaṇṭā*). Although no formal proof exists that Vajrayāna was practiced in Cambodia during the tenth century, it is well indicated in a recently found inscription from 1066.

66. BHATTACHARYA 1971.
67. *IC* 1: 102 and 139, CCLXXV. See also FILLIOZAT 1981, 86.
68. BHATTACHARYA 1961, 31–34. (At 32, read "maternal uncle" for "son," and eliminate "but who...")
69. BHATTACHARYA 1961, 98–99.
70. BHATTACHARYA 1973.
71. CŒDÈS, "Les Inscriptions," 1908, 232 and 246, XXXIII. Also CŒDÈS 1952, 473.
72. *IC* 6: 195–211.

During the eventful period that followed the reign of Jayavarman V in 1001, Viṣṇuism gained adherents among the royal family and the high dignitaries.[73] One dignitary, a Satvāta (Bhāgavata, Pāñcarātra) who had earlier served under the reign of Jayavarman V and was the "principal spiritual master" and a "highly honored counselor" to Jayavīravarman, has left an inscription dated 1006 that sets forth, among a number of concepts, a complex Pāñcarātra dogma.[74] There also flourished at this time a syncretism between Śivaism and Viṣṇuism on the one hand, and between Śivaism and Buddhism on the other.[75]

Sūryavarman I was for a long time thought to have been Buddhist on account of his posthumously given name of *Nirvāṇapada.* The assumption was challenged, however, in 1961. The epigraphy represents this monarch as a fervent supporter of Śivaism, and the name *Nirvāṇapada* is in no way incompatible with being Śivaite.[76] Perhaps the name is even an illustration of the very synthesis of Śivaism and Buddhism, which the epigraphy of his reign indicates.[77]

A syncretic Buddhism of the Mahāyāna school was therefore practiced. In the distant province of Lopburi or Lavo, in present-day Thailand, an inscription in Khmer mentions "bhikṣu mahāyāna sthavira." For a long time this was thought to refer to "monks belonging to both schools of Buddhism," namely, Mahāyāna and Sthaviravāda (Pāli for Theravāda).[78] But if one credits the Chinese pilgrims who visited India several centuries earlier, it is more likely to refer to a monastic community that practiced the Mahāyāna doctrine while observing the disciplinary code (*Vinaya*) of the Theravāda school (or *mahāyānasthavira,* if we join the last two words).[79]

From the death of Sūryavarman I in 1050 until the accession in 1113 of Sūryavarman II, the builder of Angkor Vat, a Viṣṇuite temple, Śivaism remained the dominant religion.[80] A remarkable inscription from 1100 propounds for the first time in Cambodia a doctrine characteristic of the *Āgama* (page 44). Assuming two different aspects, Śiva's energy (*śakti*) first strengthens the bonds of the soul then frees the soul from them. The strengthening or "maturing" of the bonds, which have existed for all eternity, is intended solely to help beings bring their intrinsic capabilities to full fruition. When the bonds are ripe, the "Energy of Grace" comes down to break them. Śiva himself takes on the form of a guru to perform the initiations (*dīkṣā*), which induce different states in individuals, proportional to their capacities.[81] These initiations, often mentioned in Cambodian epigraphy, comprise the most characteristic aspect of Agamic Śivaism.[82]

Viṣṇuism also underwent something of a revival. The epigraphic record shows that Jayavarman VI (1080–1107) had a marked predilection for this branch of Hinduism.[83]

A major document, recently discovered—in an outlying area, it is true, 15 miles (25 km) south of Nakhon Ratchasima in northeastern Thailand—proves the existence of Vajrayāna, the Diamond Vehicle, in the Buddhism of ancient Cambodia. The inscription, dated 1066 (the last year in the reign of Udayādityavarman II), mentions, among other significant things, above the five cosmic Buddhas a sixth Buddha, Vajrasattva, the Adamantine Being, presiding above the others and containing them all.[84] In 1108, in the same region, the temple of Phimai (Vimāya)[85] would be founded, whose iconography also confirms the presence of Vajrayāna.[86]

An inscription from 1067, in turn, reveals the remarkable syncretism that existed between Śivaism and Buddhism. It relates the raising of a Śiva *liṅga,*

73. Bhattacharya 1961, 34–35.
74. Bhattacharya 1961, 99.
75. Bhattacharya 1961, 35.
76. Bhattacharya 1961, 36 with note 3.
77. Bhattacharya 1961, 35–36. See below, page 27.
78. Cœdès 1929, 10. See also Cœdès 1964, 253.
79. La Vallée Poussin 1930, 20–39. Also Wang 1992, 65–72.
80. Bhattacharya 1961, 37.
81. Bhattacharya 1961, 64–65.
82. Bhattacharya 1961, 72.
83. Bhattacharya 1961, 37.
84. Prapandvidya 1990.
85. Cœdès 1924, 345–352.
86. Boeles 1966, 2: 14–29.

an image of Viṣṇu, an image of Brahmā, and an image of the historical Buddha associated with the "Bamboo Park," a famous site near Rājagṛha in eastern India where the Buddha stayed. The four divinities are described by the inscription as forming a Śivaite tetralogy (*śaivī caturmūrti*).[87] Earlier, a Khmer inscription from the tenth century had mentioned the Buddha and the Hindu trinity in juxtaposition (page 37), without specifically enlarging the triad to include the Buddha.[88] Finally, in the reign of Jayavarman VI, Buddhism found followers in the royal family.[89]

Sūryavarman II (1113–c. 1145) was Viṣṇuite and the temple of Angkor Vat is his creation. Yet the epigraphy of his reign shows that Śivaism was still the predominant religion. The king himself appears in it as a worshiper of Śiva. The Bhadreśvara Śiva from Liṅgaparvata (Vat Phu) continued to be regarded as the Kambujas' national god (page 38). Restoration of this sanctuary, begun in the last years of Jayavarman VI, was finished in the reign of Sūryavarman II. Between 1118 and 1139, several images were erected there by royal authority. And the Śivaite temple of Īśvarapura (Banteay Srei) was also restored during that reign, having originally been built by Jayavarman V's famous spiritual master, Yajñavarāha.[90] The rise of Viṣṇuism in Cambodia, eventually resulting in the construction of Angkor Vat, was in all likelihood linked to its rise in India and Java during the same period.[91]

An inscription dated 1129, finally, ratifies the syncretic meshing of Śivaism and Buddhism alluded to above. It speaks of the gifts which a Śivaite has offered to Śiva, Viṣṇu, and the Buddha of the "Bamboo Park," and it specifies that the latter was identified with Śiva.[92]

The last great king of Cambodia, Jayavarman VII (1181–c. 1220), received his Buddhist faith from his father, Dharaṇīndravarman II, successor to Sūryavarman II. He married two sisters in succession, the second after the first had died. They were descended from an old Buddhist family and seem to have exerted great influence over him.[93] This internal development was presumably unconnected to the exodus of scholars from the Buddhist centers in Magadha in eastern India, following their expulsion by the conquering Turks.[94] On the doctrinal level, the Buddhism of Jayavarman VII differed not at all from the Buddhism that had prevailed in Cambodia since the second half of the tenth century.

At the center of Mahāyāna Buddhism is the ideal of the Bodhisattva, a Buddha-to-be. As distinct from the saints of an earlier Buddhism who aspired only to their personal salvation (though this was not the thinking of the Buddha himself), the Bodhisattva, while free from all bonds, renounces Nirvāṇa as he has not yet preached the Doctrine to all the beings in all the worlds. (This is one of the reasons why the adherents of this branch of Buddhism called it the Greater Vehicle, Mahāyāna, as distinct from what they called the Lesser Vehicle, Hinayāna.)

But at the same time there developed a complex Buddhology. In early Buddhism, Gautama Śākyamuni, the Buddha ("enlightened"), was neither a divine incarnation nor the superhuman founder of a religion, but a man who had realized his true human condition and achieved the absolute and suprapersonal Being that each man is in the inmost depth of his being, above and beyond his empirical individuality (page 45). A distinction was thus made between the material, "stinking body," which is subject to birth, age, and death, and an absolute "body" (*dharmakāya, brahmakāya*). The terms *dharma* and *brahman,* which refer to the Absolute, are borrowed from the tradition of the

87. BHATTACHARYA 1961, 37–38.
88. ROESKE 1914, 3: 641.
89. BHATTACHARYA 1961, 37.
90. BHATTACHARYA 1961, 38–39.
91. CŒDÈS 1964, 297. See also GONDA 1975, 26.
92. BHATTACHARYA 1961, 39.
93. BHATTACHARYA 1961, 40.
94. Contrary to, for instance, FILLIOZAT 1981, 69–70.

Fig. 5
Angkor Thom. The Bayon, towers with faces. Late twelfth to early thirteenth century

Upaniṣads (page 37). Starting from this distinction, Mahāyāna Buddhism, and especially its idealist school (page 45), developed the theory of the three "bodies" of the Buddha: the absolute body (*dharmakāya*); the body of bliss (*saṃbhogakāya*), which the saintly assemblies of Bodhisattvas contemplate while absorbed in mystic concentration; and the artificial body (*nirmāṇakāya*), represented by the historical and other Buddhas. The *dharmakāya* is also called *svābhāvikakāya,* "essence body." Sometimes the *dharmakāya,* which is composed of "transcendent attributes" (*dharmas*), is distinguished from a separate *svābhāvikakāya,* the genuine, ineffable Absolute, the plenitude of the Self, the ultimate Principle of the Universe. It is this theory of the three or four "bodies" of the Buddha that prevails in the Buddhist speculations of Sanskrit inscriptions dating from Jayavarman VII's reign and those that preceded it.[95]

It was also in strict adherence to the doctrine of the idealist school that Jayavarman VII was inspired in his social works, by a concept that one of his sons expressed in the Ta Prohm inscriptions:

"Though the Self was divided in various ways in various beings, he (the king) has achieved its unity, since he has taken into his compassionate self the joys and sorrows of those who participate in the Self."[96]

The 102 hospitals founded by the king, distributed throughout his country and open to all social classes, were placed under the protection of the Buddha Bhaiṣajyaguruvaidūryaprabha, "the Master of Remedies, with the radiance of beryl," who "gives peace and health to those who simply hear his name," and of two Bodhisattva, one with the radiance of the sun, the other with the radiance of the moon, Sūryavairocana and Candravairocana.[97] In India there survives a Sanskrit text (*Sūtra*) composed in honor of this triad, which is still very popular today in China, Japan, and Tibet. The doctrine of the Self professed by Jayavarman VII is as much Hindu (Vedantic) as it is Buddhist, and is also cited by Hindus in the Sanskrit epigraphy of Cambodia.

Was a Buddharāja (Buddha-king) ever substituted for the *devarāja* (god-king)? And what do the four colossal faces on the temples of Jayavarman VII represent? We do not know, as there is no text to enlighten us.

Be that as it may, the break in the Hindu tradition during the reign of Jayavarman VII was more apparent than real. The old Hindu cults continued. All the local cults, whether Hindu or Buddhist, were reunited in the Bayon, a veritable pantheon that functioned both as the kingdom's center and its image in small. On the annual feast day at Preah Khan of Angkor, Buddhist and Hindu images were brought in from different temples. The king and his dignitaries erected numerous Hindu images at Preah Khan and Banteay Chmar. The princes and Queen Indradevī, who composed Sanskrit poems, found inspiration in Hindu mythology, and Queen Jayarājadevī, for her part, worshiped Śiva, Viṣṇu, and the Buddha. The old Hindu families retained their traditional privileges. A later text informs us that Cambodia was still "full of excellent scholars of the Veda." Hearing this, a Brahman from Narapatideśa (Burma) went there to display his knowledge. King Jayavarman VII made him his chaplain.[98]

Nonetheless, after the death of this king, a wave of fundamentalist Hindu feeling erupted. "The restoration of the Śivaite orthodoxy very likely triggered the iconoclastic fury that was vented on the monuments from Jayavarman VII's reign. Many reliefs of the Buddha on temple walls and pillars were scratched out as a result and replaced by *liṅga* or ascetics in prayer."[99] Inscriptions reveal that a priestly class devoted to the cults of Śiva and Viṣṇu existed at this time.[100]

95. *IC* 6: 197 and 202, I–V; 2: 203 and 204, I. See also FINOT 1903, 22 and 29, I. Also CŒDÈS 1906, 49 and 70. And *IC* 7: 125 and 126, B; II, 163 and 173, I.
96. BHATTACHARYA 1973, 39.
97. FINOT 1903, 18–33.
98. BHATTACHARYA 1961, 40–41.
99. CŒDÈS 1964, 384. See also FILLIOZAT 1981, 98.
100. BHATTACHARYA 1961, 41.

Fig. 6
Buddha from the Bayon. This statue occupied the temple's main sanctuary. It was discovered in 1933 during excavations at a depth of forty-five feet (140 cm) on the axis of the central tower. Sandstone. Height 360 cm

After the Thai invasions, a new religion took root—Singhalese Buddhism (Theravāda)—which has made Cambodia what it is today. In 1296, the Chinese envoy Zhou Daguan found it solidly implanted in Cambodia. He cites the fact that *bonzes* were referred to by a Siamese title (*chugu,* "sire"), proving that Cambodia had received this new form of Buddhism from the Thai. But in conjunction with the *bonzes,* the Chinese envoy mentions Brahmans he calls *banqi* (*paṇḍita*), and a group of Śivaites he names *basiwei* (*tapasvin,* "ascetics"?). The new religion soon found its way to the court. King Śrīndravarman (1296–1307) was converted to it and abdicated, very possibly because of a confrontation with the Hindu opposition. It is to him we owe the Pāli inscription dated 1309.[101]

The last Sanskrit inscription from Cambodia dates from the reign of Jayavarmaparameśvara (1327–?). "Imbued with Śivaite mysticism, the inscription proves that, in a country where Singhalese Buddhism had certainly made great strides, Hinduism had found a last refuge in the court of Jayavarman VII's successors."[102]

101. BHATTACHARYA 1961, 41.
102. CŒDÈS 1964, 412. See also CŒDÈS 1962, 183.

There, then, in broad strokes is a sketch of the religious history of ancient Cambodia, with a few remarks on the doctrines.

Two characteristic traits of these religions have long been singled out: the "personal cults" and the "tendency to syncretism."[103] Yet neither one nor the other properly represents the transformation that the Indian religions underwent in their passage to Cambodia.

The custom of giving divine images the name of the founder, or of his parents or spiritual masters, living or dead, by tacking on *-iśvara* or *-svāmin* according to whether the image was of Śiva or Viṣṇu, is one that is well-documented in India since at least the fourth century.[104] The founder thus acquired merits and glory, passing it on to others as well. Furthermore, the Indian concept identifies the worshiper with the Divinity, erasing all distinctions between adorer and adored. After death, the worshiper enters the realm of that Divinity, or assimilates with it or attains complete Deliverance—"from which there is no return." This explains the Cambodian custom of giving monarchs posthumous names such as *Viṣṇuloka* ("he who lives in the realm of Viṣṇu"), *Parameśvara* (Śiva), and *Kaivalyapada* or *Nirvāṇapada* (page 46) ("he who makes Deliverance his abode"), as well as the custom of erecting statues of people in the guise of this or that divinity.

The subject of "personal cults" has not yet been exhausted. There are many Indian documents that have not been considered, and Cambodian documents that have not been understood.[105]

The question of syncretism, on the other hand, is now clear.[106] Ancient India was not always free of religious conflicts, nor was Cambodia, as we noted earlier. But from very early on in India, a syncretic tendency arose that stood in opposition to sectarian tendencies. The tales of Hindu mythology place Śiva and Viṣṇu on the stage; they fight and are reconciled, declaring their fundamental identity. The theoretical underpinning of their identity was supplied by the concept of the trinity (page 37). Despite the sectarian elevation of one or another of these gods to the rank of Supreme God, they are theoretically identical since they are all emanations of the Absolute—"one form, three gods," say the Sanskrit poets of India.

The sectarian point of view, in this case Śivaite, is reflected in Cambodia as in India in the iconography of the *trimūrti* and the arrangement of the temples dedicated to the *trimūrti*—Śiva, sprung from the heart of the Supreme Śiva and representing him fully, is in the center, while Brahmā and Viṣṇu, who issued from his sides, are on the right and left, respectively. On the other hand, all distinctions seem to disappear from the texts either when a Śivaite foundation places itself under the protection of Viṣṇu, or conversely a Viṣṇuite foundation places itself under the protection of Śiva, or again when Śiva and Viṣṇu are both invoked as the Supreme Deity.

The enlargement of the Hindu trinity to include the Buddha does not seem to have any parallel instances in India, though it is attested to in Indonesia.[107] But Indian texts never tire of saying that the same Principle is worshiped by followers of the different religions, including Buddhism, under different names and forms.[108]

In the context of Śivaite and Buddhist monism (pages 44, 49), there was hardly any difference between the two religions at the highest metaphysical level. It is, therefore, perfectly comprehensible that in a Sanskrit inscription from Cambodia, dated 1041, Śiva is invoked on one face, the Buddha on the other, and in terms that bring them closer to each other. Śiva, the Absolute,

103. Cœdès, "Les Peuples," 1962, 209.
104. Bhandarkar 1931–1932, 1–9. See also Sircar 1942, I, 269–271.
105. See Finot, "Inscriptions," 1925, 351, CCVII.
106. Bhattacharya 1961, 151–159. See also Bhattacharya, "Notes," 1965.
107. Ensink 1978, 183.
108. Bhattacharya, "Religious Syncretism in Ancient Cambodia" (1997), to be published.

one in his essence, takes on multiple forms; but, though multiple, he is, in reality, "empty" of any empirical determination. The Buddha, though in himself beyond the distinctions inherent in our thinking, assumes four "bodies (page 409)."[109]

The inscriptions in Sanskrit and Khmer provide scattered information on Hindu and Buddhist rituals. These have never been studied. Yet one would doubtless achieve some interesting results by comparing them with the rituals described in Indian texts (many of them published in the last thirty-five years), and with the rituals still to be seen in India, Bali, and Nepal.

Temple administration, by contrast, is relatively well known, though the subject has not been studied in the last forty years. Forms of administration seem to have been inspired by models prevalent in South India, adapted to local socioeconomic conditions.[110]

Various aspects of religious life have already been examined. Another that deserves notice is the favor enjoyed by asceticism and yoga, particularly among Śivaites, Śiva being regarded as the first among ascetics. In epigraphy there is often mention of grottoes where asceticism was practiced. The temple of Vat Phu was also a special place for asceticism.[111] Speculations on the syllable *oṃ* occupy a large place in the Sanskrit inscriptions of Cambodia.[112]

Finally, a remarkable trait in the Hinduism of Cambodia is the faith that it proclaims toward the Veda, a faith that, though more or less theoretical in nature, is the criterion of orthodoxy in Hinduism.[113]

109. *IC* 7: 125–126.
110. BHATTACHARYA, "Some Aspects," 1955, 193–199.
111. BHATTACHARYA 1994, 228.
112. BHATTACHARYA 1961, 67–69, 74–76, 98.
113. BHATTACHARYA 1967, 199–222.

Khmer Epigraphy

Saveros Pou

These days the term "Cambodia's cultural heritage" immediately evokes an image of its ancient art—the glorious, universally admired monuments and the abundant and complex iconography. This image, a true one, applies both to visitors, who are proud to have access to another region of cultural wonders, and, of course, to Cambodians themselves. But the image is incomplete. An important part of that heritage, which escapes the attention of visitors and even most Cambodians, is the literary heritage. It comprises documents belonging to two groups, both very different in nature: texts carved in stone, or inscriptions (*silācārik, aksar thma*); and texts written by hand either on palm leaves bound together in bundles (*satrā*) or on strips of stiff paper pleated like an accordion (*krāṃṅ*) and other folios. This second group has barely been explored and therefore merits urgent attention. Nonetheless, this essay will focus on the first group, consisting of the lapidary inscriptions that collectively constitute the epigraphy of Cambodia.

As old as the country itself—about fourteen centuries—this epigraphy can be divided into two groups: those written in Sanskrit and those written in Khmer. The two languages are different in all respects, belonging to different language families (Indo-European and Mon-Khmer respectively), different language types, and different historical traditions. They coexisted until the thirteenth century, at which time Sanskrit was no longer used. It should be noted that a few epigraphic texts from the late periods were composed in Pāli, another Indo-European language, but they are so few in number that they have no weight in the mass of inscriptions known today. It can be said that virtually the entire epigraphic heritage consists of texts in Sanskrit and Khmer, which, after study, reflect two different forms of thought. As a vehicle for ideas, each language requires a specialized proficiency on the part of scholars, in both their education and their methods of research. For this reason, I will leave the Sanskrit inscriptions to Indianists and, as one who has made a particular study of Khmer, concentrate on the inscriptions in that language, though keeping in mind that Sanskrit and Khmer play complementary roles in epigraphic science. Before approaching Khmer texts, however, a few general comments are in order.

I. The Epigraphic Documents

The work of collecting stone inscriptions by means of rubbings started more than a hundred years ago. Most of the rubbings were brought to Paris, where they were gradually classified, catalogued, and studied. In spite of a century of sorting and classifying, it is impossible to tell exactly the number of inscriptions inventoried, let alone the total number of inscriptions extant. The texts, inscribed on monuments erected by the Khmer over the course of their long history, are today dispersed in several countries, namely Cambodia,

Thailand, Laos, and Vietnam. It is understandable that collecting proceeded without any active coordination between countries; even within a country, collecting was primarily due to chance or the simple curiosity of visitors. This is particularly true in Cambodia itself, where efforts have been scattered since the political reopening of the country. If a numerical estimate is requested despite this chaotic situation, a figure rounded up to fifteen hundred might be accurate.

With rare exceptions, Cambodian inscriptions are mystical, if not religious. Those who authored or commissioned them had no interest in history and made no effort to disguise the fact. Even in inscriptions rich in historical allusion, sometimes covering several centuries (genealogical records, for instance), the one thought unquestionably present was to "glorify" certain ideas, persons, or actions. Over the centuries, the Khmer continued to follow the same line of reasoning and behavior, engraving in stone—and so perpetuating—a record of their meritorious actions or their pious works (*puṇya* or *dharma*), that they might be respected by all forever, "so long as the sun and the moon shall last." The sacred nature of the sites on which the carvings were to be made can be deduced from this literary mystique. They include the base of statues, steles, various parts of temples (walls, doors, porticoes, windows, pillars) belonging to every religious movement (ancient Brahmanic temples, called *prāsād,* and post-Angkor Buddhist monasteries, called *vatt*).

Ancient Cambodian texts also refer to inscriptions on portable surfaces or "virgin leaves" (*rikta*), made either of a "folded" paper (*pnat*) or of gold or silver, and kept in treasure rooms called *kanloṅ*. This kind of inscription, being vulnerable on several counts, has survived neither the climate nor the destructive hand of man, unlike the lapidary inscriptions.

The sacred sites mentioned have always been worshiped by all, without regard to religion or sect, and some have become famous in epigraphy as sites of pilgrimage, in particular Vat Phu (Laos), Prasat Neak Buos, Phnom Sandak, Phnom Bakheng, Preah Vihear, and Angkor Vat. The inscriptions on these monuments date from up to several centuries after their construction, indicating their continued use by pilgrims (*saṃvaḥ vraḥ* and *saṃbaḥ braḥ* in Old and Middle Khmer respectively). Even after Theravāda Buddhism became definitely established in the fourteenth century, pilgrims continued to visit the ancient holy sites. Some pilgrims even had engravings made on these Brahmanic sites to record their passage, their devotion, the meritorious Buddhist acts they had accomplished there; all were expressions of their deep "faith" in the Buddha (*saddhā*). Two of the most famous examples are Phnom Bakheng (sixteenth-century texts) and Angkor Vat (sixteenth- to eighteenth-century texts).

The inscriptions vary greatly in length, from one or two words to hundreds of lines or even stanzas, as in the case of ancient Sanskrit poems. Some rubbings appear remarkably well preserved, while others have worn areas causing gaps in the texts.

From the beginning of its history, Cambodia has inherited from India religions as well as a rich mythology, various kinds of knowledge or arts, called *śāstra,* and the means to express these ideas graphically in the form of an alphabet and writings. The Indian alphabet, far from being a Cambodian prerogative, was implanted directly or indirectly in all the so-called Indianized countries of Southeast Asia. In Cambodia itself, the Sanskrit alphabet took root and has never gone out of use during the whole of Cambodian history; it has therefore been preserved *mutatis mutandis* up to the present day.

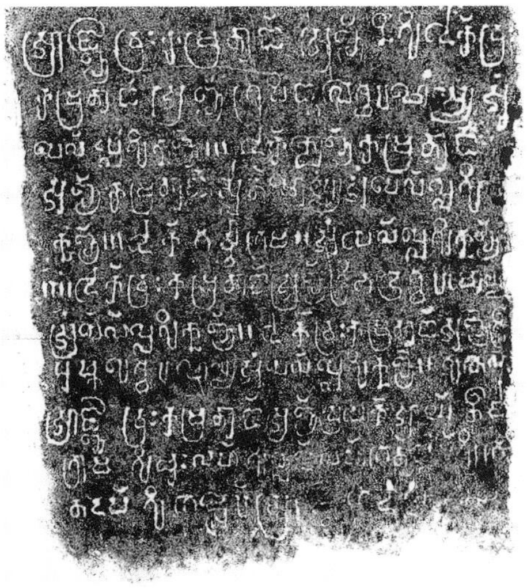

Fig. 1
Pre-Angkor stele from Tuol Neak Ta Bak Ka (Kandal), K. 940

Fig. 2
Lolei. Southwest tower, eastern entrance, north door pier (detail). Late ninth century

Two types of characters were introduced from India in the earliest historical times, namely the south Indian Cālukya-Pallava (fig. 1) and the north Indian Nāgarī writing. On the evidence of the inscriptions, the first was the more widely used from the early days until the middle of the ninth century. The second appears only in a few Sanskrit inscriptions; it had no real influence on the Cambodian calligraphic tradition. The south Indian type, which actually played a historical part, was known and used across all the former territory of the Khmer.

Toward the end of the ninth century there appeared another type of calligraphy at Roluos (the Preah Ko, Bakong, and Lolei monuments) east of Siem Reap. It is sometimes used jointly with the Nāgarī script and is called Kamvujākṣara (the writing of Kambuja or the Kambujans). Some of the inscriptions from that period even place heavy emphasis on this calligraphic creation (*nirmita*), which they ascribe to the Khmer king:

kamvujendreṇa nirmitam . . . kamvujākṣara

Some scholars have taken the term literally and refer to a "Cambodian writing" distinct from the "Indian" writing of earlier times. This view, which is neither structurally nor historically correct, requires some amendment. At first glance, it is true, Kamvujākṣara is a superb creation, characterized by a simpler form of letters with enhanced curves, a care for spacing and proportion, and a remarkable aesthetic effect (fig. 2). A writing such as this was bound to arouse feelings of creative pride in the king and his learned entourage, just as it arouses a sense of admiration in the modern viewer. But objectively speaking, Kamvujākṣara was not created out of whole cloth because it consists of modifications to the existing Cālukya-Pallava script. It therefore belongs within the orderly development of calligraphy in Cambodia,

Fig. 3
Inscription from Prasat Trau (Siem Reap), twelfth century, K. 249

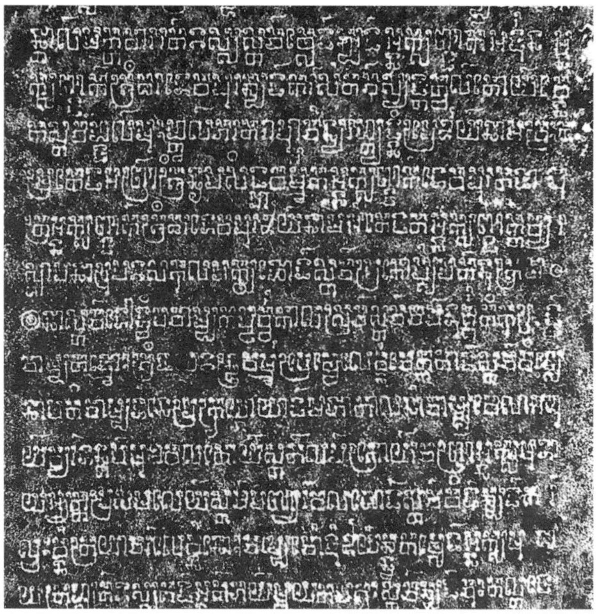

Fig. 4
Inscription from Banteay Chmar, twelfth century, detail (Battambang), K. 227

representing one of its phases. As such, it served as a very successful model for generations of later scribes (figs. 3 and 4) and is therefore an ancestor of the middle period scripts of the fifteenth to eighteenth centuries (fig. 5), from which the modern Aksar mūl writing is descended. As Cambodian paleography has not yet been examined as a whole, only a structural and evolutionary approach is likely to succeed.

The inscriptions also bear the indelible mark of another crucial element of civilization that originated in India, the notion of time and its reckoning. An Indian calendar was adopted and, like the alphabet, has remained in use to the present day. In other words, the majority of epigraphic texts have dates that, from the earliest times, correspond to the *śaka* era, which began in A.D. 78. How the dates are expressed varies according to the linguistic nature of the texts. In the case of Sanskrit texts composed of beautiful *kāvya* verses, dates are formally given by year alone, with the numbers indicated by symbols that are widely known in Indian culture. Zero is air, or ether; one is the moon; three is the Rāmas; seven the mountains; eight is the eight forms of Śiva, and so on. In Khmer texts, a more direct, pragmatic, and detailed expression of the date is made possible by the more flexible nature of the prose. First, the year of the *śaka* era is written out, using either numbers or letters, followed by the day (*vāra*), the month (*māsa*), the lunar phase (*parvan*), and the constellation (*nakṣatra*). These terms derive from the Sanskrit lexicon, except those for the lunar phases, which are Khmer, namely *knet* for the two weeks of lunar brightness and *rnoc* for the two weeks of lunar darkness.

In the tenth century, a new element in calendrical reckoning appeared: the names of animals of the twelve-year cycle well known throughout Asia (Rat, Ox, Tiger, among others) were expressed in highly archaic Khmer. This fashion gradually came into general use and eliminated the reference to the planetary constellations, as the word *nakṣatra* came to apply to all the animal names of the cycle.

In general, therefore, the dates of the texts are clearly specified, a fact whose importance for the study of history and philology cannot be overstated. It is true that certain texts are undated, either because of damage to the stone or for purely internal textual reasons. This does not constitute a major problem for scholars, however, as alternate methods of dating by comparing several texts exist. By bringing paleographic criteria to bear and juxtaposing diverse related events, undated texts can be placed fairly accurately in time.

Dating according to the *śaka* era continued until the eighteenth century, despite the arrival of Theravāda Buddhism in the fourteenth century. In actuality, it was used in conjunction with the newly adopted "Buddhist" era (*Buddhasakarāj*), which begins at the *parinibbān,* in 543 B.C. The system of dating therefore became more cumbersome than it had previously been, and was not really simplified by the phasing out of the *śaka* era. For one thing, a new era was introduced from the Theravāda Buddhist countries to the west called the "little era" (*cullasakarāj*), beginning in 638, and the animal cycle had by then become firmly established.

Aside from these extrinsic modern additions, the Cambodian calendar has remained Indian in principle as well as in application and vocabulary.

Stone inscriptions were almost invariably intended to glorify the *puṇya,* a term that refers both to "meritorious acts" and to the "merit" that results from such acts. This was true all through historical times, for though religions came and went, the mentality of the devotees remained the same. Only the content of ritual and the modes of expression changed in the transition from Brahmanism to Theravāda Buddhism.[1]

In ancient Cambodia, religious foundations were known by the Khmerized Sanskrit term *sthāpanā,* and each foundation had its own set of prescriptions and ritual, called *kalpanā.* The donor had the right to share (*oy, jvan*) his *puṇya* with whomever he chose. Empowered by his merits, he would accompany his account with a vow directed at future visitors, in the form of a blessing (*vara*) on the benevolent and a curse (*śāpa*) on all others.

1. The following text is a very simple extract from K. 341, one of the first pre-Angkor inscriptions at Prasat Neak Buos:

> 622 *śaka*: [Here is the] order of [the king] to offer lands to the lord Śrī Śivapāda. [Boundaries of these lands.] Those who worship the lord, beginning with the devout souls Poñ Myaṅ and Poñ Bhuvanāditya, those who have joined with them as [in the cult] of the lord Śrī Vijayeśvara, those who serve our lord Śrī Śivapāda: they will be rich in asceticism from this world to the next, they will be monks endowed with supernatural success, with power, with compassion, with renown, and will assure absence of fear to those who seek refuge with them. The set of offerings to Śrī Śivapāda begins with: servants, oxen, buffalo, carts, boats, plantations, plots of land, woods, rivers, channels [. . .], rice paddies, hillocks, pastures, ponds, and lakes. They will raise the deans of the monks charged with the cult of our lord. Those who take away [all this], who steal, who pillage, they will reside in hell for as long as the sun and moon shall last, they will fall into it and know great suffering there in the company of their compeers. May it be done! (Translation by George Cœdès, revised by Saveros Pou)

Fig. 5a
Inscription from Prasat Kambot (Kompong Thom), fourteenth century, K. 144

Fig. 5b
Inscription from Vat Romlok, sixteenth century, detail, K. 27

The composite term *varaśāpa* can, in Khmer, designate these antithetical aspects of a vow.[2]

The scenario remains virtually unchanged in post-Angkor Buddhist texts from Cambodia. The inscriptions, which by the sixteenth century were written almost exclusively in Middle Khmer, speak of *sāṅ* instead of *sthāpanā,* and of *rantāp* instead of *kalpanā.* Two additional notions seem to have been very important to the devout. The first, stressed with great fervor and conviction, is "true speech" (*satya/saccaṃ*). If a narrative should deviate from strict veracity it cannot operate on the mystical or moral plane—in a word, without truth there is no *puṇya.* The second consists of a kind of accounting of the different acts, good and bad, committed by an individual. Only a positive balance, called an advantage of merits (*ānisaṅs*), can guarantee that a vow will be carried out. A preliminary declaration is therefore necessary: a profession of one's pure faith (*saddhā*) in the teachings of the Buddha and the Triple Jewels; and a true speech or, in the terms of the inscriptions themselves, a "resolve of truth," *satya-adisthān* and, more frequently, *satyapraṇidhān,* thanks to whose "ardent power" (*tejaḥ*) alone the vows of the devout can be formulated and realized. This explains why I have adopted *satyapraṇidhān* as the generic name for all votive texts in Middle Khmer.[3]

As a corollary, the inscriptions give great importance to the "witnesses" to the meritorious work and the veracity of the account. They are called *sāksī* or *bejñān,* and are represented by human beings in the donor's entourage, sometimes in numerous assemblies, or by venerated invisible beings such as gods and *devatā,* with the Buddha himself at their head.

II. Epigraphic Scholarship

If the process of collecting inscriptions was at first guided by chance, it was also chance, rather than a program of planned research, that prompted the first study of the texts. A set of rubbings, among the first to have been collected, fell into the hands of an eminent Indologist from Leiden by the purest concatenation of circumstances. His name was Hendrik Kern, and it happened during the last quarter of the nineteenth century. Kern had no trouble at all deciphering the characters of the texts, which are related to those used in southern India, and recognizing the language as Sanskrit. His studies of the texts were published in The Netherlands in Dutch starting in 1879 and were translated into French in the *Annales d'Extrême-Orient.*

The Pioneer Era

Epigraphic studies were therefore instigated by a great Sanskritist and soon pursued by other no less eminent Sanskritists. Kern's writings had a tremendous impact in France. They awoke not only the curiosity of French Sanskrit scholars but also their sense of scientific duty and, in the case of Auguste Barth and Abel Bergaigne, a real determination to embark on a long-term work of great scope. Such a study required scholarship, the essential qualities of dedication and faith, and, on a practical level, teamwork. Once these conditions were met, nothing could stand in the way of the scholars confronting the enormous challenges of this enterprise.

2. A more grandiose *sthāpanā*, established by the royal entourage, is extracted here from the famous, eleventh-century inscription at Sdok Kak Thom, K. 235:

> His Majesty Paramaśivapada [Yaśovarma (sic) I], in founding the city of Śrī Yaśodharapura, brought the royal God from Hariharālaya for installation there. He then organized foundations [*sthāpanā*] at Vnaṃ Kantāl [Phnom Bakheng], [in the course of which] the Brahman Śivāśrama erected a *liṅgam* in the central part. Having participated in the royal foundations, he informed the king that he [personally] wished to accomplish the same. To this pious end, he solicited lands from the king. The Brahman Rudrālaya, his ancestor, came to discuss this subject with him and informed him that the land of the *varṇa* Vijaya. . ., which was ownerless, lay next to Bhadragiri, which belonged to him. The Brahman Śivāśrama then solicited this land from His Majesty Paramaśivaloka and on it founded the villages Bhadrapattana and Bhadravāsa. His Majesty Paramaśivaloka presented him with a *liṅgam* of two cubits, unused since the foundations of Vnaṃ Kantāl, so that he might install it at Bhadrapattana. A statue of Bhagavatī was then erected in the village of Bhadravāsa, which was part of the land of Bhadrapattana. As an honorarium [*daksina*], the king made him a gift of a quantity of goods, beginning with *vat khlās*, cult accessories, and other numerous goods, two hundred servants, rice fields [. . . .] (Translation George Cœdès and Pierre Dupont, revised by Saveros Pou)

3. The following extract from an inscription at Angkor Vat, IMA 34, was written at the end of the seventeenth century:

> This is the profession of the generosity and veracity of a great dignitary and his wife. [. . . .] Both, having meditated on impermanence, prostrated themselves to take leave of His Majesty our master, from whom they had received the order to come and build [at Angkor] a *triśūr* with three arrows as an offering to the august Triple Jewel. [. . . .] At the time the *triśūr* was installed, in Phalgun of 1618 *śaka*, year of the Rat, a recitation of the sacred verses of the *Dharmacakra* was solemnly performed, lasting three days. On Thursday, the ninth day of the waxing moon, the *triśūr* was erected, and on Friday, the tenth day of the waxing moon, its installation was completed. [. . . .] "The power deriving from our merits" [they then said] "is directed toward our benefactors. We ask to be reborn at the same time as the lord [Bodhisattva] [Śrī] Śrīāryametrī, to enter the holy order and take refuge in the teachings of the Lord, and to see our wishes come true as have those professed by the Buddhas of the past. When we have quit this existence and are reborn, we ask to have magical arts as effective as those of Braḥ Īśūr. In this life, we have lost our younger siblings and two children. May we never be separated from each other in the future! May our families be forever established in the teaching of the Lord!" If this text contains faults, may the Venerable ones [monks] help us to rectify them. This inscription was completed in Bhadrapad, on Thursday, the ninth day of the waning moon.
> (Translation by Saveros Pou)

Barth and Bergaigne had all the qualities expected of Indianists in their day, with respect to both language and culture. They were equipped with a solid competence in paleography, which allowed them to make a relatively fast and successful start in the study of the Sanskrit inscriptions. To help them with the Khmer portion of the epigraphy, they obtained the collaboration of Étienne Aymonier, who in some sense represented a link between France and Cambodia. Originally a colonial administrator, Aymonier differed from the India scholars in that he had no scientific training. He was an autodidact who had zealously converted to scholarly research and must be ranked among the finest of the type. A tireless worker and a careful explorer, he acquired the Khmer language while in Cambodia with a thoroughness that was quite extraordinary for his time. He also strictly adhered to the scientific rules imparted to him and always retained a great respect for science and the Indologists working in Paris.

The lesson for this and future generations is the admirable collaboration that persisted between the Paris Sanskritists and Aymonier, which is clearly manifested in their writings, and which was based on shared convictions, on mutual respect and confidence, and on constant cooperative relations.

Barth and Bergaigne published dozens of Sanskrit inscriptions and in so doing produced a rough outline of Cambodia's history, concentrating above all on the genealogy of the rulers, which they were able to ascertain through the texts. Concurrently, Aymonier performed a colossal quantity of work, reading numerous rubbings of inscriptions written in Old Khmer (sixth to fourteenth centuries) and in what is now called Middle Khmer (sixteenth to eighteenth centuries). He then attempted to synthesize his findings in two important works. The first is a pioneering description of Old Khmer (1883) that, though now outdated, marks an epoch. The second is a description of Cambodia in light of the inscriptions he had gathered and studied. A voluminous work, written with minute care, it was published as *Le Cambodge* (1900–1904), and became one of the basic reference works in Khmerology.

The Golden Age of Epigraphic Studies

Can it be chance again that caused scholars to follow at a steady pace one after another in this field of research? The answer may be best left to the individual to decide. What is important to stress is that two great scholars emerged; they were experts on the epigraphy of the Indochinese peninsula who were equipped with solid academic educations and an unusually high level of knowledge on a broad range of cultural subjects.

The first, Louis Finot, a renowned Sanskrit philologist, did not restrict himself to the Sanskrit of Cambodia—or of Champa—but ventured into the study of Old Khmer texts, with the aim of making the history and spirituality of these countries better understood through examinations of their writings and works of art. Finot's work on Old Khmer is certainly, by today's standards, inadequate and riddled with flaws, but these are qualities inherent in any pioneering work. And Finot, though active before the great flowering of Southeast Asian linguistics, advanced Khmer epigraphy a step beyond the work of Aymonier.

The second scholar, George Cœdès, proved very different. His education was Indo-European, and he had no trouble in learning the languages of Southeast Asia, in particular Khmer and Thai, to virtual perfection. In addition to his linguistic competence, he was a person of extraordinary qualities—

tremendous conviction and dynamism in his work, exceptional flair, and a remarkable respect for people and things. He studied both Sanskrit and Khmer texts, and published them in a practically steady stream starting in 1904, providing articles for journals as well as books, including his eight-volume *Inscriptions du Cambodge* (1937–1966), which is known throughout the world. As to the field of Old Khmer, Cœdès helped epigraphy make giant strides thanks to the great number of inscriptions he made publicly available, pointing out at every step the essential information they contained and feeding these in turn into the domain of his research, which included virtually all the archaeology and history of Southeast Asia.

Starting in the 1960s, an enormous field of well-worked research, made eminently fertile, appeared more open and promising than ever before. Cœdès, a philologist and historian, was the dominant figure in his sphere during that period. Although he had never taught at a university, he provided a beacon for young scholars eager to explore new areas using epigraphy. The most successful work in this vein was Kamaleswar Bhattacharya's study of religious materials, *Les Religions brahmaniques de l'ancien Cambodge d'après l'épigraphie et l'iconographie* (1961).

The Khmer Linguistic Approach

The historical-philological approach, however, was interrupted even before the death of George Cœdès in 1969 and was never resumed in the same form nor with the same energy. This may seem paradoxical, as the science was advancing rapidly and in a positive or "democratic" direction. It was beginning, particularly in linguistics and in other areas of the humanities, to offer new and promising ideas, and techniques better than those used in the past.

Under the circumstances, however, it was not surprising to see epigraphy take a new turn. Recent trends in research cropped up in another form: namely, re-examining the object of study and the processes it created in a new light. In the eyes of the modern linguist, epigraphic texts are as much about the speech, fraught with messages, of men of the past. Their content is thus language, in this case Khmer, belonging to a human community now more than fourteen hundred years old. The linguist wants first to describe the language according to the rules, then to study its evolution during this great span of time.

For all these reasons I was drawn, as a linguist already versed in Modern Khmer, to examine and then to study in depth the Khmer of post-Angkor texts, the previously mentioned *satyapraṇidhān*. This form of Khmer turns out to be remarkably valuable in that it represents a true bridge between Modern Khmer and the Old Khmer known through the work of philologists; hence, it has been named Middle Khmer.

The description of epigraphic Middle Khmer obviously required using related documents, which include other kinds of contemporaneous Khmer texts, and the basic lexicon of the other languages in the Mon-Khmer family. These various tools contributed enormously to deciphering Middle Khmer during the 1970s, and the good effect this had on the entire study of epigraphy later proved incalculable. It has been possible to re-examine and re-evaluate all the work done on Old Khmer. Most of the gaps in the texts were filled in, and the errors in transcription and interpretation corrected; this has resulted in a very clear improvement in the landscape of Khmer epigraphy.

The approach, in short, allows a more active resumption of the task of deciphering the texts and a deeper study of numerous new inscriptions.

The upshot of this enterprise was the revelation of a great number of historical facts that had either been misunderstood or totally unsuspected. On the methodological level, topics of study leapt to scholars' eyes along with the knowledge that their course could be followed through the centuries to the modern era. The concrete form this took was the exploration of the semantics and grammar of Old and Middle Khmer, which allowed for the decoding of many new messages in the inscriptions and, in particular, for the retracing, from actual documents, of spiritual and social aspects of the ancient Khmer community.

Another factor that surfaced concurrently provided a new and crucial phase in Khmerology; it was also the result of fortuitous circumstances. Young scholars appeared on the scene, eager to learn for themselves about ancient Khmer culture from an analysis of the texts. And, a course of epigraphic study was instituted under my direction at the university level, in this case at Paris III, as a response to the aspirations of these young researchers and as a means of education. In short, a systematic course of teaching and an expansion in research involving both the teacher and the taught came to fruition with the production of the *Old Khmer-French-English Dictionary* (Pou, 1992).

III. Outlook for the Future

A great distance separates the historical-philological and the modern linguistic approaches to epigraphy, both in time and in technique, even though there has been no break in the study of inscriptions and their use.

Thanks to the first, the historical framework of Cambodia was established, and fields for research into an ancient community were revealed. The second, taking advantage of this framework and an unusually favorable conjunction of scientific developments, has made an even larger contribution. The linguistic approach has made it possible to penetrate the texts more deeply and to understand their message far better than was possible in the past. At the same time, epigraphy has been opened to young scholars, who since the 1980s have had a means of obtaining a crucial basic education in the discipline. The result has been that well-defined topics of study have been proposed, whose questions can now be addressed with firsthand documents. These combined efforts have been vindicated by the publication of papers on a number of specific subjects, including kingship and its related institutions; the spiritual eclecticism historically manifest in Khmer culture and, as a corollary, the concept of the sacred; the role of the earth, both as an economic resource and as a mystical entity; and the early character of Khmer music and dance.

With this knowledge in hand, it is possible—even recommended—to go back and study the general questions of history; two crucial areas not yet fully understood are the nature of Cambodian society and its economy in ancient and medieval times. And epigraphy has proved indispensable to any historical research on Cambodia. It is gratifying today to see that neither the manpower nor the technical means are lacking for Khmer epigraphy to continue and develop, as long as it is supported by instances of superior research. History and linguistics combined will make it possible to resume under more favorable conditions the work left by Cœdès, and to see the connection between ancient Cambodia and modern Cambodia in a better light.

Nandin and His Avatars

Ang Chouléan

Fig. 1
Śivapada. Theat Ba Chong (Stung Treng). Sandstone. Height 32 cm. National Museum of Cambodia, Phnom Penh

Nandin, Vehicle and God

The gods of India, and therefore of ancient Cambodia, have specific vehicles. Some of these vehicles seem to have acquired their own prestige very early on, even to the point of figuring in sculpture independently. Garuḍa is usually seen carrying his master Viṣṇu, but he may also appear as the central or sole figure in a decorative lintel, or on the corner of a supporting wall. He is also seen in three-dimensional sculpture of a sometimes rather imposing size. In more recent centuries, Garuḍa has been among the protagonists of much dramatic literature (fig. 4, page 16).

Śiva's mount, Nandin, demands special attention. Since ancient times in Cambodia, the power of association has been such that the bull could be considered to command as much magic as the supreme god who rode him.[1] Just as the footprints of Śiva (*Śivapada*)[2] were sculpted (fig. 1), so were the footprints of Nandin, at least according to epigraphy.[3] In any case the association is so close that Śiva is sometimes called Vṛṣadhvaja or Vṛṣadhvajeśvara (the god who has a bull as his attribute).[4]

In his rich plastic representations,[5] Nandin is sometimes seen carrying Śiva and the couple of Śiva and Umā. But he is also represented as a god in his own right. In the principal temples of the Roluos group, he is portrayed so frequently and with such prominence that one of the temples is named Preah Ko (divine bull). The same name is given to other monuments in other parts of Cambodia.

The cult of Nandin seems to have changed from the Middle Period in Khmer history, not in a Śivaite context, but in a Theravāda Buddhist one. For the purposes of this essay, the important point about the Nandin of ancient Cambodia is that he has magical knowledge and powers. This characteristic or quality surfaces regularly throughout Khmer religious history. What will be shown here is that political history as well as religious history has been punctuated by Nandin's emergence and exaltation.

The Myth of the Emerald Buddha in Indochina

The cult of the "Emerald Buddha" holds an important place in Buddhist Indochina. He is venerated less as the universal Buddha, the Supreme Master (*paramaguru*) in total Extinction (nirvana) who bequeathed to us only his Teachings (*sāsanā*), than as a specific idol endowed with extraordinary powers of beneficence and magic, ready to grant even the most difficult wishes. He is also the guardian spirit or palladium of the kingdom possessing him. Therefore, he is situated between the universal Buddha and the multitude of

1. Bhattacharya 1961, 82; see also Pou 1993, 157.
2. An example is the piece shown at the National Museum in Phnom Penh (inventory: Ka.1756/C.11.1/D.27).
3. Bhattacharya 1961, 82.
4. Pou 1993, 143–177.
5. Boisselier 1966, *Manuel*, 306–307.

local Buddhas, each with its own personality, of the kind found in a great number of Buddhist monasteries.[6]

Of all known texts that deal with this subject, the *Chieng Mai Chronicle* has garnered the most attention.[7] It dates the discovery of the famous statue hidden in stucco at Chieng Rai to the first half of the fifteenth century. From a historical point of view, however, not a lot of credit can be given to this text, which, among other things, sets the time of the statue's installation as far back as the Milinda and Nāgasena period! The idol followed an extraordinary route through different kingdoms of Asia, particularly in Indochina. Finding the origin of the Emerald Buddha and the beginning of his travels is an impossible enterprise[8] if sources like the *Chieng Mai Chronicle* are not blindly believed. What is most interesting is the existence of such texts, which, supporting and at the same time born of oral traditions, extend below cultural beliefs.

The dark green jasper statue, now housed at Vat Phra Keo in Bangkok, is the object of great veneration, both by the people and the royal court. A replica with the same name is displayed just as piously in the Silver Pagoda of the Royal Palace in Phnom Penh. It must be said, though, that until recent years the site was visited less for worshiping the statue than for admiring the complex itself. That situation recently changed when another important statue was installed: a superb pre-Angkor Nandin. Why its presence has added so much to the royal pagoda's prestige will be seen later. In any case the situation differs from Bangkok, where it is really the jasper statue that excites the fervor of Buddhists, and the admiration of foreign and domestic tourists.

At Vat Ho Phra Keo in Vientiane, there remains only the bitter memory that the building, a former *vihāra,* once housed the famous idol.

Cambodia and the Myth of the Emerald Buddha

The *Chieng Mai Chronicle* is not the only chronicle known, but it seems to be the only one that focuses exclusively on the Emerald Buddha. Similar versions of the story are known in Cambodia,[9] where the idol-palladium is described as following the same route through India, Sri Lanka, Angkor, Laos, and Ayuthayā. The main purpose of these chronicles is to relate "history," or more precisely, the succession of reigns and events, where much is made of legends and the supernatural. The episodes concerning the Emerald Buddha arise in this context.Whatever the version of the story, Thai or Cambodian, the Emerald Buddha is associated with the *Tripiṭaka,* the sacred Buddhist texts. This is an important point, as will be seen later.Yet in Cambodia, a popular fable, more or less concerning the Emerald Buddha, is much better known than the chronicles. Its motive is not "historical," and this is why it is so interesting—it is innocent of the constraints of official style. On the contrary, it is full of the emotional fervor of a people, the Khmer, free to produce a myth that is partially historic, mostly legend, but above all totally coherent. The Emerald Buddha is just a secondary figure here. He is present only to create a connection between the Khmer tradition and that of neighboring countries. The Khmer myth, both written and oral, is called *Preah Ko and Preah Keo* (the Divine Bull and the August Crystal).

6. For Buddhas and other Indian gods with local flavor, see ANG 1995, 217.
7. NOTTON 1932, and SCHUR NARULA 1994.
8. It is fairly certain that the Thais took it from the Laotians. According to the *Chieng Mai Chronicle*, it happened in the last quarter of the eighteenth century; Laotian sources, however, place its removal to the aftermath of the sack of Vientiane in 1827. See also DEYDIER 1952, 94.
9. See MAK PHOEUN 1984.

Here is the abridged story:

A peasant couple lived in abject poverty in the Lovek region. The pregnant wife had to resist her food cravings, particularly for acidic fruits, which, according to an astrologer that the couple had consulted, could kill her if she ate them.[10] During her last month of pregnancy she had an irresistible urge to eat some of the green mangoes that were growing on a tree right next to their house. She insisted that her husband pick one for her. He tried to distract her from the subject by a variety of means, finally claiming that some urgent errand required him to go to another village. The woman, who couldn't wait any longer, decided to climb the tree herself to get a piece of fruit. She fell and died on the spot. Her stomach exploded and a calf came out. The calf went to find his father, who returned home immediately. On returning, they realized that a second child, a human boy, was in the womb.

The villagers saw this event as a bad sign, and chased away the father and his two children, who went to live on the edge of the forest. A few years later the father died, leaving his children Preah Ko (divine bull) and Preah Keo (august crystal)[11] orphaned. But Preah Ko was a supernatural being endowed with extraordinary powers. Each time his little brother was hungry this thoughtful animal, a ruminant, would regurgitate his own food for him. The village children spied on them every day and soon realized the extent of Preah Ko's powers. They told their parents, who came, encircled the two brothers, and then tied the bull to a tree. When they tried to disembowel him, thinking the source of his magical powers was in his stomach, Preah Ko easily escaped them by flying away, taking with him Preah Keo, who held tightly onto his tail.

At that time Ream Cheung Prei, the king of Cambodia, had seven daughters whom he wanted to marry off. He allowed them to choose their own husbands[12] from among the sons of the mandarins whom he presented to them. Only the youngest, Neang Peou, refused to make a choice. One day, while bathing in a pond, she saw Preah Keo, who was dressed in leaves, and instantly took to him. She gave him a scarf to cover his body. Her father chased her out of the palace at the insistence of her six older sisters, who were ashamed of her behavior. So she went to live with Preah Keo, whom she married, and Preah Ko.

Hearing of the existence of this bull with great powers, the king of Siam decided to capture him. In fact, it was the palace astrologer who suggested he be captured and taken to Ayuthayā. The capital, and all of Siam, would become prosperous simply through the bull's presence. So the king of Siam challenged the king of Cambodia to three fights with different animals, with their countries as the stakes. The first combat was a cockfight. The Khmer king's astrologer predicted that Siam would win unless Preah Ko intervened. The king had this news delivered to Neang Peou, who begged her husband Preah Keo to convince Preah Ko to participate in the fights, which he did. He changed himself into a cock and won the fight for Cambodia. The second fight was between elephants. Again Preah Ko intervened, and again Cambodia won. The third and last fight was a fight between bulls.[13]

Preah Ko realized that this time his foe would be a mechanical bull[14] disguised as an ordinary bull, and that destiny had chosen Cambodia to lose. He secretly advised Preah Keo and Neang Peou to grab his tail

10. The cravings of pregnant women are known to be very "cultural." In many Southeast Asian cultures, a craving for acidic foods is common among pregnant women.
11. The official but seldom used complete name is Preah Keo Morokot (divine emerald).
12. Indian practice known as *svayaṃvara*.
13. The logic of this three-part bet is hard to understand. But it does not make a difference as far as the myth is concerned.
14. Ko Yon (*go yantra*).

tightly if he lowed three times during the fight. And indeed, the mechanical bull was immune to the blows that Preah Ko dealt it, so he lowed three times and then flew away with the young couple. The Siamese had foreseen that he might flee and quickly deployed a troop to follow him in flight. Neang Peou was exhausted and fell, dying at once, in the region of Battambang. Her body petrified immediately. Seeing his wife fall, Preah Keo also let go. To prevent his brother's death, Preah Ko then let himself go into a free fall to support Preah Keo's body. Once on the ground the brothers had many adventures but were unable to escape the area surrounded by the Siamese. For their part, the latter themselves used magic and inexorably drew the encirclement tighter. Finally the Siamese caught the brothers[15] and took them to their country.

There is no need to decode the myth; the political subtext is self-evident: Cambodia's ruin is explained by another country's capture of their palladium. This seized statue is not of a Buddha or a Buddhistic character, but of a bull, the Holy Bull of the old Khmer Brahmanistic tradition. It is there, in fact, as a message. The impoverishment of Cambodia—dare I say, its decadence—would be the direct consequence of the abandonment of Brahmanism. However, that is not the point. What is most important to point out is the Brahmanic nature of the palladium, because the evidence shows that the bull is directly associated with Nandin. Preah Keo, who is neither emerald nor divine in the story, cuts a pale figure and could be removed without making a difference.

The fall of Lovek, a historical fact, took place at the end of the sixteenth century. The three earthen levees forming successive protective walls that are still visible today and the thick bamboo forest described in the chronicles were not enough to stop the Siamese. The fall of Lovek had a political and, above all, a psychological effect that was disastrous; Cambodians still talk passionately about it. This is not my subject either, however, but is simply pointed out to show the living nature of the myth and the variety of representations that have come out of it.

Fig. 2
Traleng Keng monastery, "Temple of the Sacred Bull." Offering of fresh grass for Preah Ko

Representations

The myth is so popular that, in addition to texts recorded on palm leaves, it has been represented in plastic form practically everywhere.

In Lovek, of course, the representation of the myth is at its most spectacular. The Traleng Keng monastery, which probably dates back as far as the reign of Ang Chan, toward the middle of the sixteenth century, has not one temple (*vihāra*) but two. Besides the famous cruciform temple that gives its name to the monastery, Traleng Keng[16] has a second temple in its northeast quadrant, the Temple of the Divine Bull. Its altar occupies a wide space. It contains statues of the Buddha as well as sculptures of the characters from the myth: Preah Ko, of course, with Preah Keo, Neang Peou, and the brothers' parents. Directly behind the temple is the pond where Neang Peou liked to bathe. Many other objects and vestiges remain as testaments to the myth, such as the Kandaol tree, a scion of the generation to which Preah Ko was once attached.[17] On holy days,[18] one of the masters of ceremony of the temple goes out to pick fresh grass from the neighborhood to offer the Divine Bull (fig. 2).

15. Certain versions tell only of Preah Ko's capture.
16. Traleng Keng means "cross, crossing." In the middle of the temple is a large bronze crowned Buddha, upright and looking in the four cardinal directions. Or, in a more accurate description, there are four Buddhas with their backs to each other, suggesting the omnipresence of the Master. European scholars noticed its power immediately; Adolph Bastian was undoubtedly the first to write about it (1865).
17. This detail is not mentioned in the story recounted here.
18. Each month has four: every eighth and the last days of the two fifteen-day periods of the lunar months of the traditional calendar.

More images and practices relating to the myth could be described, but the ones already mentioned are sufficient to demonstrate the living nature of the cult. Traleng Keng is the most spectacular example, but the myth is represented more or less throughout Cambodia. The following examples are some of the other sites found around Phnom Penh.

Oudong Hill is the site of a number of different foundations; among them are two chapels on the peak, one sheltering Preah Ko and the other Preah Keo. After an obscure period of about a decade, Oudong took Lovek's place as the capital, the latter having been leveled by the Siamese. It is thus logical that the two chapels were placed on the hill, which had long been the site of religious foundations.

Thon Mon Hill[19] is about twelve miles (20 km) south of Phnom Penh. The modern-day temple situated on the summit of the hill has two parts. Immediately to the south of the principal *vihāra* and built on the same foundation is a small sanctuary called, as at Traleng Keng, the Temple of the Divine Bull. In the middle of the building the tile work gives way to an elongated rock that rises about twelve inches (30 cm) above the ground. Three grooves are visible on the top of the rock, which were supposedly left by Preah Ko himself as a signal for his brother Preah Keo, who was hunting for him after they were separated during their attempted escape from the Siamese. In the 1960s and 1970s, the rock itself sufficed as a symbol of the myth of Preah Ko and Preah Keo. About ten years ago a cement statue of the Divine Bull was installed. It portrays him with his legs apart and his head tilted to one side, as if ready to make the grooves with his horn. Behind him there is also a statue of Preah Keo, and against a wall of the temple is a bed with two pillows, one for each brother.

Sa-ang Hill, located not far from the preceding hill, is also the site of a monastery. The principal *vihāra* and the other usual buildings are at the base of the hill; a small chapel on the hilltop is dedicated to the Divine Bull. Inside are cement images of Preah Ko and Preah Keo.

Kien Svay Krau is about nine miles (15 km) south of Phnom Penh. Among the numerous buildings and installations in this monastery is a chapel, also called the Divine Bull. Several episodes from the myth previously cited are painted on the wall, and in the middle of this small structure are cement representations of Preah Ko and Preah Keo. An interesting event took place in this monastery: It was occupied by a garrison of Vietnamese soldiers shortly after their invasion of Cambodia in 1979. One night a Vietnamese soldier thought he saw a luminous sphere descending onto the spot where the present chapel would later be built. At the moment when it touched the ground the light seemed to take on the form of a bull. The next day, the soldier reported what he had seen to the local people. No more was needed to give birth to their conviction that Preah Ko had come to reside there. The news spread quickly and, despite the lack of religious freedom at the time, they began to construct the chapel and the necessary idols. As would be normal everywhere henceforth when a statue of Preah Ko was made, holy texts and other religious and magical objects were carefully enclosed in the stomach of the animal. For several years a medium has come to the chapel on special occasions for séances of possession by Preah Ko. While in a trance, he gets down on all fours and lows like a bull. People come all day long, every day, to consult the auguries through a form of bibliomancy called *cāk' kaṃbī*. A direct rapport exists between the magical powers of the bull, manifest in the

19. For more on this location, see ANG 1993, 195–196.

different objects—including the texts—enclosed in his stomach, and the belief in the magical efficacy of the manuscript *(kaṃbī)* available to the client.

Finally, there is Svay Chrum on the east bank of the Mekong, just upstream from Phnom Penh. The *vihāra* belonging to the monastery of this name has twenty-one mural panels inside. They represent different episodes in the story of Preah Ko and Preah Keo, though nothing here shows any particular veneration of Preah Ko. This is worth underscoring in light of the myth's political message: the murals were painted only about six years ago, at the beginning of a period when it was good form to adopt Thai fashions and manners.

More examples of chapels devoted to Preah Ko, still in the Phnom Penh area, can be cited. Phnom Ta Mau is about twenty-two miles (35 km) to the southwest, and the monastery of Sre Ampil is about fifteen miles (25 km) to the southeast. Two very important points must be mentioned: First, Preah Ko is always the central personage and the idol to be venerated; Preah Keo is no more than hinted at. The memory of the Emerald Buddha is now so far dulled that Preah Keo is not even painted green! Second, Preah Ko is always associated with magic, and, more specifically, with sacred or mystical texts. All practices surrounding him, especially divination (as will be shown), prove this association.

I should also like to note in passing that the third eye found on ancient Nandin is seen on modern versions of Preah Ko in the form of a lozenge, which is interpreted as a star.

Preah Ko, Reminder of Suffering

The historico-political nature of the myth of Preah Ko and Preah Keo has recently resurfaced in contemporary history. In the early 1960s the Thai army defied international law and took possession of the famous Preah Vihear temple. The royal Khmer government took all possible diplomatic and legal steps to reappropriate the precious temple and the occupied portion of their territory. They succeeded. At the same time, it undertook a campaign to raise national consciousness. Among the various methods can be evinced a long presentation of the myth of Preah Ko and Preah Keo by the famous National Theater troupe, which performed the story in several episodes for entire evenings on the radio. Needless to say, the episode relating the flight and subsequent capture of Preah Ko by the Siamese left many audience members with tears in their eyes.

Preah Ko, Eternal Idol

In 1983, a superb seventh-century statue[20] of Nandin (fig. 3) made from a silver-rich alloy was found by accident at the Tuol Kuhea archaeological site in the Koh Thom District near the Vietnamese border.[21] Rumors, some completely preposterous, immediately began to circulate about the supernatural nature of Preah Ko, who had at last reappeared though he had suffered damage in places.[22] The celebrity of the statue, which was completely justified from an archaeological, historical, and artistic point of view, was such that it was immediately transported to Phnom Penh to be housed beneath the

20. A seventh-century inscription tells of the erection of a silver Nandin at Sambor Prei Kuk (BHATTACHARYA 1961, 88). It is probable that similar statues were constructed elsewhere.
21. See LAN SUNNARY 1991, 77–121.
22. His tail and right ear were broken, and the tip of his left ear was folded forward.

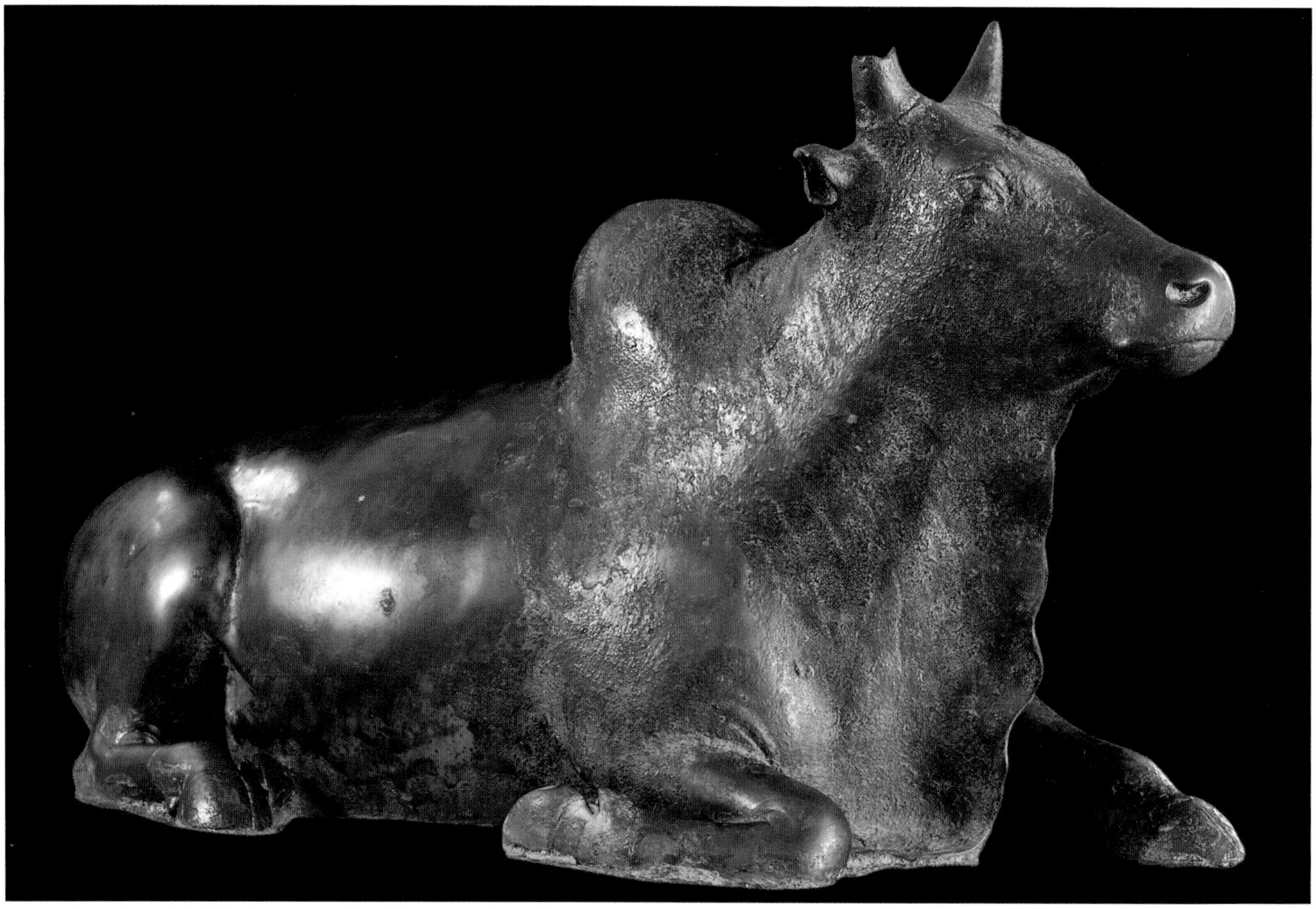

Fig. 3
Nandin/Preah Ko from Tuol Kuhea. Bronze-silver. Height 80 cm, width 130 cm. Silver Pagoda, Phnom Penh

Throne Room of the Royal Palace, which was then a museum. The devout came from all over to view the statue. Chance willed that not long after, a white marble Buddha seated in meditation, sculpted in the Burmese style, was found in a pond near the edge of the capital.[23] It was natural to install the statue a few meters behind Nandin. The Buddha added nothing to the power of the seventh-century Nandin, except that one now had the duo of Preah Ko and Preah Keo once again reunited as in the myth. Apparently the anachronistic differences in style, provenance, and materials—the basic incoherence—were unimportant. The fact that the two rediscovered characters were there created coherence in itself.

Once the museum again became the Royal Palace, the idol had to be moved so that the public could worship it. The word idol is singular because only Nandin was removed from the room, demonstrating yet again the dominance of Preah Ko and the accessory, even derisory, position of Preah Keo. Nandin's new home is without doubt the most appropriate: the holy statue is installed in the heart of the Silver Pagoda compound, in a small building called Ho Preah Trai (Chapel of the Divine *Tripiṭaka*), where the *Tripiṭaka* collection on palm leaves is kept. Given his association with sacred texts and thus with supernatural power, Nandin resumes here the vocation he has always had.[24] Considering that the official chronicles, those of Chieng Mai and others, link the Emerald Buddha with the *Tripiṭaka,* one can affirm that the Khmer tradition has replaced this Buddha with Nandin the Bull. The bull, an important figure in Brahmanism, appears as a sort of guardian of Buddhism in the Middle Period and today.[25]

Earlier it was stated that the Emerald Buddha replica in the Silver Pagoda sanctuary does not receive the kind of veneration given the one in Bangkok, and that most of the visitors come to admire the pagoda itself. Now the situation has changed. People come to admire the guardian of the sacred Buddhist texts as well. Bovine in form and divine in nature, this guardian statue was made in the seventh century by and for Śivaites. What a splendid witness is this Nandin who spans thirteen centuries of political and religious history.

23. Its owner, now dead, had left the country. The Khmer Rouge had tossed the statue into the pond next to the owner's house in 1975.
24. Remember that manuscripts are enclosed in the stomach of cement sculpture depicting Preah Ko.
25. For a period of time, a ridiculously small statue of Buddha was placed next to Nandin (fig.4) simply to suggest his connection with the Emerald Buddha. This Buddha, which is certainly not green, is no longer in the chapel.

Preah Ko: The Passion

All the organizers of the present exhibition had hoped to include the Nandin of Tuol Kuhea for many reasons: its age and therefore its historical and religious resonance, its unequaled beauty, and the chance to restore some of the damages that time has dealt it. We had hoped to present it as a living idol, one symbolizing the link between ancient and modern Cambodia.

Without doubt we failed to fully estimate the psychological impact of removing the statue, even temporarily, from Cambodia. The request was met with a perfectly legitimate refusal, which underlines yet again the living nature of Nandin / Preah Ko today. Everything considered, it is no surprise that the request aroused so much passion.

Glory to the memory of its creators, the Khmer of the seventh century. In the image of the Nandin of Tuol Kuhea, may all other Preah Ko reaffirm to future generations their deep roots in the Khmer soul.

Fig. 4
Silver Pagoda, "Chapel of the Tripiṭaka." Preah Ko and Preah Keo. Note the ridiculous nature of Preah Keo compared with the majestic Preah Ko

The Figure of Hevajra and Tantric Buddhism

Wibke Lobo

Within Mahāyāna Buddhism, the Tantric path to enlightenment, to which the cult of Hevajra (fig. 1) belongs, sets very particular intellectual and spiritual demands. It flourished in Cambodia between the tenth and thirteenth centuries, only to disappear with the collapse of the Angkor empire, but in Tibet it still remains a living tradition. The surviving sacred texts recommend that only those who have previously studied the other teachings of Theravāda and Mahāyāna should apply themselves to Tantra. The unusual feature of this path lies in the speed with which enlightenment and hence the Buddhahood may be reached. An initiate who practices the Tantric method with serious application can even manage to achieve this goal while a mortal.

This is only possible, however, under the guidance of a religious teacher. More than is the case with all other branches of Buddhism, sympathetic, sensitive instruction by a competent teacher is regarded as an essential requirement for success. He alone is entitled to lead the initiate step by step along the path to knowledge of the highest truth. He must be in a position to make a correct estimate of his pupil's current physical and psychic condition and to determine subsequent practical exercises on that basis.

Principal among these is meditation. It is the most important aid toward the gaining of knowledge. But in the course of meditation, powers that slumber deep in the human psyche may also be aroused, and, if falsely directed, may exert a destructive rather than beneficial effect. The teacher will only then transmit profound truths to his pupil when he is sure the latter is capable of appreciating them. This is one reason why Tantra is considered an esoteric doctrine. It cannot be permitted to exist in the public realm because misuse by the uninitiated could have fatal consequences. Yet it is not so much a secret discipline as a highly elitist, religious one. The pupil must show himself to be both worthy and capable and also prepared to subject his vocation to the test over and over again, before induction into the next higher stage. He is required to demonstrate a steadfast tenacity in pursuit of his goal. The height to which he can advance depends upon his own potential.

The differing practical, intellectual, and spiritual capacities of adepts are subdivided into four categories; the same terms are also applied in classifying the most important Tantric texts. These are the Action Tantra (*kriyā-tantra*), the Performance Tantra (*carya-tantra*), the Yoga Tantra (*yoga-tantra*) and the Supreme Yoga Tantra (*anuttara-yoga-tantra*). They describe the outer and inner activities of Tantric practice that are regarded as being of merit, and they range from the simple cleansing of the body and pursuit of prescribed religious rites of Action Tantra, to the meditation on complex philosophical concepts and religious mysteries in Supreme Yoga Tantra.

The method of meditative immersion makes great demands on the adept. He learns to sharpen his understanding step by step. He must control the constant flow of thought that the human brain normally generates, which is deflected this way and that by sense impressions and emotional

Opposite, Fig. 1
Hevajra. Bronze. Height 30 cm. Baphuon style, second half of the eleventh century (cat. 99). National Museum of Cambodia, Phnom Penh

associations, so that his whole mental energy can be focused on his chosen deity. He has selected this deity, the chief deity of the *maṇḍala* to which he has been initiated, according to his own needs, because he believes this is the one best suited to the progress of his enlightenment. A person who has chosen Hevajra meditates on a *maṇḍala* that displays this chief deity at its center.

The special feature of Tantric meditation is the aspiration toward identification of the initiate with this deity. By visualizing its appearance and attributes, the initiate gradually transfers to himself the characteristics and essential being of the deity. Before he can achieve complete identification, he must experience the void (*śūnyatā*). That is to say, he has then reached a spiritual state in which he is free of prejudice, illusion, and thinking in categories. All concepts embedded in the given facts of the phenomenal world no longer have any validity for him. The distinction between subject and object has been removed, so he and the deity are identical. This state of consciousness is characterized by wisdom and compassion for all living beings. These are the two components of Buddhahood. "Buddha" literally means the Enlightened One.

The path of enlightenment consists of five stages: purification of the mind; meditation; experience of the void; identification with the deity; achievement of wisdom and compassion = Buddhahood. Buddha is a title that describes the condition of spiritual perfection, while "deity" is generally used to indicate the personifications of religious mysteries and experiences gained through meditation.

Enlightenment is the precondition for no longer having to be reborn and for entering into nirvana. To attain this goal, an immeasurably long period of wandering from existence to existence is normally required. However, this process can be accelerated by the Tantric method, as mentioned above. But as in the other schools of Buddhism, enlightenment can only be attained from a starting point in human existence. No distinctions are made between the possibilities open to men and women. Teachers and pupils can be either male or female.

Tantra is widely believed to embrace permissive sexual practices, which cause doubts as to the serious nature of this religious path. Apart from the fact that erotic metaphors are frequently misunderstood, it is also the case that the eroticized version of Tantra is only one path among many variants. Such a path can readily be abused.

The recognition and overcoming of the polarities that determine our world are the principal concerns: the cosmic polarities of microcosm and macrocosm, the existential one of life and death, and the psycho-social ones of honor and shame, love and hate, happiness and misfortune. In the eroticized variant, one of the most important polarities experienced by all human beings is that between man and woman. In their union this polarity can be erased, for in the ecstasy of the act of love a couple loses the consciousness of duality and difference. The image of sexual union is commonly used to render intelligible the spiritual state of liberation from all polarities. This plays a great part in Tibetan Tantra especially, as witness the many paintings and statues of gods and goddesses in the Yab-Yum (father-mother) pose. No portrayals of this kind are found in Cambodian art, however, where sexual images as metaphors for spiritual processes do not occur in the iconographic tradition.

Cambodian inscriptions on stone provide evidence that the Tantric method was already being practiced in the tenth century and was held in high esteem. One of the most important Sanskrit inscriptions bearing information on the subject is that of Vat Sithor, Province of Kompong Cham, dating from the year 968 A.D.[1] Along with eulogies to King Jayavarman V, praise is bestowed upon the deeds of the religious teacher, Kīrtipaṇḍita, who expended great energy in spreading both exoteric and esoteric teachings of Buddhism throughout the land. He is commended for practicing yoga, bringing sacred texts from abroad, and setting up statues of Buddha, Prajñapāramitā, Lokeś, and Vajrin (cat. 59). In one of the verses it is explicitly stated that veneration is to be accorded to the priest who is familiar with the mystery of thunder (*vajra*) and bell (*ghaṇṭā*).

Vajra and *ghaṇṭā* are the most important ritual implements of a Tantric priest. He holds them in his hands while performing ceremonies, and with them describes solemn ritual gestures. They are always used together. In the left hand he holds the bell; in the right hand the *vajra* (he who is hard/mighty; thunderbolt; or sheaf of lightning flashes). Since early antiquity in India, lightning flashes have been used to indicate the explosive force of energy and brilliance unfolding to the highest degree. Thus the *vajra* already had the character of a mythical weapon, itself indestructible but possessing potency in the highest degree. In Buddhism it became the symbol for the indestructibility of *dharma* (doctrine—as expounded by the Buddha) and the infinite force of spiritual enlightenment that penetrates all things, making them transparent and thus enabling recognition of the highest truth.

The simultaneous qualities of hardness and transparency were also attributed to the diamond, which combined with *vajra* in a symbolic unity. The Tantric branch of Buddhism is therefore often known as Vajrayāna, that is the way of the *vajra* (diamond). The ringing of the bell accompanies Tantric ceremonies, spreading abroad the sacred syllables intoned by the priest.

The sharp points of the *vajra* and the swelling body of the bell result in a formal opposition symbolic (cat. 106) of male and female energy. The intermingling of the two on the terrestrial level is the source of life; on the cosmic level it means the neutralizing of the polarities referred to above. *Vajra* and bell in this way symbolize spiritual perfection, the essence of the highest Buddha, the Ādibuddha. During the performance of ritual acts, his function is taken over by the priest. In Tantra one of the names of the Ādibuddha is Vajrasattva. He is always portrayed with two arms, holding *vajra* and bell in his hands (fig. 2). In spite of his high status, he does not seem to have played any great role in the practice of the cult, for the few figures in bronze or stone known to come from Cambodia are quite coarsely fashioned, lacking any artistic inspiration. While the goal of Tantra is to understand the nature of the Buddha Vajrasattva, in order to attain that nature, images of deities like Hevajra served as focal figures for meditation.

Quite a number of bronze and stone Cambodian Hevajra figures of the eleventh to thirteenth centuries have survived. Some are of outstanding artistic quality,[2] leading to the conclusion that Hevajra must have had considerable significance at this time. Apart from the figures themselves, little is known about the nature of his cult in Cambodia. No manuscripts from the Angkor empire have been preserved, and Indian writings, and versions of these translated into Tibetan, are the closest sources.

The most important source is the *Hevajratantra*.[3] A text such as this is very difficult to understand as its pronouncements are coded. In addition, tantric teachers did not commit the most essential truths to writing, but passed them on to their pupils orally. All interpretation by the uninitiated can

1. *IC* 6: 195-211 (collection de textes et de documents sur l'Indochine III).
2. It would not be difficult to assemble some forty or so from museums and private collections. See W. LOBO, "Reflections on the Tantric Buddhist Deity Hevajra in Cambodia," *Southeast Asian Archaeology 1994. Proceedings of the 5th International Conference of the European Association of Southeast Asian Archaeologists*. Ed. by P. -Y. Manguin (in press).
3. For the *Hevajra-Tantra*, see SNELLGROVE 1959.

Fig. 2
Vajrasattva.
Provenance unknown.
Bronze. Height 27 cm.
National Museum of Cambodia, Phnom Penh, Ka 5420

therefore only have provisional, experimental status. A layman is not in a position to grasp the whole truth and must keep this fact in mind. One can only attempt to decode partially the puzzle of the images and texts.

Among the defining characteristics of the Cambodian Hevajra belong his eight heads arranged on three levels, his sixteen arms holding various attributes, and his dance posture (cats. 99–102). In the *Hevajratantra* the god himself describes his appearance: "I have eight faces, four legs, and sixteen arms, and trample the four Māra underfoot. Fearful am I to fear itself, with my necklace made of a string of heads and dancing furiously on a solar disk. Black am I and terrible with a crossed *vajra* on my head, my body smeared with ashes, and my mouths sending forth the sound HŪṂ. But my inner nature is tranquil and holding Nairātmyā in loving embrace, I am possessed of tranquil bliss. My front face is black, the one to the right is like white jasmine, the one to the left is red and fearful, and the one to the rear is distorted. The remaining faces are like those of bees, and there are twenty-four eyes, and so on."[4]

4. SNELLGROVE 1959, v, 7–12.

A few verses describe the attributes: "The skulls in his right hands contain these things in this order: an elephant, a horse, an ass, an ox, a camel, a man, a lion, and a cat. Those in the left are: Earth, Water, Air, Fire, Moon, Sun, Yama, and Vaiśravaṇa." (Yama is the god of death; Vaiśravaṇa the god of wealth).

The Indian text *Niṣpannayogāvalī* gives a different manifestation of Hevajra; in addition to the one just described, one of the attributes is called Kapāladhara (skull-bearing) Hevajra and the other Śastradhara (weapon-bearing) Hevajra.[5] The Khmer artists must have based their Hevajra figures on these text passages, as both variants are found in their art.[6] Some attributes are different from those given in the texts, for instance, so far no Hevajra has been found dancing in the embrace of his Prajña Nairātmyā.[7] In contrast to the the Indian and Tibetan examples, the Cambodian Hevajra is always dancing alone, except for the six or eight goddesses who can form a circle around him at a certain remove (cats. 102, 105). This suggests, as mentioned above, that the erotic variant of the Hevajra cult had no significance in Cambodia. Moreover, Cambodian Hevajra do not show frightening traits such as hair standing on end, round eyes, fangs for teeth, and skulls for body ornament, but are beautiful and smiling. The stylistically elegant and original Khmer solution for portraying the eight heads is an arrangement in three rows, with the lowest one bearing three heads, the central one four and the top one a single head. Specific religious and philosophical considerations underlie this arrangement.

Hevajra is the personification of enlightenment in the Here and Now. Attaining it is not solely an intellectual process, but also a sensuous experience. The body and the senses are necessary instruments for the spirit in search of truth, but ultimately they are transcended. "So the Enlightened One is neither existence nor non-existence; he has a form with arms and faces and yet in highest bliss is formless," says the *Hevajratantra*.[8]

The struggle for enlightenment is a dynamic process. More specifically, it is a dramatic inner struggle against illusion, bondage, and the lust for life. To express this, orthodox Buddhism hit upon the metaphor of the subjection of Māra by Buddha Śākyamuni; Tantric Buddhism points up the dynamics of this dramatic event by showing Hevajra dancing upon the four Māra (cat. 99). They represent the circumstances of *Saṃsāra*, that is, the world of phenomena, characterized by constant rebirth, misery, and transitoriness. By dancing, he liberates himself from these chains.

The Tantric ritual is the path to enlightenment. The pupil is guided along the way by his teacher. The gradual process of identification is brought about by transference. For example, the pupil meditates upon the attributes held in Hevajra's hands by first subjecting them to close scrutiny, but then detaching himself from the concrete image and visualizing all the details with his eyelids closed. After appropriate practice, he will be able to retain the precise image in his mind's eye. He will see the animals such as elephant, horse, dog etc. in the god's right hands and know that they symbolize certain supernatural powers (*siddhi*). By imagining himself consuming their flesh, he transfers their strength to himself. In this way he acquires the same supernatural powers as are possessed by Hevajra.

The attributes can also refer the pupil to yoga techniques, which will help him on his path. This is the case with the heavenly bodies of sun and moon and with the four elements of earth, water, fire, and air held in the left hands. In the correspondence between micro- and macrocosm typical of Tantra, they refer to the lateral channels of energy (*nadis*) and the central circles of

5. NIṢPANNAYOGĀVALĪ, Chap. 5 and 8. See MALLMANN 1975, 185.
6. A fine bronze figure of the weapon-bearing Hevajra dating from the early thirteenth century is located in the National Museum in Bangkok. Illustrated in KRAIRIKSH 1979, 62, 145.
7. Sanskrit "prajña" means "wisdom." She is personified as a female figure because the Sanskrit word has feminine gender. In Mahāyāna and Tantrayāna Buddhism she symbolizes the wisdom of a Buddha. Nairātmyā is here used as a proper name and means "Without-Self-Being"; that is, she has no individual self because the wisdom of Buddha belongs in the realm of the Absolute.
8. SNELLGROVE 1959, ii, 43.

energy (*cakras*) in the inner *maṇḍala* of the human being. By practicing a particular set of exercises, the flow of energy in them can be so influenced that mental power is enhanced. From the *Hevajratantra* we learn that one of these techniques is the repeated recital of mantra.

Mantra are sacred syllables, which in most cases do not possess a meaning that can be translated, but are related to the passage of breath and the various points of articulation of sounds in the cavity of the mouth and throat. One of the most important mantra is OṂ. It is a combination of A, U, and M. A is articulated with the lips parted. To pronounce the U, the lips must shape a narrower opening, and for the M they must be completely closed. From the pronunciation of A via that of U through to M lie all the sounds that can be articulated. Hence OṂ includes everything that can be uttered in any conceivable language. In its extreme concentration it is a universal word, the quintessence of language.

In the system of sound mysticism for both Brahmans and Buddhists, the mantra OṂ is the most sacred syllable. The Indian poet Rabindranath Tagore said: "OṂ is the symbolic word for the infinite, the perfect, the eternal. The sound as such is already perfect and represents the wholeness of things."[9]

In Tantric Buddhism, which is frequently also called Mantrayāna (way of the mantra) because of the significance of mantra, OṂ symbolizes exactly this: the experience of the Absolute. It ascends from the limitation of the three-dimensional world, but must take that world as its starting point. OṂ must have a counterpart in the Here and Now and this is expressed by the mantra HŪṂ, where the H is to be articulated deep in the throat. "OṂ is like the sun, but HŪṂ is like the soil, into which the sun's rays must descend in order to awaken the dormant life."[10]

HŪṂ is the mantra of the god Hevajra. He says of himself: ". . . my mouths sending forth the sound HŪṂ. . . ." Just as the earth absorbs the rays of the sun, so does HŪṂ contain OṂ. It combines individual and absolute, time and timelessness. HŪṂ is the synthesis of the five pieces of wisdom personified by the five Tathāgata. They are a particular class of Buddhas who can only be experienced through meditation.[11] The five Tathāgata are again to be found in Hevajra's heads on the upper and middle levels (fig. 3). It is usual for the group of five to be subdivided into four plus one, because four signifies the extension in the horizontal plane of the four cardinal points of the compass—that is why the heads look in four directions—while the fifth direction symbolizes the vertical extension into the zenith. The Tathāgata Vairocana looks to the zenith, Akṣobhya to the east, Ratnasambhava to the south, Amitābha to the west, and Amogasiddhi to the north. The number 5 is the sign for cosmic totality. The Tathāgata have their microcosmic counterparts in the upper energy centers of the human body and in certain psychic qualities.

The disciple of Tantra identifies himself with the five Tathāgata, not only by the process of meditation but through the agency of the various rites of consecration (*abhiṣeka*) performed on him by his teacher. These are described in the *Hevajrasekaprakriyā*.[12] With the water containing the essence of Akṣobhya, the disciple is brought into union with him; with the diadem placed on his brow, he is joined to Ratnasambhava; the *vajra* given into his right hand aligns him with Amitābha; the bell in his left hand does likewise for Amoghasiddhi. As the teacher lays his hand upon the pupil's head, thought of as Vairocana, he bestows upon him the sacred *vajra*-name.

Fig. 3
The eight heads of Hevajra
Hevajra as a universal being (Body of the Law)
Vairocana, Akṣobhya, Ratnasambhava, Amoghasiddhi, Amitābha (Body of Beatitude)
Buddha, Lokeśvara, Vajrapāṇi (Body of Metamorphosis)

9. Lama Anagarika Govinda 1973, 46.
10. Lama Anagarika Govinda 1973, 131.
11. Lama Anagarika Govinda 1973, 186–189.
12. Finot 1934, 39.

In this way the initiate learns that the five Tathāgata with their cosmic and terrestrial correspondences form a unity that also includes him. This all-embracing unity is personified, according to the particular persuasion being followed, as Vajrasattva, Vajradhana, Samantabhadra, or Ādibuddha. For the initiate following the way of Hevajra, no distinction is made between Vajrasattva and Hevajra (fig. 3). His enlightenment comes about through the mystery of body, speech and mind. These are the three components of a human being that are raised to the universal through the process of meditation, such that the body becomes the universe, speech becomes perfected wisdom, and the mind becomes an all-embracing compassion for all living creatures.[13]

We do not know what Hevajra's three lowest heads signify. Tantric texts from Java and Japan, deriving ultimately from ancient Indian sources, explain that the process of the gradual unfolding of the Ādibuddha in the three-dimensional world has eight aspects or stages. He first reveals himself in the five Tathāgata and then in the triad of Buddha, Lokeśvara, and Vajrapāṇi.[14] These last are manifest in the three lowest heads. The triad and the group of five together embody Hevajra in his quality as Vajrasattva, that is, in his universal, absolute aspect. This form is expressed in his name: "By *HE* is proclaimed great compassion, and wisdom by *VAJRA*," says the *Hevajratantra* (Pt. I, Chap. 1, Verse 2). These are mystical relationships, not literal translations. The eight heads of Hevajra thus express in a subtle way the doctrine, of great significance for Mahāyāna and Vajrayāna Buddhism, of the three bodies of a Buddha (also described as three classes of Buddha). This refers to the three qualities of being that the Enlightened One has realized within himself:

1. The primordial, supra-individual germ from which all things spring, and which is present in every living being. It is also defined as the pure Buddha-nature and called body of *dharma*. Here it is personified as Vajrasattva.
2. A spiritual perfection that gives rise to all inspiration and in which the realities of microcosm and macrocosm are united. It is called body of bliss and is here personified in the five Tathāgata.
3. A human body in which (a) the pure Buddha-nature and (b) the spiritual perfection are transformed into visible form. This body is called body of transformation and it is manifest in the Buddha of the triad.

The grouping of Buddha, Lokeśvara, and Vajrapāṇi has been mentioned in inscriptions on stone in Cambodia since the tenth century.[15] The three are also to be met with as bronze figures mounted on a single base, so that we are justified in regarding them as a single ritual entity, representing one aspect, that is, the body of transformation, of the universal Hevajra.

The eight-headed Hevajra is also occasionally depicted with other Buddhist deities. One example is to be seen on a four-sided stele given the shape of a temple (*caitya*) in miniature form (cat. 59). The relief carving on one of the four sides shows him standing erect rather than dancing. He has three heads, above which is a two-tiered pyramid, having one row of four niches surmounted by a single niche. In these niches the five Tathāgata are seated. This is an interesting iconographic variation on the eight heads of Hevajra. Unfortunately, this *caitya* does not have an inscription, although many do, which would tell us the names of the deities depicted.

13. Lama Anagarika Govinda 1973, 206.
14. *Sang Hyang Kamahāyānikan* from Java and *Mahāvairocanasūtra* in Japanese translation. Analyzed by Pott 1966. It is true these texts do not speak of Hevajra, but of Bhaṭāra Buddha and Mahāvairocana. However, since Hevajra is regarded as Universal Being by his followers, it seems legitimate to apply the system of development to him.
15. For example in that of Bat Chum. See Coedès, *Les Inscriptions*, 1908.

Fig. 4
Hevajra *maṇḍala* (compare cat. 102)

Strangely enough, the search for the name "Hevajra" in Cambodian inscriptions has proved fruitless, while "Vajrapāṇi" is frequently encountered.[16] Since many figures of Hevajra exist, the question arises as to whether he might have had another name. In the Sanskrit version of the *Hevajratantra* he is several times invoked as Vajrin[17] and this expression is also to be found in a few inscriptions from Cambodia, for example, in the one from Vat Sithor mentioned earlier (n. 1). It is commonly assumed that Vajrin and Vajrapāṇi are synonymous, but the meaning of the two words may be differentiated along the lines that Vajrin embodies the essence of the *vajra*, whereas Vajrapāṇi—literally translated: "He who holds the *vajra* in his hand"—is the guardian of the *vajra*.[18] Hevajra simply means "Hail, *Vajra*"; that is, the solemn invocation of the *vajra* became the name of the god. It seems entirely possible that in Cambodia he was called Vajrin.

Unfortunately, most of the figures portraying him in stone and bronze have been torn from their original settings and come down to us as separate pieces. But a few representations demonstrate that as the central god of a *maṇḍala*, he was surrounded by other deities, each of which embodied one of the many aspects of his being (cats. 102, 105).

Maṇḍala (fig. 4) are images for meditation in two or three dimensions, developed from the basic shapes of square and circle. They symbolize both the totality of the universe and that of the psycho-spiritual world of human beings. Their innermost center is the divinity and at the same time the depth of the human heart, which the person meditating seeks to approach. The steps leading to the center of the *maṇḍala* are the path that leads him to the center of his own being. The *maṇḍala* also finds interpretation "as a means to reintegration, to the discovery of and union with the indivisible self."[19] The Tantric method accompanies the seeker along this difficult path.

16. Boisselier, "Vajrapāṇi," 1957, 2: 324–332.
17. Snellgrove 1959, Pt. II, iii, 1; Pt. II, v, 1.
18. In Sanskrit the ending [-in] means enduring attachment. I am indebted to K. Butzenberger and M. Pfeiffer of Berlin, for this comment.
19. In the interpretation of G. Tucci, cited in Essen 1989, 182.

Architecture

Fig. 1 Prasat Kompong Preah. Eighth century

The Triumphs and Perils of Khmer Architecture: A Structural Analysis of the Monuments of Angkor

John Sanday

Angkor conjures impressions of vast silhouettes outlined by dramatic sunsets, soaring towers rising from temple-mountains, a sense of power and majesty, and a building achievement of enormous scale. Henri Parmentier once said that the "construction seems to have been an annoying necessity that was done without much care, as quickly as possible, the sooner to achieve the only thing that mattered, the form that was more or less dictated by tradition." This comment leads one to begin to understand the theaterlike quality of the construction of Khmer buildings, where the end result was more important than the means of achieving it. For the Khmer, the engineering and construction technologies in use throughout contemporary Europe and parts of Asia were, for the most part, of secondary importance. The overall effect of the architecture was what counted most.

The earliest Cambodian temples, such as those at Angkor Borei, were simple brick constructions of a single tower (*śikhara*), or combination of towers, set on an unadorned platform. Later, the Khmer embellished their Indian-derived temples with profusely decorated stuccowork. The transition period from brick and stucco to stone, from a simple tower to the temple-mountain, was relatively short. This progression can be traced from the ninth-century temples at Hariharālaya (now Roluos); to the first stone temple-mountain in Angkor, around 900 at Phnom Bakheng; and culminating in Banteay Srei toward the end of the tenth century. During the following three centuries, the Khmer would produce some of the most remarkable monuments ever created.

The first temples, dating from the eighth century, were brick structures of uncomplicated design (fig. 1). This early brickwork is of excellent quality, and recent studies at the temple of Preah Ko, Roluos, have shed new light on the use of the material by the Khmer. At Angkor, the size of the bricks varies from temple to temple, making it easy to date the various stages in a temple's construction. The bricks, probably baked on site in simple kilns, are generally well burnt and of even color, with sharp arrises. To create a finely honed contiguous surface, the bricks were probably rubbed together. A simple mortar of brick dust and lime was then used as a thin jointing matrix. The brickwork is technically comparable to that found at Pagan of a similar date, and its quality is generally superior to most other Asian examples. Careful analysis at Preah Ko suggests that the brickwork was originally exposed, perhaps with a very thin color render, and only later embellished with highly decorative stuccowork. Sandstone door jambs were incorporated at the time of the original construction, but the sandstone images that appear in specially prepared niches were inserted at the same time as the stucco. The platform at Preah Ko, like the temples, was also brick.

The *śikhara* form found in almost all the Angkor monuments reveals the strong influence of Indian architecture. The stone towers are tapered, have corbeled roofs, and are capped with a stone lotus flower. The corbeled vault, common to all Khmer stone structures, was also imported from India. Projecting stones are stacked to span openings (fig. 2), and when correctly placed, they overlap to create a waterproof covering. By the tenth century, the corbeled vault was widely used in many areas in place of large beams or lintels. (It is still a mystery why the arch was never introduced at Angkor.) Despite its limitations, the corbeled vault was refined and adapted for galleries, aisles, and covered arcades. The widest span (3.5 m) is said to have been achieved in the Hall of Dancers in Preah Khan, although it ultimately collapsed. The double-pitched roof, an indigenous but less common style, occurs in subsidiary structures at Bakong and Banteay Srei where the roofs were made from stone slabs. At Preah Khan, an unusual two-story pavilion used timber rafters to create a double-pitched roof that probably supported clay tiles.

Perhaps the strongest and most pervasive Indian influence on the architecture of Angkor was not structural but symbolic: the mythology of Mount Meru derived from Indian cosmology. In architecture, this myth has been expressed either through natural phenomena, the construction of temples on top of *phnom* or hillocks, such as the temple-mountain complex of Phnom Bakheng, or by manmade structures, such as the temples of Angkor Vat and the Baphuon, where the mount is created from the material that had been excavated to form the moats and canals. In many cases the *śikhara* on the highest level form a quincunx that represent the five peaks of Meru. These towers stand atop descending platforms that symbolize the continents encircling Meru, and the entire complex is surrounded by a moat that signifies the ocean.

The scale of the temple-mountain structures challenges description. The proportions are celestial, built by humans to worship gods, and there is a conscious yet subtle use of trompe l'oeil to achieve the maximum grandeur (fig. 3). The risers are extremely high, in diminishing proportions as the steps ascend to accentuate the effect of height, and are seemingly built for giants; clearly few people were actually intended to climb them. Another subtle illusion is formed by the skillful way in which, as the stairways lead up the

Fig. 2
Corbeled vault. West gate of Angkor Thom. Early thirteenth century

Fig. 3
The pyramid at Pre Rup (961). The upper terraces, where certain trompe l'oeil effects are visible

mountain to the principal sanctuary, their widths decrease to enhance the illusion of perspective.

The Bayon temple was constructed at the end of the twelfth century when Buddhism became preeminent in Cambodia under King Jayavarman VII. The last of the temple-mountain structures to be built at Angkor, Bayon is the only building of its type devoted to Buddhism. Henceforth, the Khmer temple plan was greatly modified to suit the advent of Buddhist monastic complexes. The best known examples are Ta Prohm, which Jayavarman dedicated to his mother in 1186, and Preah Khan, which he dedicated to his father in 1191. In these architectural complexes the vertical representation of Mount Meru has been converted to a horizontal or linear plan. The central tower is dominant, although its base is raised only a few meters above the level of the outer entrances, while the continents are represented by massive laterite enclosure walls and the oceans by a moat.

A sense of these monastic complexes, so different from the temple-mountains, can only be attained from a pilgrimage through a typical site such as Preah Khan (fig. 4), which retains a tranquil and spiritual ambiance. Access for a royal procession would have been from the east, across the smallest of the Angkor *baray,* or reservoirs, the Preah Khan *baray.* Barges would have drawn up to the jetty, and the progress would have begun along the unique processional way between "bornes," stone lanterns with serene protective images of the seated Buddha. The entourage would have crossed the moat by the grand causeway flanked by larger-than-life-size sculpture of *asura* (demons), on one side, and *devata* (gods), on the other, both sides supporting a *nāga,* or serpent. Next, it would have passed through the east *gopura* (gateway) IV, one of four gates placed centrally in each of the enclosure walls, where at forty-meter intervals stand powerful *garuḍa,* symbolic guardians of the temple (fig. 5).

Within the outer wall a central path would have led through a bustling residential section, where wooden structures housed many thousands of temple attendants, and brought the procession to a cruciform platform preceding the grandiose east *gopura* III leading to the temple complex itself. The level rises slightly here, and from this point on, access to the temple would have been determined by status. Through the beautifully proportioned Hall of Dancers, a communal space, a narrow passage led to the cen-

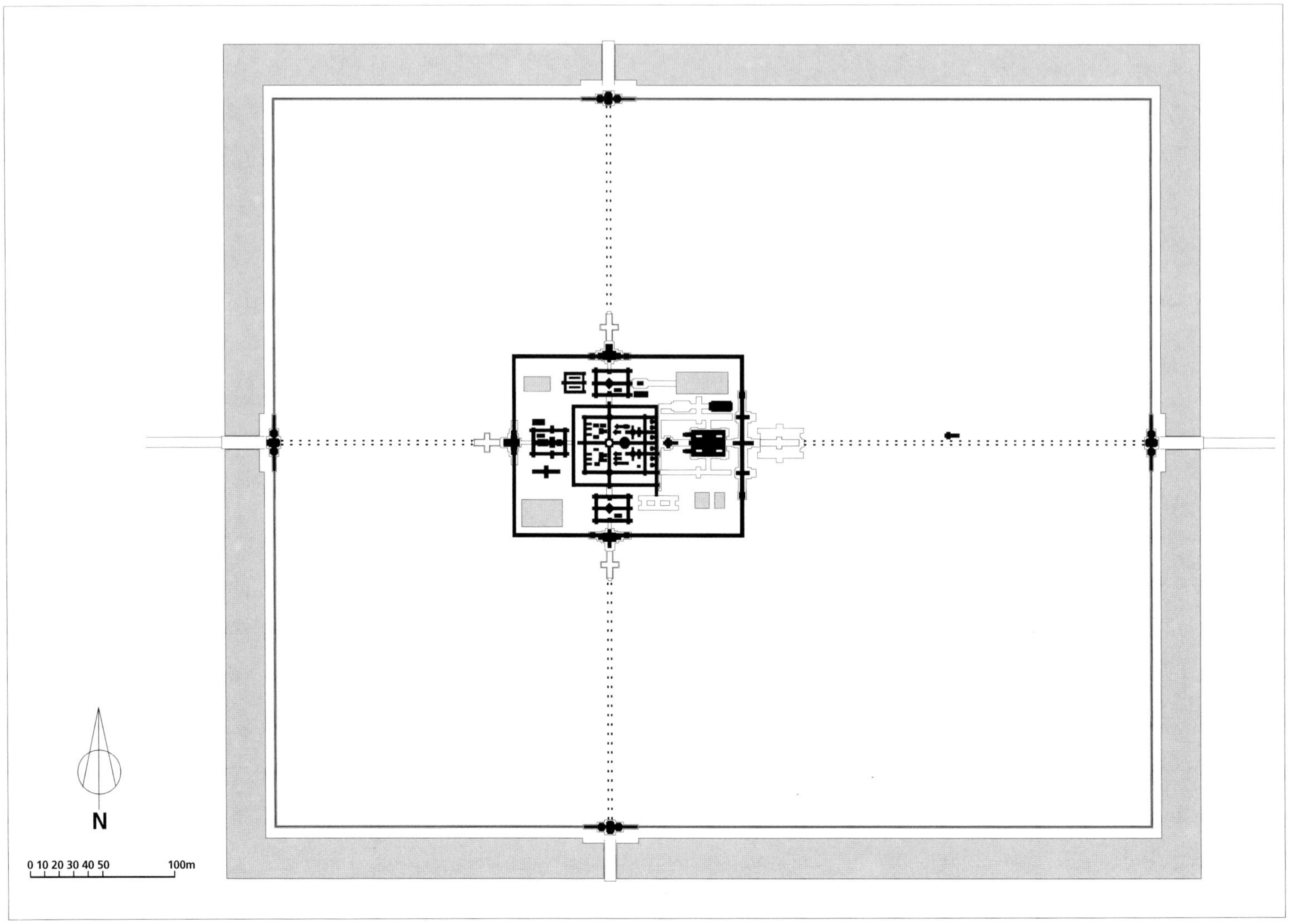

Fig. 4
Simplified plan of Preah Khan at Angkor (1191)

Fig. 5
A *garuḍa* from the exterior enclosure of Preah Khan at Angkor (1191)

tral tower and main sanctuary. Small sanctuaries allowing only individual worship (to the west, north, and south of the central sanctuary) were, at one time, enclosed by timber doors and dedicated to Viṣṇu, Śiva, and ancestor worship and Brahmā, respectively.

Prior to the brick and stone used in the temples of Angkor, timber was the most common building material for the Khmer, who excelled at carpentry. Buildings were probably framed in timber, adorned with panels of additional materials, and roofed with clay tiles or straw. The transition from wood to the more durable materials of brick or stone must have been very abrupt, though timber construction never ceased for vernacular and even royal domestic architecture. Only temples were built of permanent materials, and brick construction served as a suitable transient technology to the introduction of monumental stone construction. The early styles and structures were modest. The rapid transition from carpentry to monumental masonry is evident, and many of the intrinsic skills of carpentry can be seen in the Khmer interpretation of stone masonry. The use of sandstone for doors, windows, and as a decorative element for statuary in the temples of the Roluos group prepared the way for the eventual construction of complete temples in stone, but it is apparent that the Khmer concept of designing and building in stone was very limited, and there is no evidence of any experimental or prototypical stone construction.

The next stage of construction technology saw the introduction of laterite, a local volcanic material from a much younger substratum than the Kulen sandstone discussed below. Laterite is a volcanic conglomerate, a matrix of pebbles held together by clay. It has a honeycomb appearance and is of a darkish yellow color, in striking contrast to the gray-green tone of most Cambodian sandstone. Similar in weight and density to sandstone, laterite was used in great quantities to create the cores of the temple-mountain structures and their enclosure walls. Much of the laterite used in the construction of the temples at Angkor was doubtless excavated locally during the digging of the temple moats. When wet, after extraction, laterite is easily cut into blocks. After exposure to air and sunlight, it hardens and the color darkens, a result of the oxidization of its high iron content.

During a recent analysis of both laterite and stone, several discoveries were made. Contrary to popular belief, laterite acts as a good deterrent to rising damp, because its capillarity is very low. Also, its honeycomb composition allows for easy water drainage. Many of the platforms of the early state temples were built of huge laterite blocks creating sound and solid bases for the ethereal towers they supported. The Khmer were probably aware of laterite's properties when they used it as the core material of their monuments.

Sandstone for the monuments of Angkor was found in the Kulen hills, about fifty kilometers to the north of the site. It is a metamorphic stone from the mid-Jurassic to the mid-Cretaceous period and was extracted from well-established quarries in this extensive range, which was also a significant religious center. The quarries provided stone of various qualities and color, depending on which bed it came from.

The first state temple to be built of sandstone and laterite was the temple-mountain of Bakong, followed by that at the summit of Phnom Bakheng. Shortly afterward, the temple complex of Banteay Srei, often referred to as the jewel of Khmer art, was built about twenty-five kilometers north of Angkor. At Banteay Srei a wide variety of masonry techniques was employed, not only in extraordinary sculptural skills but also in the methods of cutting, dressing, jointing, and lifting the stones, a foretaste of the remarkable talents of later Khmer masons.

The pink sandstone of Banteay Srei is considered to be the best of the Kulen quarry in terms of color, quality, and durability. Everything about Banteay Srei is perfection: the miniature proportions are faultless; the detailed carving is supreme. Perhaps the most surprising feature is the extraordinarily fine condition of the stonework today. The carvings maintain the crispness of the day they were carved, even though they were buried deep in the jungle until the mid 1920s and underwent a complete restoration by anastylosis only in the early 1930s.

The unique sandstone in the early eleventh-century temple of Ta Keo, the "temple of crystal" at Angkor, reputedly comes from one of the deepest beds of the Kulen quarry, the "royal bed" where the strongest stone is found. The bluish-gray stone has a granitelike quality, and is said to be so hard that masons found it impossible to carve, one of the reasons put forth to explain the absence of carving at this temple. Ta Keo is, nonetheless, a mighty structure, and its uncarved state emphasizes the architectural mass and crystalline appearance.

How were these colossal monuments built, and how were the stones moved from the quarry to the site, and to their location in the structure? The transportation of these massive blocks of sandstone has been the subject of great speculation, as the stones range in weight from one to eight or ten tons. The blocks were cut and dressed in random sizes at the quarries in Kulen. At that time, it is likely that two pairs of lifting holes were drilled deep into the stones. Bamboo wedges were driven into these holes and vines were lashed between them. When swollen with water, the wedges would grip the stones tightly. The stones were probably lifted by elephant onto bamboo barges and floated down the rivers and waterways to the building sites, where, using the same system, they were lifted and stacked into the new structure. A series of ramps, presumably, enabled elephants to haul the stones close to the site. The stone would later be raised into position with something similar to a block and tackle.

Prior to stacking, wafer-thin joints between the stones were engineered by rubbing or abrading the stones, one against the other, until there was an exact match of the stones' faces. This process is depicted in one of the lesser-known bas-reliefs on the west side of the Bayon (figs. 6, 7). Afterward the stones were laid dry, ready for rough shaping by masons, whether as doors, windows, or decorative niches, or as part of a bas-relief. Ultimately, they received the fine hand of the sculptors to finish the detailed decoration. Often the lifting holes are still visible, and it appears that in several temples the holes were later disguised with stucco. It is hard to imagine how some of the ashlar stone walling with its complicated jointing pattern was achieved. The stones themselves are fitted together like patchwork: no two stones are alike nor are they laid in regular courses, so the walls have the appearance of marquetry or a giant jigsaw puzzle, with joints so tight they are almost invisible. In many places special wedge-shaped keystones were driven in to tighten the joints.

Once the stones had been stacked, the process of decorating the temple began with the shaping and carving of the structures in situ. Windows were cut, door jambs prepared in the wall slab, architraves shaped, niches carved, pilasters hewn, and, later, the decorative geometric and floral patterns were added. The more exacting task of sculpting the facade then followed. The master carver engraved an overall design onto the facade; he was followed by a team of masons who blocked out the detail. Finally, the panels were finished by a highly skilled group of sculptors. A similar process, probably involving several more stages, was no doubt used to design and carve the awe-inspiring bas-reliefs at the Bayon and Angkor Vat.

It is certain that this process was followed, as there are examples everywhere of uncompleted work. In particular at the Bayon, many of the upper registers of bas-reliefs have been left unfinished. Further proof can be seen at the uncarved temple of Ta Keo. Areas such as the back of disengaged pilasters in doorways that have been carved prior to placement, as well as some turned stone balusters inserted during preliminary construction, indicate that these structures were carved in situ. Standards of perfection demanded that even inaccessible areas be sculptured.

The persistence of the Khmer application of carpentry techniques to stonework is illustrated by the construction of stone window and door openings, especially where mitered joints have been used between vertical and

Figs. 6 and 7
Bayon. Interior gallery of bas-reliefs, west side, southern portion. Construction of a Viṣṇuite temple. Early thirteenth century

horizontal members (fig. 8). This joint is easily prepared and used extensively in timber construction, but it is a very intricate and complicated task to cut one in stone. The balusters in the window openings offer another example of stone being turned on a lathe in an identical manner to similar timber profiles.

The construction of the Khmer temple-mountains was a mammoth undertaking and must have required several thousand workers, probably slaves captured during the many cross-border skirmishes that occurred during those centuries. Assessing the time required to construct these great monuments is difficult, as there are few records, but it is probably safe to assume that temples that were started in a king's reign were either completed or abandoned before his death. On this premise, Angkor Vat was probably built in about thirty-five years under the direction of King Sūryavarman II.

During the formative centuries of the Funan and Zhenla periods, when Indian temple designs enlightened the Khmer artisans, not all the structural and technical skills associated with these monuments were absorbed. Whereas many techniques—such as detailing the corbeled vaults to prevent water penetration and translating carpentry details into stone—were expertly executed, the Indian masons' intuitive knowledge of stone construction is markedly absent in the temples of Angkor. For example, one of the principal

Fig. 8
Phnom Chisor (first half of the eleventh century), east library. The recent deterioration of the building reveals how the stones were assembled to frame a blind window

engineering defects in nearly all Khmer stone towers is the lack of bonding between courses. The individual stones were prepared with meticulous skill and accuracy, but they were often stacked with aligned vertical joints rather than staggered ones. No bonding exists between the stones, which creates an inherent weakness in the towers and is the principal reason for their collapse. Furthermore, the failure to link or bond the inner and outer walls often leads to the collapse of the decorated outer stone facade, leaving only the inner stone structure of the tower in situ. The simple expedient of bridging the joint between the inner and outer wall linings with coursed stones would have prevented this problem.

The variation of the water table has been the layman's diagnosis for the disintegration of foundations. It is true that one of the most damaging elements to the stones is the presence of water, but the severe damage to walls and column bases, especially in Angkor Vat, is not caused by moisture rising through the foundations. In general, the foundations to all the major structures in Angkor are of excellent construction and in nearly all cases there is scant evidence of their deformation despite the constant annual fluctuation of the water table—a phenomenon that has continued throughout history. At Angkor Vat, however, the chronic failure in the stonework is caused by water activating clays in the stone composition and an inherently bad design. Unfortunately, the yellowish gray stone quarried to construct Angkor Vat was of very inferior quality. Recent analysis shows that Angkor Vat sandstone contains layers of bentonite clay in its sedimentation, which expands when wet (fig. 9).

The passage of rainwater into the temple was the result of defective design, which caused water to run across the underside of beams and lintels. The problem has been exacerbated over the centuries by poor restoration and more recently by water percolation through fractures in the structures themselves. During heavy storms, rainwater pools on the platforms at wall and column bases and is drawn by capillary attraction up the exposed end grain of the stone, especially if the stones are standing in water for any length of time. This condition causes the bentonite to expand and forces the stones to delaminate. In particular at Angkor Vat, but also at many other temples, after each rainstorm end-bedded monolithic columns and wall bases of inferior quality stone are subjected to this endemic process with continuing disastrous results. In addition, many of these already stressed end-bedded monolithic columns are transferring heavy loads from the roof vaults they are supporting, and this added weight is causing many of the columns to split laterally and dangerously weaken the structures.

Fig. 9
Angkor Vat, tower at the northwest corner of the second enclosure. Expansion and delamination of the sandstone

Whereas the temple structures themselves have been well documented and their forms analyzed over the centuries, their decoration and finishes are still a subject of considerable debate. Until recently there was some speculation that the early structures may have had an exposed brick finish. There is now clear evidence and general acceptance, however, that many of the early brick structures were certainly decorated with stucco. There were several ways of providing keys to attach the stucco to the brick surface. Sometimes the surface was raked to roughen it, or sometimes holes were drilled into the bricks in a random pattern to provide fixing elements. Stucco vestiges can still be found in some of these holes, which should not be confused with the holes drilled for lifting purposes.

The irregularly spaced holes for stucco adhesion are also distinct from the more regularly arranged holes drilled in the interior walls of later stone temples, such as Preah Khan and Ta Prohm. Their principal central sanctuaries are believed to have been lined with bronze sheets or plaques that were probably embossed or engraved and gilded, then attached to timber frames or directly to the walls by plugs inserted into the holes.

There is still much debate on the original finish of the stone structures as well. In many cases evidence exists of a plaster coating over the stone, and indeed, examples of monochrome-painted surfaces are also decipherable on both interior and exterior walls. Were these surfaces ever decorated, in addition, with wall paintings? In February and March of 1996, much of this speculation was laid to rest. At the temple of Preah Ko an exacting program of conservation is being undertaken by an international group of specialists under the aegis of the Royal Angkor Foundation (RAF). The team's research has recently revealed a sequence of external decoration methods and discovered specimens of internal wall decoration. This research has established that, for a period following the temples' original construction, the brickwork was covered with a thin red-colored skim coating only. Later, alterations were made to set the sculpted stone *dvārapāla* (guardians) in place and to add a highly decorated stucco finish (fig. 10). As part of their investigations into interior wall finishes, the RAF team also found the first evidence of painted wall decoration, high up on the interior of the central west tower, a discovery that confirms the use of plaster and polychrome in the Angkor period.

As if challenged by this find, specialists undertaking detailed studies of interior wall surfaces at Preah Khan were quick to announce their discovery of fragments of paintings in the Viṣṇu temple complex of that site. These discoveries are the first examples that have so far come to light of painted decoration at Angkor and will no doubt provoke a more careful scrutiny of other temples within the whole historic site. The chemistry of the pigments of the wall paintings is unknown as yet, but analysis is in process in Germany and more information should be available soon.

For almost a hundred years the École française d'Extrême-Orient (EFEO) has been conducting archaeological research and maintaining many of the monuments at Angkor. After the recent subsidence of turmoil in Cambodia, many governments and international organizations have joined with the EFEO to assist Cambodia in the enormous challenge of safeguarding the historic site of Angkor. Many projects developing appropriate conservation technology are under way, supported by many countries. Besides the recent assistance provided by the Archaeological Survey of India at Angkor Vat and its nomination and acceptance on the World Heritage List (through UNESCO's contribution with the preparation of the Zoning and Environmental Masterplan), generous technical and financial support is being provided by the Japanese, Indonesian, German, and Italian governments. In addition, two private foundations, the World Monuments Fund (WMF) and the RAF, have been working at Angkor, thanks to generous private donations. WMF, a not-for-profit organization based in New York, has pledged support for a ten-year program of training and technical assistance at Preah Khan. Consultants from many nations have participated in research to study conditions at the monuments of Angkor and to develop conservation technology appropriate to the prevailing conditions. With very limited equipment and little imported material, the WMF team has blended local traditional skill and imported technology to train both professionals and local craftsmen in

Opposite, Fig. 10
A *dvārapāla* from Preah Ko. North tower of the east row, east face, south side

some remarkable conservation interventions. In the same manner, the RAF at Preah Ko has undertaken some innovative conservation tasks for the stabilization of stucco, brick, and stone.

Although Angkor was never really lost to the world, it has certainly been the topic of several rediscoveries throughout history. The latest is taking place now with the availability of a vast archive of knowledge maintained by the EFEO and with the constant development of research technology. With this technology, researchers and architectural historians are beginning to discover new information relating to the temples' construction, decoration, and former use. It is to be hoped that the dawn of a new period of discovery and the publicity afforded by the display of Khmer art and architecture at this exhibition will encourage new patrons to assist Cambodia in the quest to save its remarkable but threatened cultural heritage.

Khmer Hydraulics

Jacques Dumarçay

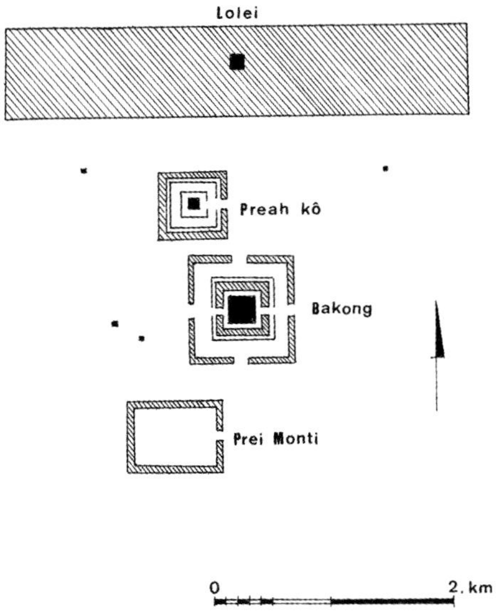

Fig. 1
SR 616. Plan of Roluos

In Asia, princes presiding over the foundation of a state almost always based their authority on the management of water. Prosperous agriculture was key to the development of Khmer civilization, and irrigation practices ensured an annual harvest despite the vagaries of the climate. In a system dating from prehistoric times and in use throughout the Indus civilization, reserves were most often accumulated behind a simple river dam. What distinguishes the Khmer is to have transformed and developed this basic system of water management, only to return to it in the thirteenth century.

In Cambodia, two kinds of reservoirs exist: those that use an excavation or natural depression, moats in particular, and those that retain water above ground behind elevated dikes, large reservoirs called *baray*. The origins of this system are hard to determine. One of the first reservoirs was the southern *baray* at Vat Phu, in present-day Laos, which was built at the end of the eighth century. But it was only later, in the Angkor region, with the beginnings of a centralized Khmer state, that irrigation assumed its full importance.

Java no doubt influenced Cambodia in certain of its architectural forms, as well as a system of irrigation whose main surviving elements lie on the slopes of the Kulen Plateau. These consist of simple river dams that form a reservoir. In Java, the triumph of the Buddhism of the Śailendra dynasty considerably weakened the Hindu Sañjayas, who were probably responsible for Javanese suzerainty over Cambodia.[1] Taking advantage of this situation, a young Khmer prince, who would be crowned King Jayavarman II in 802, freed his country from vassalage to Java and established his capital in the Roluos region (fig. 1).

Jayavarman II first built a dam at Lolei in the last decades of the eighth century. This dam, 2.4 miles (3.8 km) long, obstructed the natural course of the small streams descending from the Kulen Plateau. The system soon became inoperable, and the need became apparent for two dikes perpendicular to the original and then, to the north, another parallel to it. Thus, the principle of the *baray* was born. Water entered through a short aqueduct crossing the north dike, near the northeast corner of the artificial lake.

In the latter part of the ninth century, the Lolei reservoir, which irrigated the Roluos region, was starting to show signs of silting. King Indravarman, forced to find a site for a new *baray*, chose a spot on the east side of Angkor (fig. 2). This vast expanse of water, the eastern *baray*, measuring 4.3 by 1.4 miles (7×2 km), was fed by the Siem Reap River before it was diverted in canals.

Work on the eastern *baray* was not completed until the reign of King Yaśovarman, who took credit for the entire construction around 890. The *baray* at Lolei remained partially operable, however, and Yaśovarman built the four temples on the island in its center, which were consecrated in 893.

1. The editors wish to point out that some scholars have differing views about the relationship between Java (Javā) and Cambodia at that time.

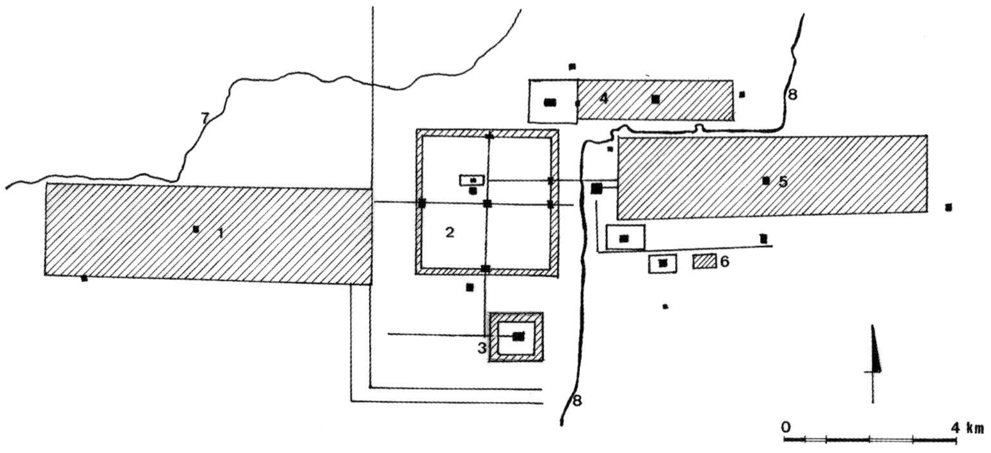

Fig. 2
SR 621. The main reservoirs at Angkor:
1 Western *baray*
2 Angkor Thom
3 Angkor Vat
4 Neak Pean
5 Eastern *baray*
6 Srah Srang

Gradually, sand started to fill the eastern *baray*, probably one reason that Angkor was briefly abandoned for the city of Koh Ker. Yet serious renovations were made during the court's absence, since, immediately upon return of the capital to Angkor, King Rājendravarman ordered the completion of the East Mebon in the middle of the reservoir (952).

At the end of the tenth century, the entire east region of Angkor underwent extensive modifications with the simultaneous construction of a number of monuments and basins. Bat Chum, for example, was a triple Buddhist sanctuary surrounded by a moat and overlooking a small *baray*. The first stage of Srah Srang also dates from this period. Its vast basin must have been used at first to supplement the eastern *baray*, which was again starting to silt up and threatened to become unusable. Work was undertaken on a new project to the west of this site, the western *baray*, which would no longer be fed by the Siem Reap River but by a smaller stream, the *stung* (*sdiṅ*) O Klok. In the center of this large reservoir, and directly tied to its function, a temple of an entirely new architectural order was erected: the West Mebon. The structure consists of a basin surrounding an island, on which stands the sanctuary proper. The monument has a shaft in the form of an inverted *liṅga* (fig. 3). The part with the circular cross-section is at the lowest level, with the octagonal part above it; there is no square portion, as that element of the traditional *liṅga* is usually hidden. The water, therefore, took on the form of the visible portion of the *liṅga*. The shaft was filled through a bronze pipe that communicated with the *baray*, passing underneath the dike linking the temple to the edge of the basin. The basin itself was surrounded by a wall, pierced by windows and, on the axes and laterally, doors with small pavilions over them. As it mounted up the shaft, the water rising up different elements of the *liṅga* indicated the current irrigation capacity of the *baray*.

At the time this work was in progress, water covered only one third of the eastern *baray*. When it became totally unusable, the Siem Reap River was deflected into the north branch of the perimeter canal, then channeled in a straight line south for the first time (fig. 4, element a), only returning to its original course beyond Angkor.

The eastern *baray*, where water had begun to reemerge, was partly inundated again in the southwest corner, with a new outlet feeding a small canal raised between two dikes (fig. 4, element b). In the meantime, during the reign of Sūryavarman II, construction began on Angkor Vat, the moats of which may have made use of natural depressions.

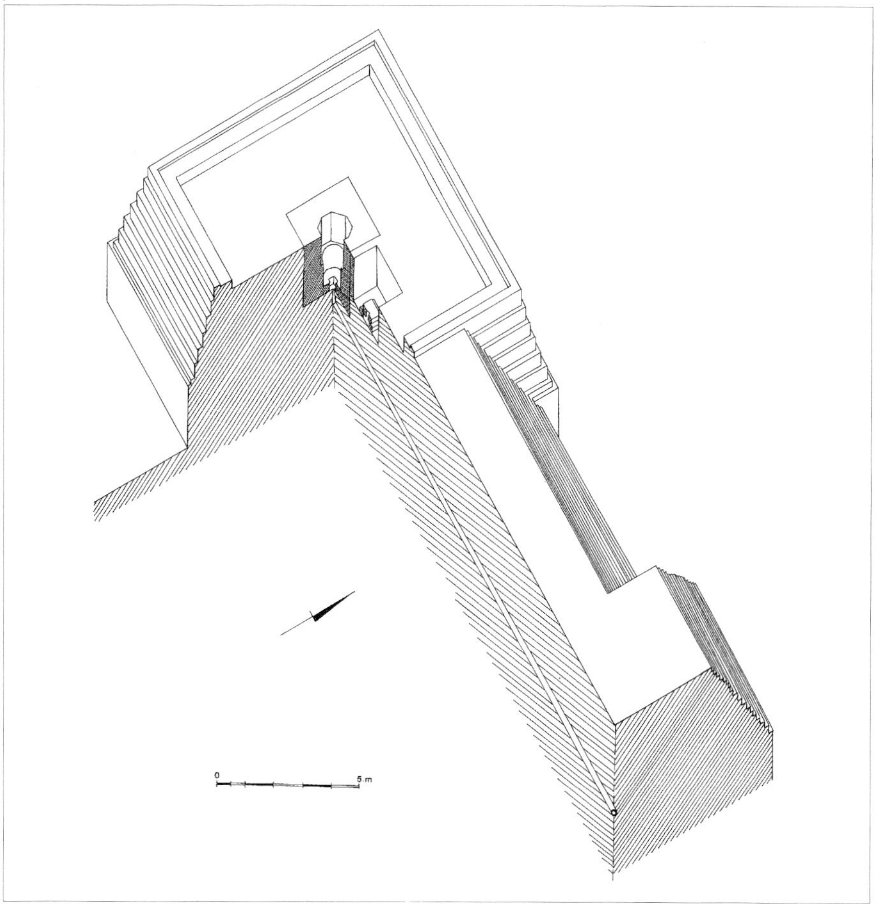

Fig. 3
SR 617. Axonometric section of the central island of the West Mebon

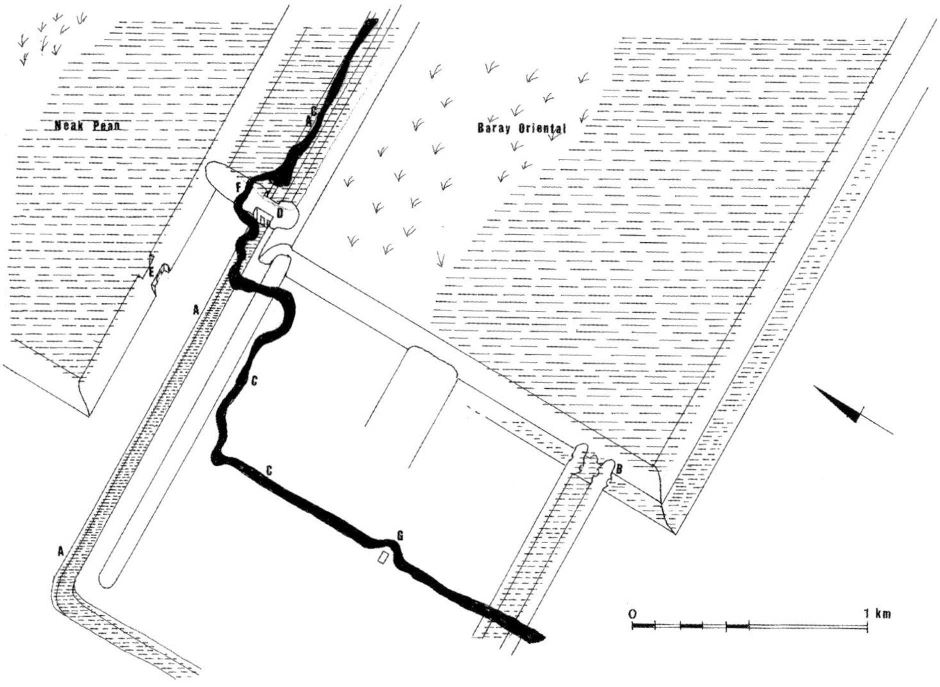

Fig. 4
SR 619. Two channelings of the Siem Reap River:
A first channel
B outlet of the eastern *baray* with use of the resurgence of water
C second channel
D bridge dam on the Siem Reap River
E bridge dam incorporated into the south dike of Neak Pean
F area of break in dike
G area of break in west abutment of the Spean Thma

Baray Oriental = eastern *baray*

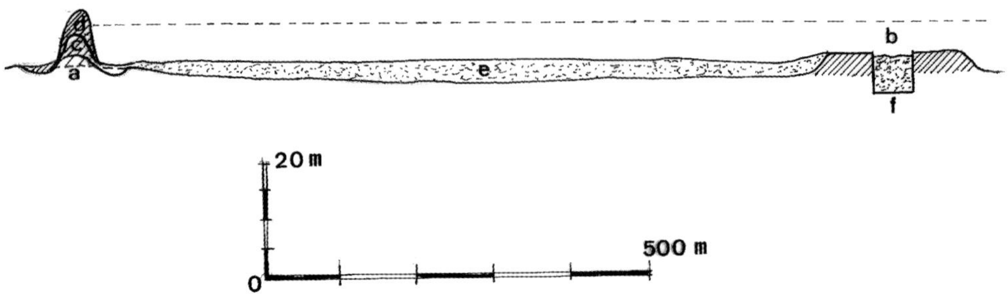

Fig. 5
SR 620. North-south half-section of western *baray*:
a first dike level
b location of central island
c second dike level
d third dike level
e level of maximum silting of the *baray*
f level of silting of the basin of the central island
The vertical and horizontal scales are not proportional

The western *baray* began, in turn, to fill up. To maintain it, the dike was raised and the West Mebon on the central island was submerged (fig. 5).

After Jayavarman VII's victory over the Chams in 1181, the site of Angkor was entirely redesigned. The urban expansion was such that a new wave of settlements entailed large-scale construction. In addition, the irrigation system had deteriorated, particularly the western *baray*, so a new reservoir had to be built, the Neak Pean *baray*. A temple similar in function to the West Mebon, though Buddhist, was installed in its center (figs. 6, 7). This new reservoir was probably fed by a partial diversion of the Siem Reap River, which continued to flow through the perimeter canal north of the western *baray*. Because of the construction of Angkor Thom, the canal leading south was, in turn, rerouted eastward (fig. 4, element c), thereby cutting across the canal distributing the renewed water supply from the eastern *baray*, which by this time had probably been out of service for about ten years.

The Neak Pean *baray* is associated with the temple of Preah Khan, which served early on as a temporary city during the building of Angkor Thom. The latter city, with its ramparts, moats, internal canals, and central temple (the Bayon), was finished about 1190, and the king left Preah Khan to live in his renovated palace.

The Neak Pean *baray* may have proved inadequate, as the western *baray* dike was raised a final time (fig. 5, element d). The reservoir, though never filled beyond two-thirds capacity, was nonetheless considerable in size.

Almost at the same time, the entire east portion of the site was wholly transformed by the construction of two very large complexes, the temples of Ta Prohm and Banteay Kdei. The great basin of Srah Srang was entirely renovated for the occasion (fig. 8). In spite of all the construction, the western *baray* was becoming gradually unusable and the O Klok stream was diverted into the north branch of the perimeter canal, resuming, though somewhat to the west, a course parallel to its original bed. The Neak Pean *baray* was also starting to silt up, and to keep it in use, its protective dike had to be raised. In spite of the raised walls (figs. 6, elements a–b show the small laterite temples in the dike built during its construction), only the south half of the *baray* remained viable.

When the Neak Pean reservoir became unusable, the Khmer completely changed their water policy. No more *baray* were built—the one at Neak

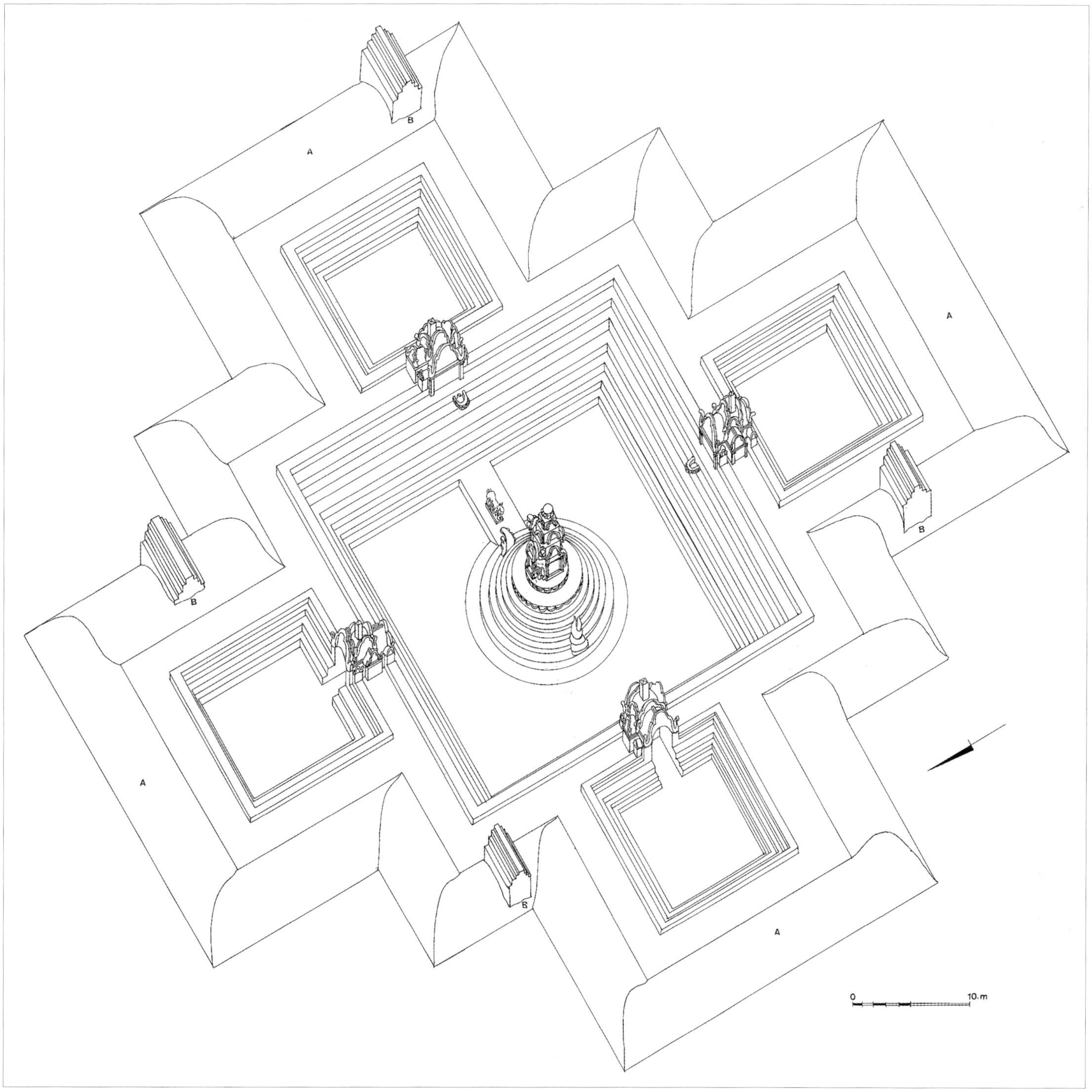

Fig. 6
SR 615. The central temple of the Neak Pean *baray*:
A dike protecting the temple after the rise in the water level
B small laterite temples set on the dike (each opens toward the east)

Fig. 8
Srah Srang

Pean is possibly the last of any size to have been established—but bridges (fig. 9) were used as dams. These fed canals that were dug into the ground rather than raised between dikes. Such a structure can be seen between the south dike of the Neak Pean *baray* and the north dike of the eastern *baray*. A dam was built there, although a bridge allowed the water of the Siem Reap River to pass (see fig. 4, element d). When the bridge was closed, the water was retained between the dikes. The Neak Pean *baray* itself was transformed into a simple dam and a bridge was placed in its south dike (see fig. 4, element e).

At a still undetermined date, but probably around 1250, the dike broke while the bridge was closed (see fig. 4, element f) and a large area to the east of Angkor Thom was flooded. In consequence, the river carved a new channel through the break in the dike, bypassing the bridge.

While the new technique of water management was only exceptionally used at Angkor, the same cannot be said for the kingdom as a whole; many bridges were built that also served as water retainers. The structures were sometimes very large. The one at Spean Praptos near Kompong Kdei, for instance, had a bridge 285 feet (87 m) long and banks faced with stone over a distance of 426 feet (130 m). Such public works clearly called for extensive maintenance, but at the same time they provided a great deal of power to the person in charge of water distribution. One consequence of this new system was the gradual breaking up of the royal power. Small potentates often lacked the resources to perform major repairs to the system and

opposite, Fig. 7
Temple of Neak Pean

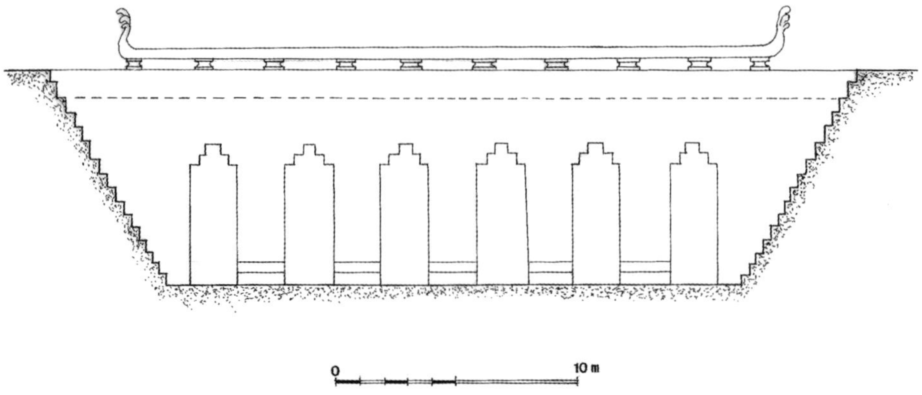

Fig. 9
SR 618. Reconstruction of a thirteenth-century bridge on the road to Angkor at Kompong Svay

therefore neglected it. This was probably one reason for the decline of Khmer civilization.

When the Khmer reoccupied Angkor at the end of the fifteenth century, their first concern again was to provide a source of irrigation. They created a dam at the Siem Reap River by constructing a bridge on the site of an earlier ruined structure. When closed, the new bridge, the Spean Thma, created a reservoir that probably extended as far upriver as the south dike of the Neak Pean *baray*. For reasons similar to those that caused the breaching of the dike in the thirteenth century, the west abutment of the Spean Thma broke and a new flood undoubtedly occurred. When the waters receded, the river did not return to its old course but went around the bridge (see fig. 4, element g), as can still be seen today.

Temple-Mountains and the *Devarāja* Cult

Helen Ibbitson Jessup

A powerful and pervasive symbol, the mountain is linked with myths of origin and perceptions of the Divine in cultures as diverse as Mesopotamian, Hebraic, and Greek, and as geographically separated as Indian and Mayan. The *kahiangan* terraces of the volcanic peaks in Java and Bali are considered holy places, while the Himalayas and Mount Olympus may offer a paradigm for the world of the gods. The mountain may be perceived as a natural phenomenon resonating with supernatural power, as, for example, in Ternate, where the ruler descends into the crater of a volcano to receive mystical guidance. In the temple-mountains of Cambodia, form and meaning drawn from both autochthonous and Indic iconography result in a microcosmic symbol.[1]

As studies of the protohistoric and historic eras in Southeast Asia indicate, the most thoroughly absorbed foreign influences were those resonating closely with existing beliefs.[2] In Cambodia, as in Indonesia, Khmer kings embraced the gods and goddesses of India, and the sacred texts and iconography of Buddhism. The royal temple-mountain, first created by the Khmer in the eighth century and not known in India, was a highly visible means of worshiping adopted deities.

Our knowledge of the society of early Cambodia is incomplete and derives in part from scattered Chinese dynastic records, while another important source is epigraphic evidence from within the Indochinese region.[3] The Chinese designation for Cambodia, Funan, signals the centrality of the mountain in early Khmer history. The word derives from an old Khmer word that the Chinese transliterated *b'iu-nâm*, from *bnaṃ* (or *vnaṃ*), in modern Khmer *phnom* (*bhnaṃ*), meaning "mountain."[4] Kings were called *kurung bnam*, meaning "king of the mountains," and the Chinese referred to "Motan" (Modan), a sacred mountain in Funan on which the god Maheśvara (Śiva) descended without ceasing.[5] It can probably be identified with Ba Phnom, the capital of Funan.[6] Sui dynasty records from before the year 589 refer to a mountain near the city of Lingjiabopo (Ling-kia-po-p'o). The mountain has been identified as Liṅgaparvata (the name for the site of Vat Phu temple in present-day Laos) and the spirit as Bhadreśvara, a reference to Śiva. By the time of the Sui dynasty records, then, the Khmer had incorporated Indian iconography, as can be inferred from the Brahamanistic names, as well as a sacred mountain setting into their national pantheon.[7] This leads to consideration of Mount Meru, one of the most sacred mountains in Hindu iconography.

Meru is the center of the Brahmanistic cosmos and the home of Indra, king of the gods. This central peak is surrounded by four others (including Mandara and Kailāsa) where cities of the gods dominate the heights and where the lower regions are the dwelling places of the *asura*, or anti-gods. Existing at the creation and transcending time and space, Meru is a world pillar, the *axis mundi,* linking the realms of gods, mortals, and creatures of the

1. The mountain may transcend the phenomenological and be abstracted as a microcosmic symbol, in examples ranging from the pyramids of Tikal to a totem embodied in royal regalia. One such, a mountain-shaped fan in the regalia of the Riau-Lingga sultans, is a symbol of the legendary appearance of their ancestors in a white light on the summit of the mountain Si-Guntang.
2. For wide-ranging studies of the cultures of Southeast Asia in the protohistoric and early historic periods see in particular SMITH and WATSON 1979.
3. Any irrefutable new interpretations, like the body of knowledge already existing, depend on the work of archaeologists, philologists, and epigraphers. Art historical interpretation, while offering valuable new insights, necessarily remains speculative without such scientific reinforcement. The most exhaustive study of the area is MALLERET 1959–1963. See also PELLIOT 1903 and Pierre Dupont, "La dislocation du Tchen-la et la formation du Cambodge angkorien (VIIe–IXe siècle)," *BEFEO* 42 (1943–1946), 17–55.
4. CŒDÈS 1968, 36. This seminal work was first published as *Histoire ancienne des états hindouisés d'Extrême-Orient*, Hanoi, 1944.
5. CŒDÈS 1968, 61, quoting *The History of the Southern Qi*. The Sanskrit word for *ku-rung bnam* is *śailarāja*, also literally "king of the mountain." It is interesting to note that the dynasty of eighth-century Java was called Śailendra.
6. BHATTACHARYA 1961, 22.
7. BHATTACHARYA 1961, 21, who also refers to *IC* 3:158.

underworld. Bosch also saw it as the cosmic tree and associated it with the lotus of creation in which Brahmā issued forth from the navel of Viṣṇu.[8] The sun is said to orbit around Meru in a clockwise direction, the basis for *pradakṣiṇā*, the circumambulation of a temple in that direction.[9] The descriptions are drawn from the sacred Brahmanistic texts, the *pūraṇa,* and also from Buddhist texts, and they offer many variants of the nature of this cosmos. One version describes Mount Meru as the central point surrounded by seven concentric continental ranges separated by seven annular oceans. Buddhist interpretation retains the Hindu definition of the realms but posits vertical layers that begin in the regions of the damned and ascend through the realms of animals, spirits, demons, and men, from what has been interpreted as the sphere of *kāmaloka,* the world of desire, to the realm of form, *rūpaloka,* and ultimately to the world of the absence of form, *arūpaloka.*[10]

Although Indra is the formal king of the gods, preeminence in power and primordial causation in the Hindu pantheon is acknowledged to reside in Śiva or Viṣṇu. These gods, who have many aspects, or manifestations, and whose mutual status is asserted according to their sectarian followers, embody two aspects of the tripartite whole, or *trimūrti,* which also includes Brahmā (see 142–143, fig. 1). In Angkor times, particularly during the reign of Sūryavarman II in the twelfth century, Viṣṇu was the deity with whom the monarch most sought to be associated; during the reign of Jayavarman VII, it was the Buddha. For most of Cambodia's history, however, the ruler's right to be considered a *cakravartin,* or spiritual and cosmic sovereign, was established by claiming an identification with Śiva.

The appropriateness of Śiva as the dominant spirit in a cult associated with the mountain is emphasized by some of the names by which this divinity is known. He is Giriśa (he who lies on the mountain); he is Girīśa (lord of the mountain); he is Giritra (protector of the mountain). By extension, his *śakti,* or consort, is Pārvatī (daughter of the mountain). His usual representation is in the form of the *liṅga,* a symbol of power and fertility manifested as a phallic column, abstracted and not yet anthropomorphized. Śiva as emanence in *liṅga* form, the exclusive co-relative for the deity in the earliest days of Brahmanism, is in fact closer to the chthonic symbols that characterize early religions, Brahmanism not excluded. As Bhattacharya has pointed out,[11] among the oldest and most revered of *liṅga* forms in India are the *svāyaṃbhuva-liṅga,* sixty-eight naturally occurring stone outcrops—frequently on mountain tops—that are considered to be natural *liṅga.* The fertility aspect of Śiva is emphasized by their direct penetration of the earth. In Cambodia, Mount Liṅgaparvata was seen as a natural *liṅga.* It was described in a seventh-century inscription at Sambor Prei Kuk as not merely a stone outcrop but also as the top of a mountain.[12]

The emergence of the architectural type known as the temple-mountain seems to have occurred within some decades of the establishment of the *devarāja* cult, but the link sometimes suggested between them is tenuous. According to the evidence of the 1052 inscription of Sdok Kak Thom, the *devarāja* was first instituted in 802 when Jayavarman II sought to establish himself as the supreme monarch of Cambodia.[13]

The inscription of Sdok Kak Thom states that the site of the *devarāja* ceremony was in the mountains of Kulen, then named Mahendraparvata, to which Jayavarman II moved his capital from Hariharālaya, the present site of Roluos, thirteen kilometers southeast of Angkor. The magic rites, which

8. Bosch 1948, 99–104.
9. Mabbett, "Symbolism," 1983, 64–83.
10. This symbolism is illustrated in the ascending terraces of one of the world's most iconographically complex monuments, the cosmic mountain of Borobudur (c. 800), where the reliefs on the lowest level depict the base life of man. This now hidden foot is surmounted by terraces lined with illustrations of the life and enlightenment of the Buddha and by *bodhisattva* stories. These, in turn, give way to circular terraces where pierced *stūpa* enclose meditating Buddha statues. These half-hidden images yield to a summit consisting of a blank *stūpa.*
11. Bhattacharya 1961, 24.
12. Bhattacharya 1961, 77.
13. This long inscription in both Sanskrit and old Khmer, on a stele carved on all four faces, dates from more than two centuries after the event, in 1052. Written by a member of a great Brahman sacerdotal family whose members had been priests of the *devarāja* cult since its inception, the text gives an overview of royal history and the continuous association of the descendants of Śivakaivalya, the first holder of the office, with the Khmer court. Translated first by Aymonier (1901) then by Finot ("L'inscription," 1915, 53–106) and later by Cœdès and Dupont (1943–1946, 57–154), the text is full of genealogical and ritual detail.

The eighth century had seen many challenges to the centrality of power (see Kulke 1986, 1–22, and Vickery 1986, 95–115) and it is not clear what the immediate background of the ruler who called himself Jayavarman II was. Although the text states that the king had come from "Javā" and sought to free the realm from its suzerainty, it is a matter of dispute in current scholarly opinion as to whether "Javā" should be read literally, as Cœdès and others believe (Cœdès and Dupont 1943–1946, note to stanza CXVIII, line 61–64), or whether the gloss of the Sanskrit is mistaken and should be interpreted otherwise, perhaps to mean an unspecified area in the Malay Peninsula or elsewhere (Jacques and Dumont 1990, 43). Whatever the true facts may be, which until further epigraphic evidence is discovered must remain a matter of speculation, it is clear that Jayavarman II, regardless of when he was consecrated (C. Jacques, in "La carrière de Jayavarman II," *BEFEO* 59 [1972], 205–220, posits an accession as early as 770), sought to be established as the unchallenged ruler of the Khmer kingdom.

seem to have included the erection of a *liṅga*, were conducted by a Brahman from Janapada[14] called Hiraṇyadāma. He made the king a *cakravartin*, or universal monarch, by reciting the holy text *Vināśikha,* teaching the rites to Śivakaivalya, a Brahman whose descendants, by the matrilineal line, would fulfill the role of priests of the *devarāja* cult.[15] Hiraṇyadāma dictated, in their entirety, four holy texts[16] in order to initiate the family of Śivakaivalya as the exclusive *purohita* (high priests) of the cult in perpetuity.

Although the temples on Mount Kulen are in a state of ruin, research by Stern and others in 1936 revealed an early temple-mountain, Krus Preah Aram Rong Chen, that may have been the site of the first *devarāja* ceremony. A stepped pyramid with three levels, with an approach by a pathway forty meters long, it was surmounted by a *liṅga* set on a cruciform stone platform.[17] This temple on Mahendraparvata was probably not, however, the first temple-mountain. That distinction almost certainly belongs to the small and today barely comprehensible temple of Prasat Ak Yum, located near the southwest corner of the western *baray* (figs. 1, 2) and having almost identical dimensions to those of Krus Preah Aram Rong Chen. It was apparently buried during the earthworks undertaken for the digging of the *baray*, and was partially cleared only in 1935.

Like Krus Preah Aram Rong Chen, Ak Yum is a three-level stepped pyramid. It seems to have been part of a settlement called Banteay Choeu that was inundated by the reservoir. The base of the lower level, an earthern mound with only the central pathways paved in brick, occupied an area of a hundred square meters and was 2.60 meters high. The second level, approached by five steps on the axes, had a brick core and was forty-two meters square and 2.40 meters high, with towers at the corners. The upper platform, completely of brick, was seventeen meters square and 1.80 meters high and was surmounted by a tower, or *prasat* (*prāsād*). What little decoration remains, in particular on the lintels, resembles the Prei Kmeng style of the second half of the seventh century, with thick garlands and foliate pendants. The dated inscriptions on the jambs on the doorways (the south face of the east doorway and the east face of the south doorway) seem to correspond with 717 and 704 respectively, which would place this building almost a century before the Mahendraparvata temple.[18]

The most puzzling feature of Ak Yum is its subterranean chamber, 2.6 meters square and about the same height, making it almost a perfect cube. It lies below the 12.25-meter shaft under the central point in the sanctuary of the upper level and is unique in Khmer architecture. The iconography of the deep shaft that is a typical feature of central sanctuaries in Cambodia probably invokes the *axis mundi* image, as the temple then penetrates both sky and earth and thus exists in all three worlds, but the function of the chamber is unknown.[19]

Despite their modest dimensions, Krus Preah Aram Rong Chen and Ak Yum are undeniably stepped pyramids and also prototypes of the temple-mountain, quite distinct from the single *prasat* or triple-grouped *prasat* on the same level that typify previous temples. They offer little, however, to prepare the student of Khmer architecture for the next example of the type, the enormous and iconographically complex temple of the Bakong dating from 881 during the reign of Indravarman I (877–889) (fig. 3). As has been mentioned above, the center of the Khmer kingdom had returned to Hariharālaya before the death of Jayavarman II in 835. His successors seem to have attempted no

14. Janapada, according to Cœdès (Cœdès and Dupont 1943–1946, note to lines 70–77), was probably Prasat Khna in Mlu Prei province.
15. We know the office continued at least until the date of the Sdok Kak Thom stele, see note 13 above.
16. Apart from the *Vināśikha*, these were the *Sammoha*, the *Nayottara*, and the *Sirascheda*, all apparently Tantric (Finot, "L'inscription," 1915, 57). These were described as "the four faces of Tumburu," Tumburu being equated with Śiva, and are thought to be equated with the four cardinal points, thus invoking protection in all directions and guaranteeing the role of the *cakravartin* (Bhattacharya 1961, 50).
17. Stern, "Le style," 1938, 144.
18. Inscriptions found at temple sites are often older than the temple itself, being reused elements from previous constructions, but Ak Yum has yielded in addition a possibly seventh-century inscription as well as bronze sculptures from the seventh or eighth century.
19. The valuable information summarized above is succinctly presented by Bruguier (1994, 273–296).

Fig. 1
Prasat Ak Yum, c. seventh to eighth century. Present vestiges

Fig. 2
Prasat Ak Yum, c. seventh to eighth century. The excavations in 1935

significant construction, but in less than a century Khmer architecture progressed from modest brick temples to the magnificent and complex structure of the Bakong. By the ninth century, then, three clearly defined architectural models were known: the single tower sanctuary, the temple comprising several towers on a common platform, and the temple-mountain.

The five-tiered pyramid of the Bakong, the first monumental temple-mountain, is surrounded by three walled enclosures and two moats that are cut by gateways framed by *gopura* structures. Several subsidiary buildings and eight significant *prasat*—their lintels and pediments offering exceptionally fine relief carving—surround the lowest level of the pyramid, which has a base measuring sixty-seven by sixty-five meters. The levels rise steeply, and the steps on all four sides are framed by pedestals with guardian lions. Massive elephants guard the corners of the first three levels, while the fourth carries twelve small sanctuary towers. The central tower, rising at fourteen meters above ground level from the highest platform, is a twelfth-century replacement of the original structure (fig. 4).

The simplest of the three temple types described above, the single tower sanctuary, was close in type to the original concepts expressed in early Khmer temples. Although its importance as an independent foundation declined, it continued to play a prominent role in the complexes associated with temple-mountains, as can been seen in the eight *prasat* that surround the Bakong.[20] The second type, a combination of *prasat* on a common platform, is most notably exemplified by the 879 complex of Preah Ko at Roluos, with two rows of three *prasat*, and by the 893 group of Lolei, which has two rows of two towers. The third type, the temple-mountain, is by far the most complex both architecturally and iconographically. In two wide-ranging and detailed studies, Stern has linked these types to a sequence of three architectural undertakings that were deemed necessary to fulfill the spiritual obligations and procedures of most Khmer monarchs.[21] He has defined three architectural projects: public works, such as reservoirs, roads, hospitals, and shelters for pilgrims; towers, frequently multiple, dedicated to both male and female sovereign and nonsovereign ancestors of the monarch; and a state temple to establish the deity with whom the king wished to be identified (the deity, most frequently in the form of a *liṅga*, was enshrined at the top of a temple-mountain).[22]

20. The number eight is significant in the iconography of Śiva, referring to the *aṣṭamūrti*, or eight manifest forms of Śiva: earth, water, fire, wind, ether, sun, moon, and the sacrificer. The spiritual importance of these aspects has been memorably captured in the poetry of the great Indian poet of the early fifth century, Kālidasā, in the benediction of the play *Sakuntala*:

The water that was first created
the sacrifice-bearing fire
the time-setting sun and moon,
audible space that fills the universe,
what men call nature, the source of all seeds,
the air that living creatures breathe—
through his eight embodied forms,
may Lord Śiva come to bless you!

MILLER 1984, 7.

21. STERN 1934, 611–616, and 1947–1950, 649–688.

22. It is tempting to see these ritual acts interpreted in terms of power plays: the engagement of the public through structures serving the common weal; the affirmation of legitimacy through structures placing the ruler in the context of a potent genealogy; the claim to universal prowess through the invocation of the spiritual might of the *devarāja*, the association of the earthly monarch with the divine.

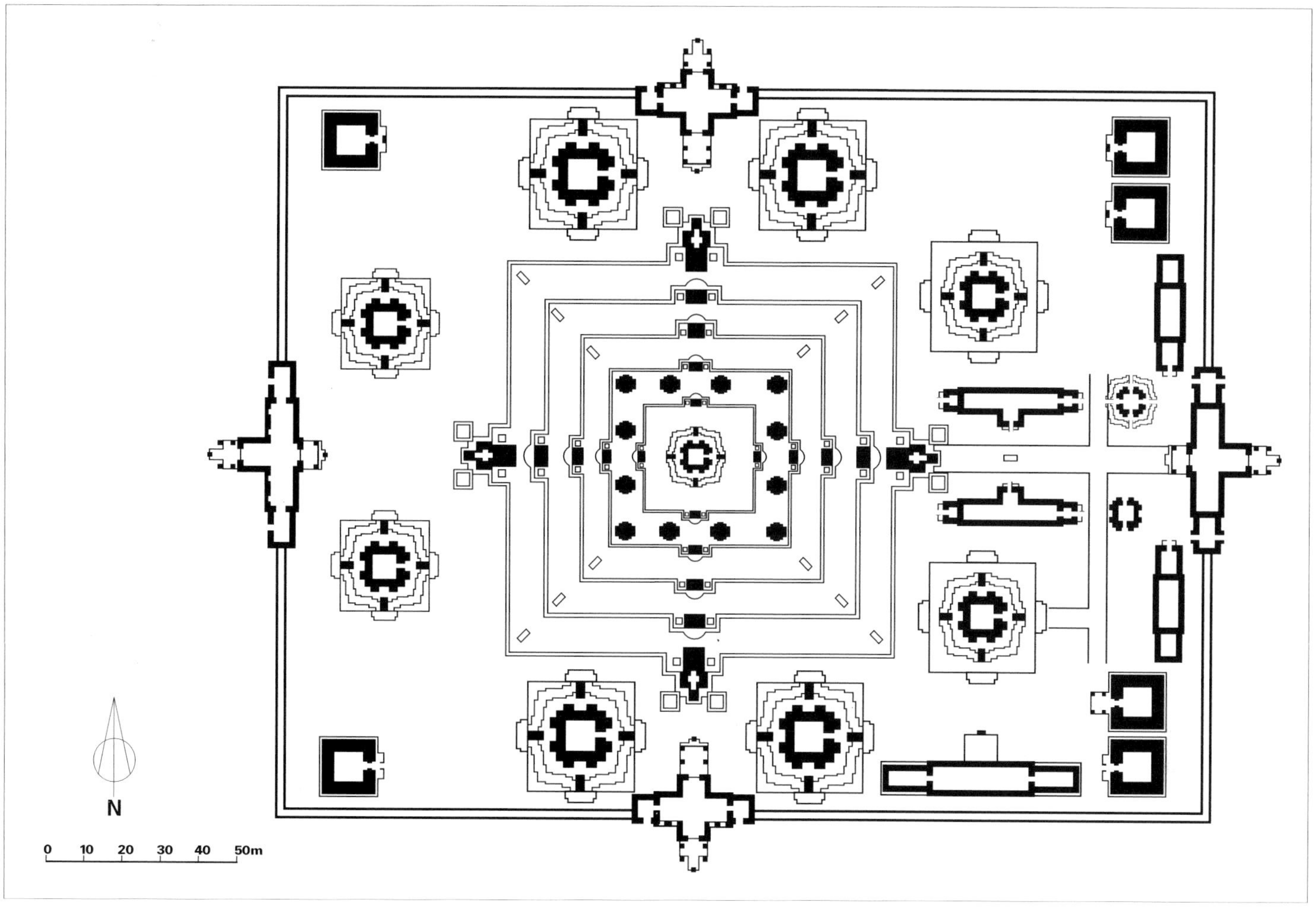

Fig. 3
Plan of the Bakong (881).
First enclosure

Probably no topic has provoked more discussion and disagreement among scholars of Cambodian culture than that of the *devarāja*. Although the conclusions are tenuous, the subject is so frequently referred to that it must be addressed.[23] While we know from the inscription of Sdok Kak Thom of the inauguration of the *devarāja*, of its association with divine blessing, legitimacy, and authority for the ruler and of the importance of its cult, it is impossible to be certain exactly what the *devarāja* really was. While the cult is popularly equated with the concept of deification of the living ruler, no inscription specifically expresses it in those terms. For Stern[24] the cult was a ritual centering on a *liṅga* bearing the name of the king with the suffix *"-īśvara"* denoting an association of the monarch with Śiva. For Cœdès it was a unique *liṅga*, to be established anew by each monarch, that could be moved from place to place and was not necessarily associated with the summit of a mountain or a temple-mountain.[25] For Bhattacharya the ceremony deified the ruler in making him a portion of Śiva by strengthening the inner essence (*moi subtil*, or *sūkṣmāntarātman*) and forging a triumvirate between *liṅga*, king, and the officiating Brahman.[26]

It is possible that an existing Khmer belief preceded Indian influences and that the Old Khmer phrase *kamrateṅ jagat ta rāja* (God who is king) required the Sanskrit translation *devarāja*. The scarcity of references does

23. See MABBETT 1969, 202–223, and KULKE 1978.
24. STERN 1947–1950, 615.
25. Introductory note C, CŒDÈS and DUPONT 1943–1946.
26. BHATTACHARYA 1961, 28.

Fig. 4
Bakong. The pyramid from the east-northeast

nothing to dispel the uncertainty.[27] The inscription of Sdok Kak Thom lists the kings between Jayavarman II and Sūryavarman I (1002–1050) who were served by the family of Śivakaivalya and states where the *devarāja* resided during each ruler's reign, from which we may assume that whether or not the *devarāja* meant an object, a ceremony, the identification of the ruler with Śiva, or a combination of all three, its presence was continuous and its importance undeniable. Further epigraphic evidence may clarify this fascinating but as yet poorly understood topic.

The creation of the three categories of construction defined by Stern—public works, ancestor temple, and state temple-mountain—remained a royal preoccupation even after written evidence of the *devarāja* cult ceased in the mid-eleventh century. Just as Indravarman I created the reservoir called Indratatāka and built the ancestor temple of Preah Ko and the temple-mountain of the Bakong, and as Indravarman's successor, Yaśovarman I, created the vast eastern *baray*, built the ancestor temple of Lolei and the temple-mountain at the top of Mount Bakheng (the first construction of Khmer royalty at Angkor), so did monarchs of a later age establish a similar range of projects.

In the three centuries between the construction of the Bakong in 881 and of the Bayon in the last part of the reign of Jayavarman VII, the rulers of Cambodia built at least nine more temple-mountains.[28] The first to be dedicated after the Bakong was Bakheng, center of the new city (Yaśodharapura, established by Yaśovarman I in about 900), which crowned the natural hill of the same name dominating the area. Even more complex in both ground plan (fig. 5) and cosmological meaning than the Bakong, this towering monument adopts the same quincunx arrangement of towers set on a platform on the highest of the five levels of the pyramid. The five peaks are symbolic of the holy Mount Meru and its four surrounding mountains, the four

27. See Sahai 1970, 43, for a summary of the textual references to the *devarāja* and *kamrateṅ jagat ta rāja*.
28. Several temples at Preah Pithu, to name just one other site, could also be considered as temple-mountains, though no specific connection is known with a particular monarch and though they are not usually mentioned in discussions of temple-mountains. One could also cite the temple of Phnom Chisor to the south of Phnom Penh.

directions of space also being invoked. The five levels of the pyramid support sixty small towers and its base a further forty-four, for a total of one hundred and nine, including the sanctuary tower.[29]

The next temple-mountain to be built was outside Angkor, at the time when Jayavarman IV and his son Harṣavarman ruled the kingdom from a capital established at Koh Ker (Chok Gargyar) between 921 to 928 and approximately 944.[30] Distinguished by a proportionately high single central sanctuary tower, the chief monument of Koh Ker, Prasat Thom, was fifty-five meters square at its base and dedicated (between 921 and 928) to the divinity Tribhuvaneśvara. With the accession of Rājendravarman (944–968) the capital was reestablished in Yaśodharapura. The new monarch, who was more concerned than most Khmer kings about his genealogy,[31] instigated the construction of not one but two temple-mountains.[32] His *devarāja* Rājendreśvara was installed in the five-tower pyramid of the East Mebon temple, which was consecrated in 952 on an island in the eastern *baray*. Pre Rup, built to the south of the *baray*, was consecrated in 961 (fig. 6) and housed the divine image, or *liṅga*, Rājendrabhadreśvara.

Why two temple-mountains were constructed during the same reign is a question that scholars have not so far been able to answer, though Stern has suggested that the Mebon might have been considered, in defiance of the usual practice of reserving pyramid structures for temple-mountains, as an ancestor temple.[33] He also raised the possibility of Pre Rup's being a funerary

29. The scholar Filliozat noted the numerology of the towers of the Bakheng, suggesting that the thirty-three towers on each of its four sides can be equated with the thirty-three gods (the *Trayastrimsa*) who are the inhabitants of Meru according to Indian belief. He also sees the ensemble as symbolizing the cosmic revolution around the polar axis represented by the central tower (see FILLIOZAT 1947–1950, 532). The image of the towers is not straightforward, in fact, and the impression of thirty-three towers would have depended on ignoring the corner towers that would have formed part of the contiguous side, so the theory is not altogether convincing.
30. 928 is the date when Jayavarman IV officially became king of the realm, after the death of his nephews Harṣavarman I and Īśānavarman II who had continued to rule in Yaśodharapura, but he had been ruling what must have been a breakaway polity from 921.
31. BRIGGS 1951, 123–125.
32. Baksei Chamkrong (948), a single-tower pyramid whose proportions, albeit on a far smaller scale, recall those of Prasat Thom, was completed during Rājendravarman's reign, but it had in fact been initiated in 921 by Harṣavarman I, son of Yaśovarman I, and did not serve as a temple-mountain.
33. STERN 1947–1950, 676.

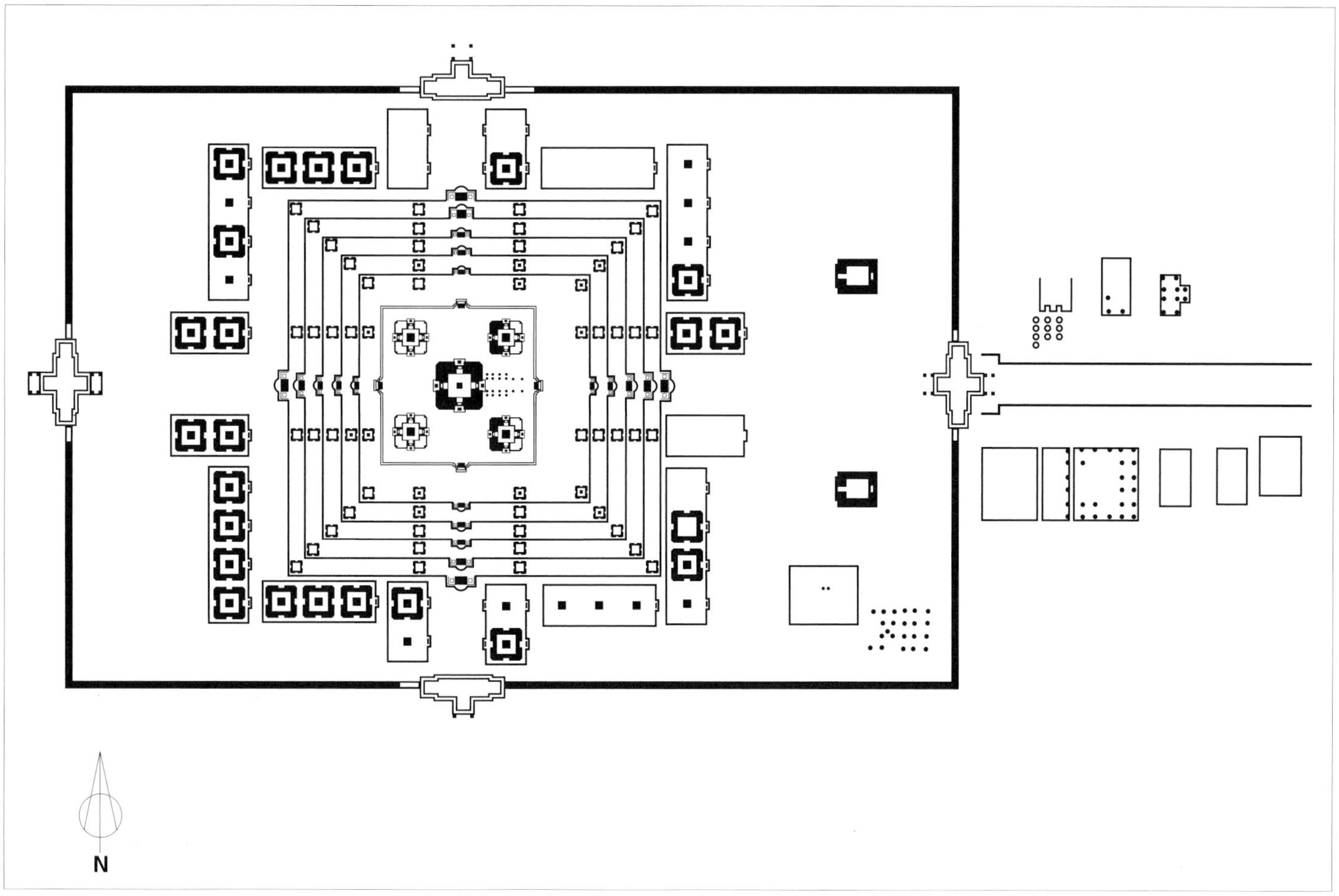

Fig. 5
Plan of the Bakheng. Early tenth century

temple as well as the sanctuary for the *liṅga* Rājendrabhadreśvara.[34] Scholars concede, however, that the temples were used both before and after the king's death, thus precluding their exclusive use as funerary monuments.

Pre Rup is a quincunx structure on a larger scale than the East Mebon.[35] Built of reddish sandstone, it is flanked by nine long narrow buildings that seem to prefigure the surrounding galleries of later monuments. Its coloration enables the temple to refract the light of the setting sun with a warm glow that provides one of the most indelible memories of Angkor. Both temples are distinguished by the exceptionally refined carving of the lintels and pediments as well as the *dvārapāla* (guardian) figures sculpted in the niches of the sanctuary towers.

Ta Keo, begun toward the end of the tenth century in the reign of Jayavarman V (968–1001), is almost entirely faced in sandstone and offers the first example of an elevated gallery, though its function remains a mystery as there is no way of entering it. With five levels of considerably varying height, the pyramid has exceptionally high and shallow steps and consequently has a particularly steep ascent. These proportions, combined with the careful diminution of scale of the steps, lend this monument a massive dignity that makes it one of the most imposing of all the temple-mountains. Though the central tower is taller than the four surrounding ones, the five towers appear similar in height because they are set closer together than usual. Lacking relief decoration and the detailing of the summit towers, Ta Keo, with a name variously translated as "the ancestor Keo" or, in the form Prasat Keo, "crystal tower," is generally considered to be unfinished, possibly because Jayavarman V died before its completion. No record is known of the dedication of a chief image in the central sanctuary and it is unclear whether or not the summit towers were constructed by his successor. The simplicity of its planar surfaces (whether owing to omission or design), and the clarity of its design are factors in the gleaming appearance of this temple-mountain (figs. 7, 8).

After the death of Jayavarman V, the brief reign of Udayādityavarman I was followed by a contest for the throne between Jayavīravarman and Sūryavarman I (1002–1050) that continued for almost a decade. After the consolidation of his authority, however, Sūryavarman constructed a palace with fortified walls. Inside it he reconstructed an existing temple to create a small temple-mountain, the Phimeanakas, that is considered to have been a royal chapel (fig. 9). According to the Chinese delegate Zhou Daguan, who visited Angkor in 1296 and 1297, the Phimeanakas was also the probable site for the ritual allegedly performed every night by the Khmer monarch. To ensure the continuity of the kingdom, the ruler was obliged to couple with a *nāgīnī*, a princess of the kingdom of the *nāga* who took the form of a woman.

The huge western *baray*—more than eight kilometers long by two kilometers wide—might have been dug during the reign of Sūryavarman I, or was perhaps either constructed or completed by Udayādityavarman II. The great temple-mountain of the Baphuon, with a foundation laid in about 1060, was constructed as the state temple of the latter monarch (figs. 10, 11). Approached by an elegant causeway, the Baphuon has magnificent gateways and is surrrounded by galleries on three of its levels. Its present dismantled state, a consequence of anastylosis begun before the devastation of the 1970s and later, prevents a clear reading of the structure of the Baphuon today. The inscription of Lovek tells us, however, that the king, knowing that a mountain of gold (*Hemadri-Meru*) rises in the middle of the

34. STERN (1947–1950, 677) makes the suggestion that the name of the temple, Pre Rup, which means "turn the body" (a practice associated with funeral rites), reinforces the possibility of its being a funerary monument. It is interesting to note that the practice of turning the body still exists in the cremation ceremonies of Bali.
35. For dimensions of the temple-mountains, see GLAIZE 1944.

Fig. 6
Pre Rup (961). View from the south-southwest

Fig. 7
Ta Keo. One of the corner tower sanctuaries of the quincunx

Fig. 8
Ta Keo. Late tenth to early eleventh century. View from the west

Fig. 9
Phimeanakas. First half of the eleventh century, the pyramid perhaps earlier. View from the east

dwelling of the gods, created a mountain of gold (*Svarnadri*) in the center of his own city.

Ankgor Vat, the supreme manifestation of the temple-mountain, occupies an area 1,300 by 1,500 meters. Its complex but perfectly proportioned plan and its magnificent vertical ordering create a harmonious whole that has never been surpassed as the architectural expression of a microcosmos. Detailed analysis of its structure and iconography have been presented in numerous publications and it is not feasible even to summarize them in this essay. In no other temple are the delineations of hierarchy or the spiritual meaning of space clearer. The successive levels are defined with distinctive spatial transitions—from gallery to courtyard, from courtyard to sweep of steps, from steps to sanctuary—that establish each stage yet articulate it with the next. In no other monument is the visitor more acutely aware of the interplay of light and shadow. Solid structures are articulated with open areas through the mediation of elements like windows, balusters, and gallery columns that span the transition from mass to space. The intimacy of covered halls alternates with the limitless vision of the open sky. Finally, after the climber's emergence into the generous and brilliant expanse of the upper terrace, the ultimate ascent leads to the mysterious dark sanctuary, protected on all sides by the crown of interlaced matter and void, with columns and balusters punctuating the exterior and interior spaces. Throughout, plane and mass are highlighted by masterpieces of

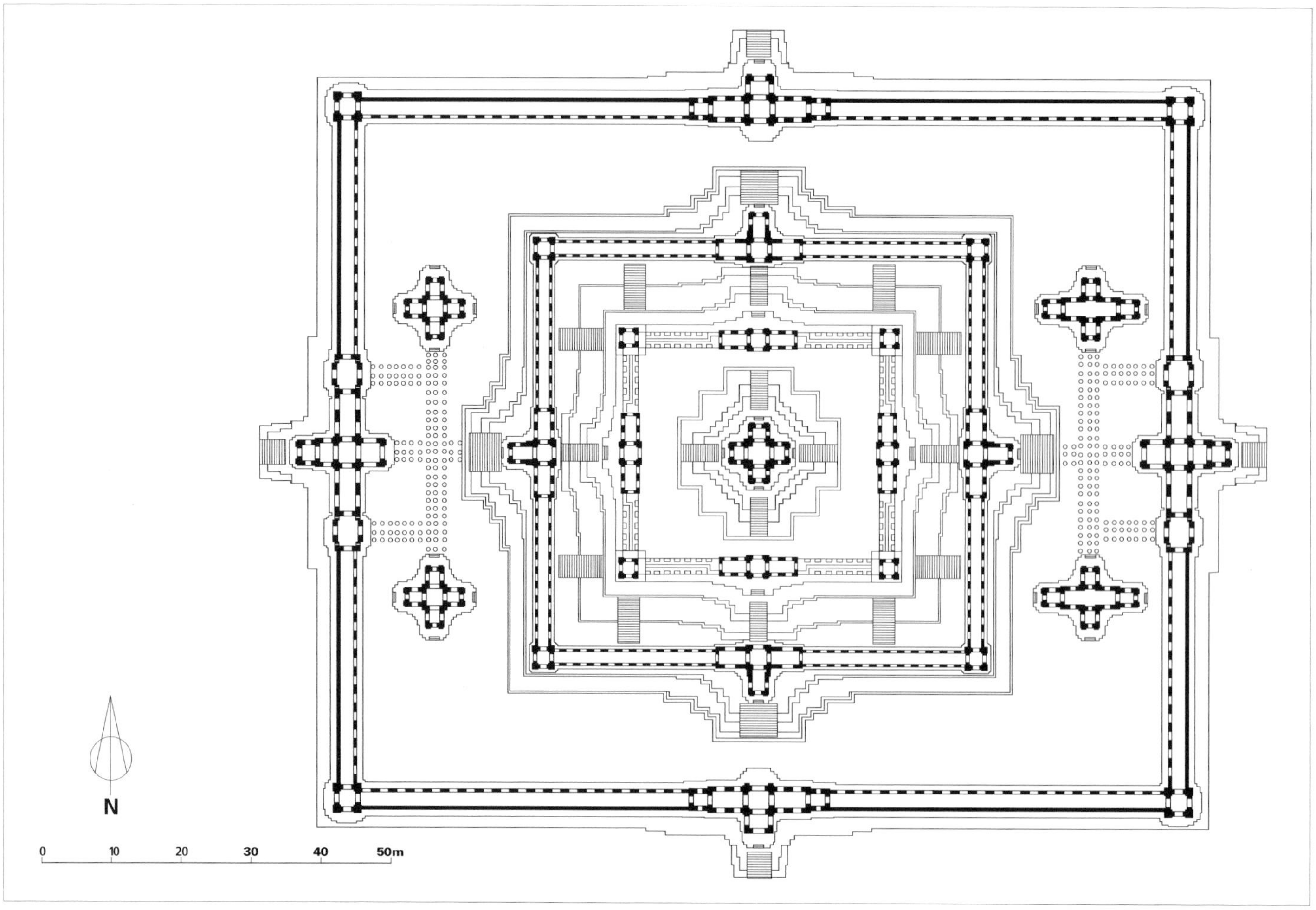

Fig. 10
Plan of the Baphuon. Third quarter of the eleventh century

Fig. 11
The Baphuon. Third quarter of the eleventh century. View from the east

Opposite, Fig. 12
Angkor Vat. First half of the twelfth century. Aerial view

Fig. 13
Angkor Vat. First half of the twelfth century. View from the northwest (taken from Phnom Bakheng)

relief carving. Though figures and scenes are individually memorable, they are always integrated into the rhythm of a flawless spatial modulation.

It has been argued that Angkor Vat's orientation to the west suggests that it was intended as a funerary monument, but whether for the mortal remains of a king or for relics deemed holy through some perceived connection with a divinity is a question that has vexed scholars for many years.[36] Some suggest that Angkor Vat and other Viṣṇuite temples at Angkor open to the west because that is the direction dominated by Viṣṇu.[37] Whatever might have been its designation, no other structure so perfectly embodies the majesty of the celestial mountain, the abode of the gods, as this apogée of Khmer architecture (figs. 12, 13).

Probably no Khmer monarch more abundantly fulfilled the triple royal architectural responsibility than Jayavarman VII (1181–c. 1218). He was famous for the large number of roads, bridges, hospitals, and pilgrims' rest-houses constructed on his orders throughout his extensive realm. His ancestor homage inspired not one but two huge ancestor temples. The first, Ta Prohm, was dedicated in 1186 to the honor of his mother, identified with Prajñāpāramitā, and possibly to two other people, one of whom was almost certainly his guru, according to stanza XXXVII of the inscription. Preah Khan, the second, followed in 1191 and was dedicated to the king's father. His third obligation was dedicated as the overpowering temple-mountain of the Bayon. In a highly complex maze of galleries, terraces, and chapels, ecumenical and syncretic representations of gods of all cults and creeds proliferate in this Buddhist monument under the imposing gaze of the face sculpted on all sides of the myriad towers (fig. 14). The identity of the face is uncertain, though both Brahmā and Avalokiteśvara have been suggested. A similar stern but benign face, whose identity is uncertain, also looks down from the gates of the royal city, Angkor Thom.[38] Whether or not there was an association of Jayavarman VII with the Buddha similar to that of previous monarchs with Śiva (or possibly of Sūryavarman II with Viṣṇu) remains a speculation.

The date and the complex plan of the Bayon challenged interpretation for many decades, but scholars today agree that is was built during the reign of Jayavarman VII in the last years of the twelfth century or the early years of the thirteenth as the microcosmic center of the city of Angkor Thom. It was the last of the great temple-mountains. Although lacking the imposing mass of Bakong or Ta Keo and the grand perfection and microcosmic clarity of Angkor Vat, the Bayon, with its clustered towers, enigmatic countenances, and lively and historically fertile reliefs, remains perhaps the most mysterious and intriguing of all Khmer temples.

36. Among others, see Cœdès 1933, 303–309; Przyluski 1933, 326–332; Bosch 1932, 12–17; Soekmono 1995, 33–50.
37. Possibly the most far-reaching analysis yet attempted of the symbolic and astronomical significance of Angkor Vat is presented in Mannikka 1996.
38. The interpretation of Boisselier (pp. 117–120) is at the moment the most convincing.

Fig. 14
The Bayon. Late twelfth to early thirteenth century. Aerial view

The Meaning of Angkor Thom

Jean Boisselier

In 1177, the armies of Champa captured Angkor, probably thanks to a surprise attack. The rivalry between Khmer and Cham rulers, of which this was just another episode, had flared up sporadically on the question of dynastic claims, probably since the time of Funan, and at least since the contested succession, in the seventh century, to King Īśānavarman I, ruler of Zhenla and founder of Īśānapura, known today as Sambor Prei Kuk.

The fall of Angkor in 1177 had dramatic consequences for the Khmer, though more on moral, religious, and political levels than the material—evidence of destruction during this period is virtually nonexistent. And while the Khmer ruler, a usurper, also met his death at this time, what contributed most to the ruin of Angkor was the fact that the entire mystical and religious framework on which Khmer power rested had simultaneously been destroyed.

The political system had been initiated by Jayavarman II on Phnom Kulen at the beginning of the ninth century, to ensure the entire sovereignty and inviolability of Kambujadeśa. His successors extended and perfected it, in particular Yaśovarman I, the original founder of Angkor in the late ninth century, and Rājendravarman II, who restored the city in the mid-tenth century. And this system, which had been doggedly improved over the centuries, and which linked the power of the Angkor state to the inviolability of its capital, now lay in ruins. For the enemy, whoever he was, to overrun the capital demonstrated the system's fallibility, and the power of Angkor crumbled with it.

It was on Jayavarman VII (1181–c. 1218) that the glory devolved, not of repairing the unspecified damage but of annulling the smallest effects of a degrading defeat by building a new power that was nevertheless totally linked to the past, a kingdom more powerful and extensive than ever before.

To accomplish, in record time, this real tour de force, Jayavarman VII did not attempt to restore what could not spiritually be reborn from its ruin. On the contrary, allowing the predominant Brahmanic tradition to pass into the background, he developed an entirely new spiritual framework; to do this he drew on the Buddhist cosmology and, especially, the concepts of Mahāyāna Buddhism. The royal family and the king himself were zealous followers of this religion, as is known from the inscriptions.

The king's efforts would therefore focus on showing the world (that is, Southeast Asia) that he was truly a *cakravartin*, or universal ruler, by extending his conquests to the farthest reaches and erecting religious foundations in every corner of his empire. Jayavarman's feverish construction program is often wrongly taxed with megalomania; in fact, he was simply following the example of Aśoka, the model for all Buddhist rulers.

Jayavarman's other priority was to build a capital for himself that would resemble the capital of Indra, the model for any sovereign who ruled over other kings, as Indra did over the Thirty-three Gods. The capital would rise up in the center of the kingdom just as Indra's capital rose from the summit of Mount Sumeru, an image echoed in the inscriptions: "Kambujadeśa, like to the heavens. . . . " In consequence, there is a second parallel to complement the first. Jayavarman VII, identifying himself with Indra, rules over a Kambujadeśa that is identical with Mount Sumeru and is the center of the world.

The new capital was Angkor Thom-Mahānagara, a city more than two miles square (3.3 km), surrounded by a high wall and a wide moat, with five monumental gateways. It is centered around a vast temple, the Bayon, the originality of which has long been enigmatic, and the royal palace, which is intentionally the only element to link the new capital to the first city of Angkor. It is curious that while local tradition nourished the Buddhist texts, and always recognized the essence of the complex as a scheme based on cosmology and *jāṭaka* texts, scholars and Western visitors, surprised and dazzled by the astonishing symbiosis of forest and deserted temples, have noted only its romantic and enchanted aspect, constructing at will the most astonishing interpretations to account for it—as though they were prevented by their reeling senses from examining the pertinent Buddhist texts and inscriptions.

In fact, Angkor Vat, that magisterial production of the early twelfth century, has drawn the greater share of interest since at least the seventeenth century. More classically perfect, more accessible, it also proved more easily adapted to Theravādin Buddhism and would maintain its activities despite the abandonment of the capital.

Yet while Angkor Vat may be considered the Cartesian masterpiece of Khmer architecture, Angkor Thom is incontestably the greatest expression of its genius. It offers, in three dimensions and on the scale of an entire nation, a material embodiment of Buddhist cosmology, a concept none but painters would dare try to represent.

No city, even among the most admired in India, Sri Lanka, the Indochinese Peninsula, or Indonesia, comes close to the inspired whole conceived by Jayavarman VII. Angkor Thom combines a profound knowledge of Buddhist texts with an exceptional capacity for adaptation and draws on a veritable genius for architectural sculpture.

Angkor Thom is not an architectural "miracle" as the West has conceived it, nor is it a gallery of "edifying" images of the kind that developed in the Christian world. Truly it is the world of the gods sprung rising up into the very heart of ancient Cambodia, superhuman yet without excess.

And what does Angkor Thom represent?

Their allusions to topical history aside, the inscriptions clearly state that the new capital is the city of Indra (with whom the king identifies) and of the Thirty-three Gods (identified with the princes and provincial governors under the king's rule), consisting of its royal palace, pleasure parks, and Assembly Hall of the Gods, which is none other than the Bayon. (This interpretation is not my assertion but one affirmed in the epigraphy, to the detriment of countless fantastic and farfetched theories.)

It is at the Bayon, the Assembly Hall of the Gods, that the gods gather together on certain days, while Brahmā, assuming the "ever young" form of Gandharva Pañcaśikha, multiplies his image to honor each of them.

No more faithful illustration, paintings included, has ever been realized of the description left by inspired visionaries. No less surprising is the enclosure of this city, intended to be unassailable and inviolable, on the model of Indra's city.

Fig. 1
The Bayon. Late twelfth to early thirteenth century. View from the northwest

Here we have the faithful illustration of a text which we may summarize briefly, putting it in the context of certain "historical" observations.

When Śakra (Sakka), in the form of Indra, was born in the Heaven of the Thirty-three Gods, that is, as their head or ruler, he discovered that there lived on the summit of Mount Sumeru both gods and *asura*. Deploring this promiscuity, he decided to rid his kingdom of the troublesome *asura*. Accordingly, he made them drunk and threw them down to the foot of Mount Sumeru.

The *asura* eventually found themselves in a kingdom at the very bottom of the mountain, one that was, in fact, the mirror image of the Heaven of the Thirty-three Gods. A tree grew there that reminded the *asura* whenever it flowered of the wonderful tree that grew in Indra's heaven. And it provoked in them the desire to recapture their ancient kingdom. They launched an assault on Sumeru "like a host of termites climbing up a pillar. . . . "

From this point in the story on there is a clear analogy to the attack of the Cham armies, represented by the *asura*, against the first city of Angkor, represented by Indra's city. It would inform the symbolism of the gateways at Angkor Thom, and also in large part the symbolism of Preah Khan at Angkor, whose highly complex meaning is fortunately illuminated for us by its foundation stele.

But to return to the *asura*, their attack made great headway, thanks to its element of surprise. The gods retreated in confusion and might have lost their kingdom entirely had it not been for a lucky accident.

When defeated on the ocean, Indra, mounted on his chariot, retreated. The gods collided with the young *garuḍa* who flit about in their forests. The chariot was not only stopped, it was driven back in the direction it had come and the *asura*, believing that a counterattack was under way armed with fresh reinforcements, now retreated in disorder. Unexpectedly, Indra had gained a complete victory. In commemoration there magically appeared the Palace of Indra's Victory, or Vaijayanta Prāsāda, which is Preah Khan at Angkor, "erected on the site of the victory." The great *garuḍa* on its surrounding wall recall the important part they played in the victory.

To forestall any further surprise attacks, Indra decided to establish a permanent guard from the denizens of Mount Sumeru and its neighboring realms. This accounts for the astonishing composition of gates of Angkor Thom, rather than any of the variously seductive hypotheses once proposed, the best known and least acceptable of which is that they represent the Churning of the Sea of Milk.

Both Theravāda and Mahāyāna texts—which differ on this subject only in the smallest details—relate that the task of guarding the city was assigned to a particular class of *nāga*, two families of *yakṣa* (which must not be confused with the *asura*, despite the fact that some are of terrifying appearance, for how could such irreconcilable enemies as the *deva* and *asura* be placed side by side?), and the Four Great Kings who were the guardians of the cardinal points. The guard was completed by images of Indra himself, holding the lightning in his hand and, of course, mounted on a three-headed elephant.

The great virtue of the *śilpin* and those who directed them is that they were able to take this material and transform it into the most remarkable monumental whole inspired by the Indian tradition: the *nāga* and the two families of *yakṣa*, one on either side of the causeway; the colossal faces of the Four Great Kings at each of the gates (all have the gift of ubiquity), each one facing the direction opposite him (according to the texts) to prepare for any eventuality; and the images of Indra on his three-headed elephant, Airāvata, at the corners of each of the five gates as ever-wakeful sentinels.

This quick sketch of the symbolism of Angkor Thom, without texts, is inadequate to express the greatness of this much-misunderstood art. The architects and sculptors of the reign of Jayavarman VII were undeniably possessed of genius (though there are often signs in their work of excessive haste), and those who provided them their inspiration possessed a deep knowledge of the cosmological treatises. Together they joined to create an interpretation of that cosmology which has never been equaled or surpassed.

Address given by Professor Jean Boisselier at the Siam Society, Bangkok, Thailand, on 17 November 1987.

Fig. 2
Angkor Thom. South gate. Late twelfth to early thirteenth century

Fig. 1
Banteay Srei (967-968). View of the first two enclosures from the east-northeast

The Marvel of Banteay Srei

Thierry Zéphir

The temple of Banteay Srei (fig. 1) is certainly one of the most celebrated and beautiful temples of the Angkor region, but the reader may well ask why it merits an exclusive note when temples as sumptuous and important as Angkor Vat or the Bayon are only evoked in the general course of the essays that constitute the catalogue's introduction. To this perfectly legitimate question we respond that the generous loans of the Royal Government of Cambodia have enabled Banteay Srei to be more fully represented than any other monument in this exhibition (cats. 48, 50–56). It seemed to us pertinent, therefore, to include a succinct supplementary document on this remarkable temple and the studies it has stimulated, especially since it falls outside the category of royal constructions.

Lost in the forest a dozen miles (20 km) northeast of Angkor, the temple of the ancient city of Īśvarapura, better known today as Banteay Srei, "the citadel of women," was only discovered in 1914, by a French officer of the geographic service, Lieutenant Marec. That same year, Georges Demasur, a resident architect for the École française d'Extrême-Orient (EFEO), visited the site to prepare the first description of it. Before he was able to publish his notes, Demasur died unexpectedly, and in 1916 Henri Parmentier resumed the study of the monument. In 1919 a detailed account of the temple of Banteay Srei was finally published in the article "L'art d'Indravarman,"[1] after which time the temple was once again more or less forgotten.[2]

In 1924, Parmentier and Victor Goloubew decided to clear the monument completely. The results of their work were published in 1926, along with an epigraphic study by Louis Finot, in a luxurious edition produced by the EFEO as the first volume in its series of archaeological monographs. The outer enclosures of the temple were then dated to the reign of Jayavarman V (968–1000/1001), and the monuments of the first enclosure were dated to the reign of Śrīndravarman (1296–1307), based on the epigraphic evidence available at the time and details of the monument's composition.

Like almost all Khmer temples, Banteay Srei is rich in epigraphy. In the first enclosure, inscriptions on the door jambs of the north and south sanctuaries (K. 573 and K. 574, respectively) mention images erected by relatives of a high dignitary named Yajñavarāha (the sacrificial boar). Although the inscriptions are undated, this personage is also named in an inscription on the east *gopura* (gateway) of the third enclosure (K. 568), which can be assigned to the fourteenth century as it contains a eulogy of King Śrīndravarman. Thus, the link between the guru Yajñavarāha and the donors of the images in two of the temple's main sanctuaries—family members, as one donor was Yajñavarāha's sister, Jāhnavī, and the other one of his parents, Pṛthivīndrapaṇḍita—and the fact that Yajñavarāha was the contemporary of King Śrīndravarman, led to the dating of the monuments of the first enclosure to the late thirteenth or early fourteenth century. Elsewhere it was noted that *gopura* III E—which had, besides the epigraphy attributable to

1. Parmentier 1919, especially 66–79.
2. Banteay Srei owed its return to the spotlight in 1923 to the "interest" André Malraux took in the monument. This painful story need not be delved into here, except to deplore the looting of archaeological treasures that has occurred at Angkor ever since the West discovered it, and to which Banteay Srei has unfortunately become particularly prey. An impartial account of the "Malraux affair" can be found in Dagens 1995.

the turn of the thirteenth century, an inscription from the reign of Jayavarman V (K. 570)—could only have been built in the tenth century, the later inscription having been incised subsequently. All indications accordingly pointed to there having been two periods of construction at Banteay Srei, yet certain aspects of the temple remained difficult to interpret. A study of the monument's architecture showed that the supposed fourteenth-century buildings used construction methods that had been in fashion during the tenth century, and with astonishing skill, considering that the techniques had long since been abandoned. The stone cutters also showed a remarkable talent for archaism, faithfully incising characters that had been in use in the tenth century. But the consensus, at the time, was that this was simply one of those returns to the past that are often found in Khmer art. This "duality of construction periods," to use Parmentier's expression, also provided an explanation for the narrowness of the temple's first enclosure. Its buildings—sanctuaries and "libraries"—seemed crowded together, probably because they replaced an older single tower sanctuary originally built in the tenth century.

Thus the very first studies dedicated to Banteay Srei raised a number of perplexing questions; this remarkable monument was already proving something of an anomaly.

After Parmentier discovered two new inscriptions in 1928 and 1929, the first at Prasat Sek Ta Tuy, six or seven miles (10 km) west of Beng Mealea, and the second at Prasat Trapeang Khyang, six miles (10 km) farther west, George Cœdès was able to shed new light on Banteay Srei and assign the monument in its entirety to the tenth century.[3]

A study of the inscriptions from these two Śivaite monuments revealed that the *liṅga* occupying their main shrines were *miśrabhoga* (associated or co-participant on a religious level) with the *liṅga* Tribhuvanamaheśvara[4] (great lord of the three worlds) at Banteay Srei; this association extended to the administrative level as well, because a portion of their taxes went to Banteay Srei. We should clarify that ties of various kinds sometimes existed between monuments at a considerable distance from one another. In a general sense, the monuments of ancient Cambodia were often part of a great interdependent network, and the political and religious landscape at the time of Angkor was probably as complex as that of medieval France or Italy. The consequence for methodology is that a particular Khmer monument may not itself contain all the keys to the issues it raises. An archaeological or historical problem may be insoluble as long as research focuses only on the monument in question, with the answer perhaps lying far off in time or space. But to return to Banteay Srei, the inscriptions from Prasat Sek Ta Tuy and Prasat Trapeang Khyang indicated, along with a profusion of other information, that Yajñavarāha did not live under Śrīndravarman at all but under Jayavarman V. This explains at a stroke the seemingly archaistic calligraphy and construction methods, because the buildings were now known to be nearly three and a half centuries older than originally thought. Cœdès was able to conclude at the end of his study that "the temple of Bantāy Srĕi, having now been correctly dated, can be seen to have played an important part in the evolution of Khmer art rather than to have been an anomaly. Its ties with the art of Indravarman on the one hand and with the art of Sūryavarman I (Práḥ Vihār) on the other make it a precious link in the history of ancient Cambodian architecture" (Cœdès 1929, 296). A few years later, Banteay Srei's foundation stele was "discovered"[5] in *gopura* IV E, inscribed with, among others,

3. Names of Khmer monuments are not firm and may have changed, sometimes quite recently. Thus, Prasat Trapeang Khyang is also known as Banteay Khyong, and Prasat Sek Ta Tuy as Prasat Kaña (Boulbet and Dagens 1973, 50). These names are more recent than the ones we use and may therefore be the only ones employed today (unless the names have changed again). However, the epigraphic studies we refer to use the old names and it seemed clearer to keep to that nomenclature.
4. This word referred to the main divinity of the temple of Banteay Srei: the *liṅga* in the temple's main tower shrine. Note that it is similar to the name of the main idol of Prasat Thom at Koh Ker: Tribhuvaneśvara (the lord of the three worlds). The formal analogies between this monument and Banteay Srei are, in point of fact, numerous. On this score, see Boisselier 1992, 265–275.
5. More correctly, this stele was rediscovered then, for although it had been indexed in Parmentier's first study, it had not been translated.

Fig. 2
Anastylosis of the south tower sanctuary

the consecration date of the monument's main idol: the first day of Mādhava (October–November), 967.

From 1931 to 1936, Banteay Srei was the site of another kind of research that would determine the course of study and restoration of Khmer temples. There, at the instigation of Henri Marchal, the method of restoration known as anastylosis was first used in Cambodia. This process aims at rebuilding a monument with its original materials on sound bases when it is threatened with ruin (Marchal 1933; fig. 2). Ideally suited to the mortarless structures of Khmer architecture, this technique is used today only in exceptional circumstances, when various modern methods of consolidation are no longer practicable. The results in Cambodia have been spectacular. Banteay Srei as well as Thommanon and many other monuments have benefited from this method of restoration. Recently the Terrace of the Leper King was renovated using this process, and the EFEO is currently reassembling the Baphuon, where anastylosis was interrupted at the beginning of the 1970s.

Marchal had chosen Banteay Srei because the high quality of its sandstone, its small size, and the excellent state of preservation of its carved ornaments boded well for the success of the operations. The restoration was a complete success and led to a long series of other resurrections.

Fig. 3
North tower sanctuary, west lintel. In the center, Viṣṇu mounted on Garuḍa

Fig. 4
North tower sanctuary, west lintel. Detail

Fig. 5
South library, east face. Mount Kailāsa shaken by the giant Rāvaṇa. Śiva, holding the cowering Pārvatī in his arms, steadies the mountain with his foot alone

Although anastylosis worked well for stone buildings, it clearly was not suited to brick architecture, and it was impossible to reassemble certain pediments belonging to the outer enclosures of the temple (cats. 50, 51).

Banteay Srei is an exemplary monument in historical terms and an ideal case study for epigraphic research and for restoration, yet the temple seems also to have a unique and somewhat tragic destiny.

As though the fates were in league against it and its sculptures, this "citadel of women," one of the most delicate of Khmer temples, where the refinement and subtlety of Khmer taste were expressed with the greatest virtuosity, has been singled out above all others as a target of greed and desire (figs. 3–5). The mutilated faces of certain *devatā* and *dvārapāla,* the now empty cornices of the roofs, the finial lopped off at the top of a *gopura,* the crushed fragments of the staircase guardians that could not be transferred to the National Museum of Phnom Penh in the early 1970s, the small Umā that was decapitated (cat. 56), all speak eloquently of the cruel trials that have beset this monument, as though Banteay Srei were a metaphor, almost an allegory, of torments that may lie in the past, but whose scars have not yet healed.

Sculpture

Introduction to Khmer Sculpture: General Remarks

Thierry Zéphir

Khmer sculpture, like that of other Indianized nations of Southeast Asia, belongs within a religious context. Commissioned, for the most part, by the country's elites—kings, Brahmans, dignitaries—it represents a remarkable balance between the art of the sculptor, which will be appreciable to the Westerner on first approach, and the iconographic imperatives of those who ordered it, to which the specialist will first be most readily sensitive.

Prolegomenon: The Mythology of the Images

During the first centuries of the Christian era, a number of the defining elements of Indian culture arrived in Southeast Asia. The so-called Vo Canh inscription (C. 40) confirms that Sanskrit was in use there in the second half of the third century, suggesting that the religious system for which that language was the vehicle had also been adopted.[1] However, no sculpture of so early a date has been found in Cambodia. Among the records relating to the ancient Khmer nation, the accounts left us by the Chinese provide an important introduction to the statuary, antedating any archaeological finds. The most often-cited information appears in the *Liang shu*, or *History of the Liang* (502–556), compiled in the first half of the seventh century (Pelliot 1903, 262). The text relates that the inhabitants of Funan adored "heavenly divinities made of bronze; those with two faces have four arms, those with four faces eight arms. Each hand holds something, either a child, a bird or a quadruped, or else the sun or the moon" (Pelliot 1903, 269). It is impossible to identify the divinities described in this passage, but its import is clear, providing as it does irrefutable evidence that a technically and iconographically complex statuary existed in the first half of the sixth century, the period to which the text refers. This is not to propose that the sixth century is the earliest possible date for such statuary, an assertion the present state of knowledge forbids us to make.

These images with multiple faces and arms were very probably Brahmanic divinities—a sixth-century Chinese presumably would have recognized Buddhist figures as such and not have called them "heavenly spirits." Were they made locally or did these statues come from the Indian subcontinent? For the moment, the question must remain unanswered. In the case of the Buddha, the most ancient images discovered in Southeast Asia have been found along maritime trade routes and were, in fact, imported from India, although occasionally they were locally made copies, and date from the fifth to sixth century.[2] Whether imports or copies, they represent the image of the Buddha in its very first stage of development in Southeast Asia, and Buddha images would very rapidly acquire their own particular characteristics in different regions. Though the "heavenly spirits" with several faces and arms are of an altogether different iconographic type, the way in which the models were transmitted

1. The so-called Vo Canh inscription, a stele, was discovered in the village of Phu Vinh, in Khanh Hoa, South Vietnam. It is now in the Museum of the History of Vietnam in Hanoi. On this subject, see George Cœdès, "The Date of the Sanskrit Inscription of Vo-Canh," *Indian Historical Quarterly* 16, 3 (1940), 484ff, or E. Gaspardone, "La plus ancienne inscription d'Indochine," *Journal asiatique* 241, 4 (1953), 477ff.

2. Dupont 1959, 631–636. Boisselier 1974, 65–71. We should note that no image from the Amarāvatī/Anurādhapura tradition has so far been found in Cambodia.

may have been the same, and future discoveries may well provide illustrations of the statues described in the *Liang shu.* These images must, at least in theory, have conformed to the prescriptions in the various religious texts (*śāstra, āgama, purāṇa,* etc.), and these are known from Khmer epigraphy to have been familiar, though at a somewhat later date.

The Gods Take Shape: From the Raw Material to the Finished Work

Khmer sculpture in the round does not have the same multiplicity of forms as its Indian model. The many aspects of divinity in Indian art are pared down to a few major types, most of which are readily recognizable. Yet while the names used to designate the different deities are well-known and appear frequently in the Sanskrit epigraphy, the gods and goddesses are never described in detail. Questions of iconography are, therefore, most complex, and, in many cases, the very fragmentary state of the works, especially in stone statuary, makes formal identification difficult. Virtually all the statues have lost their hands, and along with them the attributes they once held, raising a major obstacle to iconographic analysis.

Even in the earliest periods, certainly in the seventh and perhaps also in the sixth century, Khmer sculptors expressed themselves in stone with surprising mastery. The only way of accounting for this is to assume a long period of development, the stages of which are still unknown to us. But this period of maturation, which our Western (not to say Cartesian) way of thinking would lead us to expect at the beginning of any art tradition, may in fact never have occurred in ancient Cambodia. As we understand it today, Khmer art developed according to an irregular rhythm, with periods of intense vitality alternating with stagnant phases when creativity was at a low ebb. Though disconcerting, the situation may have arisen naturally from historical factors. A period of prosperity may have brought the art to its highest level, and a difficult period held it in check or even dealt it a setback. This incomplete and somewhat artificial explanation is used to account for the wonderful and truly splendid pre-Angkor sculpture of the seventh century, in comparison with the modest works generally attributed to the next century. Yet how are we to understand the fact that during the Angkor Vat period, when architecture was at its most sumptuous, sculpture seems to have been at a standstill with respect to earlier periods, in which real originality was expressed? Though it is hardly imaginable that Angkor Vat, one of the most beautiful monuments in the world, had an archaistic work as its central idol, one that repeated the forms of an existing model by rote for obscure artistic or political reasons, such is probably the case. The image has not come down to us, perhaps because its metal was melted down during turbulent times, but from what we know of the rest of the statuary of the period it is impossible to imagine it as anything but a competently made figure, devoid of originality and lacking the special quality of a masterpiece, whose incontrovertible beauty rises above technical, historical, or iconographic considerations.

While schist was sometimes used during the pre-Angkor period, the stone that artists used most consistently over the centuries for carving was sandstone. Breakage certainly occurred when sculpture fell, but most Khmer sandstones have survived fairly well (cats. 7, 71, 90). In many cases, though, the surface has been significantly altered, from a variety of causes: microscopic plants such as lichens, the proliferation of bacteria from bat droppings (the

3. For Śivaite texts, see, for example, BHATTACHARYA 1961, 46–50.

temples are a choice habitat for bats), the effects of heat and cold, the action of rainwater, and so on. In the most spectacular and damaging of these defacements, the surface layer flakes away irreparably, giving the sculpture a scaly aspect (cat. 45). Not all sandstones deteriorate in this way, however. A remarkable illustration is provided by the sculpture from the temple of Banteay Srei. The pink sandstone used for the monument and its sculpture (cats. 48, 50–55) is in a very perfect state of preservation, although it has been exposed to the same environmental conditions that have made other sandstone sculpture deteriorate (cat. 32; Delvert 1963).

Khmer sculptors apparently always used the technique known as direct carving. From the instances we have of unfinished works, it is possible to follow the various stages of the sculptural process (fig. 1). First the artist roughed out the form, then gradually refined it so as to obtain the desired lines and volumes, dictated by strict canons. These canons evolved over time, of course, and may even have varied slightly from region to region during a single period. Once the main outlines of a work had been carved, the process of finishing it began. When the images were complex—a god with many arms, for instance—the finishing would proceed almost to the point of completion before the various additional stone elements that lent the piece strength during the carving were removed. As a result, there is sculpture with a perfectly completed face or body that at the same time has roughly carved stone reinforcements linking one arm to another or struts between the projecting parts of the body and the sculpture's base or central core.

During the pre-Angkor period, the stone supports were generally not removed, especially when the figure had several arms. They often linked the front forearms to the base of the sculpture itself and were sometimes carved to represent the deity's attributes. Occasionally, the back hands are attached to the head by such supports (cat. 15). In a measure that was probably intended to provide maximum stability, sculptors also used the device of a supporting arch, which completely surrounds the figure like a halo (fig. 2). In certain exceptional works of sculpture, such as the Harihara from Prasat Andet (cat. 27), the use of such artifices has been deliberately reduced to a minimum. That incomparable work, contrary to what has often been said, has never had a supporting arch, though it did once have various reinforcements, the remnants of which are still visible at the base and on the left back arm.

Generally, sculpture was carved from a single stone. In some instances, notably in the Koh Ker style, the sculpture and the pedestal were carved from the same sandstone block. On the other hand, the T-shaped notches in certain later works possibly indicate that the arms were separately attached. One does find in the style of the Bayon and the post-Angkor period that the largest works are sometimes carved from several blocks of sandstone (cat. 116).

Almost nothing is known of the tools used in sculpting. The evidence would suggest that they were extremely effective since, at least in the most remarkable sculpture, the workmanship is nearly as precise as that of a jeweler (cat. 49).

The traces of gilding on some pieces (cat. 90) appear to be original, though in certain cases the gilding is obviously late. To our present knowledge, it is impossible to ascertain anything about polychromy.

Wood was used as well as stone in all periods, though few ancient works in wood have been preserved. The pre-Angkor Buddhas discovered in the south of what was historically the Cambodian Empire (Malleret 1959–1963, 4:pls. XXI–XXVI) constitute isolated examples, yet it is probably no acci-

Fig. 1
Unfinished statue of Viṣṇu. Angkor region. Sandstone. 122 cm. Angkor period. First half of the twelfth century. National Museum of Cambodia, Phnom Penh

Fig. 2
Harihara from Sambor Prei Kuk (shrine N 10). Sandstone. 166 cm. Pre-Angkor period. First half of the seventh century. National Museum of Cambodia, Phnom Penh

dent that they occurred within the context of Buddhist commissions. Works from the post-Angkor period, when wood was most generally used both in architecture (though few examples of it remain) and in statuary, are occasionally of exceptional quality (fig. 3, cat. 117). They prove the perennial nature of Khmer artistic traditions, long after the Angkor period.

The rare ancient figures that we have are made of a single block of wood, but it seems that sculptors often shaped their work from several pieces—the forearms of statues of the standing Buddha, for example, were generally added separately before the work was finished (Giteau 1975, 27–34).

The techniques used in decorating sculpture were various and complex (Giteau 1975, 34–37). The main ones to mention here are lacquering and gilding. First, a fairly thick layer of black lacquer was applied, which might then be recarved to mask the joins; then a thinner layer of red lacquer was added, and the gilding spread over it. An inlay of semiprecious stones, mother-of-pearl, or glass was often used to heighten the eyes, nails, and ornaments of the later figures.

According to the Chinese sources, mentioned above, metallic sculpture existed from as early as the fifth century. Starting in the seventh century, the information comes from inscriptions, which sometimes specify that the sculpture of a certain divinity was made of precious metal. The inscription on the east door of the outer gate of the south complex at Sambor Prei Kuk, dating from the seventh century (K. 440), mentions a gold *liṅga* and a silver statue of Nandin erected by King Īśānavarman I.[4] The Baksei Chamrong inscription (948; K. 286) mentions a gold image of Parameśvara ("supreme deity," one of the epithets of Śiva) presented by King Rājendravarman.[5]

Until the discovery, on 10 November 1983, of one of the most magnificent metallic Khmer statues ever found—a half-sized image of the bull Nandin—the only evidence that these statues in gold and silver actually existed came from the epigraphy. Though their existence was fairly certain, as statements made about them in a religious context had to contain some element of truth, no actual proof was at hand. The Nandin from Tuol Kuhea (Kandal), made from an alloy that has a large component of silver,[6] finally provides the expected proof and brilliantly confirms the great tradition of Khmer sculpture in precious metals.

Most metallic sculpture, however, was made of less noble material than gold or silver, whose use was undoubtedly exceptional. They are mostly of bronze, cast by the lost-wax process, but we have little information on their exact composition. The various tests conducted so far primarily indicate that a wide variety of alloys was used.

Cambodians use the term *saṃrit* to denote a copper alloy—the word, therefore, applies to bronzes—which is traditionally held to be rich in gold. *Saṃrit's* supposed richness in precious metals (gold, but also silver) makes the term applicable to sculpture such as the one from Tuol Kuhea. Might it also appropriately designate any religious or luxury objects made of metal? Chemical analyses of a sizable number of objects, especially of large pieces that are likely to have been cast according to the rules of the art, may allow us to begin answering such questions at some point in the future.

Khmer bronzes, because of their complexity, were often made in several parts (cats. 68, 77, 99, 115, among others). The various elements fit one into another and are held together by rivets. In certain pieces, a decorative element—the armband of the great reclining Viṣṇu from the West Mebon, for instance (cat. 68)—masks the join.

4. *IC* 4:5–11 (K. 440), XXXII and XXXIV.
5. *IC* 4:88–101 (K. 286), XLV.
6. According to the specialists, the patina leaves no doubt on this score. It would, all the same, be interesting to have the results of a laboratory analysis to know precisely the silver content of the piece.

Fig. 3
Adorned Buddha from Angkor Vat. Wood. 245 cm. Post-Angkor period. Sixteenth century (?). National Museum of Cambodia, Phnom Penh

Metal sculpture was probably gilded on a fairly regular basis. The inlay work has virtually disappeared (cat. 68) but seems to have owed less to decorative practices specific to bronze sculpture than to the characteristics of the predominant style, for example that of Baphuon.

Religious Art and Aesthetics: The Eye of the Beholder

Although the religious art of ancient Cambodia can be appreciated in a variety of ways, it clearly does not leave one indifferent, which is the sign of a truly great art. It can seem at different times full of grandeur or power, hieratic or majestic, peaceful or inner-directed, and in certain of its incarnations human, not to say sensual.

How did the Khmer, though, consider the works they saw taking shape under their eyes, and on whose execution they lavished such an abundance of resources?

The religious initiates, whether Brahmans or Buddhist monks, would have seen the sculpture as embodying, though in a necessarily reductive way, a set of philosophic and theological concepts the general public would never understand. The governing elites, the king in particular, might see them as an instance of spiritual power lending its strength and authority to temporal power. But how did the peasant view these images, how did they seem to the artisan, the fisherman? He must have approached them first and foremost as a believer, as a worshiper somewhat blinded by the hope of a better tomorrow. And it is very easy to imagine that both reverence and fear might be commingled in his gaze. Certain parts of the temple being off limits to common mortals, the average man could often only imagine the gods who wielded such enormous power over human lives and destinies. The people of Angkor, so touchingly brought to life in the reliefs of the Bayon, undoubtedly lingered longer over the modest picture of a domestic altar than over images of the great and inaccessible gods in the large temples of Angkor. Moreover, even when the worshiper managed to approach the door to the temple, the figure he might glimpse lay shrouded in semidarkness, its form covered in rich garments and sumptuous ornaments (fig. 4). The sculpture we admire today, the works whose every aspect we dissect in order to assign them to a particular style, these admirable gods the least fold of whose raiment and curl of whose hair is the subject of a dissertation, must feel themselves curiously denuded at present. For centuries they were protected, first by the sacred rituals, receiving every attention and respect due to them as divinities, then by the neglect or oblivion into which many of them fell. But let us not delude ourselves. The label of work of art that we readily give these eternal gods may have already been conferred on them in their own day, under a different form, while they were in their full glory. In fact we know nothing either of the status of the work of art in ancient Cambodia nor of the artist, and not a single sculptor's name has come down to us across the centuries. There are rough studies of sculpture that also exist in finished form.[7] Might these be an indication of purely aesthetic concerns, the sculptors having made several attempts before achieving perfection? We do not know. As to beauty, we can only say that it was never sought as an end in itself but because it honored the god whose image was being carved. The more successful and beautiful the work, according to criteria very different from Western ones, the more effective it would be, the more likely

7. For example, the studies of three figures comparable to the Umāgaṅgāpatīśvara group from Bakong, all of which are in storage at the Depot for the Conservation of Angkor.

Fig. 4
Relief carving from the Bayon, south interior gallery. Various persons pay homage to the god Viṣṇu, richly adorned and clothed. First half of the thirteenth century

the god would be to accept incarnation in it, and the more capable he would be of performing actions that, so one hoped, would be beneficial. The plastic embodiment of perfection, it is clear, was the outcome of a search that had very little to do with the criteria of earthly beauty. The image of man, however perfect, could in no way serve as the image of a divinity. Although the gods of Cambodia took human form, their idealized faces and stylized bodies, in a word their beauty, can only be truly appreciated with the consciousness that they are distinct from earthly perfection.

Catalogue

Seventh
to Eighth
Century

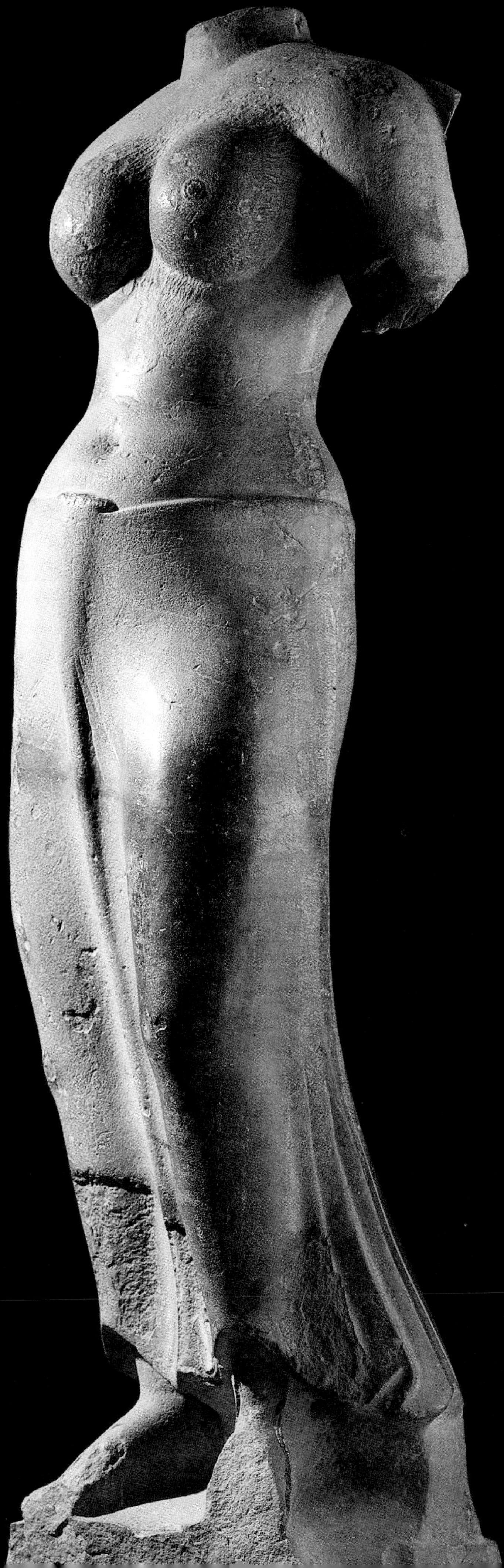

Fig. 1
"Triad" from Phnom Da (Prasat Phnom Da). Sandstone. Height 287 cm (Viṣṇu), 185 cm (Rāma), 176 cm (Balarāma). Pre-Angkor period, sixth (?) to seventh century. National Museum of Cambodia, Phnom Penh

Before Angkor: An Art in Formation

One of the dominant traits of early Khmer art, the art of the pre-Angkor period[1] (seventh to eighth century), is its diversity. The variety of its styles, sometimes within a single period, as well as the multiplicity of its plastic and iconographic traditions makes the study of this period particularly delicate. By contrast, the Angkor period (ninth to fifteenth century) is relatively monolithic in style.[2] Each of its successive sculptural styles from the ninth century to the beginning of the thirteenth—now recognizable thanks to the work of Philippe Stern, Gilberte de Coral-Rémusat, Pierre Dupont, and Jean Boisselier, among others—displays a striking unity due in large part to the highly centralized structure of the Angkor state. Nothing comparable exists in pre-Angkor art, whose complexity, profusion, and richness are its greatest qualities. One finds no repetition or adherence to conventions—original creations pour out from all sides. For a scholar the field offers uncertain ground but is at the same time particularly rewarding, upon reflexion; for the aesthete it is a source of delight continuously renewed and full of unexpected riches.

Pre-Angkor art reflects the territorial and political fragmentation of the ancient land of the Khmer. The statuary is noticeably more complex than the architecture, which was not to be the case during the Angkor period. Three major styles of pre-Angkor architecture have been defined and subdivided into a number of local variants.[3] Although a certain overlapping of styles may occur (Zéphir 1994, 159), the overall development is clear enough and can be summed up as follows (the chronology was proposed by Jean Boisselier in *Le Cambodge*):

—the Sambor Prei Kuk style (after 600 to c. 650)
—the Prei Kmeng style (c. 635 to c. 700)
—the Kompong Preah style (c. 706 to perhaps after 800)

While it is possible to fit nearly all the known monuments into this chronology,[4] it is inapplicable to the sculpture, for which two additional styles have been defined:

—the Phnom Da style (about sixth to seventh century?)[5]
—the Prasat Andet style (end of seventh to beginning of eighth century)

Although the area over which the architectural styles—Sambor Prei Kuk, Prei Kmeng, and Kompong Preah—extend roughly corresponds to the territory of the pre-Angkor times, the different schools of sculpture seem much more localized. If one simply marks the most characteristic works on a map of Cambodia, it appears that a stylistic division existed in the first half of the seventh century, corresponding to two large territories: on the one hand, the southern part of the Khmer region, where the style known as Phnom Da and its successor schools developed, perhaps as early as the sixth century (the Viṣṇuite "triad" from Phnom Da, fig. 1, cats. 7, 13–16); and, on the other hand, the central and northern part, where the style known as Sambor Prei Kuk developed (the Harihara from Sambor Prei Kuk, fig. 2, page 133 and cats. 18, 19; and the female divinity from Aranya Prathet, Boisselier 1974, page 109, fig. 72).

The Phnom Da school appears relatively homogeneous, at least with reference to its greatest masterpieces. The major works discovered in the region of Angkor Borei all belong within the iconography of Viṣṇuism. Yet other, less prestigious works as well as epigraphy indicate that Śivaite cults also existed in that region during the same period. Although the dating of

Fig. 2
Harihara, Prasat Trapeang Phong. Sandstone. Height 99 cm. Pre-Angkor period, eighth century. National Museum of Cambodia, Phnom Penh

several pieces remains uncertain—the Rāma, Balarāma, and eight-armed Viṣṇu from the National Museum of Phnom Penh—the Phnom Da school certainly represents the earliest phase of Brahmanic art in ancient Cambodia. The images of Rāma and Balarāma were discovered in a large twelfth-century tower-sanctuary alongside the imposing, almost ten-foot-tall image of Viṣṇu that evidently came from the same workshop, if not the same hand; what kind of monument originally housed them—perhaps a light shelter or a cave—is not known. These sculptures, which exhibit excellent workmanship, form a remarkable group, which is sometimes improperly called the Phnom Da triad. The highly sensitive modeling of these works combines realism and stylization. Certain details such as the double-layered clothing appear nowhere but in these decidedly original pieces, whose iconography is only very rarely found in Khmer sculpture of any period.

Only a few works can be ascribed to the style of Sambor Prei Kuk. Although small in number, the pieces, which are primarily female figures, possess very strong characteristics and amply justify their designation as a style. What forms the common element of this group, more than any details of

1. The pre-Angkor period, from a historical point of view, began in the first centuries of the Christian era. The date given here relates to the sculpture shown in the exhibition. The difficulties experienced in trying to attribute certain works in the sixth century will be discussed later (see note 5).
2. This is not meant to imply in any way that the art of sculpture failed to evolve during the Angkor period; on the contrary, each style, however different from the style that preceded or followed it, appears to have been particularly unified. This holds for the entire territory over which the Angkor empire then extended.
3. The styles of pre-Angkor architecture have been determined on the basis of the "Stern method," as adapted specifically to Khmer art. This involves the minute study of an element's morphological evolution in conjunction with the organic transformation of the element's decorative motifs (in pre-Angkor Khmer art, these primarily refer to lintels and colonnettes). Pierre Dupont, Jean Boisselier, and Mireille Bénisti have given their attention to this set of questions (see the bibliography). On the problem of local variants, or those that are so considered, see, for example, BÉNISTI 1968.
4. The Asram Maha Rosei (Ta Keo) presents certain remarkable peculiarities, both in plan and in elevation (see MAUGER, 1936, 65). It may seem an exception on this account. Its ornament, however (colonnettes and unfinished lintel), may be considered to belong to the Sambor Prei Kuk style. Note that the Asram Maha Rosei is at a great distance from the eponymous site and therefore constitutes one of the examples of the stylistic unity of architectural ornament over the whole of the pre-Angkor Khmer country.
5. Pierre Dupont dated the Phnom Da style to the sixth century, possibly extending into the seventh (see DUPONT 1955, 22–70). He also subdivided it into two phases, A and B. While Jean Boisselier at first sided with this view (BOISSELIER, *La Statuaire khmère*, 1955, 14), he came to believe, on the basis of more recent research, that the works in this style must belong to a later date. The question remains difficult to settle, particularly for the large and beautiful "triad" from Phnom Da now at the National Museum of Phnom Penh. Is it possible to draw a link with the reign of Rudravarman, one of the last kings of independant Funan? An inscription from Phnom Da, whose interpretation is sensitive and which can be dated to the twelfth or thirteenth century, seems to prove it. Pierre Dupont, however, points out that another Rudravarman, a minor king compared to the one who ruled Funan in the first half of the sixth century, is known to have reigned in the eighth century.

clothing or hair, more even than the sculptural technique, is its subtle modeling tendency toward realism. Without striving for anatomical verisimilitude, always foreign to Khmer art, the sculptors have managed to represent the body as a living, palpitating entity. Their remarkable mastery can be seen, for instance, in the nervous rendering of the abdominal musculature of the Harihara from Sambor Prei Kuk (fig. 2, page 133) or in the fullness that characterizes the mature female body in the female divinities from Koh Krieng (cat. 19) and Aranya Prathet. But the most extraordinarily realized piece is without doubt the marvelous Durgā (cat. 18) once ensconced in shrine 9 of Sambor Prei Kuk's north complex. This image, one of the great masterworks of Khmer art, carries all the emotions that a female body, at once young and brimming with inner tensions, is capable of arousing.

The second half of the seventh century (the Prei Kmeng and Prasat Andet styles) gives less impression of stylistic unity. Execution may vary widely from one work to another, and while certain sculptures of this period are among the most beautiful in all Khmer art (cat. 27), others show less skillful handling and a somewhat dry treatment, for instance, the Harihara from Kompong Speu (Dupont 1955, plate XXXV B).

The style of Kompong Preah is even more difficult to define. A great diversity, bordering on confusion, characterizes the works of the eighth century. This is no doubt related to the turbulent history of the Khmer land at that time. Certain sculptures, though of somewhat mediocre quality, nonetheless manage to prefigure the art of the ninth century, for instance the Harihara from Prasat Trapeang Phong (fig. 2).

Given these brief general comments, what picture can be formed of pre-Angkor sculpture? Aside from its diversity and technical characteristics, the important aspects to keep in mind are its formal beauty and the perfect execution of the earliest works, qualities one would expect to find at the end of a development period rather than at the beginning. Does this imply that the beginnings of Khmer sculpture are still unknown? The question is as yet unanswered. Perhaps the genius of Khmer sculptors found sure expression from the outset, remarkably enough, without the stammering and awkwardness normally associated with an art during its formation.

T.Z.

1

Head of a Buddha

Vat Romlok, Angkor Borei (Ta Keo)
Pre-Angkor period, 6th(?)–7th century
Sandstone
Height 28 cm, width 15 cm, depth 16.5 cm
National Museum of Cambodia,
Phnom Penh, Ka 1085

The Buddha's half-closed lids reflect certain conventions of beauty similar in kind to those governing Viṣṇu, whose eyes are compared to lotus buds. The curve of the Buddha's meditative eyes, which close against the illusion of the world, conforms to the curve of his mouth, which smiles discreetly and expresses a vision of inner peace. The slightly inclined head also betokens this inner vision, one evoked again six centuries later in the powerful image of King Jayavarman VII (cats. 89, 90).

As expressed so well by Charles Baudelaire, the beauty of inner peace radiates over physical beauty. One could also describe the face of this Buddha from Vat Romlok in terms of the Renaissance concept of balance, harmony, and repose: it expresses pre-Angkor classicism while still imbued with the influence of the Indian canon, particularly the art of Amarāvatī.

The cranial protuberance (*uṣṇīṣa*) is so slight as to be barely indicated—a common feature of the Amarāvatī and Anurādhapura styles—and suggests an island from which spiral waves of curly hair fan outward, a distant echo of ancient Greek and Cretan wave motifs. It should be recalled that the arrival in India of the Ionians (Yavana) after the time of Alexander the Great, gave rise in about the first century, according to certain authors, to a Buddhist iconography that used human forms: the art of Gandhāra. Prior to that, Buddhist representation had been entirely symbolic, comprising images of the *Bodhi* tree, the throne, the *Dharmacakra* (wheel of the law) and the *Buddhapāda* (footprint of Buddha) among others.

The eyebrow arch is barely suggested. The nose, which is handled in an original way, is no longer the straight nose of classical Greek art. The full lower lip and chin draw on Gupta traditions in Indian art. The model for this head appears to be a head of the Buddha from Vijiaderpuram near Bezvada, dating from the second century, which is now in the Musée Guimet.[1] That head, however, differs: eyes are open, hair curls twist in the opposite direction, and an *ūrṇā*, or symbolic tuft of hair, is in the center of the forehead.

S.S.

2

Buddha

Vat Romlok, Angkor Borei (Ta Keo)
Pre-Angkor period, 7th century
Sandstone
Height 93 cm (without tenon),
width 32.5 cm, depth 20 cm
National Museum of Cambodia,
Phnom Penh, Ka 1595

Chinese dynastic chronicles of the southern Qi and Liang record that delegations from Funan brought, as tribute, ivory *stūpa* and a coral Buddha image in 484 and 503, respectively. Such gifts reveal, if not the establishment of Buddhism in Funan at that time, at least an awareness of Buddhist iconography on the part of the Funanese ruler of the period, Kauṇḍinya-Jayavarman. The Chinese accounts indicate, however, that Brahmanism was the prevailing state religion in Funan, with a cult of the god Maheśvara, or Śiva (Pelliot 1903, 260). Khmer inscriptions of the early sixth century (Cœdès 1964, 112–120; 1989, 210–211) nevertheless provide indigenous evidence of the coexistence of Brahmanism and Buddhism in this early Cambodian era. It has not been clearly established which of these two Indian religions was the first to appear in Cambodia, but the legend of the founding of Funan by an Indian prince who married the daughter of the local *nāga*-king and became ruler suggests that Brahmanism predated Buddhism (Bhattacharya 1961, 11–17). In addition, most of the oldest known Cambodian sculpture belongs to the so-called Phnom Da style, which is iconographically predominantly Brahmanic (cats. 13, 1; page 142 fig.1). Evidence of the earliest Pre-Angkor sculpture suggests, however, that the oldest Buddhistic images were made at about the same time as their Brahmanic counterparts, that is, from the beginning of the seventh century or perhaps slightly earlier (cats. 1, 2).

Another unresolved question concerns the type of Buddhism that prevailed in that early period. Although there are inscriptions referring to Buddhist foundations, very few have references proving the existence of either the Mahāyāna (the Greater Vehicle) or Theravāda (Hīnayāna, or the Lesser Vehicle) version of the faith. References in 693 to a female deity who seems to be Prajñāpāramitā, and in 791 to an image of Lokeśvara, are among the rare epigraphic evidence of Mahāyāna practices (Bhattacharya 1961, 18). An inscription of 664 at Vat Prei Veal, formerly thought to establish the presence of Theravāda, has been refuted by Bhattacharya (1961, 16), but the Buddha of Tuol Preah Theat (cat. 4) offers epigraphic proof of this form of Buddhism.

Although inscriptions offering firm evidence of the coexistence of these two schools of Buddhism in seventh-century Cambodia may be rare, sculpture confirms the theory despite precise dating for the objects. The pantheon of beings such as the Bodhisattva Avalokiteśvara is self-evidently a Mahāyāna phenomenon, but distinguishing an early figure of the Buddha himself as either a Mahāyāna or a Theravāda image remains a challenge. Standing Buddha figures like the three early examples in the exhibition (cats. 2–4) offer iconographic evidence of neither Mahāyāna nor Theravāda characteristics, for until the appearance several centuries later of the adorned Buddha (cats. 73–76), these images, by definition, stressed the absence of materialism. Analysis, therefore, rests largely on stylistic rather than iconographic clues.

The main centers of Buddhism early in the first millennium of our era were Amarāvatī in India and Anurādhapura in Sri Lanka, and they are the likeliest sources of the earliest Buddhist influences in Funan. Subsequently, Gupta art provided a stylistic source. Angkor Borei, near the Bassac River, was one of the important centers of Buddhism in the Southeast Asian region, along with Tra Vinh, in the Plain of Reeds, and Dong Duong (significantly then called Amarāvatī) in the former Champa kingdom (in what is now central Vietnam). The first two could have been linked by the network of waterways in the Mekong delta.

This standing Buddha has some similarities with Gupta images from Sārnāth in the treatment of the features and also the upper robe, or *uttarāsaṅga*. This visibly thin and supple cloth covers both shoulders, molds closely to the body, and reveals the outline of the undergarment (*antaravāsaka*), a loosely draped hip wrap. Also visible beneath the robe are the contours of the abdomen, with the slight swelling indicating the inner spiritual breath (*prāṇa*), and a naturalistic modeling of the thighs, knees, and calves. Also characteristic of the style are the graceful hip-swayed stance (a gentle version of the Indian *tribhaṅga*), the left knee slightly bent, and the prominent and typical curls that cover the *uṣṇīṣa*, the cranial protuberance that is one of the thirty-two distinguishing features (*lakṣaṇa*) of the Buddha. Another *lakṣaṇa*, the elongated but unjeweled earlobes, demonstrates both the former princely status of the Buddha, who before his Enlightenment would have worn heavy ear pendants, and his rejection of material wealth. Characteristically for Khmer Buddha images, this example has no *ūrnā lakṣaṇa*, the small protrusion between the eyebrows often found in Indian, Indonesian, and Sri Lankan figures.

The Vat Romlok Buddha stands on two lotuses, a characteristic of Amarāvatī art. He has a slender torso and a long and elegant neck, undoubtedly a factor in the former fracture of the head, which is slightly tilted. It is not possible to determine what *mudrā*, or hand gestures, this figure once made, since both hands have been broken off, but as the elbows indicate a horizontal position of the forearms, it might have been making the gesture of *abhayamudrā* (reassurance) or *vitarkamudrā* (discussion or argumentation) with both hands (a characteristic of Dvāravatī art), or one of these gestures with the right hand while holding the edge of the *uttarāsaṅga* in the left (see cat. 3). Stylistically this Buddha resembles a spiritual and seemingly joyful wooden Buddha from Binh Hoa (the south of present-day Vietnam); the right hand of this figure shows *vitarkamudrā*, while the left is clearly raising the corner of his robe.[1]

The Vat Romlok Buddha is a compendium of the stylistic forces shaping early Cambodian statuary yet is already suffused with a spiritual quality that is distinctively Khmer. Although Boisselier dates it in the seventh century, it may, like the head from the same provenance (cat. 1), be slightly older.

H.J.

3

Buddha

Tuol Ta Hoy, Vat Phnom, Oudong
(Kompong Speu)
Pre-Angkor period, 7th century
Sandstone
Height 97 cm, width 32.5 cm, depth 32 cm
National Museum of Cambodia,
Phnom Penh, Ka 1589

The Buddha from Tuol Ta Hoy was found farther north than the images from Vat Romlok (cats. 1, 2). Though Kompong Speu is some distance from Angkor Borei, it is nevertheless connected by the Tonle Sap River to the system of the Mekong Valley waterways and would not necessarily, therefore, have been in iconographic or stylistic isolation.

This Buddha wears a monastic robe similar to the Vat Romlok example, but offers several stylistic differences. The right shoulder is bare, an interesting and possibly indigenous Khmer distinction from the norm in both Amarāvatī style, where both shoulders were typically covered, and the style of the neighboring Thai kingdom of Dvāravatī, where the left shoulder was usually bare. It is clear that his left hand, in an unusual state of preservation, holds the *uttarāsaṅga*, or outer robe. The stance is more hieratic than that of the Vat Romlok statue, the hip-swayed posture little more than a shift of weight to the proper right leg with a consequent, hardly perceptible, release of tension in the left knee. The Buddha's right hand makes the gesture of bestowing a gift, *varadamudrā*.

The treatment of the slightly fleshy abdomen, yielding to the compression of the belt of the undergarment, is more realistic, less idealized, than the representation of the torso of the Vat Romlok Buddha. The half-closed eyes, the elegant continuous contour of the brows, and the treatment of the curls are reminiscent of the art of Dvāravatī of the seventh and eighth centuries. This impression is reinforced by the expression of youthful innocence and spirituality on the Buddha's face, which is often found in Dvāravatī images but is also typical of Khmer art. Like the Buddha from Vat Romlok, this figure blends elements that derive from both Gupta and Dvāravatī art with distinctively Cambodian traits.

H.J.

4

Buddha

Tuol Preah Theat (Kompong Speu)
Pre-Angkor period, 7th century
Sandstone
Height 92.5 cm, width 31 cm, depth 22 cm
Musée national des Arts asiatiques-Guimet, Paris, MG 18891

The Buddha of Tuol Preah Theat stands stiffly, as if with locked knees, in a posture that lacks even the slight *déhanchement* of the Buddha images from Vat Romlok and Tuol Ta Hoy (cats. 2, 3). The rigid stance is softened by the benign, slightly smiling countenance and the soft modeling of the limbs and torso that are visible below his monastic garments. The right hand is raised in the gesture of argumentation, *vitarka-mudrā*. The gesture of the left hand, which is broken, can only be surmised. Buddha figures from the seventh- and eighth-century Dvāravatī kingdom in nearby Thailand, which were important in the evolution of northern Khmer style,[1] were often shown with both hands in the gesture of *vitarka-mudrā*, which may have been the case in this image. However, the slightly different arrangement of the drapery of the *uttarāsaṅga* over the forearm and the slightly different height and angle of that arm from the right one make it equally possible that the Buddha once held the end of his robe around the left wrist.

Typical of pre-Angkor art are the Buddha's almond-shaped eyes, the pronounced differentiation of the curls, and the prominence of the *uṣṇīṣa*. Also distinctively Khmer is the treatment of the feet. Like the images from Vat Romlok and Tuol Ta Hoy, the Tuol Preah Theat Buddha has feet that are still attached to the matrix of the block of stone at the heels and between the ankles, a reminder of the structural techniques of sculpture emerging from relief to fully freestanding statues (compare with cat. 13).

This Buddha offers a rare proof of its Theravādin nature. On its back is an inscription (K. 820) in Pāli (the ritual language of the Lesser Vehicle to this day in Cambodia and Thailand) of the Buddhist creed: *Ye dhammā hetuprabhavā tesaṃ hetuṃ tathāgato avaca / tesañ ca yo nirodho evaṃvādī mahāsamano.*[2] The paleology of the script establishes it as an incontestably seventh-century inscription, so it was not added posthumously, and therefore offers certain evidence of the presence of Theravāda Buddhism in Cambodia at that time.

Given the influence of Dvāravatī on Khmer Buddhism at this period, and with the certainty that the Buddha of Tuol Preah Theat is a Theravādin figure, it is possible that the images of Vat Romlok and Tuol Ta Hoy, with their numerous stylistic similarities, may also belong to this school of Buddhism.

H.J.

5

Buddha

Vat Banon (Battambang)
Pre-Angkor period, 7th–8th century
Bronze
Height 27.5 cm, width 13 cm, depth 9 cm
National Museum of Cambodia, Phnom Penh, Ga 5412

Bronze sculptures, particularly the smaller and therefore more portable ones, played an important role in the diffusion of religious iconographies in Southeast Asia. Examples of works imported from India, or faithfully copied from models from the subcontinent, are numerous in these regions. This is particularly the case with Buddha

images, whose presence marks the maritime routes along which an important maritime trade developed in the first centuries of the Christian era.[1]

Standing Buddha images with a heavy, pleated garment that leaves the right shoulder uncovered—characteristic representations of the Amarāvatī/Anurādhapura tradition—preceded, from perhaps as early as the sixth century,[2] images that are quite close but in which the Buddha wears a smooth garment, characteristic of the Budhapād school in Andhra Pradesh, India, and datable from the seventh to eighth centuries. It is to this second group that the Vat Banon Buddha belongs.[3]

Because the statue has survived in a fragmentary state, it is, unfortunately, not clear what gesture the right hand is making, whether it is in *vitarkamudrā* (discussion) or *abhayamudrā* (absence of fear). More subtly modeled than most of the works springing from the diverse tradition of Southeast Asian art and moving in its simplicity, this sculpture is not without a resemblance to the famous, very beautiful Buddha from Kota Bangun[4] in East Kalimantan, Indonesia, which is now unfortunately lost. The two pieces are aesthetically very close, but the Indonesian figure exhibits a distinctly different iconography.[5] On the Vat Banon Buddha, the *uttarāsaṅga* (overgarment) hangs freely from the left arm, while on the image from Kota Bangun it is rolled around the Buddha's wrist. Jean Boisselier believes that this detail—which shows how monks wore their robes—may have significance as a chronological marker. If so, the Vat Banon Buddha would have to be dated later than figures with the garment rolled around the wrist. This piece, therefore, could be assigned to the eighth century.

Given that comparable works in pre-Angkor art are few and that it is very possible that this Buddha was cast outside ancient Cambodia, the piece cannot be dated at present with any greater accuracy.

T.Z.

6

Buddha

Western *baray,* Angkor (Siem Reap)
Pre-Angkor period, 7th–8th century
Bronze
Height 28 cm, width 11 cm, depth 7 cm
National Museum of Cambodia,
Phnom Penh, Ga 5405

While southern India was largely responsible for the spread of Buddhism to Southeast Asia, the important role played by more northern regions should not be ignored. It was thanks to them that other iconographies and other stylistic traditions, Gupta in particular, could be introduced in Southeast Asia, presumably using the maritime routes, though an overland route through present-day Burma and Thailand is equally imaginable. These northern traditions, having been relayed by such kingdoms as Dvāravatī, would have undergone a number of changes, as seen in this Buddha, which was discovered at the northeast corner of the western *baray,* Angkor.

The Buddha is represented standing, clothed in monastic dress composed of two traditional elements: the *antaravāsaka* (undergarment), consisting of a long piece of cloth draped around the hips, and the *uttarāsaṅga* (overgarment), a sort of loose robe that here covers both shoulders. The clothing conforms perfectly to the body, without any folds, and is comparable to that of fifth-century Gupta figures of the Buddha from Sārnāth, India.

The two forearms project forward symmetrically; the lost left hand was probably in the same position as the right, performing the gesture of *vitarkamudrā*. This particular iconography originated in the Dvāravatī kingdom, on the site of what is now central and northeastern Thailand. It is likely that all pre-Angkor Buddha figures that show this characteristic (cat. 4) were more or less influenced by Dvāravatī art. In the case of this Buddha from the western *baray*, the geometric treatment of the torso is not alone in recalling the style of Dvāravatī sculpture. The face, the treatment of the hair, and the proportions of the whole induce a similar observation.

A circular hole is visible at the top of the *uṣṇīṣa*, the protuberance on the Buddha's head. Presumably, it was intended to hold a precious or semi-precious stone rather than the flame, a motif that would not appear in Khmer art until much later (see cat. 114).

Dating this statuette presents the same problems noted for the Buddha from Vat Banon (cat. 5). The lack of pre-Angkor pieces that have been dated with certainty allow it, at best, to be assigned to a period in the crux between the seventh and eighth century. Similar works in stone are no less tentatively dated, and comparing this work with them is not quite satisfactory and offers no further precision. In fact one knows that the treatment of two contemporary pieces may have been very different because of the material used. It is, therefore, a delicate matter, particularly in the highly diverse pre-Angkor period, to make rather dangerous comparisons between stone and bronze that are founded on nothing solid or verifiable and that risk obscuring the facts rather than clarifying them.

T.Z.

7

Avalokiteśvara

Tan Long (former province of Rach Gia, Transbassac), Vietnam
Pre-Angkor period, style of Phnom Da, mid-7th–early 8th century
Sandstone
Height 188 cm (with tenon), width 49 cm, depth 29 cm
Musée national des Arts asiatiques-Guimet, Paris, MA 5063

This unforgettable representation of the Bodisattva Avalokiteśvara is one of the most perfect works of sculpture in the Khmer artistic heritage. Its state of physical conservation is due both to the excellent technique of its fabrication and the protection of its site. Discovered in 1919 during ground-leveling prior to construction of a stable near the village of Tan Long, not far from Soc Trang in the vast Rach Gia Province (west of the Bassac River and south of the site of Oc Eo), the statue was buried about one and a half meters deep. Although from the front it appears to be a sculpture in the round, this figure is, in fact, fully attached in the back to its block of stone. The legs are not separated, the head is not vulnerable, and the arms are well supported by vertical columns.

The cult of Avalokiteśvara (the lord who looks down from above), also known as Lokeśvara (lord of the worlds), was widespread in Cambodia, and he was one of the most popular spiritual beings in Mahāyāna Buddhism. The earliest inscription mentioning this Bodhisattva seems to have been that of Prasat Ta Kam in 791 (K. 244; Finot 1925, 225), but sculpture of Avalokiteśvara exists, including the Rach Gia example, that predate the inscription (cats. 9, 10). Avalokiteśvara, Bodhisattva of compassion, is the representative of the Jina Amitābha, Dhyāni Buddha, Buddha of the afterlife, of intellectual power and wisdom, and is said to have been created by "a ray from Amitābha's right eye during a state of ecstatic contemplation" (Finot 1925, 229). Avalokiteśvara has many forms and is often represented in a triad with the Buddha and either Maitreya or Vajrapāṇī, or sometimes Prajñāpāramitā (cat. 95).[1] His attributes vary (as does the number of his arms) but they can include, among others, the lotus flower (*padma*), the jewel (*ratna* or *maṇi*), the vase (*kamaṇḍalu*), the book (*puṣtaka*), and the rosary (*akṣamālā*). His most characteristic mark is the presence of a small image of the meditating Amitābha Buddha in his headdress, which is particularly distinct in the Tan Long Avalokiteśvara.

Stylistically this figure shows many of the characteristics of the Phnom Da style: slight sway (*ābaṅga*) of the hip, slight projection of the left knee, long and fine nose, oval face, and cascading curls down the back and below the diadem, as well as the simple smooth garment with pleated edge and details of the belt buckle. For many years it was thought to be contemporary with other images in the Phnom Da style, of the early seventh century (Malleret 1954, 262), but now it is considered to be of slightly later date.

The sumptuousness of the Bodhisattva's jewelry—incised medallions in the diadem, earrings, wide necklace, belt, and bracelets—is unusual for this early date, when a more ascetic style typified the great icons of both Buddhism and Brahmanism.[2] The depiction of hair and face is meticulous, the eyes and lips outlined by fine incisions, the fingers delicately holding the jewel and the lotus bud, the toes carefully delineated with details of nails and (on the right foot only) the crease of the first joint.

Regardless of the regal richness of the accessories, this figure, with its elegantly arched brows, downcast eyes, and benignly curved mouth, radiates refinement, purity, and benevolence. The potentially materialistic impression of the adornment is balanced by the gentle posture and the rendering of the abdomen, shoulders, and arms as softly fleshed, the negation of threatening physical prowess. One is reminded of the canon for male beauty for the Javanese and Balinese, at least for noble characters: strength is desirable and necessary, but should conceal itself in paradoxically rounded forms and somewhat feminine curves of limbs and torso.

H.J.

8

Avalokiteśvara

Provenance unknown
Pre-Angkor period,
1st half of the 8th century (?)
Sandstone
Height 177 cm, width 30 cm, depth 20 cm
Philadelphia Museum of Art,
W. P. Wilstach Collection, W1965-1-1

If complete, this Avalokiteśvara of surpassing beauty would stand more than seven feet tall, putting it into a small group of pre-Angkor sculpture having dimensions larger than life. The head was found separately from the body in 1964, probably either in eastern Thailand or western Cambodia, at which time it was examined by Jean Boisselier (Boisselier 1981, 11). Nothing is known about its provenance. Although both arms and the attributes they would have held are missing, the identification of the statue as Avalokiteśvara is confirmed by the presence in the chignon of the meditating figure of the Amitābha Buddha (see cat. 7).

The stylized arrangement of the Bodhisattva's hair is known as a *jaṭāmukuṭa*, or crown in the form of a chignon, and it is found in sculpture, both Brahmanic and Buddhistic, throughout its evolution. The restrained treatment of the torso, the subtle indication of the short sarong-like garment, the *paridhana*, and the hieratic posture suggest the spiritual qualities of Avalokiteśvara. The creases at the base of the neck are signs of beauty and may indicate that the statue was consecrated in its destined sanctuary, while the swelling of the abdomen suggests the inner breath (*prāṇa*). The downcast gaze is consistent with the protective nature of this Bodhisattva. The unfinished nature of the back probably means that the sculpture was installed against the sanctuary wall.

For Boisselier the details of the *jaṭāmukuṭa*, where the horizontal coils of the hair are concealed by the loops of the braids, suggest a date later than the seventh century, and he draws convincing stylistic parallels between this statue and the Harihara of Prasat Andet (cat. 27) to arrive at a date in the first half of the eighth century. In particular, he finds the features of the Philadelphia piece reminiscent of the extraordinary spirituality of the Harihara, both sculptures having delicately outlined eyes, mouths, and brows, as well as a slightly upwardly tilted nose and a similar narrow and curled mustache.

Without provenance information, any further speculation must remain shrouded in doubt. It is perhaps of interest, however, to examine the nuances of expression in the Philadelphia Avalokiteśvara. The figure's youthfulness, softness of cheek, innocence of gaze, and subtle smile are also depicted in the bronzes of Prakhon Chai (cats. 11, 12) and the Dvāravatī stone sculptures that were made in the area that is now the northwestern part of Thailand at about the same period, that is, in the early eighth century.

H.J.

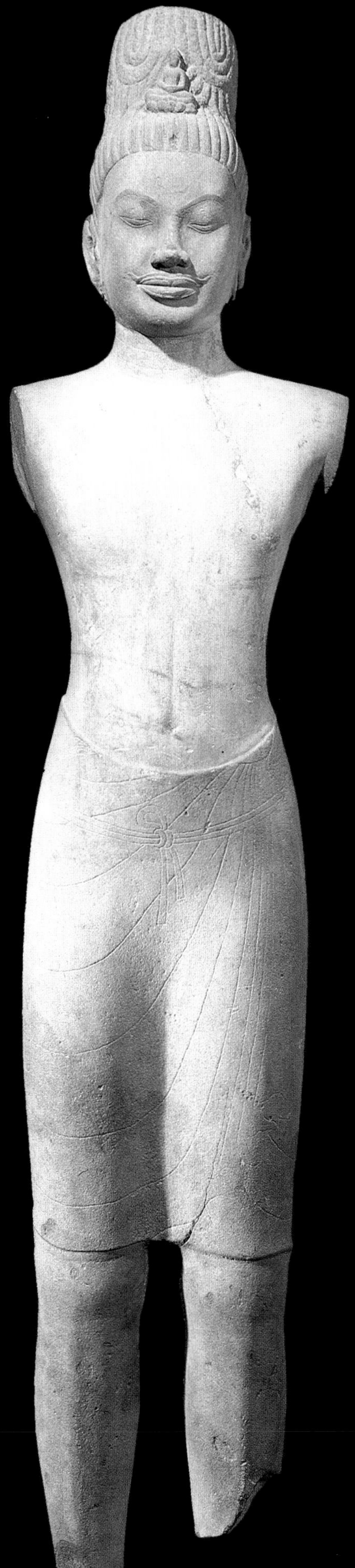

9

Avalokiteśvara

Vat Kompong Luong, Angkor Borei
(Ta Keo)
Pre-Angkor period, 7th century
Lead-tin alloy
Height 17.8 cm, width 5.7 cm, depth 4 cm
National Museum of Cambodia,
Phnom Penh, Ga 5330

Khmer sculpture of the pre-Angkor period, although endowed with its own profoundly original characteristics, derives from a variety of traditions that are not always easy to distinguish.

The Indian origin of certain aspects of clothing (cats. 13, 14) or of certain headdresses, such as Viṣṇu's cylindrical miter (cat. 15), is often suggested. But while India may have played a fundamental role in developing the iconographies, and while a family resemblance undoubtedly exists between certain Indian works of approximately the seventh century and pre-Angkor statuary, other geographical areas also received and possibly retransmitted these influences. Such is the case with Champa. This statuette of the Bodhisattva Avalokiteśvara, identifiable from the small effigy of the Amitābha Buddha at the front of the headdress, is undeniably related to Cham art of the seventh century.

The figure is shown standing, the right knee slightly flexed, in the position known as *tribhaṅga* (triple flexion), depicted here with particular ease and naturalness. The right hand does not hold a symbolic attribute. The touching thumb and index finger (the other fingers are bent) evoke the gesture of grasping, *kaṭakahasta* or *kaṭakamudrā*, but it seems unlikely that this hand could ever have held an attribute, even a detachable one. The object in the left hand is read by Pierre Dupont as a lotus bud; it could also be identified as the jewel, *maṇi* or *ratna*, that is sometimes associated, albeit rarely, with Avalokiteśvara (cat. 7).[1]

The clothing and headdress worn by the Bodhisattva are unusual in pre-Angkor sculpture. Comparable elements, however, can be found in both Khmer bas-reliefs, such as the lintel from Vat Eng Khna in the National Museum of Phnom Penh (cat. 20), and in Cham reliefs as well, such as the pedestal from Mi Son E1 in the Da Nang Museum. All are attributable to the seventh century, the probable date of this small Avalokiteśvara.

The headdress consists of a cylindrical tiara and a diadem with three small fleurons. Similar headpieces occur in certain Cham figures of Viṣṇu[2] and in works heavily influenced by Cham art.[3] Note that the hair, rendered as small curls, appears here on the temples and nape of the neck.

The short garment is draped around the hips and held in place by a simple flat belt. The free end of the cloth is tucked under the belt in front and falls freely between the legs, somewhat prefiguring the pocket fold (for example, cat. 27). To this already complex arrangement is added a double belt at the hips, knotted on the left side.

The affinities pointed out between Cham and Khmer art of the seventh century in the context of the headdress and dress of this Bodhisattva from the National Museum of Phnom Penh lead one to ask in which direction the influences could have operated. In this particular case, it is reasonable to think that Cham art influenced Khmer. It is worth pointing out, however, that neither the tiara headpiece with its flowered diadem nor the dress with a long frontal panel of cloth descending between the legs is found in Khmer art after the seventh century, while both features—elaborated—persisted in Cham art after that date in an enriched form.[4]

It is not inconceivable that the Avalokiteśvara from Vat Kompong Luong at Angkor Borei might be a purely Cham work, but the issue is difficult to resolve given the present state of our knowledge. Even taking into account the ease with which such small objects could be transported, not one of the Cham bronzes presently known is attributable to the seventh century or is comparable to this piece. Therefore, it is more likely in this case, which is far from being an isolated one, that the statuette is Khmer with characteristics that originated in another stylistic setting.

T.Z.

10

Avalokiteśvara

Phnom Ta Kream (Battambang)
Pre-Angkor period, 8th century
Bronze
Height 24 cm, width 6.8 cm, depth 6.7 cm
National Museum of Cambodia,
Phnom Penh, Ga 3548

Two practically identical statuettes of the Bodhisattva Avalokiteśvara, once kept at the Vat Po Veal Museum in Battambang, are now preserved in the National Museum of Phnom Penh. The two figures can be told apart by their workmanship, which is more supple in one than in the other, and by the rosary that the more beautiful of the two holds in his right hand.[1]

Avalokiteśvara, identified by the small Amitābha Buddha on the front of his headdress, is shown standing on a circular, lotus-shaped base in a slightly hip-swayed posture. The right hand, now lacking any symbolic attributes, must once have held a rosary (*akṣamālā*); the water bottle (*kamaṇḍalu*), traditional attribute in the iconography of a two-armed Avalokiteśvara, is held in the left hand.

The Bodhisattva wears a long dhoti, secured at the waist by a belt with a jeweled clasp. Encircling the figure's head is an oval aureole fixed to its back at shoulder level and attached to the back of the skull by a vertical pin. In an initial analysis, the base in the shape of an hourglass with lotus petals incised on it, the figure's clothing with folds indicated by a double incision, and the nimbus argue for linking this piece to Indonesian art.

Other than the jeweled belt, the Bodhisattva's only ornament is a narrow diadem decorated with three fleurons. He wears his hair in a chignon (*jaṭā*) from which two locks escape, falling symmetrically to his shoulders in a double curl. This *jaṭā,* tightly drawn in at the base, spreads out in the shape of a fan above the head. Such handling of the hair is characteristic of several works discovered on the Malay Peninsula that are considered to derive from the art of Śrīvijaya.[2] The locks of hair that unroll in curls onto the shoulders are found in identical form on a figurine likely to have come from the same source and now preserved in a private collection in Thailand.[3]

This Avalokiteśvara from Phnom Ta Kream poses the same kinds of questions as the one from Vat Kompong Luong. Here, at any rate, the question is to discover whether the work is Indonesian—in this case a work closely related to Sumatran models or deriving from the Malay Peninsula—or whether it is the product of a Khmer workshop that copied a foreign model with great fidelity. Again, it is difficult to resolve the question, though a non-Khmer origin seems more probable.

If the dates proposed for the Śrīvijaya works closely related to this statuette are accepted, it seems possible to date this Avalokiteśvara at some point in the eighth or ninth century. One should recall that it was from that time that certain Indonesian influences were felt in Khmer art. It should be made clear that these influences are of a purely iconographic or typological kind (for example, the *kāla* motif in certain lintels featuring the styles of Kulen and Preah Koh) and are not stylistic.

T.Z.

11

Maitreya

Provenance unknown
Pre-Angkor period, 8th century
Bronze, with a large component of silver
Height 46 cm, width 19 cm
Musée national des Arts asiatiques-Guimet, Paris, MA 3321

As an enlightened being, but also no doubt in the guise of the Buddha of the future, Maitreya seems to have enjoyed considerable popularity in the early phases of Khmer art. He is, with Avalokiteśvara (cats. 7–10), the most frequently depicted Bodhisattva in pre-Angkor art, especially in metal statuary.[1] Although the portable attributes that the figure once held are gone, the identification can be made without difficulty. He is recognized from the *stūpa* on the front of his *jaṭāmukuṭa,* a constant iconographic feature of Maitreya.

The Bodhisattva is represented standing, the hips flexed, the left knee slightly bent. Two arms branch out into four at the level of the elbows. The coiffure is created from locks of hair joined on top of his head to form a tall cylindrical chignon, the *jaṭā.* The locks of hair that form this complicated chignon—one that is actually common in Khmer art and that would continue to reappear with variations for several centuries—hang down in four rows of intertwined double loops. The figure wears a long dhoti, secured at the hips by a simple knotted cord, and has no ornaments. A Bodhisattva may be represented in two ways: as an ascetic, and therefore without any jewels, or as a richly adorned *cakravartin* (Le Bonheur 1972, 142, note 2). The Maitreya from the Musée Guimet apparently belongs to the first type. However, the distended earlobes are pierced. Might this imply that they once held ear pendants that have since been removed, thus placing the statuette within the second category?

The sculpture is executed in a masterful style, the face expressive and subtly modeled, the body elegant and supple. The hands and feet with their protruding heels, however, are somewhat clumsy.

Stylistically, this figure is related to a group of bronze sculptures, both Buddha and Bodhisattva figures, in which the most beautiful come from what is now northeastern Thailand: for instance, fragments such as the famous Bodhisattva from Ban Tahnot,[2] colossal in size, and possibly a representation of Maitreya. While the images of Buddha from this group are related to the Mon stylistic tradition of Dvāravatī, the Bodhisattva for their part belong in the context of pre-Angkor art. Among the figures in this group, those wearing a long garment are very rare; the Maitreya from the Musée Guimet is exceptional in this respect. The entire set of sculptures under discussion, all bronze, dates from the late seventh to the early ninth century (Bunker, 1971–1972; Boisselier 1974, 111–114). It remains difficult at the moment to date the work with any greater precision; most of the known sculptures, because of the simplicity of the dress and especially the treatment of the coiffure, are attributable to the eighth century.

The majority of these figures display a high degree of skill in the use of the lost-wax process, and a no less remarkable quality in certain alloys with high silver content, such as the one used for this statuette of Maitreya.

T.Z.

12

Maitreya

Prakhon Chai (Buriram), Thailand
Pre-Angkor period, 8th century
Bronze with silver and black stone inlays
Height 96 cm, width 35 cm, depth 26 cm
The Asia Society, New York,
The Mr. and Mrs. John D. Rockefeller 3rd Collection, 1979.63

Maitreya occupies a unique position in the Buddhist pantheon in that he is both a Bodhisattva and the Buddha who will inaugurate the new Buddhist era after the dissolution (4,500 years after its founding) of Buddhism as it was conceived by the historical Buddha, Gautama or Śākyamuni, about five hundred years before the birth of Christ. Meanwhile, he waits in heaven in the last of his ten cycles (*bhūmi*) of life on earth. Bodhisattva images usually pertain only to Mahāyāna Buddhism, but Maitreya is exceptionally accepted by Theravāda Buddhism and has been part of Buddhist philosophy from as early as the fourth century, as evinced in the *Mahāvastu*, a northern Indian text (Chutiwongs and Leidy 1994, 69-70).

The distinguishing feature of Maitreya is the presence in his *jaṭāmukuṭa* (crown of hair) of a small *stūpa*.[1] There is no textual explanation for this attribute,[2] although, like the figure of the seated Amitābha Buddha in the headdress of Avalokiteśvara, it

Fig. 1
Maitreya. Provenance unknown. Pre-Angkor period, seventh to eighth century. Bronze. Height 32.5 cm. National Museum of Cambodia, Phnom Penh

undoubtedly signifies the high status of Maitreya within the Buddhist pantheon.[3] This example, certainly one of the most beautiful Southeast Asian bronzes that exist, is one of the hoard of about three hundred found in mysterious circumstances in 1964 in a ruined temple of the Khmer type in Prakhon Chai, Buriram Province. This area, part of present-day Thailand, was once peopled by Khmer, and Khmer culture was of importance there from the earliest centuries of the pre-Angkor era in Cambodia. There have been many discussions about the genesis of the bronzes and possible influences from both Dvāravatī-Mon and Śrīvijaya / Indonesian cultures (Boisselier, *Bouddha*, 1967; Le Bonheur 1972) but current opinion tends to support the theory that, whatever their historical context might have been, the predominant stylistic traits establish their Khmer identity.

This Maitreya has many features in common with the other Maitreya in the exhibition (cat. 11) and with a Maitreya in the National Museum of Phnom Penh (fig. 1, Ga 5428), to the extent that one might suppose a common origin despite the lack of precise provenance for the other pieces. Both figures have a slender and graceful torso, and the *jaṭāmukuṭa* and simple rendering of the garment appropriate for the ascetic personification of the Bodhisattva. Each shows a technically well-resolved solution to the problem of the jointing and disposition of four arms, and the intricate modeling of the fingers reaches great beauty in the Rockefeller and Phnom Penh examples (though the rear hands of the former are less well proportioned than its front hands). All have a rich patina and all succeed in projecting benevolence and spirituality in the finely modeled features, though these are less refined in the Guimet figure than in the others. Feet and legs are often perfunctorily modeled in Prakhon Chai pieces (as in pre-Angkor bronzes in general), but the Rockefeller figure has perhaps the most naturalistic and graceful legs in all Khmer art. Details of hair tresses, eyebrows, ears, and mustache are equally perfect in this sculpture, but it is perhaps the eyes that impress as its most memorable aspect. Slightly downcast, their expressiveness enhanced by the soft texture of the stone inlays, their gaze transcends material focus and seems to reflect an inspirational insight into the divine.

H.J.

13

Kṛṣṇa Govardhana

Vat Koh, Prei Krabas (Ta Keo)
Pre-Angkor period, 6th(?)–7th century
Sandstone
Height 160 cm, width 62 cm, depth 34 cm
National Museum of Cambodia, Phnom Penh, Ka 1625

Angkor Borei (Nagara Purī) is thought to have been the center of Funan or at least of an important pre-Angkor kingdom. *Nagara*, which becomes *Angkor* in Khmer, is the Sanskrit word for city, the equivalent of the Latin *urbs* or Greek *polis*, the capital and central or unifying site of the territory, in the sense that Rome was the *urbs*, Athens the *polis*, and Constantinople at a later date the capital of the Byzantine Empire.

The most remarkable art in the Angkor Borei area, where works from all periods have been found, dates from pre-Angkor times and is still visibly influenced by Indian art. The *tribhaṅga* (triple flexion of the body), which is a characteristic feature, for instance, of the murals in Ajaṇṭā, is equally evident in the stance of this Kṛṣṇa Govardhanamūrti. The young god lifts up Mount Govardhana to provide shelter for the shepherds and their cattle against the torrential rains unleashed by Indra, the god of storms, the Indian equivalent to Jupiter / Zeus the Father. Kṛṣṇa's left arm is in alignment with his right leg and crosses the line of the head and trunk. His right hand rests on his hip and remains parallel to his left foot. The Indian *tribhaṅga* is restricted in this image to a double flexion.

Kṛṣṇa wears a short dhoti. Unlike those found in most pre-Angkor images, this dhoti with its full side panel is not designed to be knotted in the back but is held in place by a loose belt.

Although the statue is in high relief, it has a great deal in common on a technical level with freestanding statuary. The remarkable Kṛṣṇa Govardhana of the same period (from the Stoclet collection, now at the Cleveland Museum of Art, see fig. 1) offers an example of more fully freestanding sculpture.

Kṛṣṇa's head is delicately modeled, and his hairstyle is composed of the same flat curls one finds on images of Buddha.

The elegant proportions, the natural modeling, and the sense of quiet strength emanating from the god combine to give this work an undeniably classical character.

S.S.

Fig. 1. Kṛṣṇa Govardhana. Phnom Da style, pre-Angkor period, seventh century. Sandstone. Cleveland Museum of Art

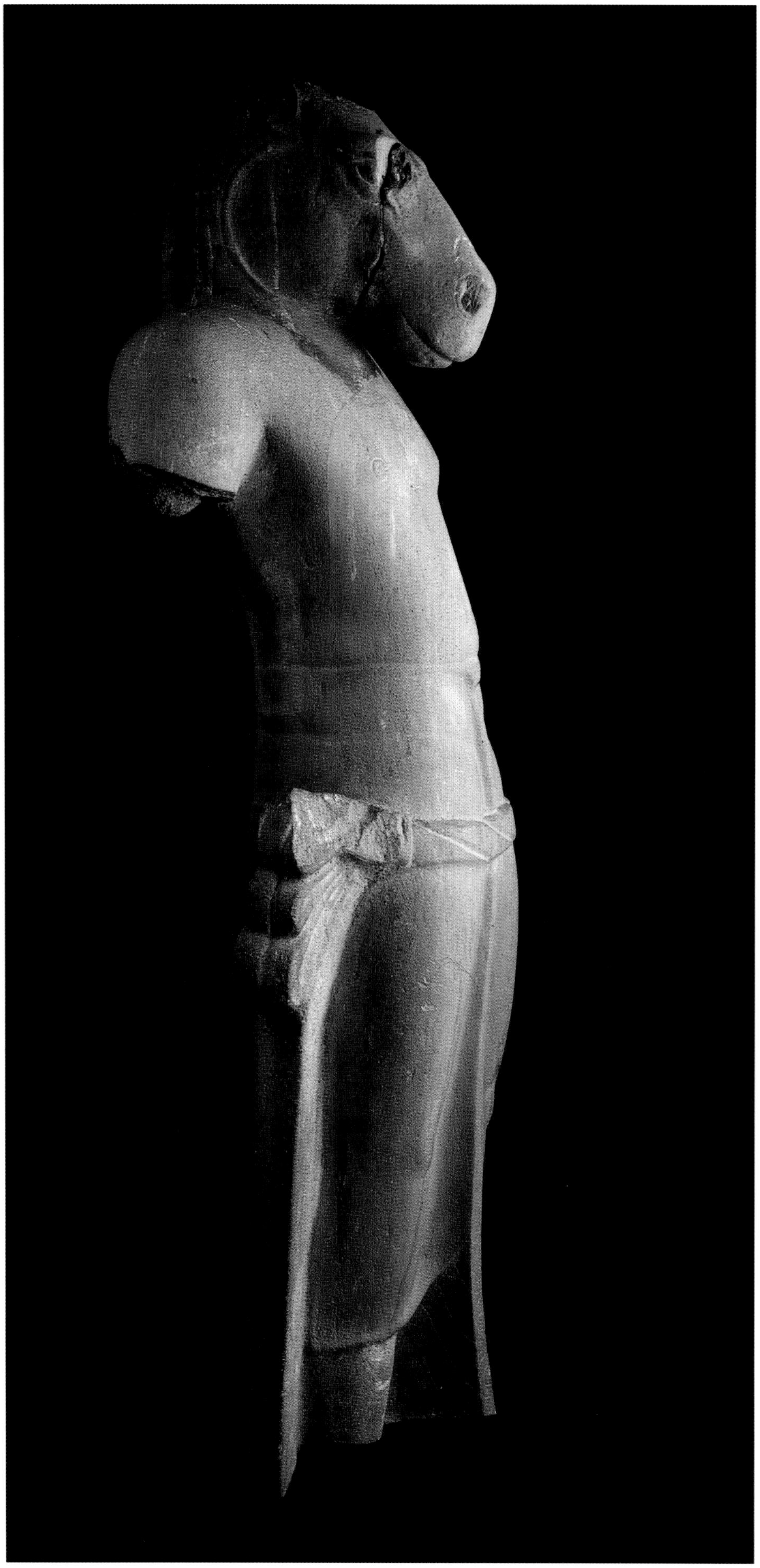

14

Vājimukha / Hayaśiras

Kuk Trap (Kandal)
Pre-Angkor period, 7th century
Sandstone
Height 135 cm, width 49 cm, depth 33 cm
National Museum of Cambodia,
Phnom Penh, Ka 1642

This imposing figure with human body and equine face (*Vāji*, "horse"; *mukha*, "face") is one of the group of early, preponderantly Viṣṇuite statues of the Phnom Da style (cat. 13) that reveal Indian influences (including those of the Gupta style). The grace of his *tribhaṅga* stance (triple-curved hip-swayed posture) and the subtlety of the rendering of his garments are characteristic of the type, but the plastic qualities revealed in the form of the sturdily braced legs, suggested below the clinging garment with its exuberantly bowed sash, the strong but sensitive horse head, in particular the delicate rendering of the nostrils and mouth, and the technical solution to the problem of the conjunction of two such disparate anatomies, lend an impressive variation to the range of the Phnom Da type.

There are two manifestations of Viṣṇu having associations with the horse. One is Hayaśiras, or Hayagrīva, known as the protector of writings for his part in rescuing the holy texts, the *Veda*, from their thieves, the demons Madhu and Kaiṭabha. He is shown on a lintel of the tenth-century temple of Banteay Srei and is mentioned in an inscription at Prasat Sankhanh during the first half of the eleventh century (Bhattacharya 1961, 118). Viṣṇuite writings (the *Bhāgavatapurān*) refer to the horse-headed being as the "all-powerful himself" who is "the color of gold." The other manifestation, the tenth avatar (*avatāra*) of Viṣṇu, is Kalkin, about whom there exists a *purāṇa* (*Kalkipurāṇa*). Kalkin, or Kalkyavatara (not mentioned in Khmer epigraphy according to Boisselier [1989, 35]), is the avatar who is yet to come, Viṣṇu's incarnation at the end of time. According to the legend, he will appear on a white horse at the end of the age of conflict, carrying a cometlike sword, to reestablish order, and will then destroy the world, after which another race will appear.

Since the horse-headed figure under discussion lacks arms and attributes, it is impossible to determine which of these avatars he represents. Regardless of the uncertainty of the iconography, however, this noble Vājimukha epitomizes the lofty qualities of both the possible avatars with a moving simplicity.

H.J.

15

Viṣṇu

Tuol Dai Buon (Prei Veng)
Pre-Angkor period, 7th century
Sandstone
Height 183 cm; width 80 cm, depth 52 cm
National Museum of Cambodia,
Phnom Penh, Ka 1597

Cambodian kings can be distinguished as official followers of Śiva, Viṣṇu or, more rarely, the Buddha, and as adherents of a specific cult, by their posthumous names, chosen by the king before his death. In spite of the identification of the kings with a specific deity, a tolerance of other sects seems to have existed during their reigns. Bhattacharya pointed out that the three faiths coexisted in Cambodia from the earliest period, that of Funan, and that the tolerance encouraged a syncretism that also accommodated indigenous cults (Bhattacharya 1961, 25–29). For most of Cambodian history Śivaism was the state religion, but Viṣṇuism also predominated in some reigns and was established in the kingdom from as early as the sixth century. An inscription of 598 refers to an image of Kapilavāsudeva, a form of Viṣṇu as supreme god. Viṣṇuism was particularly associated with the rulers of Cambodia, whereas Śivaism was less exclusive and lent itself more readily to popular participation. It was a Viṣṇu adherent, Sūryavarman II, who in the first half of the twelfth century built and dedicated to Viṣṇu the most famous of all Khmer monuments, Angkor Vat.

Viṣṇuism has more than one form; the version that predominated in Cambodia was Pāñcarātra, also known as Bhāgavata and Sātvata.[1] Central to Pāñcarātra philosophy is the belief, stated very simply, that the evolution of the universe from primordial matter is instigated by Viṣṇu, or a portion of Viṣṇu known as *puruṣa*. It is Viṣṇu who controls the cycle of creation and dissolution; he is the essence of the cosmos (in this spiritual aspect his powers are close to those of Śiva). Representation of this cycle occurs in images of Viṣṇu Anantaśāyin, or Viṣṇu in cosmic sleep on the back of the serpent Ananta who lies on the ocean (see cat. 68). Viṣṇu may also be represented on the back of his *vāhana* (mount), the mythological bird Garuḍa; he may be depicted as Trivikrama, conqueror of the three worlds (symbolized by three giant steps taken by the god); he may appear in the form of one of his twenty-four avatars, or manifestations,[2] who include Kṛṣṇa, Rāma, Balarāma, Paraśurāma, Kalkin, Hayagrīva, and Kūrma, among others. All these examples appear in Khmer sculpture, sometimes in bas-relief and sometimes in freestanding statuary, and several are represented in this exhibition (cats. 13, 51). The aspect of Viṣṇu most frequently represented in Khmer freestanding sculpture is that of the god as *cakravartin* (universal ruler, cats. 30, 31, 69, 115). The most famous example of this is the magnificent Viṣṇu from Phnom Da (see page 142, fig. 1). In this towering sculpture, where, unusually, the horseshoe arch carved out as a support structure for arms and attributes is almost intact, the god is depicted with eight arms, rare in Cambodia. Six of the eight attributes that should be carried in the hands are present, and on the basis of these, which are not limited to Viṣṇu's usual attributes but include some associated with other gods, it has been suggested that Viṣṇu is here represented as the universal king and the chief deity of the pantheon (Dupont 1955, 28; Bhattacharya 1961, 102–103). Six of the eight *dikpālaka* (deities who preside over the four cardinal and the four intermediate points of the compass, hence the entire cosmos) are represented by their attributes, Viṣṇu's miter is tall, signifying royal command, and his stance is frontal, commanding, and hieratic.

The Viṣṇu from Tuol Dai Buon (considerably to the north of Phnom Da) has four arms (*caturbhuja*). He has many of the Gupta stylistic features that are characteristic of Phnom Da sculpture: the hip-swayed stance, the supple but sturdy body and legs, the tall and simple miter, and the long braided locks. The facial expression is confident, authoritative, but benign, with downcast eyes and a faint smile on the full, finely molded lips. The sculptor in this case resorted to a support structure that leaves the upper hands and attributes connected to the head but does not continue to the ground. The lower attributes and arms are supported by simple columns of stone;[3] the lower left column is depicted as one of the god's attributes, the *gadā* (staff or mace), which stands for the power of knowledge. Only one other attribute is still present, the *cakra* (disk), symbol of power, in the upper right hand. The missing attributes would have been a ball, representing *mahī* (earth), in the lower left hand,[4] and the *śaṅkha* (conch), emanating from the element of water and signifying the origin of existence, in the upper left.

The treatment of hands, feet, and torso is realistic if somewhat heavy, with the belting of the *sampot* (*saṃbaṭ*), the short wrapped and twisted length of cloth typical of Khmer male dress, causing a slight naturalistic bulge of the flesh of the abdomen. The rings at the base of the neck are signs of beauty. This Viṣṇu radiates both majesty and benevolence.

H.J.

16

Harihara

Asram Maha Rosei, *phnom* (*bhnaṃ*)
Bakheng, Angkor Borei (Ta Keo)
Pre-Angkor period, style of Phnom Da,
7th century
Sandstone
Height 178 cm, width 65 cm, depth 31 cm
Musée national des Arts asiatiques-Guimet, Paris, MG 14910

The cult of Harihara was prevalent in pre-Angkor Cambodia, as attested by many epigraphic references (Bhattacharya 1961, 157), though almost unknown in the former neighboring kingdoms of Champa (now central Vietnam) and Thailand. This magnificent sculpture from Asram Maha Rosei, a sanctuary on a hill near Phnom Da, is the oldest known Khmer image of the deity and offers one of the clearest extant illustrations of the nature of this composite god. He comprises an equal mixture of Viṣṇu (Hari) on the proper left and Śiva (Hara) on the right.

Typical for the Phnom Da, somewhat Gupta-influenced, style is the long, slightly aquiline nose, the oval face, and the hair cascading down the back almost to shoulder-blade level, as can also be seen in the Avalokiteśvara of Tan Long (cat. 7). The impression of a slightly soft abdomen, with the stomach indented by the knotted narrow belt, as well as the slenderness of the torso, is characteristic of the style, as is the wide, strong neck and the elongated earlobes pierced to receive rings.

In Harihara figures of a later date the stylistic distinction between the Viṣṇu and the Śiva sides becomes less distinct, in most cases the Viṣṇuistic features tending to dominate, as with the example from Prasat Andet (cat. 27). Here, however, the Śiva side offers a fully developed *jaṭāmukuṭa* of braided and looped tresses twisted and arranged both horizontally and vertically (a stylistic element that identifies the sculpture as of the Phnom Da period) even though the profile has been adjusted to balance the cylinder of Viṣṇu's miter (Régnier 1966). Also typically visible for Harihara is half of Śiva's third eye in the middle of the forehead as well as the symbol of the crescent moon in his hair. Although most of the supporting horseshoe arch has been broken off and the lower hands lost, the remaining attribute on the Hara side is the upper portion of the trident proper to Śiva. One of Śiva's many manifestations is lord of the beasts, and he is appropriately garbed in a tiger skin with the head hanging over the thigh in front and the paws and tail slung behind.

The Viṣṇu side wears a *kirīta* (tall miter), from which curly locks escape to lie on the temples and tumble down the back. The garb is an understated *sampot* (*saṃbaṭ*) with graceful folds slanting across the thigh suggested by incised lines and ripples at the lower edge carved in slight relief; a free edge of the cloth is modeled in precise pleats on the central panel of the block of stone, which has not been fully carved out and thus supports the leg of Śiva. Viṣṇu's typical *cakra* (disk), is held in Hari's naturalistically jointed fingers.

The Harihara cult presumably offered its adherents the protection and spiritual inspiration of both Viṣṇuism and Śivaism, and its popularity testifies to the syncretic tendencies within Khmer civilization.

H.J.

17

Lintel

Sambor Prei Kuk, outskirts of sanctuary 7, south group (Kompong Thom)
Pre-Angkor period, style of Sambor Prei Kuk, 1st half of the 7th century
Sandstone
Height 60 cm, width 210 cm, depth 38 cm
Musée national des Arts asiatiques-Guimet, Paris, MG 18853

The chronological classification of Khmer monuments is essentially based on the study of architectural decoration. Following the work of Philippe Stern and Gilberte de Coral-Rémusat, a great number of studies, both surveys and detailed examinations, have been dedicated to these questions. Pilasters and pediments, lintels and colonnettes have evolved over the centuries at a variable rate, with some styles lasting barely a few decades and others, nearly a century.

The lintels, when they are not reused from an earlier building, are without question the most valuable chronological markers: each period in ancient Cambodian art is in fact remarkably differentiated from the periods before and after. The change from one style to another may occur either gradually, as with sculpture—in which case we speak of evolution—or in a more radical way—in which case we speak of mutation.

The beautiful brick monuments belonging to the north and south groups of the ancient religious city of Sambor Prei Kuk, to our current knowledge, are considered to be among the most ancient Khmer temples still in existence (first half of the seventh century). Within this brick architecture, the door frames, lintels, and columns were made of sandstone. Clearly, this was used to make the buildings stronger, and in some cases they are the only elements remaining.

The lintel in the Musée Guimet was discovered by Henri Parmentier on the outskirts of temple 7 of the south group of Sambor Prei Kuk, where it must once have crowned the entrance gate of this octagonal, east-facing building (fig.1, page 14).

In their composition, the most linear lintels of the Sambor Prei Kuk style are generally organized around a horizontal axis marking off the upper third of the area. It takes the form of a polylobed arch with a broad, flat ground decorated with vegetal motifs and beading, probably a copy in stone of a wooden element. Jeweled garlands and pendants are suspended below the arch; three indentations are occupied by cartouches that often contain small figures. Indra—god of storms but also guardian of the east in Hindu mythology—takes the central position here, astride his traditional mount, the elephant Airāvata. The two lateral cartouches contain *marut*, wind gods and companions of Indra. The conjunction of the arch and the atmospheric gods suggests the bridge (the rainbow) that joins the world of men to the world of the gods. As the sanctuary's entry is precisely such a passage, marking the boundary between the mortal realm and the abode of the gods, this interpretation is a natural one. The lintels, beyond their structural function, participate fully in the symbolism of the monument. At either extremity of the lintel are *makara*, figures with foliate tails who are imaginary hybrid animals from the Indian bestiary—half-crocodile, half-elephant. They are ridden by small figures, while horned lions issue from their open maws.

The composition as a whole derives from Indian art. A simpler version in which the arch has only a single indentation can be found in the sculpted decoration of the Ajaṇṭā caves in Mahārāṣṭra (fifth to sixth centuries), as well as in the Cālukya monuments of Karṇāṭaka and the Pallava monuments of Tamilnāḍu (seventh century). The Indian origin of the first Khmer lintels appears undeniable; however, the Khmer seem to have transcended this model from the beginning.

T.Z.

18

Durgā Mahiṣāsuramardinī

Sambor Prei Kuk, sanctuary 9 of north group (Kompong Thom)
Pre-Angkor period, style of Sambor Prei Kuk, first half of the 7th century
Sandstone
Height 165 cm, width 47 cm, depth 38 cm
National Museum of Cambodia, Phnom Penh, Ka 1593

The triple flexion of the body characteristic of Indian figures is expressive, in this work, of movement and quiet effort, as in the image of Kṛṣṇa Govardhanamūrti from Vat Koh (cat. 13). Here, the action is presumably violent—the goddess has just killed Mahiṣāsura—but it is suggested only by the swaying of the lower folds of her skirt. With all the powers of the gods Viṣṇu, Śiva, Brahmā, and others concentrated in her, this *śakti* (divine energy) astride a lion slew the buffalo demon, a feat no other single god could have accomplished. Durgā is not represented riding the lion or in the act of bringing down the buffalo demon, who collapsed at her feet. Khmer depictions of Durgā Mahiṣāsuramardinī are most often symbolic; the vanquished demon (missing here) is usually represented as a buffalo head carved on the pedestal of the goddess' statue. Unlike the depictions in Indian and Javanese art, the demon does not assume a human form that materializes at the level of the buffalo's severed neck.

Despite the lack of head and arms, one can sense the gesture the goddess makes as she pierces the buffalo demon with her lance. The round breasts and generous curve of the hips are indications of the youthful vigor of the goddess as she carries out her divine mission. One is almost tempted to compare her to the famous Winged Victory of Samothrace in light of the calm and completely classical equilibrium of the goddess, and her appearance of taking flight.

This statue, which was broken into three main fragments, was discovered in the north group of Sambor Prei Kuk in two separate locations almost fifty years apart. The bust, found near sanctuary 1 (N1), was brought into the National Museum of Phnom Penh in 1920, while the statue's lower part was unearthed in sanctuary 9 (N9) only toward the end of the 1960s. The work was restored, according to the museum's records, in March 1972.

S.S.

19

Devī

Koh Krieng, Sambor on the Mekong (Kratie)
Pre-Angkor period, style of Sambor Prei Kuk, 1st half of the 7th century
Sandstone
Height 127 cm, width 47 cm, depth 22 cm
National Museum of Cambodia, Phnom Penh, Ka 1621

Images in the round of pre-Angkor feminine divinities are rather rare, and the resulting lack of comparative detail makes it difficult to establish a chronological basis for them with any certainty. Despite the rarity, however, it must be said that two of the most unforgettable Khmer sculptures in existence are of goddesses of this period: Durgā Mahiṣāsuramardinī (cat. 18) and the Devī under discussion here. Both are in the style of Sambor Prei Kuk, the modern name of Īśānapura, capital of the kingdom of Īśānavarman I (615?–635). A stylistic comparison between these two figures would not be fruitful, as they are so totally different in nature, but it is perhaps useful to mention that they may both reflect a new wave of Indian stylistic influence (particularly apparent in architectural decoration) during Īśānavarman's reign, possibly as a result of the marriage of the king's daughter to an Indian Brahman called Durgāsvāmin.[1] The intricately chased buckle of the belt of the Koh Krieng Devī certainly depicts Indic motifs.

An early suggestion—based on the style of the goddess' coiffure—that the statue might represent not Devī, *śakti* (consort) of Śiva, but Lakṣmī, *śakti* of Viṣṇu, is difficult to establish in the absence of attributes. The *jaṭā*, the elaborately braided, piled, and looped coiffure, however, helps to establish the date of the work. Comparing it convincingly to that of the Harihara of Sambor Prei Kuk (page 133, fig. 2), and noting the sarong draped low on the hips in a manner typical of that style and period, Boisselier argues that the sculpture dates from the first half of the seventh century (Boisselier, *"Une statue féminine,"* 1955, 30).

Despite the frontal stance and an air of serene confidence, the figure does not project imperiousness or inaccessibility. Of all pre-Angkor Khmer feminine sculptures, as Giteau has noted (*Les Khmers,* 1965, 48–51), the Devī of Koh Krieng most compellingly suggests portraiture. The sensitivity of the facial expression and the sympathy of the gaze project an undeniable humanity. The particularization of the representation also prompts belief in a real model: a person of great beauty but not an idealized and unformed girl; she is clearly a mature woman, rather plump in stomach and hips, the creases below the full, very maternal breasts with modeled nipples not just incised beauty marks but evidence of slightly undulating flesh. The morphology is remarkably close to the characteristics of Cambodian women today, so that one is tempted to see in this Devī an inspired personification of Khmer womanhood.

H.J.

20

Lintel

Vat Eng Khna (Kompong Thom)
Pre-Angkor period, style of Prei Kmeng,
2d half of the 7th century
Sandstone
Height 55 cm, width 185 cm, depth 29 cm
National Museum of Cambodia,
Phnom Penh, Ka 1774

Documentation of the evolution of the lintel has yielded convincing parameters for the chronology of Khmer art (Dupont, *Mission au Cambodge*, 1938). This remarkable example from Vat Eng Khna, with its horizontal band of decorative vegetal elements forming a framework for figurative medallions, epitomizes one of the styles of Prei Kmeng thoroughly analyzed by Bénisti (1975, 93–100). What is at first not apparent is that almost all the decorative elements, aesthetically so well integrated into the overall composition with a masterly sense of proportion, are also tightly connected to the iconography of the two scenes represented.

The upper scene depicts the myth of the origin of the *liṅga*, or *liṅgodbhavamūrti* (Bosch 1931, 491–492; Bhattacharya 1961, 80), which concerns a quarrel between Brahmā and Viṣṇu about which was the creator of the universe. A great column appeared, surrounded by thousands of flames, which was in fact Śiva's *liṅga*. Trying to determine its ends, the gods metamorphosed. Brahmā, as a goose, flew up, while Viṣṇu, as a boar, dug down, but neither could encompass the pillar. Acknowledging after a very long time that the pillar was their superior, they offered prayers to it, whereupon Śiva appeared from the column in a form with multiple heads and limbs, his three eyes representing sun, moon, and fire, to proclaim that they were born from him and that all three gods were one, although manifest in three forms.

Śiva's head, with the column of the *liṅga* behind surrounded by flames, can be seen in the central medallion. To his right is Brahmā, three of whose four heads are visible, with geese displayed in the band that forms the architectural support of the medallions. To his left is four-armed Viṣṇu, a conch (?) in one of his left hands, with boars depicted in the horizontal band on his side. Both gods have their hands raised in the worshiping, or *añjali*, mudra.

The lower scene shows a person with a seemingly royal headdress sitting on a platform under a *maṇḍapa*, (columned pavilion). To his right and left processions of people approach, the former wearing aristocratic headdresses and carrying water pots, the latter having Brahman ascetics' *jaṭāmukuṭa* hairstyles and carrying objects that may be conches. The leading figure on each side is pouring the contents of his vessel on the head of the seated figure. Further along the procession, musicians play and dancers perform. There is a strong possibility that the scene depicts the consecration of a king (*abhiṣeka*); Bosch (1931, 494), however, suggests that the two episodes are juxtaposed to draw a parallel between the glory of Śiva and that of the king who is his representative on earth.

The figures in the lower scene are incorporated into a rhythm whose dynamics draw the eye toward the central figure. The forms are cohesive but the figures vary—arms differently disposed, bodies swayed in different directions—so that the line does not become monotonous. The hieratic nature of the personages in the top scene lends them a celestial isolation and splendor that accords well with their divine nature. The seated figures on consoles at the outer edges bridge the two scenes, anchor the overarching band to the base of the lintel, and bind the composition into a plastic unity. It is a masterpiece of iconographic and architectonic fusion.

H.J.

21

Stele

Tuol Neak Ta Bak Ka, Dangkor (Kandal)
K.940
Pre-Angkor period, 7th–8th century
Sandstone
Height 96 cm (without tenon),
width 41 cm, depth 8 cm
National Museum of Cambodia,
Phnom Penh, Ka 1760

Our knowledge of ancient Khmer culture rests in large part on the study of inscriptions, both Sanskrit and Khmer. These texts, whatever the period, essentially relate to matters of religion, and their importance in historical studies no longer needs emphasis.

The only inscriptions to survive are engraved in stone. Some are integral parts of monuments: door piers, pillars, walls, and so on; others, incised on stele, are physically independent of the monument, though just as closely associated with the temple as the former. Two chief types of stele exist: slabs, which vary in thickness and are inscribed on one or both sides; and quadrilateral blocks, which are normally inscribed on all four faces.

The stele from Tuol Neak Ta Bak Ka is incised with an eleven-line inscription in Khmer and can be dated from paleographic evidence to the pre-Angkor period. Typically for Khmer inscriptions, the text deals with the practical matters of the foundation. A dignitary, whose name is not given, orders that a certain quantity of salt be delivered to the boats of various Śivaite sanctuaries designated by the names under which Śiva was worshiped there. One finds, among others, the name of Śrī Bhadreśvara, which can certainly be connected to the god of the old Liṅgaparvata (now Vat Phu in Laos), a diety whose importance throughout Khmer history is widely acknowledged.[1] Although the Bhadreśvara of the Tuol Neak Ta Bak Ka stele cannot be positively identified as the one from Vat Phu, the similarity is worth noting.

Within a few days of its discovery in January 1948, as George Cœdès relates, the inscription was already drawing attention to itself for "the stream of visitors who came to make offerings to this stone."[2] What undoubtedly aroused interest in the stele at the time was the motif carved at the top: an image of the bull Nandin, the vehicle of Śiva, but also the god's animal form.

Nandin is shown lying down on an open lotus blossom. The image has a certain clumsy charm—the head, for instance, is too large—but is nonetheless rendered very naturally and placed adroitly within the bow-shaped line of the stele's upper edge.

T.Z.

22

Brahmanic Stele

Provenance unknown
Pre-Angkor period, style of Prei Kmeng, 2d half of the 7th century
Sandstone
Height 77 cm, width 42 cm, depth 16 cm
Musée national des Arts asiatiques-Guimet, Paris, MG 24618

The commissioning of Brahmanic works in ancient Cambodia did not concentrate solely on anthropomorphic images of the gods. The deities could also be represented by symbols or emblems that characterized and defined them in the context of an abstract iconography. The best-known and most frequent example, both in pre-Angkor and Angkor art, is the *liṅga* (cat. 23, 110), a stylized representation of Śiva's phallus as well as a symbol of the god. A divinity could also be evoked by the simple depiction of its attributes. Such is the case in this stele from the Musée Guimet representing the *trimūrti*, the three principal gods of Brahmanism.

Each of these gods is manifested by distinctive attributes. Brahmā, on the stele's proper right, is represented by the *akṣamālā* (rosary) and the *kamaṇḍalu* (Brahman's sacred water vessel) on a lotus flower. Śiva, in the center, is evoked by his *triśūla* (trident); Viṣṇu, on the stele's proper left, is depicted by Pṛthivī (the earth, rendered in Khmer iconography by a ball that replaces the grain and the lotus flower of Indian iconography), the *cakra* (discus), the *śaṅkha* (conch), and the *gadā* (club) (Bhattacharya 1961, 103–105). The group's arrangement—Śiva in the center, Brahmā and Viṣṇu on his right and left respectively—was the same as that retained during the Angkor period in sanctuaries dedicated to the *trimūrti* (cats. 37–39). The stele from the Musée Guimet is significant for its rich iconography and for demonstrating that a *trimūrti* cult already existed within the context of Śivaism—the emphasis here is certainly on Śiva, who is placed in the center—as early as the pre-Angkor period.

The symbolic attributes of the deities are set on a common pedestal inside an architectural structure. The edifice, very simple in its decoration, suggests a columned pavilion of the same type as the *maṇḍapa* for Nandin in building S2 of Sambor Prei Kuk's south group (Parmentier 1927, 2: pl. XIV). The pedestal is also based on a real model. In composition it resembles the pre-Angkor pedestals that were generally carved with vegetal motifs and on which two series of flat moldings framed a broad median band (Bénisti, "Piedestaux," 1973). As with the pavilion, the decoration has been simplified. The flat moldings, in reality covered by rich bas-reliefs, are left smooth, while the ornamentation of the median band has been reduced to a simple floral motif, framed by short pilasters with large pearls.

The *triśūla* on the Musée Guimet stele is remarkably similar to one that appears on the upper part of an inscribed stele from Vat Phu (K. 367), now at the National Museum of Phnom Penh.[1] This detail, as well as the treatment of the vegetal elements of the Musée Guimet stele, allows it to be dated to the second half of the seventh century, style of Prei Kmeng.

T.Z.

23

Mukhaliṅga

Vat Po Metrey (Ta Keo)
Pre-Angkor period, 7th–8th century
Sandstone
Height 83 cm, width 25 cm, depth 25 cm
National Museum of Cambodia,
Phnom Penh, Ka 1622

Śivaism was the main religion of Cambodia, and Śiva was generally represented by his symbol, the *liṅga*. This was particularly true of the pre-Angkor period. The *liṅga*-worship of Śivaites is tied to the myth of origin of the *liṅga* (*liṅgodbhava*), which names Śiva as the supreme god and the other two members of the *trimūrti* as his acolytes.[1] While the myth explains the *liṅga* as a column of fire whose extremities are beyond reach, it is well to remember that the *liṅga* is before all else a symbol and representation of the phallus.

Liṅga take many shapes. They can be of natural, uncarved stone (*svāyaṃbhuvaliṅga*). Some *liṅga* were carved directly and crudely into the rock; some are colossal, as with the *liṅga* from the Thma Doh (Ta Keo) sanctuary, which is six meters tall. One of the peaks at Vat Phu, whose shape suggested a *liṅga*, was chosen very early on as a site of worship and called Liṅgaparvata. Yet *liṅga* were generally more modest in scale and carved either of sandstone or some other material (*sthapitaliṅga*). While the *liṅga* in the form of a realistic phallus belonged, for the most part, to the pre-Angkor era, *liṅga* with faces (*mukhaliṅga*) belong exclusively to that period. This work provides a good example of the genre. Smaller in size than certain *svāyaṃbhuvaliṅga*, these *liṅga* may nonetheless attain respectable dimensions: the one at Phnom Bok, for example, is four meters tall.

Like anthropomorphic statues, each *liṅga* seemingly had its own identity. A king who wanted to become associated with a divinity or reside in that god's realm after his death erected a *liṅga* during his lifetime and gave it a name linking his own to some form of Śiva's: Rājendravarman consecrated a Rājendrabhadreśvara liṅga at Pre Rup, Sūryavarman I erected several Sūryavarmeśvaras in various temples, and so on.

Recent ethnology points out the parallel between the cult of the *liṅga* and the animist worship of rock spirits. But it is more than a parallel; the two represent different permutations of the same worship, the assimilation of one by the other. The *mukhaliṅga*, for instance, is the equivalent of those uncarved rocks to which a face is attributed. Probably this helped popularize the cult of the *liṅga*. After all, both cults worshiped a symbolic phallus capable of inseminating the earth and making it fruitful. The *liṅga* consequently brought together and melded the cult of the ancestors and the cult of earth spirits.

A.C.

24

Nandin

Bassak (Svay Rieng)
Pre-Angkor period, 7th century
Sandstone
Height 33 cm, width 56 cm, depth 28 cm
National Museum of Cambodia,
Phnom Penh, Ka 1584

This statue of Nandin, Śiva's mount, was unearthed during the excavation of a pre-Angkor site from the seventh century, the probable date of this work as well.

As is often the case in freestanding statuary, the animal is represented lying down. His body tilts slightly to one side, showing a close observation of reality. The horns are short (the tip of the left horn is broken). The third eye, extended by a slightly raised bump on the forehead, reflects the iconography of Śivaism and suggests Śiva himself: the eye is one of Śiva's characteristics. Nandin is not only the god's *vāhana* (mount), but also his animal form.

Unlike many other animals in Khmer sculpture, Nandin is always represented with a care for realism, demonstrated here by the sensitive and fluid modeling of the body and folds of the dewlap. As with the bas-relief image of Nandin from the Tuol Neak Ta Bak Ka stele (cat. 21), the work has a simple, naive charm. A few sober ornaments—a collar hung with bells and bracelets just above his hooves—emphasize the animal's earthly character.

Originally the statue must have been placed facing a Śiva shrine. It is impossible to tell whether it stood outdoors, like the Nandin images from the temple of Preah Ko, or whether it belonged inside a building.

A.C.

25

Skanda

Kdei Ang (Prei Veng)
Pre-Angkor period,
7th century (or earlier?)
Sandstone
Height 103 cm (without tenon),
width 48 cm, depth 21 cm
Musée national des Arts asiatiques-Guimet, Paris, MG 14900

Skanda, brother of the beloved elephant-god Gaṇeśa, is one of the more interesting gods in the Hindu pantheon. Born, according to some texts, from the semen of Śiva without the participation of a female being, he was created to conquer the evil powers of the demon Tāraka, who was attacking the gods, and became Mahāsenā, chief of the army of the gods. Śiva, in deep meditation, could not be roused for the creation until moved by the extreme ascetical meditation of Pārvatī. His seed then came forth, too scalding to be born by a living creature, and was deposited on the Himalaya, causing the birth of Skanda, which means "jet of semen," thousands of years later. Skanda was raised by six of the seven Pleiades (or the Krittikā)[1] and therefore is sometimes represented with six faces, a form that enabled him to drink the milk of all six foster mothers. This relationship accounts for one of his many names: Kārttikeya, from Kārtikka, the month when the moon is closest to the constellation of the Pleiades.

Skanda is eternally youthful, and thus is called Kumāra; he is also chaste, his only bride being the army, Devasenā. Other names include Subrahmaṇya (dear to the Brahmans), Guha (secret), Śāktidhara (carrier of the javelin) and Ṣaṇmukha (six-faced); the *Mahābhārata* mentions thirty-one names. His *vāhana*, (mount), is the peacock, Paravāṇi, the killer of snakes.[2] Skanda's emblem is a banner given by Agni, god of fire, and his attributes include bow and arrows, sword, *vajra*, and ax, as well as an invincible javelin.

The cult of Skanda is ancient, representations of him having been found on coins of the Kuṣāṇa era (second century of our era), and was important in northern India from Gupta times (fourth to sixth century). He is mentioned in a seventh-century inscription in Cambodia, in a Khmer form of the god's name, but documentation is rare and the few depictions that exist tend to be in bas-relief (Bhattacharya 1961, 136). It is significant that this Skanda and one in the National Museum of Phnom Penh (Ka 596; Dupont 1955, pl. XIV B), both come from the Angkor Borei area of southern Cambodia where Gupta influence on Khmer statuary is clearest, as seen in the Phnom Da style. Even at an early date, however, a local variation on an Indian theme could have existed, and it has been pointed out that in Cambodia, Skanda was considered as the *lokapāla*, or directional guardian, of the south (Bhattacharya 1961, 142).

Although it has been suggested that this image could be from the eighth century (Bénisti 1981, 64), both inscription evidence (Bhattacharya 1961, 142) and style[3] suggest a seventh-century date. Indeed, the rather crude carving and somewhat simplistic representation of face, fingers, hair, and garments as well as the perfunctory feather and claw details lend credence to the speculation than this Skanda may be an even older creation.

Despite the lack of evidence from attributes—the object in the right hand has been broken off, though it could have been a sword or perhaps a primitive *vajra*—the god is clearly identifiable, not only by his peacock mount (whose flaring tail forms the stele-like support for what is in effect a very deep relief rather than a freestanding sculpture), but also by the *tricīra*, (three locks of hair), that rise from his head. These locks, here formed by strands of hair twisted, rolled, and fastened with a portion of their own length, are found on young gods, most notably on Kṛṣṇa (cat. 13), and are accurate here for the depiction of Kumāra, the name for Skanda that stresses his adolescence and the one most often found, in its Khmer form, in ancient epigraphy.

For all its awkwardness and lack of refinement, the sculpture has great vitality and leaves a rather moving impression of the close relationship between god and mount.

H.J.

26

Gaṇeśa

Tuol Pheak Kin (Kandal)
Pre-Angkor period, 7th–8th century
Sandstone
Height 74 cm, width 63 cm, depth 44 cm
National Museum of Cambodia,
Phnom Penh, Ka 588

Probably no god of the Brahmanic pantheon is more popular than Gaṇeśa, best known as protector of new enterprises and surmounter of obstacles. The talismanic nature of his image is clear from the patina of most Gaṇeśa statues: like this example they have a deep polish on the round belly from the innumerable touches of those seeking patronage. Despite the benign and jolly appearance of this half-elephant, half-human figure, he is characterized by a complex iconography. There are several versions of his birth. In the *Śivapurāṇa*, one of the best-known, Śiva's consort, Pārvatī, distressed at Śiva's intrusion during her bathing ritual, created a glorious being by parthenogenesis to serve as guardian, naming him her son. When that son tried to prevent the entrance of Śiva, the enraged god decapitated him. In attempting to console Pārvatī, Śiva promised to attach to the body of the young man the head of the first living creature he met; it happened to be an elephant.

The simplicity of this charming myth masks a complicated symbolism, including reference to the microcosm and macrocosm. The syncretized god is the symbol of the unity of the small being, or man—the microcosm—with the great, the elephant—the macrocosm. The philosophy is based on the concept that categories (*gaṇa*) are fundamental to the nature of existence. Gaṇeśa means "lord of categories"; he is also "lord of obstacles," in which aspect he is called Vighneśvara. Other names for Gaṇeśa include Gaṇapati (master of categories), Vināyaka (supreme guide), and Gajānana (elephant-faced).

The *Mahābhārata* states that Gaṇeśa was the scribe of this epic, at the dictation of Vyāsa. In this connection Gaṇeśa becomes the protector of letters and god of knowledge (Bhattacharya 1961, 134). His image is found at entrances to shrines and dwellings, and invocations are made to him at the beginning of any enterprise.

In Hindu Tantrism, the symbols representing Gaṇeśa include the *yantra* (diagram of the swastika),[1] and the formula for the incantation of his twenty-eight syllables (mantra).[2] His attributes include the noose, the elephant goad, his own broken tusk, the disk, the rosary, and the *modaka* (bowl of sweets). Here, the Gaṇeśa of Tuol Pheak Kin holds a bowl in his left hand, which his trunk dips into, and his tusk in the right. Gaṇeśa's *vāhana* (vehicle) is the rat.[3]

Both epigraphy and sculpture show that the cult of Gaṇeśa was known in Cambodia from pre-Angkor times (Bhattacharya 1992, 131–134). Although the Indian Gaṇeśa usually has four arms, most Khmer examples such as the image from Tuol Pheak Kin have only two. This Gaṇeśa has all the signs of seventh-century artisanship. Notwithstanding the fantasy expressed in the flowery curves of the ears, the anatomy is accurately observed, not only of the Asian elephant skull, trunk, and slightly malicious eyes, but also of the human limbs; the lack of adornment with jewelry is also characteristic of the period.[4] Many early Khmer Gaṇeśa images are standing (Ka 1611 from Tuol Ang [Kandal] in the National Museum of Phnom Penh; Bhattacharya 1992, pl. XXVIII) but the Tuol Pheak Kin sculpture exudes an air of calm repose in his comfortably seated position. His obese benevolence indeed promises comfort and protection.

H.J.

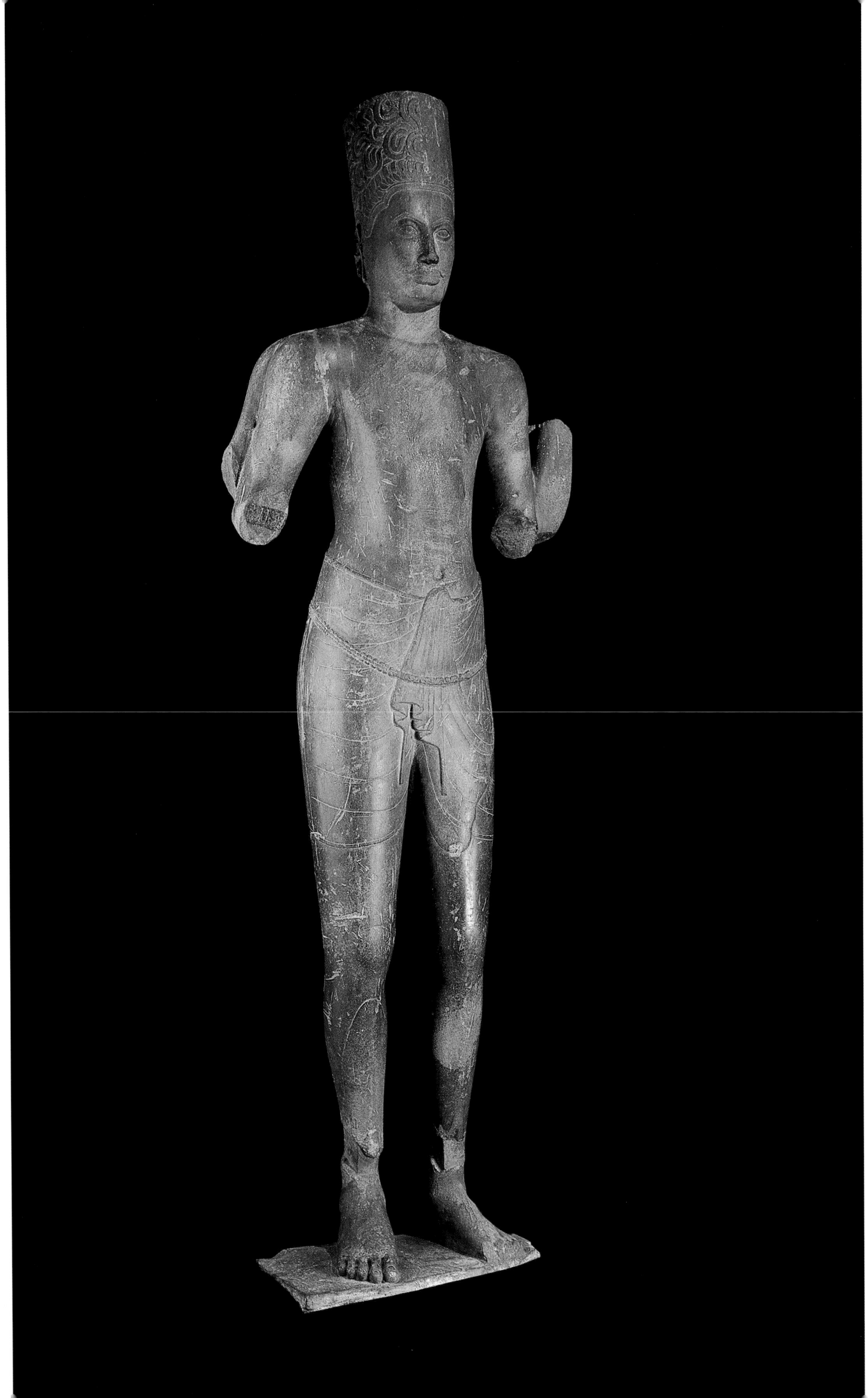

Fig. 1
Prasat Andet, late seventh century

Fig. 2
Sampot of the Harihara from Prasat Andet, detail

27

Harihara

Prasat Andet (Kompong Thom)
Pre-Angkor period, style of Prasat Andet, last quarter of the 7th century
Sandstone
Height 197 cm (without tenon), width 67 cm, depth 31 cm
National Museum of Cambodia, Phnom Penh, Ka 1635

Harihara is the syncretic representation of the gods Śiva and Viṣṇu. Śiva, whose cosmic dance creates and destroys worlds, makes up the sculpture's proper right, while Viṣṇu the preserver, who sleeps on the serpent Ananta's back in the primordial ocean during a transitional period between two cosmic eras, forms the sculpture's proper left. To represent the divine duality within one body, the Khmer artist has endowed the figure's right with half of Śiva's *jaṭāmukuṭa* (a high chignon of looping braided hair) and half of his third eye, and its left with half of Viṣṇu's cylindrical miter. The border of the headdress is decorated with a row of slanted leaves. Śiva's tresses, forming three horizontal rows, are drawn to the back. The frontal stance, rigid but for the slightly flexed left knee, heralds the hieratic tendency that would characterize Angkor statuary.

This god with a double personality once had four arms, now unfortunately damaged. He wears a short *sampot* (*saṃbat' caṅ kpin*), a length of cloth wrapped around the waist with one end passing between the legs and knotted in the back. It is held in place by a central knot and a small lateral knot toward the left hip, forming a pocket against the thigh; this fashion would continue, growing progressively more stylized, until the style of Angkor Vat in the twelfth century. The *sampot* is also held in place by a jeweled belt, made of vertical links joined by horizontal ones. The folds of the garment form a radiating pattern, and the knot in the back is fan-shaped. Although the figure's back muscles are well modeled, the pectoral muscles lack definition and there is a hint of plumpness in the stomach.

On the basis of this Harihara, Pierre Dupont established what is called the Prasat Andet style, described as follows by Jean Boisselier (1966, 242): "The *sampot* ... has a pocket to the side ... whose free end hangs down in an anchor-like shape. This garment, directly derived from the one familiar to us since style B of Phnom Da, is often simply suggested by more or less schematic incisions .... The miter is high, curves in at the temples, frames the ears, and covers the nape of the neck. Entirely masking the hair, it is edged with a band" that "may bear decorations suggestive of a primitive diadem," as in the case of this Harihara.

S.S.

28

Devī

Popel (Svay Rieng)
Pre-Angkor period,
1st half of the 8th century (?)
Sandstone
Height 106 cm, width 30 cm, depth 19 cm
Musée national des Arts asiatiques-Guimet, Paris, MG 18095

The Devī of Popel convincingly projects adolescence, in interesting contrast with the maturity that emanates from the Devī of Koh Krieng (cat. 19). The slim body has a nubile sensuality that is reinforced by her round cheeks and full, pouting lips set in an ingenuous smile. Any tendency to vapidity is balanced, however, by the delicate arch of her brow and the frank, almost challenging, gaze of her clearly delineated eyes.

Both her identity and date are uncertain. One of the chief characteristics of this divinity's dress is the looped and knotted fold of her sarong that forms a quasi pocket in relief, a feature that cannot be relied upon as a precise indication of her place in the evolution of costume style: except for the images in the Sambor Prei Kuk style, the pocket fold, either in relief or incised (cat. 29), is found on almost all pre-Angkor images. In his major study on Khmer statuary, Boisselier definitively distinguished the

traits of feminine figures in the Sambor Prei Kuk style but relegated all other pre-Angkor female sculptures to a single group. Since this research, despite recent discoveries and reassessment of previous information, there has been no further insight into the classification of these images. Dupont considered that the most beautiful figures were likely to belong either to the Prei Kmeng or to the Prasat Andet styles, while all the others could probably be ascribed to that of Kompong Preah.

Given all these uncertainties, the study of pre-Angkor, feminine sculpture is problematic. In the case of the Devī of Popel, the rather contrived slight sway of her left hip, the treatment of the incised details of the sarong and the *jaṭā*, particularly stylized, in conjunction with the attachment of her heels to the block of stone, suggest a tentative date in the first half of the eighth century.

H.J.

29

Devī

Koh Krieng, Sambor on the Mekong (Kratie)
Pre-Angkor period, 8th century (?)
Sandstone
Height 135 cm, width 52 cm, depth 21 cm
Musée national des Arts asiatiques-Guimet, Paris, MG 18094

The Devī of Koh Krieng from the Musée Guimet—not to be confused with the older sculpture of the same name from Phnom Penh (cat. 19)—presents the same dating problems as the Devī of Popel (cat. 28). The subject is clearly less youthful and is treated in a manner closer to the traditional stylization and idealization of Khmer statuary. The stance is supple but has a certain tension compared with that of the Devī of Popel, and the wide-eyed gaze is almost staring, an impression reinforced by the meticulous detailing of pupils, irises, and tear ducts.

The careful carving of the rather strange *jaṭā*, where the locks are presented in relief as distinct from the incisions used for the Devī of Popel, is more stylized than in the more naturalistic coiffure of the other Devī of Koh Krieng (cat. 19) or of the Śiva side of the Harihara of Asram Maha Rosei (cat. 16). The relief used for the Devī of Popel is abandoned for an incised representation of the pocket flap of the goddess' sarong, as well as of its folds and front pleats. It seems as though the missing feet of the Devī of Koh Krieng were cut free of the block of stone. But, it is impossible to tell whether these stylistic and technical differences constitute a chronological determinant, or whether they are simply due to the sculptor's stylistic decision. Furthermore, despite the differences between the works, they seem to belong to the same genre and are probably contemporary.

Another as yet unanswered question concerns the identity of these two divinities. In both cases, the *jaṭā* suggests a Śivaite affiliation. Many scholars, however, including Dupont, have observed that the only female images that can unquestionably be identified are those of Durgā as slayer of the buffalo demon. Durgā, as one of the manifestations of Śiva's spouse, is without doubt a Śivaite deity, yet she wears the cylindrical miter that is associated with Viṣṇuite images. This apparent contradiction is perhaps explainable in the context of her additional identity as the sister of Viṣṇu.

Should one therefore infer that feminine figures wearing the *jaṭā* represent Lakṣmī? It is hardly tenable. Rather than identifying Devī images such as this one, as well as the Devī of Koh Krieng (cat. 19) and the Devī of Popel (cat. 28), as representations of Lakṣmī, it seems preferable to describe them under the general, somewhat vague, rubric of Devī, while acknowledging that they may well represent some other goddess.

Besides Devī, Lakṣmī, and Durgā, Khmer epigraphy mentions other Brahmanic female deities, such as Sarasvatī. It is impossible to overstate the effects of the disappearance of the goddesses' attributes, in cases where they were sculpted rather than detachable; the loss will forever preclude any precise identification of these important sculptures.

H.J.

Ninth to Late Tenth Century

Fig. 1
Wrestling apes. Prasat Chen, Koh Ker. Sandstone. Height 287 cm (with pedestal). Koh Ker style, second quarter of the tenth century. National Museum of Cambodia, Phnom Penh

The Angkor Style: Echoes of the Centralized State

In 802, as the Khmer monarchy—assuming the classic form it would retain throughout the Angkor period—moved toward absolutism with the consecration of Jayavarman II-Parameśvara[1] (c. 790–a little after 830?) as *cakravartin* (universal monarch), Khmer sculpture was entering its maturity.

This period of expansion, beginning with the Kulen style (first three quarters of the ninth century), saw images gain total freedom from the constraints of the material composing them. The large sculptures discovered in 1936 (STERN, *Le Style*, 1938, 115–116, 130–135; Stern, *Travaux*, 1938, 151–173) in the monuments of Jayavarman II and his son and successor Jayavarman III-Viṣṇuloka (a little after 830?–at least 860) on ancient Mahendraparvata (present-day Phnom Kulen) no longer have the various struts and supports, notably the supporting arch, that characterized the great majority of pre-Angkor works. While the pieces thought to be the very earliest in this style retain certain of these reinforcing elements (cat. 30), the sculptures that followed take full advantage of the space surrounding them. Although Jayavarman II was Śivaite, as his posthumous name of Parameśvara indicates, the only known images in this style are of Viṣṇu. The god in majesty is represented in a highly classical style: standing, four-armed, holding his traditional attributes (earth, discus, conch, and club), and wearing the traditional cylindrical miter (cat. 31). Sculpture had gained a new freedom—though sculptors only realized its full extent later—and images began to take on a carnal fullness that would become accentuated over time, resulting in the portliness characteristic of the Preah Ko style of the last quarter of the ninth century.

The founding of the classic Khmer monarchy was the work of Jayavarman II. But it was his second successor, Indravarman-Īśvaraloka (877–at least 886), who built the first city of the Angkor type in the Tonle Sap region, Hariharālaya. Indravarman's reign saw the revival of pre-Angkor iconography and the emergence of new stylistic criteria. Some of these, such as the growing schematization of the drapery (cat. 33), can be placed in the framework of continuous evolution; others, such as the transformation of Viṣṇu's cylindrical miter into an octagonal pagoda-like structure, constitute real mutations (cat. 34). These two types of change, which may affect all or part of a work at any given moment, embody the very spirit of the development of Angkor sculpture.

The Bakheng style (first quarter of the tenth century) is a clear case of sudden mutation. The dress, both male and female, took on a new appearance, adopting a pleated cloth like that used for Scottish kilts (fig. 1). To be totally accurate, the beginnings of this change were already apparent in the female dress of the Preah Ko style (cat. 35). Aside from introducing pleated cloth for the dress, the art of the reign of Yaśovarman-Paramaśivaloka (889–beginning of 10th century) is characterized by an absolute stylization of the faces (cats. 37–40) and the bodies (cat. 41). Profoundly abstract, cold and aloof, but at the same time noble and stately, the Bakheng style, which continued through the reign of Yaśovarman's two successors, displayed more magnificently than any other the greatness of Angkor.[2]

With the Koh Ker style (second quarter of the tenth century) during the reign of Jayavarman IV-Paramaśivapada (921–928–c. 940),[3] Khmer statuary

1. The posthumous name of the king, when it is known, is included after the name of the Khmer king. This may seem to complicate things unnecessarily, but it is important. Posthumous names are as a general rule composed of the name of a divinity followed by the Sanskrit term *loka* (world). They indicate clearly which divinity the sovereign chose and specify that after his death the king will repair to the world of that god: Paramaviṣṇuloka, the posthumous name of Sūryavarman II means (the king who has gone to) "the world of the supreme Viṣṇu." The posthumous name of Jayavarman II, Parameśvara (the supreme lord)—a designation of Śiva—is exceptional because the term *loka* is absent. It does not diminish Jayavarman II's status as a Śivaite.
2. Yaśovarman's successors were Harṣavarman I-Rudraloka (by 912–at least 922) and Īśānavarman II-Paramarudraloka (by 925).
3. Jayavarman IV was already king in 921 in his city of Chok Gargyar-Koh Ker. He was consecrated as the supreme king of kings in 928. During his reign and that of his successor, the capital was no longer at Angkor but some fifty miles (80 km) to the northeast at Koh Ker.

moved toward gigantism (cat. 42), while the iconography grew more diversified (fig. 2). Sculptors displayed a certain virtuosity in increasing the number of group images, of which only one example is known from earlier periods, the Umāgaṅgāpatīśvara from Bakong (style of Preah Ko), now at the Depot for the Conservation of Angkor.[4] The formalism, geometric hieratism, and linear abstraction of the Bakheng style were replaced by a sense of movement (cat. 44) and a new softness in the modeling, particularly in the faces lit with an almost human smile (cat. 43). It should be emphasized that these developments did not signal a fundamental change in perspective, or any negation of a past that might have been judged excessively rigid. The changes ushered in by the Koh Ker style reveal, rather, an enrichment of pre-existing tendencies. Far from making three-dimensional sculpture deviate from its customary hieratism, the art of Jayavarman IV's reign represents an almost baroque phase—the last masterful flowering of a period of greatness that started with the style of Kulen and culminated with that of Bakheng—as well as a period of profound renewal. At its close, the art of sculpture, strengthened by its past experiments, could follow the new avenues opening to it.

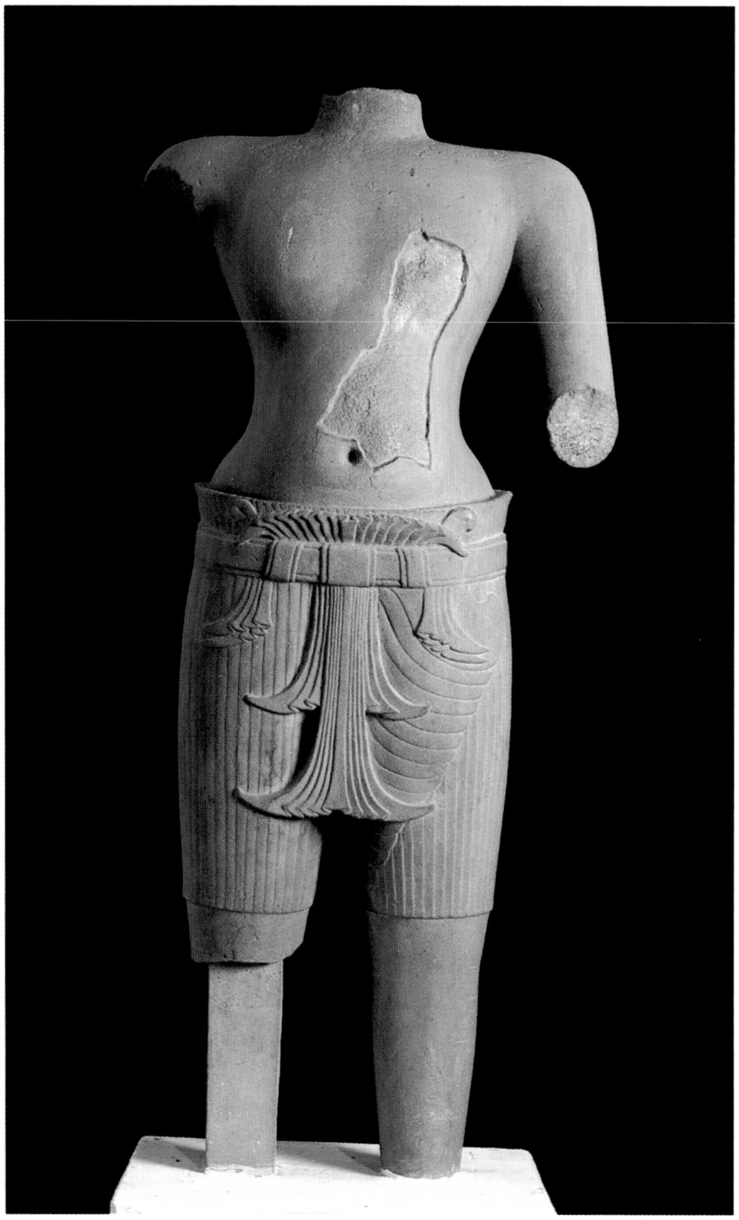

Fig. 2
Male torso. Phnom Bakheng, Angkor. Sandstone. Height 152 cm. Bakheng style, early tenth century. National Museum of Cambodia, Phnom Penh

Once the fleeting reign of Harṣavarman II-Brahmaloka (c. 940–944), a son of Jayavarman IV, had come and gone, the young king Rājendravarman-Śivaloka (944–967) reinstalled the kingdom at Angkor, moving its center toward the east into the area of the temples of East Mebon (953) and Pre Rup (961). In the return to the ancient capital, sculpture did not follow all the lessons of the Koh Ker style; the loss of movement is particularly noticeable. Only the softness of the modeling was preserved, even accentuated, in the style of Pre Rup (third quarter of the tenth century) (cat. 47). This period, though not a particularly innovative one for sculpture, was nonetheless witness to a genuine revolution in aesthetics, though at first only architectural ornament and the art of the bas-relief were affected. That revolution is called Banteay Srei. Though "revolution" may seem an overstatement, it is nonetheless true that the art of Banteay Srei, far from being a marvelous aside in the general progress of Khmer art, is one of those rare moments when a spark of genius rekindles a creative tradition that has settled too comfortably into formulaic repetition and risks coming to a dead end.

The style of Banteay Srei (c. 967), characterized by two opposite and complementary aesthetic tendencies, is essentially limited to the temple complex of that name and a few contemporary monuments that unfortunately are not as well preserved: a small temple to the east of the North Khleang, Prasat Sralao, and others. The first of these tendencies is quite traditional and applies to cult images, such as the statue of Viṣṇu that once stood in the north shrine, or the marvelous Umāmaheśvara group from the west *gopura* I (cat. 56). These figures, were it not for the site where they were uncovered, could very easily be taken for figures from the late Pre Rup or early Khleang styles. The second tendency—an innovative, even revolutionary, one—finds expression in the narrative bas-reliefs (cats. 50, 51, fig. 5, page 127) and in the architectural ornament, which is at once exuberant and inventive; its execution is never less than perfect. The plastic beauty of all the decorated surfaces of the temple is unique, whether one looks at the tapestry-like floral decoration of the front room of the central sanctuary or the stunning virtuosity of the floral scrolls on the lintels and some of the pediments. Of the two tendencies, the innovative one had a more significant impact on subsequent Khmer art. The narrative reliefs, for instance, would inaugurate one of the great chapters in Khmer art; the style was destined to flourish impressively in the erudite and elaborate compositions of the gallery of the third enclosure of the temple of Angkor Vat during the first half of the twelfth century, and in the sensitive and lively representations of the gallery of the outer enclosure of the Bayon at the beginning of the thirteenth. The art created at Banteay Srei at the instigation of Yajñavarāha, the temple's founder, constitutes one of the major contributions of Khmer art to the artistic heritage of the world.

T.Z.

4. Illustration in BHATTACHARYA 1961, pls. IIII and IV. Claude Jacques has recently proposed another identification for this group. In his view, it is not a "Śiva with his buttocks squeezed by the arms of Umā and Gaṅgā [his wives] in the form of vines," an image specifically mentioned in stanza XXIX of the stele marking the founding of the monument (see *IC*, 1: 35). The four arms of the central figure of the triad as well as the signs of removal on the base correspond, according to Jacques, to a representation of Viṣṇu. No firm conclusion can be reached on the signs of removal from the base (which could as easily correspond to Viṣṇu's club as to Śiva's trident), and the questions raised by the four arms remain unanswered given the present state of our knowledge. Although there are no known images of a four-armed Śiva in the style of Preah Ko this does not entirely preclude their existence; the general custom (perhaps abused) is to identify all four-armed sculptures that have lost their attributes as representations of Viṣṇu.

30

Viṣṇu

Protected under a rock near Rup Arak, Phnom Kulen (Siem Reap)
Angkor period, style of Kulen, 1st half of the 9th century
Sandstone
Height 190 cm (with tenon), width 57 cm, depth 26 cm
Musée national des Arts asiatiques-Guimet, Paris, MG 18860

In all periods of Khmer art the iconography in a image of Viṣṇu remains constant; that of the Viṣṇu of Rup Arak is no exception. The attributes, comprising the *cakra* (disk) in the proper rear right arm, the *śaṅkha* (conch) in the rear left arm, and the cylindrical miter confirm this identity. Although the other two arms are missing, the left front arm would certainly have rested on the club, as its remnants still exist on the sculpture's rectangular base. The front right hand would have held the globe and must have been supported by a stay similar to the kind visible in the statue of Avalokiteśvara from Tan Long (cat. 7). Various stabilizing elements recall those in the Viṣṇu from Tuol Dai Buon (cat. 15), not only the supports for the lower arms just described, but also the struts retaining the connection between the miter and the upper hands. These upper reinforcements, ubiquitous in pre-Angkor statuary, are sometimes visible in early Angkor works, and their presence in the Viṣṇu of Rup Arak establishes an early ninth-century date for this piece. The club continued as a support in stone images of Viṣṇu until much later.

Although the various reinforcing elements reveal the persistence of pre-Angkor characteristics, the Viṣṇu of Rup Arak completely accords with Angkor style in the details of his dress, with its double pleated front panel in anchor shape and its highly stylized pocket-fold draped against the left thigh. The evolution and progressively more stylized treatment of this complex front drapery can be traced from the Viṣṇu of Tuol Dai Buon, where it is realistic and legible, to this Viṣṇu, where it has become a purely decorative element. Between these two extremes one finds examples, such as the Harihara of Phnom Da of the second half of the seventh century from the National Museum of Phnom Penh (Dupont 1955, pl. VIII B), that strike a balance between the earlier naturalism and the later stylization.

The facial features of the well-preserved head seem highly particularized, as is the case with most Viṣṇu images in the Kulen style (cat. 31). Such personified treatment relates the Viṣṇu of Rup Arak to the best characteristics of the pre-Angkor tradition.

H.J.

31

Viṣṇu

Prasat Damrei Krap, north sanctuary,
Phnom Kulen (Siem Reap)
Angkor period, style of Kulen,
1st half of the 9th century
Sandstone
Height 179 cm (with tenon),
width 76 cm, depth 45 cm
National Museum of Cambodia,
Phnom Penh, Ka 882

This sculpture of Viṣṇu has many features in common with the Viṣṇu of Tuol Dai Buon (cat. 15). Although it was created about two centuries later, the god wears the same kind of high cylindrical miter that symbolizes his kingly status. Similar also is his short *sampot* (*saṃbat'*) with its end turning back below the belt to form a pocket draped against the left thigh and then falling in front in graceful pleats. His attributes, clockwise from the proper lower right hand, are the globe, the disk or wheel, the conch, and the club or mace (see cat. 15 for the symbolism of these attributes).

A comparison of the Prasat Damrei Krap Viṣṇu with the image from Tuol Dai Buon yields interesting points other than the consistency of the attributes. The influence of Gupta style apparent in the latter—slightly hip-swayed posture, long oval face, morphology of the body—has evolved toward a more hieratic form. The stance of the Prasat Damrei Krap Viṣṇu has a certain rigidity, a certain tension, that seems to imply a controlled inner power. The impression, though less humanistic and benign, is more consciously imposing. The increasing stylization of costume offers valuable dating evidence, as has been analyzed by Stern (*Le Style*, 1938, 130–135) and Boisselier (*La Statuaire khmère,* 1955). The natural fall of the front panel of the *sampot* cloth in the seventh century had become a schematic and purely ornamental device by the ninth. Unlike later images of Viṣṇu, this figure has no sculpted jewels; the pierced and elongated earlobes are empty but might once have been adorned with real pendants during rituals.

There has been a considerable evolution of facial features since pre-Angkor types. The face is squarer, while the eyes, brows, and lips are outlined with fine incised lines. The mustache emphazises the expression of the mouth, smiling slightly, rather arrogant, or at least imperious. The torso is slender but the legs retain some of the robustness of pre-Angkor pieces, while the musculature of chest and abdomen is indicated in a very restrained manner. Such features may be considered typical of Kulen style, since they are encountered in other Viṣṇu statues of the period (Boisselier 1955 pl. 28; 1966 pl. XXXIII-1). The Viṣṇu of Rup Arak is probably slightly earlier than the Prasat Damrei Krap example: Kulen-style sculpture is characterized by the disappearance of the supporting arch and the stays linking arms to head, so the Rup Arak image is probably a transitional piece utilizing such technical devices for the last time.

All the Kulen images of Viṣṇu have a highly individualized morphology. Their execution coincides with the founding of many monuments in the region to the north of the Tonle Sap (Great Lake) that would remain the center of the empire during the next six hundred years. From about 790, Jayavarman II gradually consolidated his power farther north. In 802 he consecrated a royal *liṅga* on Phnom Kulen, then called Mahendraparvata, and had himself proclaimed *cakravartin* (universal monarch). That ceremony was accompanied by the creation of the *devarāja* cult and is considered to signal the inauguration of the royal dynasty and the Angkor period in the full sense of the term.

H.J.

32

Lintel

Prasat Kok Po A, Angkor (Siem Reap)
Angkor period, style of Preah Ko,
last quarter of the 9th century
Sandstone
Height 79 cm, width 245 cm, depth 36 cm
Musée national des Arts asiatiques-Guimet, Paris, MG 18217

The undulating and looping garlands on this lintel provide a dynamic armature for the interweaving foliate and animal forms that seem always to be metamorphosing. The dynamics seem to accelerate and are only finally released at the ends of the lintel, where tricephalic *nāga* rear their highly expressive heads, and at the top, to the right and left of the central figure, where the energy seems to fly heavenward. This kind of control of architectonics and space typifies the Preah Ko style: in particular one is reminded of the astonishing variety of the lintels on the *prasat* (sanctuary towers) surrounding the central pyramid of Bakong, each having its own strong character yet according well with the form of its small sanctuary. The Prasat Kok Po lintel under discussion embodies the balance of mass and detail, of dynamic forms and solid anchoring elements, and, above all, of the ability to maintain a sense of space in spite of the proliferation of embellishment that is characteristic of the monuments of the Roluos group and the Preah Ko style.

The central figure in the scene is Viṣṇu, sitting on his *vāhana* (mount), the mythological bird Garuḍa. The dominance of the god is accentuated by the gesture (considered aggressive in Asia) of the hands placed on the hips. Garuḍa's arms echo the outward thrust of Viṣṇu's, while his hands support loops of the garland that also curves over the arms of the flanking *kāla* figures (monsters), that are disgorging long foliate pendants. The scene is imposing but not stiff, and illustrates the significant evolution of the architectonics of lintel form since the masterly hieratic classicism of the Vat Eng Khna lintel (cat. 20). Paradoxically, though the form is less hieratic, the subject matter is more so: narrative and myth have given way to iconic emphasis of divine power enhanced by such elements of diabolic force as fierce *kāla* and rearing *nāga*.

H.J.

33

Śiva

Bakong, tower 9 of the outer enclosure,
Roluos (Siem Reap)
Angkor period, style of Preah Ko,
last quarter of the 9th century
Sandstone
Height 186 cm (without tenon),
width 63 cm, depth 37 cm
National Museum of Cambodia,
Phnom Penh, Ka 1648

The style of Preah Ko is among the most hieratic of Khmer sculptural expressions. The architecture of this period established the basis for the ultimate classicism of Angkor with the construction by Indravarman of the first of the great temple-mountains, the enormous state temple of Bakong, consecrated in 881. This temple, along with Preah Ko (879) and Lolei (893, built by Yaśovarman I, Indravarman's successor, who reigned from 889 to the beginning of the tenth century), constituted the heart of Hariharālaya, the present-day Roluos. Hariharālaya was the capital of the Khmer empire until Yaśovarman founded the first Yaśodharapura, at the end of the ninth and beginning of the tenth century, on the site of Angkor proper.

During the pre-Angkor period there were very few anthropomorphic representations of Śiva, who was usually represented in the symbolic form of the *liṅga*. Such figures were numerous; some had faces (cat. 23). By the Angkor era, when the state religion was predominantly Śivaite, personified images were numerous (cats. 38, 42, 56, 57). Perpetuating a trait that had appeared during the seventh century in Harihara images, the Śiva of Bakong wears a cylindrical *jaṭāmukuṭa* composed of locks of hair, but with a stylization remote from the natural tresses depicted on the oldest statues (cat. 16, Hara portion).

The typical dress of the Preah Ko style formalized the heretofore sporadic appearance of the anchor shape of the falling front panel. Here it has a single layer, with pleats remarkably precise, as are those of the curving attachment at the back.

The modeling of the torso is opulent and generous; the *prāṇa* (inner breath), signaled by an expansion of the diaphragm, is almost perceptible. The sculpture emphasizes a tendency toward solidity that was adumbrated in late Kulen style (Stern 1938, pl. XXXVIII D) and that would be even further developed in Koh Ker style a few decades later.

The diadems encircling the brows of the deities are among new stylistic elements of the Preah Ko style that should be noted. The design is usually composed of two finely incised registers, with lozenges in quincunx arrangement in the lower band, and in the upper, small foliate elements alternating with blue lotuses.

H.J.

34

Viṣṇu

Bakong, tower 7 of the outer enclosure,
Roluos (Siem Reap)
Angkor period, style of Preah Ko,
last quarter of the 9th century
Sandstone
Height 159 cm (without tenon),
width 72 cm, depth 43.5 cm
National Museum of Cambodia,
Phnom Penh, Ka 1649

This image of Viṣṇu presents no major stylistic differences from the Śiva of the preceding entry (cat. 33); there is, however, one main distinction: all Viṣṇu's attributes, save for the conch, are conserved, whereas both of Śiva's have disappeared. Modeling of the torso, treatment of the face, proportions, and dress are identical. The differences in iconography—the crescent moon in Śiva's *jaṭā* and the third eye in his forehead, as well as his two arms, as distinct from the four of Viṣṇu, and also Viṣṇu's miter—are mandatory. With regard to the miter, however, it should be noted that the traditional cylindrical form, ubiquitous since pre-Angkor days, has evolved into a cap conforming closely to the skull and surmounted by an element, octagonal in plan, that has come to be called, for lack of a better expression, a tiered pagoda. This completely new style of headdress would remain in use through the Angkor Vat period, though its form would be modified (in the Pre Rup style of the second half of the tenth century) to a conical shape.

Although it is difficult to infer any chronological conclusion, it should be noted that the upper decorative band of the diadem comprises alternating floral elements and stems; the blue lotus flowers, while typical for Preah Ko style, have been replaced by the stems that would be characteristic in diadem design from the inception of the Bakheng style.

H.J.

35

Female Divinity

Bakong, surroundings of western *gopura* I, Roluos (Siem Reap)
Angkor period, style of Preah Ko, last quarter of the 9th century
Sandstone
Height 113 cm, width 48 cm, depth 28.7 cm
Musée national des Arts asiatiques-Guimet, Paris, MG 18862

No female image in Kulen style is known in the current state of Khmer studies. It is one of the strange accidents that sometimes determine archaeological research that this gap has deprived scholars of an important indicator in the evolution of the female image at the beginning of the Angkor period.

The stele of Bakong (K. 826, published by Cœdès, *IC,* 1:31–36) mentions several feminine images: a Durgā Mahiṣāsuramardinī, an Indranī, and, associated with Śiva, the goddesses Umā and Gaṅgā (Umāgaṅgāpatiśvara). Although the Umāgaṅgāpatiśvara seems to have been recognized (see page 191, note 4), it is impossible to connect the other feminine images from Bakong with the information provided by the foundation stele of the monument. Not one of the sculptures can be identified, since they have lost their arms and heads. Thus, in the absence of attributes and a head—which in any case would not necessarily be adequate to identify the personage—the female divinity of the Musée Guimet must remain anonymous.

Treatment of the female body in sculpture in the Preah Ko style corresponds, detail for detail, with that of male bodies: the fullness of the form approaches stoutness. The modeling, however, is subtle, and an impression of vitality and power rediates from the form of the Bakong goddess, whose legs disappear beneath a garment wrapped twice around the waist. As is true for the male *sampot* (*saṃbat*), some parts of the dress are pleated: the front panel with its folded-over upper extension fanning out in a semicircle, and the hanging triangular corner of the inner edge. This manner of draping the skirt cloth is new and would influence the Bakheng style, which followed immediately afterward.

H.J.

36

Rājendradevī in the Form of Gaurī

Lolei, southwest sanctuary tower,
Roluos (Siem Reap)
Angkor period, style of Preah Ko from the Angkor Vat period, 1st three quarters of the 12th century
Sandstone
Height 174 cm (without tenon),
width 50 cm, depth 37 cm
National Museum of Cambodia,
Phnom Penh, Ka 1645

Various inscriptions at Lolei record the names of divinities that were once found in each of the four sanctuary towers of the temple. The inscriptions, in which the calligraphy is exceptional (fig. 2, page 55), were carved at the time of the temple's consecration in 893, four years after the consecration of its founder, King Yaśovarman.

The figures in the north row of towers were erected by the monarch—according to the dedication—"for the spiritual benefit in the afterlife" of his father Indravarman and his mother Indradevī. Those on the south row were dedicated, in the same manner, to a maternal ancestor of Yaśovarman, Mahīpativarman, and to one of the wives of this great personage, Rājendradevī. It is clear that Lolei played the same part in Yaśovarman's architectural and religious program as the temple of Preah Ko did in his father's. It was not simply a monument dedicated to the ancestral spirits of the royal line but a sort of manifesto, both political and religious, demonstrating to all—perhaps to the gods in particular—the right of its founder to occupy the throne.

Among the sculptures found at Lolei, this female statue from the southwest sanctuary tower is an example, relatively rare in Khmer art (see cat. 56), of a work that can be linked not only to a particular monument but also to a particular inscription. The Sanskrit portion of the text records that the figure, who in the Khmer portion is called Rājendradevī, is a representation of Devī Gaurī, the wife of Śiva.

Although the face is unfortunately mutilated, this Devī is of great stylistic interest. The work seems at first glance to be characteristic of the Preah Ko style, because of the full form of the goddess and especially because of the type of skirt she is wearing (cat. 35). It would not be surprising if a work commissioned in Hariharālaya by Yaśovarman at the beginning of his reign should show none of the characteristics of the Bakheng style: they had probably not been formulated as yet, and the sculptors were quite naturally working in the style they knew, that of Preah Ko. Yet an attentive examination of the modeling, the costume, and the coiffure (diadem and chignon-cover) reveals features of this sculpture that one would not expect to find in the style of Preah Ko and leads to questions about its dating.

One of the remarkable traits of the female statuary from the reign of Indravarman is the wonderfully supple modeling of the bodies, which are opulent and majestic, certainly, but at the same time sensual as well as imperceptively flexed at the hip. The figure of Rājendradevī demonstrates a drier treatment and a real rigidity that would become even more pronounced in the Bakheng style (cat. 41). At this stage one might conclude, and one would be right, that the sculptors, with this work from about 893, had started down the road that would lead in the early years of the tenth century to the cold geometry of the Bakheng style, while the costume still retained the characteristics of the Preah Ko style. If the pleated portions of the skirt are examined, one must acknowledge that they do not show the regularity and perfection one finds in the styles of Preah Ko and Bakheng. Furthermore, the pleats are not carved in relief but simply incised. Such handling does not seem to correspond at all with the manner of the end of the ninth century or the first half of the tenth century. In fact, it is only found in feminine costume starting with the style of Pre Rup and continuing until the style of Angkor Vat;[1] the exception is the Baphuon style, in which the treatment is different (cat. 66). The diadem and especially the chignon-cover decorated with rows of lotus petals are also far from conforming to the normal criteria for the styles of Preah Ko and Bakheng.

From these observations it follows that the Rājendradevī from Lolei is certainly an archaistic sculpture, one could almost call it a copy, made in the style of Preah Ko at a later date. From its hieratic aspect and the rendering of the face, particularly the eyebrow arches, the work can be attributed to an artist of the twelfth century, as Albert Le Bonheur suggested. One should recall that numerous restorations were carried out at Hariharālaya in that period, starting with the main sanctuary tower of Bakong. It would therefore be no surprise if its damaged sculptures had also been replaced.

T.Z.

37, 38, 39

Heads of Brahmā, Śiva, and Viṣṇu

Phnom Bok (Siem Reap)
Angkor period, style of Bakheng,
1st quarter of the 10th century
Sandstone
Height 46 cm (Brahmā), 49 cm (Śiva),
45 cm (Viṣṇu)
Musée national des Arts asiatiques-Guimet, Paris, MG 18101, 18100, 18102

Aside from the temple of Lolei,[1] the eastern *baray*,[2] the royal city of Yaśodharapura[3] and the temple-mountain of *phnom* (*bhnaṃ*) Bakheng,[4] two temples are attributed to the reign of Yaśovarman. Both Śivaite, they stand respectively on the summits of *phnom* Bok and *phnom* Krom, one a hill to the northeast and the other to the southeast of Angkor.[5] Each of these temples, whose main buildings comprise three sanctuary towers opening to the east and west arrayed along a single north-south axis, housed a Brahmanistic triad composed of the gods Brahmā, Śiva, and Viṣṇu.[6] In ancient Cambodia, this *trimūrti* of these three gods must be understood in a Śivaite context as the polymorphic expression of a supreme Śiva, who is non-manifest and therefore not representable.[7]

After being successfully restored, the triad from Phnom Krom was returned to its original place, but it has suffered serious damage in recent years. The heads of the Phnom Bok triad, whose bodies have never been found, were for their part brought to France by Louis Delaporte in 1873. He found them buried in the earth in the interior of one of the temple annexes (perhaps one of the libraries), where they had been united at an undetermined date and where it is possible that they were worshiped as *neak ta* (*anak tā*) (local spirits).

Except for a few iconographic details, such as the third eye on Śiva's forehead, the gods' faces are treated in an identical manner. Their expression is distant and impersonal, yet benevolent, perhaps because of the discreet smile they confer on the devotee, a smile accentuated by the line of their mustaches.

The lips are accentuated by a fine incision, as are the almond-shaped eyes in which the sculptor has represented the iris. This detail, to which one must add the unusual shaping of the eyebrows to form a continuous, sharp line, point to a stylizing tendency that has already been noted in the style of Preah Ko but is still more evident here. The hairline, forming a point at the temples, and the beard, represented by stippling on the cheeks and fine, parallel striations under the chin, complete the effect of the unreality of these faces.

The diadem consists of a band decorated with lozenge and half-lozenge motifs, crowned by a row of triangular florets alternating with small flower stalks. These stalks replace the blue lotuses of the style of Preah Ko in the style of the Bakheng. The handling of the diadem gives evidence that the sculptor tried to reproduce in stone a delicately jeweled work of repoussé.

The gods Śiva and Brahmā are coiffed by a perfectly cylindrical *jaṭā* made up of small locks disposed in regular loops. Viṣṇu's headdress is the same one seen in the style of Preah Ko: a helmet surmounted by a multitiered octagonal "pagoda." Smaller than that of the Viṣṇu from Bakong (cat. 34), this *mukuṭa* is also more finely decorated and more harmoniously proportioned.

Almost metallic in quality, the polish accentuates the severity of the Bakheng style, which nowhere finds a more remarkable expression than in these three faces. Yet does not their very coldness of aspect, devoid of earthly contingencies, provide the most ineluctable proof of their divine nature?

T.Z.

40

Head of Harihara

Provenance unknown
Angkor period, style of Bakheng,
1st quarter of the 10th century
Sandstone
Height 35 cm, width 18 cm, depth 17 cm
Musée national des Arts asiatiques-Guimet, Paris, MA 6224

Images of the god Harihara, frequent in pre-Angkor art (cats. 16, 27), become extremely rare from the end of the ninth century. Excepting a famous sculpture from the temple of Bakong (DCA 4366),[1] the Harihara from the Musée Guimet—a work that recently entered the French national collections thanks to the generosity of Georges Halphen—is the only one known today dating from the Angkor period.

In the customary style of Brahmanic sculpture, each half of the god has distinct iconographic features. When one has only a head to work from, as here, Śiva can be recognized by the half-eye on the forehead and the half-*jaṭā* ornamented with half a crescent moon, and Viṣṇu by the half-*mukuṭa* headdress in the form of a tiered, octagonal pagoda.

In what appear to be the oldest images (cat. 16), the differences between the right half representing Hara (Śiva) and the left representing Hari (Viṣṇu) are particularly pronounced. Before long these differences came to be attenuated. In such sculptures as the very fine Harihara from Prasat Andet (cat. 27) and the one from Prasat Phum Prasat,[2] the garment is no longer bipartite, and the shape of Viṣṇu's headdress seems to govern Śiva's. A later work from the end of the eighth century, one of the two Harihara from Prasat Trapeang Phong (Roluos, Siem Reap),[3] is unusual in still having all its attributes; it depicts a god in whom the Viṣṇuite features are predominant: in fact, three attributes out of four belong to Viṣṇu (the conch, the club, and the earth). The formal subsumption of the Śiva half into the Viṣṇu half is also apparent in the Harihara from Bakong and in this one from the Musée Guimet, because the Śivaite half-*jaṭā* takes the form of the Viṣṇuite half-*mukuṭa*. Nonetheless, the iconography remains true to the tradition, and the first of these two figures—and very likely the second as well—belongs within a Śivaite context.

From the rendering of the face, the Musée Guimet Harihara invites attribution to the reign of Yaśovarman, at the beginning of the tenth century. The aesthetic convention is point for point comparable to those already noted in the heads of the Phnom Bok triad (cats. 37–39). The details of the headdress, however, are more finely executed: a jeweled decoration enriches Hari's neck cover, and the locks forming Hara's chignon evoke fine tresses, very similar to those of the female divinity from Phnom Bakheng (cat. 41). The richness of decoration of this headdress led Jean Boisselier to attribute the work to the style of Pre Rup. However, several details forbid assigning such a date, beginning with the *mukuṭa*, which is set on the top of the head and whose tiers are clearly defined, as in the head of the Viṣṇu from Phnom Bok. In sculptures later than the style of Bakheng, the *mukuṭa* tends to be set lower on the back of the skull and to become conical (cats. 46, 47). The composition and ornament of the diadem as well as the knot attaching it also have features similar to those in the famous triad from the Musée Guimet. Finally, the face seems very far in expression from the somewhat simpering amiability of figures from the second half of the tenth century, but very close, on the other hand, to the haughty frigidity of the rare known works in the style of Bakheng.

T.Z.

MA 6224

41

Female Divinity

Phnom Bakheng, Angkor (Siem Reap)
Angkor period, style of the Bakheng,
1st quarter of the 10th century
Sandstone
Height 140 cm, width 48 cm, depth 27 cm
Musée national des Arts asiatiques-Guimet, Paris, MG 14879

According to Étienne Aymonier, this female divinity was discovered in one of the sandstone *prasat* (*prāsād*) on the west face of the pyramid of Phnom Bakheng. If the sculpture was in fact found where Aymonier claims—which would seem to be the case—then it had very likely been moved there from its original site. Its very size prevents it from ever having been intended for one of the little temples on the pyramid itself: these buildings are much too small to have housed such a large work, and it is more likely that they contained *liṅga*. Consequently, the sculpture must have originally belonged in one of the large brick towers encircling the base of the pyramid.

This hieratic, majestic figure, unusual in size, dates back, I believe, to the founding of the monument. The hourglass shape of the deity's bust corresponds point for point with that of the very beautiful male body from the National Museum of Phnom Penh (page 190, fig. 2).

The face, unfortunately chipped, displays the "linear abstraction" and relative harshness proper to the style of Bakheng. The eyes in particular are identical to those of the heads from Phnom Bok.

The headdress, a *jaṭā*, has disappeared, but the small loops characteristic of this fashion are still visible on the top of the head. Note also that the locks of hair on the back of the head are depicted in the same manner as on the Harihara from the Musée Guimet (cat. 40).

The diadem, which is missing its entire upper portion, has two tiers of decoration, the same as that on the jeweled girdle with its pendants. This was a new element in freestanding female sculpture during the Bakheng period, though it had appeared in bas-reliefs as early as the style of Preah Ko. The skirt, whose downturned upper edge hides part of the belt in front, is entirely pleated, in accordance with a convention that first tentatively appeared in female sculpture during the Preah Ko period (cat. 35) and would continue right through the style of Angkor Vat. The pleats are perfectly executed and reinforce the strict geometry of the figure, whose haughty bearing is not animated by even the slightest flexion of the hips.

Although George Cœdès has interpreted the mark on the deity's forehead as a Viṣṇuite sign, her precise identity is impossible to determine. In any case, the sign might only have been added long after the goddess' consecration and may not correspond to her original nature.

T.Z.

42

Hand from a Colossal Statue of Śiva

Prasat Kraham, Prasat Thom, Koh Ker (Kompong Thom)
Angkor period, style of Koh Ker, 2d quarter of the 10th century
Sandstone
Height 50 cm, width 19 cm, depth 28 cm
National Museum of Cambodia, Phnom Penh, Ka 1868

The many monuments at the site of Koh Ker have yielded large numbers of sculptures that date for the most part to the second quarter of the tenth century (cats. 43, 44), a period when this remarkable site was the capital of the Khmer empire.

Prasat Thom, a vast state temple, was consecrated to Śiva, the chosen deity of Jayavarman IV (928–c. 940); it is to such a monumental statue of Śiva with five heads and ten arms,[1] shown in an attitude of dance, that this hand belongs. The figure stood approximately twice the height of a man and, along with other sculptures, occupied a place inside the imposing east *gopura* (gatehouse) of the third enclosure of the complex. The sculpture had survived a fire and been broken into countless fragments (figs. 1, 2)—Henri Parmentier maintained that the damage to the statue was the work of looters who had hoped to find some sort of treasure in its enormous pedestal. It could not be restored. A number of its remarkable parts were nonetheless transported to the museum in Phnom Penh in 1923[2] and 1952.[3]

The iconography of the statue is problematic. As Jean Boisselier has suggested, this "'dancing' Śiva with five heads and ten arms ... can be considered a Sadāśiva."[4] This then, is a major aspect of the god, a representation of the cosmic type. The difficulty in identification resides essentially in the fact that images of Śiva with five heads and ten arms—of which a number exist in bronze—are not in a dance attitude. Furthermore, the representations of a ten-armed dancing Śiva, such as the one from the *gopura* I east of the temple of Banteay Srei (fig. 3), have only one head. Whatever the precise identity of the Śiva, whose colossal hand now resides at the National Museum of Phnom Penh, it is worth noting that the work is unique in Khmer sculpture and seems to have no equivalent, either in bas-relief or in bronze statuary.

The attribute on which this left hand rests can be considered the pommel of a club. The objects still identifiable in the statue's other hands (see note 2) could belong to Śiva, but the club is not ordinarily associated with this god. Two explanations come to mind: the iconography may have been idiosyncratic and unfamiliar elsewhere; or (and the suggestion should not be rejected a priori, though it springs from considerations that are practical rather than iconographic) the club was intended to assure the stability of an unusually monumental and complex work as one of a number of struts; a club would have been particularly suited to this function.

T.Z.

Fig. 1
Bust of Śiva from Prasat Kraham at the time of discovery

Fig. 2
Hands of Śiva from Prasat Kraham at the time of discovery

Fig. 3
East pediment of *gopura* I east of Banteay Srei. Dancing Śiva

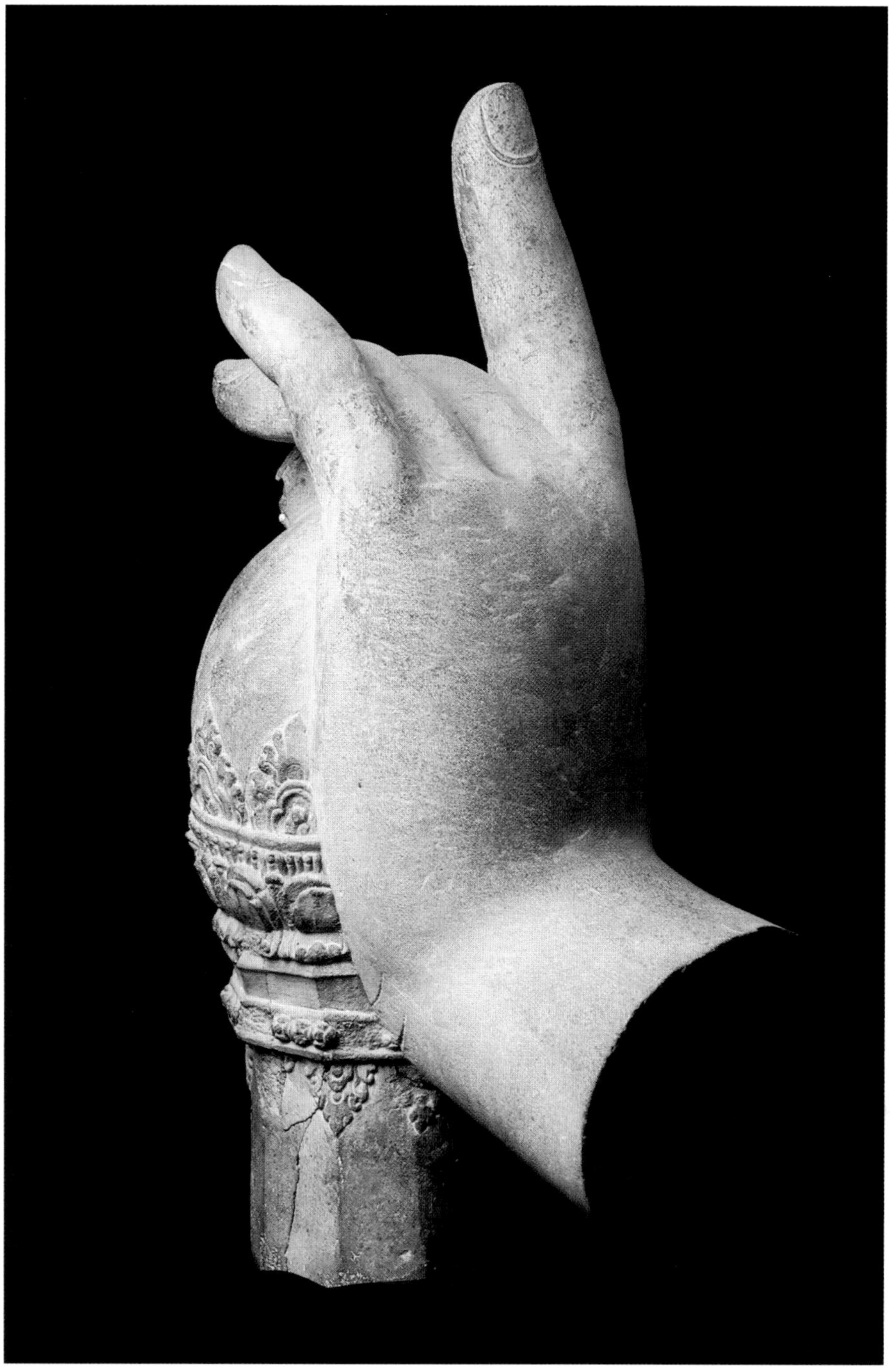

43

Dancing Female Divinity

Prasat Kraham, Prasat Thom, Koh Ker (Kompong Thom)
Angkor period, style of Koh Ker, 2d quarter of the 10th century
Sandstone
Height 135 cm, width 80 cm, depth 32 cm
Musée national des Arts asiatiques-Guimet, Paris, MG 18096

One of the most constant traits of Khmer sculpture over the centuries is its hieratic character. At some points, particularly in pre-Angkor art (cats. 14, 27), the sculptors nevertheless animated their figures by a discreetly hip-swayed posture, except when the iconography demanded a more pronounced movement, as in representations of Kṛṣṇa Govardhana (cat. 13).

But the style of Koh Ker—one of the most original in all Khmer art, formed at a time when the capital was not at Angkor but some fifty miles (80 km) to the northeast—introduced a new sense of movement into sculpture.

This statue of Devī dancing was discovered by Louis Delaporte in 1873 in *gopura* III east of Prasat Thom at Koh Ker, a structure also known as Prasat Kraham (the red temple) for its red brick.

According to Henri Parmentier,[1] "a pedestal bearing two feet in a dance position and the lower edge of a large panel of cloth in the form of a double anchor" as well as "a hand in the gesture of a female dancer" were unearthed at the Koh Ker excavation in 1933. Although it has never been possible to bring these feet and this hand together with the statue from the Musée Guimet, it seems certain that they belong to her. Some idea of the complete sculpture, at least as far as the legs are concerned, can be gained from looking at the bronze dancing female divinity from the Musée Guimet (cat. 103). The position of the arms is more uncertain, but it seems likely that they were symmetrical, judging from the rough finish of the garment to the right of the arms on either side.

Given where this sculpture was found—near a colossal statue of Śiva (cat. 42), himself perhaps in an attitude of dance[2]—it probably represents a particular aspect of Śiva's *śakti* within the highly complex Śivaite iconography of Koh Ker.

The face, unfortunately chipped, proclaims a clearly relaxed and smiling expression. It is modeled with the subtlety that was one of the characteristic innovations of the style of Koh Ker.

The *jaṭā* presents a new and original composition: the locks of hair are braided and arranged in horizontal layers. The unusually rich handling of the various elements can also be seen in the hair at the back of the head, where the braided locks alternate with slender coils (of hair?) that end in pompons.

Unlike numerous other sculptures of the time,[3] Devī is represented here without any jewelry except a diadem, whose composition outdoes that of the style of the Bakheng: the main decorative band of diamond-shaped florets is bordered by two fine strings of pearls. The pleated garment is handled with unusual mastery. The pleats are wide and regular, signaling a remarkably sure hand. Notice the width of the corolla-like fold hiding the belt in front as well as the delicacy of the bracketed clasp in the back.

T.Z.

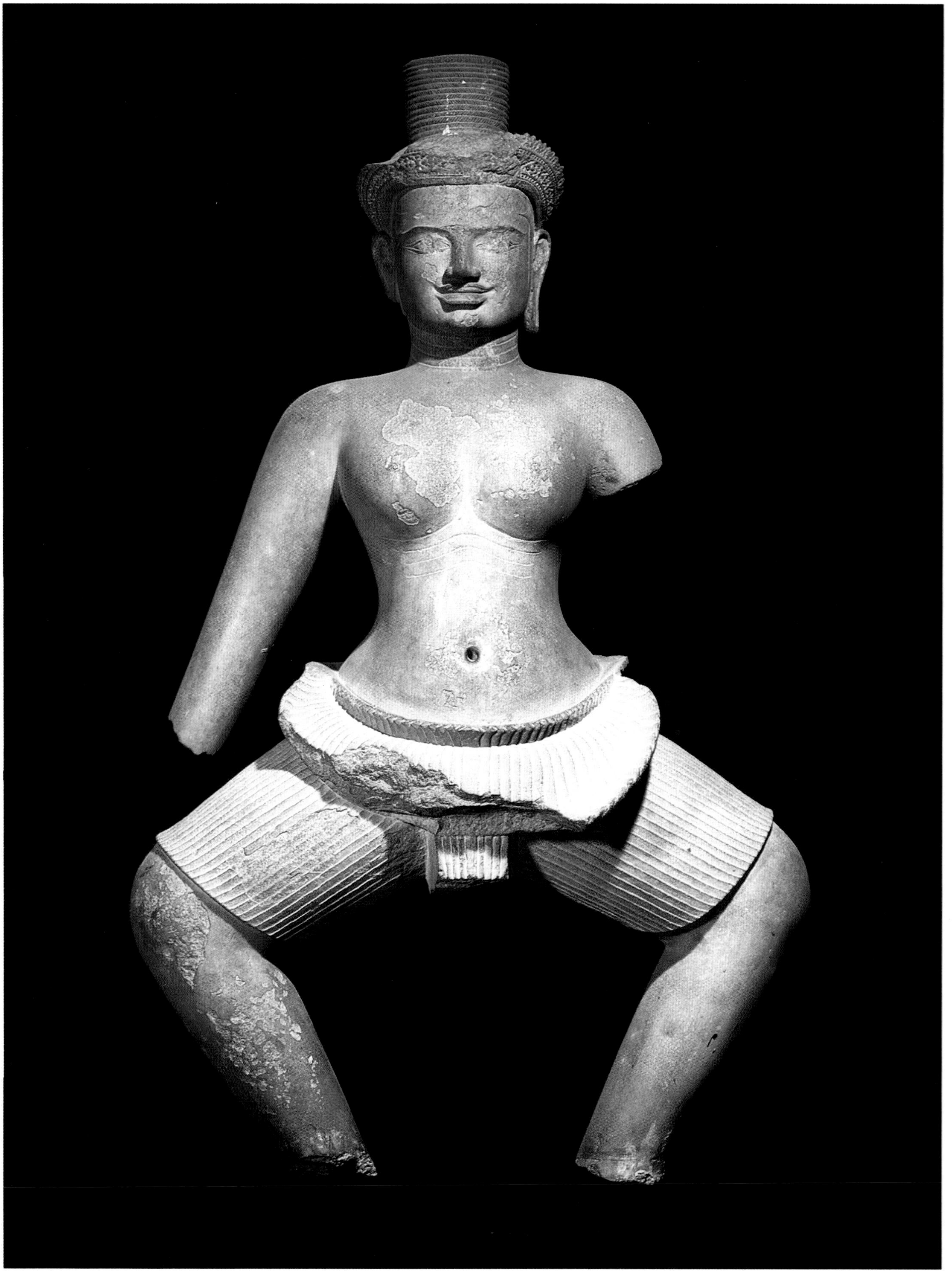

44

Wrestlers

Prasat Thom *gopura* II west, Koh Ker
(Kompong Thom)
Angkor period, style of Koh Ker,
2d quarter of the 10th century
Sandstone
Height 79 cm, width 83 cm, depth 39.5 cm
National Museum of Cambodia,
Phnom Penh, Ka 1657

The hieratic, frontal aspect of the Bakheng style was gradually abandoned at Koh Ker, where the sense of movement and "dynamic equilibrium," to use Jean Boisselier's phrase, harked back in spirit to certain pre-Angkor works (cat. 13). One of the defining characteristics of the art of Koh Ker is monumentality. This group of two male wrestlers evokes the combat between Sugrīva and Vālin, represented in the group from Prasat Chen (page 188, fig. 1) and often featured on the lintels and pediments of Banteay Srei, except that the absence of the tails of the two ape-heroes from the *Rāmāyaṇa* prevents any such identification here. The statue is damaged but still renders the interlocking holds of the wrestlers with great assurance and realism (fig. 1). The modeling provides accurate anatomical information and remains, according to Boisselier (1966, 248), "substantially similar to that of Bakheng."

One of the wrestlers wears the short, vertically pleated *sampot* (*saṃbat' caṅ kpin*) characteristic of the style of Bakheng, while his opponent wears a similar *sampot* but without the pleats and held in place by a jeweled belt from which hang pendants of a lanceolate, leaflike form. The knot of this wrestler's *sampot* has the fan shape that was classic since the style of Preah Koh. The belt with its long pendants first appeared on the female divinity from Bakheng now in the Musée Guimet (cat. 41).

S.S.

Fig. 1
The wrestlers (with pedestal) at the time of their discovery

45

Brahmā

Vat Baset area (Battambang)
Angkor period, style of Koh Ker,
2d quarter of the 10th century
Sandstone
Height 137 cm, width 110 cm, depth 84 cm
Musée national des Arts asiatiques-Guimet, Paris, MG 18098

Brahmā was rather rarely represented alone in three-dimensional Khmer sculpture. His images are generally found in company with Śiva and Viṣṇu in representations of the *trimūrti* (cats. 37–39). In bas-reliefs as well, he is rarely featured as the principal divinity.[1] He appears fairly often, on the other hand, as a subordinate figure in representations of the great Śivaite myths, such as the one about the origin of the *liṅga* (cat. 20), or in the context of Viṣṇu Anantaśāyin, seated on the lotus emerging from Viṣṇu's navel.

In conformity with the Indian tradition, the god is here shown with four faces (*caturmukha*) and one will recall that from his four mouths issued the four *Veda*. His symbolic attributes have all disappeared, with the exception of the remnant of the *akṣamālā* (rosary) that he holds in the upper right hand. It is very likely that the *kamaṇḍalu* (bottle) and the *puṣtaka* (book) were among the god's attributes, the first one at the very least. The ring of large pearls encircling the four *jaṭās* at a third of their height seems a specific iconographic feature of Brahmā in Cambodia.

The full proportions, the decorative detail of the diadem, and the representation of the ornaments (ear pendants, necklace, belts around torso and abdomen, armbands, bracelets), make it possible without contest to attribute this work to the style of Koh Ker, though it does not come from the eponymous site. Étienne Aymonier claims that he "came across it in a small wood between Baset and Ta Ke Pong," far to the west of Koh Ker in the province of Battambang.

The heavy modeling, almost flaccid, and sanctimonious expression of the faces lead one to consider this a provincial work, distinctly inferior in quality to the superb sculpture at Koh Ker itself.

The strange square base on which the god is seated, decorated with lotus petals, presents an anomaly due, perhaps, to the work's provincial origins. The pedestals of Brahmā images are in fact circular and decorated with a frieze of *haṃsa* (geese), his vehicle, as the many fine examples from Brahmā sanctuaries attest,[2] in contrast to the pedestals of the other Hindu gods, which are generally square.

T.Z.

46

Vājimukha / Hayaśiras

Sambor Prei Kuk, sanctuary 7,
north group (?) (Kompong Thom)
Angkor period, style of Pre Rup,
3d quarter of the 10th century
Sandstone
Height 146 cm, width 54 cm, depth 43 cm
Musée national des Arts asiatiques-Guimet, Paris, MG 18099

The tenth-century style of Pre Rup (see also Varuṇa, cat. 47) evolved after the return of Rājendravarman II to Angkor following the Koh Ker interim. It retains much of the detailing of the Bakheng and Koh Ker styles that preceded it: the pleated *sampot* with double, anchor-form front panel and folded-over top edge and the richly ornamented diadem, tied at the back of the head and encircling the elaborately layered, pagoda-like octagonal crown (*mukuṭa*) mandated by iconography. The crisp detailing of the headdress and garment of this lively image has a precision that contrasts pleasingly with the smooth modeling of the torso, the expansive protrusion of the upper abdomen lending a solidity and presence to the work. If compared with the other Vājimikha in the exhibition (cat. 14), the statue from the Musée Guimet exudes a forthright strength and stockiness that is quite different from the spirituality, grace, and restrained energy of the Phnom Da piece. The lips and nostrils are treated with sensitivity, as are the fantasized ears, but the relationship of the equine head to the human neck is perhaps not quite so convincingly resolved as in the pre-Angkor piece.

As with the earlier example, this horse-headed being cannot be identified with any certainty with either Hayaśiras or Kalkin, the two equine avatars of Viṣṇu, because he lacks identifying attributes. The imposing bearing and rich accoutrements of the image leave little doubt that this is a powerful divinity, but a possible identification with a guardian figure cannot be entirely ruled out.

H.J.

47

Varuṇa

Prasat Kuk Don (Siem Reap)
Angkor period, style of Pre Rup,
3d quarter of the 10th century
Sandstone
Height 77 cm, width 40 cm, depth 40 cm
National Museum of Cambodia,
Phnom Penh, Ka 1579

In the most ancient Vedic traditions, Varuṇa was the sovereign of the world beyond and of the divine law. He had magic power and created the forms of the visible world. He meted out judgment and punishment, and was seen as a somewhat despotic wielder of magic. Later, in the *Mahābhārata*, his domain was more specifically described as the oceans, in particular the western ocean, and the waters under the earth. The Prasat Kuk Don sculpture depicts him in his function as *dikpālaka*, or guardian of one of the four points of the compass, in Varuṇa's case, the west. Varuṇa's *vāhana* (mount or vehicle) is the *haṃsa* (goose, also the mount of Brahmā), as in this image, or sometimes the *nāga* or the *makara*. His attributes include the *paśa* (noose or halter), possibly once held in his right hand but now broken off. The stele of Pre Rup, in the year 961, mentions the installation of a *liṅga* with eight directional guardians (*dikpālaka*) (Bhattacharya 1961, 138), though an inscription from the thirteenth century associates these spatial guardians with the cult of Nandin, the bull who is Śiva's *vāhana*. These examples testify to the longstanding importance of cosmological associations in Khmer religion and art.

Both in size and beauty this representation of Varuṇa is outstanding. The place where it was discovered sheds no light on what cult the image might have been connected with, though it seems reasonable to think that it was probably part of a *dikpālaka* series. The magnificent patina of this image, the precision of the carving of the jeweled diadem and the breast ornaments of the geese, as well as the refined treatment of the pleats of Varuṇa's *sampot* and of the birds' beaks and feathers are typical of the perfection of Pre Rup art. This is not only manifest in freestanding sculpture, but also distinguishes the contemporary architecture, particularly in the lintels and pediments of the temples of the East Mebon and Pre Rup itself.

H.J.

48

Antefix, Architectural Element in *Prasat* Form

Banteay Srei (Siem Reap)
Angkor period, style of Banteay Srei, c. 967
Sandstone
Height 95 cm (with tenon), width 38 cm, depth 38 cm
National Museum of Cambodia, Phnom Penh, Ka 1822

One of the characteristics of Indian temple architecture is the frequent device of reproducing on a building a series of increasingly reduced miniaturized versions of the form of the whole structure (Michell 1988). Orissan temples, for example, or those in Tamilnāḍu, often include towers where the construction is formed by clustered shapes, each of which rhymes with the tower itself. This practice was also followed in Khmer temples, including Banteay Srei. Not only are the doorways and *gopura* facades surmounted by concentric lobed arcatures but on the three main *prasat* (*prāsād*), or towers, that surmount the sanctuaries of the central enclosure, small versions of the *prasat* are disposed as antefixes at the corners of each of the four redented false stories (Mazzeo and Antonini 1978, 79). Like the false stories themselves, their dimensions diminish as the height increases.

The present example of this type of architectural model demonstrates very clearly the construction principle of the towers, including the rhyming arcatures of the doorways. The form of the antefixes offered a guideline to the original construction of the collapsed *prasat* and provided a useful model during the anastylosis of Banteay Srei in the 1930s.

Banteay Srei's intricate carving and the complete integration of motif and form is brilliantly captured in this perfect architectural element.

H.J.

49

Lintel

Prasat Sralao, central sanctuary
(Siem Reap)
Angkor period, style of Banteay Srei,
3d quarter of the 10th century
Sandstone
Height 82 cm, width 186 cm, depth 44.5 cm
National Museum of Cambodia,
Phnom Penh, Ka 1819

Nowhere in Khmer art was the architectural plane more completely decorated than at Banteay Srei and monuments of the same style. In this lintel from Prasat Sralao, the entire surface has been carved. It says much for the mastery of form commanded by the sculptors of this apogee of Khmer art that the effect is nevertheless not uncontrolled, and that the parts never overwhelm the whole. The integration of small animal forms into the foliate structure is done with great asssurance and charm. See, for example, the inventive way that the beak of the *garuḍa* at both ends of the composition disgorges the trunk of the *nāga* which is in turn extended by shapes that are transposed into leaves, while tendrils on the dominant horizontal garland develop into small triple *nāga* heads lurking in the foliage. The kneeling figures surmounting the lintel are set in arcaded niches that pleasingly echo the ogive surrounding the central figure, Viṣṇu riding Garuḍa. On a smaller scale still, two rows of raised petals frame the main scene. Although the iconography of the characters depicted is clear, the scene does not seem to have a narrative content.

It is instructive to compare the Viṣṇu on Garuḍa in the lintel from Prasat Sralao with the central motif of the Prasat Kok Po lintel (cat. 32). The ninth-century figures are pre-

sented frontally, marking the center of the composition. The tenth-century lintel presents Viṣṇu in a very different light. His four arms do not merely radiate, as is customary in a sculpture in the round, but are animated asymmetrically to suggest motion as he brandishes his attributes. The deity's straddling of Garuḍa is very realistic, and the sculptor has convincingly rendered the muscular tension of the god's limbs braced against the bird's chest and shoulder. Garuḍa himself is flying, his legs invisible, presumably behind him, his tail arching backward, and his richly jeweled belt in free fall, while his clawed hands brace the god's legs to maintain his position. The entire composition has a rhythm and lyricism that typify Banteay Srei carving, a perfection that has survived almost intact because of the high quality of the sandstone medium.

The elaborate details of the conical crown and diadem, of the pectoral jewelry and ear pendants, in the same style for both god and *vāhana*, as well as of the god's pleated *sampot* conform to the types seen on reliefs in the Banteay Srei temples themselves (cats. 50, 51)

H.J.

50, 51

Pediments

Banteay Srei (Siem Reap)
Angkor period, style of Banteay Srei, c. 967
Sandstone

50
Pediment (west?) of the west *gopura* of the second enclosure
Height 196 cm, width 242 cm
National Museum of Cambodia, Phnom Penh, Ka 1660

51
Pediment of west porch of east *gopura* of the third enclosure
Height 195 cm, width 269 cm
Musée national des Arts asiatiques-Guimet, Paris, MG 18913

When discussing Banteay Srei (citadel of women) it is difficult to know which of its perfections to address first. Founded by Yajñavarāha, a Brahman who was influential in the reign of Rājendravarman and who became the guru of Jayavarman V, and by his younger brother Viṣṇukumāra, the temple complex was dedicated in 967. Because the quality of the pink sandstone used to face its brick towers was exceptionally fine, the crisp detail of the carving has survived in excellent condition. The miraculously inventive relief in the niches, door frames, lintels, pediments, and roofs is executed with exuberance, yet also with a refinement that never overwhelms the elegant proportions of the small buildings. The graceful figures of *dvārapāla* and *devatā* (masculine and feminine celestial guardians, respectively) in the niches define the canon of the Banteay Srei style, while the cult figures (cat. 56) and, to a lesser extent, the lively animal guardians on the plinths (cats. 52–55) show continuity with the style of Pre Rup.

For sheer mastery of composition and iconographic brilliance, however, nothing in Khmer art surpasses the pediments of the *gopura* (gateway) and library buildings. Most are in situ, but the two pediments discussed here came from parts of the temple that were too damaged to be reconstructed during the anastylosis carried out by H. Marchal (1931–1936). The Musée Guimet pediment came from the west porch of the east gateway of the third enclosure, that is, before the visitor arrives at the central sanctuary; the National Museum of Phnom Penh's piece probably faced west on the west gate of the second enclosure, and therefore was behind the central enclosure. Although these two pediments were never visible together, they both conform closely to the aesthetic that determines the harmony of the monument.

It has been pointed out (Bhattacharya 1961, 32) that the iconography of Banteay Srei is syncretic, a reflection of the religious tolerance in Cambodia during that period, and that although the founders of the temple were Śivaite, as was the king, one of the central sanctuary *prasat* is Viṣṇuite and much of the subject matter of the narrative reliefs treats Viṣṇuite themes. That is the case with both the pediments under discussion here, since both depict episodes in the *Mahābhārata*, an epic whose chief deity is Viṣṇu, particularly in his avatar of Kṛṣṇa.

The pediment from the National Museum of Phnom Penh presents some of the chief protagonists in the *Mahābhārata*: the five Pāṇḍava brothers and their enemies (the one hundred Kaurava brothers who have usurped the kingdom of the Pāṇḍava), as well as Kṛṣṇa and his older brother Balarāma,[1] allies of the Pāṇḍava. Bhīma, the warrior brother of fabled strength, leaps in the air to strike the Kaurava Duryodhana. Both combatants wield the mace, one of

Viṣṇu's attributes, whose use they learned from Balarāma. Watching Bhīma from the viewer's right are Yudhiṣṭhīra (the model of the just king), Arjuna (renowned hero irresistible to women), and the twins Nakula and Sahadeva. Kṛṣṇa, on the viewer's extreme left, is trying with his four arms to restrain Balarāma, holding a plow, from intervening in the struggle: although a supporter of the Pāṇḍava, Balarāma is angry that Bhīma is betraying the rules of honorable combat. The vitality of Bhīma's leaping figure with belt ends flying, the tension in the braced legs of Duryodhana, the rhythm of the limbs of the gods, and the anchoring counterpoised block of the seated Pāṇḍava combine to create a balanced, dynamic composition. The spatial vitality of the blank surface that isolates Bhīma and the rhyming movements of the small flying figures above show the hand of a master sculptor.

The Musée Guimet pediment features the same small flying deities in its apex, while a central, ovoid tree flanked by two smaller trees creates a forest background for the struggle between two *asura* (antigods or demons), Sunda and Upasunda. They are vying for possession of the *apsaras* (celestial spirit) Tilottamā, a beautiful being created by the gods to arouse rivalry and provoke a contest between the *asura* brothers in the hopes of bringing an end to the destruction that they have wreaked on the world. The central group is flanked by two groups of figures in Brahmanic ascetic garb seated *à la javanaise* (with one knee raised). The pediment shows the same mastery of dynamics in the relationship between the brothers, one with mace raised high, the other with the weapon dropped behind the back in counterpoise; one is frontal, one seen from behind, creating an interesting depth perspective. Tilottamā, leaning on her left knee, inclines her head to the right and thus belongs to both sides of the scene while forming the axis of the composition. As with the Phnom Penh example, the disposition of figures within the triangular space is unerring.

Both pediments enclose the narrative scene with an undulating frame of dramatically rearing, flame-shaped foliate forms terminating at the lower corners in magnificent rearing *nāga* with multiple heads.[2] Details of *sampot*, jewelry, and headdresses form the basis for chronological identification.

H.J.

52, 53, 54, 55

Guardian Figures

Banteay Srei (Siem Reap)
Angkor period, style of Banteay Srei, c. 967
Sandstone

52
Guardian with Lion Head
Height 83 cm (without tenon),
width 51 cm, depth 43 cm
National Museum of Cambodia,
Phnom Penh, Ka 786

53
Guardian with Raptor Head
Height 86.5 cm (without tenon),
width 52.5 cm, depth 47 cm
National Museum of Cambodia,
Phnom Penh, Ka 801

54
Guardian with Monkey Head
Height 88.6 cm (without tenon),
width 50 cm, depth 41 cm
National Museum of Cambodia,
Phnom Penh, Ka 701

55
Guardian with *Yakṣa* Head
Height 90 cm (without tenon),
width 50 cm, depth 43 cm
National Museum of Cambodia,
Phnom Penh, Ka 722

The tradition of placing guardian figures in the form of animals and mythological creatures at strategic places flanking gateways, balustrades, and steps was widespread in Cambodian temples. Lions and elephants are perhaps the most memorable as freestanding figures: one thinks of the imposing silhouettes of elephants at the corners of the Bakong and the East Mebon and of the lions of Pre Rup, among others. *Nāga*, *kāla* heads, and *garuḍa* are unforgettably integrated into the architecture of Angkor Vat and the Bayon. Perhaps the guardians of greatest character, however, are those that protected the inner enclosure of the small and perfect temple of Banteay Srei.

While most of the original figures are missing, some still exist. Because they were vulnerable to the vandalism and theft that threaten all Khmer monuments, the Banteay Srei guardians were brought to the National Museum for safekeeping during the turbulent years of the 1970s and 1980s.

Only three of the creatures have animal heads; the fourth, from the north enclosing wall of the west staircase leading to the sanctuary tower, is a *yakṣa*, a genie whose bulging eyes and bared fangs make his fierce nature clear.

The three animal figures—lion (from the east side of the south sanctuary tower), monkey (from the south side of the entrance structure of the central sanctuary), and the raptor, who is a *garuḍa* (from the east side of the north sanctuary tower)—

are strongly anthropomorphic, having human torsos and limbs, with the exception of the *garuḍa*, who has wings, tail, feathered legs, and clawed feet. None is particularly convincing as a fierce guardian, except perhaps the lion, whose fangs are menacingly bared. All save the *garuḍa* wear a short *sampot* (*saṃbat*) in a pleated fashion typical of Pre Rup, while the *garuḍa* and monkey have richly jeweled diadems and elaborately profiled *mukuṭa* also typical of that style.[1] The weapons of all four guardians have been broken off except in the case of the *garuḍa*, who seems to be holding a *vajra*; he somewhat resembles a *garuḍa* figure from Prasat Thom of Koh Ker (Jacques 1990, 69). The locations of the four creatures do not seem to be based on any of the known relationships between certain beings and specific cardinal directions. For example, the *garuḍa*, who is Viṣṇu's mount and, according to legend, lives in the south,

was found on the east face of the north tower; this happens to be the sanctuary dedicated to Viṣṇu. The monkey, if related to the monkey general Hanuman (one of the heroes of the *Rāmāyaṇa*) could be expected to face northwest, the direction of Vāya, god of wind and the father of Hanuman; in fact he faces south. However, it is impossible to know whether the figures were in their original places when scholars first observed them.

The guardians have accoutrements that suggest nobility and they were probably minor divine figures, inhabitants of Kailāsa, the abode of Śiva, a theory borne out by the scenes represented on the pediments on the north "library" at Banteay Srei. Iconographic uncertainty notwithstanding, these creatures strongly establish their dynamic personae on intrinsic stylistic qualities.

H.J.

56

Umāmaheśvara

Banteay Srei, *gopura* I west (Siem Reap)
Angkor period, style of Banteay Srei, c. 967
Sandstone
Height 65.5 cm (without tenon),
width 51 cm, depth 43 cm
National Museum of Cambodia,
Phnom Penh, Ka 1797

This group of Śiva and Umā, or Umāmaheśvara, is a popular one in Khmer iconography. Forming the couple are the daughter of the mountain, Umā / Pārvatī, and the lord of the mountain, Girīśa, another name for Śiva. They are sometimes represented riding on the back of Nandin the bull, and sometimes on Mount Kailāsa in the scene in which Rāvaṇa, possessed by an insane pride, shakes the mountain on which the god lives, spreading panic among the forest animals and ascetics.

Here, the god and goddess are wearing, respectively, a short *sampot* (*saṃbaṭ*) lacking the anchor-like fold in front, and a long *sampot* with vertical pleats and a wide, downturned frontal flap. Their belts are smooth, and the knot at the back of Śiva's *sampot* has the traditional fan shape.

The god, whose right hand rests on his raised left knee and holds a blue lotus (fig. 2), is in the same position as the Varuṇa from Prasat Kuk Don (cat. 47). Under the breasts of the goddess are incised four "beauty folds," and three folds appear on the neck of the god, who has a mustache and a beard continuous with his hair, as well as a third, vertical eye on his forehead. The goddess' legs are folded to her left while her right hand rests in the middle of the god's back. His left hand meanwhile encircles his wife's hip. Śiva sits in royal ease, in a position called *sukhāsana*. Although Pārvatī's head (fig. 1) was unfortunately stolen during the 1970s, both deities wear their hair in a high chignon of horizontally coiled tresses, their foreheads framed with a rich diadem tied in the back; the *jaṭā*, as the chignon is called, is crowned by a four-petaled flower motif. Proceeding from bottom to top, the diadem consists of two rows of pearls, a band of lozenge-shaped flowers, a third row of pearls, and a row of small, lanceolate leaves. The god's cylindrical chignon is not as tall as those in the Preah Ko and Bakheng styles; rather, it is closer to the style of Koh Ker.

The god's position, seated in *sukhāsana* with Umā on his left thigh, is similarly found in bas-relief on lintels or pediments where Śiva and Pārvatī are shown riding Nandin. Jean Boisselier (1966, 249–250) assigns this famous image to the style of Banteay Srei, observing that it continues the styles of Koh Ker (with the horizontally coiled tresses of the *jaṭā*) and of Pre Rup (the costume).

The disparity in size between Śiva and his spouse is remarkable but not in any way exceptional. While Śiva appears entirely natural in his proportions and his general attitude, the goddess seems in an awkward position, particularly in the way her legs are represented.

S.S.

Fig. 1
The Umāmaheśvara image before the head of the goddess was stolen

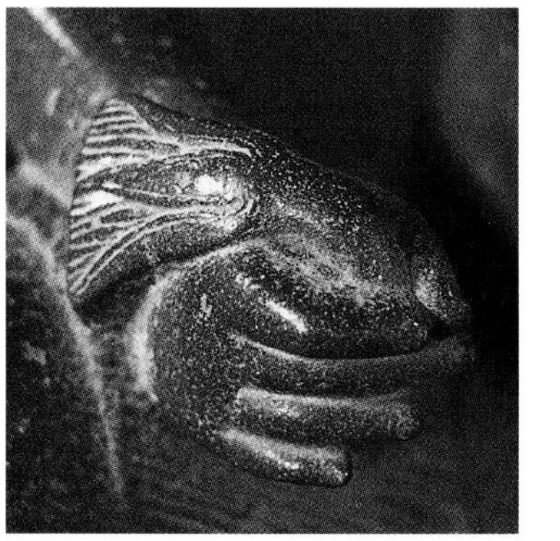

Fig. 2
Detail of Śiva's hand, holding a blue lotus

Late Tenth to Late Twelfth Century

Opposite, Fig. 1
Head of a deity. Provenance unknown. Baphuon style, mid-eleventh century. Sandstone. Height 22 cm. Chartres Museum

The Angkor Style: Archaism and Innovation

The Khleang style (last quarter of the tenth century), long somewhat uncertain in outline, now appears as a bridge between the art of Pre Rup, the final and greatly softened manifestation of the hieratic spirit of the first Angkor art, and the art of the Baphuon, heir to the art of Banteay Srei. The style flourished during the reigns of Jayavarman V–Paramavīraloka (968–1000/1001), a son of Rājendravarman, and of Jayavīravarman (1002–1010/1011?).[1] The architectural ornament of the Khleang style is clearly distinct from the ornament of Pre Rup, but the same cannot be said of the sculpture. While the modeling is perceptibly more supple and the faces are softer, prefiguring the refined style of the Baphuon, the sculpture is never wholly free of a somewhat stiff frontality, and the faces show no marked character. In some cases, the only indications that a work is in the Pre Rup style rather than the Khleang is the arrangement of the clothing or the ornamentation of a diadem.

Softness and grace characterize the style of the Baphuon, which lasts for most of the eleventh century (fig. 1). Drawing on the developments of the previous half-century, while remaining innovative in the fullest sense of the term, the art of the Baphuon introduced a number of new elements. The first striking aspect is a clear reduction in the size of the figures. This rule, as so often happens, is challenged by a major exception, namely, in the bronze art of the period (cat. 68). Aside from being smaller in size, the bodies are different in proportion, having a more elongated line, and a hip sometimes juts out (cat. 66). The youthful faces wear a definite smile. The outlines of the eyes, lips, and, where they occur, the mustache and beard (always limited to the chin), are marked by incisions. The greatest transformation, however, is in the dress. A new fashion makes its appearance: the hips are closely molded in finely pleated cloth (cat. 65). A similar treatment of pleated cloth appears on bas-reliefs as early as Banteay Srei, notably in certain male figures.[2] The specific aspects of the Baphuon style were formulated during the long reign of Sūryavarman I–Paramanirvāṇapada (1002/1010–1011–1050), attaining its mature phase during the reigns of Udayādityavarman II (1050–1066), who commissioned the Baphuon and probably the West Mebon, and of Harṣavarman III–Sadāśivapada (1066–1080). Given that this style survived for an exceptional length of time—almost a century—it is not surprising that it shows a certain internal evolution, particularly noticeable in the jewelry and dress of the figures, while faces retain their characteristic appearance over the entire period. It is important to emphasize, lest the ever-changing reality of Khmer art be falsified, that the figures from the late Baphuon style are closer to the acknowledged aesthetic of the twelfth century than to the original and inventive style of the period at its height in the mid-eleventh century.

The start of the Angkor Vat style (end of the eleventh century to the third quarter of the twelfth century) coincides with the accession of Jayavarman VI–Paramakaivalyapada (1080–1107), whose inscriptions state that he was unrelated to the kings who had preceded him on the throne and a native of the city of Mahīdarapura, which was perhaps located on the northern borders of the Khmer Empire. It was apparently at the end of the eleventh century that the characteristic elements of the completely classical architecture of the first half of the twelfth century were established, notably with the founding of the beautiful temple of Phimai, in what is now Thailand, shortly before 1107. In 1113, Sūryavarman II–Paramaviṣṇuloka (1113–to at least 1145), as ambitious a conqueror as he was an exceptional builder, seized power, which at the time was "in the service of two masters."[3] Khmer architecture certainly found its finest expression during

1. The historical situation at the end of the tenth century and the beginning of the eleventh is particularly confusing. Jayavarman V probably died in 1000 or 1001. King Udayādityavarman I, who was consecrated in 1001, apparently remained on the throne only a few months, perhaps without ever having reigned in Angkor. In 1002, inscriptions mention two rival kings: Jayavīravarman and Sūryavarman I. Without delving into too much detail, we may simply say that Jayavīravarman retained the throne at Angkor until about 1010–1011, when he was supplanted by his rival, Sūryavarman I. This king subsequently gave an earlier date for his consecration as universal king than the actual date when he became sole ruler of the Khmer Empire and established his court at Angkor (1010–1011), using instead the date when he began his contest for royal power with Jayavīravarman in 1002.
2. That the art of bas-relief seems generally to have anticipated sculpture is a fact that frequently comes to one's attention, as though a period of latency were necessary before statuary could adopt certain innovations. This remarkable fact has been explained by the greater freedom enjoyed by bas-relief over sculpture in the round: sculptors of the former were not subject to the same severity and strict iconographic imperatives that governed the latter.
3. Ban That stele, face C, stanza XXXII. The two "masters" in question were Dharaṇīndravarman I–Paramaniṣkalapada (1107–1113), elder brother of Jayavarman VI, and a sovereign whose name is not known. See Louis Finot, "L'inscription de Ban That," *BEFEO* 12, 2 (1912).

his reign in the Viṣṇuite temple of Angkor Vat, but sculpture, paradoxically, was much less handsomely served. In explaining certain remarkable characteristics of Khmer art, writers have often mentioned the curious "procedure of borrowing from the styles of the past" (Coral-Rémusat 1954). According to this view, sculptors consciously took inspiration from decorative motifs and iconographic themes that had fallen into disuse to enrich their personal repertory, of whose impoverishment they were aware! If this hypothesis seems complicated—it would appear more appropriate to speak of archaism—it is nonetheless true that Khmer art is sometimes to be understood from this perspective, especially in the case of sculpture in the round; the style of Angkor Vat provides a particularly good example. After the remarkable sweetness of eleventh-century statuary, no doubt somewhat at odds with the grandeur required of an art that was meant to function as a manifesto and reflection of the political power of the empire, sculpture returned, perhaps consciously, to an aesthetic close to that of the first half of the tenth century, but without ever achieving the haughtiness or the cold and superhuman perfection of the earlier art. Flawless in execution (cats. 70, 71), the Brahmanistic images bring back the hieratic and somewhat geometric modeling of the Bakheng style, without falling to the level of servile copies. The Buddhist statuary, with diversified iconography, is much more seductive in appearance (fig. 2).

The Buddha is frequently represented, standing (cat. 75) or protected by the *nāga* Mucilinda, on whose body he is shown in the seated meditation posture (cats. 73, 74, 76). The emergence of this latter iconographic type seems to hark back to the style of the Khleang (cat. 59). Its development can be followed during the eleventh century (cat. 60) before its participation, in the twelfth, in the flourishing of this iconography, more specifically Khmer than any other. T.Z.

Fig. 2
Female deity with multiple heads and arms. Provenance unknown. Style of Angkor Vat, mid-twelfth century. Sandstone. Height 61.5 cm. Musée national des Arts asiatiques-Guimet, Paris

57

Śiva

Provenance unknown
Angkor period, style of the Khleang,
late 10th–early 11th century
Sandstone
Height 107 cm, width 33 cm, depth 19 cm
Musée national des Arts asiatiques-Guimet, Paris, MA 3431

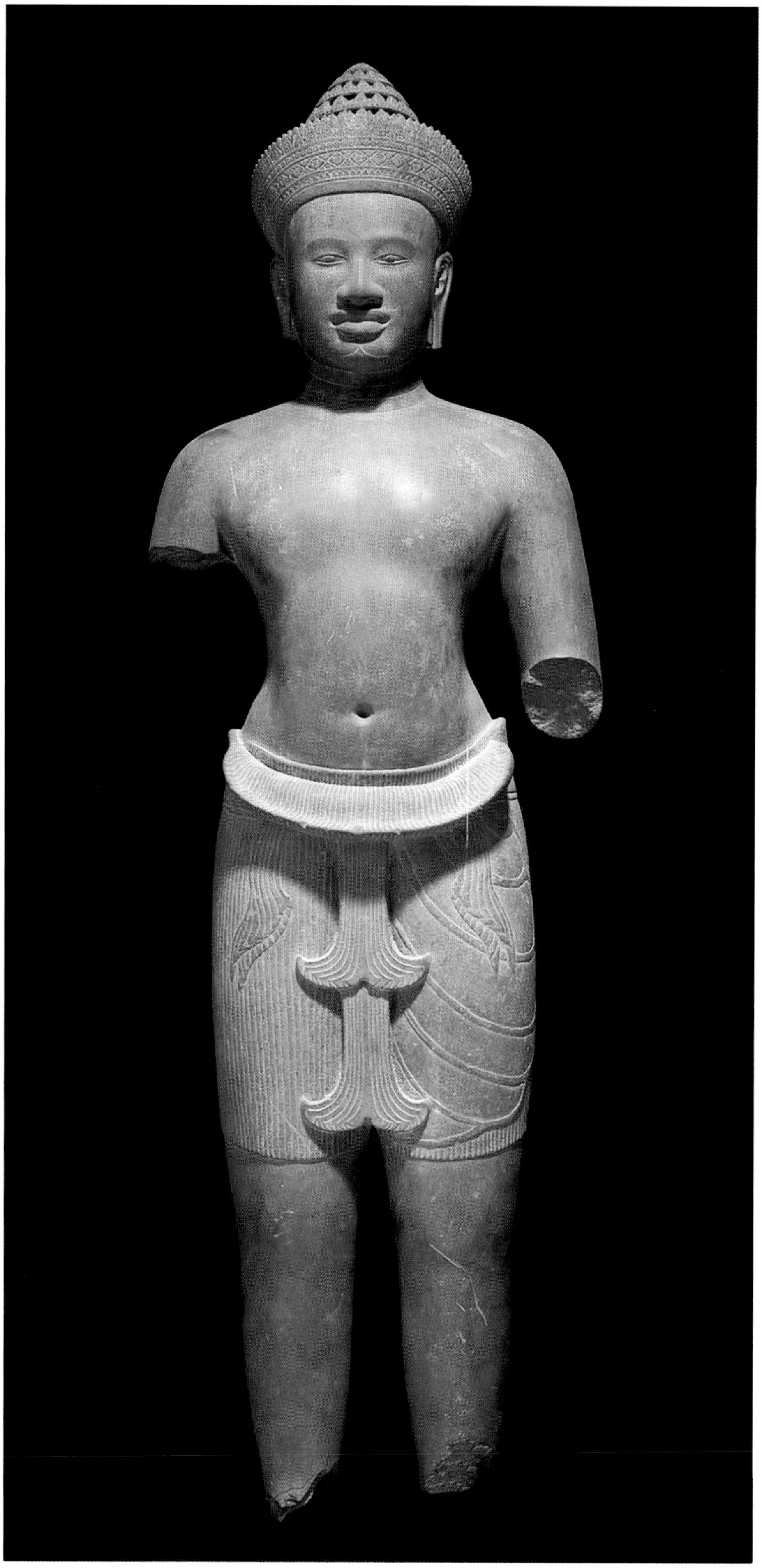

The Khleang style was produced in the rapidly changing society that encompassed the end of the reign of Jayavarman V (968–1001) and the reigns of Udayādityavarman I and Jayavīravarman. It was a turbulent period of power struggles and uncertainties, particularly toward the end. The architecture of the time includes the completion of the temple-mountain of Ta Keo and the construction of the *gopura* of the royal palace of Angkor Thom, as well as two buildings of uncertain function to the east of the palace that have given the name Khleang (emporium) to the style.

The Khleang period shares certain characteristics with the Pre Rup and Baphuon styles, which preceded it. The Śiva of the Musée Guimet, convincingly established as a Khleang production in the exhaustive analysis of Le Bonheur (1974), has traits such as the pleated *sampot* with folded-over top, the jeweled diadem, and the conical layered *mukuṭa* that relate to Pre Rup while exhibiting some of the anatomical qualities—a growing suppleness and humanization—that are reminiscent of Banteay Srei. In addition, the treatment of the dress predicts Baphuon style in the flurry of pleats springing from the fastening at the back of the *sampot*, and the elaborate arrangement looks forward to the spectacular butterfly-like adornments of Baphuon sculpture. The latter characteristics are what led Le Bonheur to propose a date late in the Khleang period for this Śiva.

Given the absence of arms and hence of attributes, the identification of the statue as Śiva rests primarily on the presence of the third eye shallowly incised on the forehead; Le Bonheur discusses other possible identities (Harihara or Lokeśvara) but rejects them on convincing grounds. The sculpture is remarkable for its tactile qualities: the stone has a patina of great allure, admirably controlled to suggest the smoothness of the skin that seemingly glows with health on a body of youthful grace and subtle anatomical accuracy. The stance, while not rigid in the sense of Bakheng statuary, is hieratic, and the overall impression is iconic. There is a lack of warmth in the gaze, perhaps because the curl of the lips is somewhat disdainful, but the nobility is unquestionable.

H.J.

58

The Nine *Deva*

Provenance unknown
Angkor period, style of the Khleang, last quarter of the 10th century
Sandstone
Height 45 cm, width 136 cm, depth 24 cm
Musée national des Arts asiatiques-Guimet, Paris, MG 14898

A group of nine divinities, collectively known to specialists as "the nine *deva*," enjoyed great popularity in Khmer art from the pre-Angkor period onward. Louis Malleret inventoried more than forty such groups, partial or complete, dating from the seventh to the thirteenth century. Once thought to be the *navagraha*, the nine seizers of Indian astronomy and astrology,[1] they have come to be called the nine *deva* after the work of Kamaleswar Bhattacharya and Malleret.

The first and last two figures in each series can be identified, respectively, as Sūrya and Candra (the Sun and Moon), and Rāhu (the ascending node of the moon or demon of eclipses) and Ketu (representing all comets and meteors). The other five divinities are more difficult to identify.

Viewed as a representation of the *navagraha*, these figures would be, from the left after Sūrya and Candra, the five planets that were then known to astronomers: Aṅgāraka[2]/Mars (the Firebrand), Budha/Mercury (the Sage), Guru[3]/Jupiter (the Master), Śukra/Venus (the White), and Śani/Saturn (the Slow). The problem of identifying the planets with the five divinities is complicated, all the more so because, with one exception, no known text names these groupings. The figures have different mounts from one series to another, as well as different symbolic attributes. Even identifying the various elements is further made difficult, and in some cases impossible, by the fragmentary state of many of the groups. Even if the mounts and attributes can be identified, there is still the question of whether they conform with the Indian texts that describe the *navagraha*. This agreement is far from certain, but as Debala Mitra has pointed out,[4] the question has been too little studied and there are too many Indian texts and images still to be analyzed to be able to claim that the disparate or apparently inconsistent nature of the Khmer groups prohibits their being considered as representations of the *navagraha*. Whatever perspective we adopt, the question will not be settled in the present state of knowledge.

According to the hypotheses of Bhattacharya and Malleret, the five divinities in the center do not represent the planets but certain of the *dikpāla*, the guardians of space, as well as several important Brahmanic gods. Accordingly, the nine *deva* from the Musée Guimet would be Sūrya, in a chariot pulled by two horses; Candra, on a pedestal; Yama (guardian of the south), on an ox; Brahmā, on a *haṃsa*; Indra (guardian of the east), on an elephant; Kubera (guardian of the north), on a horse;

Agni (guardian of the southeast and of the divine fire), on a ram; Rāhu, half visible in a swirl of clouds; and Ketu, astride a lion. (Their arguments for identifying these divinities are beyond our scope here; readers should consult the works cited in the bibliography.) Yet one of the figures, the fourth from the left, has been incorrectly identified as Brahmā. The figure rides a winged creature, recognizable as a *haṃsa*, the goose or wild duck that is Brahmā's mount. But aside from the fact that this figure does not have four heads, as Brahmā certainly would (or three in a bas-relief, the fourth being hidden, behind), his attribute is the *pāśa*, or "halter," which is certainly appropriate to Brahmā but no less so for Varuṇa, the guardian of the west.[5] Texts disagree about Varuṇa's mount; the *purāṇa* generally assign him a *makara*, but he is also linked with the *haṃsa* (Bṛhatṣamhitā). This mount is often given to him in Khmer bas-reliefs (e.g., the west lintel of the south sanctuary tower of the temple of Banteay Srei), and that, four times repeated, is what justifies the consideration of the male personage of Prasat Kuk Don as an image of Varuṇa (cat. 47). In light of this, the fourth personage in the Musée Guimet series, and in almost all the others, should be identified not as Brahmā but as Varuṇa. This would also introduce the guardian of the fourth cardinal point, the west, into the series, where, in all logic, he cannot but figure.

This piece, unfortunately very damaged, was executed with great care. It dates to the last quarter of the tenth century and represents the Khleang style, based on an analysis of the costumes (to the extent they are visible), the modeling of the figures, the representation of the animals, and the architectural elements behind the divinities. The work is comparable to another group of nine *deva* from a building at Prasat Ak Yum and now housed at the Depot for the Preservation of Angkor. That group is unusual in having an inscription, dated 1001, which confirms the dating of the Musée Guimet *deva* group.[6]

T.Z.

59

Caitya—Buddhistic Monument

Kbal Sre, Yeay Yin, near Phnom Srok (Banteay Meanchey)
Angkor period, style of the Khleang, late 10th century
Sandstone
Height 230 cm, width 76 cm, depth 76 cm
Musée national des Arts asiatiques-Guimet, Paris, MG 17487

Monolithic monuments like this one are called *caitya* (sanctuaries), because they resemble small *stūpa* and miniature temples.[1] They are always cut from a single stone and vary in size between 1.3 and 2.3 meters. All the *caitya* of the Angkor period were created within the context of Mahāyāna Buddhism. This one, found near Phnom Srok, is one of the earliest known examples. Three other monoliths of similar appearance were found in its vicinity. An inscription records how such monoliths were erected at all four points of the compass,[2] thus serving to mark off a sacred precinct from its secular surroundings.

This *caitya* is of great beauty and extremely interesting in its structure. Rising above the three-tiered base, which is entirely devoid of ornament, is a central section profusely decorated with human figures and other motifs, while smooth surfaces dominate the upper parts. This top section resembles a stoneware vase surmounted by a cone; both are octagonal and embedded in a blooming lotus with sixteen petals. The number eight refers to the four cardinal points and the four intermediate directions, thus symbolizing cosmic totality. The sixteen lotus petals are possibly a metaphor for the sixteen voids. It is certainly highly significant that the topmost section is free of any figured embellishment. It is to be associated with the body of the *stūpa* and its flamelike pinnacle.[3] The *stūpa* is the emblem of nirvana, that is, it stands for liberation from the bonds of the material world, which is the goal of every Buddhist. The way to nirvana is shown by the figures in the central section: the Buddha protected by the *nāga*, Vajrin,[4] Prajñāpāramitā, and Lokeśvara. Within Mahāyāna Buddhism they represent the most important paths to liberation. With their aid, believers seek to escape from the physical world, symbolized here by the square base.

a

b

c

d

The reliefs of the *caitya* from Phnom Srok have great significance for the iconography of Angkor art because they embody the earliest representations of these divine images of perfection. The Buddha protected by the *nāga* (a), Prajñāpāramitā, and Vajrin here make their first appearances, although they do so in forms no longer to be found at a later date. The Buddha, for example, sits on a serpent throne consisting of only two coils of the snake's body, whereas subsequent versions always display three coils.[5] His entire expression is that of a *yogin* charged with concentrated energy, and he represents the Yoga path to nirvana (cat. 76).

Proceeding in a clockwise direction, the next deity is Vajrin (b), who stands for the Tantric path. Of his three heads, only the one facing forward is fully formed. The two facing the sides end at the profile of the nose. With their heavily arched eyebrows, round, protuberant eyes, and canine fangs, the forward and left-facing images present a fearsome aspect, whereas the face on the right is gentle and peaceful. All three heads bear identical diadems, with their hair arranged in identical cone-shaped structures. Separated from them by a narrow band of lotus petals is a two-tiered structure, consisting of four niches on the lower level and one above. In each of these sits a tiny Buddha. These are the five Tathāgata (Jina), who play a major role in Tantric meditation. Together with the three heads of the deity, they clearly form a single unit, as they are all contained within one large, overarching niche. This is a highly significant variant of the three-tiered structure of the eight heads of Hevajra as seen somewhat later in the bronze figures of the subject. There the five Tathāgata are realized as four heads plus one; here they are shown as small, complete figures. Attention has never been drawn to this aspect of the deity, who has always been identified as the Bodhisattva Vajrapāṇi. Indeed, it would seem that at that time the iconography of Hevajra and Vajrapāṇi was not clearly separated. The four attributes preserved in what were originally six hands (*vajra,* knife, wheel, and bell) are appropriate to either deity. The fearsome facial expression, however, is more commonly associated with Vajrapāṇi.

In regard to the five Tathāgata, it is here argued that the deity should be considered as an early form of Hevajra, who is mentioned a number of times in inscriptions under the name of Vajrin.

Continuing in a clockwise direction, the next figure is Prajñāpāramitā (c), who originally seems to have had five heads built up on three levels. The three on the lowest level and the fourth on the middle level have been preserved, but there is only a fragment to indicate the fifth head at the top, unless it was located behind the fourth, looking backward. At the point where the break starts, a chignon displaying a small figure of the Buddha was originally situated. The five heads correspond to the ten arms. Apart from the lowest left hand, which gestures as if to grant a wish, the hands have been destroyed. Prajñāpāramitā is the personification of the perfect wisdom of the supreme Buddha (cat. 95). She represents the path to salvation through study of the sacred texts.

The figure in the fourth niche is the Bodhisattva Lokeśvara (d). He was of great importance as early as the pre-Angkor period, and a whole series of iconographic variants of him exist. In many cases he displays characteristics typical of Brahmanic gods, among them the cylindrical crown of plaited hair and the mustache, but his distinguishing element is the tiny Buddha figure, of which only slight traces remain, at the front of his crown of hair. Like Vajrin and Prajñāpāramitā, apart from the ear ornaments shaped like lotus buds, he is not wearing any body ornament. His characteristic attribute is the lotus in his lower right hand. Here the flower has been broken off, but the stalk is still recognizable. The upper right hand is holding a rosary, as can be deduced from the remaining fragment of a circle. The attributes on the left side have not been preserved, but comparisons with other Lokeśvara figures make it clear that they must have been a book and a flask of nectar (cat. 95). Lokeśvara embodies the infinite compassion felt by the Enlightened One for all beings in the world. He stands for the path of devoted love.

W.L.

60

Buddha Protected by the *Nāga*

Peam Cheang plantation (Kompong Cham)
Angkor period, style of the Baphuon,
2d half of the 11th century
Sandstone
Height 114 cm (without tenon),
width 64 cm, depth 40 cm
National Museum of Cambodia,
Phnom Penh, Ka 1680

The compelling image of the Buddha seated on the coils of the *nāga*, its outspread hood sheltering the figure meditating in *samādhī* pose, is found more frequently in Cambodia than anywhere else in Asia. In both stone (cats. 73, 74, 94) and bronze (cats. 76, 95), such sculpture was common during the Angkor Vat period, despite its being an epoch when Viṣṇuism dominated official religion, and particularly during the Bayon period, when the Buddhist Jayavarman VII was king. This Buddha on *nāga*, dating from the Baphuon period, is one of the earliest Khmer examples known.

The popularity of the image in Cambodia may perhaps be explained by the importance of the *nāga* in Khmer mythology,[1] not only in the legend of Kauṇḍinya, the Brahman ancestor who married the daughter of the *nāga*-king, but also that of the ritual relationship between the king and the *nāgī* princess Somā in the Phimeanakas temple (see page 111). The iconography of this Buddha, however, relates to the story of the *nāga* Mucilinda, who, during a torrential rainstorm that lasted seven days, emerged to shelter the Buddha meditating on the sixth day after his enlightenment (cat. 76).[2]

Compared to later versions of the subject (cats. 73, 74), this sculpture radiates intense spirituality through a restrained and simple image. He is starkly unadorned save for a narrow motif encircling his forehead and a stylized cover on his *uṣṇīṣa.* Although the subtle volumes of the stomach and chest are clearly shown, the Buddha is wearing a thin robe on his upper body. The edge of a garment encircles the base of the neck and creates a vertical division where it lies on the upper torso; it is possibly also indicated at the wrists, as the tapering of the forearms is not legible or as refined as might be expected in relation to the proportions of the upper arms. The undergarment is indicated by a line just below the umbilicus and seems to end above the ankles; since the feet are not very clearly indicated, the details are not certain.

The stone is exceptionally dark and the knees have a gleaming patina as if from the constant rubbing of devotees. The elegant, slender proportions of the Buddha and of the sculpture as a whole reveal the stylistic tendencies of Baphuon art and its ability to depict the volumes of the human body with great sensitivity. The meditative bliss of the subject is totally convincing, both in the relaxed attitude of the limbs and the gentle composure of the face, softer and more aware than that of the Sisophon Buddha

(cat. 73), for all its perfection. The treatment of the eyes is particularly moving. Outlined with fine almond-shaped extensions that lend them a rare expressiveness, they have incised pupils that, remarkably for Khmer sculpture, seem not to stare but to allow the viewer to see the soul, revealing the exalted spirituality of the Buddha in profound meditation.

H.J.

61

Stele

Palhal (Battambang)
K 449
Angkor period, style of the Baphuon,
Ka 1069
Sandstone
Height 106 cm (without tenon),
width 56 cm, depth 23 cm
National Museum of Cambodia,
Phnom Penh, Ka 1823

The stele of Palhal is among the relatively restricted number of illustrated steles. The inscriptions comprise a more or less complex iconographic motif, associated, or not, with the text. It may be a symbol, such as the trident of the pre-Angkor stele of Vat Phu (Boisselier 1966, pl. XXX/3), or a more complex motif, such as the Umāmaheśvara group carved in high relief on the lower part of this stele. Śiva and Pārvatī appear on a small jutting pedestal above the base of the stele, which is decorated with lotus petals. The goddess is in an unusual position, kneeling on her husband's left thigh rather than sitting (cat. 56). Śiva's face has the characteristics of the Baphuon style, the modeling natural and supple, the proportions broad, lips full, chin cleft. The coiffure is also characteristic of eleventh-century art. The locks of hair, in groups of three, are brought together on the top of the head into a slightly bulbous *jaṭā*, held at the base by a string of pearls. As often with bas-relief, certain jewels, in this case ear pendants, have been represented.

The text is written in two languages. There are two lines of Khmer text and thirty-six lines of Sanskrit on the front face (A), and twenty-five lines of Sanskrit and seven of Khmer on the back face (B). The letters, rather shallowly carved, are of medium calligraphic quality, a far cry from the perfection of the inscriptions at the end of the ninth and first half of the tenth century, in every way incomparable in the field.

George Cœdès published this inscription twice, each time calling attention to "the extraordinary incorrectness of the Sanskrit text." The first two lines on face A refer to the main object of the inscription, namely, the erection of a Śrī Tribhuvaneśvaradeva *liṅga* in 991 *śaka* (1069). A few lines of invocation to the gods follow, then a long genealogy of the donors[1] and a list of the gifts bestowed on the powerful family during the reigns of all the various kings succeeding to the Khmer throne up to Harṣavarman III, in whose reign the inscription was carved (end of face A and almost all of face B). It provides a remarkable example of *vaṃśa* (genealogical descent in Sanskrit) and has been mined by historians for important historical, geographic, and general cultural information. The end of the Sanskrit text mentions the erection of "two *liṅga* with two bulls" and of an "image of Parameśa with a Devī." After the usual imprecations against anyone who fails to respect the foundation, the inscription ends with a few practical details concerning the distribution of the donors' property after their deaths, and a list of those who work for the foundation.

T.Z.

62

The Nine *Deva*

Provenance unknown
Angkor period, style of the Baphuon, 11th century
Sandstone
Height 37.5 cm, width 139 cm, depth 24 cm
Asian Art Museum of San Francisco, Gift of Ed Nagel, B 71. S 9

Meticulous studies by Bhattacharya and Malleret have convincingly established that the mysterious and fascinating groups of nine divinities such as this sculpture and that in catalogue 58 are not, as they traditionally have been identified, *navagraha*. *Navagraha* means nine planets, or "nine seizers," and was thought to refer to nine planetary deities. These personages include Sūrya, the sun, in a horse-drawn chariot; Candra, the moon, on a pedestal; Aṅgāraka, Mars, on a goat; Budha, Mercury, on a bird; Bṛhaspati, Jupiter, on an elephant; Śukra, Venus, on a horse; Śani, Saturn, on a buffalo; Rāhu, the ascending node of the moon, on turbulent clouds; Ketu, comets and meteors, on a lion.

While it is clear that the two figures farthest left, Sūrya and Candra, and the two figures farthest right, Rāhu and Ketu, are correctly identified, the five remaining figures present a problem, because their mounts and attributes do not, in most cases, conform to the other *navagraha*. Bhattacharya suggests that the nine *deva* refer, rather, to an invocation of the protectors of the points of the compass: *dvārapāla*, who number four, or *dikpālaka*, who number eight, with the ninth direction being the nadir or the zenith. He identifies the five central personages, from left to right, as Yama (south, god of the underworld, on a buffalo), Brahmā (northeast, on a goose, or *haṃsa*), Indra (east, on an elephant), Kubera (north, on a horse), and Agni (fire, southeast, on a ram). Zéphir (cat. 58) believes that the fourth from left should be Varuṇa, guardian of the west, since he too has the goose for a mount and there is no indication of the four faces that characterize Brahmā.

Both Malleret and Bhattacharya give several variations that may occur, particu-

larly when the figures form part of a bas-relief, considerably exacerbating the identification problem. In the absence of clear details of attributes and mounts, which is the case with the San Francisco piece, it is very difficult to suggest with any certainty who any of the characters may be beyond the two left and two right figures, who obviously conform to the traditional iconography.

It is interesting to compare this frieze with catalogue 58. The latter is an older piece and has more recognizable details for the deities' mounts, though the faces are more damaged. One of the chief differences is that it does not have so developed an architectural setting as does the frieze from San Francisco. It is on the basis of the style of the armatures, niches, half-columns, and capitals that a Baphuon period date seems appropriate for the San Francisco frieze. A photograph of a fragment of a nine *deva* frieze from the museum in Ho Chi Minh City illustrates an architectural setting remarkably similar to the San Francisco example. Malleret (1960, 215–216, fig. 7) dates the fragment as mid-eleventh century on the basis of the triple-branched lotus stems above the pillars. Another feature making a Baphuon date likely is the treatment of the personages. The technique of rendering the surfaces of the foliage and architectural detail round in profile is one of the devices that characterize the plastic quality of Baphuon art.

H.J.

63

Lintel

Vat Baset (Battambang)
Angkor period, style of the Baphuon,
last quarter of the 11th century
Sandstone
Height 70 cm, width 152 cm, depth 33 cm
Musée national des Arts asiatiques-Guimet, Paris, MG 18218

The Baphuon style is notable in its architectural decoration for luxuriant vegetal motifs with deeply carved details, and for narrative scenes on lintels.

The horizontal branch that dominates the composition of the lintel from Vat Baset is disgorged by a *kāla* in the lower central area. The branch rises and spreads laterally, terminating in *nāga* heads that spit out *haṃsa* figures, an unusual motif for this period. The representation of the mountains in a form of layered plaques is also unusual and supports the theory that this lintel is a provincial piece and should probably be dated late in the eleventh century. This impression is offset by the details of dress, which is closer to that of Angkor Vat than that of the Baphuon. It is probably a transitional creation, or one that was made during the Angkor Vat period yet retained the older stylistic traits precisely because it was provincial.

Several scenes from the *Rāmāyaṇa* are depicted: on the left, a meeting of Rāma and his brother Lakṣmaṇa with Sugrīva, the monkey king unjustly dispossessed of his throne by his brother, Vālin; in the center, the mortal combat between Vālin and Sugrīva during which Rāma, to assure the victory of the latter, fires an arrow in the former's back; to the right, the death of the repentant Vālin, mourned by his wives. The episodes are from Book IV of the *Rāmāyaṇa*, the book of Kiṣkindhā (*Kiṣkindhākāṇḍa*), in which an alliance is sworn between Rāma and the monkey people, who

will help him regain his wife Sīta, captured by the demon Rāvaṇa.

The scenes show many of the elements of vivacity and precision that characterize the bas-reliefs of the Baphuon, along with a certain charming naivety, a quality that is found not only in the carving on the Baphuon itself but also in another temple of the same period: Prasat Khna Sen Keo 261 in Preah Vihear.

H.J.

64

Lintel

Prasat Pen Chung (Kompong Thom)
Angkor period, style of the Baphuon,
c. mid-11th century
Sandstone
Height 71 cm, width 138 cm, depth 15 cm
National Museum of Cambodia,
Phnom Penh, Ka 1826

During his childhood and adolescence, Kṛṣṇa had to withstand many attacks from demons, generally in animal form: Dhenuka, the demon ass; Ariṣṭa, the demon bull; Keśin, the demon horse; and so on. These creatures were the incarnation of various aspects of evil and were endowed with extraordinary powers. One, the serpent Kāliya, was particularly formidable. Choosing to live in the Yamunā River, Kāliya had poisoned its waters. At the request of the people living near the river, Kṛṣṇa resolved to rid the world of this terrible serpent; after a fierce battle, Kāliya was vanquished and tranquillity returned to the banks of the Yamunā.

The central scene of this lintel from Prasat Pen Chung represents Kṛṣṇa at the very moment when he is about to triumph over the evil serpent and express his joy. In contrast with Indian iconography, where Kṛṣṇa is shown dancing on a defeated Kāliya, Khmer art commemorates the actual combat. The issue is not in doubt, however, and one could even interpret Kṛṣṇa's position as tearing Kāliya apart.

The composition of the central scene has great dynamism, and the sinuous curves of the vegetal decoration have an almost baroque energy. The dancing limbs of Kṛṣṇa seem to dictate the composition of the whole.

The supple modeling of the god's body, the treatment of his face, his costume, and her jewelry conform to the criteria of the Baphuon style at its height during the mid-eleventh century. In spite of the fantastic nature of the theme, the scene retains the intimate character that is pervasive in the bas-reliefs of this period in Khmer art.

H.J.

65

Male Divinity

Provenance unknown (Battambang ?)
Angkor period, style of the Baphuon, 11th century
Sandstone
Height 60 cm, width 25 cm, depth 12 cm
National Museum of Cambodia, Phnom Penh

If Banteay Srei style represents the peak of Khmer plastic invention and liveliness, and if Angkor Vat sculpture epitomizes the noble and hieratic, Baphuon style suggests grace and elegance with an unsurpassed perfection and restraint. It extends throughout most of the eleventh century, from the reign of Sūryavarman I until that of Jayavarman VI, and this youthful standing figure demonstrates many qualities of the Baphoun style. The smaller scale itself is typical, and the carving of the *sampot* shows the deep frontal scoop that characterizes both male and female costume of the period. The rear bow with its fantastic butterfly arrangement is another characteristic of the style, which is notable for the subtlety of its decorative details and the absence of grandiose proportions. Even when (rarely) an image is executed on a large scale, as with the reclining Viṣṇu from the West Mebon (cat. 68), the effect is not of overwhelming majesty but of spiritual power and benevolence.

The modeling of the body is also typical of Baphuon figures. The limbs are rounded and the remaining knee very accurately rendered, as are the central depression of the chest, the swelling of the pectoral muscles, and the detailing of the umbilicus. The outlining of the eyes, the delicately arched brows, and full and sensitive lips are all to be found in most Baphuon figures, as is the dimpled chin. Apart from the exuberance of the rear bow, the costume is restrained, without jeweled belt, while the profile of the diadem relates well to the overall silhouette and the line of the carefully rendered ears.

Identification of the statue is difficult, because no arms or attributes remain. The fact that it has a conical *mukuṭa* and once had four arms suggests that it might be a Viṣṇu image, but if so, it depicts a youthful and spiritual god rather than a *cakravartin*.

H.J.

66

Female Divinity, possibly Lakṣmī

Prasat Trapeang Totung Thngay (Siem Reap)
Angkor period, style of the Baphuon, 2d half of the 11th century
Sandstone
Height 102 cm (without tenon), width 26 cm, depth 25 cm
National Museum of Cambodia, Phnom Penh, Ka 1830

In its frontality, this female divinity seems to continue the hieratic tradition of the Khleang style. The hollowed eyes were once inlaid with precious or semiprecious stones. The eyebrows are delicately drawn. The mouth with full lips, slightly parted, is sensual. The face, almost round, conforms to a criterion of beauty that refers to the full moon, and the neck is incised with beauty folds. The breasts are firm and somewhat like those of the Durgā Mahiṣāsuramardinī of Sambor Prei Kuk (cat. 18), though closer together, a sign of youth. The slender waist, heightened by the outline of the skirt, contrasts with the wide shoulders. The hips are not as ample as those of the Durgā. The musculature of the back is skillfully modeled. The finely pleated skirt rises behind and dips forward below the navel and knotted in front, one end of which hangs over the jeweled belt. The top and bottom of the belt are fringed with pearls, and between them, separated by pearls, are square flower motifs. The pendants are analogous to those on the belt of one of the wrestlers from Prasat Thom at Koh Ker (cat. 44).

The forearms and hands of the goddess extend forward. The left hand is broken, but the wrist and fingers of the right hand make the gesture of *kaṭakahasta;* the hand likely once held a detachable lotus of a precious material.

The *jaṭāmukuṭa* of the figure is complex and appears artificial. The locks of hair alternate toward the back with bands of pearls. The chignon proper is held in place at the base by a large circular tress, divided into four parts so that bands of pearls alternate with locks of hair.

Works in the style of the Baphuon have been described by Jean Boisselier (1966, "Manuel," 174, 252) in the following way: "Featuring a costume that seems inspired by the 'new' fashions of Banteay Srei, the statues are generally smaller and tend to have a certain elegance. The figures are elongated, with wide shoulders and narrow pelvis, though the head is often somewhat large. In certain of the female images, one again finds the old slightly flexed posture. . . .The soft, somewhat sensual faces hark back to Banteay Srei; the chin is often cleft. At the waist, the sarong describes the same curve as the *sampot.* The vertical edge reappears, still pleated, its lower end widening into a 'fishtail.' The fastening bow, at first very reduced in scale, recalls Banteay Srei; toward the end of the style it tends to elongate considerably, announcing the style of Angkor Vat. . . .The belt, at first a simple smooth band, becomes enriched with fastening laces, then an incised decoration, and finally with pendants. . . ." Compared to the divinity of Vat Mahā (Boisselier, *La Statuaire,* 1955, pl. 57a), which stands in the same position with both hands broken, this female divinity, with her coiffure, folded-over skirt with fastening bow, and gold belt with pendant, represents a more developed type.

S.S.

67

Viṣṇu (?)

Provenance unknown
Angkor period, style of the Baphuon, last quarter of the 11th century
Bronze
Height 88 cm, width 35 cm, depth 15 cm
Musée national des Arts asiatiques-Guimet, Paris, MA 1339

The scooped front of the finely pleated *sampot* of this bronze figure is almost a caricature of the characteristic line of Baphuon sculpture and the chief basis on which to assign it to that period. Baphuon statues are also noted for their slenderness, and in this context as well the image conforms to the principle of the canon while surpassing it in execution, particularly in the length of the legs. Many late Baphuon pieces exhibit belts with jeweled pendants and again, the detail is exaggerated here, as are the pendants and central gems of the rib-level belt, necklace, and upper arm bracelets.

Without attributes, the figure's identity cannot be established. The four arms could justify a speculation that it represents Viṣṇu, but there is no headdress, although there is a rough area on the crown of the head that may indicate a missing chignon. It is possible that a diadem and crown could have been cast separately, and have now been lost, or that the figure was presented with these accessories made from precious metal; this theory is perhaps supported by the presence above the left ear of a small loop that might have been a fastening device.

While the details of the face are finely cast—the nose in particular is highly refined, as are the details of the ears, brows, and unusually full mustache—there are many imprecise areas on the *sampot* and the back, whether from uncontrolled casting (the likelier reason) or corrosion during later years is not certain.

Although its somewhat arrogant expression and the rigidity of the posture deprive this figure of the grace expected of Baphuon art, it nevertheless has a commanding presence that transcends its scale and somewhat provincial characteristics, in particular the elongation of its proportions.

H.J.

68

Viṣṇu Anantaśāyin

West Mebon, Angkor (Siem Reap)
Angkor period, style of the Baphuon, 2d half of the 11th century
Bronze
Height 122 cm, width 222 cm, depth 72.5 cm
National Museum of Cambodia, Phnom Penh, Ga 5387

Certainly one of the most monumental works of sculpture ever created in Cambodia, and also one of the largest bronze figures ever cast in Southeast Asia, this Viṣṇu reclining in cosmic sleep (Viṣṇu Anantaśāyin) would have extended at least six meters. In the great Viṣṇuite creation myth, representations of which were widespread in Cambodia (Bénisti 1965), the god reclined on the serpent Ananta ("without end"), who was floating on the ocean during one of the cosmic intervals, or *kalpa*. From Viṣṇu's navel sprang a lotus plant, in the heart of which sat Brahmā, who then set the cycle of creation in motion once more. According to Vedic myth, Viṣṇu, Ananta, and ocean are all aspects of the same reality, parts of the primordial waters whose chaos gives rise to the universe.[1] In some contexts the lotus stem develops three branches that become the three gods of the *trimūrti*: Viṣṇu, Śiva, and Brahmā (Bhattacharya 1961, 109–110).

The figure was cast in several parts—the joints of the arms are clearly visible—and

Fig. 1
Bronze fragments found with the bust of Viṣṇu. National Museum of Cambodia, Phnom Penh

Fig. 2
The bust of Viṣṇu at the time of its discovery in 1936

Fig. 3
Aerial view of the West Mebon

would probably have had precious metals inserted into the hollows of the brows, eyes, and mustache. Holes in the head indicate that the god probably wore a detachable diadem. The statue would have been placed in water, which accounts for its location in the Mebon temple in the western *baray*, the huge reservoir created by Udayādityavarman II in the mid-eleventh century, where it was rediscovered by archaeologists in 1936.

As is well known, the Chinese envoy Zhou Daguan visited Angkor in 1296 and in his memoirs described the sight of what he took to be a Buddha figure with water flowing from its navel. While he mislocated the site (thinking it was the eastern *baray*) and interpreted Viṣṇu as Buddha, his account of the fountain function of the navel seems to be borne out by subsequent research.

The surface of this piece has many original repairs and has suffered from its years buried underground. Damage and the loss of more than half the sculpture do not negate the extraordinary power of the god, however, and it is easy to comprehend why Viṣṇu Anantaśāyin was a cult figure. From a distance the benign countenance radiates eternal comprehension. When one stands close the image emits an almost palpable magnetism and one senses the latent energy captured by the maker, who must not only have been a remarkable artist but also, one is sure, a true follower of Viṣṇu as supreme god.[1]

H.J.

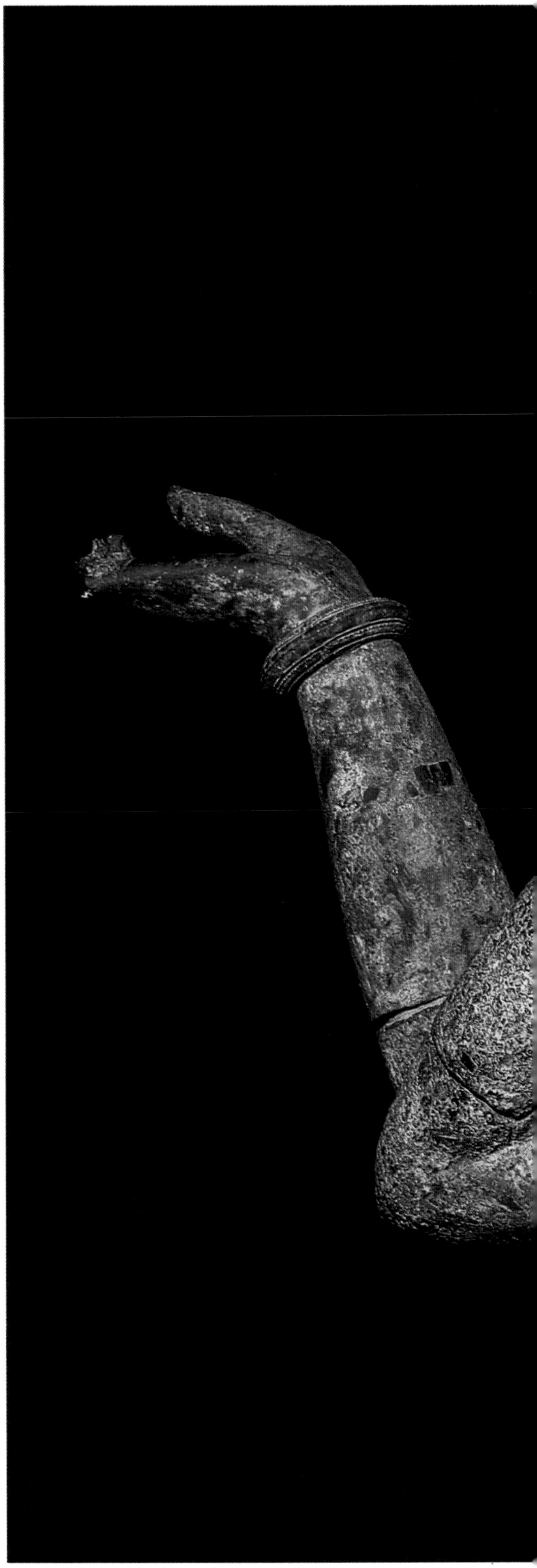

69

Viṣṇu-Vāsudeva-Nārāyaṇa

Kapilapura, Angkor (Siem Reap)
Angkor period, style of Angkor Vat,
1st half of the 12th century
Bronze
Height 43.5 cm, width 18 cm, depth 11 cm
National Museum of Cambodia,
Phnom Penh, Ga 5291

Few Brahmanic religious images from the Angkor period have caused as much confusion as this four-armed god, standing in an upright posture. In his hands he bears, clockwise from lower right, an orb, a disk, a conch, and a mace, the typical attributes of Viṣṇu (cat. 31). But his head, with the third eye on the forehead and the high crown of hair in which the Sanskrit symbol for "oṃ" is set, seems to be displaying the characteristic signs for Śiva. This duality has generally suggested that he be interpreted as Harihara, the fusion of Viṣṇu and Śiva into one image. Between the sixth and the tenth centuries, Harihara enjoyed great prominence in Cambodia, as may be seen from the numerous surviving works of sculpture depicting him. In accordance with Indian iconography, images of Harihara were always split vertically into a Śiva half and a Viṣṇu half (cat. 16). However, with this bronze figure and all others of its type,[1] the dividing line runs horizontally, between head and trunk. This salient distinction must have a deep-rooted origin; it is not very likely that an iconographical tradition of almost a thousand years underwent a sudden change. One might more readily imagine that Harihara came to lose status as other divinities with their own representations in conformity with the Khmer canon became more prominent.

Around the tenth century the Pāñcarātra were the most important Viṣṇuite sect in Cambodia. In the important inscription of Thvar Kdei dating from this time, the essential tenets of their doctrine are summarized.[2] As it is there related, their highest god unites in his person three aspects, that of omnipresent Nārāyaṇa, the universal soul Vāsudeva, and Viṣṇu Lokapāla.

All three aspects are present in this bronze figure, as can be ascertained from the details of its realization. The inscription of Thvar Kdei says that Nārāyaṇa will grant absolute liberation (from the cycle of rebirth) to those who practice yoga and know how to utter the syllable "oṃ." It is explicitly stated that "oṃ" is the proper image of Nārāyaṇa, which sheds light on the reputedly Śivaite head, revealing it to be, instead, the aspect of Nārāyaṇa. Its dominant features, namely, the third eye, the crown of hair, and the written symbol "oṃ," are not primarily signs of Śiva, but those of a *yogin*. Śiva bears them because he has been revered as a master of yoga since the earliest days of Indian antiquity. In Cambodia, however, other Brahmanic and Buddhist deities have also been depicted as *yogin*.

In further study of the inscription of Thvar Kdei, the Vāsudeva and Viṣṇu aspects become obvious.

It is said of Vāsudeva that his four arms are the characteristic manifestations of his universal *ātman* (world soul), an unmistakable reference to the *vyūha* doctrine, which is of fundamental importance in Pāñcarātra philosophy. It postulates that the absolute (Nārāyaṇa) is manifested in four emanations, which, in turn, bring forth the material world. The four arms of Vāsudeva, according to the inscription, stand for these four emanations.[3]

The material world is represented finally by the god in his aspect as Viṣṇu. The square base he stands on is the symbol of the world as created and ordered by him. His four attributes of orb, disk, conch, and mace are associated with the protectors of the four cardinal directions. Viṣṇu as Lokapāla (protector of the world) is the manifestation of God in this world.

In his highest form embracing all three aspects, he may be likened to the *yupa* (sacrificial post) that symbolizes the world-axis. The association of the *yupa* with a sprouting tree putting forth new shoots (*visakha*) is also found in the Pāñcarātra texts. The trunk is the column that supports the world, while the spreading crown is the totality of the cosmos. The tree is frequently cited as a metaphor for the cosmic aspect of God, representing both the stable, indivisible basis of the world, as well as the diversity of creation.

Viṣṇu, standing erect as a column, his four arms indicating the four cardinal directions, transmits this message to the person meditating on his image. In pursuit of the process of visualization, the meditator can move from the superficial figure to the underlying mystical level. Then, the body of the god is transformed into a lotus stalk enfolding the column within and issuing above into bud or blossom. Such a flower is visible on the tip of the god's crown of hair. Frequently, as in this example, the bud is abstracted to a cone, but there are similar bronzes that show the full-blown rosette of the lotus, which focuses on the infinitude of the cosmos (cat. 115). In this context, lotus bloom, stalk, and square symbolize, respectively, primordial nature, pure creation, and the physical world (see fig. 1).

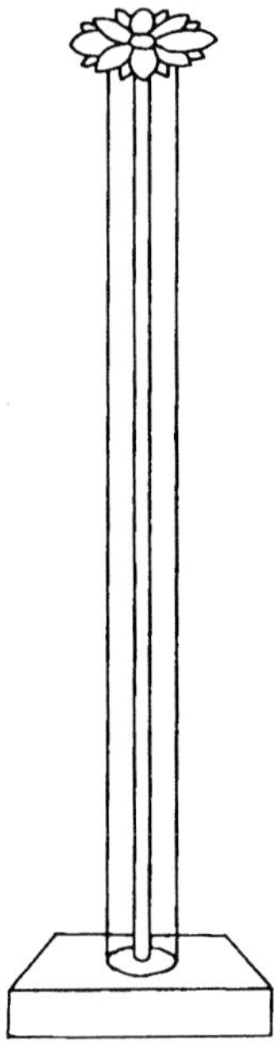

Fig. 1
Primordial nature, pure creation, phenomenal world

It is only against the background of this broad spectrum of interlocking meanings that one can begin to realize how much imaginative profundity and creative power go into the fashioning of such a cult image.

The bronze figure was found in a small chamber, sealed off by a sandstone slab, in a ruined building. It was housed within a cylindrical copper receptacle, with a number of other small bronze objects and pieces of gold leaf. Those excavating the site who discovered the treasure conjectured that they were accessories for ritual processions.[4]

W.L.

E.594

70

Viṣṇu

Vat Khnat, Angkor (Siem Reap)
Angkor period, style of Angkor Vat,
1st half of the 12th century
Sandstone
Height 101 cm, width 26 cm,
depth 25 cm
National Museum of Cambodia,
Phnom Penh, Ka 1810

From the beginnings of Khmer art through the style of Angkor Vat, it is customary to identify four-armed masculine images wearing *mukuṭa* (a cylindrical tiara in the pre-Angkor period, an octagonal, later conical, head covering in the Angkor era) as images of Viṣṇu (cats. 15, 34, among others). This identification seems certain, even if, as here, the hands and the attributes once held are missing.

This sculpture presents the rather dry modeling, with archaizing tendencies, that characterizes sculpture in the Angkor Vat style of the first half of the twelfth century.

The impersonal face is carefully treated. The eyes are underlined by an incision extended in a slight curve to the temples; numerous works in Angkor Vat style show this particularity (cat. 71). The slightly waving brows hark back to the continuous and almost sharp appearance they had in the tenth century, notably in the Bakheng style (cats. 37–40), and show the same tendency to archaism as the modeling and the proportions of the figure. In general, beards and mustaches are less systematically represented in this style than in the past; this Viṣṇu, for example, has neither.

The costume, with some difference in detail—the double anchor-shaped panel still falls to the lower edge of the *sampot*—is close to that of the Pre Rup style (cat. 46). The jewelry, on the other hand, including the belt, follows its own evolution; although it does not outdo the models in Baphuon style, it nevertheless does not look to the past. The belt, in particular, shows a new motif, constant from then on, consisting of a double row of ovals enclosed by two strings of small beads.

It is hard to explain why, after the style of the Baphuon, sculptors returned to a concept of statuary that was perhaps more grandiose—while works generally maintained the reduced dimensions that were established in the course of the eleventh century—but surely less original.

T.Z.

71

Female Divinity

Angkor (Siem Reap)
Angkor period, style of Angkor Vat,
1st half of the 12th century
Sandstone
Height 86.5 cm, width 23.5 cm, depth 20 cm
National Museum of Cambodia,
Phnom Penh, Ka 1867

The style of Angkor Vat is not generally considered one of the high points in Khmer sculpture. True, placed between the engaging sweetness of the art of the Baphuon and the moving spirituality of the Bayon style, the sculpture of the first three-quarters of the twelfth century seem somewhat lifeless and repetitive. In fact, the sculpture of the period is fixed in an archaizing current, resuming with less strength and grandeur—in a word, less genius—formulas elaborated some two centuries earlier in the style of the Bakheng. From an abundant and stereotyped production some remarkable works nevertheless emerged, such as this female divinity, whose greatest quality is perfection of technique.

Unusually well-preserved, the sculpture is exceptional in having both of its hands. The symbolic attributes they once held were detachable, as was common for those not carved in stone, and were probably made of metal.[1] Though they are most unusual in being palm upward, the position of the hands does not preclude the possibility that they may have held two lotus flowers, which might identify this divinity as a Lakṣmī.

A weak echo of the statuary from the beginning of the tenth century, the face is young and impersonal, the expression distant, the gaze somewhat fixed as befits a superhuman deity.

The skirt's wide, downturned top edge and long, decorative front panel (derived from the folded panel of the Baphuon style ending in a "fishtail" motif) are entirely characteristic of the Angkor Vat style. The pleats are incised in the manner of the period, but other ornamental details—the many fine jewels, in particular—are carved in shallow relief. While the sculptors of the Angkor Vat period—those who made the cult images, not those who decorated the monuments—may have lacked invention, they were undoubtedly skilled as craftsmen.

T.Z.

72

Viṣṇuite Votive Monument

Preah Khan (Kompong Svay)
(Kompong Thom)
Angkor period, late style of Angkor Vat, early style of the Bayon, 3d quarter of the 12th century
Sandstone
Height 105 cm, width 41 cm, depth 41 cm
Musée national des Arts asiatiques-Guimet, Paris, MG 18104

The cult of Viṣṇu, of which there is continuous evidence in Khmer art, was particularly important during the reign of Sūryavarman II, who chose Viṣṇu as his patron deity.

This Viṣṇuite monument, brought back from Preah Khan by Louis Delaporte in 1873, constitutes a sort of brief catalogue of the deity's iconography.

Given the limited information surrounding its discovery, even assuming the work was found in its original spot, it is difficult to determine which is the monument's main face, the one the worshipers were to see first. From a formal viewpoint, the multilobed pediments, the volutes of which end in many-headed *nāga*, offer no help on this score—the variations in height and width are minimal and entirely a function of the images they contain. As none of the forms represented depends directly or indirectly on those surrounding it, the question of the monument's orientation may have no real bearing either.

The lower portion of the monument is identical on all four sides, consisting of fifteen rows of seventeen miniature images, all similarly representing a standing four-armed Viṣṇu (*caturbhuja*) carrying his traditional attributes: the club, clearly visible in the lower left hand, and, presumably, the ball representing the Earth in the lower right hand, with the disk and conch in the upper right and left hands, respectively. This arrangement is the one most generally found from the pre-Angkor period onward whenever Viṣṇu is represented in his major form (cats. 31, 34).[1] The total number of miniature figures, 255 per side and 1,020 in all, undoubtedly represents a perfect sum according to the rules of a numerology, the meaning of which are lost (or not yet rediscovered). The reiteration of Viṣṇu's image is in itself a way of expressing Viṣṇu's omnipresence and supremacy in all the worlds.

Of the four aspects of Viṣṇu represented on the pediments of the upper section, the eight-armed image is perhaps the most important (a). Three of his symbolic attributes can be identified with certainty: the disk (upper right hand), the conch (upper left hand), and the club (lower left hand). While it is highly likely that the Earth was in the lower right hand, the other attributes are impossible to identify. From what we know, it seems inappropriate to compare this image with the cosmic forms of Viṣṇu, such as the famous Hari Kambujendra from Phnom Da (fig. 1, p. 142)[2] or the eight-armed Viṣṇu from Prasat Kravanh (fig. 4, p. 44), because of the widely different attributes these remarkable and rare forms of Viṣṇu possess in comparison with those of the relatively common eight-armed figures of the twelfth century, such as this one.

Proceeding clockwise, the first image is that of the classic four-armed Viṣṇu (b) bearing his traditional attributes. Next comes a representation of Viṣṇu Anantaśāyin (c), which is unfortunately damaged. The god reclines on the back of a dragon, a hybrid animal associated with the realm of water and very likely the same as the serpent Ananta/Śeṣa, on which Viṣṇu is said to rest between cosmic eras. The twelfth-century Khmer sculptors have represented the dragon as a *gajasiṃha,* or elephant-lion—note the animal's short trunk—with a serpentlike body. According to an iconographic system that still awaits explication—chronology alone does not account for the differences between the images—Viṣṇu Anantaśāyin can be represented reclining on a multiheaded *nāga*; reclining on a multiheaded *nāga,* which itself rests on a dragon (perhaps symbolizing the ocean); or reclining on the dragon alone, as here.

The goddess Śrī, whose head is missing, massages her husband's legs on the left side of the composition. Above the god is a lotus stem with three (?) flowers or three (?) buds. It would be logical, given the cosmological implications of the creation myth of Viṣṇu Anantaśāyin, for Brahmā to appear on the central flower, but the work is broken in that spot and it is not possible to confirm it. Although rare, several images of the reclining Viṣṇu in which Brahmā does not appear are known; these are considered, for want of a better explanation, as "simple" representations of the "Sleep of Viṣṇu" (Bénisti 1965, 101).

As for the reclining Viṣṇu from the votive offering in the Musée Guimet, its category cannot be assigned with any certainty.

The fourth pediment contains an image of Viṣṇu on his mount Garuḍa (d). The iconography is traditional, but the dynamism of the image is specific to the styles of Angkor Vat and the Bayon.

While erosion of the sandstone has made the details fairly hard to read, the work probably belongs to a transitional phase between the mature style of Angkor Vat and the style of the Bayon. The Garuḍa is still similar in portrayal to those of the first half of the twelfth century, those in the so-called Gallery of the Heavens and Hells at Angkor Vat, for instance, yet the dragon wearing an impressive collar with two tiers of pendants can be found again on a pediment of the temple of Preah Khan (1191). Note also that Viṣṇu's headdress consists of a cylindrical *jaṭā*, as often found in the style of the Bayon, not the conical *mukuṭa* typical of the Angkor Vat style.

T.Z.

a

b

c

d

73

Adorned Buddha Protected by the *Nāga*

A cave in the Sisophon region
(Banteay Meanchey)
Angkor period, style of Angkor Vat,
1st half of the 12th century
Sandstone
Height 88.5 cm, width 43 cm, depth 27 cm
National Museum of Cambodia,
Phnom Penh, Ka 985

The diadem worn by this beautiful adorned Buddha protected by the *nāga* has the same decorations as the diadems worn by Śiva and Umā in the Umāmaheśvara image from Banteay Srei (cat. 56)—the lower register, bordered by narrow bands of pearls, consists of a diamond-shaped ornament and the upper register of lanceolate leaves. It is slightly more flared than the diadem on a comparable piece from the Musée Guimet (cat. 74) and partly masks a somewhat shorter, conical *mukuṭa*. The present Buddha is more adorned than the Buddha in the style of the Baphuon from Peam Cheang (cat. 60), who wears only the jeweled *mukuṭa,* and less so than the one from Preah Khan (Kompong Svay) in the style of Angkor Vat (cat. 74), adorned with numerous jewels.

The *nāga's* body consists of three coils, traditional since the style of the Baphuon. Its oval, seven-headed hood allows us to date the piece to a transitional phase between the style of the Baphuon and the mature style of Angkor Vat: clearly less slender than the hood of the *nāga* from the Peam Cheang image, but also not so broad as those in the Buddha images from Preah Khan (Kompong Svay).

The face is square, the eyebrows meet at the bridge of the nose, and the eyes, most unusually, are half-closed. The slight smile is less natural and sensual than the smile of the Buddha from Peam Cheang—not to mention the smiles of pre-Angkor Buddhas or of slightly later Buddhas in the style of the Bayon. Whereas the style of the Baphuon leaned more toward naturalism, there was a clear tendency in the style of Angkor Vat toward stylization, manifested here in the way the seven-headed *nāga* is depicted. The six heads on either side look toward the central head, in accordance with custom, but the nostrils are particularly telling in this context, as is the strange double spiral on the serpents' cheeks, which is found neither in the Buddha from Peam Cheang nor in the Buddhas from Preah Khan (Kompong Svay).

The bare torso of this Buddha is comparable in its modeling to the Buddha from Thma Puok in the Phnom Penh museum, but palpably different from the Peam Cheang Buddha, whose muscles and even bones were quite accurately suggested.

Jean Boisselier has written about adorned Buddhas protected by the *nāga* in the style of Angkor Vat (the present image, it will be noted, does not have all of the typical features): "The same type of adorned Buddha exists in the Lopburi school, though its *mukuṭa* is somewhat different and seems to herald in certain aspects the *mukuṭa* that evolved in the style of the Bayon. The torso still appears entirely bare, with nothing to suggest the *uttarāsaṅga*. The *antaravāsaka* forms a roll at the waist, and while sometimes provided with a belt, it only rarely features a central, vertical flap of cloth (Buddha from the Sisophon region, National Museum of Phnom Penh...). In the school of Lopburi, however, this flap appears from the style of the Baphuon onward (Buddha on *nāga* from Vat Mahādhātu, Ayuthayā Museum).... Closed eyes are the exception (Buddha from the region of Sisophon)."

S.S.

74

Adorned Buddha Protected by the *Nāga*

Preah Khan (Kompong Svay)
(Kompong Thom)
Angkor period, style of Angkor Vat, 1st half of the 12th century
Sandstone
Height 111 cm, width 68 cm, depth 37 cm
Musée national des Arts asiatiques-Guimet, Paris, MG 18127

Although there is mention of Buddhism throughout the period of Angkor art, only a handful of Buddhist sculpture (all Buddha images) is known to date from the period extending from the beginning of the ninth century to the middle of the tenth. It is as though Buddhist production went into suspended animation during that relatively long period.

Subsequently, after a somewhat timid start in the Pre Rup period, but in gathering

numbers and with greater variety in the Khleang, images of the Buddha and of certain Bodhisattvas (cat. 59) were again made in quantity, to the point where they can be usefully studied alongside contemporary Brahmanic images. Yet it is only with the style of the Baphuon, in which the Buddha is generally shown seated in meditation (*samādhi*) on the *nāga* Mucilinda, that Buddhist statuary reassumes an important place in Khmer sculpture (cat. 60).

The iconographic type of the Buddha protected by the *nāga* refers, in the first instance, to a well-known incident in the life of Śākyamuni that took place during the sixth week after his enlightenment.[1] In Cambodia, however, this theme does not simply refer to a moment in the Buddha's life, but has a wider and more profound meaning. The *nāga* played a key role in the mythical origin of the Khmer kings, and the symbolic importance of the *nāga* in Cambodia is obviously not unconnected with Khmer devotion to this iconography.

The present sculpture, which is characteristic of the style of Angkor Vat, presents a very richly adorned Buddha, unlike the preceding work in which only the *uṣṇīṣa*-cover and the diadem were represented. The ornaments do not differ typologically from those worn by Brahmanic figures: an *uṣṇīṣa*-cover with incised decoration similar to the conical *mukuṭa* of the Hindu gods and goddesses, a diadem, ear pendants, a pectoral necklace with pendants, arm bands, bracelets, anklets, and, in certain images, a jeweled belt. Similarly, the rendering of the face and the modeling of the body, with their archaistic geometrical form, are in every way comparable to the contemporary Brahmanic statuary.

The serpent's body on which the Buddha is seated consists of the traditional three coils. The *nāga*'s heads are arranged in a pointed arch, curved somewhat inward at its base, and exhibit a sobriety quite different from the decorative, fantastic aspect of the *nāga*-balustrades (cats. 82, 83) and finials (cat. 80), whose symbolic weight was obviously very different.

The questions raised by the iconography of the adorned Buddha protected by the *nāga* are complex. The meaning of the adornment itself is not well understood. The most widely accepted explanation is that it represents a way of emphasizing once again the preeminence of the Buddha, who thus wears the insignia of royalty in the spiritual realm just as monarchs do in the temporal. Besides the fact that some Buddhas are more heavily adorned than others—might there be an attempt to create iconographic differences between the images?—it is not certain that such an explanation applies to all images of the adorned Buddha on *nāga*. In certain sculptures, bronze works especially (cat. 76),[2] the Buddha holds a mysterious object (a jewel, a lotus bud, an alms bowl?) in his hands; where the object has been tentatively identified as a medicinal flask, the particular Buddha represented has been imagined to be the "master of remedies," Bhaiṣajyaguru. This interpretation, however, is based on the epigraphy of Jayavarman VII's reign (on steles at hospitals) and is perhaps not entirely applicable to earlier periods, before that monarch's special type of Buddhism gained currency. Whatever the Buddha's identity, whether the historical Śākyamuni or another, this type of image achieved archetypal status in Cambodia; no other depiction of the Buddha is more specifically Khmer. Neither in India nor the other Indianized states of Southeast Asia did this type achieve the same popularity.

The traces of lacquer still found on the work do not appear to be original, though this cannot be put to formal proof. They would seem rather to be "embellishments," added as many as several centuries after the sculpture's completion.

T.Z.

75

Adorned Buddha

North library, third enclosure,
Angkor Vat (Siem Reap)
Angkor period, style of Angkor Vat,
2d half of the 12th century
Bronze
Height 79 cm, width 29 cm, depth 14 cm
National Museum of Cambodia,
Phnom Penh, Ga 2081

This Buddha is one of the larger works in bronze to come down to us from the twelfth century.[1] The craftsmanship is of a remarkably high quality, with both diadem and body ornament delicately modeled. The face is compelling in its beauty. The body is well-proportioned and the abdominal and thigh muscles are clearly articulated under the transparent garments. Robe and undercloth cling so closely to the body that they can only be recognized by the waistband, the panels of material projecting at the sides, and the hems arranged in small pleats. The stylized drapery does not correspond to garments found in the real world.

The damage visible on the head and arms does not detract in any essential way from the effect of this impressive bronze. Originally there would have been a conical hair-knot rising from behind the diadem (cat. 70). It was cast separately, together with the top of the skull, then attached later. Illustrations from earlier publications show the lower arms still intact.[2] They were reaching forward, both hands in the gesture of dispelling fear (*abhayamudrā*). It is not entirely clear what significance believers in the Angkor period attached to both hands performing this gesture. It later gained widespread popularity in Thailand and is still interpreted today as showing the Buddha's ability to calm the ocean.

Judging by its style, the bronze must have originated in the second half of the twelfth century. Its chronological proximity to the Angkor Vat style is clearly discernible in the fashioning of the diadem and the body ornament. But the delicate sweetness of the features, the elegant grace of the body, and the draping of the robe, with the chains and pendants hanging from the belt buckle to the feet, are characteristic of bronzes from Lopburi, northwest of Angkor.[3] The mark on the Buddha's forehead, composed of a circle and a flame symbolizing his spiritual energy, is occasionally found in bronzes of the late twelfth century.

From the earliest representations of the Buddha Śākyamuni in human form, around the dawn of our era, the rule generally held that he be depicted without any ornament whatsoever, as he had renounced the worldly values of wealth and beauty for spiritual perfection. However, in the ninth and tenth century, within the ambience of Nālandā, a center of Mahāyāna Buddhism in eastern India, figures of the Buddha were created that were lavishly adorned with crowns and jewelry. This type achieved great prominence in the eleventh and twelfth centuries in Southeast Asian cultures of Pagan (Burma) and Angkor, as may be judged from the many examples that have been preserved. Bejeweled and unadorned Buddhas now existed side by side, both of which might be regarded as Śākyamuni.[4] Paul Mus discussed this phenomenon in a seminal article published in 1928,[5] in which he shows that the doctrine of the three bodies of a Buddha—*dharmakāya, saṃbhogakāya,* and *nirmāṇakāya*—must be

analyzed to arrive at an explanation. In Cambodia, the image of the Buddha seated on the *nāga* was used for his *dharmakāya* form, which shows him as Ādibuddha (cat. 76). But his *saṃbhogakāya* form is the Buddha adorned with crown and jewels, for in this form he is regarded as a king. In him the transcendental form of Śākyamuni is made manifest. In his *nirmāṇakāya* form he took on the figure of the mendicant preacher Śākyamuni, who embodies the transformation of the pure Buddha nature into a mortal human being. In this aspect he is shown with no adornment at all.

The conception of the Buddha as a king is encountered in many passages of Khmer epigraphy. One example is provided by an inscription from Bat Chum, which states: "The Buddha resplendent has attained the imperishable royal status of enlightenment. This king of kings now disports himself in his gorgeous palace—Nirvāṇa."[6]

W.L.

76

Adorned Buddha Protected by the *Nāga*

Silver Towers (Bahn-it), Binh Dinh, Vietnam
Angkor period, style of Angkor Vat, 3d quarter of the 12th century
Bronze
Height 46 cm, width 26.5 cm, depth 14 cm
National Museum of Cambodia, Phnom Penh, Ga 3296

During the twelfth century, Buddha protected by the *nāga* became the most important cult image for Mahāyāna Buddhism in Cambodia. He is always depicted in the posture of meditation, with legs tucked under and hands folded in his lap. The *nāga* forms a throne with the three coils of its body and then rears up behind Buddha, spreading its hood with the seven heads resembling the crown of a tree. Indeed, the entire image is reminiscent of representations of the Buddha under the Tree of Enlightenment, well known from ancient India. But this was certainly not the only source of inspiration for the Khmer artists. There were statues of Hindu gods, many of which had been depicted with *nāga* hoods since about the fifth century, that may have served as models. When the motif was taken up in Cambodia, Hindu and Buddhist belief systems had blended into an indivisible conglomerate, and the *nāga* had for some centuries already enjoyed paramount importance as a protective power in temple architecture. In reality a dangerous creature, the cobra assumes a protective function by the presence of divine energy in the temple, which transforms it into an agency of good. The Enlightened One, too, by virtue of his energy and inner peace, is able to transform the serpent into a protective servant.

This is the motif behind the legend of the newly enlightened Buddha Śākyamuni, who was sheltered during a thunderstorm by Mucilinda, king of the *nāga*. For a long time, the image of the Buddha on the *nāga* was taken to be an illustration of the Mucilinda story. But the fact that such a statue was placed in the central shrine of the Bayon temple as the main cult image,[1] as well as its position in the triad (cat. 95), suggests it must have had more far-reaching significance in the context of Mahāyāna Buddhism. This assumption is supported by various inscriptions invoking the Buddha as he in whom the three bodies are manifested, namely, the law (*dharma*), serene bliss (*saṃbhoga*), and perception (i.e., transformation or *nirmāṇa*).[2] These three bodies distinguish the highest Buddha nature, which represents the primordial and undivided cosmic power in which all Buddhas and Bodhisattvas had their origin. There is speculation about whether the three coils of the serpent's body are symbolic of the three worlds in which the Buddha is triumphant, as asserted by his epithet from the inscriptions of Trailokyavijaya.[3] Possibly they also allude to the three jewels (Buddha, Dharma, Saṃgha) invoked in the first three verses of the inscription of Preah Khan.[4]

The serpent as symbol of the primordial energy of the highest god is also familiar from Hindu iconography, and in Cambodia, too, it was frequently depicted in the image of Viṣṇu reclining on the body of the *nāga* (cat. 68). Other considerations may have played a role in the pictorial realization of the highest nature of the Buddha. He is sitting on the *nāga* in the posture of meditation, while the serpent rears up, rising above his head; this action can be associated with yoga techniques for raising the sleeping energy of *kuṇḍalinī* in order to use it for spiritual enlightenment. This is the primal, vital energy with which it is possible to achieve the highest state of spiritual perfection. These thoughts, which gradually evolved in India over many centuries, were quite at home in Cambodia; there had, after all, always been a steady transmission of ideas between the two countries. Cambodian scholars traveled to India and returned with *anuttarayoga* texts.[5] Given the great significance that yoga must have had for the initiates, it would be strange if the image of the erect serpent had not been brought into association with the awakening of cosmic energy. In this connection it would also be possible to recognize a system of mystic numbers in the seven heads and three coils, for they can be linked to the set of seven centers of energy (*cakra*) in the human body and to the three highest of these in the throat and head, where enlightenment takes place.[6]

A statue of Buddha protected by the *nāga* was the main cult image of the Bayon temple, and Jayavarman VII identified himself with it. The medicine-box placed in the hands of this Buddha refers to the king's great desire to heal the sufferings of his people. He is Bhaiṣajyaguru, who possesses the effective remedy for physical and spiritual distress.

Among the many representations of its type, this bronze is one of the finest. The damage to its leg and the pedestal do not detract from its energy and serenity in any serious way.

The image has an interesting history, for it was found far removed from the center of the Khmer Empire. Along with other Mahāyāna Buddhist cult images, it was located in the so-called Silver Towers of Binh Dinh in central Vietnam. After its discovery it was first taken to the museum of the École française d'Extrême-Orient in Hanoi and finally brought to Phnom Penh.[7]

Binh Dinh is the former Vijaya of the Champa kingdom, where Mahāyāna Buddhism had been the favored religion of various kings from the tenth century onward. Between 1190 and 1203, Jayavarman VII went to war against Champa several times and installed his relatives or intimates as kings in Vijaya. From 1203 to 1220 Champa became a province of the Khmer kingdom, although subsequently the Khmer left the country. It may be assumed that the bronze was taken to Vijaya during those years.[8] All the other cult-images found with it are in the Bayon style, so the most likely date would seem to be after 1203, but the Buddha protected by the *nāga* must be earlier, because stylistically it belongs to Angkor Vat. The soft facial modeling, the rhomboid, slightly slanting eyes, and the gentle smile suggest a date at the end of this period. The medallions in the center and on the sides of the diadem also support this view.

The Buddha on the *nāga* is here depicted simultaneously as monk and king. His sumptuous jewelry is worn over the top of the smooth robe, which leaves the right shoulder bare but hangs down over the left side of the chest to end in a narrow shoulder flap. His knot of hair is built up in stages behind the broad diadem as if it were part of a king's crown. The contrast between the ornamented head of the *nāga* and the smooth body surface of the Buddha creates a strong formal tension, and the protruding cobra heads with their indented neck rings add a sense of movement.

With the creation of this bronze, the artist has succeeded in achieving something quite unusual. He has understood how to lend a delicate individual nuance to the prescribed iconography. Around each coil of the serpent's body a lotus stalk winds its way, then stretches up at the back of the hood, dividing into smaller shoots to end in a tiny crown of blossoms on the head of the topmost *nāga*. The medallions on the seven bodies resemble blossoms on a tree. The tree being referred to is made clear by the form of the hood. It has the outline of the heart-shaped leaf of the Bodhi tree (*Ficus religiosa*), under which the Buddha Śākyamuni received enlightenment. Thus, here are combined in the subtlest way symbols of tree, lotus, and snake, which have maintained their importance for more than one thousand years. The fascinating thing about such a work of art is that the traditional motifs of old survive and are enriched by additional meanings until all finally come together in an image of unique depth and focus.

W.L.

77

Finial—Adorned Buddha Protected by the *Nāga*

River near the village of Kas Prag,
Banteay Cha (Kompong Cham)
Angkor period, style of the Bayon (?),
late 12th–early 13th century
Bronze
Height 49.5 cm, width 20.5 cm,
depth 6.2 cm
National Museum of Cambodia,
Phnom Penh, Ga 5593

Most bronzes of the Angkor period, unless quite small, were cast in several parts, and the different elements were then assembled with iron rivets. The present finial,

bearing an adorned Buddha protected by the *nāga,* was constructed in this way. The Buddha is represented in a posture of meditation, with legs crossed and right hand on left, in his lap, palms upturned. The nature and symbolic import of the object resting on the Buddha's hands (a jewel?) is still in question, however it is fairly often represented, particularly in bronzes.

In keeping with the traditional iconography of these images, the *nāga* has seven heads, and his triple-coiled body serves as the Buddha's throne. The heads, larger toward the center than the outside, form an arch, somewhat horseshoe-shaped; the central head faces outward and the six lateral heads are turned toward it in three-quarters view. Each bears a finely detailed crest formed like the teeth of a comb, which relates it to the finial in the shape of a three-headed *nāga* from the Musée Guimet (cat. 80). The similarities end there, however, as the heads of the Musée Guimet *nāga* present a complex and fantastic variant with open mouth, forked tongue, and visible teeth, while the faces on this finial have rounded snouts that bring them closer to cult images in stone or bronze of the Buddha protected by Mucilinda (cats. 73, 74, 76). In type, therefore, the present *nāga* belongs between this latter sort, the simplest that can be found after the development of the style of Angkor Vat, and the *nāga*-shaped finials from chariot shafts and palanquins that often appear in the bas-reliefs of the twelfth century. These variations in representation do not seem to represent a chronological evolution; they reflect, rather, a hierarchy of use, with the most complex forms reserved for the humbler applications.

The object's function is not in any doubt. It was intended to fit on the end of a pole. The stem is decorated toward the top with a frieze of small supporting lions, suggesting that the work was made during the Bayon period, when that motif was frequently used.

It is impossible to specify whether the object belonged on the end of a chariot shaft or the carrying pole of a palanquin, or even on a piece of furniture. Given the iconography, however, it is certain that it belonged to the realm of the sacred.

It is worth noting that there is another exactly comparable piece in the National Museum of Phnom Penh (Inv. 2883, former Groslier cat. E653, former Boisselier cat. E/II 40.19). The present finial is, therefore, one of a pair.

A.C.

78

Support for a Mirror—Kneeling Female Figure

Bayon, Angkor Thom (Siem Reap)
Angkor period, style of Angkor Vat,
1st half of the 12th century
Bronze
Height 39 cm, width 24 cm, depth 15.5 cm
National Museum of Cambodia,
Phnom Penh, Ga 5476

This bronze, one of the most beautiful and famous in the National Museum of Phnom Penh, holds its own as a freestanding sculpture as much as the statues of deities.

The female figure kneels in a position often found in freestanding sculpture and bas-relief, with right knee raised and the left touching the ground. Both arms are held up symmetrically at head height, the position of the hands indicating that they once held a detachable object. The object must have been flat, judging from the shape of the headpiece. Its transversal flattening provides a notch in which the object (either a mirror or a screen, possibly inscribed) could be placed. There is also a longitudinal groove in the palm of the right hand that must have been used to secure the object.

Stylistically, this statue belongs to the art of Angkor Vat through its costume, the type of its jewelry, and the somewhat geometric aspect of its proportions, accentuated by the position of the forearms, practically raised at right angles. The modeling of the face, however, is softer than in contemporary stone sculpture, a fact that can often be noted in bronze works, which are fashioned by modeling rather than carving. The diadem (actually a crown since it is not attached at the back of the head) also differs in certain details from the diadems in stone works, with its small open flowers above the ears and simplified bands of decoration; the simplification is understandable, given the size of the piece.

A.C.

79

Perfume Censer or Oil Lamp (?)—Kneeling Female Figure

Danrun (Banteay Meanchey)
Angkor period, style of the Bayon (?),
late 12th–early 13th century
Bronze
Height 16.5 cm, width 6.5 cm, depth 6.5 cm
National Museum of Cambodia,
Phnom Penh, Ga 5467

This delicate figurine was probably used as a perfume censer or possibly oil lamp in a temple or private chapel. There are still traces of apparent burning in the four-petaled lotus flower on the figure's head.

This female figure assumes the position of a worshiper, kneeling and seated on her heels, hands joined in *añjali* to indicate prayer or reverence. No accurate typology has been established for altar furnishings of this kind, which are extremely diverse. There is a male figure in the collection of the Musée Guimet, earlier in date but extremely corroded, which may have been intended for the same purpose. That figure, however, holds the receptacle above its head in a gesture resembling that of the female mirror- or screen-bearer from the National Museum of Phnom Penh (cat. 78), and in consequence shows formal points of difference with the female figure under discussion. These small bronzes, more than any other kind, must have allowed the sculptor to give free rein to his creative imagination.

Dating pieces of this kind can be quite difficult. Though the adornments seem characteristic of the style of Angkor Vat (the necklace, ear pendants, and, to a lesser extent, the diadem), the costume seems to indicate a slightly later date, particularly its rear fastening. In any case, the object must be attributed to a date from the twelfth to the early thirteenth century.

A.C.

80

Finial for a Shaft in the Shape of a Three-Headed *Nāga*

Banteay Srei (Siem Reap)
Angkor period, style of Angkor Vat,
1st half of the 12th century
Bronze
Height 33 cm, width 12 cm, depth 6 cm
Musée national des Arts asiatiques-Guimet, Paris, MG 18889

The bas-reliefs of the Bayon are famous for the information they provide on such varied fields as mythology, history, and the daily life of men great and small—princes and monks, as well as merchants and fishermen. The bas-reliefs of Angkor Vat are just as rich, though more specifically oriented toward religion, the illustration of episodes in the Hindu epics, and the evocation of certain myths.

A few examples of the many kinds of objects depicted in these compositions have actually been unearthed by archaeologists. Such is the case, in particular, with the carved ends of palanquins and other finials that have been found in great numbers. The three-headed *nāga* from the Musée Guimet, one of the most elegant of its kind, belongs to the latter category. Pure in line and restrained in its decoration, it is one of the most beautiful bronze works from the Angkor Vat period in the twelfth century.

The technique used to make this work is equally remarkable. Like all Khmer bronzes, it was produced by the lost-wax process. Though it would take a scientific analysis to determine it for certain, it seems that some elements—the forked tongue and crest on each of the heads, for instance—were soldered on after the bodies and the heads had been cast.

From the decided curve of the bodies, the bulge of the heads behind, and the bracket design of the crests, this *nāga* can be linked to the *nāga* balustrades of the temples of Phimai and Phanom Rung in Thailand, and can be assigned a date in the first half of the twelfth century.

T.Z.

Architectural Sculpture

81

Lion

Preah Thkol, Preah Khan
(Kompong Svay) (Kompong Thom)
Angkor period, style of the Bayon,
late 12th–early 13th century
Sandstone
Height 146 cm, width 70 cm, depth 56 cm
Musée national des Arts asiatiques-
Guimet, Paris, MG 18109

The large, freestanding animal sculptures that in most Khmer temples welcome visitors—along the causeways linking different enclosures, flanking the staircases and even the doorways—are among the great achievements of ancient Cambodian sculpture. The typology of the animals varies according to their place in the temple. Lions are frequently represented, though they do not exist in Cambodia.[1] They generally appear as guardian figures on the walls flanking a stairway, and sculptors were pleased to depict them in a variety of poses: seated;[2] standing on four legs and, more rarely, walking (fig. 1);[3] or even rearing up on hind legs in a menacing attitude (fig. 2).

This lion from Preah Thkol, lofty in bearing and rigid in stance, displays an extreme stylization of volume and line. Clearly the sculptor did not draw his inspiration from a live model.

The animal, standing squarely on almost cylindrical legs, answers primarily to the requirements of a guardian: the eyes bulge and stare at the visitor; the mouth, exposing its sharp teeth and fangs in a terrifying grin, is ready to bite.

The mane is rendered by a series of small curls that give the impression of a detachable hood; the hair of the chest is similarly treated as an ornamental breastplate. Finally, the beast wears a variety of jeweled ornaments that complete the fantastic picture: a heavy necklace, a belt with pendants in the form of claws, and bracelets.

The tail, now missing, is likely to have been a separate element, probably made of metal. The details of the ornaments, particularly in the decoration of the necklace, make it possible to attribute this lion to the style of the Bayon (late twelfth to early thirteenth century).

T.Z.

Fig. 1
Walking lion. Lolei, Roluos (Siem Reap), in situ. Late ninth century

Fig. 2
Rearing lion. Preah Thkol, Preah Khan (Kompong Svay, Kompong Thom). Late twelfth to early thirteenth century. Musée national des Arts asiatiques-Guimet, Paris

82

Balustrade End with a Seven-Headed *Nāga*

Terrace in front of the Royal Palace,
Angkor Thom, Angkor (Siem Reap)
Angkor period, style of Angkor Vat,
1st half of the 12th century
Sandstone
Height 110 cm, width 75 cm, depth 34.6 cm
Musée national des Arts asiatiques-Guimet, Paris, MG 18106

The *nāga*, a many-headed cobra with an outspread hood, is closely associated with the realm of water, its natural habitat, which it has come to symbolize.[1] It appears principally in the form of a "*nāga* balustrade" along access causeways or around the terraces beside entrances to monuments.[2]

This remarkable work displays the purity of line and attention to decorative detail characteristic of the style of Angkor Vat during the first half of the twelfth century. The seven heads of this *nāga*, diminishing in size as they fan outward, form an elegant ogival arch radiating from the body of the snake. The backs are accurately depicted as covered in scales, and the necks are banded.

A symbol of water, the *nāga* also performs the role of a guardian in Khmer art. For this reason, the sculptor has given him a terrifying expression, just as with the lion in the preceding entry: the eyes bulge and the mouth is open. The sharp teeth and flattened, slightly upturned nose (quite similar to a lion's muzzle) are unusual and distinctive in a snake.

Each of the heads is crowned with a large and elegant headpiece, which, from the back, resembles a policeman's cap. The headpiece in the form of leafy scrolls is present (though in miniature) on the oldest known *nāga* sculpture. In the style of Angkor Vat, it acquires a new decorative value. Khmer ornamental art often closely interweaves vegetal and animal elements, and its architectural sculpture is no exception to this rule.

T.Z.

83

Balustrade End with *Nāga* and *Garuḍa*

Preah Thkol, Preah Khan
(Kompong Svay) (Kompong Thom)
Angkor period, style of the Bayon,
late 12th–early 13th century
Sandstone
Height 180 cm, width 185 cm, depth 85 cm
Musée national des Arts asiatiques-
Guimet, Paris, MG 18107

The *nāga* is often associated in Khmer art with its hereditary enemy, the *garuḍa*, a mythological animal that is half-man and half-raptor.[1]

During the period of the Bayon style, the ends of *nāga* balustrades underwent a profound change. The many-headed serpent of the earlier styles was replaced by a skillful arrangement comprising, from bottom, one *nāga*, generally three-headed, straddled by a *garuḍa* controlling a second *nāga* with six or, toward the end of the period, eight heads. This composition was prefigured toward the end of the Angkor Vat period, when a small *garuḍa* was sometimes represented lost in the vegetal scrolls of the central *nāga*'s crest. This detail is characteristic, for instance, of certain *nāga* from the temple of Banteay Samre.

The evolution of this motif within the style of the Bayon has been well described by Philippe Stern (Stern 1965, 35–37). The present work can therefore be attributed to the style's first period, when a second *garuḍa* appears behind the principal motif. The *nāga*'s body rests on a band decorated with lotus petals, supported by blocks carved with lion columns. The blocks, which existed at the time of Angkor Vat, were not then ornamented with animal figures but with a simple vegetal decoration.

This work, rich in iconography and remarkably executed, lacks the formal elegance of the preceding work.

T.Z.

84

Elephant

Preah Damrei, Preah Khan
(Kompong Svay) (Kompong Thom)
Angkor period, style of the Bayon,
late 12th–early 13th century
Sandstone
Height 132 cm, width 137 cm, depth 54 cm
Musée national des Arts asiatiques-
Guimet, Paris, MG 18108

The elephant never enjoyed the popularity in Khmer art of the lion and the *nāga*. Appearing first toward the end of the ninth century on the tiers of the pyramid at Bakong (881), elephants are essentially found in the temple-mountains of the tenth century, only reappearing sporadically thereafter.[1]

This work was discovered in 1873 by Louis Delaporte at the top of the pyramid of Preah Damrei, a monument adjoining Preah Khan at Kompong Svay and erected during the first phase of the style of the Bayon. The sculpture, in fact, gave its name to the monument on which it was found, since the Cambodian words *braḥ taṃrī* (*preah damrei*) mean "sacred elephant." Despite this, it originally belonged elsewhere. Along with other sculpture of this type, it was designed to stand at the corner of one of the tiers of the pyramid, perhaps symbolically guaranteeing its stability.

The animal, wearing a band around its forehead as well as a necklace and bracelets, holds a bundle of aquatic plants in its trunk. Like the *nāga*, the elephant is associated with the realm of water. On its back is a saddle blanket, secured by a realistic set of ropes and hung with bells.

From the decoration on the jewels, it is possible to attribute the work to the style of the Bayon: the open flower motif of the bracelets, for instance, appeared at that time; in the earlier style of Angkor Vat, the bracelets were decorated with a series of juxtaposed ropelike petals.

Curiously, the sculpture is unfinished at the back. We propose the hypothesis that the sandstone block from which the sculpture was carved was set in place while the figure was still only roughed out. The finishing was to have been performed at that time, but because of insufficient space between the block and the retaining wall of the next tier of the pyramid, the work remained unfinished.

T.Z.

85

Dvārapāla

Preah Thkol, Preah Khan
(Kompong Svay) (Kompong Thom)
Angkor period, style of the Bayon,
late 12th–early 13th century
Sandstone
Height 268 cm, width 95 cm, depth 59 cm
Musée national des Arts asiatiques-
Guimet, Paris, MG 24614

One of the important works brought back to France by Louis Delaporte following his 1873 mission to Cambodia, the *dvārapāla* from Preah Thkol belongs in the realm of architectural sculpture (see also cats. 81–84). The sculpture in this category, placed around the outside of a monument to serve both as greeters and defenders, functioned within a very different symbolic register from the divinities worshiped inside the sanctuaries. The *dvārapāla*, "guardians of the gate," were specifically intended to protect the principal entries. The worshiper, therefore, typically encountered them after having traveled the length of the access causeways lined with *nāga* balustrades and ascended the entrance stairs flanked with lions.

The earliest known *dvārapāla* are situated on either side of the entrance gate into Prasat Toc 144 (Kompong Chhnang), a small brick temple dating to the seventh century. Carved in bas-relief, they are the first of a long series of guardians produced between the seventh and thirteenth centuries. The finest examples of the genre, dating from the last quarter of the ninth century, are in the temples of Preah Ko (879) and Lolei (893) (fig. 10, p. 91).

According to Jean Boisselier, freestanding *dvārapāla* first appeared in the tenth century, in the style of the Pre Rup (Boisselier 1966, 296). Only sporadically encountered thereafter, they were to find particular favor under the reign of Jayavarman VII.

Iconographically, *dvārapāla* were designed in pairs and were generally differentiated by their ornaments and weapons. The guardian on the proper right of the door generally wore a genial expression and held a trident (fig. 1); the one on the left had a fierce expression and was armed with a club (fig. 2). The *dvārapāla* from Preah Thkol belongs to the second category. Only the handle and lower portion of his club have survived. The snakes he wears for armbands and especially his disk-shaped ear pendants are emblematic of terrifying creatures, as are his bulging eyes and knitted brow. But the conical *mukuṭa*, or chignon-cover, decorated as it is with rows of lotus petals, is ordinarily reserved for figures of a peaceful nature.

This work presents both the qualities and the faults that are characteristic of the style of the Bayon. The modeling of the face is sensitive and expressive, showing a tendency toward realism, but the body is overly heavy and the legs particularly massive. The short garment with its incised folds is summarily treated, as was often the case at that time, while the ornaments are executed with great care. Around the base of the guardian's neck one can see an element that first appeared under Jayavarman VII, a necklace decorated with open flowers.

T.Z.

Fig. 1
Fierce *dvārapāla*. Banteay Kdei, Angkor. Late twelfth to early thirteenth century

Fig. 2
Benign *dvārapāla*. Preah Khan, Angkor. Approximately 1191

86

Nāga

Causeway on the dike in front of *gopura* IV east, Preah Khan, Angkor (Siem Reap)
Angkor period, style of the Bayon, late 12th–early 13th century
Sandstone
Height 218 cm, width 181 cm, depth 75 cm
Set of five blocks
Musée national des Arts asiatiques-Guimet, Paris, MG 24616

Three great architectural complexes from the Bayon period possess the famous and impressive array of large, three-dimensional sculpture popularly known as the "Giants' Causeway."[1] These causeways, leading to the gate of the outer enclosure of these complexes and crossing their moats, represent the final evolution of the "*nāga* balustrade" or parapet along the processional path to the monuments.

The symbolism of these astonishing ensembles is complex and can be interpreted from several points of view.

Paul Mus[2] has shown that the *nāga* is equivalent to the rainbow in Khmer mythology, where it represents, as in many other mythologies, the bridge between the world of men and the world of the gods. The *nāga* balustrades are then readily interpreted as symbolizing a rainbow, the devotee's passage from the secular to the divine realm.

In the case of the Giants' Causeways, the initial symbolism is overlaid by an allusion to the myth of the Churning of the Sea of Milk. In this myth, which appears in the *Bhāgavatapurāṇa,* among other texts, the gods (*deva*) and demons (*asura*) undertake to produce the elixir of immortality (*amṛta*) by churning the Sea of Milk, using Mount Mandara as a paddle and the snake Vāsuki to spin it. Lining the causeways are thus two sets of fifty-four giants, those on one side being demoniac in appearance, the *asura*, and those on the other being benevolent, the *deva*, holding the body of a gigantic seven-headed *nāga*, Vāsuki.

According to Jean Boisselier, it is also possible to analyze the motif from a more general perspective, one that is perhaps more consonant with the Mahāyāna Buddhism of Jayavarman VII, though it does not at all exclude the earlier interpretations. In this view, the giants represent the different categories of lesser gods responsible for defending the capital of Jayavarman VII, king of kings on earth, the equivalent to the city of Indra, king of the gods in heaven.[3]

The *nāga* of the Giants' Causeways are definitely in the style of the Bayon, from the start of its second period (Stern 1965, 29–30), yet they are never shown straddled by a *garuḍa*; they return to a typology that appeared during the time of the Angkor Vat style.

Gilberte de Coral-Rémusat divides the *nāga* of the Angkor Vat style into two broad groups. The first, which is further subdivided into three types, is characterized by a fan of heads that form a pointed arch and are visible only from the front (cat. 82). The differences between the three subtypes mainly concern the contour of the ogival halo, whether more or less indented, and the decorations that embellish it (Coral-Rémusat 1951, 99–100). The second group is radically different in that the heads of the *nāga* can be seen symmetrically from both front and back. Such *nāga* appear, for instance, on the raised causeway linking the third gallery enclosure to the western entrance pavilions, or on *gopura* IV west, at Angkor Vat. Establishing a relative chronology for these two groups is difficult, because both, at times, occur within the same monument without apparent differences in treatment. It may well be that the variety of *nāga* found at Angkor Vat reflects concerns of a hierarchical order rather than any chronological development.

At any rate, the *nāga* of the Giants' Causeways conform to the complex and innovative design characteristic of the second group in the style of Angkor Vat, in which the many heads are figured both from the front and rear.

On a more general level, these mythological animals perpetuate a form that first appeared at the end of the eleventh century: the mouths are open and lined with small, sharp teeth, the eyes bulbous under wrinkled brows, the noses flattened and slightly uptilted. The heavy pectoral ornament, however, is a new element.

At the gateways to Angkor Thom, the noses of the *nāga* were transformed into little trunks, whereas at Preah Khan, where the *nāga* motif seems to have originated, this detail had not yet appeared.

T.Z.

87

Bust of a "Giant"

Causeway elevated on dike in front of *gopura* IV east, Preah Khan, Angkor (Siem Reap)
Angkor period, style of the Bayon, late 12th–early 13th century
Sandstone
Height 129 cm, width 118 cm, depth 50 cm
Set of two blocks
Musée national des Arts asiatiques-Guimet, Paris, MG 18103 (head) and MG 24615 (torso)

This bust of a giant belongs to one of the fifty-two pseudo-*deva* (not counting the many-headed figures at the head and tail of the procession) lining the south side of the causeway, elevated on a dike, leading to *gopura* IV, east of Preah Khan at Angkor. Like the other statues in the series, this colossus stood on braced legs and helped support the body of the *nāga*.

The giant's expression is relaxed and smiling, though this is not the case with all the figures in the series. Perhaps the sculptors intended to differentiate between one *deva* and another, which would explain why this giant's third eye, represented vertically in the middle of his forehead, is not common to all.

On his head the *deva* wears a low diadem and a conical chignon-cover decorated with rows of lotus petals, a common Bayon-style ornament. The jeweled bands forming a cross on his torso and the necklace encircling the base of his neck first appeared in three-dimensional sculpture in that period. The other ornaments are less characteristic.

Although the work is considerably eroded, its modeling heralds the trend toward realism that particularly distinguishes the art of Jayavarman VII's reign and marks its break with the past.

T.Z.

Late Twelfth to Early Thirteenth Century

Opposite, Fig. 1
Head of the Buddha. Pedestal of the Buddha of Tep Pranam. Bayon style, late twelfth to early thirteenth century. Sandstone. Height 41 cm. National Museum of Cambodia, Phnom Penh

The Bayon Style

As far as is known at present, the last inscription to mention Sūryavarman II dates from 1145, but it is likely that his reign continued for several years beyond that.[1] Of the intervening years before the rule of Jayavarman VII/ Mahāparamasaugatapada (1181–1218?), the history is confusing. A king named Yaśovarman (the second with this name since the founder of Yaśodharapura, at the beginning of the tenth century) ascended the throne at an unknown date, probably after 1150, and ruled until 1165. He was then "stripped of his kingship" by one of his "servants"—a term to be understood in the broadest sense—who ruled as Tribhuvanādityavarman until 1177. This date is fateful above all others in Angkor history; in that year the "usurper" Tribhuvanāditya was, in turn, overthrown by the Cham monarch Jaya Indravarman, whose armies sacked the Khmer capital.

The architecture and statuary of this turbulent period seems to have been unmarked by profound changes. The elements that characterized the art of Sūryavarman II's reign persisted, particularly in the realm of architectural ornament, as can be seen in the ruins of parts of the provincial temple of Preah Khan at Kompong Svay.[2]

With the work of liberation undertaken by Jayavarman VII after the fall of Angkor, the Khmer Empire reached its climax. George Cœdès, the great master of epigraphic studies, defined the importance of this monarch: "one of the greatest sovereigns of Cambodia, he who enlarged his country to its furthest limits, incorporated for a time the kingdom of Champa, and covered his capital and states with a prodigious collection of monuments."[3] A follower of the Mahāyāna sect of Buddhism, Jayavarman VII made it the state religion, though he refrained from eliminating all that had gone before.

Innovative in many respects, the architecture of the new era—the towers with faces and the giants' causeways among them—is basically a continuation of the earlier tradition, though a certain lack of care is appreciable. Many of the decorative reliefs show signs of hasty execution, the plan of the monuments is often confused,[4] and even the construction methods, while on the whole close to those used earlier, show a decline. This loss in quality is connected with the inordinate scale of an architectural program that perhaps lacked the means of fulfillment.

The statuary, above all, changed in response to the new religious concerns that influenced not only the iconography, naturally enough, but also, in a more unexpected way, the aesthetics. The cult images were now expected to embody and transmit the spiritual essence of the very complex form of Buddhism prevalent in Angkor Cambodia in the late twelfth and early thirteenth centuries, a Buddhism of which Jayavarman VII presented himself the virtuous champion.

Reflecting a more earthly and human ideal of beauty than the grandiose Brahmanic art of the previous centuries, the style of the Bayon (late twelfth to early thirteenth century) corresponds in time to the reign of the powerful monarch. The statuary again became lifelike, and, without being able to form a hypothesis on this subject, one may well ask at what school the sculptors learned their art. Nothing seems to have prepared the way for their subtle technique, blending as it does a tempered realism—the musculature is now discreetly but accurately suggested (cat. 98)—with an intense expressiveness—the faces show spiritual focus, serenity of soul, and, sometimes, physical suffering (cats. 89, 90, 92). The realism and expressiveness of the period

1. Cœdès 1964, 297.
2. For more on this complex monument, see the bibliography. It is probably in the region of Preah Khan at Kompong Svay (present province of Kompong Thom)—this monument must have belonged to an important fief—that the future Jayavarman VII waited for the opportune moment to "seize the kingship."
3. Cœdès 1947, 177.
4. The confusion went so far that plans for the temples and even certain of the structures were modified while under construction. See Stern 1965.

of Bayon is never intended to externalize feelings, however, even the most guarded or deeply religious. The genius of Jayavarman VII's artists, to whom we owe the famous "Angkor smile" (fig. 1), is to have been able to translate in plastic terms, beyond the passionless quietude of the Buddhist faith, the mystery of salvation at the heart of a religion governed by principles, apparently contradictory, about the impermanence of all things and compassion for all beings.

The profound upheavals set in motion by the reign of Jayavarman VII were to last, however, only a short time. Far from heralding a new dawn for Khmer art and thought, the trends of that period signaled both the high point and the twilight of a certain vision of the kingship. From the reign of the second king after Jayavarman VII, Jayavarman VIII/Parameśvarapada (1243–1295), a Śivaite reaction occurred. In the iconoclastic crisis that ensued, innumerable Buddha images were destroyed, originally carved for the monuments of the ruler who held that "the suffering of the people is the suffering of the king." The Brahmanic cults, which had certainly not disappeared under Jayavarman VII, though they had evidently taken second place, were reinstated, while the Khmer Empire grew progressively weaker. Its rulers had to face numerous attacks on their borders, particularly from the Thai, until 1431, the traditional date given for the abandonment of Angkor as a capital.

T.Z.

88

Lower Register of a Pediment

Bayon, Angkor Thom (Siem Reap)
Angkor period, style of the Bayon,
late 12th–early 13th century
Sandstone
Height 60 cm, width 276 cm, depth 33 cm
Musée national des Arts asiatiques-Guimet, Paris, MG 18142

This relief formed the lower element of a pediment and represents nine *apsaras*, or celestial dancers. The central dancer wears a higher crown than her eight companions and has a very long garland around her neck, but is otherwise the same as the others who flank her. Each dancer stands on one foot, on the toes, and raises the knee that faces the center, so the scene is symmetrical. The brief skirt, with its elaborate low-slung belt with rich pendants and a long rear sash, resembles the costume in a series of similar friezes in the Hall of Dancers at Preah Khan.

The relief is very deep and the handling of the vulnerable slender portions has been well controlled. The dynamism and rhythm of the composition is aesthetically pleasing, but perhaps the most interesting aspect of the frieze is that the gestures (hands bent backwards and fingers curving almost parallel with the forearm) and the postures (pronounced turnout and flexed foot) are identical with the technique and choreography of classical Khmer dance today. Such persistence of style is one of the strongest arguments for the continuity of Khmer culture even after the apogee of the empire had long passed.

H.J.

89

Head of Jayavarman VII

Preah Khan (Kompong Svay)
(Kompong Thom)
Angkor period, style of the Bayon,
late 12th–early 13th century
Sandstone
Height 41.5 cm, width 29 cm, depth 31 cm
National Museum of Cambodia,
Phnom Penh, Ka 989

When his royal majesty King Jayavarman VII, king of kings (*rājādhirāja*) and universal monarch (*cakravartin*), chose to have himself represented it was in the humble attitude of a worshiper. All the works produced during his reign bear the stamp of his compassion, and he was hailed as "he who has gone where the great followers of the supreme Buddha reside," as indicated by his posthumous name, Mahāparamasaugatapada. Yet his was also the power that had subdued many kingdoms and he had extended his empire north to the borders of China and reached the seas to the south and the oceans to the west.

Just as Avalokiteśvara radiates compassion to the four points of the compass, Jayavarman VII took the liberty of multiplying his own image throughout the four corners of his realm. Two nearly complete statues have survived showing the king seated in an attitude of humility. One was discovered at Krol Romeas near Angkor Thom (fig. 1), the other in the temple of Phimai in present-day Thailand. The king's head is slightly lowered and the eyes are closed in deep meditation. It is in this humility and physical deprivation that his greatness is expressed.

This head, discovered at Preah Khan, Kompong Svay (Kompong Thom), is alive with contradictions: its meditative sweetness contrasts with a powerful physique and an expression that betrays an iron will.

Was it weariness from the wars and massacres needed to establish a large empire and maintain its independence, civil peace, and political stability that led Jayavarman VII to take refuge in Buddhism? Did he seek the Triple Jewel—the Buddha, the law, and the community of monks—so that peace might come to all beings? Was it from remorse or a sudden realization that "the king suffered from the ills of his subjects more than from his own; for it is the suffering of the people that causes the suffering of kings and not their own"? (hospital edict, Say-fong stele). For whatever reason, the tone of the empire changed, and different themes and iconography appeared. Rather than the customary glorification, the monarch was now cloaked in humility, even humanity, with a view to re-establishing his ties with the people. Some sixty centuries earlier another *rājādhirāja*, another *cakravartin*, Emperor Aśoka, having subjugated the Kaliṅga, also took refuge in Buddhist law, for the same political reasons.

Without doubt, this head from Preah Khan is one of the great masterpieces in the National Museum of Phnom Penh. The sculptor has ably and simply rendered the fullness of the face and the softness of its volumes and contours. The mustache, modest and slightly upturned, suggests youth. The king's hair, indicated by fine, regular incisions, is swept up in back to form a simple knot, which is not to be confused with the Buddha's *uṣṇīṣa*. The forms are simple, in keeping with the simplicity of the royal personage, who appears without any of the insignia or decorations of his rank. All the king's power and wealth are expressed in the eyes, which are closed to the impermanence of earthly things. Jayavarman radiates internal power and riches. The peacefulness so sweetly expressed in his meditative smile is the very treasure the people seek.

The back of the king's sacred head, from the nape of his neck to his knot of hair, is flat; in most mortals, this area is curved. This trait adds to the sense of physical power in the work. The nose is short, the dilated nostrils indicating an inner tension. The play of contrasts is striking. While the king appears slightly older in the full-figure image from the National Museum (note that the mustache is missing), the principles governing his representation are the same (fig. 1).

This sculpture was discovered at the beginning of 1958 by M. Lucien, at a time when Professor Jean Filliozat was in residence in Cambodia as director of the École française d'Extrême-Orient. It was first taken to the Depot for the Conservation of Angkor, after which Madeleine Giteau arranged for its entry into the National Museum of Phnom Penh.

S.S.

**Fig. 1
Jayavarman VII. Angkor. The head was found within the enclosure of Angkor Thom, near the Gate of the Dead. The body was found near the north gate of Angkor Thom, outside the enclosure (Krol Romeas). Late twelfth to early thirteenth century. Sandstone. Height 135 cm. National Museum of Cambodia, Phnom Penh**

90

Head of Jayavarman VII

Provenance unknown
Angkor period, style of the Bayon, late 12th–early 13th century
Sandstone
Height 42 cm, width 25 cm, depth 31 cm
Musée national des Arts asiatiques-Guimet, Paris, P 430 (on deposit from the Musée Maritime de Marseilles)

Occasionally in Khmer art, the Bayon style produces rare works that can be considered portraits. Thus, the physiognomy of certain members of the royal family and, above all, that of the king himself, are known to us, at least so it is thought. The inscriptions of the reign often allude to the consecration of images "in the likeness of" a particular person, living or dead. One seeks in vain in the faces of this period the diversity one would have the right to expect from such a perspective. However, the art of Jayavarman VII is realistic, without doubt, but in a tempered way. The modeling is more lively and sensitive than in the past, but the sculptors hardly went beyond that, except when it specifically concerned the king and possibly one of his wives (cat. 92). Several portraits of Jayavarman VII are known.[1] The complete works present the monarch in an attitude of respect, sitting with legs crossed, torso leaning forward. Such images certainly belong in a symbolic context different from that of cult images, Buddha or others. Perhaps it was a concern for the pious Jayavarman VII to fix in stone for eternity the exact image of his humble devotion before the Buddha. The question needs to be researched further, in any case.

This head, which is possibly from Angkor (Cœdès 1960, 191) belongs to the series of presumed portraits of Jayavarman VII. The king is here shown looking visibly older than in other works of the same nature (cat. 89). The sculptor clearly never intended to depict the marks left by the passing years on the king's face. The process would, in fact, have been unthinkable in the context of Khmer art, even during the period of the Bayon when a certain degree of realism was in order. The man's maturity is betrayed by certain subtle details of the modeling, which transform his physiognomy. The mouth is imperceptibly turned down at the corners, the lower half of the face is slightly heavy, and the expression, which is softer and more relaxed than in other royal portraits, indicates a model who has grown less willful but more serene. The slight differences between the various portraits of Jayavarman VII may indicate that they were executed at different periods in the king's life.

The sandstone from which the portrait is carved is quite dark and retains a handsome gloss. A few traces of gilding, possibly original, can still be seen on the face.

T.Z.

91

Head of the Buddha

Angkor (Siem Reap)
Angkor period, style of the Bayon, late 12th–early 13th century
Sandstone
Height 39 cm, width 27 cm, depth 27 cm
Musée national des Arts asiatiques-Guimet, Paris, MG 17482

This head, obviously recarved, represents the Buddha in what is incontestably the style and iconography of the reign of Jayavarman VII: flat curls of hair bordered by a binding strip and a cranial protuberance covered by a conical *mukuṭa* decorated with rows of lotus petals.

The masklike face, with its realistic and strongly individualized features, clearly belongs to the highly distinctive style of the Bayon. The closed eyes, for instance, are characteristic of all the Buddhist images from this period.

The flattened nose, the broad and willful jaw, the full, almost pudgy cheek permit a comparison between this face and the pseudo-portraits of Jayavarman VII himself. A head from the National Museum in Phnom Penh (fig. 1, p. 296), also a depiction of the Buddha and also recarved or carved in two phases, proceeds with somewhat greater refinement from the same principles of representation.

It is tempting to follow George Cœdès in identifying these images as part of a group of sculpture referred to in an inscription from Preah Khan.[1] One stanza mentions twenty-three[2] and another twenty-five[3] Jayabuddhamahānātha erected by the king in shrines throughout his realm (respectively, stanzas CXV-CXXI of the Preah Khan stele at Angkor, end of face C and beginning of face D; and stanza CLIX of the same stele, face D). Though tentative, the identification is supported by the custom, first noted in the style of the Bayon, of giving certain images the features of a particular person, either living or dead (cat. 92), in conjunction with an emerging art of realistic portraiture (cats. 89, 90).

T.Z.

92

Tārā (?), Kneeling

Preah Khan, Angkor (Siem Reap)
Angkor period, style of the Bayon,
late 12th–early 13th century
Sandstone
Height 130 cm, width 51 cm, depth 52 cm
Musée national des Arts asiatiques-Guimet, Paris, MG 18043

Just as there is sculpture in which the barely idealized features of Jayavarman VII are recognizable (cats. 89, 90, and possibly 91), there are also at least four images (which should probably include certain heads without bodies) that seem to have been carved in the likeness of Jayarājadevī, his first and greatly loved wife.[1]

The "biography" of the princess, her innumerable good deeds, and her generosity, are the subject of the Phimeanakas stele (K. 485),[2] erected by her erudite and pious older sister Indradevī, who herself became Jayavarman's queen after Jayarājadevī's death, "whose good deeds... have earned her glory in all the worlds."[3]

The face, meditative and almost severe in its geometric purity, expresses the gentle serenity of an unruffled faith in the Buddha and his law. From the slender body, some have deduced that the queen, who died young, had a lung ailment or congenital malformation. This may be slightly farfetched, as this unusual body shape can be found in most of the female images dating from the end of the twelfth to the beginning of the thirteenth century, even those whose faces least resemble the figure thought to represent the queen.

In addition to its characteristic facial expression, the work accords fully with the art of Jayavarman VII's reign, as in its subtle modeling, both delicate and realistic, its stylized treatment of the locks of hair, its chignon-cover with its rows of lotus-petal ornaments, its dress with florets and wide zig-zag panels, and a jeweled belt with pendants.

This image and its "sisters" have long posed questions of iconography that still await a definitive answer. There are two conflicting hypotheses. The first suggests that the figure's hands, which reach forward, might once have held a book. The image could then be identified as Prajñāpāramitā, the "perfection of wisdom" and mother of all the Buddhas, a very high-ranking figure in the pantheon of Mahāyāna Buddhism. In fact, when Jayavarman VII built a temple for the spiritual benefit of his mother, Ta Prohm (1186), it was dedicated to Prajñāpāramitā. The second hypothesis suggests that the hands were joined at chest height in an attitude of prayer or perhaps holding a lotus, in which case the image could be a representation of Tārā, the companion of the Bodhisattva Avalokiteśvara. In both cases the figure of the Amitābha Jina on the front of the chignon-cover is consistent with the proposed identification, but the kneeling posture of the image, which corresponds more closely to the attitude of a worshiper, is not consistent with the picture of Tārā or Prajñāpāramitā in Khmer iconography. It is thus impossible in the absence of the arms and a knowledge of the attribute or attributes they once held to determine the identity of this figure.

The work is unfinished, as is often the case in Khmer art. The circular base has only been roughed out, and it seems worth noting that the bases of the other complete statues of this type have been left in a similar state, as have the full-body portraits of Jayavarman VII.

T.Z.

93

Prajñāpāramitā (?) as a Child

Bush north of Angkor Thom (Siem Reap)
Angkor period, style of the Bayon,
late 12th–early 13th century
Sandstone
Height 94.5 cm, width 32.5 cm, depth 16 cm
National Museum of Cambodia,
Phnom Penh, Ka 1691

The Bayon period covers the years of Jayavarman VII's reign, during which the new capital, Angkor Thom, was centered around the temple of the Bayon. Iconography also evolved at that time, tied to the new state religion of Mahāyāna Buddhism, but it was a complex form of this religion that established a synthesis of sorts between Brahmanism and Buddhism. Within this context, a new aesthetic also appeared. Compassion was made the central element of the king's philosophy, a fact that was carved in stone: "The people's suffering causes the king to suffer, and not his own." Having warred incessantly to restore the Khmer monarchy, the sovereign sought a return not only to civil peace but to the emotional and spiritual peace that only Buddhism could provide. Along with compassion, all the Buddhist virtues were extolled, intelligence or *prajñāpāramitā* chief among them. In its highest and largest sense, this term was understood to mean consciousness, understanding, perception, and wisdom. As these concepts were incarnated by royal personages, George Cœdès was led to identify certain sculpture as portraits of Jayavarman VII (cats. 89, 90) and one of his wives (cat. 92), erected throughout the empire. This statue of a child with babyish features presumably issued from the same kind of preoccupation. Might it be a member of the royal family? The treatment of the face with its smile and closed eyes suggests a link with the famous image of Jayavarman VII from the National Museum of Phnom Penh (fig. 1, p. 300).

The child's garment consists of a skirt, with a large triangular fold in front, decorated with floral ornaments; it is held in place at the waist by a wide jeweled belt. Jean Boisselier, who refers to this long *sampot* as a sarong, describes it in these terms: "The sarong is no longer made of pleated material, but is decorated with florets familiar from the bas-reliefs of Angkor Vat. The downturned edge has practically disappeared, the borders are defined by a narrow braid, and the front flap is folded over on itself and extends to a triangular point, remarkably like a shark's fin. The *sarong* is held by a wide jeweled belt with simply incised pendants. . . " (Boisselier 1966, 258). Philippe Stern defines "three distinct types (of costume) corresponding to the three periods of the style." The first and earliest is directly derived from the style of Angkor Vat (oldest parts of Ta Prohm at Angkor) and can be seen worn by *devatā* in the bas-reliefs; the second and third, which make general use of the "shark-fin" front flap, are derived from elsewhere. The costume worn by this child belongs to the third category, and the sculpture would seem to date from the style of the Bayon at its fullest flowering.

S.S.

94

Buddha Protected by *Nāga*

Preah Khan (Kompong Svay)
(Kompong Thom)
Angkor period, style of the Bayon,
late 12th–early 13th century
Sandstone
Height 111 cm, width 68 cm, depth 37 cm
Musée national des Arts asiatiques-Guimet, Paris, MG 18126

This very fragmentary sculpture—the Buddha's legs as well as the *nāga*'s lower body and five upper heads are missing—is representative of the idealized and expressive art of the reign of Jayavarman VII. As with many images of Buddha from the eleventh to the early thirteenth century, the deity is shown seated in meditation on the *nāga* Mucilinda (cats. 73, 75). The serpent's seven heads were once arrayed in a sort of halo around the serene and meditative face of the Buddha.

The hair, edged on the forehead with a thin band, is coiled in large flat curls to the right and left, a style specific to the art of Jayavarman VII. The *uṣṇīsa*-cover consists of rows of lotus petals, as is customary in the Bayon period. Unlike most images in the style of Angkor Vat (cat. 74), the Buddha is virtually unadorned—aside from the jeweled belt with large pendants—in keeping with his ethic of renunciation.

Khmer sculptors have always shown consummate mastery at representing *samādhi* (cat. 60), and this work renders in a remarkable way the body's relaxation under the discipline of meditation: the upper body is straight, the arms perfectly relaxed, the hands one atop the other in the lap as though forgotten. This particular state of the body is complemented, in the style of the Bayon, by a peaceful and smiling expression, a sense of absolute detachment, total introspection, and perfect stillness. Generally, the eyes are half-closed or even shut.

This work, discovered by Louis Delaporte at Preah Khan, Kompong Svay in 1873, is nevertheless unusual in its treatment of the eyes, which are undeniably open. In addition, their outline and the iris have been indicated by incised lines, drawn with an uncertain hand. This detail, to which can be added the similarly clumsy incisions outlining the lips, seems to indicate that the sculpture was reworked after its consecration or was finished only after the reign of Jayavarman VII, according to the stylistic criteria proper to post-Bayon Buddhist art.

T.Z.

95

Buddhistic Triad

Prei Monti, Roluos (Siem Reap)
Angkor period, style of the Bayon, late 12th–early 13th century
Bronze
Height 49.5 cm, width 41.5 cm, depth 16 cm
National Museum of Cambodia, Phnom Penh, Ga 2424; Ga 5470 (Prajñāpāramitā)

With the increasing significance of Mahāyāna Buddhism in the course of the twelfth century, the triad of Buddha, Lokeśvara, and Prajñāpāramitā occupies an increasingly central position in artistic activity until, in the reign of Jayavarman VII, it becomes one of the most important icons of all.

This bronze is among the largest and finest works of its kind. It seems to have only been discovered at the beginning of the 1960s, as B. P. Groslier refers to it as a recent find.[1] The three figures are mounted on a common plinth, but were cast separately. Each stands on its own base plate, which is fixed to the pedestal with a pin. Beneath the central figure on the upper surface of the pedestal, a written character is inscribed. It can be interpreted as the Sanskrit word *urū*, meaning great or excellent, and is, thus, obviously a reference to the Buddha.[2]

As befits his significance, the Buddha in the center is taller than his companions. His throne is formed by the three coils of a *nāga*, which then rises behind his back, spreading wide its hood with the seven heads to create a mandorla-like backdrop. This *nāga* throne identifies the figure as Ādibuddha, who was enlightened before the beginning of time and is the personification of the most fundamental principle of Buddhism. The lotus in full bloom, which forms the cushion on which he sits, symbolizes his perfection. This highest essence of the Buddha combines in his person two components: infinite compassion for all beings in the world and complete wisdom. Both are personified here in the figures of Lokeśvara (compassion) and Prajñāpāramitā (wisdom). Thus, the triad does not present three different persons but a single being in his most important aspects. The little medicine-box in his hands shows that this Buddha is represented in his quality as Bhaiṣajyaguru, the Buddha of healing, who can cure the ills of the world. He not only has the power to heal physical illnesses, but can also alleviate spiritual anguish.

Lokeśvara, on his right, stands erect on a square base. He can be identified by the small Buddha figure in his crown of hair and by the attributes in his hands. The two lower ones reveal him to be a pure, eternal being. The lotus flower in his right hand signifies his liberation from the cycle of rebirth; the flask in his left contains the nectar of immortality. The raised hands indicate to the faithful the path to salvation. The string of beads on the right is a rosary. By shifting the beads, the prayers as they are spoken are mechanically counted. In this way the person praying can concentrate entirely on the sacred syllables or words and thus accumulate good *karma*. The raised left hand is holding a palm-leaf manuscript, which contains the written version of a sacred text. By studying such texts, a believer can accumulate the knowledge that will eventually lead to enlightenment.

The eight-petaled lotus flower on Lokeśvara's crown of hair, his erect posture, and the square base form a symbolic unity that reveals his cosmic nature to the initiate (see cat. 69).

The somewhat smaller and elegant figure of Prajñāpāramitā on the left of the Buddha has only two arms. The lotus flower that Lokeśvara holds in his right hand, she holds in her left, while the book is in her right hand. Clearly, symmetry was a more important consideration for the artist than iconographical accuracy. In Prajñāpāramitā's case the attributes bear a meaning similar to those of Lokeśvara. The lines on her throat, below the breasts, and beneath the navel are marks of beauty. She is wearing a calf-length wraparound skirt, held in place by a broad ornate belt and folded into a decorative panel in the front. Skirt and breasts declare her to be female, but in body ornamentation, features, and hairstyle she is no different from the Buddha. Like him and Lokeśvara she bears the third eye upon her forehead as a sign of her spiritual perfection. Prajñāpāramitā is frequently referred to in the inscriptions as mother of the Jina (Buddha), because she personifies wisdom from which enlightenment is born (Buddha, "the enlightened one"; Jina, "the conqueror").

The triad can definitely be ascribed to the Bayon style. The oval form of the faces, the continuous undulating line of the eyebrows, the obliquely slanted eyes, and the straight wide mouth are typical of the era at the close of the twelfth century. Moreover, it is not unusual in that period to represent the Buddha like any other divine being, clad in nothing but *sampot* and body ornament instead of the monk's robe.

In the case of standing male figures in the Bayon style, the kneecap is often emphasized by a semicircular line, as seen here. The *sampot* is very short and the pattern of the material consists of alternating strips, plain and incised. The hair, incidentally, often receives the same treatment.

The closed eyes and introspective expressions show that this triad was intended as a piece for meditation. It assisted the faithful in forming an image in their minds of the essence of the highest Buddha. This process was rendered easier by personifying his two most important components in separate figures.

The idea of representing complex religious relationships by a group of related figures was not in itself something new, but in Cambodia the triad was enriched in the age of Jayavarman VII by aspects that caused it to become an icon of unique profundity. Inscriptions relate that Lokeśvara was regarded as the deified form of Jayavarman's deceased father, while Prajñāpāramitā represented the apotheosis of his deceased mother.[3] The temples of Preah Khan and Ta Prohm, which contain their statues, were dedicated to them. In George Cœdès' view, Jayavarman VII identified himself with the Buddha seated on the *nāga*, which was the central cult image of the Bayon.[4] These three temple precincts formed an architectural triad within the sacral topography of Angkor.

In bronzes of this kind various levels of physical and spiritual existence are concentrated into one image: that of the highest manifestation of the Buddha, that of the royal family, and that of monumental temple architecture.

W.L.

96

Lokeśvara

North Khleang, Angkor Thom (Siem Reap)
Angkor period, style of the Bayon,
late 12th–early 13th century
Bronze
Height 44 cm, width 20 cm, depth 12.5 cm
National Museum of Cambodia,
Phnom Penh, Ga 5340

"O Victorious Lokeśvara, living incarnation of the Tree of Paradise!" Such is the invocation to the Bodhisattva in one of the first verses of the inscription from Preah Khan.[1]

One has the impression that the image of a handsome, sturdy tree was the inspiration behind the fashioning of this bronze. The four arms are the branches spreading out to the four cardinal directions, and the remarkably solid, almost columnar legs form the trunk of the tree. This large, splendidly bejeweled figure demonstrates the manner of depicting the Bodhisattva typical for the period from the late twelfth to early thirteenth century. His cult reached its apogee during the reign of Jayavarman VII (1181–after 1218). He was then not only to be found as a member of the triad grouping—with the Buddha and Prajñāpāramitā—but also gained great significance as an autonomous deity.[2]

Toward the end of the twelfth century, Lokeśvara, "lord of the world," unites in his person a broad spectrum of aspects. The long history connecting him to Śiva can be seen in his hairstyle, as the hair is shaped into the cylindrical crown typical of *yogin*. In this case, however, the hair of both head and crown is composed of small spiral curls, instead of the strands found with his image in the Prei Monti triad (cat. 95). This reveals a merging with the iconography of the Buddha, where such curls have played an emblematic part since ancient times. Furthermore, his erect posture, four arms, and the lotus in full bloom on the top of his crown of hair associate him with Viṣṇu. On the terrestrial plane, these are emblems of the king who is the ruler of the world; on the spiritual level, they indicate the primordial energy from which all that exists takes its being. Those who are capable, through the power of meditation, of reaching beyond the physical world to a comprehension of the mystic dimension, will perceive in his erect bearing the *yupa,* the axis of the world, to which the stalk of the lotus inclines as it grows to unfold its blossom at the top. It is the mystic image for primeval, pure nature (see cat. 69).

At the end of the twelfth century, Lokeśvara, Nārāyaṇa, and Sadāśiva share this symbolism developed from the iconography of Viṣṇu. But internal cohesiveness continues to be confronted by external differences, making each of them unique. Among the individual characteristics, the attributes held in the hands are of primary importance. They have not been preserved in their entirety in the case of this Lokeśvara, but from comparisons with other bronzes of the same type it is known that a lotus and a nectar flask were to be found in the lower hands, with a string of beads and a book in the upper ones (see cat. 95).

In many of his inscriptions, Jayavarman VII has it published abroad that his father, Dharaṇīndravarman II, took on the form of Lokeśvara after his death.[3] Statues like this bronze figure, therefore, may be taken as the apotheosis of the dead king. They embody the great compassion the king feels for his subjects. "The suffering of the people is the pain of kings" is the approximate equivalent of a saying that has come down to us from Jayavarman VII. He had hospitals built to alleviate the people's suffering, and Lokeśvara gradually came to be the patron and protector of these hospitals alongside the Buddha Bhaiṣajyaguru. He was imputed with the power to cure sickness, especially leprosy.[4]

For the faithful he was a figure of light. That is why the Buddha Amitābha, he of the immeasurable radiance, is always depicted in Lokeśvara's crown of hair in the guise of his spiritual father (see cat. 95). While his image can no longer be found on this bronze, no doubt it once occupied the shallow niche at the front of the crown in a form pressed from sheet gold. The band holding it, which once encircled the crown of hair, was held in place by means of the hole still visible at the back.

From behind one can distinguish some old repairs made to the arms and back. It is possible that these covered up openings that once served to anchor a mandorla.

W.L.

97

Cosmic Lokeśvara with Radiating Arms

Provenance unknown
Angkor period, style of the Bayon, late 12th–early 13th century
Bronze
Height 38.5 cm, width 26 cm, depth 14 cm
Musée national des Arts asiatiques-Guimet, Paris, MA 5940

At the end of the twelfth century the art of Angkor produced some astonishing iconographic innovations. Impulses stemming from the Buddhist pictorial tradition of India and Central Asia were adopted and adapted to shape an unmistakable Khmer iconography.[1] The image of Cosmic Lokeśvara must be among the most original of these creations, and the many statues in stone and bronze bear witness to his great importance during the reign of Jayavarman VII. A series of eight colossal bas-reliefs in stone in the west gallery of the temple of Banteay Chmar glorify his various aspects.[2]

This bronze figure is among the few examples carved fully in the round that show him almost complete.[3] His feet have been destroyed, but in contrast to most stone sculpture of the subject, all eight arms with their attributes have been preserved (see cat. 98). By referring to the eight major directional points, they imply his omnipresence. The attributes in his hands show that he has absorbed into his cosmic form both Brahmanic and Vajrayāna-Buddhist elements. In his proper right hands he is holding, from bottom, a seated divinity, a book, an elephant goad, and a *vajra;* in his left hands, from bottom, he holds a sword, a flask of nectar, a string of prayer beads, and a wheel or disk. Book, nectar flask, and prayer beads are standard attributes of Lokeśvara, but *vajra,* elephant goad, wheel, and sword are only found in representations of his cosmic aspect. The *vajra* is the symbol for the indestructibility of Buddhist doctrine; the elephant goad is meant to put unwilling believers firmly on the right path; the sword cuts to pieces those evil qualities such as hate, envy, and delusion, which bind human beings to the cycle of rebirth; the wheel shows the link between Lokeśvara and Viṣṇu;[4] and the seated divinity has been interpreted as Prañā, wisdom personified.[5]

The same sequence of attributes is also to be found on one of the eight reliefs of Banteay Chmar,[6] where Lokeśvara is preaching the Buddhist doctrine of release to the Brahmanic god Śiva and his wife Umā and prophesying to them that they will achieve Buddhahood. The subject shows a scene from the *Kāraṇḍavyūhasūtra,* a didactic text in praise of Lokeśvara, in which his

superiority over all other deities is extolled.

The text also supplies a key to understanding the curious iconography of Cosmic Lokeśvara. It is there stated that he bears the whole universe in his body. Every pore of his skin constitutes a world of its own filled with every kind of living being.[7] His radiant spiritual power, symbolized by the Jina Amitābha (the victor, whose light is infinite) in his crown of hair, quickens in all these beings the Buddha nature that dwells within them. This is why miniature Buddha figures cover his body (see cat. 98), or appear as ornaments, decorating his neck, upper arms, wrists, chest, hips, and ankles, as in this bronze. The eight Buddhas around his hips, like his eight arms, refer to the eight major directions, thus symbolizing the entire scope of cosmic totality.

The bronze was first described in print in 1992 by A. Le Bonheur.[8] It presents a fascinating mix of transcendent calm and energetic power, which is the hallmark of the great works of art of the Bayon style.

W.L.

98

Lokeśvara with Radiating Arms

Preah Thkol, Preah Khan (Kompong Svay) (Kompong Thom)
Angkor period, style of the Bayon, late 12th–early 13th century
Sandstone
Height 113 cm, width 64 cm, depth 22 cm
Musée national des Arts asiatiques-Guimet, Paris, MG 18139

Avalokiteśvara, or Lokeśvara as he is often called in the inscriptions,[1] has been represented more often in sculpture than any other Bodhisattva in Khmer art.

In essence associated with the idea of compassion, he is primarily invoked as a protector and as the savior of suffering humanity. Many Mahāyāna *sūtra* exalt this major component of his personality.[2] Frequently found during the pre-Angkor period (see cats. 7, 9, 10), Avalokiteśvara seems to disappear for a time—along with the rest of Buddhist statuary—from the thoughts of those who commissioned sculpture and perforce from the repertory of sculptors, only to reappear in the second half of the tenth century after a fairly long absence.[3] From then on, images of Avalokiteśvara became more numerous and more complex until the reign of Jayavarman VII, when his cult experienced unprecedented popularity.[4]

During the period of the Bayon, when only the superhuman form of Lokeśvara with more than two arms seems to have been retained, the iconography of the Bodhisattva became remarkably diverse, with the most complex images being sculpted in bas-relief in the south part of the west gallery of the great provincial temple of Banteay Chmar (Banteay Meanchey). Alongside relatively simple representations with one head and four arms can be found others with as many as sixteen heads and thirty-two arms (Boisselier 1965).

In freestanding sculpture, a highly complex and original form of Avalokiteśvara developed, one found only in Khmer statuary. Known as the Avalokiteśvara with radiating arms, it was shaped by the sculptor's chisel with particular eloquence and skill. The Bodhisattva is represented with a single head and eight arms (cat. 97). His body, cosmic in aspect, is covered almost entirely with miniature images of the Buddha, as though they issued from every pore of his skin. The metaphor is clearly meant to express the Bodhisattva's compassion in all the worlds. In addition to the Buddhas on his torso, arms, and *jaṭā*,[5] all of whom are shown in the meditation position, Avalokiteśvara is encircled at the waist by eight two-armed and cross-legged divinities—these are probably associated with the cardinal directions, reinforcing the idea of a cosmic image—while a ninth divinity, more difficult to interpret, is pictured on his heart.

The *Kāraṇḍavyūhasūtra* is often mentioned as a possible source for these complex images of the Bodhisattva, yet other texts may also have provided the basis in literature for representations of the Avalokiteśvara with radiant arms.

Though damaged, this Avalokiteśvara with radiating arms is one of the finest of those that survive. The face, with its highly refined features, displays the intense spirituality typical of the art of Jayavarman VII; the body, admirably modeled, is more slender and elegant than that of any other known image of the Bodhisattva. Note the particularly realistic treatment of the legs, which, exceptionally for sculpture in the Bayon style, are heavy without being unduly so. Only the very fine Avalokiteśvara with radiating arms from Preah Khan at Angkor, now in the National Museum of Phnom Penh, can rival this work for the beauty of its face.

T.Z.

99

Hevajra

Banteay Kdei, Angkor (Siem Reap)
Angkor period, style of the Bayon,
2d half of the 11th century
Bronze
Height 30 cm, width 14.5 cm,
depth 6.5 cm
National Museum of Cambodia,
Phnom Penh, Ga 5331

This bronze figure was found on 14 February 1922 in a small shrine inside the monastery of Banteay Kdei (the citadel of the cells), on the western shore of the royal baths of Srah Srang. The monastery was constructed in several stages during the second half of the twelfth century. Several schools of Mahāyāna Buddhist belief coexisted within its walls.

Hevajra is the chief deity of the Tantric path to enlightenment, a particularly demanding path, requiring a high degree of religious knowledge and intellectual acuity.[1] The deity is the personification of enlightenment in the here and now. Among his most important attributes is his dance pose, which symbolizes the dynamics of the process of enlightenment as an inner battle between the powers that cling to the conditions of the three-dimensional world and those that seek to break free of them. The small human figure being trampled by the deity represents that bondage; his dance, liberation from it. The grooves on the arms and legs of the small figure multiply the limbs: it is not, in fact, one individual, but the four Māra, personifications of the four chief evils preventing enlightenment. The technique of suggesting multiplicity through simple grooves is also to be found in the treatment of Hevajra's legs. They are each divided into two by a median line, signifying that he has not two but four legs, just as his right and left feet are doubled, each displaying ten toes. This formal device is typically Khmer, permitting an iconographically correct depiction without in any way detracting from the elegance of the dance pose.

In his hands, Hevajra holds the full complement of attributes ascribed to him by the Tantric texts. On the right are to be found, reading from bottom to top: elephant, horse, ass or dog, camel, human being, *sarabha* (a fantastic beast), and a cat. They represent the various supernatural powers of the deity. The left hands are holding a number of undifferentiated human figures. According to the texts, these are personifications of the four elements of earth, water, fire, and air, and the heavenly bodies of sun and moon. They have their correspondences on a microcosmic level in the lateral channels of energy (*nāḍi*) and the central circles of energy (*cakra*) within the person. Through certain prescribed practices a *yogin* can so control the flow of energy through these channels that his mental powers are enhanced. The two small figures in the top two left hands are the gods of wealth and death, bearing witness to Hevajra's power over riches and mortality. All sixteen attributes repose upon cups fashioned from skulls, which can probably be related to the sixteen voids. A person meditating must cleanse the mind of prejudice and preconceptions, that is, create an emptiness or void to employ the mind in a totally unconstrained way so as to advance spiritual development.

The eight heads are built up on three levels, with the lowest one comprising three heads, the middle one four, and the highest having but one. Middle and top together represent the group of the five Jina (also called Tathāgata), which are important figures for the adept to identify with in the course of meditation. The three lowest heads may be taken to represent the triad of Buddha, Lokeśvara, and Vajrapāṇi in the process of the gradual unfolding of the Absolute in the three-dimensional world. All the heads display a third eye in their foreheads, the sign of a *yogin* who has the power to discern the eternal truth behind the transitory things of this world.

The slender pyramid of heads slightly inclined to one side, the arms fanned out like wings, the slim body, and the vigor of the dancing legs lend the figure a rhythmic elegance.

Stylistic markers indicate that the bronze is considerably older than the building in which it was found. In particular, the draping of the *sampot,* which follows a v-shaped line from above the hips to a point deep below the navel, points to the Baphuon style of the eleventh century.

The piece was cast in six parts: the upper five heads, the lower three heads with body and prostrate Māra, the right arms, the left arms, the sash, and the lotus pedestal.

W.L.

100

Hevajra

Provenance unknown
Angkor period, style of the Bayon,
2d half of the 12th century
Bronze
Height 30.7 cm, width 20.7 cm, depth 9 cm
Staatliche Museen zu Berlin,
Museum für Indische Kunst, Inv. II 1138

Powerful and yet elegant, expressing vigorous movement yet also serenely at rest, awe-inspiring but at the same time friendly: such is the fascination exerted by this bronze figure. It would seem to have been fashioned in accordance with one of the verses of the *Hevajratantra:* "He is possessed of the nine emotions of dancing: passion, heroism, loathsomeness, horror, mirth, frightfulness, compassion, wonderment and tranquillity."[1]

This Hevajra is one of the outstanding works of art produced by Tantric Buddhism in Cambodia in the second half of the twelfth century.[2] There are few other images of gods which can match him for all-round beauty. Particular care has been taken with the modeling of the sash of the *sampot* at the back. A flower-shaped buckle secures the gathered folds of material, and flowers also adorn the free-flowing ends of the sash. The eight heads are constructed on three levels in the manner typical for Hevajra, with the gaze directed forward, behind, and to the sides. They signify his all-embracing Buddha nature (see pp. 71–78, fig. 1; cat. 99). The third eye is placed firmly in bold modeling on each of the heads. The

three eyes symbolize the mystery of body, speech, and mind. Like wide-spread wings, the sixteen arms frame the deity poised on one leg, lending him stability. All his attributes have been preserved, as they were cast together with the hands. They display the sequence that is customary with Khmer Hevajra. Beginning in each case with the lowest hand, one can discern on the proper right: elephant, horse, dog, bull, unidentified, personage in human form, lion, and fabulous beast. On the left, apart from the orb at the bottom, all the hands hold a figure in the shape of a human being. The animals symbolize the deity's magic powers (*siddhī*), while the small figures and the globe represent his microcosmic and macrocosmic aspects. In addition to these attributes, he is also holding skull cups in his hands. They stand for the sixteen voids that distinguish a completely purified mind (see cat. 99).

Even the details of the body ornament are intended to communicate important messages to believers, as we learn from the *Hevajratantra:* "The crown is worn for the adoration of one's guru and master and chosen divinity. Earrings are worn to indicate one's deafness to evil words spoken against one's guru and *vajra*-holder. The necklace suggests the mantras intoned, the bracelets one's renunciation of harming living beings, the girdle one's service of the *Mudrā*. The body should always be signed with these signs of the Five Buddhas."[3]

The powerful physique with firmly outlined pectoral muscles, the short *sampot*, and the decorative sash at the back all show an affinity with the Bayon style, but the modeling of the face, the mouth, the horizontal cast of the eyes, and the crown of hair capped with a lotus bud are strong reminders of the Angkor Vat style. The bronze may have been cast during a period of transition.

W.L.

101

Hevajra

Royal Palace, Angkor Thom (Siem Reap)
Angkor period, style of the Bayon,
late 12th–early 13th century
Bronze
Height 22.5 cm, width 12 cm, depth 7 cm
National Museum of Cambodia,
Phnom Penh, Ga 4170

During the course of excavations undertaken in 1950 by the École française d'Extrême-Orient in Angkor Thom, this bronze figure came to light in the ruins of the palace of Jayavarman VII. B. P. Groslier, leader of the project, dated it to around 1220, at the end of the Bayon style.[1]

This is the most ornate of the known images of Hevajra. The deeply incised lines of the eyes and their lids, the broad mouth, and the pointed shapes of the diadem and body ornament lend a disturbing accent to its undeniably expressive power. Anyone meditating on this figure will feel more keenly the savage and awe-inspiring quality that is also a part of Hevajra's nature than is the case with other representations of the deity.

The iconographic features appropriate to Khmer Hevajra are faithfully delineated here, as if following the texts to the letter. All sixteen attributes have been preserved, because they were cast in one piece with the hands and arms. They are the same as with all other Hevajra. The middle row of the eight heads built up in the form of a pyramid has an unusual arrangement. The faces are offset with those of the bottom row, so that they face out toward the intermediate points of the compass (see pp. 71–78, and cat. 99).

Many Hevajra are posed in the dance, supported on the left leg with the right one raised. Here it is the opposite. It is hard to say whether this detail is meant to signal a subtle shift in meaning or is simply to be ascribed to chance. The small prostrate figure he is standing on is clearly characterized as a representation of the four Māra by its multiple heads, while the viewer must imagine the fourth head as turned downward and therefore not visible.

The features, the over-large and powerful legs, the cruciform navel, and the fringe of pearls on the lower hem of the *sampot* indicate that this bronze is a work in the Bayon style.

W.L.

102

Miniature Shrine of Hevajra

Provenance unknown
Angkor period, style of the Bayon,
late 12th–early 13th century
Bronze
Height 20.5 cm, width 16 cm, depth 16 cm
National Museum of Cambodia,
Phnom Penh, Ga 2494

There must have been many groups of figures showing Hevajra with eight *yoginī,* but this piece, never before published, is the only one known. Unfortunately it has not been preserved in its entirety. What is missing is the superstructure of the tower that rose above the open pavilion of columns and was attached to it by means of the two lugs still visible. The probable appearance of the original shrine when complete may be deduced from certain bronze molds and the terra-cotta impressions struck from them.[1] The two-dimensional image that is outlined on these plaques can here be seen in three dimensions.

The shrine consists of several parts, separately cast. The square-stepped base, rising in four tiers with redented corners, forms a single unit, with the large lotus flower of eight petals inside. The square and the circle of the flower are the basic elements of a *maṇḍala,* the innermost center of which is formed by the god. The pavilion of columns rising from this base defines the space where the god can manifest himself. Entrance portals in each of the four cardinal directions indicate that this space is the entire universe. *Nāga* heads above the columns protect the entrances from all forms of evil. In each of the four tympani there sits one small figure, indistinguishable from the others, with his hands folded in the gesture of meditation. In Cambodian art this does not necessarily signify Jina Amitābha, who is identified by the gesture in Javanese art. So it is doubtful whether the figure can be identified at all as an individual being or whether it is not rather to be taken in a general sense as a spiritual protective deity for each of the four cardinal directions. The tower piece is missing, so it is no longer known which gods were represented on its higher levels or what relationship there was between them and the figures in the tympani.

The gilded figure of Hevajra, cast in one piece, is dancing on top of a high lotus pedestal. His left foot is treading on a prostrate human figure with three visible heads. Longitudinal grooves on the legs stand for multiplicity. This clearly points to the four Māra, with the fourth head and body turned downward and hence not visible. While the deity is dancing on his left leg with the right one raised, the *yoginī* dancing in a circle round him have the opposite leg raised. Although this combination may have conveyed a subtle message to initiates, to us its significance remains mysterious.

Hevajra's sixteen arms fan out like wings. Together with the lower faces and the raised foot, they form a circle with his navel at its center. In this way the complexity of the forms is drawn into an imaginary frame and so brought into harmony. Most of his right hands have been broken off, but those on the left have been preserved. All seem to be holding the same oval-shaped attribute, which is possibly meant to represent a cup made from a skull. Khmer Hevajra can be seen either with all sixteen hands holding empty skull cups without attributes, or just displaying the gesture of holding something. They symbolize the sixteen voids, a spiritual state of purity which forms one of the stages on the path to enlightenment.

Hevajra's short *sampot* has a semicircular folded-over panel at the front and is decorated behind with a beautiful butterfly-shaped sash crowned with a flower. This preference for an ornamental treatment of the sash ends seems to be typical of the era spanning the close of the twelfth to the beginning of the thirteenth century. (It is also present in the Hevajra bronzes, cats. 100, 101.)

The tier of eight heads is controlled by the body's dance gesture and inclines slightly to the left. All the faces have a benevolent expression and bear the third eye on their foreheads as a sign of their ability to perceive the absolute truth lying behind the changing forms of the phenomenal world. (For a discussion of the structure and significance of the heads, see cat. 99.)

Originally there was a *yoginī* dancing on each of the eight lotus petals on the base, fully modeled in the round. Unfortunately, only six remain. The number eight alludes to the four cardinal points of the compass and the four intermediate directions to which they belong. They are emanations of Hevajra and personify inner powers that can be acquired through the practice of yoga techniques. It is their task to do battle against evil and ignorance throughout the entire universe. In the *Hevajratantra,* the most important text for this cult, they are given their names and their attributes are described. Although the attributes are only partially preserved in the case of the small figures on this shrine, individual *yoginī* can still be identified on the basis of their relationship to the central figure. Since it may be assumed that Hevajra faces east, it must be Gaurī dancing in front of him (missing), opposite her to the west is Vetālī (right hand, a noose; left hand, a skull cup), to the south is Caurī (right hand, a knife?), to the north is Ghasmarī (missing). The intermediate stations are taken up by Pukkasī to the northeast (right hand, a figure; left hand, a trident), Śavarī to the southeast (?), Caṇḍālī to the southwest (right hand, a drum; left hand, a bud), and Ḍombinī to the northwest (right hand, an animal?; left hand, a fish).[2] All the *yoginī* have pointed chignons, are adorned with diadems, and are wearing short *sampot* with long triangular-shaped sashes. The tips of the upward-curving lotus leaves they are dancing on, together with the sashes and chignons, repeat the same basic shape and thus form a vertical line that is intersected by the diagonals of arms and legs. This pattern may contribute to the feeling of serene harmony in spite of the vigorous movement.

W.L.

103

Dancer

Provenance unknown
Angkor period, 12th–14th century
Bronze
Height 21 cm, width 15 cm, depth 5.5 cm
Musée national des Arts asiatiques-Guimet, Paris, C 6500

Displaying vigorous energy, yet controlled to the fingertips: such is the immediate impression this dancer makes on the observer. The flying panels of her *sampot* form a charming counterpoint to the erect carriage of upper torso and head. The legs, spread apart and with knees flexed, make the figure look more powerful than graceful. The angular planes of the face are still strongly reminiscent of the Angkor Vat style, but the large almond-shaped eyes and the slanting eyebrows can be noted on many of the bronzes of the Bayon style. Even though the dancer may be found to be lacking in the fine modeling of features, diadem, and body ornament, she still radiates a powerful aura.

Her height of twenty-one centimeters makes her far taller than all the known images of *yoginī* grouped as dancers around deities like Hevajra (see cats. 102, 105), or the Tantric form of Prajñāpāramitā.[1] It is unlikely that she belongs in the company of such divine beings, especially since she is not bearing any attributes. She is, rather, to be associated with the dancers (*apsaras*) depicted on many of the bas-reliefs on the walls and columns of the temples of Jayavarman VII.

Sacred dances had an important function at that time. Even to the present day they are still performed for important ceremonies such as initiations within the context of Vajrayāna Buddhism. Through miming the hand and body gestures of a god, the dancers strive to identify themselves with that deity. As they dance, they picture

themselves as the god, attempting to penetrate to the divine center deep in their own being, their own Buddha nature. The performance constitutes a process of unfolding of the self; its goal the awakening of wisdom and compassion in their own inward being.

W.L.

104

Prajñāpāramitā with Eleven Heads

Provenance unknown
Angkor period, 2d half of the 12th century
Bronze
Height 15 cm, width 13 cm, depth 4 cm
National Museum of Cambodia,
Phnom Penh, Ga 5333

This small bronze figure packed with vibrant energy can be assigned to the second half of the twelfth century on stylistic grounds. The wide, angular face is still highly reminiscent of the Angkor Vat style, but the pattern of the ankle-length skirt, consisting of alternating smooth and ribbed panels, is common to many bronzes of the Bayon style.

Prajñāpāramitā in her eleven-headed form achieved great renown at the end of the twelfth century. She is depicted in widely differing versions; most of them show her standing or dancing. A sitting figure such as this, with the legs tucked under (*sattvaparyankāsana*) and the ramrod straight back of a *yoginī,* is rare.[1] The way her eleven heads are arranged here is not otherwise known. Of the seven lower heads, only the forward-looking one is shown fully frontal, the other six appear in profile. On the upper level, the four faces direct their gaze to the four cardinal directions. The small Buddha figure in her crown of hair depicts the Jina Amitābha, the victor whose light is infinite. This is an iconographic sign that she shares with the Bodhisattva Lokeśvara (cat. 95), which symbolizes her radiant spiritual power that sheds its light over all things.

Corresponding to the eleven heads are eleven pairs of arms that surround her like spread wings. Unfortunately, it is not possible to identify with any accuracy the elongated attributes in her hands, some of which seem to have the form of lotus buds (?). It is also not at all clear whether the only object resembling a disk, held in her seventh right hand (counting from below), is supposed to be a mirror. Tantrism regards the mirror as reflecting the Void (*śūnyatā*) as well as objects, and is therefore a symbol of comprehensive wisdom.

The word Prajñāpāramitā has a comprehensive meaning, denoting the highest wisdom of a Buddha, the path that leads to that wisdom, and the instructional texts describing in minute detail the spiritual training to be followed on this path. The deity personifies all of this simultaneously. Her many iconographical variations indicate her manifold aspects. One or another of them will predominate in depictions of her, according to the particular ritual context. As a member of a triad (cat. 95) she has a different meaning from that of the eleven-headed form. In the former role she symbolizes the highest wisdom of the Buddha, in the latter she seems rather to be involved with spiritual training on the way to such wisdom. Her eleven heads may well correspond to certain spiritual processes. To decipher their meaning, both the Cambodian inscriptions and the extensive Prajñāpāramitā literature need to be consulted. These still require closer analysis to arrive at a better understanding of the sculpture.

The application of particular numbers plays a great part in this literature. For example, mention is made of the Four Bases of psychic power, the Seven Limbs of Illumination, the Eight-fold Path, and the Ten Powers of the Tathāgata. The number eleven is also frequently mentioned. In chapter sixteen of the *Prajñāpāramitāsūtra,* for example, the Eleven Insights are expounded upon, such as the insight of how not to inflict suffering, and the insight that all acts of perception and all physical events are inconstant.[2]

In the *Abhisamayālaṃkāra,* which summarizes the content of the instructional texts of Prajñāpāramitā in extremely abridged form, mention is made of the eleven elements that characterize the omniscience of a Bodhisattva in connection with the path to enlightenment.[3] Moreover, there are eleven features that mark the activities of a Bodhisattva along this path.[4] Further examples could be adduced. What remains to be examined is how far they can be brought into association with the eleven heads of this deity. Whatever the answer, Prajñāpāramitā performs the functions of a Bodhisattva: for the interim she renounces her own claim to enlightenment, and therefore Buddhahood, in order to help believers find the true path. She is an ideal model and at the same time gives help to those in need. Whoever meditates upon her image will use the attributes in her hands and her eleven heads to visualize her qualities and powers with the aim of self-purification and the perfecting of spiritual capacities.

W.L.

105

Ritual Conch

Angkor, shore of the Tonle Sap
Angkor period, 12th–13th century
Bronze
Height 28 cm, width 11 cm (conch)
Height 10 cm, width 11.5 cm (tripod)
National Museum of Cambodia,
Phnom Penh, Ga 5484, 5485

Ritual implements dating from the twelfth century whose form echoes that of a sea-snail (triton) shell are referred to as conches; the Sanskrit term for them is *śaṇkha*. Like real conch shells, they were used either as ladles to dip and pour libations of holy water or as wind instruments to produce the sacred sound "oṃ" (see pp. 71–78). This conch clearly belonged to the latter category, for its spiral apex ends in a carefully worked mouthpiece surrounded by the rosette of a full-blown lotus consisting of eight petals. The sound is produced in a chamber formed by a separately inserted cross-piece.[1]

The conch is decorated according to a fixed design that recurs in almost all the known examples, whether they are vessels or instruments. The apex imitates the spiral turns of the shell, the curving belly is left entirely smooth, the tongue-shaped portion bears depictions of figures in relief, while the entire opening is rimmed by a decorative border. During ritual performances, the conch was laid horizontally on a tripod stand that concealed the lower belly section. This possibly explains why this part was left undecorated.

It is remarkable how many conches are decorated, like this one, with a miniature relief of the Tantric deity Hevajra (cats. 99–101). Here he is dancing in front of a circular disk, at the center of a wider circle formed by other dancing figures. His iconographic signature, the eight heads built up on three levels, can be clearly distinguished. As distinct from the roughly contemporary miniature bronze shrine (cat. 102), there are not eight but six *yoginī* surrounding him. They cannot, therefore, be attributed, as in the former case, to the four cardinal directions and four intermediate points. The *Hevajratantra*, the primary literary source for understanding the cult of Hevajra, describes in several chapters the number, appearance, and function of the *yoginī*. In connection with the spheres of purification and the means that a meditator may employ to aid in spiritual cleansing, the emanations of six *yoginī* are named: "Gaurī is for form, Caurī is for sound, Vetālī is for smell, Ghasmarī is for taste, Bhūcarī is for touch, Khecarī is for thought."[2] Those who can visualize these figures cleanse their minds and sense perceptions. Presumably it is the above *yoginī* who are depicted on this conch.[3]

Although the tripod stand dates from the same period as the trumpet, it did not originally belong with it and its provenance is unknown. Small praying figures have been worked into the petal-shaped spikes forming a wreath around the upper edge. The three curved feet emerge from the mouths of monster masks and take the form of stylized *garuḍa*.

W.L.

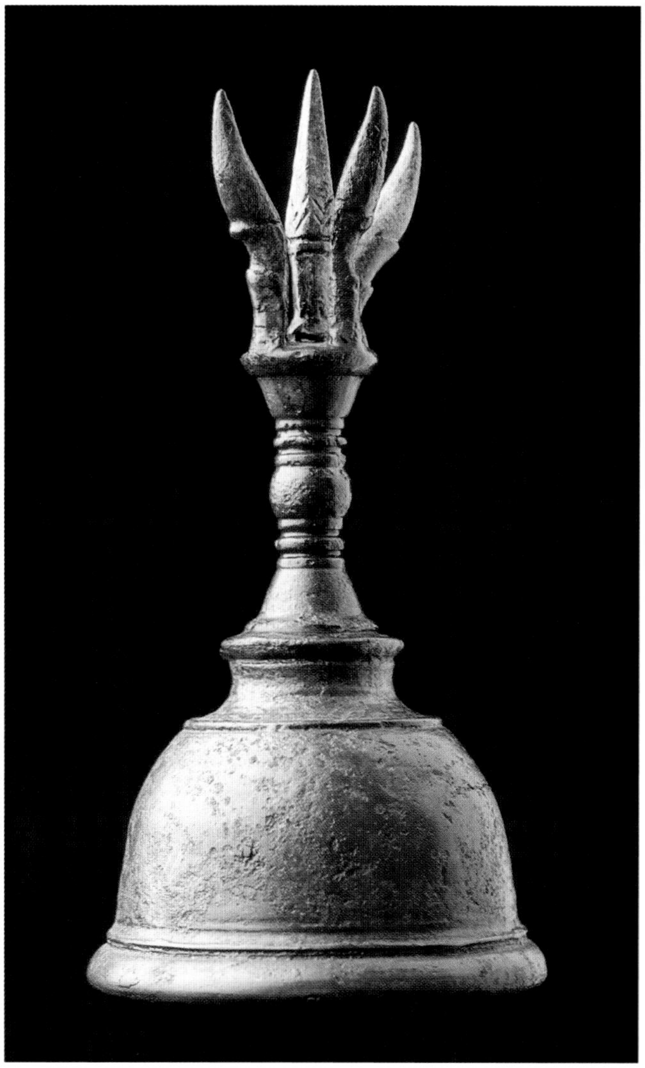

106

Vajra and *Ghaṇṭā*

Sra Moch, Mongkolborei
(Banteay Meanchey)
Angkor period, 12th–13th century
Bronze
Height 13.8 cm (*vajra*); 14.1 cm (*ghaṇṭā*)
National Museum of Cambodia,
Phnom Penh, Ga 5483 (*vajra*);
Ga 5481 (*ghaṇṭā*)
[*ghaṇṭā* not in exhibition]

In 1921, in the course of work at a construction site, a number of bronze artifacts were unearthed that bear all the signs of having originally belonged together on a Buddhist altar. Apart from two small figures, the find included the shell of a sea-snail, used as a container for holy water, along with its tripod stand, a *ghaṇṭā* (bell), and two *vajra*.[1]

In Vajrayāna Buddhism, *vajra* and bell are the most important ritual implements of a priest. They are always used together. The *vajra* is held in the right hand and the bell in the left, and the priest performs solemn gestures with them while chanting appropriate *mantra*.

As an attribute of the Vedic rain god Indra, the *vajra* originally symbolized the elemental powers of thunder and lightning.[2] In Vajrayāna Buddhism it later assumed the role of one of the most important religio-magical symbols and was assigned to various deities as an attribute. While it retained its character as a dispenser of light and energy, the immediate link with the forces of nature was relegated to the background. Instead, it came to be associated with the diamond, as the precious, transparent, yet at the same time extremely hard gemstone is better suited as a symbol of the essential indestructible nature of Buddhist teaching than the uncontrollable forces of nature. The purity and sharp cutting edge of the diamond are equated with the brilliance and penetration of the doctrine. Likewise, it symbolizes the intellectual penetration of the enlightened person who is capable of recognizing and annihilating such inner adversaries as greed, hate, and delusion. An inscription from Bat Chum handed down from the tenth century describes the *vajra* as a flame that sweeps aside the barriers on the path to enlightenment by consuming all sins in its fire.[3]

The function of the *vajra* is that of a ritual scepter. Its form reflects its symbolic import. The round central section is to be thought of as a seed, the smallest unit of matter from which the cosmos develops.[4] The immanent energy it contains is expressed in motion, as represented in the form of a spiral or, as here, in a series of rings. This energy is the driving force behind creation, as represented by the cups and petals of lotus flowers. By opening out at both ends of the *vajra*, they make manifest the polarity within all being (e.g., male/female, happiness/misfortune). From the circle formed by the four petals spring four curving rays, identified with the four cardinal directions; the space they encompass is the physical world. The fifth ray, originally found in the center as is the case with the bell, is no longer there. It is always fashioned as a straight rod because it points to the zenith. The five directions of north, south, east, west, and zenith symbolize cosmic totality. On a spiritual level they are identified with the five transcendental Buddhas, also known as Tathāgata or Jina, who personify the wise insights of the enlightened mind.

The handle of the bell also ends in a five-pointed *vajra*. However, one of the points is missing. The points and the swelling body of the bell present a contrast in form, which is of deep symbolic significance. They reference the male capacity for penetration and the female characteristic of enclosure, but both have developed from the same original seed, represented by the round swelling in the middle of the handle, thus showing that they form a unity.

The swelling body of the bell is not only an instrument for producing sound, but also a symbol of the uterus in which human life develops. Cosmic life, on the other hand, as taught by the sound-mystics of Mahāyāna Buddhism, began with a sound spreading out in waves and causing inert primal matter to vibrate until the increasing energy finally released the creative process.[5] So the ringing of the bell and its uterine shape are macro- and microcosmic references to the primal source of all life. The bell's *vajra*-handle reinforces this symbolism, for the five rays, the Tathāgata, which are assigned to the five cardinal directions on the macrocosmic level, are aligned with the five elements on the level of the microcosm. Every time the bell is rung, they are set in action and their powers are manifested as sound.

While various decorations on Nepalese, Tibetan, and Javanese bells reflect this profound symbolism, Khmer bells are always left unadorned.[6] In their simplicity, they concentrate on the essential message while at the same time largely locking it away in a secret code.

The mystery of *vajra* and *ghaṇṭā* is referred to in Cambodia for the first time in an inscription from Vat Sithor of 968,[7] but no examples of these implements have been preserved from that time. The oldest extant pieces date from the twelfth century. The two examples found in Sra Moch are the only elements known to be a pair.

W.L.

107

Standing Lakṣmī

Preah Ko, Roluos (Siem Reap)
Angkor period, style of the Bayon, late 12th–early 13th century
Sandstone
Height 188 cm (without tenon), width 59 cm, depth 45 cm
National Museum of Cambodia, Phnom Penh, Ka 1698

The distinctive aesthetic that prevails in the style of the Bayon was due in part to the new religious concerns prompted by Jayavarman VII's choice of a different form of Buddhism as the state religion. The sculptors of that period also had a propensity for individualizing their sculpture at the request of those who commissioned them, a remark that should not be taken as an unqualified endorsement of the notion of realistic portraiture.

Certain strange formal characteristics appear frequently in both Buddhist and Brahmanistic sculpture in the Bayon. This Lakṣmī from Preah Ko is a good example of the change. Identifiable by the lotus buds she holds in her hands, the deity has the high forehead, narrow shoulders, small bosom, and general slenderness that recall the statues of Tārā (?) kneeling that scholars have often described as "portraits" of the devout queen Jayarājadevī, the beloved wife of Jayavarman VII. But is it proper to speak of a "portrait" in this case?

The stele from Phimeanakas (K. 485),[1] which provides important information on the reign of Jayavarman VII, documents that Indradevī, who was Jayarājadevī's older sister and who replaced her in the king's heart after her death, had "many likenesses of Śrī Jayarājadevī [erected] in every town, along with likenesses of herself and the king." What figures these refer to is unfortunately not specified. As it is generally admitted that the so-called kneeling Tārā images could be "portraits" of the dead queen, there is no reason not to make the same claim for other statues with the same characteristics. One objection might be that Lakṣmī is a Brahmanic divinity, while Jayarājadevī was a devout Buddhist. This is certainly true, but religions in ancient Cambodia were never strictly distinct, and besides, as the stele from Phimeanakas points out, Jayarājadevī originally belonged to the Brahmanic faith and was led to Buddhism by her sister; she made many large donations to both Hindu and Buddhist sanctuaries. It is not out of the question, then, for likenesses of Śrī Jayarājadevī to have been consecrated in Hindu sanctuaries after her death. The subject is, of course, open to debate.

Stylistically, the Lakṣmī from Preah Ko fulfills expectations for a work from the reign of Jayavarman VII. She wears a chignon-cover decorated with lotus petals and a skirt with florets and a long, incurved, triangular front panel.

In general, unlike Buddhist images, whose eyes are closed or half-closed, the Brahmanic images in the Bayon style have their eyes open. This detail speaks to the difference in spirit between the two religions: the internalization and humility of Buddhism, on the one hand, and the pride, even haughtiness, and grandeur of Brahmanism on the other.

T.Z.

108

Brahmanic Triad

Provenance unknown
Angkor period, style of the Bayon,
late 12th–early 13th century
Bronze
Height 24.5 cm, width 24 cm, depth 8.5 cm
National Museum of Cambodia,
Phnom Penh, Ga 2283

The three deities are standing on a common altar, but they were cast as separate pieces. Each figure has its own square base, which locks into the altar. The slightly raised outer edge and the drainage spout at the side of the altar top show there was provision for ritual washing of the figures with holy water.

The four-armed god in the center is readily identified as Viṣṇu by his attributes. From below his proper right to below left he is holding an orb, a disk, a conch, and a mace (cat. 115). Although his central importance is emphasized by the expanded middle section of the altar, the fact that all three figures are about the same size speaks for their equality. Śiva stands on his right with a rosary and a lotus bud (?) in his right hand and the trident that usually identifies him in his left. The corresponding place on the other side is filled by Devī, who holds a lotus bud in each hand.

Facial expression, body ornament, and costume clearly have all the characteristics of the Bayon style, so the altar can be dated to the late twelfth or early thirteenth century. Its external configuration is modeled on the pattern of the Buddhist triads (cat. 95). Viṣṇu takes the place of the Buddha on the *nāga,* Śiva that of Lokeśvara, and Devī that of Prajñāpāramitā. In the inscriptions, Viṣṇu, Śiva, and Devī are occasionally mentioned together. One example is the inscription of Trapeang Don On from 1129.[1] A donor who is not explicitly identified reports on the gifts he has made. In 1095, it is said, he had an Īśa (a Śiva) set up; in 1109 a Viṣṇu and a Devī were erected, and he made provision that for their worship a sacred fire and a certain amount of rice per day would be supplied.

Even if the inscription does not directly refer to this particular bronze triad, it is informative in the present context. The fact that the statues of Śiva, Viṣṇu, and Devī were donated by the same person and accorded the same degree of worship demonstrates the endeavors of the Khmer of the Angkor period to stress the essential equality of the great gods.

A bronze triad from Prei Veng, which is stylistically very close to this one, shows a further iconographic variant. Standing to the right and left of the four-armed Viṣṇu at the center are a male and a female figure who are likewise four-armed and hold the same attributes as Viṣṇu: orb, disk, conch, and mace.[2] Other triads have unexpected divine configurations, which can be explained with the aid of the short donor inscriptions on many shrines of the age of Jayavarman VII.[3] While these relate to the images of the gods that were originally presented to the shrine, they do not always mention their names, but frequently refer instead to the names of the donors in a family triad of father, mother, and son or daughter. From this one may conclude that the donors had depicted themselves in the images of the gods with whom they identified. So the son, for example, who is always depicted at the center, can appear as Viṣṇu, while the father can be Śiva or Viṣṇu, depending on which god he has chosen for himself.

At the end of the twelfth century, personal identification with a deity was one of the most basic elements of religious practice in both the Tantric-Buddhist as well as the Tantric-Brahmanic tradition.

W.L.

109

Gaṇeśa

Provenance unknown
Angkor period, style of the Bayon,
late 12th–early 13th century
Bronze
Height 25.5 cm, width 23.5 cm,
depth 15 cm
National Museum of Cambodia,
Phnom Penh, Ga 2320

The elephant-headed god is sitting in the attitude of a *yogin* on a triangular bronze plate, which was originally attached to a larger base by means of lugs.

From ancient times Gaṇeśa has been recognized by his paunch, a characteristic reaching back to the Indian legend, according to which his father Śiva permitted him to be the first to partake of the offerings of food presented by believers. His triangular navel is frequently found in Bayon-style bronzes, while his short *sampot* is also a mark of the Bayon style. Folded over and pleated in the front, the cloth conceals his splendid belt, which is only visible from behind. Its elegant pendants, flower-shaped buckle, and the end panels of cloth, carefully arranged to fan out at top and bottom, create a decorative effect. There is a snake coiled around his plump chest and waist, and the bracelets on his upper arms are also augmented by snakes. The rhomboid-shaped ornament adorning his forehead is reminiscent of a third eye. What is missing above the diadem is the former crown of hair, which was presumably cone-shaped. It was cast separately from the head and was, therefore, more easily broken off and lost.

Only three of the attributes held in his four hands have been preserved. The lower right hand is grasping a round object, which, in view of the decoration of beaded rim and blossom it bears, can hardly be taken for the sweet (*modaka*) Gaṇeśa used to hold following Indian practice in the pre-Angkor period, but which is rarely found in the age of Angkor.[1] The meaning of this object thus remains obscure. In the upper right hand he is holding his own broken-off tusk, which is consequently missing from his right jaw. His upper left hand seizes hold of a small snake, which is knotted into the shape of a noose. The attribute in the lower left hand has not survived. Clearly it was something to be inserted in the opening formed by the thumb and index finger.

Statues of Gaṇeśa have been documented since the seventh century (cat. 26). In inscriptions of the Angkor period the god is also called Vighneśvara, lord of obstacles. The natural endowments of this largest of all land animals underlie the concept behind the name. The obstacles may be physical or mental; he can either construct them or dismantle them. Gaṇeśa is also esteemed as patron of the arts and sciences. As the son of Śiva, he was originally a member of the Brahmanic pantheon, but he also won for himself great significance in Buddhist Cambodia. To the present day he has remained one of the most popular of gods and is especially efficacious in the sphere of magical practices.[2]

As there are no texts preserved from the Angkor period to transmit his myths, it is hard to reconstruct the legends woven around his remarkable hybrid figure in those days. Presumably in the seventh century they were still strongly shaped by Indian tradition and only gradually came to assume their specifically Khmer character. Whether the stories told about him today in Cambodia reach back in essence to Angkor times has not as yet been examined. But in discussing this question, it is very instructive that in spite of a variety of narrative material, the fundamental elements essentially agree with those of the ancient Indian legends.[3] What is involved here is the transformation of a human being into something new. He loses his identity because his head is struck off. But his death is not final, since he receives a new head, that of a passing elephant, and by the power of magic he is brought back to life. He gains not only a new identity, but also intelligence and magical knowledge: the powers of man and animal unite in this new being. He does not symbolize a duality, but the essential unity of nature and culture. The act of violence is an initiation, a passage into another stage of life. The mutilation this involves is symbolized by the broken-off tusk.

According to ancient Indian custom, an initiate receives a string made of three threads to be placed across his upper body on the left side. With Gaṇeśa this takes the form of a snake with a body built up in three layers. The sloughed skins of the snake reflect the rebirth arising from the initiation. But the knotted snake in his left hand is the noose that binds human beings to the cycle of rebirth if they fail to subject themselves to this process of transformation. Such thoughts play a considerable role in both Brahmanic and Buddhist religions, and it is this that explains Gaṇeśa's significance across the boundaries of the religions.

W.L.

110

Liṅga

Provenance unknown[1]
Angkor period, 10th–13th century
Milky quartz, silver, bronze
Height 11.5 cm, width 14.5 cm,
depth 10 cm
National Museum of Cambodia,
Phnom Penh, Ga 3557

Although stone *liṅga* are the best known, inscriptions also mention *liṅga* of gold, pewter, and precious stone. The present example calls for two observations: its very small size suggests an idol that was kept on a family's household altar, with the added advantage of being easily transportable; and the materials and delicate workmanship declare this to be a precious object.

The pedestal is made of bronze and was probably gilded originally. The *liṅga* is carved of milky quartz, its rounded top perfectly cylindrical and its base solidly sunk into the pedestal. The different parts of the latter are monolithic as the entire pedestal was cast as a unit. The tip of the *snānadronī,* though difficult to make out in its present state, was "realistically" represented.

A thin ring of silver encircles the base of the *liṅga,* covering its junction with the pedestal. (For the symbolism of the *liṅga,* see cat. 23.)

A piece of this sort is difficult to date accurately. The molding on the pedestal allows us at best to assign it to the Angkor period (tenth to thirteenth century).

A.C.

111

Sadāśiva

Provenance unknown
Angkor period, transitional style
between Angkor Vat and the Bayon,
2d half of the 12th century
Bronze
Height 34 cm, width 18 cm, depth 8.5 cm
National Museum of Cambodia,
Phnom Penh, Ga 2682

It was not uncommon to depict Śiva with five heads in the later stages of the Angkor period. Best known are the bronze figures, but stone sculptures and reliefs have also been found.[1] Most pieces can be dated to the twelfth century. This bronze displays defining characteristics of the styles of both Angkor Vat and the Bayon. The severity of the angular features and the straight line of eyes and eyebrows are often encountered in the bronzes of the Angkor Vat style. The sturdy legs and the decoratively gathered folds of the sash ends of the *sampot*, however, point to the Bayon style, which tends toward an ornate treatment. The bronze was possibly cast during the transitional phase.

Śiva's five heads are arranged on two levels, four heads below and a single head above. Incised in the flat top of the crown of hair on the uppermost head is the pericarp of a lotus.

Cambodian inscriptions occasionally refer to multiheaded forms of Śiva. The inscription of Sdok Kak Thom, for example, reports on the importation of four Tantric texts (*śāstra*) from India during the reign of Jayavarman II at the beginning of the ninth century.[2] According to the inscription, they are said to be represented by the four faces of Tumburu (Śiva).

The identification of the faces with sacred texts can also be transferred to the five-headed Śiva. In view of the fact that each of his five mouths is uttering a *śāstra*, it is clear why each of his ten hands is raised in the gesture of teaching. In each case, thumb and index finger form an O, thus intimating that Śiva is engaged in expounding divine truths.

The image of the five-headed Śiva comprises far more than this, however, for it is deeply rooted in Indian theories of cosmogony. The inscription of Phnom Sandak dating from 1110 proves that these theories were familiar in Cambodia. It makes covert allusion to the five-headed god by praising Śiva as the highest being, commencing his

unfolding in the physical world with Vāma.[3] This cryptic statement can be decoded with the aid of the Indian Śaivāgama and the Śaivasiddhānta. They teach that Sadāśiva has his origin in the highest, absolute principle of Śiva (Paramaśiva), which is without form. Sadāśiva possesses the qualities of both nonform and form, for from him emanate the five entities, namely, Vāmadeva, Sadyojāta, Aghora, Tatpuruṣa, and Īśāna, who are represented by the five heads, with Īśāna uppermost. The number five implies the zenith as well as the four cardinal directions. The five emanations are also regarded as embodiments of the five primordial elements of earth, water, fire, air, and ether, besides being the five heavenly directions. They thus have both micro- and macrocosmic aspects. In a progressive unfolding from the transcendental to the material, the five-headed Śiva develops into the god Maheśvara. He is the manifestation of Śiva in this world. As all living beings take their origin from him, he is the essence of the power of generation.[4]

In Cambodian epigraphy, Sadāśiva is occasionally referred to by the name Sadeśa, literally "the everlasting lord."[5]

The square base, erect posture, and pericarp of the lotus on the crown of hair is also seen in other Brahmanic and Buddhist deities (cats. 69, 96). They are part of the fundamental vocabulary of archetypal symbolism. The square has been the symbol of the material world since ancient times. Its ideal form reflects in Brahmanism the perfection of divine creation, and in Buddhism the regularity of nature. The erect posture of the many-armed god mirrors both the column and the tree, both of which symbolize the world axis that guarantees the cosmic order. With its strong trunk and spreading branches, the tree also communicates the notion of God as eternally unchanging and at the same time all-embracing, projecting himself outward into the diversity of creation.

The lotus has always been a symbol of purity and detachment. As a concluding motif to the crown of hair, it marks the transition into the sphere of the absolute, the realm of the purest and highest form of God. In yoga, too, the perfectly liberated mind, which is capable of recognizing this absolute state of God, is symbolized by a lotus on the head.

W.L.

112

Pediment

Preah Pithu, Angkor (Siem Reap)
Angkor period, style of the Bayon or slightly later, 1st half of the 13th century
Sandstone
Height 87 cm, width 134 cm, depth 33 cm
Musée national des Arts asiatiques-Guimet, Paris, MG 18912

This relatively small pediment is on a scale that accords with the size of the small Preah Pithu temples that are situated to the north of the northern Khleang in the central zone of Angkor Thom. The temples, several of which resemble temple-mountains, date from several periods, but mostly the twelfth and thirteenth centuries. Though not very well known, their decoration is quite fine, and they are notable for their reliefs, of which this is an excellent example. Of extraordinary depth, the carving presents some of the subjects, especially the central female figure, all but in the round.

A comprehensive interpretation of the iconography has been given by Banerjee (1964) and can be summarized as follows. The episode is known as the *tapahktista Pārvatī* and is recounted in a poem (Song V) in *Kumārasambhavan* by the famed poet Kālidāsa, who drew on ancient texts.[1] The relief depicts two scenes in chronological sequence from the viewer's right. The central figure is Pārvatī (here known as Aparnā because she has been fasting) performing extreme penance in order to be the worthy bride of Śiva. She occupies the linking position between the two incidents in the story. On her left, dressed as a Brahman ascetic, stands a figure who is trying to attract her attention by reviling Śiva, while an attendant kneels at his feet to plead with him to desist. Pārvatī, in a gesture expressed by the sculptor with compelling realism, raises her arms and plugs her ears with her fingers to block out the words. The irritating ascetic is none other than Śiva himself, who has been testing the devotion of Pārvatī. In the second incident, Pārvatī kneels, still central, with an ecstatic look on her face, while her attendant pays homage to Śiva, who has revealed himself in his kingly glory and presents himself as Pārvatī's suitor. Above, two *apsaras* fling garlands on the participants.

The remaining elements of the vegetal decoration on the superstructure of the pediment do not offer sufficient evidence for the firm dating of this piece. The figures themselves are more instructive. The modeling of the faces and bodies is not very explicit, but the costumes of the Brahman and of Śiva, and the coiffures of Śiva and Pārvatī, indicate a Bayon date at the earliest, and probably a later one.

The lower edge is bordered with a row of schematic worshipers' heads executed with none of the naturalistic vigor and plastic mastery of the narrative panel itself.

Any sound dating of this pediment awaits more profound research into the bas-reliefs on the monuments of the time of Jayavarman VII and later reigns.

H.J.

Thirteenth Century and Later

Opposite, Fig. 1
Head of the Buddha.
Preah Palilay, Angkor Thom.
Second half of the thirteenth century.
Sandstone. Height 52 cm.
Musée national des Arts asiatiques-Guimet, Paris

Post-Angkor Art

Beginning perhaps as early as the late twelfth century, but more certainly during the thirteenth and fourteenth centuries, Theravāda Buddhism became established in Cambodia on a vast scale. A few disparate facts signal this major turning point in Khmer culture: the very probable sojourn of one of Jayavarman VII's sons in Sri Lanka between 1180 and 1190 to study ancient Buddhism;[1] the account by Zhou Daguan in the late thirteenth century (1296) that seems to indicate that Theravāda Buddhism had made great progress at that time;[2] and, finally, in 1308, the earliest Pāli inscription in Cambodia.[3] The adoption of Theravāda Buddhism was clearly accompanied by the definitive abandonment of Brahmanism. The Mahāyāna Buddhism of Jayavarman VII had effortlessly blended with the political and religious views of the state religion of Śivaism, which had been espoused by most of his predecessors, and created no break in the historical and cultural continuity of Angkor Cambodia. This was not the case with the shift to Theravāda Buddhism, the principles of which were fundamentally different from those of Brahmanism. This change is illustrated in statuary by the appearance of an expression of "humble gentleness" on the faces of Buddha images (fig. 1).

Relatively little is known about the period that followed the style of the Bayon. An infinitesimal number of monuments date from this time, among them the temple of Mangalārtha, the "last" Angkor monument, which has been dated to the thirteenth century. The main undertaking seems to have been completing the decoration of already existing religious foundations, for example, some of the bas-reliefs from the interior gallery of the Bayon and some decorative elements from the Preah Pithu temples. Any new foundations seem to have been built of wood, which explains why none has survived. During this period, called the "post-Bayon" because there is not a single monument after which to name it, a new type of Buddha image came into being (cat. 113) that has not been dated with any accuracy (second half of the thirteenth to the fourteenth century?). Perhaps we should search in the Lopburi school—a provincial school of Khmer art situated in territory that is now Thailand—for both the stylistic and iconographic origins of these very important images, which provide a link between the Angkor and post-Angkor periods, descend from the first and anticipate the second.

Post-Angkor art begins, according to the traditional chronology, with the abandonment of Angkor after the city was captured by the Thai armies of Ayuthayā in 1431. The hard reality of the events of that year—the Khmer defeat was accompanied by a heavy tribute, both material and human—could only lead to the final weakening of the Khmer kingdom. The abandonment of the capital, too exposed to restless and ambitious neighbors, became inevitable and was brought about by a protracted war in the face of pressure from the Thai armies, a pressure that had scarcely let up since the founding of the kingdom of Ayuthayā in 1350.

Post-Angkor art, like pre-Angkor art before it, is defined in the same terminology as the great Angkor period, the beginnings of which are sought in one and the echoes in the other. So the historical caesura of 1431, rather artificial in terms of art, is used more for narrative convenience than for accurate, concrete stylistic facts. The reality of the evolution of Khmer art after the Bayon period is completely different: there was probably no break in continuity between Angkor and post-Angkor art. The facts at our disposal are simply too restricted to show clearly the progressive shift from one to the

1. Cœdès 1964, 323.
2. Pelliot 1951, 14-15.
3. Cœdès 1936, 14-21.

other, a shift that was also attended by a marked loss of vitality that, given the difficulties of the time, was perfectly understandable.

This period in Khmer art has been relatively little studied.[4] It is true that many of its works have disappeared—they were most often made of wood and did not survive the tropical climate of Cambodia—and that many of those that have survived are disappointing, either because of their poor condition or because they are of little interest other than for their iconography.

A few extant masterpieces (cat. 117), however, make us regret the loss of this heritage. Though less brilliant than the art bequeathed by the pre-Angkor and Angkor periods, it is nonetheless remarkable; the sculpture, including the many images of the adorned Buddha (cat. 116), shows certain affinities with the Thai art of the kingdom of Ayuthayā. These affinities can be explained both by the fact that post-Angkor Cambodia and Thailand shared a religion, Theravāda Buddhism, and also that the kingdom of Ayuthayā had achieved political preeminence in continental Southeast Asia starting in the mid-fourteenth century. Khmer works of this period are generally more severe than contemporary Thai works, however, and one senses clearly, particularly in the types of jewelry, their relationship to the great art of Angkor.

In its continuity with the so-called post-Bayon period and despite the profound changes in mentality that appear there, the post-Angkor period is a worthy successor to the earlier periods of grandeur and display, according to its techniques and new modes of expression. If one needed proof, the very beautiful statue of the kneeling worshiper from Angkor Vat (cat. 117), on its own, confirms the continuity in excellence demonstrated by Khmer sculptors throughout more than "a millennium of glory."

T.Z.

4. The most significant, on the subject of statuary, is GITEAU 1975.

113

Buddha

Preah Khan, north wing of *gopura* III east, Angkor (Siem Reap)
Angkor period, post-Bayon style, 2d half of the 13th–14th century
Sandstone
Height 178 cm, width 66 cm, depth 29 cm
Musée national des Arts asiatiques-Guimet, Paris, MG 18048

It was in the thirteenth century, apparently, that Theravāda Buddhism brought about the creation of a new type of Buddha image. These sculptures are collectively known as "Commaille Buddhas," after their discoverer Jean Commaille, the first French curator of the monuments at Angkor, who disappeared in 1916 under dramatic circumstances. These Buddhas were the first to draw widespread attention in the West. Their plasticity, at once supple and monumental, and the smiling, natural faces struck a more familiar chord with early scholars than the works now recognized as being more ancient, but which, being more highly stylized, were then considered "of inferior artistry."

The broad and delicately modeled face echoes the style of the Bayon, but the expression is entirely different. More relaxed and even prepossessing, it seems to betray a different set of religious concerns. The elegantly curved eyelids are lowered, directing a benevolent gaze toward the worshiper. The spirituality emanating from the face of this Buddha is above all else human and belongs to our world.

The hair consists quite properly of small curls, evenly covering both the head and the *uṣṇīṣa,* which is almost conical in memory of the earlier *uṣṇīṣa*-covers (cat. 91).

The *antaravāsaka* is held at the waist by a wide, flat, unornamented belt and clings to the Buddha's heavy legs. The sheer *uttarāsaṅga* closely molds to the shape of his body, but can be seen where it is not in contact with it. This distinguishes it from many older Buddha images where nothing indicates its presence (cats. 60, 73, 74, 94).

Using a technique characteristic of Dvāravatī art but appearing frequently in Khmer art after the Bayon period, the forearms were attached separately. The hands were very likely in a symmetrical position, without doubt in the gesture called *abhayamudrā,* or absence of fear.

T.Z.

114

Buddha

Kong Pisei (Kompong Speu)
Angkor period, style of the post-Bayon, 14th century
Bronze
Height 85 cm, width 28 cm, depth 12 cm
National Museum of Cambodia, Phnom Penh, Ga 2057

At the end of Jayavarman VII's reign, Buddhist commissions, in keeping with the imperatives of Theravāda Buddhism, were first directed toward the production of relatively simple works. That is what the representations of the Buddha of post-Bayon type, both in freestanding and bas-relief art, seem to reveal. Adorned Buddhas—already less numerous in Bayon style (cat. 95) than in that of Angkor Vat (cats. 73–76)—were rarely made. They only reappeared in great numbers, probably under the influence of Thai schools of art, after Angkor was abandoned by the monarchy in the first half of the fifteenth century (cat. 116).

Like the preceding "Commaille" Buddha (cat. 113), the bronze Buddha from Kong Pisei, from the iconographic and stylistic perspective, belongs to the still quite badly defined outlines referred to as "post-Bayon." This fringe period in Khmer art is far from having received the attention it deserves. One should be able to trace in it, as with Angkor styles from the tenth to the beginning of the thirteenth centuries, the evolution—perhaps the degeneration—of Brahmanic sculpture, which was then in its final phase in Cambodia, as well as the establishment and development of the specific iconography and aesthetic of Theravāda, the fulfilled formulas of which would characterize the art of the post-Angkor period.

If the beautiful face of the Kong Pisei Buddha relates in its proportions and sensitive modeling to the tradition of "Commaille" works—as can be noted for the body—it is also clearly distinct in some details. The eyes, for example, are treated simply, in tapering almond shape; the eyelids no longer have the characteristic and accentuated curve they had in the "Commaille" pieces. The lips are less full, and the smile is fixed in a more distant expression, close to that of most post-Angkor Buddhas.

The curls of hair seem miniaturized and simplified to the extreme, and are covered with a thick coating of lacquer, which may or may not be original. The special treatment of the curls is found in many metal works of the U Thong school in Thailand (from approximately the middle of the thirteenth to the middle of the fifteenth century), all composite styles.[1] The presence of the flame (*rasmi*) at the top of the *uṣṇīṣa*—a Sri Lankan influence in both Khmer and Thai sculpture toward the end of the thirteenth century—allows a more precise connection with style B of U Thong, which is characterized by precisely this element.

The simple monastic garment completely molding the form of the body offers no differences from that of the "Commaille" Buddha images: the *uttarāsaṅga* covers both shoulders and reveals through its transparency the *antaravāsaka* held at the waist by a wide flat belt.

If one really wishes to maintain a date in the second half of the thirteenth century or even the beginning of the fourteenth for the "Commaille" Buddhas, the Buddha of Kong Pisei, which seems logically to fit between those pieces and post-Angkor images, and taking account of what was said above, could belong to the fourteenth century. In any case it indicates the path to post-Bayon sculpture and introduces interesting information about the connections between Khmer and Thai art on the eve of the abandonment of Angkor.

Khmer Buddhist art after the Bayon period seems to have developed for rather a long time quite independently from Thai art and could have played a compelling role in the formation of the Thai art of Ayuthayā in its first manifestations of the U Thong school[2] (styles A and B).

T.Z.

115

Viṣṇu-Vāsudeva-Nārāyaṇa

North Khleang, Angkor Thom (Siem Reap)
Post-Angkor period, 16th century (?)
Bronze
Height 67 cm, width 22 cm, depth 21 cm
National Museum of Cambodia,
Phnom Penh, Ga 5457

The precise dating of this large, remarkably handsome bronze statue continues to present a puzzle to scholarship. The only thing experts can agree on is that it dates from the post-Angkor period.[1] This is a general term for the era after the conquest of Angkor by the Siamese in 1431, as a consequence of which the Khmer kings moved their capital to a location near what is today Phnom Penh. This implies that the bronze was cast at the earliest in the fifteenth century. It was fashioned in a curiously mixed style. The upper garment, which extends to the calves in two wraparound layers, is not familiar from figures of Khmer masculine deities, but it is known in bronzes originating in Thai workshops. On the other hand, both the cloth folded over in a semicircle beneath the navel and the broad belt are typically Khmer (cat. 68). However, nothing is known from either Thai or Khmer sources to compare with the ornamental treatment of the edges of the garment that hang down in front and back.[2] The broad flat necklace bears some resemblance to the splendid neck ornaments of the late Angkor period. Its triangular shape is typical of figures from the fifteenth to sixteenth centuries. The features, however, are again comparable to the bronzes of the Bayon style (thirteenth century). In the bas-reliefs of the southern gallery of the Bayon there are also parallels for the curious treatment of the hairstyle, where the strands of hair are passed upward through a pearl-studded band and a hollow cylinder at its center, and are then allowed to fall back again on the outside.[3] The shape of the hands and, above all, the way the fingers are disposed once again reveals a strong influence from Thailand.

In spite of the mixture of various stylistic elements, however, this bronze is without question a masterpiece. No other similar piece has yet been found to cast light on its origins. It was discovered in the North Khleang opposite the royal palace in Angkor Thom. It could have been placed in the building at that period in the sixteenth century when Angkor again briefly, in the reign of Ang Chan, became the royal seat and attempts were made to revive the greatness of the Khmer tradition. In this context the role of Viṣṇu as protector of the world may have gained renewed significance, for he was the ideal model for the king who performed the same function within his realm. There is no contradiction in the fact that at this time Theravāda Buddhism was the state religion. There were always Brahmans at the Buddhist courts, too, who had the duty of carrying out certain rituals associated with kingship.

Viṣṇu's attributes bear witness to his function as divine creator and protector of the world. Except for the orb in his lower right hand, which is peculiar to Southeast Asia, they are the same as those familiar from images of Viṣṇu in India since the earliest centuries A.D. The disk in his upper right hand, stylized here into a ring, had associations both with the sun disk and the discus as weapon. In Vedic times (third to second century B.C.) Viṣṇu was closely connected with the sun, the light and warmth of which make life and fertility possible. At the start of the Christian era, his aspect as a mighty king who carries his discus into battle against the enemies of law and order received greater emphasis. From about 600 the notion of the wheel of time, whose passage knows neither beginning nor end, was added as a new symbolic dimension of the disk. The conch in his upper left hand is both a container for holy water and also a wind-instrument for forming the sacred sound "oṃ." It symbolizes Viṣṇu's connection to the primordial ocean and to Nārāyaṇa, a link which can be traced back to the *Ṛgveda*. Viṣṇu's role as creator has close associations with water, as shown by the representation of him as Anantaśāyin (cat. 68). The mace in his lower left hand is short and carried upright. This has only commonly been so since the twelfth century. The earlier heavy form that emphasized its character as a weapon (cat. 31) gave way to the more peaceful image of a royal scepter. But in either form it signifies power and symbolizes Viṣṇu's ability to subject all beings to his will.

Although this bronze did not come into existence until several centuries after the Viṣṇu of Kapilapura (cat. 69), it still bears the same meaning as a representation of the highest god in his three aspects of Viṣṇu-Vāsudeva-Nārāyaṇa. While it is true that he does not bear the third eye on his forehead, the treatment of the hair behind the broad diadem is clearly a stylized version of the way the strands of hair of a *yogin* are bound into a high chignon. Its curious shape leads to further speculation. The hemispherical dome of the skull inside the diadem, which incidentally was also cast separately from the hairpiece, is totally smooth, like a polished surface. The upward-drawn strands of hair clearly come only from the center of the skull, which is otherwise clean shaven. Those who found the bronze in the North Khleang report that the hollow, cylinder-shaped center of the hairpiece contained pieces of gold leaf and rock crystal.[4] Such offerings are also found in reliquaries and *stūpa*. Was the bell shape of the hair crown also meant to evoke a *stūpa*?[5] It is quite possible that Brahmanic and Buddhistic elements are here intertwined.

W.L.

116

Bust of an Adorned Buddha

Provenance unknown
Post-Angkor period, 15th–16th century
Sandstone
Height 83 cm, width 49 cm, depth 32 cm
Musée national des Arts asiatiques-Guimet, Paris, MG 17825

The bust of this adorned Buddha is among the rare post-Angkor sculptures in stone. Often very large in size, these figures were generally composed of several stone blocks skillfully cut and assembled (Le Bonheur, *Cambodge*, 1989, 235, no. 150, and 245).

Following a tradition that first became widespread in the Angkor Vat period, the diadem around the Buddha's forehead is organized in horizontal bands. Although it lacks the more or less pronounced wings of the Thai images, the diadem is comparable to those found on adorned Buddhas of the Ayuthayā school. The chased pectoral necklace preserves ornamental elements from the twelfth century (cat. 74), in particular the bands of decoration and the large central flower.

The dominant pattern in both the diadem and the necklace is of vegetal scrolls with arabesque-like curves, replacing the diamond-shaped florets typical of the Angkor period. The outer border of the necklace as well as the inner band decorated with chevrons, though more simply rendered, owe their inspiration directly to the foliate pendants with incurving points and the intertwined rope motifs characteristic of the jewels in the style of Angkor Vat.

The conical *uṣṇīṣa*-cover, its surface embellished with incised motifs or relief carvings of lotus petals, typical of twelfth- and early thirteenth-century images, is gone. Replacing it is an unadorned domed head-covering surmounted by a kind of bulb with a tapering point, also plain, such as one finds in Ayuthayā art of the fifteenth and sixteenth centuries.[1]

As is often the case in post-Angkor statuary, the facial expression is serious, even severe. Without having either its grace or its gentleness, this Buddha's face can be compared with that of the worshiper from the National Museum of Phnom Penh (cat. 117) with its relatively flat frontal plane, its long, narrow mouth, and almost closed eyes.

There are few comparable works dated with any certainty, but this bust can be safely attributed to the fifteenth century, or the sixteenth at the latest.

Remnants of a coating, perhaps lacquer, form several large areas on the face and are probably the work of the faithful or monks who "maintained" the appearance of the figure when it was still an object of worship.

T.Z.

117

Worshiper

Angkor Vat (Siem Reap)
Post-Angkor period, 15th (?)–16th century
Wood
Height 91 cm, width 44 cm, depth 53.5 cm
National Museum of Cambodia,
Phnom Penh, Ga 315

Angkor was never, in historical terms, truly deserted. This is particularly true of the temple of Angkor Vat, where bas-reliefs in the northeast quadrant of the third enclosure are known to have been carved at a late date. In the middle and late sixteenth century, under the reign of Ang Chan, the site was reoccupied and new foundations created. Various works, among them the reclining Buddha from the east face of the Baphuon, are attributable to this period.

Various seated and kneeling postures are represented in Angkor iconography. A figure in meditation is generally shown sitting cross-legged (cat. 95), and in the case of an ascetic generally with the knees drawn up and held by a belt (Boisselier 1956, pl. IX). An attitude of homage is portrayed by a kneeling posture, hands joined in *añjali* (*sampaḥ* in Khmer), the buttocks resting on the heels (cat. 79), or in a very similar posture with one knee raised (cat. 78).

The image of a kneeling worshiper (more accurately, a seated one), his legs generally tucked under him on the right side, is therefore an innovation specific to the post-Angkor period, at least as an iconographic convention to express meditation, prayer, or humble homage to a divinity or cult object. Though wood was the material of choice during the post-Angkor period, there is a sculpture from Vat Tep Pranam at Udong (Giteau 1975, photo 21) that seems to be the equivalent in stone of the present worshiper from Angkor Vat.

The full, slightly elongated face is modeled with subtlety—the lips are fine, the nose slightly aquiline, the eyes almost slanted. The headdress has been transformed here into an enclosing head-cover, the upper portion of which has the aspect of a stylized lotus bud. The figure wears a short *sampot* held at the waist by a richly decorated belt with a long frontal panel, perhaps of embroidered cloth. Despite certain resemblances to the art of Ayuthayā, particularly in the jewelry and iconography, the face is typically Khmer. The peace and serenity manifested in its features, and the veneration naturally elicited by its great age, have rendered this statue of a worshiper, whose air of humility befits the Buddha's disciples, an object of worship in its own right. The spirit of Theravāda Buddhism, stripped of all metaphysical speculations and focused on a moral attitude, is admirably conveyed in this work. The former grand vision of the divine, embodied in the imposing monuments of Angkor, have given way to a natural modesty in which man is the measure. Paradoxically enough, mildness has gone hand in hand in Cambodia with an uncertain political future.

S.S.

Notes and Bibliographic References

1
(Inv. 1646, B 152 Groslier cat., B 101.16 Boisselier cat.)
• Notes
1. MG 17003, most recently published in Béguin 1992, 25.
• Selected bibliography
AAK 1924–1926, pl. IV
Bénisti 1981, 63 fig. 6, 64
Boisselier 1955 (1), pl. 86
Boisselier 1978, 260, ill. 124
Giteau 1960, 8–9, ill. 2
Groslier 1925 (1), 305, pl. 29 A
Groslier 1931, pl. III

2
(Inv. 1644, B 150 Groslier cat., B 10.8 Boisselier cat.)
• Notes
1. The sculpture is in the collection of the Historical Museum of Ho Chi Minh City (see *L'Art de L'Asie du Sud-Est* 1944, 498 fig. 433). Formerly dated fifth century, it seems likelier to be from the early seventh, or possibly late sixth century. Two other wooden Buddha figures may be older: an extremely eroded but tall and elegant Buddha and a statue from Dong Thap, both shoulders covered and making the gesture of *abhayamudrā*.
• Selected bibliography
Boisselier 1955 (1), pl. 88A
Boisselier 1966, 270–271, pl. XLI-3
Giteau 1960, 7–8, ill. 1
Groslier 1924–1926 (1), 211 fig. 57, 213, pl. III
Groslier 1925 (1), pl. 28B (without head)
Parmentier 1927, 325–326, fig. 117 (without head)

3
(Inv. 6449, B 878 Groslier cat., B 10.43 Boisselier cat.)
• Selected bibliography
L'Art bouddique 1990, 42 no. 3
Boisselier 1967 (2)
Brown 1996, 19–28
Canberra 1992, 38–39, cat. 4
Snellgrove (ed.) 1978, 163, fig. 118

4
• Notes
1. See Brown 1996, 19–65.
2. Cœdès, *IC* 4:108. *Mah vagga* I, 23/5, translated by Thānissaro Bikhu, Metta Forest Monastery. In French, translated by A. Barth, it reads "Les conditions qui proviennent d'une cause, d'elles le Thathagata a dit la cause, d'elles aussi ce qui est la suppression. Telle est la doctine du Grand Ascète."
• Selected bibliography
Boisselier 1955 (1), pl. 88B
Boisselier 1966, 270
Boisselier 1978, 260 no. 26
Dalet 1935, 156–157, pls. XXXII a, b
Dalet 1936 (1), 192–193, pl. LXVIII-2
Dupont 1955, pl. XLV B
Monod 1966, 126 fig. 47, pl. 127
Naudou 1973, ill. 269
Rarities of the musée Guimet 1975, no. 18, 47, ill. 52
Zéphir 1994, 162 fig. 440, 499

5
(Inv. 1019, E 215 Groslier cat., E/I 102.1 Boisselier cat.)
• Notes
1. See Dupont 1959, 631–636 and pls. LVI–LXIV.
2. The Buddhas of this tradition hold a fold of the upper-garment in the left hand and make the *vitarkamudrā* (discussion-of-the-doctrine gesture) with the right. See for example Boisselier 1974, 68–69 and 224 ill. 35 (Sungai Golok Buddha, Narathiwet, Thailand, H.R.H. Prince Bhanubandhu Yugala, Bangkok); and *Divine Bronze, Ancient Indonesian Bronzes from A.D. 600 to 1600* (Leiden, 1988), 53, no. 1 (Buddha from Kota Blater, East Java, Indonesia, Rijksmuseum, Amsterdam); A. Le Bonheur, "L'art du Champa," in *L'Art de l'Asie du Sud-Est* 1994, 258, and fig. 128 (bronze Buddha from Dông-du'o'ng, Quang-nam, Vietnam, Historical Museum of Ho Chi Minh City).
3. The statue was turned over to Henri Parmentier by the superior of the Banon Pagoda (Battambang) in February 1921, at which time it entered the National Museum of Phnom Penh.
4. See Thierry Zéphir, "A propos de quelques images javanaises du Buddha," in *Les ors de l'archipel indonésien* [exh. cat., Réunion des musées nationaux] (Paris, 1995), 50–53 and ills. 1 and 2.
5. See Boisselier 1991, 169–177, and pl. I.
• Selected bibliography
Boisselier 1966, 326 note 4
Dupont 1955, pl. XLV A
Giteau 1965 (1), 122, 123, pl. XII
Groslier 1925 (1), 297–314, pl. 30 B
Groslier 1931, 48, pl. XI-3
Zéphir 1994, 498 fig. 436

6
(Inv. 5929, E 1299 Groslier cat., E/I 10.118 Boisselier cat.)
• Selected bibliography
Boisselier 1966, 270–271, 326 note 4
Giteau 1965 (1), 117, 122, pl. XI
Zéphir 1994, 498 fig. 437

7
• Notes
1. See also the *caitya* (cat. 59), where the Buddha on *nāga* is accompanied by all three personages.
2. A bronze sculpture in the exhibition, however, shows another early example of an adorned Avalokiteśvara: cat. 9 has three medallions in his diadem.
• Selected bibliography
Béguin 1992, 64
Bénisti 1969, 109–111, 117 fig. 18
Boisselier 1955 (1), pls. 12, 15 B
Boisselier 1957 (1), 268–272, 269 fig. 11
Boisselier 1966, 238, 303, pl. XXXI-2
Boisselier 1978, 253 nos. 86–87
Dagens 1993 (3), 311 (ill.)
Duflos 1991, 99, 100 fig. 7
Finot 1925 (2), 237–238, pl. 16
Fort Worth 1996, no. 54, 60–61
Le Bonheur 1988 (2), 107
Le Bonheur 1989 (2), 123–125
Malleret 1942, 37–38, pl. IX
Malleret 1954, 249–262
Zéphir 1994, 497 fig. 428

8
• Selected bibliography
Boisselier 1967 (1), 296 fig. 17
Boisselier 1981, 11–24, figs. 1–5, 11

9
(Inv. 4430, E 988 Groslier cat., E/I 11.13 Boisselier cat.)
• Notes
1. Mallman 1948, 270.
2. Such as the reclining Viṣṇu from the pediment of Mi Son E1 now in the Museum of Cham Sculpture at Da Nang, see Boisselier 1963, fig. 9.
3. Such as the reclining Viṣṇu from the lintel at Tuol Baset (Battambang) now at the Vat Po Veal Museum, see Giteau 1965 (1), 50, fig. 15.
4. The standing Viṣṇu from Da-nghi, now in the Museum of Cham Sculpture at Da Nang, presents a remarkable example of a work in which the dress and headpiece perpetuate earlier traditions until about the eighth or ninth century. One would seek in vain for such an example in contemporary Khmer art.
• Selected bibliography
Boisselier 1955 (1), 279, pl. 103 B
Boisselier 1966, 303, 327 note 1
Dupont 1955, 138–139, and pl. XXII A
Giteau 1965 (1), 122–125
Groslier 1966, 52 and ill. 22

10
(Inv. ?, former 279 Vat Po Veal Museum)
• Notes
1. This work is not the one featured in the present exhibition. A very good reproduction of it can be found in Giteau 1965 (1), 127, pl. XIII.
2. M.C. Subhadradis Diskul, "Srivijaya Art in Thailand," *The Art of Srivijaya* (Paris, 1980), figs. 3 and 20.
3. Diskul 1980, fig. 20.
• Selected bibliography
Giteau 1965 (1), 125–126

11
• Notes
1. There has been recorded, to my knowledge, only one representation of Maitreya in stone dating from the pre-Angkor period. Even then it is a statue of Viṣṇu transformed into Maitreya at an undetermined date during the pre-Angkor period. On this subject, see Malleret 1959–1963, 4:39–40, 183–184, and pl. XXXVIII.
Among the bronze representations of Maitreya are a statuette from Prasat Ak Yum (Dupont 1955, pl. XXX fig. A) and several works of sculpture discovered on the Korat plateau and in Buriram Province, Thailand, some of which would seem to belong to the famous group of Mahāyāna bronzes clandestinely discovered at Prakhon Chai, Buriram Province, in 1965 (*Masterpieces of Bronze Sculptures* 1973, figs. 15 and 25; Boisselier 1974, 111–114 and ills. 73, 74, and 151; Chutiwongs and Leidy 1994, 12, no. 1).
2. See Boisselier 1967 (1), figs. 10, 11, 12, 13, and 14, showing the work before restoration (since Boisselier's article was written, the work has moved—it is now preserved at the National Museum in Bangkok); and *Treasures from the National Museum Bangkok* (Bangkok, 1987), 25, and ill. 31, showing the work after restoration.

• Selected bibliography
Boisselier 1971, 369–371
Boisselier 1993, 32 (ill.)
Duflos 1991, 98–99 and fig. 4
Fort Worth 1996, 61, no. 55
Le Bonheur 1972, 129–154
Masterpieces of Bronze Sculptures 1973, fig. 13
Zéphir 1994, 162, 498 fig. 432

12
• Notes
1. A *stūpa* is a structure comprising a domed base with a rodlike spire rising from its zenith. Its purpose is to protect a relic of the Buddha, homage to which draws pilgrims to the site.
2. See Chutiwongs and Leidy (1994, 70–72) for the legend of the monk Kasyapa and the *stūpa* in which he is buried on Mount Kukkutapada, where it is foretold that Maitreya will go, at the end of the current Buddhist era, to receive from the monk the robes of the Buddha that will authenticate Maitreya's role as the Buddha of the future.
3. Since a *stūpa* contains relics of the Buddha, it is a holy place whose configuration in Maitreya's headdress suggests the links between Buddha and Maitreya; one can only speculate about its possible additional symbolism. The implication could be, perhaps, that the relationship is based on the assumption that when the first era of Buddhism ends (as Buddha's physical existence has ended, with his relics enshrined in the *stūpa*), Maitreya will become the guardian of the holy relics and what they represent.
• Selected bibliography
Béguin 1986, 23
Boisselier 1967 (1)
Bunker 1971–1972, 68 fig. 19
Chutiwongs and Leidy 1994
Le Bonheur 1972, 129–154

13
(Inv. 3602, B 376 Groslier cat., B 31.5 Boisselier cat.)
• Selected bibliography
Bénisti 1981,64 fig. 7
Bhattacharya 1961, 113, pl. XXII
Boisselier 1955 (1), pl. 3
Boisselier 1956 (1), 29–30, pl. III
Canberra 1992, 32–33, no. 1
Duflos 1988, 36, 37 fig. 1
Dupont 1955, pl. I fig. A
Frédéric 1964, 235, 243 fig. 258
Giteau 1960, 9–10 and ill. 3
Giteau 1965 (1), 22 fig. 3, 35–36
Giteau 1992, xlix
Groslier 1966, figs. 24–25
Groslier 1968, 213 fig. B
Malleret 1942, 74, pl. XIX
Zéphir 1994, 161, 497 fig. 427

14
(Inv. 2052, B 253 Groslier cat., B 31.2 Boisselier cat.)
• Selected bibliography
Boisselier 1955 (1), pl. 1
Boisselier 1956 (1), 29–30, pl. III
Boisselier 1978, 254 no. 90
Duflos 1988, 35 fig. 3
Dupont 1941, 243–244, 252–253, pl. XXXIII
Dupont 1955, pl. XIX A
Giteau 1960, 13–14
Groslier 1966, 52, figs. 24–25
Groslier 1924–1926 (1), 207, fig. 56, 209
Groslier 1931, pl. XX
Malleret 1942, 62, pl. XVIII
Zéphir 1994, 161, 497 fig. 431

15
(Inv. 3371, B 343 Groslier cat., B 30.15 Boisselier cat.)
• Notes
1. The name of the Pāñcarātra sect is derived from the Sanksrit *pañca*, or five. The cult is concerned, among other principles, with the Five Elements, and requires the performance of five rites five times a day (Bhattacharya 1961, 97).
2. Some sects claim that there are more than twenty-four avatars of Viṣṇu.
3. The 1996 conservation of the Viṣṇu from Tuol Dai Buon has removed the clumsy and extraneous elements added during the original reconstruction, and has restored this masterpiece to its full glory.
4. In India the attribute symbolizing the earth is not the ball, as in Cambodia, but the lotus, another symbol of the earth (as well as of the ocean). Its eight petals are associated with the eight spatial directions.
• Selected bibliography
Bhattacharya 1961, pl. XIV
Boisselier 1955 (1), pl. II-2, pl. 10
Boisselier 1956 (1), 33–34, pl. IV
Boisselier 1966, 237 fig. 55 d, 238
Boisselier 1978, 254, no. 88
"Chronique," *BEFEO* 34 (1934), 749, pl. XVIII
Dupont 1955, pls. X A and B
Giteau 1960, 13
Parmentier 1935 (1), 29–30, pl. V

16
• Selected bibliography
AAK 1921–1923, 1 pl. IV
Aymonier 1901–1904, 1:200
Béguin 1992, 63 (ill.), 64
Bhattacharya 1961, pl. XXXI
Boisselier 1955 (1), pl. 7
Boisselier 1978, 253, no. 84
Cœdès 1910, 31, no. 3
Coral-Rémusat 1951, 89, pl. XXX no. 104
Czuma 1974, 121, fig. 8
Duflos 1991, 96, 97 fig. 2
Dupont 1955, pls. II A and B
Goloubew 1925
Le Bonheur 1986, 3 fig. 2
Lunet de Lajonquière 1902–1911, 1:14 fig. 54, 15
Mazzeo and Silvi Antonini 1972, 27–28
Monod 1966, 123, 124 (ill.), 125
Musée national des Arts asiatiques-Guimet 1993, 26
Parmentier 1927, 245, 317, fig. 110
Safrani 1977, 61
Stern 1939, 230–231, fig. 178
Zéphir 1994, 161, 495 figs. 417–418
Zimmer 1960, 515, fig. 514

17
• Selected bibliography
Bénisti 1970, fig. 26
Boisselier 1966, 146, 147 fig. 33-*a*
Boisselier 1978, 239, no. 29
Boisselier 1986, 177
Coral-Rémusat 1951, 41–42, pl. VI-fig. 13
Duflos 1988, 35 fig. 4
Dupont 1952, 31–83, fig. 5
Groslier 1961, 73 fig. 10, 74
Groslier 1968, 214–215 fig. E
Le Bonheur 1989 (1), 26 fig. 9, 29
Monod 1966, 149–150, fig. 65
Parmentier 1927, 60, fig. 6-A
Zéphir 1994, 158, fig. 80

18
(Inv. 635, B 30 Groslier cat., B 712.1 Boisselier cat.)
• Selected bibliography
Boisselier 1955 (1), pl. 13
Boisselier 1955 (2), 20 fig. 1, 28–29
Dagens 1993 (1), 293
Dupont 1955, pl. XXIII B
Giteau 1960,16–17
Giteau 1965 (1), 47 fig. 13, 48
Giteau 1992, li
Groslier 1924–1926 (1), 202–203 fig. 49, pl. IX A
Le Bonheur 1989 (1), 24 fig. 6
Parmentier 1927, fig. 88
Zéphir 1994, 158, 201 fig. 79

19
(Inv. 786, B 45 Groslier cat., B71.1 Boisselier cat.)
• Notes
1. This topic is discussed by Boisselier (1955 [2], 19 and 13), who in addition analyzes information and suggestions on the subject made earlier by Stern and Cœdès.
• Selected bibliography
Bhattacharya 1961, pl. VII
Boisselier 1955 (1), pl. XV fig. 1, pl. XXI fig. 4, pl. XXIX fig. 1, pl. 14
Boisselier 1955 (2), 21 fig. 2, 29–31
Boisselier 1956 (1), 37–38, pl. V
Boisselier 1966, 237 fig. 55 b–e, 239
Boisselier 1978, no. 89, 254
Boisselier 1986, 178, fig. 2
Dupont 1955, pls. XXIV B, XXV B
Frédéric 1964, 248, 257 fig. 277
Frédéric 1994, 364 (ill.), 365
Giteau 1960, 17–18
Giteau 1965 (1), 48, 49 fig. 14, 50–51, 200 no. 4, 202 no. 10, 212 no. 40
Groslier 1961, 59 (ill.), 74
Groslier 1921, fig. 224
Groslier 1924–1926 (1), 205–206 fig. 54, 215
Groslier 1931, pl. XXV
Lunet de Lajonquière 1902–1911, 1:xciv, xcv fig. 44 (copy from the Musée du Trocadéro), 192
Parmentier 1912, 16 (under no. 13.2 [s.1])
Parmentier 1927, fig. 89

20
(Inv. 834, C 44 Groslier cat., C 30.17 Boisselier cat.)
• Selected bibliography
Bénisti 1970, figs. 111–112
Bhattacharya 1961, pl. I
Boisselier 1956 (2), 199 fig. 1
Boisselier 1966, pl. XXXII-1
Bosch 1931
Dupont 1952, 45 fig. 12, 52–60
Dupont 1955, pl. XXVII
Giteau 1965 (1), pl. I
Parmentier 1927, 88, fig. 34
Zéphir 1994, 160, 494 fig. 413

21
(Inv. 4951, D 103 Groslier cat., D/I 38 Boisselier cat.)
• Notes
1. The summit of the mountain above Vat Phu was used for cult worship probably even before the Indianization of the Khmer land. The site was then used by Śivaites and became something of a national Khmer sanctuary. See Bhattacharya 1961, 20–22 and 38–39.
2. *IC* 5:73.
• Selected bibliography
IC 5:73–74 (K. 940)
Giteau 1966 (1), 148

22
• Notes
1. The inscription appears in A. Barth, "Stèle de Vat Phou," *BEFEO* 3 (1902), 235–240. This inscription dates to the second half of the seventh century and contains an encomium to Jayavarman I, as well as an ordinance on the subject of Liṅgaparvata, the ancient name of Vat Phu hill in what is now Laos.
A good reproduction of the decorated portion of this stele is reprinted in Boisselier 1966, pl. XXX-3.
• Selected bibliography
Cœdès 1910, 30, no. 162, pl. VIII

23
(Inv. 2947, C 118 Groslier cat., B 41.8 Boisselier cat.)
• Notes
1. The base, which is square, represents Brahmā; the octagonal middle section represents Viṣṇu; and the circular upper one, Rudra. Together these comprise the supreme form of Śiva.
• Selected bibliography
Canberra 1992, 42–43, no. 6

24
(Inv.?, B 86 Groslier cat., B 48.1 Boisselier cat.)
• Selected bibliography
Canberra 1992, 36–37, no. 3
Commaille 1902, 267
Giteau 1960, 5–6
Giteau 1965 (1), 41 fig. 10
Lan Sunnary 1991, 94 note 28, fig. 1
Lunet de Lajonquière 1902–1911, 1:69, fig. 69
Parmentier 1912, 22 (as no. S 19.1)

25
• Notes
1. There are seven stars in the constellation of the Pleiades, but one is invisible and is omitted from the myth.
2. The snake represents the cycle of the year; the peacock is also the slayer of time.
3. For traces of Gupta style, note in particular the Phnom Da–like, isolated, fat curls and the long ear-lobes. Dupont suggests the seventh century and Le Bonheur even proposes the sixth as a possible date for this Skanda's creation.
• Selected bibliography
Aymonier 1901–1904, 1:241, 246
Bénisti 1981, 64 fig. 8
Boisselier 1966, 291, pl. XLVIII-1
Boisselier 1978, 255 no. 95
Cœdès 1910, 32 no. 7
Lunet de Lajonquière 1902–1911, 1:53 fig. 64

26
(Inv. 2033, B 251 Groslier cat., B 51.6 Boisselier cat.)
• Notes
1. The swastika, exhibiting development in multiple directions, shows the progress from the center, the unity, to the periphery, but the movement is deflected so that the external point does not reveal the direction of the center. This is perhaps related to the belief common in the Indicized areas of Indonesia that the forces of evil can travel only in straight lines, and that the inner core of a space can be protected by a baffle such as a step or wall that precludes direct access.
2. A. Okada and P. Mukherjee, *Ganesh, La Mémoire de l'Inde* (1955), 117–120.
3. The rat is significant because his domain is the interior of places; it offers another metaphor for the contest between malice and intelligence. The interdependence of the immense being with the minuscule, of course, recalls Aesop's fables.
4. Later Gaṇeśa images are richly adorned with jewelry and diadems; see cat. 109.
• Selected bibliography
Bhattacharya 1961, pl. XXVII
Dupont 1955, pl. XXI D
Giteau 1960, 6
Groslier 1931, pl. XXXIII-1

27
(Inv. 669, B 113 Groslier cat., B 45.1 Boisselier cat.)
• Selected bibliography
Boisselier 1955 (1), pl. II fig. 3, pl. XXIX fig. 2, pl. 17-8
Boisselier 1956 (1), 41–42, pl. VI
Boisselier 1966, 241 fig. 56 g, 242
Boisselier 1978, 254 figs. 92–93
Boisselier 1981, 18–19 figs. 9–10
Boisselier 1986, 178, 180 fig. 1
Coral-Rémusat 1951, 89, pl. XXX, no. 105
Dupont 1955, pls. XXXIII A, XXXIV A
Frédéric 1964, 248, 260 fig. 281
Giteau 1965 (1), 55–56 figs. 17–18, 204 no. 16, 210 no. 34
Giteau 1992, xlix
Groslier 1924–1926 (1), 206 fig. 56, 207, 215
Groslier 1931, pl. XXIII
Groslier 1961, 71 (ill.), 77
Groslier 1968, 213 fig. C
Malleret 1942, 79, pl. XXV
Naudou 1978, 29 fig. 16
Parmentier 1927, 268, 317–318, fig. 87 (photograph of the Musée Guimet cast)
Stern 1932, 515–516, pl. lxviii a
Stern 1939, 231 fig. 179
Zéphir 1994, 162, 206 figs. 85–87, 497 fig. 430
Zimmer 1960, figs. 517–519

28
• Selected bibliography
Aymonier 1901–1904, 1:252
Boisselier 1966, 242, pl. XXXII-2
Boisselier 1978, 255 no. 97
Cœdès 1910, 7 no. 3
Dupont 1934, 60 nos. 1–2, pl. III fig. b
Dupont 1955, pls. XXXIX A and B
Le Bonheur 1986, fig. 3
Lunet de Lajonquière 1902–1911, xciv, xcv fig. 45
Mazzeo and Silvi Antonini 1972, 32
Monod 1966, 125–126
Parmentier, 1927, 245, 322
Stern 1939, 229–230, fig. 177
Zéphir 1994, 499 fig. 439
Zimmer 1960, fig. 516

29
• Selected bibliography
Béguin 1992, 64, 65 (ill.)
Boisselier 1955 (1), pl. 24-B
Coral-Rémusat 1951, 89, pl. XXX no. 103
Cœdès 1910, 9, no. 14, pl. II
Dupont 1934, 60–61, nos. 1–3
Dupont 1955, pl. XXXII A and B
Groslier 1968, 213 fig. A
Lunet de Lajonquière 1902–1911, 1:192
Monod 1966, 125–126 fig. 46
Parmentier 1927, 213–214, 245, 302 fig. 103, 321–322
Rarities of the Musée Guimet 1975, 48, no. 20, 54 (ill.)
Zimmer 1960, figs. 512–513

30
• Selected bibliography
Béguin 1986, 24
Béguin 1992, 67
Boisselier 1955 (1), pls. IV-3, 26
Boisselier 1967 (1), 296 fig. 18
Coral-Rémusat 1951, 90, pl. XXXI no. 106
Dagens 1989, 168 (ill.)
Dalet 1936, pl. XLIV A-B
Groslier 1968, 215 fig. H
Malleret 1942, 74, pl. XXII-2
Monod 1966, 48
Naudou 1978, pl. IV fig. 3, pls. 26, 29 A
Zéphir 1994, 164, 499 fig. 442

31
(Inv. 6176, B 846 Groslier cat., B 30.30 Boisselier cat., D 311.93 former Louis Finot Museum, Hanoi)
• Selected bibliography
Boisselier 1955 (1), pl. 27
Boisselier 1978, 255 nos. 98–99
Boisselier 1986, 182 fig. 2
Giteau 1960, 21
Groslier 1966, 73 fig. 31
Marchal 1939, 61

32
• Selected bibliography
Béguin 1986, 26
Le Bonheur 1986, 6–7 fig. 7
Monod 1966, 151 fig. 67, 152
Musée national des Arts asiatiques-Guimet 1993, 28
Stern 1938 (1), 143, pl. XLVII
Zéphir 1994, 212 fig. 91

33
(Inv. 5703, B 789 Groslier cat., B 40.5 Boisselier cat.)
• Selected bibliography
Boisselier 1955 (1), pl. 33
Boisselier 1956 (1), 49–50, pl. VIII
Boisselier 1966, 244, pl. XXXIV-1
Boisselier 1978, 256, no. 100
Boisselier 1986, 187 fig. 1
Giteau 1960, 23–24
Frédéric 1964, 280, 298 fig. 296

34
(Inv. 5638, B781 Groslier cat., B 30.26 Boisselier cat.)
• Selected bibliography
Alvares 1992, 30–31, 32 fig. 4
Bhattacharya 1961, pl. XVI
Boisselier 1955 (1), pl. V fig. 3
Boisselier 1966, 246, 247 fig. 57-e
Cœdès 1962 (1), pl. IX (right)
Giteau 1960, 22–23
Zéphir 1994, 168–169, 503 fig. 455

35
• Selected bibliography
Le Bonheur 1986, 7 fig. 6
Monod 1966, 128, 158, 159 fig. 74

36
(Inv. 2887, B 289 Groslier cat., B 42.4 Boisselier cat.)
• Notes
1. The majority of female garments are in the style of Angkor Vat: smooth and decorated with florets.
• Selected bibliography
Boisselier 1955 (1), 285–287, pl. 35 A
Dupont 1936 (1), 424–425, pl. XLIX A
Giteau 1960, 24
Giteau 1965 (1), 66
Groslier 1931, 80, pl. XXVII-1,
Jacques 1988, 68 (ill.)
Parmentier 1919, 42, pl. IV B
Zéphir 1994, 170, 503 fig. 454

37, 38, 39
• Notes
1. The four sanctuary towers of the temple of Lolei, whose name outlives the former name of the royal city of Hariharālaya, were consecrated in 893. Built on an island in the approximate center of the Indratatāka, the brick towers of Lolei were raised to benefit Yaśovarman's ancestors in the next world (compare cat. 36).
2. Angkor's eastern *baray*, which appears in ancient inscriptions as Yaśodharatatāka, was both a useful public work that served to irrigate the rice paddies and a sacred basin. Measuring 4.3 miles (7,000 m) from east to west and 1.1 miles (1,800 m) from north to south, it remained the largest reservoir at Angkor until the western *baray* was built some 150 years later.
3. The name of Angkor's first capital, Yaśodharapura (the city where glory resides), is a reminder of the name of its founder. According to one theory, disputed by Groslier 1979, the city measured four kilometers on each side and was surrounded by an earthen levee, or perhaps two, as well as by a system of moats, with only the southwest corner of this arrangement, long ago transformed into rice paddies, not entirely disappearing in the course of the site's successive transformations.
4. The city of Yaśodharapura was in all likelihood organized around *phnom* (*bhnaṃ*) Bakheng. On top of this hill, some two hundred feet (60 m) in height, Yaśovarman built a temple-mountain of considerable symbolic complexity (see Filliozat 1944, 527–554). The central tower of this temple (there were 109 in all) contained the *liṅga* Yaśodhareśvara. On Phnom Bakheng, see also Dumarçay, *Phnom Bakheng*, 1971.
5. On these two temples dedicated to the *trimūrti*, see Glaize 1963, 262–268.
6. Originally, the image of Brahmā was in the south sanctuary tower, the one of Śiva in the central tower, and the one of Viṣṇu in the north tower.

7. See Bhattacharya 1961, 60, 67–68, 126, pls. XXV–XXVI.
• Selected bibliography
Béguin 1986, 28 (ill., Brahmā)
Boisselier 1955 (1), 107, pl. XXII-2 (not 3 as stated in the caption), pls. 40 A (Śiva) and 40 B (Brahmā)
Boisselier 1966, 246–247, 290, pl. XXXIV-2 (Brahmā)
Boisselier 1978, 256, no. 104 (Brahmā)
Cœdès 1910, 20 nos. 88 (Śiva), 87 (Brahmā), and 89 (Viṣṇu)
Coral-Rémusat 1951, 91, pl. XXXVI-fig. 124 (Śiva)
Croizier 1875, 100, no. XI (Śiva); 98–99, no. VI, 113 (pl.) (Brahmā); 101, no. XII (Viṣṇu)
Delaporte 1880, 125 (ill., Śiva); 126, 341 (ill., Brahmā); 126 (Viṣṇu)
Dupont 1934, 69, nos. 2–6 (Śiva); 68, nos. 2–5 (Brahmā); 69, nos. 2–7 (Viṣṇu)
Dupont 1936 (1), 415–426, pls. LIII-A (Śiva) and LIII-B (Brahmā)
Monod 1966, 131 (triad)
Musée national des Arts asiatiques-Guimet 1993, 23, 28, 29 (ill., Śiva)
Zéphir 1994, 171–172, 503 figs. 457 (Śiva), 456 (Brahmā), and 458 (Viṣṇu)

40
• Notes
1. See Boisselier 1952, 253–256. The head of this sculpture was stolen several years ago, see *Cent objets disparus* 1993, 94.
2. A work now in the National Museum of Phnom Penh (Ka 1770; former B 877 [Groslier cat.], B 45.8 [Boisselier cat.], inv. 6447 for the body; former B 874 [Groslier cat.], B 451.2 [Boisselier cat.], inv. 6403 for the body). This sculpture represents an important benchmark in pre-Angkor art, for it can be dated to around 706 thanks to the inscription of Prasat Phum Prasat.
3. A work now in the National Museum Phnom Penh (former B 829 [Groslier cat.], B 45.3 [Boisselier cat.], D 311.76 [former Louis Finot Museum, Hanoi], inv. 6159).
• Selected bibliography
Boisselier 1989, 44–49
Zéphir 1994, 172, 214 figs. 95–96

41
• Selected bibliography
Aymonier 1901–1904, 3:75, 76 fig. 11
Boisselier 1955 (1), pls. XV-5 and 39 A
Cœdès 1910, 34, no. 19
Dupont 1934, 66, no. 2-2
Dupont 1936 (1), 415–426, pl. LVI-B
Monod 1966, 128
Stern 1927, 151–152, pl. 22-B

42
(Inv. 1818, B 214 Groslier cat., B 403.3 Boisselier cat.)
• Notes
1. In his *La statuaire khmère et son évolution* (1955), 198, Boisselier mentions an eight-armed statue. Yet Parmentier's description of the extant fragments leaves no doubt that the statue in fact had ten arms.
2. In particular, four other hands that are almost complete: a left hand holding a circular shield; a left hand holding a cranial orb; a right hand holding a halter; a right hand holding the hilt of an unknown attribute; and a fragment of a left hand holding a human head (the dimensions of this fragment, which, regrettably, could not be seen at the National Museum of Phnom Penh, would seem to identify it as one of Śiva's hands).
3. In particular, one of the four lower faces, as well as a right hand holding the handle of an unknown attribute.
4. Boisselier 1966, 1:287. See also Bhattacharya 1961, 85–87, on the subject of the dancing Śiva and the five-headed and ten-armed forms of this god.
• Selected bibliography
Bhattacharya 1961, 87
Boisselier 1955 (1), 198
Boisselier 1966, 248, 286
Canberra 1992, 48–49, no. 8
Frédéric 1964, 282, 303 fig. 305
Giteau 1960, 30
Giteau 1965 (1), 73
Groslier 1931, 94, pls. XXXIV-3 and 4
Parmentier 1939, 41–43, pl. XVIII A

43
• Notes
1. Parmentier 1939, 44–45.
2. Parmentier mentions the "splayed thighs" of the Śiva figure, which seems to indicate a similar attitude to the Devī's. The position would in any case correspond to that of the dancing Śivas carved in bas-relief on certain lintels and pediments, for instance on *gopura* I east of the temple of Banteay Srei.
3. The reason sculptors of the Koh Ker period were compelled to represent jewelry (necklaces, abdomen belts, bracelets, ear pendants) more often than their predecessors seems to be that the treasury was low. As the inscriptions confirm, the ornaments were generally of metal—gold, silver, or gilt bronze—and a scarcity of these metals could effectively explain the more frequent representation in stone. And yet there is no other evidence that the Khmer empire was experiencing difficulties of this nature at this time. Perhaps it is wisest simply to see the fact as another instance of the originality of the Koh Ker style.
• Selected bibliography
Béguin 1986, 29 (ill.)
Béguin 1992, 69
Cœdès 1910, 19–20, pl. VII
Croizier 1875, 96, no. IV
Delaporte 1880, 99 (ill.), 100
Dupont 1934, 70, nos. 2–8
Dupont 1936 (1), 415–426, pl. LIX
Groslier 1968, 217 fig. N
Monod 1966, 130–131
Parmentier 1939, 44–45

44
(Inv. 4947, B 759 Groslier cat., B 702.56 Boisselier cat.)
• Selected bibliography
Boisselier 1955 (1), pl. XXIX fig. 5, pl. 46
Boisselier 1956 (1), 61–62, fig. XI
Canberra 1992, 52–53 no. 10
Giteau 1960, 28
Giteau 1965 (1), 61 fig. 25, 73
Parmentier 1939, 50, pls. XXIII A and B
Zéphir 1994, 507 fig. 469

45
• Notes
1. The east lintel of Prasat Neang Khmau at Koh Ker has one of the rare solitary representations of Brahmā. See Parmentier 1939, pl. XXXVI A.
2. For instance, the pedestal in the south sanctuary tower at Phnom Krom.
• Selected bibliography
Aymonier 1901–1904, 1:403, fig. 75
Aymonier 1901–1904, 2:298
Boisselier 1955 (1), pl. 42 A
Boisselier 1966, 283
Boisselier 1993, 18 (ill.), 19
Cœdès 1910, 29, no. 156
Dagens 1989, 68, 69 (ill)
Dupont 1934, 67–68, pl. V
Dupont 1936 (1), 415–426, pl. LVII
Groslier 1968, 216 fig. L
Le Bonheur 1988 (2), 108 (ill.)
Monod 1966, 130, fig. 50
Stern 1927, 13–15, 151, pl. 18

46
• Selected bibliography
Aymonier 1901–1904, 1:372
Béguin 1992, 70
Boisselier 1966, 249, pl. XXXV-1
Cœdès 1910, 9 no. 15
Dupont 1934, 66–67 nos. 2–3, pl. III fig. C
Goloubew 1927, fig. 10
Le Bonheur 1974, pls. 4–5
Le Bonheur 1986, 10 fig. 9
Le Bonheur 1989 (1), 46 fig. 21
Lunet de Lajonquière 1902–1911, 1:xcvii, 233, fig. 47
Monod 1966, 128, 130 fig. 49
Parmentier 1927, 245
Rarities of the Musée Guimet 1975, 49 no. 23, 57 ill. 23
Zéphir 1994, 179, 507 fig. 471
Zimmer 1960, fig. 520

47
(Inv. 6188, B 850 Groslier cat., B 731.8 Boisselier cat., D 311.65 former Louis Finot Museum, Hanoi)
• Selected bibliography
Boisselier 1966, 293, pl. XLVIII-2
Canberra 1992, 56–57 no. 12
Marchal 1939, 81–82

48
(Inv. 2144, C 96 Groslier cat., C 36.16 Boisselier cat.)
• Selected bibliography
Canberra 1992, 62–63 no. 14
Giteau 1966 (1), 100–101
Mazzeo and Silvi Antonini 1978
Michell 1988
Parmentier 1939

49
(Inv. 5727, C 346 Groslier cat., C 30.32 Boisselier cat.)
• Selected bibliography
Giteau 1966 (1), 59–60

50
(Inv. 5467, C 317 Groslier cat., C 32.10 Boisseilier cat.)
• Notes
1. Balarāma was the seventh avatar of Viṣṇu and also an incarnation of Śeṣa, or Ananta, the serpent on which Viṣṇu rested during cosmic sleep.
2. The form of the tree behind the combatants is reminiscent of the *kekayon* or *gunungan* (tree-form and mountain-form, in their Javanese version) placed in the center of the scene for a shadow play performance. The shadow play is still performed in Cambodia today, particularly episodes from the *Rāmāyaṇa* (in its Khmer version of the *Reamker*) and the *Mahābhārata*, and it is interesting to speculate about the connection between the elements of the architectural legacy and the evolution of the puppet forms.
• Selected bibliography
Boisselier 1966, 250, pl. XXXV-3
Boisselier 1978, 237 no. 22
Broman 1976, 36 (ill.)
Canberra 1992, 64–65 no. 15
"Chronique," *BEFEO* 35 (1935), 487, pl. LXXII
Cœdès 1935
Coral-Rémusat 1951, 78–79, pl. XXV no. 91
Giteau 1960, 32–33, ill. 13
Giteau 1965 (1), 69 fig. 31, 79–80, 238 no. 119
Giteau 1966 (1), 72 (ill.), 76–77
Giteau 1976, 47, 48 ill. 20, 269
Groslier 1961, 119 (ill.)
Le Bonheur 1989 (1), 63 ill. 34, 71 no. 34

51
• Selected bibliography
Auboyer 1968, pl. XXIX
Béguin 1986, 31
Béguin 1992, 50 (ill.), 71–72
Cœdès 1932 (2)
Coral-Rémusat 1951, 78–79, pl. XVII no. 57
Le Bonheur 1986, 12–13, fig. 10
Monod 1966, 146–147 fig. 64, 148–149

Musée national des Arts asiatiques-Guimet 1993, 23 (ill.)

52, 53, 54, 55
• Notes
1. One can also mention in this connection, however, the coiffure of the *yakṣa*. As has been pointed out by Coral-Rémusat (1940, 100), there seems to have been a tendency toward archaism in the sculpture of Banteay Srei. The *yakṣa*'s head silhouette suggests a diadem, but the profile is shaped by large, isolated spiral curls such as those found on Phnom Da sculpture three centuries earlier; it could therefore also be considered an example of the trend to revive past idioms.
• Selected bibliography
Most publications about Khmer art and architecture deal with Banteay Srei. The four guardian figures are discussed here in the context of the architecture and symbolism of the monument. The general bibliography contains further references. For the iconography of the creatures, see:
Bosch 1959
Boisselier 1992

56
(Inv. 870, B 24 Groslier cat., B 43.1 Boisselier cat.)
• Selected bibliography
Bhattacharya 1961, 83, pl. II
Boisselier 1955 (1), pl. XXIV fig. 1, pl. 49 A
Boisselier 1978, 257, no. 106
Boisselier 1986, 197 (ill.)
Canberra 1992, 58–59 no. 13
Cent objets disparus 1993, 6 (ill.)
"Chronique," *BEFEO* 18 (1918), 64
Dagens 1989, 154 (ill.)
Duflos 1988, 52 (ill.)
Finot, Goloubew, and Parmentier 1926, 6, 51–52, pls. 44 A and B
Giteau 1960, 31–32, 67, ill. 11
Giteau 1965 (1), 64, fig. 28
Giteau 1976, 191 fig. 117, 260
Groslier 1931, pl. XXIX
Groslier 1961, 114 (ill.)
Groslier 1988, pl. 23
Le Bonheur 1989 (1), 64 ill. 37, 72
Parmentier 1919, 79, pl. XII
Zéphir 1994, 181, 221 fig. 102, 507 fig. 470

57
• Selected bibliography
Le Bonheur 1974, 179–204
Zéphir 1994, 182 fig. 491, 512

58
• Notes
1. See, for example, R. Billard, *L'astronomie indienne* (Paris, 1971).
2. Also Maṅgala.
3. Also Bṛhaspati (the lord of prayer).
4. Mitra 1965, 13–37.
5. The attribute of our personage is certainly stylized and could correspond to a kind of mirror. However, Kamaleswar Bhattacharya firmly identifies it as the halter. See, for example, the piece from Tuol Don Srei at the National Museum of Phnom Penh (Malleret 1960, 222, fig. 12) or the series from Prasat Neang Khmau, also kept in Phnom Penh (Malleret 1960, 213, fig. 6).
6. *IC* 5:59 (K. 752). Malleret 1960, 213, fig. 4.
• Selected bibliography
Bhattacharya 1956, 183–193, fig. 1
Cœdès 1910, 44, no. 104, pl. XII
Dupont 1934, 78–79, nos. 3–7
Malleret 1960, 218, 228
Monod 1966, 158

59
• Notes
1. Finot 1925 (2), 251
2. Finot 1925 (2), 252. The inscription concerned is that on the *caitya* of Thma Puok, dating from the year 989.
3. Boisselier 1966, 98. On the form of the *stūpa*, see Marchal 1954.
4. So named in the inscription of Thma Puok; see note 2.
5. Dupont 1950, 43, 45, figs. 2–3.
• Selected bibliography
Boisselier 1966, 98, 302–304, pls. XV-3, XLII-3
Boisselier 1978, 237 no. 18
"Chronique," *BEFEO* 22 (1922), 329
Dupont 1934, 92 nos. 3–35
Finot 1925 (2), 252–254, pl. 25
Monod 1966, 157, 159 fig. 73
Zéphir 1994, 182, 566 figs. 492–495
Zimmer 1960, fig. 566

60
(Inv. 3456, B 364 Groslier cat., B 10.20 Boisselier cat.)
• Notes
1. It is notable that the Indic imagery that most successfully pervaded the cultures of Southeast Asia was connected to those countries' fundamental chthonic symbols, such as the *nāga* (in Indonesia as well as in Cambodia), the mountain, and the tree (Jessup 1990, 49–71).
2. For a complete account of the iconography see cat. 76.
• Selected bibliography
Boisselier 1955 (1), pl. 93
Boisselier 1956 (1), 81–82, pl. XVI
Boisselier 1966, 272, pl. XLIII-1
Boisselier 1978, 261 no. 130
Dupont 1950, 55 fig. 12 (wrong caption)
Giteau 1960, 36–37
Zimmer 1960, figs. 558–559

61
(Inv. 770, D 25 Groslier cat., D /I 9 Boisselier cat.)
• Notes
1. Their ancestor, the royal priest Śivakaivalya, was a well-known figure living in the time of Jayavarman II, who is himself mentioned in the inscription under his posthumous name, Parameśvara. On the subject of Śivakaivalya, see, for example, the Sdok Kak Thom inscription, published, for one, by Cœdès and Dupont 1943–1946, especially 57–134. The Sdok Kak Thom stele, in the National Museum of Bangkok, is illustrated, for example, in Siribhadra, Moore, and Freeman 1992, 201.
• Selected bibliography
Boisselier 1952, 247
Boisselier 1955 (1), 292
Boisselier 1966, 287
Canberra 1992, no. 21, 78–79
Cœdès 1913, 27–36, pls. XI (face A)–XII (face B)
Finot 1932, 255–259, pl. XX
Giteau 1966 (1), 134–135
Groslier 1921, 2, pl. IIC
Groslier 1931, pls. XXXV-1, 96
IC 2:141 ff (K. 449)
Parmentier 1913, 43

62
• Selected bibliography
Bhattacharya 1956, 183–194
Bhattacharya 1958 (1), 220
Bhattacharya 1964, 91–94
Malleret 1960, 205–230

63
• Notes
1. From the eighth century, the arch imitating wood in previous lintels was replaced by a foliate roll that is, in fact, a stylized and explicit lotus rhizome.
2. The stylization is not unlike the treatment of *wadasan*, or rock motifs, in Chinese painting and porcelain.
• Selected bibliography
Cœdès 1910, 34 no. 23
Dupont 1934, 76–77 nos. 3–4
Monod 1966, 153

64
(Inv. 1352, C 77 Groslier cat., C 30.19 Boisselier cat.)
• Selected bibliography
Boisselier 1966, 154, 155 fig. 38-b
Boisselier 1978, 246 no. 53
Canberra 1992, cat. 22, 80–81
Giteau 1966 (1), 47–48, 63 (ill.)
Groslier 1931, pl. XXXVI-3

65
(Inv. A 34 B seems to be an inventory number from the Museum of Vat Po Veal, Battambang)
• Selected bibliography
Canberra 1992, cat. 19, 74–75

66
(Inv. 4949, B 761 Groslier cat., B 32.9 Boisselier cat.)
• Selected bibliography
Boisselier 1955 (1), pl. 57 B
Boisselier 1956 (1), 73–74, pl. XIV
Boisselier 1960, 236 fig. 4
Boisselier 1986, 202 fig. 2
Canberra 1992, cat. 20, 76–77
Frédéric 1964, 286, 315 fig. 325
Giteau 1960, 35–36
Giteau 1965 (1), 87, cat. 27, 207
Giteau 1976, 168 fig. 104
Le Bonheur 1989 (1), 89 fig. 31
Zéphir 1994, 514 fig. 501

67
• Selected bibliography
Giteau 1965 (1), 119 fig. 74, 134
Monod 1966, 136
To our knowledge, this piece must have been published by A. K. Coomaraswamy at the beginning of the century, but we have not yet been able to find out in which book or article.

68
(Inv. 5456, E 1229 A, B, C Groslier cat., E/I 30.17 Boisselier cat.)
• Notes
1. The similarity of this account of creation through the formation of order from chaos to the Judeo-Christian theory in Genesis is a reminder that primordial myths tend to be universal.
• Selected bibliography
Béguin 1986, 31
Boisselier 1955 (1), pl. XXXII, fig. 2, pl. 106
Boisselier 1956 (1), pl. XV, 77–78
Boisselier 1966, 327, 338, pl. LVII-2
Boisselier 1967 (1), fig. 4
Broman 1976, 36 (ill.)
Canberra 1992, cat. 17, 68–71
Coral-Rémusat 1938, 172–173, pl. LVI no. 9
Frédéric 1964, 286, 316 fig. 326
Giteau 1965 (1), 134, 135 pl. XV
Giteau 1976, 120, 265, 119 ill. 69
Giteau 1992, L
Groslier 1961, 129–130, 130 (ill.)
Le Bonheur 1989 (1), 8 ill. 5, 16 no. 5, 78 ill. 46, 93 no. 46
Mazzeo and Silvi Antonini 1972, 89
Zéphir 1994, 186, 227 fig. 109
The number Ga 5387 in the Phnom Penh Museum also includes various elements (Inv. 5457, formerly E 1230 Groslier cat., formerly E/I 30. 18 Boisselier cat.): A to J and thirty small fragments that belonged to this piece.
A: fragment of the lower back with smooth *sampot* and jeweled belt, profile of a left leg. L.: 100 cm
B: front part of a leg, slightly bent. L.: 94 cm
C: fragment of a leg. L.: 100 cm
D: fragment with a pendant (shoulder?). H.: 27 cm L.: 29 cm

E: fragment with a pendant, fitting together with D. H.: 14 cm L.: 10 cm
F, G, H, I, J: unidentified fragments.
Respectively L.: 30 cm, 20 cm, 14.5 cm, 15 cm, 11 cm. The dimensions of the thirty small fragments are not indicated on the inventory index cards.

69
(Inv. 2388, E 594 Groslier cat., E/I 50.1 Boisselier cat.)
1. A particularly fine comparable piece is located in the Museum für Indische Kunst, Berlin (Inv. no. II 1139). See Lobo 1997 (2).
2. Cœdès 1954, 132–139.
3. In the case of Indian statues, they are symbolized by the four heads of Viṣṇu: the forward-facing human head, the lion's head growing from the right shoulder, the backward-facing demon head, and the boar's head springing from the left shoulder.
4. *BEFEO* 24 (1924), 654, pl. XXV.
• Selected bibliography
Boisselier 1955 (1), pl. 107 B
Boisselier 1978, 258 no. 114
Canberra 1992, cat. 23, 82–83
"Chronique," *BEFEO* 24 (1924), 645, pl. XXV
Groslier 1931, pl. XXXVII-1

70
(Inv. 1868, B 232 Groslier cat., B 30.7 Boisselier cat.)
• Selected bibliography
Boisselier 1952 (2), 241, fig. 31
Boisselier 1955 (1), pl. X-1, 51, pl. 62 A
Boisselier 1956 (1), 88 fig. XVII, 89–90
Boisselier 1966, pl. XXXVII-1
Boisselier 1978, 258, no. 113
Giteau 1960, 39
Giteau 1965 (1), 90
Groslier 1931, pl. XXVII-2, 80
Le Bonheur 1989 (1), 123, 125 fig. 35
Zéphir 1994, 191, 520 fig. 527

71
(Inv. 6187, B 849 Groslier cat., D 311.57 ex-Museum Louis Finot, Hanoi, B 71.11 Boisselier cat.)
• Notes
1. It is also possible that the attributes were real, at least in the case of the flowers.
• Selected bibliography
Boisselier 1952 (2), 239, pl. XIV
Boisselier 1955 (1), pl. 64 B
Marchal 1939, 81

72
• Notes
1. In the very oldest images, other arrangements of the symbolic attributes may be found, but they remain very rare. See Bhattacharya 1961, 105–106.
2. On Hari Kambujendra, see, for instance, Bhattacharya 1965.
• Selected bibliography
Bénisti 1965, 104, note 1
Bhattacharya 1961, 111
Cœdès 1910, 10, no. 19, pl. VIII
Croizier 1875, 114, no. XXXV
Delaporte 1880, 69, 359–360 (ill.)
Dupont 1934, 95, nos. 3–39
Monod 1966, 157

73
(Inv. 1353, B 128 Groslier cat., B 10.7 Boisselier cat.)
• Selected bibliography
AAK 1924–1926, 2:pl. VI
Boisselier 1955 (1), pl. 94
Boisselier 1956 (1), 85–86, pl. XVII
Boisselier 1966, 274, pl. XLIII-2
Boisselier 1978, 261, no. 131
Boisselier 1986, 207 (ill.), 208
Canberra 1992, cat. 24, 84–85
Dupont 1950, 54, 55 fig. 10
Giteau 1960, 39–40, ill. 14
Groslier 1931, pl. VII, 1–2

74
• Notes
1. The Buddha was meditating under the bodhi tree when a violent storm broke out. So absorbed was he in his meditation that he did not realize that the nearby waters of Lake Mucilinda were about to swallow him up. But the *nāga* of the lake, also called Mucilinda, coiled himself around the Buddha and shielded him with his heads (seven, in classical mythology), thus protecting the Buddha from the waters.
2. In the case of stone images where this attribute is missing, we may well wonder whether the attribute was not detachable as with so many others in Khmer art.
• Selected bibliography
Aymonier 1901–1904, 1:333, fig. 27
Cœdès 1910, 11–12, no. 24
Croizier 1875, 94–95, no. II
Delaporte 1880, 349
Dupont 1934, 80, nos. 3–9
Dupont 1950, 52 note 28
Le Bonheur 1989 (1), 123, 126 fig. 36
Monod 1966, 137
Zimmer 1960, fig. 561

75
(Inv. 5933, E 1302 Groslier cat., D32.140 ex-Museum Louis Finot, Hanoi, E/I 10.119 Boisselier cat.)
• Notes
1. An almost identical bronze figure is located in the National Museum in Bangkok. Woodward 1980, 163 fig. 3.
2. Boisselier 1955 (1), pl. 113 B.
3. Boisselier 1966, 275, pl. XLIII, 3, and Woodward 1979, 72–83, esp. figs. 1 and 11.
4. This is clearly demonstrated by the many stone stele and terracotta plaques, showing as their central figure a Buddha, either adorned or unadorned, surrounded by scenes from the life of Śākyamuni.
5. Mus 1928, 153–278.
6. Cœdès 1908 (2), 247, inscription C, 1. The translation by Cœdès from the Sanskrit into French reads as follows: "Le Buddha resplendit... ayant obtenu la royaut impérissable—la Bodhi—, ce roi suprème se réjouit dans son palais splendide—le Nirvana."
• Selected bibliography
Boisselier 1950 (2), 304–305, pl. VII
Boisselier 1955 (1), pl. 113 B
Boisselier 1966, 274–275, pl. XLIII-3
"Chronique," *BEFEO* 34 (1934), 746, pl. XIV
Marchal 1939, 89

76
(Inv. 5952, E 1320 Groslier cat., D 32.107 ex-Museum Louis Finot, Hanoi, E/I 10.125 Boisselier cat.)
• Notes
1. Discovered in 1933 by G. Trouvé. Cœdès 1941, 262.
2. In the inscriptions of Prah Khan and Ta Prohm, Cœdès 1941, 283.
3. Chutiwongs 1984, 390, note 86.
4. Cœdès 1941, 283–284.
5. Inscription of Vat Sithor, paragraph XXIX. Cœdès 1954, 205.
6. Lama Anagarika Govinda 1973, 140–143.
7. Boisselier 1963, 326.
8. Maspero 1928, 164–169.
• Selected bibliography
Boisselier 1963, fig. 222, 225
Groslier 1961, 166, 167 (ill.)
Marchal 1939, 98

77
(Inv. 2884, E 654 Groslier cat., E/II 40.20 Boisselier cat.)

78
(Inv. 1143, E 291 Groslier cat., E/I 61.1 Boisselier cat.)
• Selected bibliography
Boisselier 1955 (1), pl. 109
Broman 1976, 36 (ill.)
Canberra 1992, cat. 25, 86–87
Frédéric 1964, 288, 322 fig. 335
Giteau 1965 (1), 141, 144, 147 pl. XVII
Groslier 1921, pl. XXVII
Groslier 1931, 108 pl. XLI, 109 (ill.)
Jacques and Dumont 1990, 33
Zéphir 1994, 521 fig. 532

79
(Inv. 2320, E 563 Groslier cat., E/I 61.3 Boisselier cat.)
• Selected bibliography
Canberra 1992, cat. 26, 88–89
Giteau 1965 (1), 150
Groslier 1931, 56 pl. XV-2, 57 ills. 2–3

80
• Selected bibliography
Béguin 1992, 73
Boisselier 1966, 339
Boisselier 1978, 263, no. 141
Le Bonheur, 1989 (1), 123, 127 fig. 37
Monod 1966, 139, 140 fig. 58
Musée national des Arts asiatiques-Guimet 1993, 24 (ill.)
Zéphir 1994, fig. 535

81
• Notes
1. The oldest sculpture of lions in the round now known belong to the Kulen style (first to third quarters of the ninth century). See, for example, the lions of the main sanctuary tower of the central complex at Sambor Prei Kuk, reproduced in Coral-Rémusat 1951, pl. XLII, fig. 149.
2. For example, the great lions at the foot of the *phnom* (*bhnaṃ*) Bakheng, reproduced in Jacques 1990, 58.
3. For example, at the temple of Lolei at Roluos, reproduced in Jacques 1990, 56.
• Selected bibliography
Boisselier 1966, 312, pl. LIV-fig. 4
Boisselier 1967 (1), 320–321, fig. 29
Cœdès 1910, 13, no. 36
Croizier 1875, 109, no. XXVIII
Delaporte 1880, 375
Dijon 1996, 76 no. 16
Dupont 1934, 124, nos. 4–34
Monod 1966, 142–143, fig. 61, 143

82
• Notes
1. The *nāga*, a product of the realm of water, is also associated with prosperity in the agricultural societies of Southeast Asia. In Cambodia, where water is present everywhere, either naturally or artificially, the *nāga* plays a prominent role in legends relating to the mythical origins of the kings.
2. The earliest examples of *nāga* sculpture in the round currently known are those of the temple of Bakong, consecrated in 881.
• Selected bibliography
Cœdès 1910, 24, no. 123
Croizier 1875, 110, no. XXXI
Dijon 1996, 73 no. 17
Dupont 1934, 96, nos. 3–41
Monod 1966, 144–145, 144 fig. 62
Rarities of the musée Guimet 1975, 49 no. 24, 58 fig. 24.
Safrani 1977, 61

83
• Notes
1. *Garuḍa* is well known as the vehicle to the god Viṣṇu. Freestanding sculpture of *garuḍa* is rare in Khmer art. The most spectacular examples are those from Bakong—of which we have only the base—and from Koh Ker, one of which is in the National Museum in Phnom Penh (fig. 4, p. 16). In both cases, the *garuḍa* are depicted in dynamic attitudes behind a gigantic body of

a *nāga* resting directly on the ground, in an association with the same symbolism seen in the balustrades with *nāga* and *garuḍa* from the Bayon period.
• Selected bibliography
Cœdès 1910, 13, no. 34
Coral-Rémusat 1951, 100–101 [Note: An error having crept into the identification of the illustrations, the *garuḍa* on a *nāga* of pl. XL-fig. 143 is not MG 18107]
Croizier 1875, 110, no. XXX
Delaporte 1880, 335
Dijon 1996, 74 no. 18
Dupont 1934, 121–122, nos. 4–29
Monod 1966, 145, fig. 63, 144

84
• Notes
1. For example, at the corners of the terraces of pyramids of the East Mebon (953) and Pre Rup (961).
• Selected bibliography
Boisselier 1966, 310
Boisselier 1967 (1), 321–325, fig. 33
Cœdès 1910, 15, no. 45
Croizier 1875, 110–111, number XXXII
Delaporte 1880, 85
Dijon 1996, 75 no. 19
Dupont 1934, 72, nos. 2–12
Lunet de Lajonquière 1902–1911, 1:252, and fig. 136
Monod 1966, 145

85
• Selected bibliography
Cœdès 1910, 14, no. 38
Croizier 1875, 111–112, no. XXXIII
Delaporte 1880, 74, ill. 75

86
• Notes
1. Preah Khan of Angkor, consecrated in 1191, and, of somewhat later date though still in the reign of Jayavarman VII, the great provincial temple of Banteay Chmar and the city of Angkor Thom.
2. See Paul Mus, "Angkor in the Time of Jayavarman VII," *Indian Arts and Letters* 11, 1, 65 ff.
3. On this subject, see Le Bonheur 1989 (1), 195–196.
• Selected bibliography
Cœdès 1910, 26, no. 135
Croizier 1875, 106–107, no. XXIV

87
• Selected bibliography
Beguin 1992, 74
Cœdès 1910, 26, no. 136
Croizier 1875, 106–108, no. XXIV
Dijon 1996, 77 no. 20
Dupont 1934, 120–121, nos. 4–27
Monod 1966, 170

88
• Selected bibliography
Aymonier 1901–1904, 3:150, fig. 22
Béguin 1992, 78
Cœdès 1910, 24 no. 117
Croizier 1875, 118–119 no. LII
Dagens 1989, 69
Delaporte 1880, 142
Dijon 1996, 79 no. 23
Dupont 1934, 117 nos. 4–20
Le Bonheur 1986, 16–17 fig. 17
Monod 1966, 167 fig. 81, 168

89
(Inv. 6334, B 857 Groslier cat., B 191.7 Boisselier cat.)
• Selected bibliography
Auboyer 1959, figs. 2–3
Boisselier 1978, 259 fig. 118
Canberra 1992, cat. 29, 94–95
Cœdès 1960, 191–193, 192 fig. 8, 193 figs. 9–10
Dagens 1989, 17
Dagens 1993 (2), 312
Frédéric 1964, 293, 337 fig. 361
Giteau 1960, ill. 17
Giteau 1965 (1), 93 pl. IX, 102–105, 105 figs. 64–65
Giteau 1992, LIII
Groslier 1961, 168, 170 (ill.)
Jacques and Dumont 1990, 130 (ill.)
Stern 1965, 172–174, 189–194, figs. 198, 198 bis–199
Zéphir 1994, 492 fig. 405

90
• Notes
1. In addition to this piece, two other heads are known (cat. 89 and a head intercepted in Battambang in 1989 as it was on its way to the art market) as well as a complete statue, unfortunately without the arms, in the National Museum of Phnom Penh (fig. X, p.X). A complete statue, also without the arms, is in the Archaeological Museum of Phimai in Thailand; finally there is a body without a head at That Luang of Vientiane in Laos (personal communication from M. A. Le Bonheur).
• Selected bibliography
Béguin 1992, 77
Cœdès 1960, 188–191, 190 figs. 6–7
Fort Worth 1996, no. 61, 65
Foucher 1912 (2), 218, pl. XV
Monod 1966, 161
Rarities of the musée Guimet 1975, 49–50 no. 25, 59 fig. 25
Stern 1965, 170–175, 189–194, fig. 200

91
• Notes
1. Cœdès 1947, 197–199.
2. Cœdès 1942, 295–296.
3. Cœdès 1942, 298.
• Selected bibliography
Cœdès 1960, 196–197, 196 fig. 13
Dupont 1934, 116, nos. 4–18, pl. VII b
Le Bonheur 1989 (1), 196 fig. 51, 222
Monod 1966, 161 fig. 77, 163
Naudou 1973, 271 (ill.).
Stern 1939, 234, fig. 182 (center)
Stern 1965, 172–174, 189–194
Zimmer 1960, fig. 560

92
• Notes
1. Other than the present piece (discovered at Preah Khan in Angkor in 1929), a kneeling figure apparently representing the same person was discovered at Phimai near one of the two complete statues of Jayavarman VII that we know of; an image of the same kind comes from the *dharmaśālā* of Preah Khan at Angkor, where it was discovered in 1927; and finally, one was found in the brush on the outskirts of Angkor Thom, not far from the place where the complete statue of Jayavarman VII now in the National Museum of Phnom Penh was discovered. See Cœdès 1960, 193–194.
2. *IC* 2:161–181.
3. *IC* 2:178, stanza LXXV of the Phimeanakas stele.
• Selected bibliography
Béguin 1992, 76 (ill.), 77
Boisselier 1955 (1), pl. XXVI-2 (without the image of Amitābha and mistakenly designated as the Lakṣmī from Preah Koh), pl. 77 B
Boisselier 1966, 257, fig. 62b (without the image of Amitābha and by mistake designated as the Lakṣmī from Preah Koh), 258, nd pl. XXXVIII-2
Boisselier 1978, 259, no. 120
"Chronique," *BEFEO* 29 (1929), 515
Cœdès 1960, 193–194, 195 fig. 11
Cœdès 1962 (1), pl. X (on the right)
Dagens 1989, 19 (ill.), 108
Dagens 1993 (2), 312–313, 312 (ill.)
Duflos 1991, 96, 97 fig. 3
Dupont 1934, 125–126, nos. 4–37, pl. VIII
Finot 1931, 32–33, pl. II B
Fort Worth 1996, 65–66, no. 62
Giteau 1965 (1), 101, 199 (ill. cat. 3)
Giteau 1976, 206–208, 208 fig. 126
Jacques 1988, 71 (ill.)
Le Bonheur 1989 (1), 196, 223 fig. 53
Monod 1966, 161–163, 164 fig. 78
Stern 1939, 234–235, fig. 183
Stern 1965, 170–175, 189–194, fig. 189
Zéphir 1994, 196, 520 fig. 529

93
(Inv. 4999, B 770 Groslier cat., B 12.4 Boisselier cat.)
• Selected bibliography
Boisselier 1952 (4), 265, pl. XXIV B
Boisselier 1955 (1), pl. 74
Boisselier 1956 (1), 101–102, pl. XXI
Canberra 1992, cat. 32, 100–101
Cœdès 1947, ill. opp. p. 54
Cœdès 1960, 182, 183 fig. 1
Giteau 1960, 48–49, ill. 19
Giteau 1965 (1), 100 fig. 63, 102

94
• Selected bibliography
Béguin 1992, 74, ill. 75
Cœdès 1910, 12, no. 25, pl. III
Croizier 1875, 93–94, no. I
Dagens 1989, 169 (ill.)
Delaporte 1880, 250
Dupont 1934, 114–115, nos. 4–15
Fort Worth 1996, 64 no. 60
Groslier 1924–1926 (2), 100, pl. 17 B
Monod 1966, 137, 138 fig. 57
Naudou 1973, ill. 133
Zimmer 1960, fig. 557

95
(Inv.? Prajñāpāramitā alone, Ga 5470, also former 7193 DCA)
• Notes
1. Groslier 1966, 244–245 fig. 142, 280.
2. Text of the inscription kindly provided by Saveros Pou, Paris.
3. Cœdès 1941, 260–261.
4. Cœdès 1941, 262.
• Selected bibliography
Groslier 1966, fig. 142

96
(Inv. 2387, E 593 Groslier cat., E/I 11.9 Boisselier cat.)
• Notes
1. Cœdès 1941, 284. The translation into French recorded there is as follows: ". . .Lokeśvara est victorieux, vivante incarnation de l'arbre du Paradis."
2. Finot 1925 (2), 227–256.
3. Chutiwongs 1984, 319.
4. Chutiwongs 1984, 319–320.
• Selected bibliography
Boisselier 1955 (1), pl. 110 B
Groslier 1931, pl. XVII

97
• Notes
1. Chutiwongs 1984, 47, 48, 327.
2. Boisselier 1964, 73–83, figs. 1–3, 6 photos.
3. An entire figure, almost identical and nearly contemporary, is located in the temple of Bot Brahm in Bangkok. There is a similar one, though of later date, in the royal palace in Phnom Penh. Illustrated in Cœdès 1923, pl. XXXII (Phnom Penh), pl. XXXIII (Bangkok).
4. The bronze figure in the royal palace in Phnom Penh (see note 3) is carrying a conch as well as a wheel, thus revealing a distinct tendency towards "Viṣṇuisation." Cf. Le Bonheur 1992, 113.
5. Boisselier 1964, 78.
6. Boisselier 1964, fig. 3, ill. 3.
7. Extract from the *Kāraṇḍavyūha*, trans. Mallmann 1948, 43–45.
8. Le Bonheur 1992, 112–113.

• Selected bibliography
Le Bonheur 1992, 112–113, 55 (ill.)
Musée national des Arts asiatiques-Guimet 1993, 24 (ill.)

98
• Notes
1. Linguists disagree on the meaning of "Avalokiteśvara." Interpretations include: "He who looks down from above," "He who looks with compassion," and "The greatly compassionate." The other names by which the Bodhisattva is known are easier to translate: "Padmapāni," or bearer of the *padma* (pink lotus), which is in fact an epithet of Avalokiteśvara, and especially "Lokeśvara," or lord of the world, the name most often used in Khmer epigraphy.
2. See Finot 1925 (2), 227–256; and Boisselier 1965 (1), 73–89.
3. While the virtual absence of images from the ninth century and the first half of the tenth is conceivably due to the vagaries of preservation, Buddhist commissions nonetheless declined enormously during that period.
4. The Bodhisattva was given numerous forms in both contemporary relief carvings and freestanding sculpture. He frequently appears in triads alongside the Buddha and Prajñāpāramitā, and it is to him that Jayavarman VII consecrated the temple city of Preah Khan at Angkor (1191), which he built for the spiritual well-being of his father.
5. Where complete figures survive, the bracelets, anklets, and rings on each toe are also carved with a series of miniature effigies, often of the Buddha.
• Selected bibliography
Boisselier 1966, 303, pl. LII-2
Cœdès 1910, 14, no. 42, pl. IV
Croizier 1875, 95–96, no. III
Dagens 1993 (2), 312–313, 312 (ill.)
Delaporte 1880, 78
Dupont 1934, 131, nos. 4–49
Fort Worth 1996, no. 59, 63–64
Le Bonheur 1989 (1), 199, 225 fig. 56
Monod 1966, 165, 166 fig. 79

99
(Inv. 1426, E 329 Groslier cat., E/I 13.1 Boisselier cat.)
• Notes
1. Lobo 1997 (1).
• Selected bibliography
AAK 1921–1923, 1:pl. XXV, XXVI
Boisselier 1955 (1), pl. 111
Boisselier 1967, fig. 1
Boisselier 1978, 258 no. 115
Boisselier 1986, 211
Canberra 1992, cat. 33, 102–103
Frédéric 1964, 290, 328 fig. 344
Giteau 1965 (1), 139 fig. 85, 146
Giteau 1976, 26 ill. 11, 271
Groslier 1931, pl. XII
Le Bonheur 1989 (1), 226 fig. 57
Stern 1965, fig. 202
Zéphir 1994, 521 fig. 534
Zimmer 1960, fig. 563

100
• Notes
1. *Hevajratantra*, II, v, 26: Snellgrove 1959, 111.
2. Lobo 1997 (1).
3. *Hevajratantra*, II, vi, 3–4: Snellgrove 1959, 114.

101
(Inv. 6294, E 1510 Groslier cat., E/I 13.17 Boisselier cat.)
• Notes
1. Cf. Groslier 1974, 200, ill. 42.
• Selected bibliography
Groslier 1961, 183 (ill.), 184

102
(Inv. ? former 7192 A et B DCA)
• Notes
1. There is a bronze mold in the collection of the National Museum of Phnom Penh, Ga 5651; see Groslier 1931, pl. XLVI. Another mold of this type is to be found in the collection of the National Museum in Bangkok; see Boeles 1966, fig. 4.
2. Boeles 1966, 21.

103
• Notes
1. Such images are extremely rare. In a private collection in Berlin there is a bronze, as yet unpublished, showing Prajñāpāramitā in the dance, surrounded by eight *yoginī.*
• Selected bibliography
Dupont 1934, 106–107 nos. 3–70
Monod 1966, 139, 140 fig. 59, 141

104
(Inv. 2074, E 468 Groslier cat., E/I 12.4 Boisselier cat.)
• Notes
1. A comparative piece is illustrated in Cœdès 1923, pl. XXXV, 3.
2. *The Large Sutra on Perfect Wisdom*, Conze 1975, 156.
3. Obermiller 1988, 65–66.
4. Obermiller 1988, 69, note 4.
• Selected bibliography
Canberra 1992, cat. 31, 98–99
Giteau 1965 (1), 150
Groslier 1931, pl. XV-1

105
(conch: Inv. 1064, E 229 Groslier cat., E/II 10.2 Boisselier cat.; tripod: Inv. 1062, E 227 Groslier cat., E/II 14.5 Boisselier cat.)
• Notes
1. Groslier 1931, 110, pl. XLII.
2. *Hevajratantra*, 1:IX. Snellgrove 1959, 79–80.
3. Boisselier (1966, 333–334) considers the *yoginī* as proof of the use of the conch as a receptacle for holy water. This is hard to believe in view of the hole at the end of the spiral.
• Selected bibliography
AAK 1921–1923, 1:pl. XXI-B
Boisselier 1966, 333–334, pl. LVIII-2
Canberra 1992, cat. 34, 104–105
Giteau 1965 (1), 145 fig. 87
Giteau 1976, 229 ill. 138
Groslier 1931, pl. XLII-1
Zéphir 1994, 521 fig. 531

106
• Notes
1. Groslier 1921–1923, 226, pl. 11. Groslier does not mention the identity of the figures. To judge from the extremely unclear illustration, they could well be Lokeśvara and Prajñāpāramitā.
2. In literal translation, the Sanskrit word means "he who is hard (mighty)."
3. Cœdès 1908 (2), 237.
4. Lama Anagarika Govinda 1973, 62–64.
5. Lama Anagarika Govinda 1973, 25–27. Cf. in a Christian context: "In the beginning was the Word, and the Word was with God, and the Word was God. . . And the Word was made flesh."
6. Boisselier 1966, 335.
7. Cœdès 1954, 195 ff.
• Selected bibliography
AAK 1921–1923, 1:226, pls. D–E

107
(Inv. 5640, B 783 Groslier cat., B 32.10 Boisselier cat.)
• Notes
1. *IC*, 2:161–181.
• Selected bibliography
Boisselier 1952 (4), 261–273, pl. XXV B
Boisselier 1955 (1), pl. 73 B
Boisselier 1956 (1), 105–106, 104 fig. XXII
Boisselier 1966, 295
Cœdès 1960, 194, 195 fig. 12
Giteau 1960, 49

108
(Inv. ? former 4861 A, B, C, D, DCA)
• Notes
1. Bhattacharya 1961, 147, and Cœdès 1951, 180–192.
2. Cœdès 1947–1950, 147–150, pl. XXXIII-1 (National Museum of Phnom Penh, E 120, Groslier cat.).
3. Cœdès 1947–1950, 97–119.

109
(Inv. ? former 7671 DCA)
• Notes
1. Bhattacharya 1961, 134.
2. Pou 1987–1988, 346.
3. Ellul 1980, 69–154.

110
(Inv. ? former 222 DCA?)
• Notes
1. The place of provenance of this object was certainly recorded in its curator's file report, but it has not been possible to find this report—though this does not necessarily mean it has disappeared for good. Many objects now in the National Museum of Phnom Penh were not photographed at the time of their accession, and without their old accession numbers it is presently impossible to determine their origin in all cases. (The number 222 on the pedestal does not correspond to number 222 in the Groslier catalogue.) Once the museum's entire inventory has been computerized, the task will of course become possible. Among the objects for which information is missing are the following: objects accessioned long ago but not photographed (in several cases, the description alone is insufficient); objects accessioned in the 1960s or later for which no curator's report was made, or for which the curator's report was lost; objects brought to the museum in the early 1970s for safekeeping (the deposit records, if any existed, have been lost), many of which came from the Depot for the Conservation of Angkor or from provincial museums such as those in Battambang.

111
(Inv. ? former 7210 DCA)
• Notes
1. Bhattacharya 1961, 87, fig. XXV.
2. Bagchi 1929.
3. Filliozat 1981, 91–92.
4. Mitra 1933. Srinivasan 1987, 338–340.
5. For example, in the inscription of Prasat Chrung southeast, K. 597. See Filliozat 1981, 71.

112
• Notes
1. Banerjee informs us that the episode is recounted in the *Brahmāpurāṇa*, the *Kālikāpurāṇa*, and the *Śivapurāṇa* (1964, 80).
• Selected bibliography
Banerjee 1964
Béguin 1992, 79
Monod 1966, 170

113
• Selected bibliography
Boisselier 1955 (1), pls. XIX-4 89, 96 B
Boisselier 1966, 277
Boisselier 1978, 262, no. 136
"Chronique," *BEFEO* 28 (1928), 516
"Chronique," *BEFEO* 30 (1930), 225
"Chronique," *BEFEO* 31 (1931), 645 no. 7
Dupont 1934, 113–114, nos. 4–14
Dupont 1935, 63–75, pl. XXV-1
Le Bonheur 1988 (1), 98–100, 99 (ill.)
Le Bonheur 1989 (1), 243, fig. 59
Monod 1966, 165–166, fig. 80
Stern 1965, fig. 204

114
(Inv. 3362, E 795 Groslier cat., E/I 10.93 Boisselier cat.)

• Notes
1. See Boisselier 1974, 162–170, and particularly ill. 121.
2. The influence of the Khmerized art of Lopburī has long been recognized in the matter. Perhaps one has not sufficiently taken into account, however, the possible contribution to the formation of the U Thong school by Buddist art that developed within the already reduced frontiers of the Khmer Empire in the thirteenth and fourteenth centuries.
• Selected bibliography
Boisselier 1955 (1), 282–283, pl. 113 A
Boisselier 1966, 277
Boisselier 1967 (1), 283, 293 fig. 8
Boisselier 1986, 227
Dalet 1936 (2), 195, pl. LXVIII-1
Giteau 1965 (1), 152, pl. XVIII, 153

115
(Inv. 2389, E 595 Groslier cat., E/I 30.8 Boisselier cat.)
• Notes
1. Giteau 1975, 308.
2. Giteau 1975. Giteau considers a Cham influence possible.
3. Giteau 1975.
4. *BEFEO* 25 (1925), p. 217, pl. XXXc.
5. On the form of the *stūpa* in Cambodia, see Marchal 1954.
• Selected bibliography
Groslier 1931, pl. XL
Giteau 1975, 308, pl. XLII, ill. 116

116
• Notes
1. For example, the very beautiful head of an adorned Buddha, the so-called Camondo head (EO 1622) in the Musée Guimet. The *uṣṇīṣa*-cover consists of several tiers but is otherwise of the same type as the one on the stone bust presently being considered.
• Selected bibliography
Dupont 1934, 138, nos. 5–7

117
(Inv. 3459bis, J 186 Groslier cat., J 11.4 Boisselier cat.)
• Selected bibliography
Boisselier 1955 (1), pl. 85
Boisselier 1956 (1), 113–114, pl. XXIV
Frédéric 1964, 294, 341 fig. 368
Giteau 1960, 57, ill. 20
Giteau 1965 (1), 182–184, 182 fig. 98, 185 pl. XXIII.
Giteau 1975, 140–141, ill. 22, pl. XXI fig. a–d
Groslier 1961, 191 (ill.), 192
Jacques and Dumont 1990, 164
Le Bonheur 1988 (1), 100 (ill.), 101
Le Bonheur 1989 (1), 244, 243 fig. 60
Zéphir 1994, 248 fig. 127

Glossary

A

• *Abhayamudrā:* Buddhist gesture signaling the absence of fear: right hand raised, palm out.
• *Abhiṣeka:* a ritual for the consecration of a king; an annointing ritual.
• *Ācārya:* a spiritual teacher, deeply learned in the sacred texts.
• *Ādibuddha:* the supreme and original Buddha.
• *Agni:* deity of fire; guardian (*dikpālaka*) of the southeast.
• *Airāvata:* a three-headed elephant, Indra's mount; like the *apsaras,* Dhanvantari (the physician of the gods), Śri / Lakṣmī (the goddess of beauty and fortune) and others, Indra's mount was born out of the churning of the Sea of Milk.
• *Ak Yum:* Brahmanistic temple built in the seventh to eighth centuries south of the western *baray*; the first temple mountain.
• *Akṣamālā:* rosary used for Buddhist and Hindu prayers.
• *Akṣar mūl:* script of modern Khmer.
• *Akṣobhya:* (the imperturbable, the unshakable), one of the five Jina (the East), usually shown in *bhūmisparśamudrā.*
• *Amarāvatī:* early center of Buddhism in India.
• *Amitābha:* (infinite light), one of the five Meditation Buddha or Jina (victors) of Mahāyāna Buddhism, appears in Avalokiteśvara's headdress.
• *Amoghasiddhi:* (the incorruptible, whose success is infallible), one of the five Jina (the North), usually represented in *abhayamudrā.*
• *Amṛta:* the nectar of immortality derived by the *deva* and *asura* from the churning of the Sea of Milk.
• *Ananta:* (without end), also *Śeṣa* (who stays), mythological snake on whose back Viṣṇu sleeps between cosmic cycles or *kalpa.*
• *Anavatapta:* mythological Himalayan lake of Buddhist cosmology; around its circumference, four "aspects" (lion, horse, elephant, and bull) give rise to four rivers that water the four cardinal points.
• *Ang Chan I:* (r. 1516–1566).
• *Angkor:* (royal city, from the Sanskrit *nagara*), current name for the site that functioned as the Khmer capital from the early tenth century to 1431, the date traditionally given for its abandonment.
• *Angkor Borei:* (the royal city that is a holy city), current name for a site thought to be one of the capitals of Funan.
• *Angkor Thom:* (the royal city that is large), current name for the walled city built on the site of Angkor by Jayavarman VII at the end of the twelfth century.
• *Angkor Vat:* (the royal city that is a temple), current name for the temple of Viṣṇu built in the twelfth century at Angkor by King Sūryavarman II; this most imposing of Angkor's temples was reconsecrated as a Buddhist shrine at an indeterminate date, possibly in the sixteenth century.
• *Antaravāsaka:* a garment, worn by the Buddha and Buddhist monks, consisting of a long flowing cloth wrapped around the hips.
• *Apsaras:* (who walks, or glides, over the waters), heavenly nymph, born of the churning of the Sea of Milk.
• *Arjuna:* (white), one of the five Pāṇḍava brothers, the main protagonists, along with the hundred Kaurava brothers, of the *Mahābhārata.*
• *Arūpa:* formlessness.
• *Āsana:* (seat, throne), a term used in combination to designate the different positions of the body in Indian iconography.
• *Asram Maha Rosei:* (from the Sanskrit *āśrama mahā ṛṣi,* hermitage of the great ascetic), a pre-Angkor temple in the southern province of Ta Keo.
• *Āśrama:* hermitage.
• *Asura:* (demon), a divine being antagonistic to the gods.
• *Ātman:* self, soul.
• *Australoid:* the most ancient population of Southeast Asia, related to the aboriginals of Australia.
• *Avalokiteśvara:* (compassionate lord, or lord who looks down from above), also *Lokeśvara* (lord of the world), one of the greatest Bodhisattva, who wears an image of the Amitābha Buddha in his headdress; in Cambodia he is most often represented with two or four arms, and his attributes are most often the lotus flower (he is sometimes called lotus-bearer, Padmapāṇi), the rosary, a water pitcher, and a manuscript; during the reign of Jayavarman VII (r. 1181–1218?), he was sometimes represented with eight arms in his cosmic aspect, his body covered with numerous small images of the Buddha said to emanate from his pores—this form, sometimes called radiating, expresses the Bodhisattva's universal compassion.
• *Avatāra:* (avatar), descent of a divinity to earth, divine incarnation.

B

• *Bakheng:* Śivaite temple of the beginning of the tenth century built by Yaśovarman I in Yaśodharapura (later Angkor) on Mount Bakheng.
• *Bakong:* Śivaite temple built in 881 by Indravarman I in Hariharālaya.
• *Balarāma:* (Rāma the plowman), Kṛṣṇa's brother, also considered an avatar of Viṣṇu's; his attribute is the plow, which he used to bring the course of the Yamunā, one of India's sacred rivers, closer to him so that he could bathe in it; in the *Mahābhārata,* he teaches the Pāṇḍava how to wield a club.
• *Ban Chiang:* site of Neolithic and Bronze Age culture in the northeast of Thailand.
• *Banteay Chmar:* large provincial temple-city of the reign of Jayavarman VII, unusual for its bas-reliefs of historical scenes and its complex representation of Avalokiteśvara.
• *Banteay Kdei:* (the citadel of cells), Buddhist temple built in the late twelfth to early thirteenth century in Angkor by Jayavarman VII.
• *Banteay Srei:* (the citadel of women), Śivaite temple built in 967 to 968 by the Brahman Yajñavarāha about fourteen miles north of Siem Reap.
• *Baphuon:* Śivaite temple of the third quarter of the eleventh century built in Angkor Thom by Udayādityavarman II.
• *Baray:* a reservoir (not excavated) that retains water between strong dikes; *baray* were primarily intended to store water—for irrigating rice paddies and supplying households—for the dry season; *baray* are sometimes considered symbolic representations of the ocean.
• *Bayon:* Buddhist temple of the late twelfth to early thirteenth century built in Angkor Thom by Jayavarman VII.
• *Beng Mealea:* (pond of Mealea), ruined temple in the style of Angkor Vat (first half of the twelfth century), located sixty miles (100 km) east of Angkor; its plan is similar to Angkor's, but without the

pyramid.
• *Bhadreśvara*: (benevolent lord), an epithet of Śiva's, and the patron deity of the temple of Vat Phu in present-day Laos.
• *Bhāgavata*: devotees of Kṛṣṇa as supreme god, Pāñcarātra, Satvata.
• *Bhaiṣajyaguru*: (the master of remedies), Buddha of medicine.
• *Bhavapura*: (city of life), capital of a pre-Angkor kingdom founded by King Bhavavarman I at the end of the sixth century.
• *Bhavavarman I*: (protected by life), king from the late sixth century.
• *Bhūmi:* earth in its divine form, one of Viṣṇu's consorts.
• *Bhūmisparśamudrā:* Buddhist gesture of touching the earth or calling the earth to witness: left hand in the lap, palm up.
• *Bodhi:* (enlightenment), the ultimate stage of consciousness.
• *Bodhisattva*: (enlightened being), in Theravāda Buddhism, the historical Buddha before he attained enlightenment; in Mahāyāna Buddhism, the Bodhisattva are spirits who have reached the rank of deities but have put off entering *nirvāṇa* to help other souls achieve release.
• *Bola:* clay ball serving as a missile.
• *Brahmā*: one of the gods of the *trimūrti*, the triple godhead in the Brahmanic religion; he is the creator god, the ancestor of all worlds, and is depicted with four arms and four faces, through which he authored the four *Veda;* his attributes include the rosary, whose beads represent the letters of the Sanskrit alphabet, the water pitcher, and the manuscript; in Buddhism, the Brahmā gods are said to reside in the highest celestial spheres; they are the upholders of the articles of faith.
• *Brahman*: a member of the highest, or priestly, Indian caste; all brahmans are not priests, however, nor all priests brahmans.
• *Brahmanism*: or Hinduism, Indian religion having its source in the Vedism imported to India in the latter half of the second millennium BC by the Aryans, mixed with the local animist and earth cults; the supreme godhead in the Brahmanic religion is one, a creator, identified with different names in different sects (Śiva, Viṣṇu, and others); according to the cyclical conception of time in India (and other Indianized countries), the individual soul migrates from life to life, either rising or falling, and ultimately will be reunited with the universal soul of creation.
• *Brāhmī*: ancient script of southern India, read from left to right, that gave rise to numerous scripts within and beyond India.
• *Bronze*: alloy of metals including copper and tin.
• *Buddha*: (enlightened one), epithet usually applied to the founder of the Buddhist religion; in Mahāyāna Buddhism; however, it designates not only the historical Buddha but also all the spiritual beings in the high pantheon, including Vajrasattva / Vajradhara, the first Buddha, and the five Jina (victors, over illusion): Amitābha, Vairocana, Ratnasambhava, Amoghasiddhi, and Akṣobhya.
• *Buddhasakarāj:* (Buddhist era), beginning in 543 B.C.
• *Buddhism*: religion founded in the sixth century B.C. by the Buddha (enlightened) Śākyamuni (sage of the Śākya clan); he preached a nonviolent way of life, one that was respectful of all living things and that used meditation as the basic path to salvation; Buddhism was adopted by every country in Southeast Asia, but under varying forms: Theravāda (the path or opinion of the ancients), the original form of Buddhism (also Hīnayāna, or Lesser Vehicle), which offered salvation only to monks, while the laity had first to acquire sufficient merit in their successive lives to escape *saṃsāra*, the hellish wheel of reincarnation; Mahāyāna (Greater Vehicle), or great progress (along the path of enlightenment), which held out the hope of more rapid salvation, thanks to the intercession of the compassionate Bodhisattva; Vajrayāna (diamond path), also Tantric Buddhism, whose magical observances allowed for the possibility of deliverance within a single lifetime.

C

• *Caitya:* a holy place or building in the Indian religions, and by extension a votive monument in Buddhism or Brahmanism.
• *Cakra:* wheel or disk, symbol of the sun, attribute or weapon of Viṣṇu; in Buddhism, designation of the wheel of law.
• *Cakravartin:* (who holds the moving wheel), universal ruler, a supreme monarch in the Indian tradition.
• *Cālukya-Pallava*: South Indian script used in earliest Cambodian epigraphy; Indian script used in the Cālukya-Pallava period.
• *Candra*: (brilliant), moon god.
• *Caturbhuja:* (four-armed), usually used in reference to Viṣṇu.
• *Champa*: land of the Chams.
• *Chams*: the ancient peoples of Champa (present-day central and south Vietnam), who are affiliated with the people of Indonesia.
• *Chedi:* Thai pronunciation of *cetiya* (Pāli form of *caitya*).
• *Chok Gargyar*: ancient name for the present site of Koh Ker.
• *Corbeled arch*: stacked arch without a keystone, the method adopted by the Khmer in the construction of their temple roofs and towers.
• *Cullasakarāj:* (little era), period in the Buddhist calendar beginning in 638.

D

• *Ḍākinī:* term in Tantric Buddhism designating a kind of *yoginī.*
• *Dao-thinh*: Dôngsonian site in northern Vietnam celebrated for its large bronze jars with motifs of boats armed with warriers wearing feathered headdresses and lids decorated with copulating couples.
• *Deva:* god.
• *Devarāja*: divinity (Śiva, probably in the form of a *liṅga*) in whose name Jayavarman II founded a ritual closely linked to the royal power.
• *Devatā:* feminine divinity.
• *Devī*: (goddess), in Brahmanism, the *śakti* (energy) of a god, but commonly refers to Devī, wife of Śiva, whose many forms include Pārvatī (daughter of the mountain), Umā (light), Durgā (inaccessible one), and Kālī (black one).
• *Dharaṇīndravarman I*: (protected by the Indra), Khmer ruler (1108–1113) whose posthumous name was Paramaniṣkalapada.
• *Dharma:* cosmic law, the world order in India's religions; also, pious words and deeds.
• *Dharmacakramudrā:* Buddhist gesture of turning the wheel of law: both hands raised in front of chest, fingertips touching to make wheel shape.
• *Dhoti:* loin cloth.
• *Dhyānamudrā*: Buddhist gesture of meditation: hands lying on top of each other in lap, palms up.
• *Dikpālaka:* guardian of one of the eight subpoints of the compass.
• *Dīkṣā*: initiation.
• *Dông-son*: site in the Thanh-hoa region in northern Vietnam that gave its name to the brilliant indigenous culture of the end of the Bronze Age and the beginning of the Iron Age; particularly noted for large bronze ritual drums.
• *Durgā*: (inaccessible one), an epithet of Devī's, particularly in her combat against the demon-buffalo Mahiṣāsura; Viṣṇu's sister; Durgā's attributes are the discus and the conch, among others.
• *Dvārapāla:* guardian of the gates.
• *Dvārapālikā:* female guardian of the gates.
• *Dvāravatī:* Indianized Buddhist kingdom located in ancient times in central and northeast Thailand.

E

• *Elephant Terrace*: terrace in front of the royal palace in Angkor Thom, built by Jayavarman VII late in the twelfth century; so-called from the reliefs of elephants and

garuḍa that decorate its walls.
• *Emerald Buddha*: jasper image of the Buddha taken to Thailand and now kept in the temple in the royal palace; replica housed in royal palace in Phnom Penh.

F
• *Funan*: name given by the Chinese to a large southern kingdom in Southeast Asia that existed during pre-Angkor times; Oc Eo was one of its important centers.

G
• *Gadā:* mace or club.
• *Gajasiṃha:* (elephant-lion), a mythical Indian animal with the body of a lion and the head of an elephant.
• *Gaṇa:* category.
• *Gaṇeśa*: god with the head of an elephant, a son of Śiva and Pārvatī.
• *Garuḍa*: mythological bird, hereditary enemy of the *nāga* and the traditional mount of Viṣṇu; *garuḍa* are often depicted as half human and half bird of prey.
• *Gaurī*: (who is clear), one aspect of a consort of Śiva's.
• *Ghaṇṭā:* bell.
• *Giriśa*: (who lies on the mountain), an epithet of Śiva's.
• *Girīśa*: (lord of the mountain), an epithet of Śiva's.
• *Giritra*: (protector of the mountain), an epithet of Śiva's.
• *Gopura:* entrance pavilion, gate, of a city or temple; *gopura* were often shrines as well.
• *Govardhana*: mountain in the Mathurā region of India, lifted by Kṛṣṇa like a gigantic umbrella over the heads of the region's people and flocks to protect them from a storm caused by Indra.
• *Guru:* spiritual teacher.

H
• *Haimavatī*: (daughter of the Himalaya), epithet of the *śakti* (spouse) of Śiva; see Pārvatī, Devī.
• *Haṃsa:* heavenly goose or duck of mythology, the mount of Brahmā and Varuṇa.
• *Hanuman*: a monkey general, featured in the *Rāmāyaṇa*, and the commander of the monkey army.
• *Harihara*: composite god, half Viṣṇu (on the left), half Śiva (on the right), often represented in the pre-Angkor period.
• *Hariharālaya*: (abode of Harihara) town in the ninth century that was the Khmer capital before Yaśodharapura / Angkor; today the site is known as Roluos, in the province of Siem Reap.
• *Harṣavarman I*: (protected by happiness, r. 912–922), posthumously named Rudraloka.
• *Harṣavarman II*: (r. 940–c. 944), posthumously named Brahmaloka.
• *Harṣavarman III*: (r. 1066–1080?), posthumously named Sadāśivapada.
• *Hayagrīva*: (having the neck of a horse), a form of Viṣṇu's; in this guise, with a horse's head (see also Kalkin), he fought two demons who had stolen the *Veda*.
• *Hevajra*: an important divinity in later forms of Mahāyāna Buddhism and Tantrism whose image appears primarily during the reign of Jayavarman VII; the god is represented as having eight heads and sixteen arms, and dances on one leg, trampling the four Māra.
• *Hīnayāna*: (Lesser Vehicle), see Buddhism, Theravāda.
• *Hinduism*: see Brahmanism.
• *Hoabinhian*: from the eponymous site of Hoan-binh in northern Vietnam, center of Mesolithic culture characterized by tools made from single-faced pebbles.
• *Huntian / Houen-t'ien* (EFEO script): mythological founder of Funan according to Chinese texts.

I
• *Indra*: (master), the king of the gods, the god of storms and guardian of the east; like Jupiter, his attribute is the thunderbolt (*vajra*); his mount is the three-headed elephant, Airāvata.
• *Indradevī*: (goddess of the master), one of the wives of Jayavarman VII; she commissioned the Phimeanakas stele, which has yielded much information on the reign of Jayavarman VII.
• *Indratatāka*: (basin of Indra), the *baray* at Hariharālaya (present-day Roluos).
• *Indravarman I*: (protected by Indra, r. 877–after 886), his posthumous name was Īśvaraloka.
• *Indreśvara*: (lord of Indra), *liṅga* worshiped in the temple of the Bakong.
• *Īśāna*: (the lord who is big), one of Śiva's names.
• *Īśānavarman I*: (protected by the master, Śiva, r. 616–628), pre-Angkor king.
• *Īśānavarman II*: (reigned in 925), his posthumous name was Paramarudraloka.
• *Iśvara*: (lord), epithet often applied to Śiva.

J
• *Jaṭā:* piled chignon of the ascetics; numerous gods, Śiva among them, wore their hair in this style.
• *Jātaka:* (birth), moral tales of the previous lives of the Śākyamuni Buddha.
• *Jaṭāmukuṭa:* crown formed by plaited and piled locks of hair; particularly applies to Śivaite images.
• *Jayarājadevī*: (goddess of the king of victory), the first wife of King Jayavarman VII; a devout Buddhist, she died young; several sculptures of a kneeling woman in the attitude of a worshiper are thought to be her portraits.
• *Jayatatāka*: (basin of victory), the *baray* of Preah Khan at Angkor; in its center is the temple of Neak Pean.
• *Jayavarman*: (protected by victory), name of many Khmer kings.
• *Jayavarman I*: (r. 2d half of 7th century), pre-Angkor king.
• *Jayavarman II*: (r. 790–after 830?), the founder of the great Khmer royal line; his posthumous name of Parameśvara (supreme lord) is one of Śiva's names, indicating that the king was personally a Śivaite.
• *Jayavarman III*: (r. 830?–after 860), his posthumous name was Viṣṇuloka.
• *Jayavarman IV*: (r. 928–c. 940), his posthumous name was Paramaśivapada.
• *Jayavarman V*: (r. 968–1000 or 1001), his posthumous name was Paramavīraloka.
• *Jayavarman VI*: (r. 1080–1107), his posthumous name was Paramakayvalyapada.
• *Jayavarman VII*: (r. 1181–1218?), his posthumous name was Paramasaugatapada.
• *Jayavarman VIII*: (r. 1243–1295), his posthumous name was Parameśvarapada.
• *Jayavīravarman*: (protected by the hero of victory, r. 1002–after 1006).
• *Jina*: epithet of the Buddha and the five cosmic (*dhyāni*) Buddha of the four cardinal points plus the zenith; vanquishers of illusion; see also Tathāgata.

K
• *Kailāsa*: mythical mountain in the Himalayas, the private abode of Śiva.
• *Kāla*: (black one), originally an epithet of Śiva's, the term refers by extension to a decorative motif that has protective powers and is often found in the central portion of a lintel over a doorway.
• *Kāliya*: a mythological snake, one of Kṛṣṇa's opponents in battle.
• *Kalkin*: the Viṣṇu-to-be, who will be incarnated in the form of a man with the head of a horse; he will come to bring the world to an end and to prepare for a new golden age.
• *Kalpa:* cosmic cycle.
• *Kalpanā:* set of prescriptions and benefits of religious foundations in Cambodia; see also *rantāp*.
• *Kāma*: (desire, love), the god of love, whom Śiva blasted with his third eye; Kāma had tried to lure Śiva from his ascetic devotions by showing him his passionate face.
• *Kamaṇḍalu:* water vessel.
• *Kambu*: a mythical figure, the epony-

mous ancestor of the Cambodians.
• *Kambujadeśa*: country of the Kambuja, or Cambodians.
• *Kamrateṅ jagat ta rāja:* Khmer phrase for *devarāja*.
• *Kamvujākśara*: script first used at the end of the ninth century in Cambodia, a Khmer modification of Nāgarī meaning the writing of the Kambujas (Cambodians).
• *Kanloṅ:* treasure room.
• *Karma:* effect of one's deeds on one's present or future.
• *Kārttikeya*: one of the names for Skanda, god of war; see also Kumāra.
• *Kauṇḍinya*: Brahman said to have founded the royal line in the myths of Funan's origin.
• *Kāvya*: Sanskrit verse type.
• *Ketu*: planetary deity of comets and meteors, one of the *navagraha*.
• *Khleang*: (emporium), two buildings, North Khleang and South Khleang, of the late tenth or eleventh century, opposite the royal palace of Angkor Thom; possibly used to receive visiting dignitaries.
• *Kirītamukuṭa:* crown or miter.
• *Kjökkenmödding:* mound of shells.
• *Koh Ker*: present name for the ancient site of Chok Gargyar, the Khmer capital between 928 and 944.
• *Krāṃṅ:* accordion-folded paper texts.
• *Kravan*: Viṣṇuite temple built in Angkor in 961 by Harṣavarman I.
• *Kṛṣṇa*: (dark), an avatar of Viṣṇu's; born in Mathurā in the north of India, he was exchanged at birth with the son of a shepherd in order to escape his uncle, Kamsa, who wanted his death; after a lively youth among the *gopī* (herdswomen), he recovered the throne taken from him by Kamsa; in the *Mahābhārata*, he teaches the *Bhagavadgītā*, one of the fundamental texts of Indian thought.
• *Kubera*: guardian of the north and of the earth's treasure.
• *Kulen*: mountain, north of Siem Reap, where the first *devarāja* was installed in 802; sculptural style of the early ninth century; source of much of the sandstone used for the construction of Angkor temples.
• *Kumāra*: youth; see Kārttikeya and Skanda.
• *Kūrma*: (tortoise), an avatar of Viṣṇu's; when the *deva* and *asura* were churning the Sea of Milk, using Mount Mandara as a pivot, the mountain sank under the waters; Viṣṇu took the form of a turtle and supported Mount Mandara on his back so that the sea could be churned and *amṛta* made.
• *Kurukṣetra*: (field of the Kuru), battlefield where the final encounter between the Pāṇḍava and Kaurava took place in the *Mahābhārata*.

L

• *Laang Spean*: grotto in the Battambang region occupied at the end of the Paleolithic period and during the Mesolithic period.
• *Lakṣaṇa:* distinguishing physical traits of the Buddha.
• *Lakṣmaṇa*: brother of Rāma.
• *Lakṣmī*: see Śrī.
• *Laṅkā*: dwelling place of Rāvaṇa (the island of Sri Lanka or Ceylon) and the site of the decisive battle of the *Rāmāyaṇa*.
• *Linyi*: name given by the Chinese to an important Southeast Asian kingdom, Champa.
• *Liṅga:* (sign, symbol), the phallus of Śiva, symbol of his creative power, and the form in which the god is most often represented in the temples dedicated to him; the *liṅga* stands for fertility and prosperity, the more so as it is fitted within the *yoni* (womb) in the stylized form of a vulva; the *liṅga* is also a pillar, a sort of *axis mundi*; in Cambodia the *liṅga* is often tripartite, in reference to the *trimūrti*: the base is square in section, Brahmā; the median portion octagonal, Viṣṇu; and the top circular, Śiva.
• *Liṅgapura*: (city of *liṅga*), the Sanskrit name for the present site of Koh Ker.
• *Liuye, Lieou-ye* (EFEO script): (willow leaf), the local princess won by Kauṇḍinya when he landed on Khmer shores (as the Chinese texts refer to her).
• *Lokapāla:* collective name of the four Great Guardian Kings of the world in Buddhism who watch over the four cardinal points; not to be confused with the *dikpāla* / *dikpālaka*, guardians of the cardinal and intercardinal points in Brahmanism.
• *Lokeśvara*: see Avalokiteśvara.
• *Lolei*: Śivaite temple of 893 built by Yaśovarman I as an island in Indratatāka.
• *Lopburi*: site in central Thailand where many vestiges of provincial Khmer art can be found; school of provincial art active from the eleventh to the early thirteenth century.

M

• *Mahābhārata:* (great exploits of the Bhārata), one of two great Indian epics (the other is the *Rāmāyaṇa*); it tells the story of two rival but related clans, the Pāṇḍava and Kaurava, and of Kṛṣṇa's intercession as Arjuna's charioteer; the *Bhagavadgītā*, one of the main texts of Brahmanism, is Kṛṣṇa's discourse to Arjuna on disinterestedness and love of the holy.
• *Mahāyāna*: see Buddhism, Mahāyāna.
• *Mahendraparvata*: (mountain of great Indra), ancient name of Phnom Kulen.
• *Mahendravarman*: (protected by great Indra, r. beg. of 7th century), pre-Angkor king.
• *Maheśvara*: (lord who is great), one of Śiva's many names.
• *Mahiṣa*: (buffalo), demon (Mahiṣāsura) in the form of a buffalo whom Durgā battled.
• *Maitreya*: (friendly), Bodhisattva who is to be the next human incarnation of the Buddha; he will appear only after the teachings of Śākyamuni, the historical Buddha, are forgotten.
• *Makara:* aquatic animal of Indian mythology; in Khmer art, the *makara* is part crocodile, part elephant, and sometimes part lion; its tail is often a leafy scroll.
• *Maṇḍala:* (discus, circle; also area, territory), diagram deriving from the Indian conception of the universe and giving material form to the realm of a divinity; in two or three dimensions, it is used as an aid in meditation.
• *Mandara*: mountain used by the *deva* and *asura* in churning the Sea of Milk.
• *Mantra:* Buddhist or Hindu formula for an incantation to evoke a deity.
• *Māra*: demon of illusion.
• *Marut:* wind gods in Indra's retinue.
• *Māyā:* illusion, dream.
• *Mebon, East*: Śivaite temple built in 953 (?952) by Rājendravarman as an island in the eastern *baray*.
• *Mebon, West*: Brahmanistic (Viṣṇuite?) temple built in the second half of the eleventh century as an island in the western *baray*.
• *Mekong*: the most important river in Cambodia and several neighboring countries.
• *Merā*: wife of Kambu, the eponymous mythical ancestor of the Cambodians.
• *Meru*: cosmic mountain, the axis of the world in Indian cosmology, the abode of thirty-three gods, and the site of Indra's and Brahmā's city.
• *Mlu Prei*: site in northern Cambodia comprising three prehistoric sites of the Neolithic and Bronze Ages.
• *Modaka:* sweet, bowl of sweets; particularly associated with Gaṇeśa.
• *Mon*: peoples formerly living in southeast Burma and central and northeast Thailand.
• *Mucilinda*: *nāga* who protected the Buddha while he meditated beside Lake Mucilinda, whose waters swelled in a storm and threatened to drown him.
• *Mudrā:* (seal), gesture of the hands; the *mudrā* may signal different episodes in the life of the Buddha (early or Theravāda Buddhism) or different Jina (Mahāyāna Buddhism).
• *Mukhaliṅga: liṅga* with a representation of a face.
• *Mukuṭa:* hairstyle or headdress; principally the *jaṭāmukuṭa*, or piled hair of the ascetics, and the *kirītamukuṭa*, a jeweled crown.

• *Mūrti:* (aspect, form), shape assumed by a god.

N

• *Nāga:* (snake), represented as a cobra, the symbol of water and the guardian of subterranean treasure in Indian mythology; the *nāga* is the archenemy of the *garuḍa* and a central figure in Cambodian culture.
• *Nagara:* Sanskrit word for city, royal capital; in the Khmer language it becomes *nokor*, then Angkor.
• *Nāgarī*: Indian script that evolved about the sixth to seventh century; the script used for Sanskrit in India today.
• *Nāgī:* female counterpart of *nāga*.
• *Nandin*: (happy), a white bull, Śiva's mount, and the animal form of this god.
• *Narasiṃha*: (man-lion), an avatar of Viṣṇu's; the demon Hiraṇyakaśipu received the promise that he could be killed neither by day nor night, neither by a god, a man, nor an animal, and neither on earth nor in the sky; he therefore lorded it over gods and men with impunity; Viṣṇu took the form of a man-lion (neither animal, man, nor god) and killed the demon at twilight (neither day nor night), holding him on his legs so that he was neither in the air nor on the ground.
• *Navagraha:* (nine seizers), group of deities representing the stars, planets, and celestial events; said to have influence over the destinies of men; see Rāhu, the ninth of this group.
• *Neak Pean*: (the entwined serpents), Buddhist temple built in the second half of the twelfth century by Jayavarman VII as an island in the *baray* of Preah Khan.
• *Nirvāṇa:* (nirvana; extinction, vanishing), ending of the chain of existence, particularly in Buddhism; in Hindu religions *mukti*, release.

O

• *Oc Eo*: archaeological site in southern Vietnam, once a thriving center of Funan.
• *Oudong*: a capital of post-Angkor Cambodia.

P

• *Padma:* lotus.
• *Padmapāṇi:* Bodhisattva, one of Avalokiteśvara's forms; associated with his attribute, the lotus.
• *Pāṇḍava*: the five sons of Pāṇḍu, a hero of the *Mahābhārata*.
• *Paramarāja I*: (king who is supreme, r. 1566–1576).
• *Paramaviṣṇuloka*: (who has rejoined the realm of the supreme Viṣṇu), posthumous name of Sūryavarman II.
• *Parameśvara*: (supreme lord), an epithet of Śiva's, posthumous name of Jayavarman II.
• *Paraśurāma*: Rāma with an ax.
• *Pārvatī*: (daughter of the mountain), see Devī.
• *Pāśupata*: Śivaite sect.
• *Phimai*: provincial temple in present-day Thailand, twelfth century.
• *Phimeanakas*: Brahmanistic temple of the first half of the eleventh century, or perhaps partly earlier; functioned as a royal chapel in the grounds of the royal palace at Angkor Thom.
• *Phnom:* hill, mountain.
• *Phnom Da*: hill in the province of Ta Keo, holy site of the pre-Angkor city of Angkor Borei; also, a style of pre-Angkor sculpture.
• *Phnom Loang*: Neolithic and Bronze Age site in southern Cambodia.
• *Phnom Penh*: (hill of lady Penh), founded in the fifteenth century, became the capital only in 1867 during the reign of King Norodom (1859–1904).
• *Pnat:* folded paper.
• *Pradakṣiṇā:* circumambulation of a temple in a clockwise direction.
• *Prajñā:* knowledge, wisdom, intelligence; in Tantric Buddhism, the feminine element of the divine couple.
• *Prajñāpāramitā*: (perfection of wisdom), mother of all the Buddhas; a group of texts important in Mahāyāna Buddhism; may be represented as a goddess personifying the Word; she is sometimes considered a familiar spirit of the god Avalokiteśvara.
• *Prāṇa:* inner breath, control of spiritual strength, life force.
• *Prāsād:* Brahmanic temple.
• *Prasat:* tower-shrine.
• *Prasat Andet*: pre-Angkor shrine of the late seventh century; also, the eponymous monument of the style.
• *Pre Rup*: Brahmanic temple built in 961 by Harṣavarman I in Angkor.
• *Preah Khan*: (sacred sword), Buddhist temple of 1191 dedicated to the father of Jayavarman VII in Angkor.
• *Preah Ko*: (sacred bull), Śivaite temple of 879 built by Indravarman I in Hariharālaya; also, hero of a Khmer myth with his brother, Preah Keo (sacred crystal).
• *Preah Pithu*: group of Buddhist temples, of the twelfth century and later, in Angkor Thom.
• *Preah Vihear*: Brahmanistic temple, in the northwest of Cambodia, built in the eleventh century by Sūryavarman I.
• *Prei Kmeng*: (forest of the child), temple to the west of Angkor's western *baray*, the eponymous monument of the pre-Angkor style covering the second half of the seventh century.
• *Puṇya:* pious words or deeds and their results.
• *Purāṇa:* collection of Brahmanic texts.
• *Purohita*: (*baku*, in Khmer), high priest, chaplain.
• *Pustaka:* book.

R

• *Rāhu*: (demon of the eclipse), an *asura* who was denounced by the Sun and the Moon just as he was about to drink the *amṛta* after the churning of the Sea of Milk; throwing his sharp-edged discus, Viṣṇu decapitated him, and only Rāhu's head became immortal; ever since, Rāhu has pursued the two celestial bodies for revenge, and he sometimes manages to devour them; the eclipse occurs while they are in the demon's mouth.
• *Rājendrabhadreśvara*: (beneficent lord of the king's Indra), deity (Śiva) worshiped in the temple of Pre Rup.
• *Rājendradevī*: (goddess of the king's Indra), name belonging to a number of female historical personages, among whom is the second wife of Jayavarman VII.
• *Rājendravarman*: (protected by the king's Indra, r. 944–967), his posthumous name was Śivaloka.
• *Rājendreśvara*: (lord of the king's Indra), divinity worshiped in the West Mebon.
• *Rāma*: (charming), an avatar of Viṣṇu's, legendary hero of the *Rāmāyaṇa*; his favorite weapon is the bow, and he is known as the prince of archers.
• *Rāmāyaṇa:* one of the two great Indian epics (the other is the *Mahābhārata*); the *Rāmāyaṇa* tells the story of prince Rāma, who, aided by the monkey people, undertakes to recover his kingdom and his wife Sītā, abducted by the demon Rāvaṇa.
• *Rantāp:* (Middle Khmer word for *kalpanā*), set of prescriptions and benefits of religious foundations.
• *Ratnasambhava*: one of the five Jina (South).
• *Rāvaṇa*: a main character in the *Rāmāyaṇa*; a demon living on the island of Lanka and the abductor of Rāma's wife Sītā.
• *Rikta:* portable inscription; virgin leaves.
• *Royal palace*: walled enclosure in Angkor Thom with elaborate *gopura* of the eleventh century, contains the foundations of residential buildings, ceremonial bathing pools, and the Phimeanakas, the royal chapel.
• *Ṛṣi*: sage.
• *Rudra*: (howler), a terrible form of Śiva.
• *Rudravarman*: (protected by Rudra, r. 1st half of 6th century), pre-Angkor ruler.

S

• *Sadāśiva*: five-headed supreme form of Śiva.
• *Saddhā:* pure faith.

• *Śaka:* Indian chronology commonly used in Southeast Asia, including Cambodia. The era is said to have begun in 78 or 79, five hundred years after the birth of the Buddha.
• *Śaksī:* (also *bejñān*), witness to a meritorious deed.
• *Śakti:* energy, personification of the female aspect of a god, spouse of a god.
• *Śākyamuni:* the sage of the Śākya clan; one of the names for the historical Buddha.
• *Samādhi:* state of concentration (mental and physical) through which one attains a transcendent awareness.
• *Saṃbat'can kpin:* see *sampot.*
• *Sambor Prei Kuk:* (hillock in the forest of Sambor), pre-Angkor site whose most important remains date back to the seventh century; the style of the same name.
• *Saṃgha:* monastic community.
• *Saṃghāṭi:* overgarment, worn by the Buddha, which may be draped over both shoulders or carried in accordion folds over the left shoulder.
• *Sampot:* (cloth) kilt, worn short around the waist and pulled between the legs.
• *Samrong Sen:* site, in the Tonle Sap region, of the shell mounds known as *kjökkenmöddinger.*
• *Saṃsāra:* the phenomenal world, rebirth.
• *Saṃvaḥ vraḥ, saṃbaḥ braḥ:* (Old and Middle Khmer respectively), pilgrim.
• *Sāṅ:* (Middle Khmer word for *sthāpanā*), a religious foundation.
• *Śaṅkha:* shell.
• *Sarasvatī:* (goddess of knowledge), wife of Brahmā.
• *Sarong:* Indonesian word for a long strip of cloth worn around the body.
• *Śāstra:* knowledge, arts.
• *Satrā:* palm-leaf manuscript.
• *Satya:* true speech.
• *Satyapraṇidhān:* post-Angkor Khmer texts.
• *Sdok Kak Thom:* site of an eleventh-century temple in the Prachinburi Province, Thailand, whose ruins yielded the stele of the same name.
• *Śeṣa:* serpent supporting Viṣṇu on the cosmic ocean during cosmic sleep; see Ananta.
• *Siddhārta:* name of the Buddha.
• *Siddhi:* supernatural powers.
• *Śikhara:* temple tower of northern Indian style.
• *Silver Pagoda:* structure in the royal palace in Phnom Penh.
• *Sītā:* (furrow), wife of Rāma in the *Mahābhārata.*
• *Śiva:* (beneficent), one of the gods of the *trimūrti,* the destroyer god; according to the cyclical conception of time prevalent in India and the Indianized countries, Śiva is the destroyer but also the creator; he is most frequently represented in the form of a *liṅga*; his characteristics include a third eye on the forehead (the eye of knowledge) and symbolic attributes such as the trident, the vase, and the rosary.
• *Śivakaivalya:* priest instructed by the Brahman Hiraṇyādama in the rites for the installation of the *devarāja*; first of a family entrusted to be *purohita* (high priests) of the *devarāja* cult, a responsibility that was inherited by the maternal line.
• *Śivapada:* also *Śivapāda,* Śiva's footsteps.
• *Skanda:* (god of war), son of Śiva and Pārvatī; he is normally shown riding a peacock and holding a lance.
• *Soma:* in the Funanese myth of origin, the *nāgī* subjugated by Kauṇḍinya.
• *Srah Srang:* royal bathing place built in Angkor at the end of the twelfth century by Jayavarman VII.
• *Śrī / Lakṣmī:* (fortune, beauty), a consort of Viṣṇu's, born of the churning of the Sea of Milk; in each hand she holds a lotus flower.
• *Sthāpanā:* (Sanskrit/Khmer), religious foundation; also, see *sāṅ.*
• *Stung:* water course.
• *Stūpa:* Buddhist monument, originally a rounded sepulchral mound; the Buddha's remains were placed in a *stūpa*; over the centuries the *stūpa* acquired a commemorative and votive character but might also contain the ashes of an important, religious or lay, person.
• *Sugrīva:* monkey hero in the *Rāmāyaṇa;* Rāma helped him to defeat his brother in the struggle to determine who should be king of the monkeys.
• *Sūrya:* sun god.
• *Sūryavarman I:* (protected by Sūrya, r. 1002/1010–1049), his posthumous name was Paramanirvāṇapada.
• *Sūryavarman II:* (r. 1113–at least 1145), builder of the temple of Angkor Vat; his posthumous name, Paramaviṣṇuloka, indicates that he was one of the few Angkor rulers to choose Viṣṇu as his protective deity.
• *Svāyaṃbhū:* self-existent.
• *Svāyaṃbhuvaliṅga:* naturally occurring stone outcrops considered to be *liṅga.*

T
• *Ta Keo:* (the ancestor Keo, or, as Prasat Keo, the tower of crystal), Śivaite temple built in Angkor late in the tenth or early in the eleventh century by Jayavarman V (and, possibly, by Sūryavarman I).
• *Ta Prohm:* (the ancestor Brahmā), Buddhist temple of 1186 in Angkor dedicated to the mother of Jayavarman VII.
• *Tantra:* Tantric scripture, Esoteric Buddhist doctrine.
• *Tārā:* a female spirit of Mahāyāna Buddhism, a counterpart to the Bodhisattva Avalokiteśvara.
• *Tathāgata:* (he who has proceeded as he should, he who has acquired that which is so—the truth), term for any Buddha achieving total enlightenment; the five great Buddha of wisdom; also, see Jina.
• *Tep Pranam:* Buddhist temple, fifteenth or sixteenth century.
• *Theravāda:* see Buddhism, Theravāda.
• *Tīrtha:* bathing place, holy place.
• *Tribhaṅga:* stance with triple flexion, or S-shaped curve of the torso.
• *Tribhuvanāditya:* (sun of the three worlds, in power in 1166), usurping king, killed in 1177 when the Chams captured Angkor.
• *Tricīra:* triple lock of hair characteristic of young Brahmanistic gods, especially Kṛṣṇa.
• *Trimūrti:* (threefold form), in Śivaism, the gods Brahmā, Viṣṇu, and Śiva (actually Rudra, a horrific form of Śiva), conceived as an emanation of the supreme Śiva, who is himself nonmanifest and therefore incapable of representation.
• *Tripiṭaka:* body of Buddhist texts.
• *Triśūla:* trident; one of Śiva's attributes.
• *Trivikrama:* cosmic form of Viṣṇu as the conqueror of the Three Worlds, incarnated as the dwarf Vāmana.

U
• *Udayādityavarman I:* (protected by the rising sun, reigned in 1001).
• *Udayādityavarman II:* (r. 1050–1066).
• *Umā:* (light), see Devī.
• *Umāmaheśvara:* (lord who is great and Umā), representations of Śiva and Pārvatī in which they clasp each other around the waist.
• *Ūrṇā:* characteristic sign of great men and the Buddha in particular, tuft of hair between the eyebrows generally represented as a dot in the middle of the forehead.
• *Uṣṇīṣa:* (what is at the summit), in Buddhist iconography, the cranial protuberance on the Buddha's head, seat of his transcendent knowledge.
• *Uttarāsaṅga:* garment of the Buddha, a wide piece of cloth worn as a mantle, generally covering the shoulders.

V
• *Vāhana:* mount, or vehicle, of a god.
• *Vairocana:* (the illuminator), one of the five Jina (the zenith).
• *Vajra:* thunderbolt, lightning, diamond; weapon and attribute of Indra; ritual object held by certain Tantric beings and used in Tantric rites along with the *ghaṇṭā* (bell).
• *Vajradhara:* one of the names of the Ādibuddha.
• *Vajrapāṇi:* bearer of the *vajra,* name of a major Bodhisattva.
• *Vajrasattva:* one of the names of the

Ādibuddha.
• *Vajrayāna*: (the way of the diamond), see Buddhism.
• *Vāmana*: the demon Bali oppressed the world; Viṣṇu appeared before him as Vāmana, a Brahman dwarf, and asked Bali to repay his services for a religious observance by giving him all the land he could cover in three steps; at the moment of receiving his compensation Viṣṇu changed into a cosmic being and recaptured all the universe in three strides; in this form Viṣṇu is called Trivikrama.
• *Varadamudrā:* Buddhist gesture of bestowing a gift: hand projecting downward, palm forward.
• *Varaśāpa:* antithetical term for aspects of a wish composed of *vàra*, (blessing) and *śāpa* (curse).
• *Varuṇa*: (god of the waters), guardian of the west; in Khmer art he is most often shown astride a *haṃsa*, and he carries a noose or halter.
• *Vāsuki*: *nāga* who helped the *deva* and *asura* to churn the Sea of Milk to obtain the elixir of life; also, one of Śiva's attributes.
• *Vat:* temple.
• *Vat Phu*: temple in present-day Laos, seat of Bhadreśvara.
• *Vatt:* post-Angkor Buddhist monastery.
• *Vāyu*: god of winds, guardian (*dikpālaka*) of the northwest.
• *Veda:* (knowledge), set of texts written in an archaic form of Sanskrit; Vedism, the forerunner of Brahmanism, is defined by these texts.
• *Vinayaka*: name associated with Gaṇeśa.
• *Viṣṇu*: one of the three gods of the *trimūrti*; he is the savior god, reincarnated age after age to save the world; his usual attributes speak to his status as a sovereign: discus, conch, club, and earth, represented in Khmer iconography as a ball.
• *Viṣṇupada:* also *Viṣṇupāda*, Viṣṇu's footprint.
• *Vitarkamudrā:* Buddhist gesture of argumentation: right hand raised, thumb and index finger forming a circle.

Y

• *Yajñavarāha*: Brahman *guru* of Jayavarman V; instigator of Banteay Srei.
• *Yakṣa:* low-ranked divinities, protectors and owners of riches.
• *Yama*: judge of the dead and the guardian of the south in Brahmanic mythology.
• *Yamunā*: goddess, the personification of the Yamunā (Jumna) River.
• *Yantra:* geometrical diagram to aid meditation.
• *Yaśodharapura*: (city supported by glory), Sanskrit name for Angkor during the Angkor period.
• *Yaśodharataṭāka*: eastern *baray* of Angkor.
• *Yaśodhareśvara*: deity worshiped at Phnom Bakheng.
• *Yaśovarman I*: (protected by glory, r. 889–beg. 10th century), his posthumous name was Paramaśivaloka.
• *Yaśovarman II*: (r. after 1150–1165).
• *Yoga*: meditative practices of Buddhism.
• *Yogin:* follower of Yoga.
• *Yoginī:* female follower of Yoga; minor female divinity in Tantric Buddhism, especially found dancing in groups of six or eight around Hevajra; in Hindu mythology, sorceress, ogress, and protector of children.

Z

• *Zhenla*: name given by the Chinese to a Southeast Asian kingdom, ancestor to the Khmer empire, straddling the northern portion of present-day Cambodia and Laos.
• *Zhou Daguan*: Chinese traveler who visited the Khmer capital from 1296 to 1297; his account, still extant, is the oldest known description of the site of Angkor.

Bibliography

AAK:
Art et archéologie khmers

BEFEO:
Bulletin de l'École française d'Extrême-Orient

IC:
Cœdès, G. *Inscriptions du Cambodge*. 8 vols. Hanoi and Paris, 1937–1966

ISCC:
Barth, A., and A. Bergaigne. *Inscriptions sanscrites de Campā et du Cambodge*. Paris, 1885–1893

BSEI:
Bulletin de la Société des Études Indochinoises

A

Alvares, S. "L'iconographie du temple de Bàkong de sa fondation au XIIIe siècle." *Histoire de l'art* 20 (1992), 27–38

Ang, C. "Recherches récentes sur le culte des mégalithes et des grottes au Cambodge." *Journal Asiatique* 281, 1–2 (1993), 185–210

Ang, C. "Le sol et l'ancêtre. L'amorphe et l'anthropomorphe." *Journal Asiatique* 283, 1 (1995), 213–238

Ang, C., E. Prenowitz, and A. Thompson. *Angkor Past, Present, and Future*. 1996

Angkor. L'art khmer au Cambodge et en Thaïlande. Archeologia Dossier Histoire et archéologie 125 (March 1988)

d'Ardenne de Tizac, H. "Statuaire siamoise et statuaire khmère." *Revue des Arts Asiatiques* 2, 1 (1925), 35–41

L'Art bouddhique. Paris, 1990

L'Art de l'Asie du Sud-Est. L'art et les Grandes Civilisations 24. Paris, 1994

Auboyer, J. "Un torse khmer du XIe siècle." *Oriental Art* 3, 1 (1950), 20

Auboyer, J. "Trois portraits du roi Jayavarman VII." *Arts Asiatiques* 6, 1 (1959), 70–74

Auboyer, J. *Les Arts de l'Inde et des pays indianisés. Les neuf muses*. Paris, 1968

Auboyer, J. "L'art khmer du IXe au XIIIe siècle." *Cahiers de civilisation médiévale* 14, 2 (April-June 1971), 119–129

Aymonier, E. *Textes khmers*. Saigon, 1878

Aymonier, E. "Quelques notions sur les inscriptions en vieux khmêr." *Journal Asiatique* (April-June, 1883), 441–505; (August-September, 1883), 199–228

Aymonier, E. "La stèle de Sdok Kak Thom." *Journal Asiatique* 9, 17 (1901), 261–271

Aymonier, E. *Le Cambodge*. I, *Le Royaume actuel*. II, *Les Provinces siamoises*. III, *Le Groupe d'Angkor et l'histoire*. Paris, 1901-1904

B

Bagchi, P. C. "On Some Tantric Texts Studied in Ancient Kambuja." *The Indian Historical Quaterly* 5 (1929), 754–769

Banerjea, J. N. *The Development of Hindu Iconography*. Calcutta, 1956

Banerjee, N. R. "An Unidentified Sculptural Panel at the Musée Guimet, Paris." *Arts Asiatiques* 10, 1 (1964), 87–90

Bareau, A. *Bouddha. Philosophes de tous les temps collection*. Paris, 1962

Barrett, D. "The Later School of Amaravati and Its Influences." *Indian Art and Letters* 28 (1954), 41–53

Barth, A. "Bulletin critique des religions de l'Inde." *Revue de l'histoire des religions* 5 (1882), 227–252

Barth, A. *Oeuvres*. Vol. 1. Paris, 1914

Bastian, A. *Die Völker des Östlichen Asien*. Leipzig, 1866

Bayard, D. T. *Southeast Asian Archaeology at the XV Pacific Science Congress* (University of Otago Studies in Prehistoric Archaeology 16). Otago, 1984

Béguin, G. *L'Art du sud-est asiatique*. Paris, 1986

Béguin, G. *L'Inde et le monde indianisé au Musée national des Arts asiatiques-Guimet*. Paris, 1992

Bellugue, P. "L'anatomie des formes et la sculpture khmère ancienne." *AAK* 2 (1924–1926), 253–302

Bellwood, P. S. *Prehistory of Southeast Asia. The Cambridge History of Southeast Asia*. Vol. 1. 1985

Bénisti, M. "Le *stūpa* monolithe du musée national de Phnom Penh." *Arts Asiatiques* 8, 1 (1961), 57–66

Bénisti, M. "Illustration de quelques procédés de sculpture khmère." *Arts Asiatiques* 9, 1–2 (1962–1963), 99–105

Bénisti, M. "Représentations khmères de Viṣṇu couché." *Arts Asiatiques* 11, 1 (1965), 91–117

Bénisti, M. "Note d'iconographie khmère—4: au sujet d'un linteau de Vat Baset." *BEFEO* 53–2 (1967), 513–516

Bénisti, M. "Recherches sur le premier art khmer—1: les linteaux dits de Thala Borivat." *Arts Asiatiques* 18 (1968), 85–101

Bénisti, M. "Recherches sur le premier art khmer—2: la 'bande à chatons,' critère chronologique?" *Arts Asiatiques* 20 (1969), 99–120

Bénisti, M. *Rapports entre le premier art khmer et l'art indien*. 2 vols. (Mémoires archéologiques 5). Paris, 1970

Bénisti, M. "Recherches sur le premier art khmer—3: aux confins des styles de Prei Kmeng et de Kompong Preah." *Arts Asiatiques* 23 (1971), 93–134

Bénisti, M. "Recherches sur le premier art khmer—4: piédestaux décorés." *Arts Asiatiques* 26, 1 (1973), 191–224 [1]

Bénisti, M. "Recherches sur le premier art khmer—5: la face de monstre." *Arts Asiatiques* 28, 2 (1973), 119–138 [2]

Bénisti, M. "Recherches sur le premier art khmer—6: linteaux inédits et linteaux méconnus." *Arts Asiatiques* 30, 1 (1974), 131–172

Bénisti, M. "Note d'iconographie khmère—10: premières représentations de Sri Laksmi." *BEFEO* 61, 2 (1974), 349–354

Bénisti, M. "Note d'iconographie khmère—11: la dalle de Ba Kan aux deux faces sculptées." *BEFEO* 63 (1976), 375–387

Bénisti, M. "Recherches sur le premier art khmer—7: le problème de Sambor S. 1." *Arts Asiatiques* 33 (1977), 25–56

Bénisti, M. "Une sculpture khmère inédite." *Arts Asiatiques* 36 (1981), 62–65

Bhandarkar, D. R. "Mathura Pillar Inscription of Candragupta 2: G. E. 61." *Epigraphia Indica* 21 (1931–1932), 1–9

Bhattacharya, K. "Étude sur l'iconographie de Banteay Samrè." *Arts Asiatiques* 2, 4 (1955), 294–308 [1]

Bhattacharya, K. "The Pancaratra Sect in Ancient Cambodia." *Journal of the Greater India Society* 14, 2 (1955), 111–116 [2]

Bhattacharya, K. "La secte des Pāśupata dans l'ancien Cambodge." *Journal Asiatique* 243, 2 (1955), 479–490 [3]

Bhattacharya, K. "Some Aspects of Temple Administration in the Ancient Khmer Kingdom." *Calcutta Review*, 3d series, 134 (1955), 193–199 [4]

Bhattacharya, K. "Notes d'iconographie khmère, 1–2–3–4: le lion, vāhana d'Indra et de Viṣṇu, interprétation du simhasana?-Les 'neuf Deva'-Le rhinocéros, vāhana de Skanda?-Le 'Triomphe' de Viṣṇu." *Arts Asiatiques* 3, 3 (1956), 183–193

Bhattacharya, K. "Notes d'iconographie khmère, 5–7: Viṣṇu Trivikrama-Le Barattement de la mer de Lait-Le Soleil et la Lune." *Arts Asiatiques* 4, 3 (1957), 208–220 [1]

Bhattacharya, K. "Notes d'iconographie khmère, 8: Śiva dansant." *Arts Asiatiques* 4, 4 (1957), 293–298 [2]

Bhattacharya, K. "Notes d'iconographie khmère, 9–10: Abhiseka de Lakṣmī-Une série de 'Neuf Dieux.'" *Arts Asiatiques* 5, 3 (1958), 217–220 [1]

Bhattacharya, K. "An Unpublished Gaṇeśa Image from Cambodia." *Artibus Asiae* 21 (1958), 269–270 [2]

Bhattacharya, K. *Les Religions brahmaniques dans l'ancien Cambodge, d'après l'épigraphie et l'iconographie* (EFEO 49). Paris, 1961

Bhattacharya, K. "Hari Kambujendra." *Artibus Asiae* 27, 1–2 (1964–1965), 72–78

Bhattacharya, K. "Notes d'iconographie khmère, 11: les Navagraha et les 'Neuf Divinités.'" *Arts Asiatiques* 10, 1 (1964), 91–94

Bhattacharya, K. "Notes d'iconographie khmère, 12: Les images de Lakṣmī à Prasat Kravan." *Arts Asiatiques* 11, 2 (1965), 45–52 [1]

Bhattacharya, K. "Sur une stance d'une inscription sanskrite du Cambodge." *Journal Asiatique* 253 (1965), 407–409 [2]

Bhattacharya, K. "Notes d'iconographie khmère, 13–14. Viṣṇu Anantasayin-Les images de Lakṣmī à Prasat Kravan." *Arts Asiatiques* 13 (1966), 111–113 [1]

Bhattacharya, K. "Liṅga-Kośa." In *Essays Offered to G. H. Luce* (Artibus Asiae, suppl. 23), 2:6–13. Ed. B. Shin, J. Boisselier, and A. B. Griswold. Ascona, 1966 [2]

Bhattacharya, K. "Le védisme de certains textes hindouistes." *Journal Asiatique* 255 (1967), 199–222

BHATTACHARYA, K. "Religious Speculations in Ancient Cambodia. Śaiva Speculations." In *R. C. Majumdar Felicitation Volume*, 78–97. Ed. H. B. Sarker. Calcutta, 1970
BHATTACHARYA, K. "Note sur le Vedānta dans l'inscription de Prè Rup (Cambodge)." *Journal Asiatique* 259 (1971), 91–101
BHATTACHARYA, K. *L'Ātman-Brahman dans le Bouddhisme ancien* (EFEO 90). Paris, 1973
BHATTACHARYA, K. "The Present State of Researches on the Sanskrit Epigraphy of Cambodia: Some Observations." In *Amṛtadhārā, Professor R. N. Dandekar Felicitation Volume*, 475–484. Ed. S. D. Joshi. Delhi, 1984
BHATTACHARYA, K. *Recherches sur le vocabulaire des inscriptions sanskrites du Cambodge* (EFEO 167). Paris, 1991
BHATTACHARYA, K. "Some Observations on the Sanskrit Epigraphy of Cambodia." In *Corolla Torontonensis, Studies in Honour of Ronald Morton Smith*, 225–228. Ed. E. Robins and S. Sandahl. Toronto, 1994
BHATTACHARYA, K. *Religious Syncretism in Ancient Cambodia* (in preparation)
BHATTACHARYYA, A. K. "The Theme of Churning of the Ocean in Indian and Khmer Art." *Arts Asiatiques* 6, 2 (1959), 121–134
BIARDEAU, M. *L'Hindouisme. Anthropologie d'une civilisation*. Paris, 1981
BIZOT, F. "Les ensembles ornementaux illimités d'Angkor." *Arts Asiatiques* 21 (1970), 109–149
BIZOT, F. "La consécration des statues et le culte des morts." In *Recherches nouvelles sur le Cambodge*, 101–139. Paris, 1994
BOELES, J. J. "Two Yoginīs of Hevajra from Thailand." In *Essays Offered to G. H. Luce* (Artibus Asiae, suppl. 23), 2:14–29. Ed. B. Shin, J. Boisselier, and A. B. Griswold. Ascona, 1966
BOISSELIER, J. "Évolution du diadème dans la statuaire khmère." *BSEI*, n. s. 25, 2 (1950), 149–170 [1]
BOISSELIER, J. "Note sur deux Buddha parés des galeries d'Angkor Vat." *BSEI* n. s. 25, 4 (1950), 299–306 [2]
BOISSELIER, J. "Garuḍa dans l'art khmer." *BEFEO* 44, 1 (1951), 55–87
BOISSELIER, J. "Ben Mala et la chronologie des monuments du style d'Angkor Vat." *BEFEO* 46, 1 (1952), 187–226 [1]
BOISSELIER, J. "Précisions sur la statuaire du style d'Angkor Vat." *BEFEO* 46, 1 (1952), 227–252 [2]
BOISSELIER, J. "Le Harihara de Bakon." *BEFEO* 46, 1 (1952), 253–256 [3]
BOISSELIER, J. "Réflexions sur l'art du règne de Jayavarman VII." *BSEI*, n. s. 27, 3 (1952), 261–273 [4]
BOISSELIER, J. *La Statuaire khmère et son évolution* (EFEO 37). Saigon, 1955 [1]
BOISSELIER, J. "Une statue féminine inédite du style de Sambor." *Arts Asiatiques* 2, 1 (1955), 18–34 [2]
BOISSELIER, J. *Tendances de l'art khmer. Commentaires sur vingt-quatre chefs-d'œuvre du musée de Phnom-Penh*. Paris, 1956 [1]
BOISSELIER, J. "Arts du Champa et du Cambodge préangkorien. La date de Mi-so'n E-1." *Artibus Asiae* 19 (1956), 197–212 [2]
BOISSELIER, J. "À propos d'un bronze cham inédit d'Avalokiteśvara." *Arts Asiatiques* 4, 4 (1957), 255–274 [1]
BOISSELIER, J. "Vajrapāṇi dans l'art du Bayon." *Proceedings of the 22nd Congress of Orientalists*. 2:324–332. Leiden, 1957 [2]
BOISSELIER, J. "La statuaire préangkorienne et Pierre Dupont." *Arts Asiatiques* 6, 1 (1959), 59–69 [1]
BOISSELIER, J. "Le Viṣṇu de Tjibuaja (Java occidental) et la statuaire du Sud-Est asiatique." *Artibus Asiae* 22 (1959), 210–226 [2]
BOISSELIER, J. "Un torse khmer du Musée oriental de Venise." *Artibus Asiae* 23 (1960), 233–238
BOISSELIER, J. "Note sur les bas-reliefs tardifs d'Angkor Vat." *Journal Asiatique* (1962), 244–248
BOISSELIER, J. "À propos de l'identification d'un 'Acala' cham." *Arts Asiatiques* 9, 1–2 (1962–1963), 81–86
BOISSELIER, J. *La Statuaire du Champa. Recherches sur les cultes et l'iconographie* (EFEO 54). Paris, 1963
BOISSELIER, J. "Précisions sur quelques images khmères d'Avalokiteśvara. Les bas-reliefs de Banteay Chmar." *Arts Asiatiques* 11, 1 (1965), 73–89 [1]
BOISSELIER, J. "Récentes recherches archéologiques en Thaïlande." *Arts Asiatiques* 12 (1965), 125–174 [2]
BOISSELIER, J. *Manuel d'archéologie d'Extrême-Orient*. Part I, *Asie du Sud-Est*. Vol. 1. *Le Cambodge*. Paris, 1966
BOISSELIER, J. "Notes sur l'art du bronze dans l'ancien Cambodge." *Artibus Asiae* 29, 4 (1967), 275–334 [1]
BOISSELIER, J. "Le Bouddha de Tuol-Ta-Hoy et l'art bouddhique du Sud-Est asiatique." In *Annales de l'Université Royale des Beaux-Arts 1. Phnom-Penh* 1967 [2]
BOISSELIER, J. "Les linteaux khmers du VIIIe siècle. Nouvelles données sur le style de Kompong Preah." *Artibus Asiae* 30 (1968), 101–144
BOISSELIER, J. "Recherches archéologiques en Thaïlande, 2." *Arts Asiatiques* 20 (1969), 47–98
BOISSELIER, J. "Pouvoir royal et symbolisme architectural: Neak Pean et son importance pour la royauté angkorienne." *Arts Asiatiques* 21 (1970), 91–108
BOISSELIER, J. "Un bronze d'époque préangkorienne." *Revue du Louvre* 6 (1971), 369–371
BOISSELIER, J. "Travaux de la mission archéologique française en Thaïlande (July-November 1966)." *Arts Asiatiques* 25 (1972), 27–90
BOISSELIER, J. *La Sculpture en Thaïlande*. Fribourg, 1974
BOISSELIER, J. *The Heritage of Thai Sculpture*. New York and Tokyo, 1975
BOISSELIER, J. "Asie du Sud-Est-Cambodge." In *La Grammaire des formes et des styles-Asie*, 227–265. Fribourg, 1978
BOISSELIER, J. "The Avalokiteśvara in the Museum's Wilstach Collection." *Bulletin of the Philadelphia Museum of Art* 77, 333 (1981) 11–24
BOISSELIER, J. *Il Sud-Est Asiatico*. In *Storia Universale dell'arte-Sezioneseconda-Le Civiltà dell'Oriente*. Turin, 1986
BOISSELIER, J. "Une tête angkorienne de Harihara." *Arts Asiatiques* 44 (1989), 44–49
BOISSELIER, J. "Mahisasuramardini." *Orientations* (Feb. 1990), 40–42
BOISSELIER, J. "Un Buddha de bois préangkorien et ses affinités indonésiennes." *BEFEO* 78 (1991), 169–177
BOISSELIER, J. "1. La signification d'Angkor Thom. 2. Prasat Thom de Koh Ker et Banteay Srei. 3. Oc-èo." *Renaissance culturelle du Cambodge* 6 (1992), 259–284
BOISSELIER, J., *La Sagesse du Bouddha*. Paris, 1993
BOSCH, F. D. K. "Notes archéologiques, 2. La *liṅgodbhavamurti* de Śiva en Indochine." *BEFEO* 31 (1931), 491–498
BOSCH, F. D. K. "Notes archéologiques, 4. Le temple d'Angkor Vat." *BEFEO* 32 (1932), 12–17
BOSCH, F. D. K. *De Gouden Kiem*. Amsterdam and Brussels, 1948
BOSCH, F. D. K. "On Some Groups of Yaksa Figures in Indonesian and Khmer Art." *Artibus Asiae* 22 (1959), 227–239
BOUILLEVAUX, C. E. *Ma visite aux ruines cambodgiennes en 1850*. Saint-Quentin, 1863
BOULBET, J. "Des femmes Bu Dih à quelques apsaras originales d'Angkor Vat." *Arts Asiatiques* 17 (1968), 209–218
BOULBET, J. *Le Phnom Kulen et sa région* (EFEO Collection de textes et documents sur l'Indochine 12). Paris, 1979
BOULBET, J., and B. DAGENS. "Les sites archéologiques de la région du Bhnam Gulen (Phnom Kulen)." *Arts Asiatiques* 27 (1973)
BRIGGS, L. P. "Les missionnaires portugais et espagnols au Cambodge (1555–1603)." *BSEI* 25 (1950), 5–29
BRIGGS, L. P. *The Ancient Khmer Empire*. Philadelphia, 1951
BROMAN, B. M. "The National Museum of Cambodia." *Arts of Asia* (Jan.-Feb., 1976), 30–37
BRONSON, B. "Patterns in the Early Southeast Asian Metal Trade." In *Early Metallurgy, Trade and Urban Centres in Thailand and Southeast Asia*, 63–114. Ed. I. Glover, P. Suchitta, and J. Villiers. Bangkok, 1992
BROWN, R. *The Ceramics of South-East Asia. Their Dating and Identification*. Singapore and Oxford, 1988
BROWN, R. L. *The Dvāravatī Wheels of the Law and the Indianization of South East Asia*. Leiden, New York, and Cologne, 1996
BRUGUIER, B. "Sur quelques procédés de liaison utilisés dans l'architecture cambodgienne ancienne." *BEFEO* 78 (1991), 179–202
BRUGUIER, B. "Le prasat Ak Yum." In *Recherches nouvelles sur le Cambodge*, 273–296. Ed. F. Bizot. Paris, 1994
BUHOT, J. "L'Art khmer. L'art des origines à nos jours." *Les arts de l'Extrême-Orient*. 2:373–377. Paris, 1933
BUNKER, E. C. "Pre-Angkor Period Bronzes from PraKon Chai." *Archives of Asian Art* 25 (1971–1972), 67–76

C

The Cambridge History of Southeast Asia. Ed. N. Tarling. 2 vols. Cambridge, New York, and Oakleigh, 1992
CANBERRA 1992. Michael Brand and Chuch Poeurn. *The Age of Angkor. Treasures from the National Museum of Cambodia* [exh. cat., The Australian National Gallery] (Canberra, 1992)
Cent objets disparus. International Council of Museums (ICOM)-École française d'Extrême-Orient. Paris, 1993
CHAKRAVARTI, A. *The Sdok Kak Thom Inscription*, part II (Calcutta Sanskrit College Research Series 112). Calcutta, 1980
CHANDLER, D. P. *The Land and People of Cambodia*. Philadelphia, 1972
CHANDLER, D. P. "Royalty Sponsored Human Sacrifices in Nineteenth Century Cambodia." *Journal of the Siam Society* 62, 2 (1974), 207–222
CHANDLER, D. P. *A History of Cambodia*. Boulder, Colorado, 1983; Sydney, 1992
CHANDLER, D. P., and I. MABBETT. *The Khmers*. Oxford, 1995
CHUTIWONGS, N. "The Iconography of Avalokiteśvara in Mainland South East Asia," dissertation, Rijksuniversiteit, Leiden, 1984
CHUTIWONGS, N., and D. P. LEIDY. *Buddha of the Future: An Early Maitreya from Thailand* [exh. cat., The Asia Society Galleries] (New York, 1994)
CŒDÈS, G. "La stèle de Ta-Prohm." *BEFEO* 6 (1906), 44–81
CŒDÈS, G. "La stèle de Tep Pranam." *Journal Asia-*

tique (March-April 1908) [1]
Cœdès, G. "Les inscriptions de Bàt Cum." *Journal Asiatique* 10, 12 (1908), 213–254 [2]
Cœdès, G. "Catalogue des pièces originales de sculpture khmère conservées au musée Indochinois du Trocadéro et au musée Guimet." *Bulletin de la Commission archéologique de l'Indochine* (1910), 19–62
Cœdès, G. "Les bas-reliefs d'Angkor Vat." *Bulletin de la Commission archéologique de l'Indochine* (1911), 170–220
Cœdès, G. "La stèle de Pàlhàl. Études cambodgiennes 11." *BEFEO* 13, 6 (1913), 27–36
Cœdès, G. "Essai de classification des documents historiques cambodgiens conservés à la bibliothèque de l'École française d'Extrême-Orient." *BEFEO* 18, 9 (1918), 1–28
Cœdès, G. *Bronzes khmers* (Ars Asiatica 5). Paris and Brussels, 1923
Cœdès, G. "Études cambodgiennes 17. L'épigraphie du temple de Phimai." *BEFEO* 24 (1924), 345–352
Cœdès, G. *Inscriptions du Cambodge publiées sous les auspices de l'Académie des inscriptions et belles-lettres.* 6 vols. Paris, 1926–1937
Cœdès, G. *Recueil des Inscriptions du Siam,* 2. Bangkok, 1929; 2d ed., 1961
Cœdès, G. "Études cambodgiennes 25. Deux inscriptions sanskrites du Fou-nan." *BEFEO* 31 (1931), 1–12
Cœdès, G. "Études cambodgiennes 30. À la recherche du Yaśodharāśrama." *BEFEO* 32, 1 (1932), 84–112 [1]
Cœdès, G. "Un nouveau tympan de Banteay Srei." *BEFEO* 32, 1 (1932), 81–84, pl. 3 [2]
Cœdès, G. "Angkor Vat temple ou tombeau?" *BEFEO* 33 (1933), 303–309
Cœdès, G. "The Central Image of the Bayon of Angkor Thom." *Journal of the Indian Society of Oriental Art* 2 (1934), 8–10
Cœdès, G. "Une scène du Mahābhārata figurée sur un fronton de Banteay Srei." *Revue des Arts Asiatiques* 9, 4 (1935), 225–227
Cœdès, G. "La plus ancienne inscription en pāli du Cambodge." *BEFEO* 36 (1936), 14–21
Cœdès, G. "A New Inscription from Fu-Nan." *Journal of the Greater India Society* 4 (1937), 117–121
Cœdès, G. "La stèle du Preah Khan d'Angkor." *BEFEO* 41 (1942), 255–301
Cœdès, G. *Pour mieux comprendre Angkor.* Paris, 1947
Cœdès, G. "Études cambodgiennes 39. L'épigraphie des monuments de Jayavarman VII." *BEFEO* 44 (1947–1950), 97–119
Cœdès, G. "Un Yantra récemment découvert à Angkor." *Journal Asiatique* 240 (1952), 465–477
Cœdès, G. "Nouvelles données épigraphiques sur l'histoire de l'Indochine centrale." *Journal Asiatique* 246 (1958), 125–142
Cœdès, G. "Le portrait dans l'art khmer." *Arts Asiatiques* 7, 3 (1960), 179–198
Cœdès, G. *Les Peuples de la péninsule indochinoise.* Paris, 1962 [1]
Cœdès, G. "La date d'exécution des deux bas-reliefs tardifs d'Angkor Vat." *Journal Asiatique* (1962), 235–243 [2]
Cœdès, G. *Angkor: An Introduction.* Trans. E. Gardiner. Hong Kong, 1963
Cœdès, G. *Les États hindouisés d'Indochine et d'Indonésie.* Rev. ed. Paris, 1964
Cœdès, G. *The Indianized States of Southeast Asia.* Ed. W. F. Vella. Trans. S. Cowing. Hawaii, 1968
Cœdès, G. *Articles sur le pays khmer.* 1. Paris, 1989. 2. Paris, 1992
Cœdès, G., and L. Finot. *Notes d'épigraphie.* (*BEFEO* 15) Paris, 1915
Cœdès, G., and P. Dupont. "Les stèles de Sdok Kak Thom, Phnom Sandak et Prah Vihar." *BEFEO* 43 (1943–1946), 57–134
Colless, B. E. "The Ancient Bnam Empire: Fu-nan and Po-nan." *Journal of the Oriental Society of Australia* 9, 1–2 (1973), 21–31
Commaille, J., "Les ruines de Bassac." *BEFEO* 2 (1902), 260–267
Commaille, J., and G. Cœdès. *Le Bàyon d'Angkor Thom. Bas-reliefs publiés par les soins de la Commission archéologique de l'Indochine, d'après les documents recueillis par la mission Henri Dufour, avec la collaboration de Charles Carpeaux.* Paris, 1910, 1914
Conze, E., trans. *The Large Sūtra on Perfect Wisdom with the divisions of the Abhisamayālakāra.* Berkeley, Los Angeles, London, 1975
Cooler, R. M. "Sculpture, Kingship, and the Triad of Phnom Da." *Artibus Asiae* 40, 1 (1978), 29–40
Coomaraswamy, A. "Catalogue des pièces khmères conservées dans les musées d'Amérique du Nord." *Art et Archéologie khmers* 2 (1924–1926), 235–240
de Coral-Rémusat, G. "L'activité archéologique en Indochine." *Revue des Arts Asiatiques* 12, 4 (1938), 170–183
de Coral-Rémusat, G. *L'Art khmer. Les grandes étapes de son évolution* (Études d'art et d'ethnologie asiatiques 1). 1st ed. 1940; 2d ed. Paris, 1951
de Coral-Rémusat, G. "Le procédé des emprunts aux styles passés dans l'art khmer." *Arts Asiatiques* 1, 2 (1954), 118–128
Cowan, C. D., and O. W. Wolters, eds. *South-East Asian History and Historiography: Essays presented to D. G. E. Hall.* Ithaca, 1976
de Croizier. *L'Art khmer. Étude historique sur les monuments de l'Ancien Cambodge avec un aperçu général sur l'architecture khmère et une liste complète des monuments explorés suivi d'un catalogue raisonné du Musée khmer de Compiègne.* Paris, 1875
Czuma, S. "A Masterpiece of Early Cambodian Sculpture." *The Bulletin of the Cleveland Museum of Art* 41 (April 1974), 119–127

D
Dagens, B. "Étude iconographique de quelques fondations de l'époque de Sūryavarman Ier." *Arts Asiatiques* 17 (1968), 173–208
Dagens, B. "Étude sur l'iconographie du Bàyon (frontons et linteaux)." *Arts Asiatiques* 19 (1969), 123–167
Dagens, B. "Les linteaux décoratifs du Prasat Cha Chouk." *BEFEO* 57 (1970), 91–97
Dagens, B. *Angkor—la forêt de pierre* (Découvertes 64). Paris, 1989
Dagens, B. "L'Asie du Sud et du Sud-Est." *Atlas de l'art Universalis* (1993), 292–293 [1]
Dagens, B. "De Nālandā à Angkor ou les théologiens au service du roi." *Atlas de l'art Universalis* (1993), 312–313 [2]
Dagens, B. "Le voyage en Orient ou à chacun sa beauté." Atlas de l'art Universalis (1993), 310–311 [3]
Dagens, B. *Angkor: Heart of an Asian Empire.* New York, 1995
Dalet, R. "Quelques nouvelles sculptures khmères." *BEFEO* 35 (1935), 147–158
Dalet, R. "Notes sur les stèles en édifice avec personnages dans les baies." *Revue des Arts Asiatiques* 10, 1 (1936), 37–41 [1]
Dalet, R. "Iconographie bouddhique khmère." *Revue des Arts Asiatiques* 10 (1936), 192–198 [2]
Delaporte, L. *Voyage au Cambodge. L'architecture khmère.* Paris, 1880
Delvert, J. *Le Paysan cambodgien.* Paris and The Hague, 1961
Delvert, J. "Recherches sur l'érosion des grès des monuments d'Angkor." *BEFEO* 51, 2 (1963), 453–534
Delvert, J. *Le Cambodge.* Paris, 1983
Deydier, H. *Introduction à la connaissance du Laos.* Saigon, 1952
Dijon 1996. *Âges et visages de l'Asie. Un siècle d'exploration à travers les collections du musée Guimet* [exh. cat., Musée des Beaux-Arts de Dijon] (Dijon, 1996)
Duflos, M. C. "L'art préangkorien." In *Angkor-L'Art khmer au Cambodge et en Thaïlande.* Archeologia. Dossiers Histoire et Archéologie 125 (March 1988)
Duflos, M. C. "Cambodian and Thai Masterpieces." *Orientations* 22, 5 (May 1991), 96–101
Dumarçay, J. *Ta Kev. Étude architecturale du temple* (EFEO Mémoires archéologiques 6). Paris, 1971 [1]
Dumarçay, J. *Phnom Bakheng. Étude architecturale du temple* (EFEO Mémoires archéologiques 7). Paris, 1971 [2]
Dumarçay, J. *Documents graphiques de la Conservation d'Angkor, 1963–1973.* Paris, 1988
Dumarçay, J. *Histoire des retenues d'eau khmères.* 1994
Dumarçay, J., and B. Ph. Groslier. *Le Bayon. Histoire architecturale du temple* (EFEO Mémoires archéologiques 3; 3, 2). Paris, 1967 and 1973
Dupont, P. "Catalogue des collections indochinoises." *Bulletin de la Commission archéologique de l'Indochine, 1931–1934.* Paris, 1934
Dupont, P. "Art de Dvāravatī et art khmer. Les Buddha debouts de l'époque du Bàyon." *Revue des Arts Asiatiques* 9, 2 (1935), 63–75
Dupont, P. "L'art du Kulên et les débuts de la statuaire angkorienne." *BEFEO* 36 (1936), 415–426 [1]
Dupont, P. "La statuaire en ronde bosse dans l'Asie du Sud-Est." *Revue des Arts Asiatiques* 10, 2 (1936), 97–106 [2]
Dupont, P. "Mission au Cambodge. Recherches archéologiques sur le Phnom Kulên 1, à Angkor et à Battambañ." *BEFEO* 37 (1937)
Dupont, P. "Les monuments de Phnom Kulên." *BEFEO* 38 (1938), 199–208 [1]
Dupont, P. "Mission au Cambodge. Recherches archéologiques sur le Phnom Kulên 2." *BEFEO* 38, 2 (1938), 426–438 [2]
Dupont, P. "Variétés archéologiques, 1.-Viṣṇu mitrés dans l'Indochine occidentale." *BEFEO* 41 (1941), 233–254
Dupont, P. "Les Buddha sur *nāga* dans l'art khmer." *Artibus Asiae* 13, 1–2 (1950), 39–62
Dupont, P. "Les premières images brahmaniques de l'Indochine." *BSEI* 26 (1951), 131–140
Dupont, P. "Les linteaux khmers du viie siècle." *Artibus Asiae* 15, 1–2 (1952), 31–83
Dupont, P. *La Statuaire préangkorienne.* Ascona, 1955
Dupont, P. "Variétés archéologiques 3.-Les Buddha dits d'Amaravati en Asie du Sud-Est." *BEFEO* 49, 2 (1959), 631-636

E
Ellul, J. "Le mythe de Gaṇeśa: le Gaṇeśa cambodgien, un mythe d'origine de la magie." *Seksa khmer* 1–2 (1980), 69–153

ENSINK, J. "Śiva-Buddhism in Java and Bali." In *Buddhism in Ceylon and Studies on Religious Syncretism in Buddhist Countries,* 178–198. Ed. H. Bechert. (Abhandlungen der Akademie der Wissenschaften in Göttingen, philologisch-historische Klasse, Dritter Folge, 108) Göttingen, 1978

ESSEN, G.-W., and T. T. THINGO. *Die Götter des Himalaya. Buddhistische Kunst Tibets. Die Sammlung G.-W. Essen.* Munich, 1989

F

FILLIOZAT, J. "Le symbolisme du monument du Phnom Bakhen." *BEFEO* 44 (1947–1950), 527–554

FILLIOZAT, J. "New Researches on the Relations between India and Cambodia. *Indica* 3, 2 (1966), 95–106. Reprinted in *Laghupraban-dhāṛ, choix d'articles d'Indologie,* 454–465. Leiden, 1974

FILLIOZAT, J. "Les symboles d'une stèle khmère du VIIe siècle." *Arts Asiatiques* 16 (1967), 111–117

FILLIOZAT, J. "Temples et tombeaux de l'Inde et du Cambodge." *Comptes rendus de l'Académie des inscriptions et belles-lettres* (1979), 40–53

FILLIOZAT, J. "Sur le śivaïsme et le bouddhisme du Cambodge, à propos de deux livres récents." *BEFEO* 70 (1981), 59–99

FILLIOZAT, J. *Les Philosophies de l'Inde.* 3d ed. Paris, 1987

FINOT, L. "Deux nouvelles inscriptions de Bhadravarman I, roi de Champa." *BEFEO* 2 (1902), 185–191

FINOT, L. "Notes d'épigraphie 2. L'inscription sanskrite de Say-fong." *BEFEO* 3 (1903), 18–33

FINOT, L. "L'inscription de Prah Khan." *BEFEO* 4 (1904), 672–676

FINOT, L. "L'inscription de Sdok Kak Thom." *BEFEO* 15 (1915), 53–106 [1]

FINOT, L. "Inscriptions d'Aṅkor." *BEFEO* 15 (1915), 289–410 [2]

FINOT, L. "Dharmaçalas au Cambodge." *BEFEO* 15 (1915), 417–422 [3]

FINOT, L. *Notes d'épigraphie indochinoise.* Paris, 1916

FINOT, L. "Arts et archéologies khmers. 2." *BEFEO* 17 (1917), 360–372

FINOT, L. "Inscriptions d'Aṅkor." *BEFEO* 25 (1925), 289–409 [1]

FINOT, L. "Lokeśvara en Indochine." In *Études asiatiques publiées à l'occasion du 25e anniversaire de l'EFEO par ses membres et ses collaborateurs,* 1:227–256. Paris, 1925 [2]

FINOT, L. "L'archéologie indochinoise-1917–1930." *Bulletin de la Commission archéologique de l'Indochine, 1917–1930* (1931), 1ff

FINOT, L. "Stèles historiées du Cambodge." In *Études d'orientalisme publiées par le musée Guimet à la mémoire de Raymonde Linossier,* 1:255–259. Paris, 1932

FINOT, L. "Manuscrits sanskrits de Sādhana's retrouvés en Chine. Première partie: Hevajrasekaprakriyā." *Journal Asiatique* (1934), 19–48

FINOT, L., V. GOLOUBEW, and H. PARMENTIER. *Le Temple d'Īśvarapura* (EFEO Mémoire archéologique 1). Paris, 1926

FINOT, L., V. GOLOUBEW, and G. CŒDÈS. *Le Temple d'Angkor Vat* (EFEO Mémoires archéologiques 2). Paris, 1927–1932

FORT WORTH 1996. *The Path to Enlightenment. Masterpieces of Buddhist Sculpture from the National Museum of Asian Art, Musée Guimet, Paris* [exh. cat., Kimbell Art Museum] (Fort Worth, 1996)

FOUCHER, A. "Matériaux pour servir à l'étude de l'art khmer, 1, Bronzes." *Bulletin de la Commission archéologique de l'Indochine* (1912), 215–218 [1]

FOUCHER, A. "Matériaux pour servir à l'étude de l'art khmer, 2, Deux têtes de statues en pierre." *Bulletin de la Commission archéologique de l'Indochine* (1912), 217–218 [2]

FOUCHER, A. "Matériaux pour servir à l'étude de l'art khmer, 3, La collection Moura." *Bulletin de la Commission archéologique de l'Indochine* (1913), 93–103

FRANKFORT, H. *The Birth of Civilization in the Near East.* London, 1951; 3d edition 1954

FRÉDÉRIC, L. *Sud-Est asiatique, ses temples, ses sculptures.* Paris, 1964

FRÉDÉRIC, L. *The Art of Southeast Asia: Temples and Sculpture.* New York, 1965

FRÉDÉRIC, L. *Les Dieux de Bouddhisme. Guide iconographique.* Paris, 1992

FRÉDÉRIC, L. *L'Art de l'Inde et de l'Asie du Sud-Est.* Paris, 1994

FREEMAN, M., and R. WARNER. *Angkor: The Hidden Glories.* Boston, London, and Melbourne, 1990

G

GARNIER, F. *Voyage d'exploration en Indochine effectué par une commission française présidée par le capitaine de frégate Doudart de Lagrée.* Paris, 1873

GITEAU, M. "L'expression de la sensibilité dans l'art khmer." *Arts Asiatiques* 2, 3 (1955), 209–228 [1]

GITEAU, M., "L'expression de la sensibilité dans l'art khmer," *Arts Asiatiques* 2, 4 (1955), 242–250 [2]

GITEAU, M. "The Boar Aspect of Viṣṇu in Khmer Art." *Artibus Asiae* 19 (1956), 234–239

GITEAU, M. *Guide du Musée national de Phnom-Penh 1, Sculpture.* Phnom Penh, 1960

GITEAU, M. "Note sur un *garuḍa* récemment entré au Musée national de Phnom-Penh." *Arts Asiatiques* 8, 3 (1961), 215–226

GITEAU, M. *Les Khmers. Sculptures khmères-Reflets de la civilisation d'Angkor.* Fribourg, 1965 [1]

GITEAU, M. "Une représentation de la Bhiksatanamurti de Śiva à Angkor Vat." *Arts Asiatiques* 11, 1 (1965), 131–137 [2]

GITEAU, M. *Guide du Musée national de Phnom-Penh II. Mobilier en pierre, éléments d'architecture, inscriptions.* Phnom Penh, 1966 [1]

GITEAU, M. "Note sur une école cambodgienne de statuaire bouddhique inspirée de l'art d'Angkor Vat." *Arts Asiatiques* 13 (1966), 115–126 [2]

GITEAU, M. "Note sur les frontons du sanctuaire central de Vatt Nagar." *Arts Asiatiques* 16 (1967), 125–139

GITEAU, M. "À propos d'un épisode du Ramakerti représenté à Vatt Pubi (Siem Reap)." *Arts Asiatiques* 19 (1969), 107–121

GITEAU, M. "Battambang: le musée de Vat Po Veal." *Nokor Khmer* 3 (1970), 70–79

GITEAU, M. "Note sur quelques pièces en bronze récemment découvertes à Vatt Deb Pranamy d'Oudong (Utun)." *Arts Asiatiques* 24 (1971), 149–159

GITEAU, M. *Iconographie du Cambodge postangkorien* (EFEO vol. 100). Paris, 1975

GITEAU, M. *Angkor. Un peuple—un art.* Fribourg, 1976

GITEAU, M. "Le musée de Phnom Penh." *Connaissance des arts,* ex-series (March 1992), 48–53

GITEAU, M. "Note sur Kumbhakarna dans l'iconographie khmère." *Arts Asiatiques* 50 (1995), 69–75

GLAIZE, M. "Le gopura de Prah Palilay." *BEFEO* 40 (1940), 363–370

GLAIZE, M. *Les monuments du groupe d'Angkor.* Saigon 1944. Paris, 1963; reprint 1994

GLOVER, I. "Large Bronze Urns in Southeast Asia: Some New Finds and a Reassessment." In *Southeast Asian Archaeology 1990. Proceedings of the Third Conference of the European Association of South-East Asian Studies.* Ed. Ian Glover. Hull, 1992

GOLOUBEW, V. "Le Harihara de Maha Rosei." *Études asiatiques publiées à l'occasion du 25e anniversaire de l'EFEO par ses membres et ses collaborateurs,* 1:285–295. Paris, 1925

GOLOUBEW, V. "Le cheval Balāha." *BEFEO* 27 (1927), 223–238

GOLOUBEW, V. "Phnom Baken et la ville de Yaçovarman." *BEFEO* 33 (1933), 319–344

GONDA, J. "The Indian Religions in Pre-Islamic Indonesia and Their Survival in Bali." In *Handbuch der Orientalistik.* Ed. B. Spuler. Leiden and Cologne, 1975

GOPINATHA ROA, T. A. *Elements of Hindu Iconography.* Delhi, 1985

GOUDRIAAN, T. *The Vāśikhatantra.* Delhi, 1985

GROSLIER, B. Ph. *Angkor. Hommes et pierres.* Paris, 1956

GROSLIER, B. Ph. *Angkor et le Cambodge au XVIe siècle, d'après les sources portugaises et espagnoles.* Paris, 1958

GROSLIER, B. Ph. *Indochine carrefour des arts.* Paris, 1961

GROSLIER, B. Ph. *Indo China: Art in the Melting Pot of Races.* Baden-Baden and London, 1962

GROSLIER, B. Ph. *Indochine* (Archaeologia Mundi 8). Paris and Munich, 1966

GROSLIER, B. Ph. *Inscriptions du Bayon.* (J. Dumarçay and B. Ph. Groslier, *Bayon* 2). Paris, 1967

GROSLIER, B. Ph. *Angkor. Hommes et pierres.* Paris, 1968

GROSLIER, B. Ph. "Travaux archéologiques." *Travaux et Perspectives de l'École Française d'Extrême-Orient en son 75e anniversaire.* Paris, 1976

GROSLIER, B. Ph. "La cité hydraulique angkorienne: exploitation ou surexploitation du sol?" *BEFEO* 66 (1979), 161–202

GROSLIER, B. Ph. "L'Asie du Sud-Est." In *Histoire de l'art. L'art asiatique—4000 ans de chefs-d'œuvre,* 60–116. Paris, 1988

GROSLIER, B. Ph., and J. ARTHAUD. *Angkor: Art and Civilization.* London, 1966

GROSLIER, G. *À l'ombre d'Angkor. Notes et impressions sur les temples inconnus de l'ancien Cambodge.* Paris, 1916

GROSLIER, G. *Recherches sur les Cambodgiens, d'après les textes et les monuments depuis les premiers siècles de notre ère.* Paris, 1921

GROSLIER, G. "L'art du bronze au Cambodge." *AAK* 1 (1921–1923), 413–423

GROSLIER, G., "Introduction à l'étude des arts khmers." *AAK* 2 (1924–1926), 167–234 [1]

GROSLIER, G. "Troisième recherche sur les Cambodgiens, 2: Essai sur le Buddha khmer." *AAK* 2 (1924–1926), 93–112 [2]

GROSLIER, G. "Note sur la sculpture khmère ancienne." *Études asiatiques publiées à l'occasion du 25e anniversaire de l'EFEO par ses membres et ses collaborateurs.* 2 vols. Paris, 1925 [1]

GROSLIER, G. "La femme dans la sculpture khmère ancienne." *Revue des Arts Asiatiques* 2, 1 (1925), 35–41 [2]

GROSLIER, G. *Les Collections khmères du musée Albert-Sarraut à Phnom-Penh* (Ars Asiatica 16). Paris, 1931

GUY, John. *Ceramic Traditions of South-East Asia.* Singapore and New York, 1989

H

Hall, D. G. E. *A History of South-East Asia.* London

and Basingstoke, 1955. 3d ed. 1968

HALL, K. R., and J. K. WHITMORE, eds. *Explorations in Early South-East Asian History: The Origins of South-East Asian Statecraft.* Ann Arbor, 1976

HIGHAM, C. *The Archaeology of Mainland Southeast Asia: From 10,000 BC to the Fall of Angkor.* Cambridge, 1989

I

INSTITUT BOUDDHIQUE. *Silacarik Nagar Vatt (Inscriptions d'Angkor Vatt).* Phnom Penh, 1938. Reprinted Paris, 1984

J

JACQ-HERGOUALC'H, M. *L'armement et l'organisation de l'armée khmère aux XIIe et au XIIIe siècles, d'après les bas-reliefs d'Angkor Vat, du Bàyon et de Banteay Chmar.* Paris, 1979

JACQUES, C. "Notes sur l'inscription de la stèle de Vat Luong Kau." *Journal Asiatique* 250 (1962), 249–256

JACQUES, C. "Supplément au tome 8 des inscriptions du Cambodge." *BEFEO* 58 (1971), 177–196

JACQUES, C. "'Funan,' 'Zhenla': The Reality Concealed by These Chinese Views of Indochina." In *Early Southeast Asia,* 371–379. Ed. R. B. Smith and W. Watson. Oxford, 1979

JACQUES, C. "Le pays khmer avant Angkor." *Journal des Savants* (January-September 1986)

JACQUES, C. "Le roi khmer." In *Angkor—L'Art khmer au Cambodge et en Thaïlande,* 67–70 Archeologia. Dossiers Histoire et Archéologie 125 (March 1988)

JACQUES, C., and R. DUMONT. *Angkor.* Paris, 1990

JESSUP, Helen Ibbitson. *Court Arts of Indonesia.* New York, 1990

JESSUP, Helen Ibbitson. "Spirit of Place: The Genius of the Khmers." In *Kenro Izu. Light over Ancient Angkor,* 26–29. New York, 1996

K

Kāraṇḍavyūha. Mahāyānasūtrasaṃgraha. Part 1 (Buddhist Sanskrit Texts 17), 258–308. Ed. P. L. Vaidya. Darbhanga

KERN, Hendrik. "Opschriften op oude bouwwerken in Kambodja." *Bijdragen tot de Tal-, Land- en Volkenkunde* (1879), 268–272

KHIN SOK. "L'inscription de Preah Thom du Kulen." *BEFEO* 67 (1980), 133–134

KRAIRIKSH, P. *The Sacred Image. Sculptures from Thailand.* Cologne, 1979

KRAMRISCH, S. *The Hindu Temple.* Delhi and Varanasi, 1980

KULKE, H. *The Devaraja Cult* (Data Paper 108, Southeast Asia Program, Cornell University). Ithaca, 1978

KULKE, H. "The Early and Imperial Kingdoms in Southeast Asian History." In *Southeast Asia in the 9th to 14th Centuries,* 1–22. Ed. D. G. Marr and A. Milner. Singapore, 1986

L

LAMA ANAGARIKA GOVINDA. *Foundations of Tibetan Mysticism.* New York, 1973

LAN SUNNARY. "Étude iconographique du temple khmer de Thommanon (Dhammananda)." *Arts Asiatiques* 25 (1972), 155–198

LAN SUNNARY. "Le Nandin de Tuol Kuhea (Duol Guha)." *Khméritude* 1 (1991), 77–121

de LA VALLÉE POUSSIN, L. "Notes bouddhiques. 18. 'Opinions sur les relations des deux Véhicules au point de vue du Vinaya.'" *Académie royale de Belgique. Bulletins de la Classe des Lettres et Sciences politiques* 5, 16 (1930), 20–39

LE BONHEUR, A. "Un bronze d'époque préangkorienne représentant Maitreya." *Arts Asiatiques* 25 (1972), 129–154

LE BONHEUR, A. "Un Śiva inédit du style des Khleang." *Arts Asiatiques* 30 (1974), 179–204

LE BONHEUR, A. *Art khmer.* 2d ed. Paris, 1986.

LE BONHEUR, A. "L'art postangkorien." In *Angkor–L'Art khmer au Cambodge et en Thaïlande.* Archeologia. Dossiers Histoire et Archéologie 125 (March 1988) [1]

LE BONHEUR, A. "Où voir de l'art khmer en France?" In *Angkor—L'Art khmer au Cambodge et en Thaïlande.* Archeologia. Dossiers Histoire et Archéologie 125 (March 1988) [2]

LE BONHEUR, A. *Cambodge. Angkor. Temples en péril.* Paris, 1989 [1]

LE BONHEUR, A. "Une statue khmère célèbre entre au musée Guimet: 'L'Avalokiteśvara Didelot' (VIIe siècle environ)." *Arts Asiatiques* 44 (1989), 123–125 [2]

LE BONHEUR, A. "Activités du Musée national des Arts asiatiques-Guimet-Acquisitions-Asie du Sud-Est." *Arts Asiatiques* 47 (1992), 110–113

LE BONHEUR, A. "Activités du Musée national des Arts asiatiques-Guimet-Acquisitions-Asie du Sud-Est." *Arts Asiatiques* 48 (1993), 136–140

LE BONHEUR, A. "Activités du Musée national des Arts asiatiques-Guimet-Acquisitions-Asie du Sud-Est." *Arts Asiatiques* 49 (1994), 92–95

LE BONHEUR, A., and J. PONCAR. *Des Dieux, des Rois, des Hommes. Les bas-reliefs d'Angkor Vat et du Bayon.* Geneva, 1995

LEE, Sherman. *Ancient Cambodian Sculpture.* New York, 1969

LÉVI, S. "Les 'marchands de mer' et leur rôle dans le bouddhisme primitif." *Bulletin de l'Association des Amis de l'Orient* 3 (1929), 19–39. Reprinted in *Mémorial Sylvain Lévi,* 133–144. Paris, 1937

LÉVY, P. *Recherches préhistoriques dans la région de Mlu Prei* (EFEO 30). Hanoi, 1943

LEWITZ, S. "Textes en khmer moyen. Inscriptions modernes d'Angkor, 3." *BEFEO* 57 (1970), 99–126

LOBO, W. "Reflections on the Tantric Buddhist God Hevajra in Cambodia." *Southeast Asian Archeology 1994. Proceedings of the 5th International Conference of the European Association of Southeast Asian Archaeologists.* Hull, 1997 [1]

LOBO, W. "Viṣṇu-Vāsudeva-Nārāyana. A Late Twelfth Century Khmer Bronze." In *Living a Life in Accord with Damma: Papers in Honour of Professor Jean Boisselier on his Eightieth Birthday.* Ed. Kh. Sri-Aroon, N. Eilenberg, M. C. S. Diskul, R. L. Brown. Bangkok and Los Angeles, 1997 [2]

LUNET DE LAJONQUIÈRE, E. *Inventaire descriptif des Monuments du Cambodge.* 3 vols. (EFEO 4, 8, 9). Paris, 1902–1911

LUONG NINH. "Oc Eo và Phù Nam." *Khao cô hoc* 1 (1987), 47–59

LUONG NINH. "Van hoa Oc Eo và van hoa Phù Nam." *Khao cô hoc* 3 (1993), 22–35

M

MABBETT, I. W. "Devaraja." *Journal of Southeast Asian History* 10, 2 (Sept. 1969), 202–223

MABBETT, I. W. "*Varnas* in Angkor and the Indian Caste System." *Journal of Asian Studies* 36, 3 (1977), 429–442 [1]

MABBETT, I. W. "The 'Indianization' of Southeast Asia: Reflections on the Prehistoric Sources." *Journal of Southeast Asian Studies* 8, 1 (March 1977) [2]

MABBETT, I. W. "Cosmography, Architecture and Ritual in Hindu-Buddhist Culture." *South Asia* 6, 1 (1983), 44–53 [1]

MABBETT, I. W. "The Symbolism of Mount Meru." *History of Religions* 23, 1 (1983), 64–83 [2]

MABBETT, I. W., ed. *Patterns of Kingship and Authority in Traditional Asia.* London, Sydney, and Dover, New Hampshire, 1985 [1]

MABBETT, I. W. "Introduction: The Comparative Study of Traditional Asian Political Institutions." In *Patterns of Kingship and Authority in Traditional Asia,* 1–23. London, Sydney, and Dover, New Hampshire, 1985 [2]

MABBETT, I. W. "Divine Kingship in Angkor." *Acarya-Vandana, D. R. Bhandarkar Birth Centenary Volume,* 277–285. Ed. S. Bandyopadhyay. Calcutta, n.d.

MAHĀ BIDUR KRASSEM. *Inscriptions modernes d'Angkor.* Reprint Paris, 1984

Mahabharata. Excerpts translated from the Sanskrit by J. M. Peterfalvi; commentaries, summary, and glossary by M. Biardeau. Paris, 1986

MAJUMDAR, R. C. "Holy Kurukṣetra in Laos." *Journal of the Asiatic Society of Bombay,* n. s. 34–35 (1959–1960), 22–26

MAK PHOUEN. *Chronique royale du Cambodge (des origines légendaires jusqu'à Paramarāja Ier)* (EFEO Textes et documents sur l'Indochine 13). Paris, 1984

MALLERET, L. *Pour comprendre la sculpture Bud-dhique et Brahmanique en Indochine.* Saigon, 1942

MALLERET, L. "L'art et la métallurgie de l'étain dans la culture d'Oc-Eo." *Artibus Asiae* 11, 4 (1948), 274–284

MALLERET, L. "La statue de Lokeśvara de la collection Didelot." *Arts Asiatiques* 1, 4 (1954), 249–262

MALLERET, L. "Objets de bronze communs au Cambodge, à la Malaisie et à l'Indonésie." *Artibus Asiae* 19 (1956), 308–327 [1]

MALLERET, L. "La statue de Gaṇeśa de Rochefort-sur-mer." *Arts Asiatiques* 3, 3 (1956), 211–224 [2]

MALLERET, L. "Ouvrages circulaires en terre dans l'Indochine méridionale." *BEFEO* 49, 2 (1959), 409–434

MALLERET, L. "Quelques poteries de Sa-Huynh dans leurs rapports avec divers sites du sud-est de l'Asie." *Asian Perspectives* 3 (1959), 113–120

MALLERET, L. *L'Archéologie du Delta du Mékong.* 4 vols. 1, *L'Exploration archéologique et les fouilles d'Oc-Eo.* 2, *La Civilisation matérielle d'Oc-Eo.* 3, *La Culture de Fou-nan.* 4, *Le Cisbassac* (EFEO 43). Paris, 1959–1963

MALLERET, L. "Contribution à l'étude du thème des neuf divinités dans la sculpture du Cambodge et du Champa." *Arts Asiatiques* 7, 3 (1960), 205–230

MALLERET, L. "Bossus et nains dans la sculpture en Extrême-Orient." *Arts Asiatiques* 20 (1969), 121–133

de MALLMANN, M.-Th. *Introduction à l'étude d'Avalokiteśvara.* Paris, 1948

de MALLMANN, M.-Th. *Introduction à l'iconographie du tântrisme bouddhique* (Bibliothèque du centre de recherches sur l'Asie centrale et la haute Asie 1). Paris, 1975

MANNIKKA, E. *Angkor Wat. Time, Space, and Kingship.* 1996

MANSUY, H. *Stations préhistoriques de Somrong Sen et de Longprao.* Hanoi, 1902

MANSUY, H. "Résultats de nouvelles recherches effectuées sur le gisement préhistorique de Samrong Sen." *Mémoire de la Société Géologique Indochine* 11, 1 (1923)

MARCHAL, H. "Monuments secondaires et terrasses bouddhiques d'Angkor Thom." *BEFEO* 18, 8 (1918)

MARCHAL, H. "Le temple de Preah Palilay." *BEFEO* 22 (1922), 101–134

MARCHAL, H. "Sur le monument 486 d'Angkor

Thom." *BEFEO* 25, 3–4 (1925)
MARCHAL, H. "Notes sur L'architecture de Nak Pan." *BEFEO* 26 (1926), 1ff
MARCHAL, H. *Guide archéologique aux temples d'Angkor.* Paris and Brussels, 1928
MARCHAL, H. "Reconstruction of the Southern Sanctuary of Bantay Srei." *Indian Art and Letters* 7 (1933), 129–133
MARCHAL, H. "Notes sur les Terrasses des Éléphants, du Roi Lépreux et le Palais Royal d'Aṅkor Thom." *BEFEO* 37 (1937), 347ff
MARCHAL, H. *Musée Louis Finot. La collection khmère.* Hanoi, 1939
MARCHAL, H. *Rapport de la Conservation d'Angkor.* July, 1950
MARCHAL, H. *Le Décor et la Sculpture khmers.* Paris, 1951
MARCHAL, H. "Note sur la forme du *stūpa* au Cambodge." *BEFEO* 44, 2 (1954), 581–590, pls. 70–72
MARCHAL, H. *Les Temples d'Angkor.* Paris, 1955
MARCHAL, H. *Nouveau guide d'Angkor.* Phnom Penh, 1961
MARR, D. G., and A. C. MILNER, eds. *Southeast Asia in the 9th to 14th Centuries.* Singapore, 1986
MASPERO, G. *Le Royaume de Champa.* Paris and Brussels, 1929
Masterpieces of Bronze Sculptures from Ban Fai, Lam Plai Mat, Buriram. Bangkok, 1973
MAUGER, H. "L'asram Maha Rosei." *BEFEO* 36 (1936), 65–96
MAUGER, H. "Le Phnom Bayan." *BEFEO* 37 (1937), 239–262
MAUGER, H. "Prah Khan de Kompong Svay." *BEFEO* 39 (1939), 197–220
MAZZEO, D., and C. SILVI ANTONINI. *Civiltà Khmer.* Milan and Tokyo, 1972
MAZZEO, D., and C. SILVI ANTONINI. *Monuments of Civilization: Ancient Cambodia.* 2d ed. London, 1978
MILLER, B. S., ed. *Theater of Memory, the Plays of Kalidasa.* New York, 1984
MICHELL, G. *The Hindu Temple: An Introduction to Its Meaning and Form.* Chicago and London, 1988
MITRA, D. "A Study of Some Graha-images of India and Their Possible Bearing on the nava-Devas of Cambodia." *Journal of the Asiatic Society* 7, 1–2 (1965), 13–37
MITRA, H. "Sadāśiva Worship in Early Bengal: A Study in History, Art and Religion." *Journal and Proceedings of the Asiatic Society in Bengal,* n. s. 29, 1 (1933), 171–254
MONOD, O. *Le Musée Guimet.* Paris, 1966
MORON, E. "Configuration of Time and Space at Angkor." *Studies in Indian Art and Culture* 5 (1977)
MOUHOT, H. *Voyage dans les royaumes de Siam, de Cambodge, de Laos et autres parties centrales de l'Indochine. Le Tour du Monde.* Paris, 1863
MOURA, J. *Le Royaume du Cambodge.* Paris, 1883
MOURER, R. "Laang Spean and the Prehistory of Cambodia." *Modern Quaternary Research in Southeast Asia* 3 (1977), 29–56
MOURER, R. "Contribution à l'étude de la préhistoire du Cambodge." *BEFEO* 1993, 80, 2 (1994), 143–187
MUS, P. "Le Buddha paré. Son origine indienne. Śākyamuni dans le Mahāyānisme moyen." *BEFEO* 28 (1928), 153–278
MUS, P. *L'Inde vue de l'Est: cultes indiens et indigènes au Champa* (*BEFEO* 33 [1934], 367–410). Hanoi, 1934
MUS, P. "Le sourire d'Angkor. Art, foi et politique bouddhiques sous Jayavarman VII." *Artibus Asiae* 24 (1961), 363–381
MUS, P. *India Seen from the East: Indian and Indigenous Cults in Champa.* Ed. and trans. I. W. Mabbett and D. P. Chandler. Clayton, Victoria, 1975
Musée national des Arts asiatiques-Guimet. Paris, 1993

N

NAFILYAN, G. *Angkor Vat. Description graphique du temple* (EFEO Mémoires archéologiques 4). Paris, 1969
NAGASWAMY, R. "Reference to Śaṅkarācārya in Cambodian Inscription–Re-examined." *Journal of the Oriental Institute* (Baroda) 16, 4 (1967), 342–343
NAUDIN, G. *Le Groupe d'Angkor vu par les écrivains et les artistes étrangers.* Saigon, 1928
NAUDOU, J. *Le Bouddha.* Paris, 1975
NAUDOU, J. "La démarche de la méthode." In *Au service d'une biologie de l'art-Recherches sur les arts de l'Inde et de l'Asie du Sud-Est,* 19–56. Lille, 1978
NOTTON, C. *The Chronicle of the Emerald Buddha.* Bangkok, 1932
NOUTH NARANG, M. BUTOR, and P. GRAS. *Angkor silencieux.* Paris and Heidelberg, 1988

O

OBERMILLER, E. *Prajñāpāramitā in Tibetan Buddhism* (Classics India Religion and Philosophy Series 3). Delhi, 1988
O'CONNOR Jr., S. J. *Hindu Gods of Peninsular Siam* (*Artibus Asiae* Supplementum 28). Ascona, 1972

P

PACHOW, W. "The Voyage of Buddhist Missions to South-East Asia and the Far East." *Journal of the Greater India Society* 17 (1958), 1–22
PARIS, Pierere. "Anciens canaux reconnus sur photographies aériennes dans les provinces de Ta Kev et de Chau-doc." *BEFEO* 31 (1931), 221–224
PARMENTIER, H. "Les bas-reliefs de Banteay Chmar." *BEFEO* 10 (1910), 205–221
PARMENTIER, H. "Catalogue du Musée khmer de Phnom-Penh." *BEFEO* 12, 3 (1912), 1ff
PARMENTIER, H. "Complément à l'Inventaire descriptif des monuments du Cambodge." *BEFEO* 13, 1 (1913), 1–61
PARMENTIER, H. "L'architecture interprétée dans les bas-reliefs du Cambodge." *BEFEO* 14 (1914), 1–28 [1]
PARMENTIER, H. "Le temple de Vat Phu." *BEFEO* 14, 2 (1914), 1ff [2]
PARMENTIER, H. "Vat Nokor." *BEFEO* 19 (1919), 1–98 [1]
PARMENTIER, H. "L'art d'Indravarman." *BEFEO* 19, 1 (1919), 1–98 [2]
PARMENTIER, H. *L'Art khmer primitif.* 2 vols. (EFEO 21 and 22). Paris, 1927
PARMENTIER, H. "Examen du nivellement d'Angkor." *BEFEO* 33 (1933), 310–318
PARMENTIER, H. "Complément à l'art khmer primitif." *BEFEO* 35 (1935), 1–115 [1]
PARMENTIER, H. "La construction dans l'architecture khmère classique." *BEFEO* 35 (1935), 243–312 [2]
PARMENTIER, H. *L'Art khmer classique. Monuments du quadrant nord-est.* 2 vols. (EFEO 29 b). Paris, 1939
PARMENTIER, H. *Angkor.* Saigon, 1950
PELLIOT, P. "Le Fou-nan." *BEFEO* 3 (1903), 248–303
PELLIOT, P. "Textes chinois concernant l'Indochine hindouisée." *Études asiatiques* 2 (1925)
PELLIOT, P. *Mémoires sur les coutumes du Cambodge de Tcheou Ta-Kouan, version nouvelle suivie d'un commentaire inachevé.* Paris, 1951
PHAM DUC MANH. "'Qua' dông Long Giao (Dông Nai)." *Khao cô hoc* 1 (1985), 37–68
PICH, K., and N. SMITH. *Khmer Art in Stone.* Phnom Penh, 1993
PICHARD, P. *Pimay. Étude architecturale du temple* (EFEO Mémoires archéologiques 10). Paris, 1976
PIGEAUD, Th. G. Th. *Java in the 14th Century: Nagara-Kertāgama.* 3d ed. The Hague, 1960
PIGOTT, V., and SURAPOL NANTAPINTU. "Investigating the Origins of Metal Use in Prehistoric Thailand." In *Ancient Chinese and Southeast Asian Bronze Age Culture.* Ed. N. Barnard and F. D. Bulbeck. Taipei, 1996
POTT, P. H. *Yoga and Yantra. Their Interrelation and Their Significance for Indian Archaeology.* The Hague, 1966
POU, S. *Rāmakerti (xvie–xviie siècles),* translation and commentary. Paris, 1977 [1]
POU, S. *Études sur le Rāmakerti* (XVIe–XVIIe siècles). Paris, 1977 [2]
POU, S. *Rāmakerti* (XVIe–XVIIe siècles). Paris, 1979
POU, S. *Rāmakerti* 2. Paris, 1982
POU, S. "Notes on Brahmanic Gods in Theravādin Cambodia." *Indologica Taurinensia* 14 (1987–1988), 339–351
POU, S. *Nouvelles inscriptions du Cambodge* 1. Paris, 1989
POU, S. "Les noms des monuments khmers." *BEFEO* 78 (1991), 203–228
POU, S. *Dictionnaire vieux khmer-français-anglais: An Old Khmer-French-English Dictionary.* Paris, 1992
POU, S. "Īsūr/Īśvara, ou Śiva, au Cambodge." *Orientalia Lovaniensia Periodica* 24 (1993), 143–177
POU, S. "Viṣṇu/Naray au Cambodge." *Orientalia Lovaniensia Periodica* 25 (1994), 175–195
POU, S. "Indra et Brahmā au Cambodge." *Orientalia Lovaniensia Periodica* 26 (1995), 141–161
PRAPANDVIDYA, C. "The Sab Bāk Inscription: Evidence of an Early Vajrayāna Buddhist Presence in Thailand." *Journal of the Siam Society* 78, 2 (1990), 11–14
PRZYLUSKI, J. "La légende de Kṛṣṇa dans les bas-reliefs d'Angkor Vat." *Revue des Arts Asiatiques* 5, 2 (1928), 91–97
PRZYLUSKI, J. "Pradakṣiṇa et Prasavya en Indochine." In *Festschrift für M. Winbernitz zum 70ten Geburtstag,* 326–332. Leipzig, 1933

R

Rāmāyaṇa. Ch. Le Brun and A. Daniélou. Paris, 1985
Rarities of the Musée Guimet. New York, 1975
RÉGNIER, R. "Note sur l'évolution du chignon (*jaṭā*) dans la statuaire préangkorienne." *Arts Asiatiques* 14 (1966), 17–40
RENAN, E. *Nouvelles études d'histoire religieuse.* Paris, 1884. Reproduced in E. Renan, *Études d'histoire religieuse.* Paris, 1992
RENOU, L. *La Civilisation de l'Inde ancienne d'après les textes sanskrits.* Paris, 1950
RENOU, L. *L'Hindouisme.* 7th ed. Paris, 1979
RENOU, L., et al. *L'Inde classique. Manuel des études indiennes.* Reprint. Paris, 1985
ROESKE, M. "Les inscriptions bouddhiques du mont Koulen." *Journal Asiatique* 11, 3 (1914), 637–644
RIBOUD, M. *Angkor, sérénité bouddhique.* Paris, 1992
ROHANADEERA, M. "Telakaṭāhāgāthā in a Thailand Inscription of 761 A.D." *Vidyodaya Journal of Social Science* (University of Jayewardenepura, Nugegoda, Sri Lanka) 1, 1 (1987), 59–73
ROONEY, D. *Khmer Ceramics.* Kuala Lumpur, 1984

S

SAFRANI, N. S. H. "Rarities of the musée Guimet." *Arts of Asia* (Jan.–Feb. 1977), 59–67
SAHAI, S. *Les institutions politiques et l'organisation*

administrative du Cambodge ancien (VIe–XIIIe siècle) (EFEO 75). Paris, 1970
SALOMON, R. "Indian Trthas in Southeast Asia." In *The History of Sacred Places in India as reflected in Traditional Literature* (Panels of the 7th World Sanskrit Conference 3), 160–176. Ed. H. Bakker. Leiden, 1990
SAURIN, E. "Quelques remarques sur les grès d'Ankor." *BEFEO* 46 (1952), 619–634
SAURIN, E. *Les Recherches préhistoriques au Cambodge, Laos et Viêtnam—1877–1966* (Asian Perspectives 12, 2742). Honolulu, 1969
SCHUR NARULA, K. *The Voyage of the Emerald Buddha*. Kuala Lumpur, 1994
SEIDENFADEN, E. "Complément à l'inventaire descriptif des monuments du Cambodge." *BEFEO* 22 (1922), 55–99
SIRCAR, D. Ch. *Select Inscriptions bearing on Indian History and Civilization*, 1. Calcutta, 1942
SIRIBHADRA, S. "Note sur un bronze d'époque angkorienne représentant Prajñāparāmitā." *Art and Archaeology in Thailand* 2
SIRIBHADRA, S., E. MOORE, and M. FREEMAN. *Palaces of the Gods. Khmer Art and Architecture in Thailand*. London, 1992
SIVARAMAMURTI, C. *L'Art en Inde*. Paris, 1974
SMITH, R. B., and W. WATSON, eds. *Early South East Asia. Essays in Archaeology, History, and Historical Geography*. New York and Kuala Lumpur, 1979
SNELLGROVE, D. L. *The Hevajra-Tantra. A Critical Study*. Pt. 1. Introduction and translation. Pt. II. Sanskrit and Tibetan Texts (London Oriental Series 6). London, New York, and Toronto, 1959
SNELLGROVE, D. L., ed. *The Image of the Buddha*. Paris, 1978
SOEKMONO, R. *The Javanese Candi*. Leiden, 1995
SRINIVASAN, D. M. "Śaiva Temple Forms: Loci of God's Unfolding Body." *Investigating Indian Art*. Vol. 8. Ed. M. Yaldiz and W. Lobo. Berlin, 1987
STENCEL, R., and E. MORON. "Astronomy and Cosmology at Angkor Wat." *Science* 193 (23 July 1978)
STERN, Ph. *Le Bàyon d'Angkor et l'évolution de l'art khmer* (Annales du musée, Bibliothèque de vulgarisation, 47). Paris, 1927
STERN, Ph. "La transition de l'art préangkorien à l'art angkorien et Jayavarman II." In *Études d'orientalisme publiées par le musée Guimet à la mémoire de Raymonde Linossier*. 2:507–524. Paris, 1932
STERN, Ph. "Le temple-montagne khmer, le culte du *liṅga* et le *devarāja*." *BEFEO* 34 (1934), 611–616
STERN, Ph. "Le style du Kulên." *BEFEO* 38 (1938), 111–149 [1]
STERN, Ph. "Travaux exécutés sur le Phnoṃ Kulên (15 avril–20 mai 1936)." *BEFEO* 38 (1938), 151–173 [2]
STERN, Ph. "Hariharālaya et Indrapura." *BEFEO* 38 (1938), 175–197 [3]
STERN, Ph. "L'art khmer." *Histoire universelle des arts 4: Arts musulmans-Extrême-Orient*, 206–236 Paris, 1939
STERN, Ph. "Diversité et rythme des fondations royales khmères." *BEFEO* 44 (1954), 649–687
STERN, Ph. *Les Monuments khmers du style du Bàyon et Jayavarman VII*. Vol. 9. Paris, 1965
STERN, Ph. *Les colonnettes khmères. Au service d'une biologie de l'art. Recherches sur les arts de l'Inde et de l'Asie du Sud-Est*. Lille, 1978
STIERLIN, H. *Angkor. Architecture universelle*. Fribourg, 1970
STIERLIN, H. *Le Monde d'Angkor*. Paris, 1979
STÖNNER, H. "Catalogue des sculptures chames et khmères du musée royal d'Ethnographie à Berlin." *Bulletin de la Commission archéologique de l'Indochine* (1912), 195–198

T

THIERRY, S. *Les Khmers*. Paris, 1964
TRINH SINH. "Vài nét vê giao luu van hoa o thoi dal kim khi trong bôi canh lich su Dông Nam A (Some Features of Cultural Contacts in the Metal Age within the Historical Context of Southeast Asia)." *Khao cô hoc* 3 (1979), 49–63

V

VALLIBHOTAMA, M. *Report of the Survey and Excavations of Ancient Monuments in North-Eastern Thailand*, Part I. BE 2503. Bangkok, 1960
VALLIBHOTAMA, M. *Report of the Survey and Excavations of Ancient Monuments in North-Eastern Thailand*, Part II. BE 2510. Bangkok, 1967
VICKERY, M. "L'inscription K 1006 du Phnom Kulen." *BEFEO* 71 (1982), 77–86
VICKERY, M. "Some Remarks on Early State Formation in Cambodia." *Southeast Asia in the 9th to 11th Centuries*, 95–115. Ed. D. G. Marr and A. Milner. Singapore, 1986
VICKERY, M. "What and Where was Chenla?" *BEFEO* 80, 2 (1993), 197–212. Paris 1994
VIENNOT, O. "À propos des linteaux khmers du VIIe siècle." *Arts Asiatiques* 3, 1 (1956), 64–68

W

WANG, B. "Buddhist Nikāyas through Ancient Chinese Eyes." *Buddhist Studies Present and Future* (Tenth International Conference of the International Association of Buddhist Studies, Summary Report by Ananda W. P. Guruge), 65–72. Paris, 1992
WANG GUNGWU. *The Nanhai Trade. A Study of the Early History of Chinese Trade in the South China Sea* (*Journal of the Malaysian Branch of the Royal Asiatic Society* 31, 2 [1958])
WHEATLEY, P. *The Golden Khersonese: Studies in the Historical Geography of the Malay Peninsula before A.D. 1500*. Kuala Lumpur, 1961
WHEATLEY, P. "The Mount of the Immortals." *Oriens Extremus* 21 (1974), 97–109
WHITE, J. C. *Discovery of a Lost Bronze Age—Ban Chiang*. 1982
WOLTERS, O. W. "Khmer 'Hinduism' in the Seventh Century." In *Early South East Asia: Essays in Archaeology, History, and Historical Geography*, 427–442. Ed. R. B. Smith and W. Watson. New York and Kuala Lumpur, 1979
WOODWARD, H. W., Jr. "The Bayon-Period Buddha Image in the Kimbell Art Museum." *Archives of Asian Art* 32 (1979), 72–83
WOODWARD, H. W., Jr. "Some Buddha Images and the Cultural Developments of the Late Angkorian Period." *Artibus Asiae* 42 (1980), 155–174
WOODWARD, H. W., Jr. "Tantric Buddhism at Angkor Thom." *Ars Orientalis* 12 (1981), 57–67
WOODWARD, H. W., Jr. "The Jayabuddhamahānātha Images of Cambodia." *The Journal of the Walters Art Gallery* 52, 53 (1994–1995), 105–110

Z

ZÉPHIR, Th. "L'art khmer." *L'Art de l'Asie du Sud-Est*, 151–249. Paris, 1994
ZÉPHIR, Th. "Louis Delaporte au cœur de la forêt sacrée." In *Âges et visages de l'Asie, un siècle d'exploration à travers les collections du musée Guimet*, 58–68. Dijon, 1996 [1]
ZÉPHIR, Th. "The Progress of Rama. The Ramayana in Khmer bas-reliefs of the Angkor period." In *Silk and Stone—The Art of Asia*, 80–89. London, 1996 [2]
ZÉPHIR, TH. "Banteay Srei: le séjour de Çiva." *Angkor et dix siècles d'art khmer*, ex-series 100 *Connaissance des Arts*, 1997 [1]
ZÉPHIR, TH. *L'empire des rois khmers* (Collection Découvertes 310). Paris, 1997 [2]
ZIGMUND-CERBU, A. "À propos d'un *vajra* khmer." *Artibus Asiae* 24 (1961), 425–431
ZIMMER, H. *The Art of Indian Asia*. 2 vols. 2d ed. New York, 1960; 1st ed. 1955

Index

Terms in **bold** indicate catalogue items. Catalogue numbers are in [brackets]. Page numbers in *italics* indicate illustrations. Page numbers followed by "n" indicate notes.

Photographic credits

Agence photographique de la Réunion des musées nationaux, Paris:
pp. 166-167 (Arnaudet); p. 175 (Th. Ollivier); pp. 196-197 (Arnaudet); Fig. 2 p. 40

Ang Chouléan, Phnom Penh:
Fig. 2 p. 65; Fig. 4 p. 69

Archives photographiques du musée national des Arts asiatiques-Guimet, Paris:
Fig. 5 p. 9; Fig. 6 p. 50; Fig. 2 p. 104; Fig. 2 p. 125; Figs. 3–4 p. 126; Fig. 5 p. 127; Fig. 4 p. 137; Figs. 1–2 p. 210; Fig. 1 p. 214; Fig. 1 p. 236; Fig. 1 p. 257

Asian Art Museum of San Francisco:
pp. 248–249

The Asia Society, New York:
p. 159

Cleveland Museum of Art:
Fig. 1 p. 160

École française d'Extrême-Orient, Paris:
Fig. 5 p. 29

Laure Feugère, Paris:
Fig. 1 p. 39

Musée Albert Kahn, Boulogne-Billancourt:
Fig. 6 p. 31

Musée d'Histoire Naturelle, Lyon:
Figs. 1–2 p. 6

Philadelphia Museum of Art:
p. 155

Staatliche Museen zu Berlin, Museum für Indische Kunst:
p. 317

Ashley Thompson, Paris:
Fig. 1 p. 24; Figs. 2–3 p. 27

Thierry Zéphir, Arcy-Sainte-Restitue:
p. 1; Fig. 3 p. 17; Fig. 5 p. 18; Fig. 6 p. 19; Fig. 8 p. 20; Fig. 4 p. 44; Fig. 2 p. 55; Fig. 2 p. 82; Fig. 3 p. 83; Fig. 5 p. 85; Figs. 6–8 p. 88; Fig. 9 p. 89; Fig. 10 p. 91; Fig. 7 p. 98; Fig. 8 p. 99; Figs. 7–8 p. 110; Fig. 9 p. 111; Fig. 11 p. 112; Fig. 1 p. 119; Fig. 2 p. 183; Fig. 3 p. 210; Fig. 2 p. 232; Fig. 1 p. 280; Figs. 1–2 p. 288

All rights reserved:
Fig. 1 p. 14; Fig. 10 p. 21; Fig. 1 p. 55; Figs. 3–4 p. 56; Figs. 5a–b p. 57; Fig. 1 p. 80; Fig. 1 p. 183; Fig. 1 p. 232

All other photographs by John Gollings, St. Kilda, Australia